AMNESTY INTERNATIONAL

Amnesty International is a global movement of more than 3 million supporters, members and activists who campaign for internationally recognized human rights to be respected and protected. Its vision is for every person to enjoy all of the human rights enshrined in the Universal Declaration of Human Rights and other international human rights standards.

Amnesty International's mission is to conduct research and take action to prevent and end grave abuses of all human rights – civil, political, social, cultural and economic. From freedom of expression and association to physical and mental integrity, from protection from discrimination to the right to housing – these rights are indivisible.

Amnesty International is funded mainly by its membership and public donations. No funds are sought or accepted from governments for investigating and campaigning against human rights abuses. Amnesty International is independent of any government, political ideology, economic interest or religion.

Amnesty International is a democratic movement whose major policy decisions are taken by representatives from all national sections at International Council meetings held every two years. The members of the International Executive Committee, elected by the Council to carry out its decisions, are Bernard Sintobin (Belgium Flemish – International Treasurer), Euntae Go (South Korea), Guadalupe Rivas (Mexico – Vice-Chair), Julio Torales (Paraguay), Nicole Bieske (Australia), Pietro Antonioli (Italy – Chair), Rune Arctander (Norway), Sandra S. Lutchman (Netherlands) and Zuzanna Kulinska (Poland).

United against injustice, we work together for human rights.

First published in 2012 by
Amnesty International Ltd
Peter Benenson House
1 Easton Street
London WC1X 0DW
United Kingdom

© Amnesty International 2012
Index: POL 10/001/2012

ISBN: 978-0-86210-472-6
ISSN: 0309-068X

A catalogue record for this book is available from the British Library.

Original language: English

Printed on 100 per cent recycled post-consumer waste paper by
Pureprint Group
East Sussex
United Kingdom

Pureprint is a CarbonNeutral® company, and uses only vegetable-oil-based inks.

AMNESTY INTERNATIONAL REPORT 2012
THE STATE OF THE WORLD'S HUMAN RIGHTS

This report covers the period
January to December 2011.

Journalists interview activist artist
Ai Weiwei outside his home after he
returned from detention, Beijing, China,
22 June 2011.

CONTENTS
ANNUAL REPORT
2012

"*The butterfly for us is a symbol of the desire to realize our dreams, spread our wings… fighting with strength for our rights.*" Martha Munguía, Nicaraguan Alliance of Women's Centres

Women, girls, men and boys take to the streets in Nicaragua on the Day for the Decriminalization of Abortion in Latin America and the Caribbean, 28 September 2011.

PREFACE

"IF ANYTHING HAPPENS TO ME, KNOW THAT THE REGIME DOES NOT FEAR THE PRISONERS BUT RATHER THOSE OF YOU WHO DO NOT FORGET THEM."

Razan Ghazzawi, a Syrian blogger, detained for 15 days in Syria in December 2011

The Amnesty International Report 2012 documents the state of human rights during 2011. In five regional overviews and a country-by-country survey of 155 individual countries and territories, the report shows how the demand for human rights continued to resound in every corner of the globe.

Millions took to the streets of their towns and cities in a mass outpouring of hope for freedom and justice. Even the most brutal repression seemed unable to silence the increasingly urgent demands for an end to tyranny as people showed they were no longer willing to endure systems of governance that were not built on accountability, transparency, justice and the promotion of equality.

Resistance to injustice and repression took many forms, often inspiring acts of enormous courage and determination from the communities and individuals facing seemingly insuperable obstacles. In the face of indifference, threats and attacks, human rights defenders pursued legal challenges at the national and international level to long-standing impunity and endemic discrimination.

This report reflects an approach to tackling human rights abuses that is informed by both the challenges and the opportunities for change. As Amnesty International moves into its sixth decade, this report bears witness not only to the plight of those living in the shadow of human rights violations, but also to those who continue to be inspired to action by the principle of human dignity.

COUNTRY DATA

The facts at the top of each individual country entry in this report have been drawn from the following sources:

All **Life expectancy** and **Adult literacy** figures are from the United Nations Development Programme's (UNDP) *Human Development Report 2011*, found at: http://hdr.undp.org/en/media/HDR_2011_EN_Complete.pdf

The latest figures available were Life expectancy at birth (2011) and Adult literacy rate (percentage aged 15 and older, 2005-2010). For more information, see the UNDP website or www.uis.unesco.org

Some countries that fall into the UNDP's "high human development" bracket have been assumed by the UNDP to have a literacy rate of 99 per cent. Where this is the case, we have omitted the figure.

All **Population** figures are for 2011 and **Under-5 mortality** figures are for 2009, both drawn from the United Nations Population Fund's *State of World Population 2011* report, found at: http://foweb.unfpa.org/SWP2011/reports/EN-SWOP2011-FINAL.pdf

Population figures are there solely to indicate the number of people affected by the issues we describe. Amnesty International acknowledges the limitations of such figures, and takes no position on questions such as disputed territory or the inclusion or exclusion of certain population groups.

Some country entries in this report have no reference to some or all of the above categories. Such omissions are for a number of reasons, including the absence of the information in the UN lists cited above.

These are the latest available figures at the time of going to print, and are for context purposes only. Due to differences in methodology and timeliness of underlying data, comparisons across countries should be made with caution.

ABBREVIATIONS

ASEAN	Association of Southeast Asian Nations
AU	African Union
CEDAW	UN Convention on the Elimination of All Forms of Discrimination against Women
CEDAW Committee	UN Committee on the Elimination of Discrimination against Women
CERD	International Convention on the Elimination of All Forms of Racial Discrimination
CERD Committee	UN Committee on the Elimination of Racial Discrimination
CIA	US Central Intelligence Agency
ECOWAS	Economic Community of West African States
EU	European Union
European Committee for the Prevention of Torture	European Committee for the Prevention of Torture and Inhuman or Degrading Treatment or Punishment
European Convention on Human Rights	(European) Convention for the Protection of Human Rights and Fundamental Freedoms
ICCPR	International Covenant on Civil and Political Rights
ICRC	International Committee of the Red Cross
ILO	International Labour Organization
International Convention against enforced disappearance	International Convention for the Protection of All Persons from Enforced Disappearance
LGBT	lesbian, gay, bisexual and transgender
NATO	North Atlantic Treaty Organization
NGO	non-governmental organization
OAS	Organization of American States
OSCE	Organization for Security and Co-operation in Europe
UK	United Kingdom
UN	United Nations
UN Convention against Torture	Convention against Torture and Other Cruel, Inhuman or Degrading Treatment or Punishment
UN Refugee Convention	Convention relating to the Status of Refugees
UN Special Rapporteur on freedom of expression	Special Rapporteur on the promotion and protection of the right to freedom of opinion and expression
UN Special Rapporteur on indigenous people	Special Rapporteur on the situation of human rights and fundamental freedoms of indigenous people
UN Special Rapporteur on torture	Special Rapporteur on torture and other cruel, inhuman or degrading treatment or punishment
UN Special Rapporteur on violence against women	Special Rapporteur on violence against women, its causes and consequences
UNFPA	United Nations Population Fund
UNHCR, the UN refugee agency	Office of the United Nations High Commissioner for Refugees
UNICEF	United Nations Children's Fund
USA	United States of America
WHO	World Health Organization

Malawi police chase protesters. At least 19 people were killed and dozens, including children, were injured after police used live ammunition during demonstrations over bad governance, fuel shortages and human rights abuses in various cities. 22 July 2011.

Migrants being rescued by Italian
coastguards, Pantelleria, Italy,
13 April 2011.

AMNESTY INTERNATIONAL REPORT 2012
PART ONE: REGIONAL OVERVIEWS

12

A man in Kurchi watches military aircraft fly
overhead, Southern Kordofan, Sudan,
August 2011. Following the outbreak of
conflict in the region in June, the Sudanese
government repeatedly carried out
indiscriminate aerial bombardments, killing
and wounding civilians.

AFRICA

"Maybe this could be the year when freedom of expression and association will be respected... Maybe this could be the year when Ethiopians will no more be imprisoned for their political convictions."

Ethiopian journalist and former prisoner of conscience, Eskinder Nega, in a speech on press freedom on the eve of the new Ethiopian calendar year in September 2011. Days later he was arrested and charged with terrorism offences and treason.

The popular movements across North Africa resonated with people in sub-Saharan Africa, particularly in countries with repressive governments. Trade unionists, students and opposition politicians were inspired to organize demonstrations. People took to the streets because of their political aspirations, the quest for more freedom, and a deep frustration with a life in poverty. They protested against their desperate social and economic situation and the rise in living costs.

Many of the underlying factors which led to the uprisings in North Africa and the Middle East also exist in other parts of Africa. They include authoritarian rulers who have been in power for decades and rely on a security apparatus to clamp down on dissent. Poverty and corruption are widespread, there is a lack of basic freedoms, and large groups are often marginalized from mainstream society. The brutal suppression of demonstrations during 2011 illustrated how the region's political leaders learned little from what happened to their peers in the north.

Poverty

Africa's poverty rates have been falling and progress has been made in realizing the UN Millennium Development Goals over the past decade. But millions of people are still living in poverty, without access to essential services such as clean water, sanitation, health care and education.

Rapid urbanization means that many Africans live without adequate housing, often in slums, where they lack the most basic facilities and are at constant risk of forced eviction by the authorities. People who are forcibly evicted often lose their belongings when their homes are destroyed. Many also lose their livelihood, which pushes them further into poverty. Thousands of people were affected when mass forced evictions took place in at least five informal settlements in Nairobi, Kenya. Hundreds of people were forcibly evicted from a settlement in the Federal Capital Territory of Nigeria. Forced evictions also continued in N'Djamena, Chad, and in different parts of Angola.

Violence, including during anti-government demonstrations, was sometimes partially caused by high levels of unemployment and poverty. Anti-corruption initiatives were regularly squandered by a lack of political support. In Nigeria, for example, the President dismissed the Chairperson of the Economic and Financial Crimes Commission six months before her tenure was due to end, without explanation.

The brutal suppression of demonstrations during 2011 illustrated how the region's political leaders learned little from what happened to their peers in the north.

Political repression

Inspired by events in North Africa, anti-government protesters took to the streets in Khartoum and other towns across Sudan, from the end of January onward. They were beaten by security forces, and dozens of activists and students were arbitrarily arrested and detained. Many were reportedly tortured in detention. In Uganda, opposition politicians called on people to imitate the Egyptian protests and take to the streets, but violence marred the demonstrations. In February, the Ugandan government banned all public protests. The police and army used excessive force against protesters, and opposition leader Kizza Besigye was harassed and arrested. In Zimbabwe, a group of about 45 activists were arrested in February, merely for discussing events in North Africa. Six of them were initially charged with treason. In April, the Swaziland authorities repressed similar protests with excessive force.

Security forces used live ammunition against anti-government protesters in Angola, Burkina Faso, Guinea, Liberia, Malawi, Mauritania, Nigeria, Senegal, Sierra Leone and South Sudan, resulting in many casualties. The authorities usually failed to investigate the excessive use of force and nobody was held to account for the deaths caused.

Human rights defenders, journalists and political opponents in most African countries continued to be arbitrarily arrested and detained, beaten, threatened and intimidated. Some were killed by armed groups or government security forces. Investigations into the 2009 killing of human rights defender Ernest Manirumva in Burundi did not progress significantly. In June, five policemen were convicted for the 2010 killing of human rights activist Floribert Chebeya in the Democratic Republic of the Congo (DRC). However, concerns remained that some individuals allegedly involved in this crime had not been investigated.

Governments tried to control publicly available information in Burundi, the DRC, Equatorial Guinea, Ethiopia, Gambia, Guinea, Guinea-Bissau, Liberia, Madagascar, Somalia, Sudan and Uganda. They placed restrictions on reporting certain events, closed down or temporarily suspended radio stations, blocked specific websites or banned the publication of certain newspapers. Rwanda embarked on a process of reforms to enhance media freedom, but some media outlets that were closed by authorities in 2010 remained suspended. Two journalists were also sentenced to lengthy prison terms.

The national assemblies of Angola and South Africa debated legislation which could severely limit freedom of expression and access to information. On a more positive note, President Goodluck Jonathan finally signed the Freedom of Information Act into law in Nigeria.

Conflict

The political violence that erupted following Côte d'Ivoire's November 2010 presidential elections escalated into armed conflict during the first half of 2011. Forces loyal to Alassane Ouattara were supported by French troops and the UN peacekeeping mission. They took control of the country at the end of April and arrested former President Laurent Gbagbo and dozens of his supporters. Hundreds of thousands of people were displaced because of the conflict and many fled to neighbouring countries, particularly Liberia. Several thousand civilians were killed or injured in the economic capital, Abidjan, and in the western part of the country. Both parties to the conflict unlawfully killed hundreds of civilians in March and April in the western area of Duékoué and surrounding villages. People were targeted because of their ethnicity or their perceived political affiliation. The UN peacekeeping mission failed to adequately protect civilians in Duékoué. Forces on both sides also committed acts of sexual violence, including rape. In October, the International Criminal Court (ICC) authorized an investigation into war crimes and crimes against humanity committed by both parties to the conflict. After an arrest warrant was issued, Laurent Gbagbo was transferred to the ICC in the Netherlands in November. To preserve its credibility, the ICC should ensure that crimes committed by forces loyal to President Ouattara are also investigated and individuals prosecuted. The ICC should also investigate war crimes and crimes against humanity committed prior to the November 2010 presidential elections, as the judiciary in Côte d'Ivoire has as yet been unable or unwilling to do so.

The South Sudanese people voted overwhelmingly in favour of independence during the January referendum on self-determination. With South Sudan's independence date set for 9 July, tensions rose in

Security forces used live ammunition against anti-government protesters, resulting in many casualties.

the so-called transitional areas of Abyei, Southern Kordofan and Blue Nile. The envisaged separate referendum for Abyei did not take place as scheduled in January, and conflict erupted in May. The Sudanese Armed Forces (SAF), supported by militia, took control of Abyei, causing tens of thousands of people from the Dinka Ngok community to flee to South Sudan. Houses in Abyei town were looted and destroyed. Here too the UN peacekeeping mission, deployed in Abyei, failed to take any meaningful action to prevent the attacks and protect the civilian population. By the end of the year, no resolution had been found for the status of Abyei.

Following disagreements over security arrangements and the outcome of the state elections, the situation in Southern Kordofan escalated into armed conflict between the Sudan People's Liberation Movement-North (SPLM-N) and the SAF. Hundreds of thousands of people were displaced as a result of the insecurity and conflict. The SAF carried out indiscriminate aerial bombardments that resulted in numerous civilian casualties. The UN and various organizations including Amnesty International documented these indiscriminate attacks and unlawful killings. In one example, Angelo al-Sir, a farmer, described how his pregnant wife, two of their children and two other relatives were killed in an air strike on 19 June in Um Sirdeeba, a village east of Kadugli.

By September, the Southern Kordofan conflict spilled over into Blue Nile state, again causing tens of thousands of people to flee to South Sudan and Ethiopia. The Sudanese government essentially sealed off the Southern Kordofan and Blue Nile states from the outside world by denying access to independent humanitarian organizations, human rights monitors and other observers. The AU Peace and Security Council and the UN Security Council failed to take any concrete action to address the situation, including by not condemning the lack of humanitarian access or the ongoing human rights violations.

The conflict in Darfur, Sudan, also continued unabated, forcing more people to leave their homes. Those already living in camps for internally displaced people were targeted by the Sudanese authorities because they were perceived to be supporting armed opposition groups. Rape and other forms of sexual violence continued to be reported. Sudan still refused to co-operate with the ICC. The ICC Prosecutor requested an arrest warrant for the Minister of Defence, Abdelrahim Mohamed Hussein, for war crimes and crimes against humanity committed in Darfur.

Continued fighting in Somalia against the Islamist armed group al-Shabab took on a regional dimension when Kenyan and Ethiopian

Only very rarely were individuals held to account for committing human rights violations. As a result, people have lost confidence in law enforcement agencies and the judiciary in many countries in the region.

troops directly intervened in the conflict. Indiscriminate attacks by various parties to the conflict killed or injured thousands of civilians, mainly in Mogadishu. Hundreds of thousands of people remained displaced as a result of the conflict and insecurity. The drought in the sub-region compounded the already dire humanitarian situation, and a famine was declared in parts of Somalia. Humanitarian organizations faced immense difficulties in accessing people to provide them with emergency assistance.

No end was in sight either to the conflict in the eastern DRC. Rape and other forms of sexual violence remained endemic, and were committed both by government security forces and armed opposition groups. Other human rights abuses, such as unlawful killings, looting and abductions continued as well, primarily by armed groups. The DRC's justice system remained unable to deal with the many human rights violations committed during the conflict. Child soldiers continued to be recruited and used in various conflicts, such as in the Central African Republic, the DRC and Somalia.

Some African governments remained reluctant to ensure accountability for crimes under international law. Senegal continued to refuse to either prosecute or extradite the former Chadian President, Hissène Habré. At the end of the year, the Burundian government discussed a revised proposal for setting up a Truth and Reconciliation Commission. However, the government seemed to have insufficient political will to create a Special Tribunal, as recommended by the UN in 2005.

Justice and impunity

Many human rights violations committed by security and law enforcement forces remained unaddressed. The authorities hardly ever initiated independent and impartial investigations in reported cases of arbitrary arrests and detention; torture or other ill-treatment; unlawful killings, including extrajudicial executions; and enforced disappearances. Only very rarely were individuals held to account for committing human rights violations. As a result, people have lost confidence in law enforcement agencies and the judiciary in many countries in the region. High costs are another obstacle to accessing the formal justice system, including for people subjected to human rights violations.

Impunity for human rights violations by law enforcement officers was pervasive in Burundi, Cameroon, Republic of Congo, DRC, Eritrea, Ethiopia, Gambia, Guinea, Guinea-Bissau, Kenya, Madagascar, Malawi, Mozambique, Nigeria, Senegal, Sudan, Swaziland, Tanzania and Zimbabwe. For example, the commission of inquiry set up by the

Burundian authorities to investigate extrajudicial executions did not publish its findings. The Burundian authorities also failed to investigate allegations of torture committed by the National Intelligence Service in 2010. Another blatant example of institutionalized impunity was Sudan's rejection – during the Human Rights Council's Universal Periodic Review of Sudan in September – of recommendations to review its 2010 National Security Act and to reform the National Intelligence and Security Service (NISS). As a result, NISS agents continue to enjoy immunity from prosecution or disciplinary action for the human rights violations they have committed.

The number of people in pre-trial detention remained very high, as most countries' justice systems could not guarantee a fair trial without undue delay. Many people arrested had no access to legal representation. Detention conditions remained appalling in many countries, with overcrowding, a lack of access to basic sanitation facilities, health care, water or food, and a lack of prison staff. Detention conditions often fell below minimum international standards and constituted inhuman, cruel and degrading treatment or punishment. In one particularly gruesome incident, nine men died of asphyxiation caused by overcrowding during their detention in a National Gendarmerie facility in Léré, Chad, in September.

The trend towards abolition of the death penalty continued. Benin's parliament voted to ratify the Second Optional Protocol to the International Covenant on Civil and Political Rights, thereby confirming its intention to abolish the death penalty. In Ghana, the Constitutional Review Commission recommended that the death penalty be abolished. Nigeria's Attorney General and Minister of Justice informed an Amnesty International delegation in October that the government had introduced an official moratorium on executions. Sierra Leone's government had made a similar announcement in September. In contrast with these positive developments, Somalia, South Sudan and Sudan were among the last remaining countries in sub-Saharan Africa to still execute people – often after grossly unfair trials.

Marginalization

Refugees and migrants were particularly affected by human rights violations and abuses in many countries. Congolese nationals were again exposed to gender-based violence while being expelled from Angola. Mauritania arbitrarily arrested several thousand migrants before deporting them to neighbouring countries. Refugees and migrants were also subjected to human rights violations in Mozambique, including reported unlawful killings by law enforcement

Discrimination against people based on their perceived or real sexual orientation or gender identity worsened. Politicians often used statements or actions to incite discrimination and persecution based on perceived sexual orientation.

officials. In South Africa, refugees and migrants continued to experience violence and had their property destroyed. In December, UNHCR, the UN refugee agency, recommended that host countries take steps to terminate the refugee status of most Rwandans on their territory. Refugees and human rights organizations expressed concern about the extent to which the UNHCR had adequately articulated the rationale behind this recommendation, and also that its implementation by individual states could put large numbers of people still in need of protection at risk of being forcibly returned to Rwanda.

Tens of thousands of South Sudanese people decided to leave Sudan for South Sudan because they risked losing their Sudanese citizenship rights after South Sudan's declaration of independence. They faced numerous difficulties, including harassment before and during their journey and a dire humanitarian situation on arrival.

Violence and discrimination against women remained widespread in many countries, including as a result of cultural norms and traditions. Existing legislation institutionalizes discrimination against women in some countries. Discrimination also affected women's ability to access health care services.

Girls and women continued to be subjected to rape and other forms of sexual violence in various countries in conflict or with a large number of refugees or displaced people. These included eastern Chad, the Central African Republic, Côte d'Ivoire, eastern DRC and Sudan (Darfur). Members of government security forces were often responsible, and in most cases no investigations were carried out.

Discrimination

Discrimination against people based on their perceived or real sexual orientation or gender identity worsened. Politicians not only failed to protect people's right not to be discriminated against, but often used statements or actions to incite discrimination and persecution based on perceived sexual orientation.

In Cameroon, people believed to be in a same-sex relationship were persecuted. Scores were arrested and some, such as Jean-Claude Roger Mbede, were sentenced to lengthy prison terms. The Cameroonian government also proposed to amend the penal code to increase prison sentences and fines for people found guilty of same-sex sexual relations. In Malawi, Mauritania and Zimbabwe, men were also arrested and prosecuted because of their perceived sexual orientation. The government in Malawi enacted legislation to criminalize sexual relationships between women, and President Bingu wa Mutharika described gay men as "worse than dogs" at a political rally. In Nigeria, the Senate passed a bill further criminalizing same-sex relationships. In Ghana, the Western Region Minister called for all gay men and lesbians to be arrested.

Uganda's anti-homosexuality bill was not discussed in parliament, but it was not formally withdrawn either. David Kato, a prominent human rights defender and lesbian, gay, bisexual and transgender (LGBT) activist, was killed in January at his home. One man was arrested for the killing and sentenced to 30 years' imprisonment in November. In South Africa, civil society pressure to address violence against lesbians, gay men, bisexual and transgender people, in particular lesbian women, led to a Task Team being set up by the authorities to prevent violence based on perceived sexual orientation.

In Eritrea, people continued to be persecuted on religious grounds. Scores were arbitrarily arrested and believed to be ill-treated while in detention.

Security and human rights

Africa has become increasingly vulnerable to acts of terrorism from various Islamist armed groups. They include al-Qa'ida in the Islamic Maghreb (AQMI), which operated in various countries in the Sahel; the religious sect Boko Haram, which stepped up its bombing activities in Nigeria throughout the year; and al-Shabab, which is active in Kenya and Somalia. These armed groups were responsible for numerous human rights abuses, including indiscriminate attacks, unlawful killings, abductions and torture.

In response, some governments increased their military co-operation, including in the Sahel. Neighbouring countries also intervened militarily. Nigeria set up a Special Military Task Force to counter Boko Haram in some states. Government security forces were often responsible for human rights violations during their response to violence by armed groups. In Mauritania, 14 prisoners sentenced for terrorism activities were subjected to enforced disappearances during a transfer to an unknown location. In Nigeria, security forces responded to escalating violence in some states by arbitrarily arresting and detaining hundreds of people, subjecting people to enforced disappearance and carrying out extrajudicial executions.

Time to embrace change

Improved respect for and protection of human rights will probably not develop as quickly and dramatically in sub-Saharan Africa as in North Africa. In some places the situation might even get worse. However, factors such as sustained economic growth, demands for better governance, an emerging middle class, stronger civil society and improved access to information and communication technology will

The question is whether Africa's political leadership will embrace these changes or see them as a threat to their hold on power. In 2011, most political leaders – in their reactions to protests and dissent – were part of the problem, not the solution.

gradually contribute to a better human rights situation. The question is whether Africa's political leadership will embrace these changes or see them as a threat to their hold on power. In 2011, most political leaders – in their reactions to protests and dissent – were part of the problem, not the solution.

REGIONAL OVERVIEWS
AFRICA

"The struggle for justice doesn't end with me. This struggle is for all the Troy Davises who came before me and all the ones who will come after me."
Troy Davis, executed after spending 20 years on death row.

Martina Correia gazes towards the prison at the exact moment her brother, Troy Davis, was executed on 21 September in Georgia, USA, amid serious doubts about the reliability of his conviction. Two months later Martina Correia herself died, following a long illness.

AMERICAS

"An affront to democracy [and] an affront to the rule of law."

Brazilian State Deputy Marcelo Freixo, himself a victim of numerous death threats for
his work investigating and denouncing criminal gangs, speaking of the killing of Judge
Patrícia Acioli

On 11 August 2011, Judge Patrícia Acioli was shot 21 times outside
her home in Niterói, Rio de Janeiro state, Brazil, by members of the
Military Police. Her long track record of presiding over criminal cases
implicating Brazilian police officers in human rights violations had
made her a target of numerous death threats. In October, 11 police
officers, including a commanding officer, were detained and charged
with her killing. It was reported that, at the time of her death, Judge
Acioli had been presiding over the investigation into allegations of
extrajudicial executions and criminal activity by the policemen
involved. Her death was a serious blow to the human rights movement
in Brazil, but her tireless pursuit of justice remains an inspiration to
countless others who, like Judge Acioli, refuse to let human rights
violations go unchallenged.

The demand for human rights resounded throughout the region
during 2011 in the national courts, the Inter-American system and
on the streets. The calls for justice from individuals, human rights
defenders, civil society organizations and Indigenous Peoples
continued to gain strength, frequently bringing people into direct
confrontation with powerful economic and political interests. At
the heart of many of these conflicts were economic development
policies that left many, particularly those living in poverty and
marginalized communities, at increased risk of abuse and exploitation.

The demand for justice and an end to impunity

Many human rights cases made slow progress, obstructed by the
absence of meaningful access to justice, a lack of independence
in the judiciary, and a willingness among some sectors to resort to
extreme measures to avoid accountability and to protect vested
political, criminal and economic interests. Difficulty in pursuing

respect for rights was often exacerbated by threats against and killings of human rights defenders, witnesses, lawyers, prosecutors and judges in countries such as Brazil, Colombia, Cuba, Guatemala, Haiti, Honduras and Venezuela. Journalists trying to expose abuses of power, human rights violations and corruption were also frequently targeted in Latin America and the Caribbean.

In some countries, however, despite obstacles and frequent setbacks, there were significant advances in the investigation and prosecution of past human rights violations and a number of former de facto military rulers and senior commanders were convicted and sentenced to prison terms.

In Argentina, Reynaldo Bignone, a former army general, and Luis Abelardo Patti, a politician and former police officer, were both sentenced in April to life imprisonment for murder, abduction and torture carried out in the town of Escobar during the 1970s. In October, former navy captain Alfredo Astiz and 15 others were sentenced to prison terms of between 18 years and life for their role in 86 crimes against humanity during the 1970s. Their victims had been abducted and held at a secret detention centre in a Buenos Aires naval school (the Escuela Superior de Mecánica de la Armada, ESMA) where some died under torture while others were flung to their deaths from aeroplanes. Among those killed were French nuns Léonie Duquet and Alice Domon; human rights activists Azucena Villaflor, María Bianco and Esther Careaga, co-founders of the Mothers of the Plaza de Mayo; and writer and journalist Rodolfo Walsh.

In Bolivia, the Supreme Court convicted seven former high-ranking military and civilian officials in August for their part in the events known as "Black October", which left 67 people dead and more than 400 injured during protests in El Alto, near La Paz, in 2003. This was the first time that a trial of military officials accused of human rights violations had reached a conclusion in a Bolivian civilian court. Five former military officers received prison sentences ranging from 10 to 15 years, while two former ministers were sentenced to three years' imprisonment, later suspended.

In Brazil, President Rousseff signed into law the creation of a Truth Commission to investigate human rights violations committed between 1946 and 1988. And in Chile the number of cases of human rights violations under investigation by the courts rose to its highest level yet, after a court prosecutor submitted 726 new criminal complaints and more than 1,000 complaints filed over the years by relatives of people executed on political grounds during the military government of General Augusto Pinochet.

Navy captain Alfredo Astiz and 15 others were sentenced to prison terms of between 18 years and life for their role in 86 crimes against humanity during the 1970s.

Former President Jean-Claude Duvalier returned to Haiti after 25 years in exile to find himself the subject of a criminal investigation on the basis of complaints of serious human rights violations brought by victims and their relatives. In Colombia, retired general Jesús Armando Arias Cabrales was sentenced in April to 35 years in prison for his role in the enforced disappearance of 11 people in November 1985 after military forces stormed the Palace of Justice where people were being held hostage by members of the M-19 guerrilla group. In September, Jorge Noguera, former head of the Colombian civilian intelligence service (the Departamento Administrativo de Seguridad, DAS), was sentenced to 25 years in prison for the killing in 2004 of academic Alfredo Correa de Andreis and for his links to paramilitary groups.

Important though these cases were, they were the exception, and impunity for human rights violations remained the norm. For example, in Colombia another former DAS director, María del Pilar Hurtado, implicated in a scandal involving illegal wire-tapping and surveillance and threats targeting opponents of former President Alvaro Uribe, continued to evade justice. She had been granted asylum in Panama in 2010.

In Mexico, legal action against those responsible for grave human rights violations during the 1960s, 1970s and 1980s remained stalled. However, the Supreme Court ruled that Inter-American Court judgements against Mexico, including the requirement that alleged human rights violations by military personnel be transferred to civilian jurisdiction, were binding.

In the sphere of international justice, progress was uneven. For example, in October, the Canadian government failed to arrest former US President George W. Bush when he travelled to British Columbia, despite clear evidence that he was responsible for crimes under international law, including torture. However, in December, France extradited former de facto head of state Manuel Noriega to Panama where he had been convicted in his absence of the murder of political opponents, among other crimes.

The Inter-American human rights system

The Inter-American system, and in particular the Inter-American Commission on Human Rights, came under sustained attack from several states during 2011. For example, Brazil recalled its Ambassador to the OAS in reprisal for the Commission's ruling that work on the Belo Monte dam project should be suspended until Indigenous communities affected had been adequately consulted. Worryingly, the OAS Secretary General, José Miguel Insulza, openly supported Brazil's position and publicly called

Law enforcement practices in Brazil continued to be characterized by discrimination, human rights abuses, corruption and military-style policing.

on the Commission to review its decision in the Belo Monte case. Subsequently, the Inter-American Commission modified the precautionary measures issued in this case, no longer requiring Brazil to suspend the project pending consultation.

Ecuador, Peru and Venezuela also voiced criticisms of the Commission, accusing it of exceeding its mandate and interfering in their sovereign rights. Ecuador and Venezuela's criticisms focused on the Office of the Special Rapporteur for Freedom of Expression while Peru voiced serious criticism of the Commission's decision to refer a case related to alleged extrajudicial executions committed during the rescue of 71 hostages in 1997 (the "Chavín de Huántar" operation) to the Inter-American Court of Human Rights.

During the second half of 2011, OAS member states continued the debate over possible reforms of the Inter-American human rights system. This debate concluded with the issuing of a report that the OAS Permanent Council was due to consider in early 2012. Although the recommendations contained in the report were described as an effort to strengthen the system, in reality some of the measures proposed could have the effect of undermining its independence and effectiveness, and have a particularly serious impact on the work of the Commission and its rapporteurs.

There was evidence that in a number of cases the Dominican police had adopted a shoot-to-kill policy, rather than trying to arrest unarmed suspects.

Public security and human rights

Governments continued to exploit legitimate concerns regarding public security and high crime rates to justify or to ignore human rights violations committed by their security forces when responding to criminal activities or armed groups.

The Mexican government closed its eyes to widespread reports of torture, enforced disappearances, unlawful killings and excessive use of force by the army and, increasingly, by navy personnel, as it pursued its campaign against the drug cartels. More than 12,000 people were killed in violence attributed to criminal organizations and some 50,000 soldiers and navy marines continued to be deployed on law enforcement duties by President Felipe Calderón. There was evidence that members of the police and security forces colluded with criminal organizations in the abduction and killing of suspected members of other criminal organizations, among other crimes. The government continued to assert that abuses were exceptional and perpetrators were held to account, but in only one case were members of the military brought to justice during 2011.

On a lesser scale, a number of other countries in the region also used military personnel to carry out law enforcement duties. These included the Dominican Republic, El Salvador, Guatemala, Honduras and Venezuela, where President Hugo Chávez ordered National Guard troops onto the streets to tackle widespread violent crime.

In the face of high levels of violent crime, law enforcement practices in Brazil continued to be characterized by discrimination, human rights abuses, corruption and military-style policing operations. While certain public security projects achieved limited success in reducing levels of violence, federal government public security reforms were undermined by severe budget cuts and a lack of political will. Socially excluded communities continued to be caught between violent criminal gangs and abusive policing that often resulted in residents being treated as criminal suspects. In Rio de Janeiro the power of the *milícias* (militias) continued to grow. These criminal gangs, made up of active and former law enforcement agents, increased their hold on many of the poorest communities of Rio de Janeiro through violence and extortion, sustained by illicit financial activity and the creation of political power bases. The attack on Judge Acioli underlined the reach and confidence of these criminal gangs.

In the Dominican Republic, serious human rights violations, including arbitrary detentions, torture and other cruel and inhuman or degrading treatment, unlawful killings and disappearances, were committed by the police implementing a so-called "hard line policy" in fighting crime. There was evidence that in a number of cases the police had adopted a shoot-to-kill policy, rather than trying to arrest suspects, many of whom were unarmed.

Armed conflict

The long-running internal armed conflict in Colombia continued to inflict untold misery on civilian communities across the country. The human rights consequences of the fighting were particularly acute for rural Indigenous Peoples and Afro-descendent and peasant farmer communities, thousands of whom were forced to flee their homes. Guerrilla groups, as well as paramilitaries and the security forces sometimes acting in collusion, were all responsible for serious human rights abuses and violations of international humanitarian law.

Some of the administration's legislative measures, such as the Victims and Land Restitution Law, were important first steps in efforts to acknowledge the rights to reparation of some victims and to return some of the millions of hectares of land stolen during the course of the conflict. However, the Law excluded many victims and a surge in threats and killings targeting human rights defenders, especially those working on land restitution, raised doubts about the government's ability to make good on its promise to return land to the rightful owners.

The long-running internal armed conflict in Colombia continued to inflict untold misery on civilian communities across the country.

The Colombian administration's commitment to human rights and the fight against impunity was called into question by efforts to broaden military jurisdiction, which could allow members of the security forces to evade justice for human rights violations. President Juan Manuel Santos and the Commander in Chief of the Armed Forces also criticized the conviction of several senior military officers for human rights violations.

Counter-terror and security

At the end of 2011, nearly two years after US President Barack Obama's missed deadline to close the Guantánamo detention facility, more than 150 men were still held there.

Hopes that the US administration would follow through on its decision, announced in 2009, to bring five detainees accused of involvement in the attacks of 11 September 2001 to trial in ordinary federal courts were dashed when the Attorney General announced in April that the five would now be tried by military commission. The administration made clear its intention to seek death sentences against these five. In another military commission case, the death penalty came a step closer in September when the charges against Saudi Arabian national 'Abd al Rahim al-Nashiri were referred on for trial as capital offences.

Impunity continued for human rights violations committed under the previous administration as part of the CIA's programme of secret detention. In June, the Attorney General announced that, with the exception of two cases involving deaths in custody, no further investigations into the detentions were warranted. This despite the fact that torture and enforced disappearance were an integral part of the secret programme and that victims included the detainees currently facing unfair trial by military commission who, if convicted, could be executed.

Indigenous Peoples

Human rights violations against Indigenous Peoples remained a serious concern despite some positive advances in the region.

In many cases, Indigenous Peoples were denied their right to meaningful consultation and free, prior and informed consent over large-scale development projects, including extractive industry projects, affecting them. Peru passed a landmark law in 2011 making it mandatory to hold consultations with Indigenous Peoples before development projects can go ahead on their ancestral lands. However, this remained the exception. Despite the fact that all states in the region had endorsed the 2007 UN Declaration on the Rights of

Nearly two years after US President Barack Obama's deadline to close the Guantánamo detention facility, more than 150 men were still held there.

Indigenous Peoples, the rights it sets out were still far from being respected.

The failure to respect the rights of Indigenous Peoples had a negative impact not only on livelihoods, but also resulted in communities being threatened, harassed, forcibly evicted or displaced, attacked or killed as the drive to exploit resources intensified in the areas where they live. In Brazil, Colombia, Guatemala and Mexico, Indigenous Peoples were forced off their lands, often violently. Excessive use of force against those demonstrating for Indigenous Peoples' rights and against development projects was reported in Peru and Bolivia. Spurious charges against Indigenous leaders were a concern in Ecuador and Mexico.

There were further signs that governments were not taking Indigenous Peoples' rights seriously or showing the political will to roll back decades of entrenched discrimination. In April, the Inter-American Commission on Human Rights urged Brazil to suspend the construction of the Belo Monte dam until Indigenous communities had been fully and effectively consulted – including by having access to a social and environmental impact assessment of the project in appropriate languages – and until measures had been put in place to protect the lives of communities in voluntary isolation. Brazil argued fiercely against these precautionary measures, which were subsequently weakened by the Commission.

In Bolivia, after several weeks of protests during which scores of people were injured when the security forces used tear gas and truncheons to break up a makeshift camp, the President decided to cancel the building of a road through the Isiboro-Sécure Indigenous Territory and National Park. Indigenous protesters argued that the road had been planned in breach of constitutional guarantees on prior consultation and of environmental preservation laws.

In August, a Canadian federal audit concluded that 39 per cent of water systems in First Nations communities had major deficiencies, with 73 per cent of drinking water systems and 65 per cent of waste water systems constituting medium or high risks to health.

The rights of women and girls

States in the region failed to put the protection of women and girls from rape, threats and killings at the forefront of their political agendas. Implementation of legislation to combat gender-based violence remained a serious concern and the lack of resources available to investigate and prosecute these crimes raised questions about official willingness to address the issue. The failure to bring to justice those responsible for these crimes further entrenched impunity for gender-

In Brazil, Colombia, Guatemala, and Mexico, Indigenous Peoples were forced off their lands, often violently.

based violence in many countries and helped foster a climate where violence against women and girls was tolerated.

Violations of women's and girls' sexual and reproductive rights remained rife, with appalling consequences for their lives and health. Chile, El Salvador and Nicaragua continued to ban abortion in all circumstances, including for girls and women pregnant as a result of rape or who experience life-threatening complications in their pregnancies. Those seeking or providing an abortion risked lengthy imprisonment.

In other countries, access to safe abortion services was granted in law, but denied in practice by protracted judicial procedures that made access to safe abortion almost impossible, especially for those who could not afford to pay for private abortion services. Access to contraception and information on sexual and reproductive issues remained a concern, particularly for the most marginalized women and girls in the region.

Migrants: visible victims, invisible rights

Hundreds of thousands of regular and irregular migrants in a number of countries were denied the protection of the law.

In Mexico, hundreds of bodies, some identified as kidnapped migrants, were discovered in clandestine graves. The families of Central American disappeared migrants, carried out nationwide marches to press for action to locate their relatives and highlight the fate of many migrants. Central American migrants travelling through Mexico in their tens of thousands were kidnapped, tortured, raped and killed by criminal gangs, often with the complicity of public officials. In the case of irregular migrants, fear of reprisals or deportation meant they were rarely able to report the serious abuses they experienced.

Migrants' rights defenders came under unprecedented attack in Mexico, especially those working at the network of shelters providing humanitarian assistance to migrants.

In the USA, along its south-western border with Mexico, regular and irregular migrants suffered discrimination and profiling by federal, state, and local law enforcement officials. They faced discrimination when attempting to access justice and protection and encountered barriers to education and health care. Such barriers included policies to single out migrants for extra scrutiny, and the threat of being reported to the immigration authorities. Proposals for new anti-immigrant laws forced some students to drop out of school for fear their parents might be arrested. Anti-immigrant legislation in Georgia, Indiana, South Carolina and Utah faced legal challenges in federal courts.

The families of disappeared migrants carried out nationwide marches to press for action to locate their relatives.

In the Dominican Republic, regular and irregular Haitian migrants were victims of human rights violations, including mass and violent illegal deportations in which Dominicans of Haitian descent continued to be denied their right to Dominican nationality. Beatings and the separation of children from their parents were reported during deportations. Several states, including the Bahamas, failed to heed the UN's calls to stop deportations to Haiti on humanitarian grounds, given the continuing humanitarian crisis in Haiti triggered by the earthquake and cholera outbreak of 2010.

Death penalty

Forty-three prisoners were executed in the USA during the year, all by lethal injection. This brought to 1,277 the total number of executions carried out since the US Supreme Court lifted a moratorium on the death penalty in 1976. On a more positive note, however, in March, Illinois became the 16th abolitionist state in the USA and in November, the Governor of Oregon imposed a moratorium on executions in the state and called for a rethink on the death penalty.

Among those put to death in 2011 was Troy Davis. He was executed in Georgia in September, despite serious doubts about the reliability of his conviction. Martina Correia, his sister and a determined and fearless campaigner against the death penalty right up to her own death in December 2011, remains an inspiration to the many speaking out for human dignity and justice throughout the region and beyond: "The death penalty is an abomination. A denial of human dignity. It's not just based on colour and race but on ability to fight the system. I try to be a voice for the voiceless. I don't think I'm a special person, I just believe that my community doesn't only mean the people who live on my street – it means my global community. And when someone is killed in China or Uganda or Nigeria or Georgia or Texas, it kills a little of us."

Su Su Nway, a labour rights activist, arrives at Yangon airport, Myanmar, 16 October 2011. She was originally sentenced to 12 years and six months' imprisonment but was released after the government granted an amnesty to around 240 political prisoners on 12 October 2011.

ASIA-PACIFIC

"It's time, people of China! It's time.
China belongs to everyone.
Of your own will
It's time to choose what China shall be."

Zhu Yufu, Chinese dissident

As winds of political change blew in from the Middle East and North Africa, several governments in the Asia-Pacific region responded by increasing their efforts to retain power by repressing demands for human rights and dignity. At the same time, the success of uprisings in Tunisia and Egypt inspired human rights defenders, activists, and journalists in Asia to raise their own voices, using a combination of new technologies and old-fashioned activism to challenge violations of their rights.

Zhu Yufu, the author of the poem cited above, was detained by Chinese authorities in March. The prosecutor cited this poem as key evidence in support of the charge of "inciting subversion of state power". Zhu Yufu, who had already spent nearly nine of the last 13 years in prison for demanding greater political freedom, was just one of dozens of critics, activists, and dissidents detained and harassed by the Chinese authorities after February in what has been one of the worst political crackdowns since the Tiananmen Square protests of 1989. In addition to Zhu Yufu, the long list of those detained, placed under illegal house arrest or subjected to enforced disappearance included Liu Xia, wife of Nobel Peace Prize winner Liu Xiaobo, lawyer Gao Zhisheng and Ai Weiwei, the globally renowned artist. In several cases, Chinese authorities tortured detainees to extract "confessions" and promises to avoid using social media or speaking to journalists or others about their mistreatment.

The harshness of the crackdown was an indicator of just how worried the Chinese government was about the anonymous "Jasmine" online messages that began circulating in February, calling for Chinese citizens who were fed up with corruption, poor governance and political repression to gather peacefully and simply walk around designated areas in selected cities. As innocuous as these calls were, the Chinese government responded by banning internet searches for the words "jasmine" and "Egypt" at various points in the year. Nevertheless, tens of thousands of demonstrations occurred throughout the country as Chinese protesters sought to protect their human rights – civil, political, economic, social and cultural.

The dynamism of Chinese citizens invoking their rights contrasted with the situation in neighbouring Democratic People's Republic of Korea (North Korea), where there were no indications of an improvement in the country's horrific human rights situation after Kim Jong-un, in his late twenties, succeeded his father as absolute ruler of the country on 17 December. If anything, there were signs that the authorities had detained officials suspected of potentially challenging or questioning a smooth transition, and there were concerns that those detained would be sent to join the hundreds of thousands already suffering arbitrary detention, forced labour, public execution and torture and other ill-treatment in the country's numerous political prison camps.

Repression of dissent

Few governments in the region were as brutal as the North Korean regime in repressing the voices of their own people, but violations of the right to freely express and receive opinions continued throughout the region. Several governments deliberately crushed dissenting views. In North Korea, those deviating from official ideology could end up spending the rest their lives in a bleak and remote political prison camp. Both Viet Nam and Myanmar have criminalized free expression of dissenting views, and have intelligence agencies that are dedicated to intimidating and silencing critics.

Other countries also muzzled critics, although they relied on less overtly violent means. Continuing to hold itself as an exception to international standards on the protection of freedom of speech, Singapore briefly jailed 76-year-old British author Alan Shadrake on 1 June, having charged him with contempt of court after he criticized the judiciary for imposing the death penalty.

In India, which boasts a proud history of free speech and a vibrant media, the government sought to impose new restrictions on social media including instant messaging services. Internet media also remained under pressure in Malaysia, although it was slightly less fettered than the country's heavily censored print and broadcast media.

In Thailand, the newly elected government of Yingluck Shinawatra (sister of former Prime Minister Thaksin Shinawatra) did not put a stop

Success of uprisings in Tunisia and Egypt inspired human rights defenders, activists, and journalists in Asia to raise their own voices, using a combination of new technologies and old-fashioned activism to challenge violations of their rights.

to the aggressive enforcement of the highly problematic lèse majesté law, which prohibits any criticism of the royal family. Many of those who were targeted had posted material on the internet which prosecutors had found objectionable, or, in the case of a 61-year-old grandfather, Ampon Tangnoppakul, had allegedly sent text messages deemed offensive, earning a 20-year prison sentence.

Authorities in the Republic of Korea (South Korea) increasingly invoked the National Security Law to harass those perceived as opposing the government's policy on North Korea. At times, this resulted in absurd applications of the Law, as in the case of Park Jeonggeun, who faced detention and criminal prosecution for posting satirical snippets of North Korean propaganda.

Other critics demanding human rights and dignity in the region provoked more severe responses and, at times, paid the ultimate price for raising their voices. Pakistani journalists managed to maintain a boisterous and at times fractious media environment in the country despite a violent backlash from the government as well as from political parties and insurgent groups such as the Pakistani Taleban. At least nine journalists were killed during the year, including Saleem Shahzad, an online journalist who had openly criticized the country's powerful military and intelligence agencies. Other journalists told Amnesty International that they had been seriously threatened by the country's powerful and shadowy intelligence agencies, security forces, political parties or militant groups.

Journalists were not alone in being attacked for their opinions in Pakistan. Two high-profile politicians were assassinated for challenging the use of the highly problematic blasphemy laws: Salman Taseer, the outspoken Governor of Punjab, and Shahbaz Bhatti, Minister for Minorities (and sole Christian cabinet member).

Minority groups

Pakistan, like many other countries in the Asia-Pacific region, witnessed ongoing and serious discrimination against religious and ethnic minorities. Members of minority groups were often marginalized and in many instances were the victims of direct government harassment. In numerous cases, governments failed to uphold their responsibility to protect the rights of members of minority groups. This entrenched discrimination, aggravated poverty, slowed down overall development, and in many countries, stoked violence.

In Pakistan's resource-rich Balochistan province, security forces as well as some insurgent groups were implicated in violations, including enforced disappearances, torture and extrajudicial executions. The government did not follow through on all its promises

In North Korea, those deviating from official ideology could end up spending the rest their lives in a bleak and remote political prison camp.

to address the long-standing grievances of the Baloch community relating to distribution of income from major extractive and infrastructure projects. The province also witnessed several brutal attacks on Pakistan's Shi'a community, especially Shi'a Hazaras, many of them of Afghan origin living in Balochistan's capital, Quetta. Militant religious groups openly called for violence against the Shi'a and were allowed to operate and carry out acts of violence, such as the execution-style killing of 26 Shi'a pilgrims on 20 September. Pakistani militant groups claimed responsibility for attacks on the Shi'a even in Afghanistan, where twin bomb blasts in December killed some 70 Shi'as participating in the Ashura religious processions in Kabul and Mazar-e Sharif.

The Ahmadiyya community, a religious group mainly based in Asia that consider themselves to be adherents of Islam, faced systematic discrimination in Pakistan and Indonesia. In Pakistan, where Ahmadis are legally barred from declaring themselves Muslims, the Ahmadiyya community experienced ongoing harassment from government officials, and without sufficient protection or support, were targeted by militant religious groups. In Indonesia, the police were criticized for failing to stop a 1,500-person mob from attacking the Ahmadiyya community in the sub-district of Cikeusik in February, killing three and injuring many more. The central government allowed local regulations restricting Ahmadiyya activities to remain in force. Ahmadis in other Muslim-majority countries in the Asia-Pacific region, such as Bangladesh and Malaysia, also suffered from discrimination for their religious beliefs, with their children barred from some schools and their right to worship freely under severe constraints.

Sunni Muslims were victims of discrimination in China: the Uighur population, predominantly Muslim and ethnically distinct, continued to face repression and discrimination in the Xinjiang Uighur Autonomous Region. The Chinese government invoked the nebulous threat of terrorism and insurgency to repress civil and political rights and interfere with the religious practices of the Uighurs, while the influx of Han Chinese migrants and discrimination in their favour has rendered Uighurs second-class citizens in terms of cultural, economic and social achievement.

Other ethnic minorities in China also fared poorly. At least a dozen Tibetan nuns and monks or former monks set themselves on fire (six of them are believed to have died) in protest against the restrictions imposed on religious and cultural practices – restrictions that have heightened Tibetans' sense of alienation and deepened their grievances. In Inner Mongolia, too, ethnic tensions were high.

In Indonesia, the police were criticized for failing to stop a 1,500-person mob from attacking the Ahmadiyya community in February, killing three and injuring many more.

Widespread protests erupted across the region after a Han Chinese coal truck driver allegedly murdered an ethnic Mongolian herder.

Armed conflicts and insurgencies

Ethnic and religious discrimination and the resulting political and economic grievances were behind many of the multiple armed conflicts and long-running insurgencies that afflicted hundreds of thousands of people in the region.

The decades-old conflicts between the government of Myanmar and various ethnic armed groups flared up again significantly. Government forces fought against Karen, Shan and Kachin insurgents, displacing tens of thousands of civilians and committing human rights violations and violations of international humanitarian law that amounted to crimes against humanity or war crimes.

The Taleban and other insurgent groups in Afghanistan engaged in widespread and systematic attacks on civilians, causing 77 per cent of civilian casualties in the conflict, according to the UN. Amnesty International renewed its call for the International Criminal Court (ICC) to investigate the situation, even as international forces assisting the Afghan government began to transfer responsibility for security to Afghan government forces. Many Afghan civil society groups, and in particular women's groups, voiced concerns about being excluded from negotiations with insurgent groups, despite UN Security Council Resolution 1325, which calls for women to be meaningfully and adequately represented during peace talks.

Lower intensity conflicts continued on Mindanao island in the Philippines, as well as in southern Thailand – both areas where Muslim minority populations were historically disenfranchised and had to contend with poor economic development. There was room for hope in the Philippines, as the parties seemed to pursue peace despite a brief outbreak of violence. But in southern Thailand the situation defied easy answers as insurgents continued to target civilians with the intention of intimidating the local population and displacing Buddhists and others perceived as loyal to the central government. Thailand's central government did not meet commitments to provide accountability for violations committed by security forces, nor to provide a strategic and sustainable response to demands for greater political and economic development in the area.

Relatively low economic development, particularly for tribal Adivasi communities, and poor governance, fuelled insurgencies in several of

The decades-old conflicts between the government of Myanmar and various ethnic armed groups flared up again significantly. Government forces fought insurgents, displacing tens of thousands of civilians and committing violations that amounted to war crimes.

India's central and eastern states. Clashes between Maoist insurgents and security forces killed some 250 people. The insurgents resorted to hostage taking and indiscriminate attacks, while government forces routinely violated the rights of the local populations they were ostensibly protecting. Recognizing the problematic nature of the government's strategy, India's Supreme Court ordered the disbandment of Chhattisgarh's state-sponsored paramilitary groups allegedly responsible for serious human rights violations. The Indian Supreme Court also allowed prisoner of conscience Dr Binayak Sen to be released on bail while he appeals against his life sentence. In 2010, a Chhattisgarh district court sentenced him to life after convicting him on charges of sedition and collaborating with armed Maoists.

Indian forces in Jammu and Kashmir again came under criticism for violating human rights. Amnesty International released a report in March that focused on the misuse of administrative detentions under the Public Safety Act (PSA), prompting the state government to promise the PSA's reform. In September, the state human rights commission identified over 2,700 unmarked graves and identified 574 bodies as those of disappeared locals, belying the security forces' claim that they were militants. The human rights commission's request that the state use modern forensic testing to identify the other remains went unheeded.

Accountability and justice

Impunity for past violations haunted many countries in the region, particularly those grappling with the legacy of conflicts. The failure to provide justice complicated reconciliation efforts and often established a pattern of injustice and lack of accountability for security forces.

Sri Lanka's decades-long record of faulty special commissions to address major human rights violations continued with the work of the Lessons Learned and Reconciliation Commission (LLRC). The LLRC completed its mandate with a report that included some useful suggestions for improving the country's human rights situation, but failed to properly investigate the role of government forces in the attacks on thousands of civilians during the final stages of the conflict against the Liberation Tigers of Tamil Eelam. The LLRC's conclusions in this regard were the outcome of a deeply flawed process, and stood in contrast to the findings of the UN Secretary-General's Panel of Experts on Accountability in Sri Lanka, which concluded that there were credible allegations that war crimes and crimes against humanity had been committed by both sides. The Panel of Experts recommended establishing an independent

Impunity for past violations haunted many countries in the region, particularly those grappling with the legacy of conflicts. The failure to provide justice complicated reconciliation efforts and often established a pattern of injustice and lack of accountability for security forces.

investigation into the allegations of violations by all sides to the conflict, as well as a review of UN actions during the conflict in Sri Lanka.

The failure to provide justice helped foster a climate of impunity that saw new cases of enforced disappearances in the north and east of the island, as well as threats and attacks on journalists, critics and activists. Although the government repealed the State of Emergency, it retained the repressive Prevention of Terrorism Act and even added new regulations that allowed for suspects to be detained without charge or trial.

Cambodia's accountability process for crimes committed during the Khmer Rouge period was also compromised by government interference, as one case was closed without a full investigation and another stalled. And in Afghanistan, individuals facing credible allegations of responsibility for war crimes and crimes against humanity continued to hold senior government posts.

While those accused of human rights violations evaded accountability, many governments used flogging to punish alleged wrongdoers – a violation of the international prohibition of cruel, inhuman and degrading punishment. Singapore and Malaysia continued to impose caning for a variety of offences, including immigration violations. The Indonesian province of Aceh increasingly used caning as a punishment for various offences, including drinking alcohol, gambling, and being alone with someone of the opposite sex who is not a marriage partner or relative. And in the Maldives, the government retained the punishment of caning under pressure from its political opposition.

Migrants and refugees

Insecurity, natural disasters, poverty, and lack of suitable opportunities drove hundreds of thousands of people to seek better lives elsewhere, within the region as well as outside. While many governments in the region rely on migrant labour as a matter of basic economic necessity, many governments still fell short of protecting the rights of people who were seeking work or shelter.

At least 300,000 Nepalis migrated abroad to avoid poverty and the legacy of a long conflict. Many of them were deceived about the conditions of their employment and worked in conditions that amounted to forced labour. Although the Nepalese government put in place some laws and redress mechanisms to protect its migrant workers, Amnesty International's research documented that these measures were not properly implemented due to low public awareness and poor monitoring and prosecution of wrongdoers.

Insecurity, natural disasters, poverty, and lack of suitable opportunities drove hundreds of thousands of people to seek better lives elsewhere.

Malaysia served as a major receiving country for regional migrants, as well as a staging ground for asylum-seekers on their way to Australia. Undocumented migrants in Malaysia were often detained and imprisoned or caned. Poor detention conditions led to riots by detained migrants at the Lenggeng facility near Kuala Lumpur in April. Australia's High Court invalidated a bilateral agreement between Australia and Malaysia to "swap" 800 asylum-seekers who arrived by boat in Australia with 4,000 refugees (predominantly from Myanmar) who were in Malaysia awaiting resettlement, citing inadequate legal guarantees for refugees in Malaysia.

Steps forward

Despite serious obstacles, many human rights defenders and activists in the Asia-Pacific region were able to navigate their way towards greater respect for their rights, with success in one country serving as inspiration and encouragement in others.

In India, the Adivasi communities of Orissa gained a victory in July in their struggle to defend their way of life when the Orissa High Court found that Vedanta Aluminium's bid to expand its refinery violated the communities' rights to water, health and a healthy environment, and that the expansion would perpetrate further abuses against Adivasi communities.

Malaysia's Prime Minister announced in September that he would seek to repeal the Internal Security Act, which among other things allows for indefinite detention without charge or trial, and replace it with new security laws. The move came at least in partial reaction to the Bersih 2.0 ("Clean") movement, which saw thousands of peaceful protesters marching in Kuala Lumpur in July. The police beat protesters, fired tear-gas canisters directly into the crowds and arrested more than 1,600 people.

In March, Malaysia announced that it had signed the Rome Statute of the ICC and would seek to ratify the treaty. The Philippines ratified the Rome Statute in November.

Perhaps the most significant potential advance in terms of the region's human rights situation was the decision by the authorities in Myanmar to free more than 300 political prisoners during the year and to allow Aung San Suu Kyi to contest parliamentary elections. The authorities continued to harass and detain some dissidents and opposition activists, raising concerns that their main intention was to loosen the sanctions imposed on the country rather than to bring about genuine change. But as events in Myanmar and elsewhere have shown, it is through such

> Perhaps the most significant potential advance in terms of the region's human rights situation was the decision by the authorities in Myanmar to free more than 300 political prisoners during the year.

narrow openings that political activists and human rights defenders can make their voices heard and decide what their future will be.

REGIONAL OVERVIEWS ASIA-PACIFIC

Policemen ill-treating a political activist during a protest in Baku, Azerbaijan, 12 March 2011. A ban on demonstrations effectively criminalized protests in March and April and led to the imprisonment of many of those who organized and took part in them.

EUROPE AND CENTRAL ASIA

"I am very happy to be released. I am extremely grateful to Amnesty International, who have campaigned since the beginning. In my opinion you saved me. Thank you to all those who tweeted."

Journalist and prisoner of conscience Eynulla Fatullayev in Baku, Azerbaijan

Early one spring morning in a small village in Serbia, one of Europe's biggest manhunts came to an end. General Ratko Mladić, wanted among other things for the murder of 8,000 men and boys in Srebrenica, was finally set to face justice. Two months later Croatian Serb Goran Hadžić, the last remaining suspect wanted by the International Criminal Tribunal for the former Yugoslavia, was also detained in Serbia and subsequently transferred to The Hague.

These were landmark steps for the victims of the horrific crimes of the 1990s wars in former Yugoslavia. The long-overdue arrests held out hope for the survivors that they would finally receive the truth, justice and redress. Many, many more across the region, however, were still waiting for their own chance to see justice done, not delayed.

Freedom of expression

In a marked contrast to the hope and change unleashed across the Arab world, autocratic regimes in a number of the successor states to the Soviet Union strengthened their grip on power. They crushed protest, arrested opposition leaders and silenced dissenting voices. For many, the hope that accompanied the collapse of the Soviet Union 20 years ago must have seemed a distant memory.

In Belarus, protests following the alleged vote-rigging in 2010 were banned or dispersed, hundreds of protesters were arrested and fined and even more draconian restrictions on the freedom of assembly were introduced. Critical human rights NGOs were also targeted. In Azerbaijan, anti-government demonstrations were effectively outlawed, and attempts by a small number of government critics prompted a fresh wave of repression and intimidation. The demonstrations planned for March and April, to protest against corruption and call for greater civil and political freedoms, were unreasonably banned then violently dispersed despite their peaceful nature. As in Belarus, critical NGOs and reporters also felt the backlash, with five human rights organizations closed down and several journalists reporting instances of intimidation and harassment in the immediate aftermath of the protests.

In Central Asia, Turkmenistan and Uzbekistan continued to severely restrict the rights to freedom of expression and association. Genuine opposition political parties continued to be denied registration, and social activists were rarely able to operate openly. Critical journalists and human rights defenders were routinely monitored and risked beatings, detention and unfair trials. In Tajikistan, Kazakhstan and Kyrgyzstan there were unfair trials and cases of harassment for government critics and those who exposed abuses by public officials.

The picture in Russia was mixed. As elsewhere in the region, human rights defenders and journalists were harassed, intimidated and beaten for exposing abuses. Anti-government demonstrations were frequently banned and their organizers and participants subjected to short periods of detention or fined. Typically for the region, most mainstream media and TV outlets remained under the strong influence of national and local authorities. Despite this, civic activism continued to grow, with a variety of causes garnering widespread popular support – including the environment and combating abuses by public officials. The internet remained relatively uncontrolled by the authorities and grew in importance as a rival source of information and forum for the exchange of opinion.

Against this backdrop, the largest demonstrations seen in Russia since the collapse of the Soviet Union took place in December, sparked by widespread allegations, and numerous recorded instances, of electoral fraud in the parliamentary elections that returned Prime Minister Vladimir Putin's United Russia party to power with a significantly reduced share of the vote. Initial spontaneous demonstrations across Russia in the days immediately following the elections were routinely dispersed, with hundreds being sentenced to short periods of detention or fined. Demonstrations planned in Moscow in subsequent weeks became too big to ban – and passed off peacefully.

In Turkey, critical journalists, Kurdish political activists, and others risked unfair prosecution when speaking out on the situation of Kurds in Turkey, or criticizing the armed forces. Threats of violence against prominent outspoken individuals continued and in November new regulations came into force raising further concerns regarding the arbitrary restriction of websites.

In Azerbaijan, anti-government demonstrations were effectively outlawed, and attempts by a small number of government critics prompted a fresh wave of repression and intimidation.

People on the move

Against the backdrop of political turmoil in North Africa and the Middle East, thousands of refugees and migrants attempted the dangerous sea crossing to Europe in search of safety and a secure future, often in overcrowded and un-seaworthy vessels. According to conservative estimates, at least 1,500 people, including pregnant women and children drowned while attempting this journey. Rather than taking measures to prevent such deaths at sea, including by increasing search and rescue operations, the EU's response was to boost the ability of its external border agency, Frontex, to deter arrivals in Europe via the Mediterranean. There were reports that NATO failed to rescue people in distress at sea, despite the fact that the prevention of civilian casualties was being advanced as the primary justification for military intervention in Libya.

Those who survived the crossing often found Europe less than welcoming. Instead of a humanitarian response to a humanitarian crisis, the signature response of European states remained an approach focusing on policing borders and controlling migration flows.

Thousands of those who made it onto the Italian island of Lampedusa endured appalling reception conditions, the result of a failure on the part of the Italian authorities to respond to the growing number of arrivals.

New arrivals on the island were often left stranded, with many of them having to sleep rough with limited or no access to sanitary and washing facilities. Nor was arriving on European shores a guarantee of protection: in April, following an agreement between the Italian government and the Tunisian authorities, Italy began summary and collective expulsions of Tunisians back to Tunisia.

Many European countries, including France and the UK, refused to resettle any refugees displaced by the armed conflict in Libya, despite having been parties to that conflict under the aegis of NATO.

Across the region, states continued to violate human rights through the interception, detention and expulsion of foreign nationals, including those eligible for international protection. Detention as a tool of deterrence and control was a widespread, rather than a last, legitimate, resort.

Asylum systems frequently failed those seeking protection, including because of the resort to expedited asylum determination procedures in countries such as Finland, France, Germany, the Netherlands, Sweden, Switzerland and the UK that offered inadequate safeguards against the risk of individuals being sent back to places where they faced human rights abuses. People were returned from Turkey and Ukraine without even being able to access the asylum systems there.

REGIONAL OVERVIEWS
EUROPE AND CENTRAL ASIA

Detention as a tool of deterrence and control was a widespread, rather than a last, legitimate, resort.

Following a landmark ruling in January by the Grand Chamber of the European Court of Human Rights in the case *M.S.S. v Belgium and Greece*, European states suspended the return of asylum-seekers to Greece under the Dublin II Regulation due to the country's lack of a functioning asylum system. However, some states continued to send people back to countries such as Iraq and Eritrea, contrary to the advice of UNHCR, the UN refugee agency, and to forcibly return Roma to Kosovo despite the real risk of persecution and discrimination there.

Across the region, hundreds of thousands of people remained displaced by the conflicts that accompanied the collapse of the former Yugoslavia and the Soviet Union, often unable to return owing to their legal status – or lack of it – and discrimination in access to rights including property tenure.

While negotiating new EU asylum legislation, EU member states failed to address deficiencies in their asylum systems and in arrangements for transferring asylum-seekers back to the first EU country which they had entered.

Instead of counteracting stereotypes and prejudices that fuel intolerance and hatred, some governments and public officials actually strengthened them.

Discrimination

Although discrimination continued to affect the lives of millions of people across the region, governments failed to prioritize policies to combat it, citing other urgent needs. They quoted economic factors, in spite of many pointers that those already marginalized faced an increased risk of having the inequalities they already experienced further entrenched. Or they simply sought to walk away from their obligations, like the Dutch government, which publicly stated in July that it was the primary responsibility of citizens to free themselves from discrimination.

Instead of counteracting stereotypes and prejudices that fuel intolerance and hatred, some governments and public officials actually strengthened them. The equality body in Romania twice warned the President about anti-Roma statements on TV.

Gaps in both domestic and European anti-discrimination legislation persisted. In some cases the opportunity to bridge them was lost by reluctant public authorities or governmental coalitions concerned that offering enhanced protection might stir up political opposition. The inclusion of sexual orientation as a prohibited ground in a new anti-discrimination bill in Moldova was criticized, leading to a stalemate in its adoption. A new anti-discrimination bill in Spain failed to be adopted before the parliamentary elections in November. At the European level, the Council of the European Union pursued its discussion on the proposal for new EU-wide anti-discrimination legislation, proposed in 2008, although participants showed more interest in watering down the proposals or shelving it. In addition, existing legislation, such as the Race Directive or the Charter of Fundamental Rights, was not enforced by the European Commission, despite continuing breaches by member states.

Domestic and regional anti-discrimination standards were sometimes publicly criticized and had their legitimacy questioned. The European Court of Human Rights had played a key role in applying the discrimination prohibition enshrined in the European Convention on Human Rights and strengthening the prohibition to discriminate on specific grounds such as gender identity and sexual orientation. Past judgements of the Court, such as those finding segregation of Romani children in schools discriminatory, were not implemented in several countries such as the Czech Republic and Croatia.

Unanimous ratification of key regional human rights instruments, which would have enhanced protection, did not take place. For instance, no new country signed or ratified Protocol No. 12 to the European Convention on Human Rights, which prohibits discrimination. On a more positive note, in May the Council of Europe adopted a new Convention on preventing and combating violence against women and all forms of domestic violence, which was subsequently signed by 18 countries in the region.

While failing to strengthen domestic or European mechanisms to tackle discrimination, some governments were also keen to uphold existing or promote new discriminatory tools. Legislation, policies and practices discriminating against Roma in the enjoyment of their right to housing remained on many statute books, and Roma communities continued to be forcibly evicted in several countries across the region including France, Italy and Serbia. Legislative proposals discriminating against individuals on the basis of gender identity or sexual orientation were introduced in the Russian Federation and Lithuania.

The absence of comprehensive legal protection and a robust championing of rights by those in authority again led to adverse consequences in individual lives. Hostility and discrimination, often driven by radical-right populist parties, against ethnic and religious minorities, as well as people on the basis of their gender identity or sexual orientation, continued to be a matter of concern throughout the region. Lesbians, gay men, bisexual and transgender people, and Roma, migrants and Muslims, among others, were targeted in hate-motivated attacks. Hate crimes continued to be inadequately tackled because of gaps in legislation, poor reporting systems, inadequate investigations, or flaws in criminal justice systems and lack of trust towards the police. Entrenched prejudices and stereotypes also resulted in racially motivated misconduct by law enforcement officials.

REGIONAL OVERVIEWS
EUROPE AND CENTRAL ASIA

Discussions on general prohibitions of full face veils were pursued in many countries across the region.

Discussions on general prohibitions of full face veils were pursued in many countries across the region. Legislation came into force at the national level in Belgium and France. The accompanying debates, often based on assumptions rather than reliable data, further stigmatized Muslims. Stereotypical views of symbols perceived to be Muslim, such as the headscarf, were advocated, rather than counteracted, by public officials. The wearing of specific forms of religious and cultural symbols and dress continued to lead to discrimination against Muslims, and in particular Muslim women, in employment and education.

Counter-terror and security

European governments continued to stonewall in the face of concerted efforts to secure accountability for their alleged complicity in the CIA's rendition and secret detention programmes. Some governments released new information regarding their involvement in these operations, or were accused yet again of such complicity upon the discovery of new evidence by NGOs or the media. Others terminated or only gave lip service to anaemic investigations, proposed inquiries that failed to meet even minimal human rights standards, or simply denied any involvement despite mounting evidence to the contrary. In March, the European Parliament approved a follow-up to its 2007 report on European complicity in these CIA-led operations, in order to ensure compliance with its earlier resolutions regarding the obligation to investigate allegations of fundamental human rights abuses.

Invoking technicalities and state secrecy, Lithuania abruptly closed its investigation in January into two secret detention facilities established on Lithuanian territory by the CIA. In October, the government refused to re-open the investigation, despite credible new evidence of a potential rendition flight from Morocco to Lithuania presented by NGOs to the authorities in September. The protocol for the "Detainee Inquiry", issued by the UK government in June, met strong opposition from internationally recognized human rights experts, NGOs, and former detainees and their representatives due to concerns about government control over disclosure, secret hearings, and no provision for the meaningful participation of victims. Many groups and individuals vowed not to co-operate with the inquiry until changes had been implemented, but no modifications to the protocol had been made by the end of the year.

In August, the Polish authorities extended their investigation into the presence of a secret CIA site there, but continued to thwart access to information sought by the two named victims' lawyers and failed to reveal any information about the investigation's progress. Revelations

Invoking technicalities and state secrecy, Lithuania abruptly closed its investigation in January into two secret detention facilities established on Lithuanian territory by the CIA.

by the media in December that the location of a secret CIA site in Bucharest had been identified evoked firm denials from the Romanian authorities. They continued to reject outright claims of any involvement in the CIA operations, despite compelling evidence that Romania was deeply and willingly incorporated into these programmes.

The Finnish authorities released flight data in October and November indicating that rendition aircraft had landed on their territory and fielded calls for an independent inquiry into alleged complicity, but by the end of the year had made no decision to investigate. An investigation into alleged Danish complicity, announced in November, was limited to Greenland and would involve only a "paper review" of information previously compiled in the course of a parliamentary inquiry.

In the face of obstructions to investigations at the national level, some rendition victims submitted applications to the European Court of Human Rights, hoping for some measure of accountability there. Cases against Lithuania, Macedonia, and Poland were pending before the Court.

Counter-terrorism policies and practices across the region continued to undermine human rights protections. The use of unreliable diplomatic assurances to deport people considered a risk to national security proliferated across the region, including in Belgium, Germany, Italy and the UK. In November, the UN criticized Germany for collaborating with intelligence agencies that routinely employed forms of coercion in interrogations. Control orders and other forms of social control amounting to a deprivation of liberty were used in a number of countries, most notably the UK, as proxies for full criminal trials and the safeguards normally attendant on them.

In Turkey a vast number of cases were brought under flawed anti-terrorism laws which routinely contravened fair trial standards. Many of those prosecuted were political activists, among them students, journalists, writers, lawyers and academics. They were routinely interrogated about activities which were protected by the right to freedom of expression.

The security situation in Russia's North Caucasus remained volatile and uneven. Armed groups continued to target law enforcement and other officials, with civilians caught in the crossfire and, on occasion, deliberately attacked. Security operations across the region were often accompanied by serious human rights violations. There were reports of witnesses being intimidated and journalists, human rights activists and lawyers being harassed and killed.

The armed Basque separatist group Euskadi Ta Askatasuna announced the end of its armed struggle. In Turkey bombings by both the army and armed groups claimed the lives of civilians.

REGIONAL OVERVIEWS
EUROPE AND CENTRAL ASIA

The use of unreliable diplomatic assurances to deport people considered a risk to national security proliferated across the region.

Impunity in post-conflict situations

In spite of the arrests of the two final suspects indicted by the International Criminal Tribunal for the former Yugoslavia, progress was slow in tackling impunity for crimes committed during the wars of the 1990s. There was a lack of capacity and commitment, and some retrograde steps. In Croatia, some efforts were undertaken by the President and the judicial authorities to deal with the war-time past, but there was little action by the government. Instead, key political figures engaged in attacks on international justice, and the parliament passed a law which breached Croatia's obligation to co-operate with Serbia in criminal matters. Regional co-operation was also hampered, in the failure to dismantle legal barriers to extradition of war crimes suspects between Bosnia and Herzegovina, Croatia, Serbia and Montenegro.

Ten years after the 2001 armed conflict in Macedonia, prosecutions for war crimes cases returned from the Tribunal were annulled after parliament adopted a new interpretation of the Amnesty Law, effectively ensuring immunity from prosecution in domestic courts.

In Kyrgyzstan, despite facilitating two independent commissions of inquiry, the authorities failed to fairly and effectively investigate the violence of June 2010 and its aftermath.

Torture and other ill-treatment

Victims of torture and other ill-treatment were likewise too often failed by justice systems that did not hold those responsible to account. Obstacles to accountability included lack of prompt access to a lawyer, failure by prosecutors to vigorously pursue investigations, fear of reprisals, low penalties imposed on convicted police officers, and the absence of properly independent systems for monitoring complaints and investigating serious police misconduct.

Pockets of entrenched impunity persisted. In Uzbekistan, despite assertions by the authorities that the practice of torture had significantly decreased, and the introduction of new legislation to improve the treatment of detainees, dozens of reports of torture and other ill-treatment of detainees and prisoners emerged throughout the year. In Turkey the ground-breaking decision issued in 2010, which, for the first time in legal history, convicted state officials to long prison terms for causing death through torture, was overturned on appeal. Incidents of torture remained widely reported in Ukraine and in Russia, despite superficial police reforms in the latter.

Elsewhere, there were allegations of excessive use of force and ill-treatment as police sought to disperse protests against anti-austerity measures, such as in Greece and Spain.

> **Incidents of torture remained widely reported in Ukraine and in Russia, despite superficial police reforms in the latter.**

The death penalty

Belarus remained the region's last executioner, putting to death two men within a flawed criminal justice system which continued to shroud the process in secrecy. The executions were carried out despite a formal request by the UN Human Rights Committee for a stay so it could consider the two men's cases.

Conclusion

The arrests of Ratko Mladić and Goran Hadžić sent out a powerful message not only to those affected, but across the wider region. It was a message of hope in the face of long years of waiting, but also a message of warning to all those who thought that influential friends, powerful neighbours or opaque vested interests would – or could – protect them from the reach of justice. It was a testament to what could be achieved when individuals, civil society, governments and the international community were committed to upholding universal human rights.

However, too many people across the region still fell through the gap between the rhetoric of human rights and the reality of their implementation. Robust support for human rights was too often seen as incompatible with supporting state security or energy supply. There were challenges to the independence and authority of the European Court of Human Rights; the EU too often showed itself a toothless tiger in the face of violations committed by its member states. And individual states still failed in their primary obligation to uphold all human rights for all.

REGIONAL OVERVIEWS
EUROPE AND CENTRAL ASIA

The arrests of Ratko Mladić and Goran Hadžić sent out a powerful message not only to those affected, but across the wider region.

Yemeni rights activist and Nobel Peace Prize winner Tawakkol Karman shouts slogans as a policeman watches during an anti-government demonstration in Sana'a, Yemen, 15 February 2011.

MIDDLE EAST AND NORTH AFRICA

"We are not scared of being killed, injured or tortured. Fear does not exist any more. People want to live in dignity. So we will not stop."

Ahmed Harara, who worked as a dentist, was injured in one eye by gunshot pellets during protests in Egypt on 28 January 2011, then a second time in the other eye on 19 November 2011, leaving him blind.

For the peoples and states of the Middle East and North Africa, 2011 was a truly momentous year. It was a year of unprecedented popular uprisings and tumult, a year in which the pent-up pressures, demands and protests of a rising generation swept aside a succession of veteran rulers who, almost until they fell, had appeared virtually unassailable. Others, at the year's end, were still clinging to power but only through the most ruthless means, their futures hanging in the balance. The region as a whole was then still reeling amid the continuing tremors and aftershocks of the political and social earthquake that exploded in the first months of the year. Although much remained uncertain, the events of 2011 appeared likely to be every bit as significant for the peoples of the region as the fall of the Berlin Wall and the collapse of the Soviet empire had been for the peoples of Europe and Central Asia.

All across the Middle East and North Africa, 2011 was marked by mass demands for change – for greater liberty to speak and to act, free from the suffocating fear of state repression; for government transparency and accountability and an end to pervasive high-level corruption; for more jobs and fairer employment opportunities and the means to seek a better standard of living; for justice and human rights, including the right to live one's life and bring up one's family in dignity and security. It was in support of such demands that hundreds of thousands of people, with women conspicuous in the vanguard, thronged onto the streets of Tunis, Cairo, Benghazi, Sana'a and many other cities and towns across the region to demand change. They continued to do so despite the carnage wrought among them by government security forces. They did so with determination, resolution and naked courage, and in doing so freed themselves from the fear that their governments had for so long sought to imbue in order to keep them quiescent and in their place. For a time at least, the notion of people's power gripped the region and shook it to its core.

Initially, the protests mostly voiced popular frustration against the failure of national leaders to address people's needs and aspirations. Those leaders responded all too characteristically by sending out their riot police and security agents to crush the protests by force; they succeeded only in pouring fuel on the flames and further igniting public outrage and defiance. As protesters were shot down in cold blood, rounded up in mass arrests, tortured and abused, so the popular mood hardened. Unintimidated by the bloodshed, more and more people rallied to the streets to demand the replacement or overthrow of national leaders who had become both discredited and despised as they sought to consolidate family dynasties to maintain their grip on power. The rapid fall of Tunisia's President Zine El 'Abidine Ben 'Ali and then Egypt's President Hosni Mubarak resounded all across the region, sending a message of hope to advocates of change and reform in other states. For a time, it seemed that a new form of domino effect was taking place that would sweep out other repressive and authoritarian rulers from power. Within months, Colonel Mu'ammar al-Gaddafi's 42 years of abusive rule in Libya had been brought to an abrupt and bloody end, and in both Yemen and Syria long-standing regimes were fighting a rearguard action – literally – for their survival in the face of continuing mass demands for their demise. In Bahrain, the government used excessive force and repression to quell the protests yet ended the year committing to political and human rights reform. Elsewhere, in states such as Algeria, Jordan and Morocco, those in power were urgently promising the people reform and a greater say in government. In oil- and gas-rich Saudi Arabia and other Gulf states, rulers used their financial reserves to try to address social grievances and try to keep the people sweet.

2011 was marked by mass demands for greater liberty to speak and to act, free from the suffocating fear of state repression.

The uprisings

2011 dawned with Tunisia in ferment. For a time, President Ben 'Ali sought to quash the protests in the same way that he had crushed earlier protests in the Gafsa region in 2008, through the application of brute force. In a few short weeks, some 300 Tunisians met violent deaths but, this time, without the resolve of the protesters being diminished. On 14 January, Ben 'Ali's nerve gave way. With other members of his clan, he boarded a plane and flew away to seek safe haven in Saudi Arabia. It was an electric moment, as both governments and people across the region recognized that what had until then seemed almost unthinkable – the enforced flight of an autocratic ruler of more than 20 years – had just been achieved. For the other repressive governments of the region, Ben 'Ali's abrupt demise sounded the alarm bells; for the mass of people watching events unfold on Al Jazeera and other satellite TV stations, the Tunisian uprising inspired new hope and a sense that they too could obtain for themselves what Tunisia's people had achieved.

Within two weeks, what had occurred in Tunisia was being mirrored on an even greater scale in Egypt. Cairo's Tahrir Square had become the fulcrum and a key battleground in which Egyptians set forth their demands for change. Using the internet, social networking sites and mobile phones to help organize and co-ordinate their activities, within 18 days the protesters wrought the "25 January Revolution" and provoked the downfall of President Mubarak after 30 unbroken years in power. This they achieved in the face of extreme repression by the security forces and thugs hired by the government. At least 840 people were killed and more than 6,000 injured, with thousands more arrested, beaten or tortured. On 11 February, Hosni Mubarak announced his resignation and was replaced by the Supreme Council of the Armed Forces (SCAF). He retreated to his villa in the Red Sea resort of Sharm el-Sheikh, from where he was summoned to a Cairo court in August to stand trial for corruption and ordering the killing of protesters.

Mubarak's fall, which occurred in the full glare of the worldwide media, had the effect of spurring calls for mass protests in a rash of other cities and towns across the region. In Bahrain, starting in February, protesters belonging mostly to the country's Shi'a Muslim majority mounted peaceful demonstrations and set up a protest camp at the capital Manama's Pearl Roundabout to demand a greater say in the running of the country and an end to their alleged marginalization by the ruling Al Khalifa family. The protesters were cleared away with excessive force days later and then with even greater brutality when they resumed their protests in March. In Iran, the leaders of mass protests crushed by the government in 2009 called for new demonstrations, and were shut up under house arrest in response.

In Algeria, the government called out the security forces in large numbers to deter demonstrations but also sought to reduce tension by lifting the 19-year-long state of emergency. Oman's Sultan Qaboos bin Said promised to create thousands of new jobs and improved benefits for the unemployed, and ordered the release of detained protesters. In Saudi Arabia, the government was reported to have paid out more than US$100 billion to citizens while warning that all public demonstrations were banned. It mobilized the security forces to deploy against anyone attending a planned "Day of Rage" in Riyadh.

In Yemen, protests had begun in January, sparked by proposed constitutional changes that would enable President Ali Abdullah Saleh to remain in office for life and then hand power to his son. The protests continued throughout the year, spurred by the events in Egypt and elsewhere, while President Saleh's forces fired indiscriminately into crowds of demonstrators and he manoeuvred to try and maintain his long monopoly of power. By the end of the year, the Yemeni President's position had become seriously eroded. Nevertheless, he still clung to power as the Gulf Cooperation Council (GCC) offered him immunity from prosecution despite the grim toll of unlawful killings and other gross human rights violations committed by his forces. That he and others responsible should be afforded impunity was an affront to justice and an outrageous betrayal of the victims of his regime's crimes.

In Libya, geographically lying between Tunisia and Egypt, the events in those countries brought new hope to a population that, after 42 years under Mu'ammar al-Gaddafi, was denied freedom of speech, independent political parties, trades unions or civil society organizations. Mu'ammar al-Gaddafi had maintained power for so long by playing one section of the population against another, favouring those who he considered loyal and clamping down ruthlessly on those who expressed dissent. Formerly an international pariah for his alleged sponsorship of terrorism, in recent years he had enjoyed a blossoming rapprochement with Western democracies as Libya's oil extraction industry developed and Libya assumed a new importance as a means of transit for African refugees and migrants seeking to gain entry to Europe. Mu'ammar al-Gaddafi appeared confident and in firm control as first Ben 'Ali and then Mubarak fell, but in February anti-government demonstrations erupted into a popular revolt in Libya too. This quickly developed into an international armed conflict in which NATO became involved and culminated on 20 October in al-Gaddafi's capture and violent death as he sought to flee from his besieged stronghold in the city of Sirte. A National Transitional Council then took office but by the end of the year it had yet to establish its authority and Libya was awash with arms and armed militias which carried out reprisals against suspected al-Gaddafi loyalists and presented a continuing threat to public security.

Protesters in Egypt provoked the downfall of President Mubarak in the face of extreme repression by the security forces. At least 840 people were killed.

In Syria, where the regime headed by the al-Assad family has been in power since 1970, the first stirrings of protest in February were low key and hesitant. However, when security forces detained and reportedly abused children who had chalked up anti-government slogans in the southern town of Dera'a, they set off mass protests that rapidly spread from city to city. Caught off guard, the government closed the country to the world's media and to independent observers. It launched a crackdown of vicious intensity against unarmed protesters, using snipers on rooftops, firing into crowds and deploying army tanks in towns and villages, while all the time claiming that the killings were the work of shadowy anti-government armed gangs. By the end of the year, the UN reported, some 5,000 people, mostly civilians, had been killed while thousands more had been wounded or arrested or both. In some pockets of the country, an incipient civil war appeared to be developing between the regime's forces and soldiers who had defected to join the protests.

Syria's government tried to conceal both the extent of the protests and the violence of its response but was largely thwarted due to the courage and determination of local activists and witnesses who recorded the carnage on mobile phone cameras and uploaded hundreds of videos onto the internet. Some showed the bodies of individuals who had been tortured to death in detention and, in some cases, mutilated; among them were children.

The international response

The US and other Western governments that had long been principal allies of the autocratic leaders of Tunisia and Egypt initially failed to grasp the significance of the protests and were slow to react. Soon, however, they were hurrying to reformulate policy, now finally acknowledging the abusive nature of the regimes at risk. When Libya descended into armed conflict, they intervened decisively against Colonel al-Gaddafi, with the support of the key Gulf states, using a UN Security Council mandate to protect civilians that paved the way for a NATO air campaign which swung the balance against the Libyan leader.

In Bahrain, where the US navy's Fifth Fleet has its base, and particularly in Syria and Yemen, protesters were also in desperate need of protection from the murderous policies of their governments. The international community, however, was notably less inclined to offer them support. While the Security Council had referred Mu'ammar al-Gaddafi to the International Criminal Court, it took no such action against Syria's President Bashar al-Assad despite compelling evidence that his forces were committing crimes against humanity.

The Russian Federation, China and the governments of the emerging powerhouses of Brazil, India and South Africa all used their leverage at the Security Council to forestall effective action on Syria even as the UN's own human rights chief spoke out against the crimes being committed by the al-Assad regime. Saudi Arabia also denounced the Syrian government's crimes while denying Saudi Arabians the right to demonstrate and after sending troops into Bahrain only hours before the authorities there launched a bloody crackdown in March. Overall, it was a depressingly familiar story, with governments of all political hues continuing to operate selectively and, whatever their rhetoric, to subordinate human rights to their own perceived and partisan interests.

Conflict and intolerance of dissent

The uprisings that dominated the headlines throughout 2011 overshadowed other deep-seated problems that retained disastrous potential for human rights in the Middle East and North Africa, and beyond.

> **By the end of the year Libya was awash with arms and armed militias which carried out reprisals against suspected al-Gaddafi loyalists and presented a continuing threat to public security.**

Israel maintained its blockade of Gaza, prolonging the humanitarian crisis there, and continued aggressively to expand settlements in the Palestinian West Bank territory it has occupied since 1967. The two leading Palestinian political organizations, Fatah and Hamas, despite a reconciliation agreement signed in May remained divided and targeted each other's supporters, while Israeli forces and Palestinian armed groups mounted tit-for-tat attacks in Gaza. It was a sorry and all too familiar tale that continued to wreak a heavy cost on so many people's lives.

Iran's government became increasingly isolated internationally and tolerated no dissent at home; human rights defenders, women's and minority rights activists were among those persecuted, and the death penalty was used on an extensive scale, ostensibly to punish criminals but also to intimidate the populace. Globally, only China carried out more executions.

Elsewhere in the region, it was unclear how the withdrawal of all US military forces from Iraq would impact security there after eight years of conflict. The issue of self-determination for the people of Western Sahara still remained as a running sore, poisoning government relations in the Maghreb.

Other patterns of human rights violations remained and were both central in driving the popular uprisings and protests and also deepened by governments' responses. Arbitrary arrests and detentions, enforced disappearances, torture and other ill-treatment, unfair trials, and unlawful killings by state forces remained common and widespread across the region. Almost without exception, those in power allowed their forces to kill and torture with impunity. In Egypt, the SCAF bowed to popular demands and disbanded the State Security Investigations service, which was notorious for torture under Hosni Mubarak. Torture, however, did not cease; the army simply took it over, even subjecting some women protesters to forced "virginity testing", while also arresting and sending thousands of civilians for trial before unfair military courts. Yet thousands of Egyptians remained stubborn in the face of the new authorities' repression and continued to demand political, social and human rights changes.

Discrimination

Discrimination on grounds of gender, ethnicity, religion, national origin and other factors, such as sexual orientation, remained. To a large extent, the sense of injustice this engendered was reflected in the wave of protests, as when stateless Bidun gathered together in Kuwait to demand that they be recognized as citizens. At the same time, the turmoil also deepened divisions. In Libya, both Libyans and foreign nationals were targeted by militias because of their skin colour. There was growing fear within the Syria's complex of different faiths and communities that the country might descend into a civil war of such bitterness and hatred as the one that tore Lebanon apart from 1975 to 1990 – a war whose legacy of enforced disappearances and distrust still remains conspicuously unaddressed. In Egypt, discrimination against Copts remained rife. In Iran, religious and ethnic minorities continued to face discrimination in law and, in the case of the Baha'i minority, persecution.

Migrants, many of them originating from sub-Saharan Africa, were among the principal victims of the Libya conflict. Thousands were forcibly displaced by the fighting. Many escaped to Egypt or Tunisia but others were trapped for weeks or months and subject to racist attacks in Libya, often accused of being African "mercenaries" recruited by Colonel al-Gaddafi. Some who reached Egypt and Tunisia, many of them Eritreans and Somalis, were unable to return to their home countries for fear of persecution and at the end of 2011 were consigned to desolate desert camps to await resettlement in European or other countries where they would be safe. Still others lost their lives trying to cross the sea to Italy.

All across the region, migrant workers from poor and developing countries were abused and exploited even though, as in several Gulf states, they were the lifeblood of the economy. They were inadequately protected, if offered any protection at all, under local labour laws. Women domestic workers suffered worst of all – they were victims all

The offer of immunity from prosecution to the Yemeni President was an affront to justice and a betrayal of the victims of his regime's crimes.

too often of multiple discrimination, as women, as migrants, and as foreign nationals whose own governments frequently took little or no interest in their plight.

Economic concerns – housing and livelihoods

At the end of 2011 it was still too early to assess how Egypt's "25 January Revolution" had impacted, let alone improved, the lot of the millions of poor and marginalized residents of the country's teeming informal settlements. Many lived in areas officially designated as "unsafe" due to unstable rock formations or other hazards, without access to basic services – clean water, effective sanitation, electricity – and were liable to be forcibly evicted from their homes without adequate notice or any consultation. During the year, further forced evictions were carried out in Manshiyet Nasser, the sprawling slum-like informal settlement on the outskirts of Cairo in which over 100 residents were killed by a rock fall in 2008, under the SCAF's authority, perpetuating the policy pursued under Hosni Mubarak and rendering more families homeless.

The Israeli authorities also continued to force people from their homes – both Palestinians resident in the West Bank, including East Jerusalem, and Arab Israelis resident in officially "unrecognized" villages in the Negev and elsewhere – as they continued their policy of demolishing homes and other buildings erected without official permits that they themselves withheld. By contrast, thousands of Jewish Israelis living in settlements unlawfully established on occupied Palestinian lands received every encouragement to further expand, develop and consolidate the settlements even though these settlements are prohibited under international law. Meanwhile, Israel's blockade of the Gaza Strip continued to suffocate the local economy and prolong what is a deliberate humanitarian crisis whose heaviest impact is on the most vulnerable – children, the elderly, those needing specialist medical care not available in Gaza. The blockade constituted nothing less than collective punishment of Gaza's 1.6 million inhabitants, and breached international law.

When 24-year-old Mohamed Bouazizi set himself alight on 17 December 2010 in the Tunisian town of Sidi Bouzid, few could have predicted the regional firestorm of protest and change that his tragic and fatal act would ignite. A year later, the outburst of euphoria had all but evaporated. The early gains of the popular uprisings remained in the balance and the struggles for change in Syria, Yemen, Bahrain, Libya and elsewhere continued to levy a heavy cost in people's lives and gross abuses of human rights. Yet at the end of

Syria's government tried to conceal both the extent of the protests and the violence of its response but was largely thwarted due to the courage of local activists.

2011 there was a palpable feeling that the old discredited order was in the process of being consigned to history through the valiant and determined efforts of the people. For the peoples of the region, it appeared that the long march to freedom, justice and human rights for all had undoubtedly begun.

REGIONAL OVERVIEWS
MIDDLE EAST AND NORTH AFRICA

Women and children wait to receive medical attention at the Ahmad Shah Baba Hospital in Arzan Qimat, Afghanistan. Attacks on aid workers and doctors, especially in areas most affected by the conflict, deprived millions of health care during 2011. February 2011.

AMNESTY INTERNATIONAL REPORT 2012
PART TWO: COUNTRY ENTRIES

12

© Glenna Gordon

Cells in Liberia's Monrovia Central Prison intended for two prisoners are often crowded with up to eight inmates. Several people sleep on the floor, while others are on narrow hammocks made from empty rice bags tied to the cell bars and windows.

AFGHANISTAN

ISLAMIC REPUBLIC OF AFGHANISTAN

Head of state and government:	**Hamid Karzai**
Death penalty:	**retentionist**
Population:	**32.4 million**
Life expectancy:	**48.7 years**

October marked the 10th anniversary of the international military intervention in Afghanistan. The ongoing armed conflict between the Afghan government and its international allies on the one hand, and the Taleban and other armed groups on the other, led to record levels of civilian casualties, prompting Amnesty International to reiterate its calls for the International Criminal Court to investigate suspected war crimes and crimes against humanity. According to the UN Assistance Mission in Afghanistan (UNAMA), 3,021 civilians were killed in the conflict during 2011, with armed groups responsible for 77 per cent of civilian deaths. The judicial authorities, the police and the Afghan National Army routinely committed serious human rights violations. Arbitrary arrests and detentions continued, with systematic use of torture and other ill-treatment by the intelligence services. Afghans, particularly women and girls, were deprived of their rights to health and education. Humanitarian aid remained inaccessible for most people in areas controlled by the Taleban and other insurgent groups. The Afghanistan NGO Safety Office documented 170 attacks on NGO workers – a rise of 20 per cent compared to 2010. Violence against women and girls was widespread and went unpunished, particularly in areas controlled by insurgents. Women reporting cases of gender-based violence received little redress.

Background

Parliament was inaugurated on 26 January, four months after elections that had been marred by violence and electoral fraud. Amnesty International raised concerns over the inclusion of candidates suspected of having committed war crimes and other human rights abuses.

Nader Nadery, Fahim Hakim and Mawlawi Gharib, prominent members of the Afghanistan Independent Human Rights Commission (AIHRC), were ousted on 21 December when President Hamid Karzai failed to renew their terms shortly before the publication of a report cataloguing past human rights violations.

In July, NATO and International Security Assistance Forces (ISAF) began transferring responsibility for security in seven provinces to the Afghan government, and a second phase of security transition commenced in November in 17 provinces.

Peace talks between the Afghan government and the Taleban and other insurgent groups continued, despite the 20 September assassination of former President Burhanuddin Rabbani, ostensibly in charge of the talks, by two men pretending to be Taleban representatives. The UN Security Council de-linked the Taleban from al-Qa'ida in June, removing it from one UN sanctions list.

There were only nine women among the 70-member High Peace Council – the body tasked with negotiating with the Taleban and other armed groups. Afghan women's rights groups and civil society organizations voiced serious concerns over human rights, and women's rights in particular, fearing these could be bargained away for the sake of expedience. The Afghan government and its international allies persistently failed to implement in policy and practice UN Security Council Resolution 1325, which calls for women to be meaningfully and adequately represented during all stages of peace talks.

Abuses by armed groups

The Taleban and other armed groups targeted civilians through assassinations and abductions, and harmed civilians indiscriminately in bombings (including multiple suicide attacks), violating the laws of war and committing a raft of human rights abuses. Targeted killings of Afghan civilians, including government officials and tribal elders, working for or allegedly supporting the government or international organizations increased.

According to UNAMA, the Taleban and other armed groups accounted for 77 per cent of civilian deaths. They increasingly resorted to using improvised explosive devices in mosques, markets and other civilian areas, contributing to a substantial rise in the number of civilian casualties.

Armed groups systematically targeted aid workers, killing 31, injuring 34 and kidnapping and detaining 140.

■ On 28 June, Taleban gunmen and suicide bombers attacked the Intercontinental Hotel in the capital, Kabul, killing seven people.

- On 13 September, around 10 insurgents targeted the US Embassy, NATO headquarters and other high-profile targets in Kabul. At least 11 civilians, including students, and five policemen were killed; more than 24 others were injured. The Taleban claimed responsibility but the USA blamed the Haqqani network, believed to be based in Pakistan's tribal areas and supported by Pakistan.
- On 17 September, nine civilians, including five children, were killed when an improvised explosive device was detonated in Faryab province, north-west Afghanistan.
- On 31 October, Taleban gunmen and suicide bombers attacked UNHCR, the UN refugee agency, in Kandahar city, southern Afghanistan, killing three staff members.
- On 6 December, a suicide bomb attack on the Shi'a Muslim Abul Fazl shrine in Kabul killed up to 71 people. Another four people were killed in a near simultaneous bomb blast at a Shi'a mosque in Mazar-e Sharif. The attacks marked a serious escalation of previously rare sectarian violence. Lashkar-e-Jhangvi, a Pakistani armed group linked to al-Qa'ida and the Pakistani Taleban, claimed responsibility for the attacks which took place during the Shi'a rite of Ashura.

Violations by Afghan and international forces

ISAF and NATO continued to launch aerial attacks and night raids, claiming scores of civilian lives. According to UNAMA, at least 410 or 14 per cent of civilians were killed in ISAF, NATO and Afghan operations.
- On 20 February, the Governor of eastern Kunar province claimed that 64 civilians, including 29 children, had been killed during joint ground and air operations by Afghan and ISAF forces in the Ghazi Abad district over the previous four days. Senior ISAF officials disputed the account but agreed to a joint investigation. NATO officials later said that most of those killed were insurgents.
- On 23 March, Jeremy Morlock, a US soldier who confessed to participating in the 2010 murder of three Afghan civilians, was sentenced to 24 years in prison. He told the judge at his court martial at Joint Base Lewis-McChord, USA, that "the plan was to kill people".

Arbitrary arrests and detentions, torture and other ill-treatment

The National Directorate of Security (NDS), Afghanistan's intelligence service, continued to arbitrarily arrest and detain suspects, denying them access to a lawyer, their families, the courts or other external bodies. The NDS faced credible allegations of torturing detainees and operating secret detention facilities. NATO ceased transferring detainees to Afghan forces after a UN report, issued in October, documented the systematic use of torture by NDS officers. According to the report, prisoners had been tortured in 47 NDS and police detention facilities across 22 provinces.
- In August, family members of an Afghan man who had been detained by the NDS in Kabul for allegedly selling counterfeit currency told Amnesty International he had been arrested by the NDS in April and tortured into making a confession. The detainee, who cannot be identified for security reasons, was reportedly punched and kicked until he vomited blood and lost consciousness.

US forces continued to detain Afghans and some foreign nationals without clear legal authority or adequate legal process. Around 3,100 detainees remained held at the US Detention Facility in Parwan (outside the former detention facility at the air force base at Bagram airport). They were held indefinitely in "security internment"; some had been detained for several years. In January, the USA handed over one detention housing unit at the facility, with 300 inmates, to the Afghan authorities as part of its detainee transfer operations. The US Department of Defense stated that by May, the Afghan authorities had conducted more than 130 trials at the facility and the Afghan Justice Center in Parwan since these trials began in June 2010 (see USA entry).

Freedom of expression

Afghan journalists carried out their work despite pressure and violence, including from government institutions and other influential bodies. The NDS and the Ulema Council (Council of Religious Scholars) brought criminal proceedings against people for writing or talking about matters deemed a threat to national security or considered blasphemous.
- Three Afghan men arrested and detained in 2010 for converting to Christianity were released between March and April.

Journalists were abducted, beaten or killed in politically motivated attacks by government forces and insurgent groups. According to Nai, an Afghan media watchdog, 80 journalists were attacked and three killed. In areas controlled by the Taleban and other armed groups, journalists were actively prevented from reporting and were frequently attacked.

The government failed to fully investigate and prosecute perpetrators of attacks on journalists, human rights defenders and others peacefully exercising their right to freedom of expression.

■ On 18 January, Hojatullah Mujadedi, director of Kapisa FM radio based in the north-east, was released after four months in NDS detention in Kabul. He had been accused of acting as an accomplice to the Taleban.

■ On 6 July, Taleban members threatened Ariana TV reporter Niamatullah Zaheer in Helmand province for reporting critically on attacks carried out by the Taleban.

Violence against women and girls

Afghan women and girls continued to suffer discrimination, domestic violence, forced marriages, trafficking and being traded to settle disputes. They were frequent targets for attack by Taleban forces. According to a joint report by UN Women and the AIHRC, 56 per cent of all marriages occurred when the bride was below the age of 16. The Ministry of Women's Affairs documented 3,742 cases of violence against women from 22 March to 31 December. In a positive move in September, the Attorney General's office agreed to create six provincial offices to fight violence against women.

The police and courts often failed to address women's complaints of abuse, so that allegations of beatings, rape and other sexual violence were rarely investigated. Women trying to flee abusive marriages were detained and prosecuted for alleged offences such as "home escape" or "moral" crimes, neither of which was provided for in the Penal Code and which were incompatible with international human rights law.

■ In April, the Taleban abducted and killed a woman in Zurmat district, Paktia province. The Taleban claimed she was killed because she worked for an NGO, denying rumours that it had been an "honour" killing.

■ Gulnaz, aged 21 and serving a 12-year prison sentence in Kabul for adultery, was released in December. Lawyers have said that such charges have no basis in Afghan law. Gulnaz had been jailed in 2009 after reporting a rape to the police. She faced pressure from the court and others to marry the man later convicted of her rape.

Right to health

Targeted attacks on aid workers and government workers, particularly doctors, deprived millions of people of health care, especially in areas most affected by the conflict and those controlled by the Taleban and other armed groups. Notwithstanding improvements to maternal and child mortality ratios in certain areas of the country, conditions overall for pregnant women and young children remained dire.

Right to education

The Taleban and other armed groups targeted schools, students, and teachers. In areas occupied by these groups, many children, particularly girls, were prevented from going to school. According to the Ministry of Education, more than 7.3 million children were enrolled in school, 38 per cent of whom were girls. Official sources reported that more than 450 schools remained closed and around 200,000 children were unable to go to school due to insecurity mainly in the southern and eastern provinces.

■ On 24 May, Taleban members shot dead Khan Mohammad, headmaster of Poorak girls' school in Logar province, south-eastern Afghanistan. He had continued to teach the girls despite receiving numerous death threats from the Taleban, demanding that he stop teaching them.

Refugees and internally displaced people

Afghans accounted for the highest number of asylum applications to industrialized countries between January and June, according to UNHCR. By the end of the year, UNHCR documented more than 30,000 Afghan asylum-seekers, while around 2.7 million remained refugees in Pakistan and Iran. The total number of people displaced as a result of the conflict reached 447,647.

Those displaced internally gravitated to the larger cities, particularly Kabul, Herat and Mazar-e Sharif. Many ended up in informal settlements where they were forced to live in crowded and unhygienic conditions with little or no access to potable water, adequate shelter and health services, and under the constant threat of forced eviction. In October, the ICRC reported a 40 per cent rise in the number of those displaced by conflict in the north compared to 2010.

■ In early June, clashes between government forces and the Taleban in Faryab province reportedly displaced at least 12,000 people.

A

Death penalty

There were two executions. More than 140 people remained on death row and nearly 100 had their death sentences confirmed by the Supreme Court.

■ In June, two men – one from Pakistan, the other an Afghan national – were executed in Kabul's Pul-e-Charkhi prison, after their appeal for clemency to the President failed. The men had been found guilty of killing 40 and injuring more than 70 people – mostly civilians – in a February attack on a bank in Jalalabad city, Nangarhar province.

Amnesty International visits/reports

🚍 Amnesty International delegates visited Afghanistan from June to September.

📄 Afghanistan 10 years on: Slow progress and failed promises (ASA 11/006/2011)

ALBANIA

REPUBLIC OF ALBANIA

Head of state:	Bamir Topi
Head of government:	Sali Berisha
Death penalty:	abolitionist for all crimes
Population:	3.2 million
Life expectancy:	76.9 years
Under-5 mortality:	15.3 per 1,000
Adult literacy:	95.9 per cent

Domestic violence remained widespread and the trafficking of women for forced prostitution continued. Four demonstrators died following clashes with police. There were allegations of ill-treatment by police. Detention conditions were often poor. Homeless people with "orphan status" were denied their right under domestic law to priority with housing.

Background

Hostility between the government and opposition was exacerbated following violent clashes in January between police and demonstrators protesting over alleged electoral fraud and government corruption. Local government elections held in May led to further mutual accusations between the government and opposition, and disputes over vote counting, in particular in Tirana. The political stalemate had somewhat abated by the end of the year, and discussion of electoral reform was initiated. In October, the European Commission again concluded that Albania had not fulfilled the criteria for candidate status for EU membership.

Police and security forces

On 21 January, violent clashes broke out between police and demonstrators during anti-government demonstrations in Tirana organized by the opposition Socialist Party. Shots were fired, killing three demonstrators. A fourth died later. Arrest warrants were issued the following day for six Republican Guards (responsible for the security of public buildings) in connection with the deaths. Investigations were hampered by a lack of co-operation by the police and senior Republican Guard officers, and delays in the collection of ballistic evidence. By the end of the year, 11 Republican Guards were under investigation in connection with the deaths. More than 140 police officers and demonstrators were injured overall. Police beat dispersing demonstrators and several journalists. At least 112 demonstrators were arrested and some 30 were subsequently convicted of setting fire to vehicles, assaulting police, and breaching the security perimeter of the Prime Minister's offices. Prime Minister Sali Berisha characterized the demonstrations as an attempted coup by the Socialist Party and accused the Prosecutor General of supporting it.

Torture and other ill-treatment

Commissioners of the Ombudsperson's Office visited Tirana police stations and detention centres following the January demonstrations. They stated that detained demonstrators, two of whom bore marks of physical ill-treatment, alleged being ill-treated during arrest, and that psychological pressure had been used to make them sign self-incriminating statements. Nine complaints of police ill-treatment were reportedly filed. In February, the Internal Control Service of the State Police undertook to investigate complaints, but by the end of the year no perpetrators had been brought to justice.

■ The Ombudsperson wrote to the Prosecutor General raising the case of Reis Haxhiraj, who was allegedly severely ill-treated during his arrest in March. The Ombudsperson stated that although his injuries were clearly visible, and he had complained of ill-treatment when brought before a judge to be remanded in custody, neither the police, prosecutor, judge or hospital staff had reported his ill-treatment or initiated an investigation. His requests to contact the Ombudsperson's Office were ignored. The Prosecutor General subsequently instructed prosecutors and officers of the judicial police to collect evidence on the ill-treatment of detainees, in order to bring those responsible to justice, and an investigation was started into the alleged ill-treatment of Reis Haxhiraj.

Enforced disappearances

In December Ilir Kumbaro failed to appear at an extradition hearing before a court in London, UK. Albania had sought his extradition from the UK to face charges of torture and abduction in connection with the enforced disappearance in 1995 of Remzi Hoxha, an ethnic Albanian from Macedonia, and the torture of two other men. The judge revoked his bail and issued a warrant for his arrest, but at the end of the year his whereabouts remained unknown. Trial proceedings continued in Tirana against Ilir Kumbaro in his absence, and two other former officers of the Albanian National Intelligence Service, Arben Sefgjini and Avni Koldashi.

Prison conditions

Inmates at Lezhë and Fushë-Krujë prisons went on hunger-strike in protest against poor conditions. The Ombudsperson criticized sanitation in some prisons and remand centres, citing squalid toilets, rodents, damp cells, and the unhygienic preparation and distribution of food. The Ombudsperson also noted the poor quality of construction of recently built detention centres in Durrës, Kavaja and Korça. Remand centres and the Women's Prison in Tirana were overcrowded, and prison medical services, especially for detainees with mental illnesses, were inadequate.

Violence in the family

Domestic violence remained widespread. Shelters for women survivors were insufficient to meet demand. Reported incidents increased to 1,683 in the first nine months of the year, 260 more than for the same period in 2010. Eighty-two per cent (1,377) of the victims were women. Most incidents, including those involving violence against children, went unreported.

Domestic violence was not a specific criminal offence and, except in the gravest cases, prosecution had to be instigated by the victim. Legislation providing free legal aid for people requesting protection orders was not implemented, and despite training programmes, health workers reportedly often failed to provide certificated records of injuries. In most cases, proceedings were stopped, either because the petitioner withdrew, often due to social pressure and economic dependence on the perpetrator, or due to lack of written evidence. Perpetrators who broke the terms of protection orders were liable to fines or up to two years' imprisonment, but courts rarely imposed custodial sentences.

■ In September, Servete Karoshi was killed by her husband, who had repeatedly ignored protection orders. She had reported his continued violence but was given no effective protection.

In March, legislation was adopted to provide basic economic assistance of US$30 per month for victims for the duration of their protection order, and also for victims of human trafficking.

Trafficking in human beings

Trafficking continued, mainly of young women and girls for forced prostitution, but also children for forced begging and labour. Statistics released for 2010 showed that 12 people had been convicted of human trafficking. The US State Department Trafficking in Persons Report noted that Albania had taken concrete steps to improve anti-trafficking strategy, but stated that "widespread corruption, particularly within the judiciary, continued to hamper overall anti-trafficking law enforcement and victim protection efforts". In February, the government adopted a national action plan against human trafficking.

Housing rights – Roma

In February, some 40 Romani families fled from the site they inhabited near Tirana railway station after being attacked. In July, two men were acquitted of inciting racial hatred but sentenced to four months' imprisonment for arson. The authorities offered the Romani families a temporary site with tents on the outskirts of Tirana, but many rejected this on the grounds of health and safety and the distance from their workplaces. The families who did move to the site were still there at the end of the year, although the authorities had promised that two disused military buildings would be renovated for their use.

Housing rights – orphans

Under Albanian law, registered orphans up to the age of 30 who are homeless are to be prioritized when social housing is allocated. However, the law was very rarely implemented and many continued to live in dilapidated disused school dormitories or struggled to pay for low-grade private rented accommodation.

■ In June, Mjaftoni Xhymertaj, aged 22, and her small child were forcibly evicted by police, apparently without prior written notice or right of appeal, from her shared room in a Tirana school dormitory. She was not offered alternative accommodation. Mjaftoni Xhymertaj was raised in an orphanage, was unemployed, with poor health and in great poverty. She was subsequently permitted to return, but had no security of tenure. The conditions were severely inadequate for a young family.

Amnesty International visits/reports

🚘 Amnesty International delegates visited Albania in November.

📁 Investigation urged into Albania protest (PRE01/025/2011)

ALGERIA

PEOPLE'S DEMOCRATIC REPUBLIC OF ALGERIA

Head of state:	Abdelaziz Bouteflika
Head of government:	Ahmed Ouyahia
Death penalty:	abolitionist in practice
Population:	36 million
Life expectancy:	73.1 years
Under-5 mortality:	32.3 per 1,000
Adult literacy:	72.6 per cent

The government lifted the nationwide state of emergency in force since 1992, but maintained tight restrictions on freedom of expression, association and assembly, and on practising religious beliefs. The security forces used excessive force in dispersing some demonstrations and in response to instances of rioting; several people were killed. Detainees remained at risk of torture and other ill-treatment. Women continued to face discrimination in law and in practice and to be inadequately protected against gender-based violence, including within the family. No steps were taken to address the legacy of impunity for gross human rights abuses committed in the past. Death sentences continued to be handed down but there were no executions. Armed groups carried out attacks, killing some civilians.

Background

After mass protests and some rioting in January, demonstrations were held periodically throughout the year against food and other price rises, unemployment, poor housing conditions, official corruption and violence by the security forces. Many were called by the National Co-ordination for Change and Democracy, an umbrella group of opposition parties, trade unions and human rights organizations. The group was formed in January after protests and riots were violently suppressed by the security forces; several people were killed, hundreds were injured and hundreds more arrested.

The authorities took steps to address some of the protesters' grievances, temporarily cutting taxes on some basic foodstuffs and in February lifting the national state of emergency in force since 1992. In April, President Abdelaziz Bouteflika announced planned reforms, including new laws to liberalize elections and the media, and the appointment of a committee to reform the Constitution, but these had not been fully implemented by the end of the year, and many of the laws subsequently adopted were criticized for not going far enough.

The government permitted visits by the UN Special Rapporteurs on freedom of expression and housing but continued to block long-standing requests for visits by the UN Special Rapporteur on torture and the UN Working Group on Enforced or Involuntary Disappearances.

Freedom of expression, association and assembly

The government continued to restrict freedom of expression and to prohibit unauthorized public gatherings. Mass protests in January in Algiers, Oran and other cities were violently dispersed by thousands of riot police and other security forces, leading to deaths and injuries. In the following weeks, thousands of security forces were deployed ahead of protests called in Algiers and other cities on 12 February. The authorities also reportedly blocked access to

Facebook and Twitter in some areas to obstruct efforts to organize and co-ordinate protests.

After the state of emergency was lifted on 24 February, it became lawful to demonstrate anywhere but Algiers if prior authorization was granted. However, such authorization was often denied. Nevertheless, many unauthorized protests were staged in Algiers and elsewhere. The security forces often dispersed these using tear gas and water cannon, and arrested demonstrators. Some of those arrested were charged and tried before criminal courts for "unlawful unarmed gathering" and assaulting the security forces. Most were subsequently acquitted.

In December, the parliament passed a new media law that restricts journalists' activities in areas such as state security, national sovereignty and economic interests, and sets down heavy fines as punishment for breaking it.

Human rights organizations reported that the authorities sometimes refused to grant them permission to hold meetings. Trade union activists said they were harassed by the security forces. The government reportedly refused to approve new associations or political parties, informing applicants that they should wait for new laws to be passed. In December, the parliament passed a new law on associations giving the authorities extensive powers to suspend or dissolve NGOs and further restricting their registration and funding.

Counter-terror and security

Armed groups, particularly Al-Qa'ida Organization in the Islamic Maghreb (AQIM), carried out a number of attacks. These mostly targeted military installations but also caused civilian deaths. Over 100 alleged members of AQIM and other Islamist armed groups were reported to have been killed by the security forces, often in unclear circumstances, prompting fears that some may have been extrajudicially executed.
■ An AQIM attack on a military barracks at Cherchell on 26 August reportedly killed two civilians and 16 soldiers.

In February, a presidential decree gave the army powers to combat terrorism, at the same time as lifting the state of emergency.

Also in February, a presidential decree amending the Code of Criminal Procedures gave judges the power to refer terrorism suspects to "secure establishments" in undisclosed locations for months at a time, in effect allowing for secret detention for prolonged periods.

Those detained as terrorism-related suspects were allegedly tortured and ill-treated while held by the Department of Information and Security (military intelligence), and in some cases were detained incommunicado in what may have amounted to enforced disappearances.
■ On 18 July, Abdelhakim Chenoui and Malik Medjnoun were sentenced to 12 years in prison after an apparently unfair trial after which they were found guilty of murdering Kabyle singer Lounès Matoub years before. Both had been held without trial since 1999. Their conviction was based on a "confession" that Abdelhakim Chenoui said he had been forced to make under duress and which he later retracted.

Women's rights

Women remained subject to discrimination under the law and in practice. In particular, under the 2005 Family Code, women's rights are subordinated to those of men in matters relating to marriage, divorce, child custody and inheritance.

In May, after visiting Algeria in April, the UN Special Rapporteur on violence against women said the government had taken positive steps to advance women's rights but urged the authorities to address continuing violence against women in the family, sexual harassment, and stigmatization of unmarried single women and women living on their own.

In November, the National Assembly passed a law to increase the representation of women in parliament, but did not adopt draft proposals for a 30 per cent quota in all constituencies or for women to be placed high on electoral lists.
■ In June and July, groups of young men in the northern city of M'sila were reported to have attacked women they accused of prostitution.

Impunity – enforced disappearances

The authorities again took no steps to investigate the thousands of enforced disappearances and other serious abuses that took place during the internal conflict in the 1990s or to ensure that perpetrators were held accountable. They continued to implement the Charter for Peace and National Reconciliation (Law 06-01), which gave impunity to the security forces, criminalized public criticism of their conduct and granted amnesties to members of armed groups responsible for gross human rights abuses. Families of people who disappeared faced pressure to accept generic certificates, which stated that their relatives were dead but did not specify the date or cause of death, as a precondition for claiming compensation. The security forces dispersed demonstrations organized by families of the disappeared.

Freedom of religion or belief

Christians, including converts, continued to face prosecution for unauthorized religious activity under Ordinance 06-03 regulating faiths other than the state religion, Islam. Under the legislation, Christians continued to face hindrances building or maintaining churches. In May, the governor of the north-east province of Béjaïa ordered the closure of all churches on the basis of the law. The order was countermanded by the Minister of Interior.

■ On 25 May, a court in Cité Jamal in the city of Oran sentenced Abdelkarim Siaghi, a Christian convert, to five years' imprisonment and a heavy fine for "offending the Prophet Mohamed" after what was reported to be an unfair trial in which his lawyers were not permitted to cross-examine witnesses. He remained at liberty at the end of the year, awaiting the outcome of an appeal.

Death penalty

Courts continued to hand down death sentences, mostly against people tried in their absence for terrorism-related offences. The last execution took place in 1993.

Amnesty International visits/reports

🚌 Amnesty International delegates visited Algeria from February to March.

ANGOLA

REPUBLIC OF ANGOLA

Head of state and government:	José Eduardo dos Santos
Death penalty:	abolitionist for all crimes
Population:	19.6 million
Life expectancy:	51.1 years
Under-5 mortality:	160.5 per 1,000
Adult literacy:	70 per cent

The authorities curtailed freedom of assembly through excessive use of force, arbitrary arrests and detentions, and criminal charges. Police used excessive force resulting in deaths. Journalists faced increased restrictions. Two journalists were tried and convicted of defamation for writing critical articles. There were further forced evictions and the government failed to honour its promise to rehouse 450 families who had been previously evicted. Human rights violations continued against Congolese people expelled from Angola.

Background

A bill to criminalize cybercrime, which was criticized by civil society as a risk to freedom of expression and information, was withdrawn in May. Concerns remained that the bill would be reintroduced or its provisions incorporated into the Penal Code under revision.

Anti-government demonstrations took place throughout the year calling for the resignation of the President. A protest in September became violent after suspected members of the State Information and Security Services infiltrated the crowds and reportedly vandalized property and beat individuals, including journalists. A number of demonstrators were arrested.

In September the Provincial Government of Luanda issued a by-law indicating the areas that could be used for assemblies and demonstrations. It excluded Independence Square, where the majority of anti-government demonstrations had taken place during the year.

In June, parliament approved a law against domestic violence.

In July the President inaugurated the first phase of the City of Kilamba project comprising 20,000 new apartments, 14 schools, a hospital and 12 health posts. Other plans to build social housing in various parts of the country were announced throughout the year.

In August, immigration authorities at Luanda's international airport refused entry into Angola to delegates of various civil society organizations who were to attend the Civil Society Forum of the Southern African Development Community (SADC), planned around the SADC Heads of State Summit. Arrangements had been made for them to receive visas upon arrival at the airport. Two Mozambican journalists who were to cover the Summit were also refused entry, despite having valid visas.

In November, opposition party parliamentarians walked out of a parliamentary debate on the new Electoral Legislative package for the 2012 general elections. The National Union for the Total Independence of Angola (União Nacional para Independência Total de Angola, UNITA) stated that the package contained unconstitutional provisions. In December, the Organic Law for the National Electoral Commission was approved.

Forced evictions

Forced evictions continued, although on a smaller scale than previous years, and thousands of people remained at risk of being forcibly evicted. Some planned evictions were suspended. Thousands of families forcibly evicted in the past remained without compensation.

In June the government announced that over 450 families in Luanda whose homes were demolished between 2004 and 2006 were to be rehoused from September. This had not begun by the end of the year.

Planned demolitions in the Arco Íris neighbourhood of Lubango city centre were cancelled by the Huíla Provincial Governor in August because of inadequate conditions where approximately 750 families were to be resettled. The families had been given a month to leave their homes in June, which was extended for a further month, and were offered land in an isolated area 14km from the city.

■ In August, according to reports, municipal officials protected by armed national and military police forcibly evicted 40 families in the Km 30 neighbourhood of Viana in Luanda after the land was apparently sold to a private company. According to the local housing rights organization SOS-Habitat, the officials demolished the houses of any who were not present, destroying their belongings. Firmino João Rosário was reportedly shot dead by police when he attempted to stop the demolitions. Another resident, Santos António, was reportedly shot in the hand.

■ In October, members of the Lubango municipal administration community services, protected by National Police, demolished 25 homes belonging to families in the Tchavola area of Lubango, Huíla Province. The evictions were accompanied by arbitrary arrests and excessive use of force by the police. All those arrested were released the same day. The homes demolished belonged to families who had been relocated to the area after being forcibly evicted from March 2010 to make way for railway upgrades in Lubango.

Police and security forces

Police carried out their functions in a partisan manner, especially during some of the anti-government demonstrations. They used excessive force to disperse demonstrators, including live ammunition, dogs and an irritant spray to the eyes, and carried out arbitrary arrests and detentions.

■ In September, police officers used live ammunition during a protest by motorcycle taxi drivers in Kuito city, Bie province. Two protesters died after being shot in the head and the back, and six others were injured. The drivers were protesting against the abuse of power by police, whom they accused of confiscating the motorcycles of those who were lawfully operating in the province, as well as arbitrarily arresting and ill-treating several motorcycle taxi drivers during an operation to control their activities. No officer appeared to have been brought to justice for the excessive force and unlawful killings.

In a number of cases, off-duty police officers were accused of shooting and killing individuals. In most cases the officers had not been brought to justice by the end of the year.

■ On 12 November an off-duty police officer reportedly shot dead Francisco dos Santos with a police-issue firearm after he intervened to stop two children fighting in the Rangel neighbourhood of Luanda. According to eyewitnesses, one of the children called his father, a police officer, who arrived and started shooting before running away. Two shots hit Francisco dos Santos in the back and he died in hospital later that day. The police officer remained at large and no arrests had been made by the end of the year.

Freedom of expression – journalists

Journalists faced increased restrictions. Several were briefly detained or beaten by police or suspected members of the security services, and had their property confiscated or destroyed while covering anti-government demonstrations. Two were sentenced to imprisonment for alleged defamation.

■ In March, Voice of America correspondent Armando Chicoca was convicted of defamation and sentenced to one year's imprisonment. The charges related to two articles he had written concerning allegations of sexual harassment and corruption by the President of the Namibe Provincial Court. Armando Chicoca was conditionally released on bail in April pending an appeal.

■ In October, William Tonet, director and owner of the newspaper *Folha 8*, was convicted of defamation against three army generals in 2007. He was reportedly sentenced to one year's imprisonment suspended for two years and a fine of 10 million kwanzas (over US$100,000). William Tonet lodged an appeal but no decision had been made by the end of the year.

Freedom of assembly

Freedom of assembly was curtailed throughout the country. Police used excessive force in some instances, including dogs and firearms, to quell demonstrations and arbitrarily arrested protesters and journalists. Some were released without charge after hours or days; scores of others were tried for disobedience and resisting authority.

■ During a demonstration in March, police arrested three journalists and 20 demonstrators, saying that these were precautions to "prevent incalculable consequences". They were released without charge after a few hours. Other demonstrators were arrested in May, September and October. On 9 September police used dogs to disperse hundreds of people gathered outside a court, where 21 people were being tried in connection with a demonstration six days earlier. A further 27 people were arrested and charged with attacking security forces; the case was dismissed by a court on 19 September for lack of evidence. However, 18 of the 21 were convicted of disobedience, resistance and assault on 12 September. All 18 had their convictions overturned by the Supreme Court on 14 October and were released.

Prisoners of conscience and possible prisoners of conscience

Thirty-three members of the Commission of the Legal Sociological Manifesto of the Lunda Tchokwe Protectorate remained in prison without trial until the Supreme Court ordered their release in March, despite the repeal in December 2010 of the law under which they had been charged. They were not awarded any compensation for their unlawful detention.

Two other Commission members, Mário Muamuene and Domingos Capenda, detained in October 2010, were sentenced to one year's imprisonment for rebellion in March. They remained in prison although the sentence expired in October. They and five other prisoners – Sérgio Augusto, Sebastião Lumani, José Muteba, António Malendeca and Domingos Henrique Samujaia – went on hunger strike in May and again in October to protest against their continuing detention and poor prison conditions.

Migrants' rights

According to the International Committee for the Development of Peoples (Comitato Internazionale per lo Sviluppo dei Populi, CISP), at least 55,000 nationals of the Democratic Republic of the Congo (DRC) were expelled from Angola during the year. At least 6,000 of these reported suffering sexual violence. No one was held responsible for human rights abuses during the expulsions of Congolese migrants from Angola in past years. Following a visit to Angola in March, the Special Representative of the UN Secretary-General on Sexual Violence in Conflict expressed concern over the continued reports of sexual violence against Congolese migrants by Angolan armed forces during expulsions. The Angolan Minister of Foreign Affairs denied the allegations. In November the Special Representative called on the governments of Angola and the DRC to investigate these reports and bring the perpetrators to justice. In December, the Minister of Foreign Affairs stated that the government would co-ordinate with the UN to expel foreign nationals from the country.

Amnesty International visits/reports

🚗 Despite continued statements by the authorities that Amnesty International had never been denied visas to Angola, applications submitted in October 2008, October 2009 and November 2010 had still not been granted.

▨ Angola to forcibly evict hundreds of families (PRE01/414/2011)

ARGENTINA

ARGENTINE REPUBLIC
Head of state and government: **Cristina Fernández de Kirchner**
Death penalty: **abolitionist for all crimes**
Population: **40.8 million**
Life expectancy: **75.9 years**
Under-5 mortality: **14.1 per 1,000**
Adult literacy: **97.7 per cent**

Investigations and prosecutions of human rights violations committed during the years of military rule made significant progress. Indigenous Peoples were threatened with eviction from their traditional lands. Access to legal abortion remained difficult.

Background

President Cristina Fernández was re-elected in October. The ruling party was set to control both houses of Congress for the next two years.

In April, the crime of enforced disappearance was incorporated into the Criminal Code, in line with a recommendation by the Inter-American Commission on Human Rights in the case of Iván Eladio Torres Millacura who disappeared in 2003.

In October, Argentina ratified the Optional Protocol to the International Covenant on Economic, Social and Cultural Rights.

Following her visit to Argentina in April, the UN Special Rapporteur on the right to adequate housing expressed concern about the increasing number of violent evictions affecting residents of informal settlements, peasants and Indigenous Peoples.

Indigenous Peoples' rights

Indigenous communities continued to be threatened with eviction, despite a blanket ban on such evictions until November 2013 pending completion of a nationwide survey of Indigenous territories. Following his visit to Argentina in November, the UN Special Rapporteur on indigenous people expressed his concern about the number of forced evictions, the failure to put in place real protection of rights to land ownership, and the need for a mechanism to consult communities on projects that affect them.

■ In May, five months of protest in the centre of Buenos Aires came to an end when the national government finally met the Toba Qom Indigenous community of La Primavera, Formosa province. The government agreed tô guarantee the community's safety and initiate a dialogue to discuss land and other community rights. However, the family of community leader Félix Díaz continued to be threatened and harassed. Félix Díaz faced charges in connection with the violent dispersal by police of a roadblock mounted by the community in November 2010 in which two people, one a police officer, died.

■ In November, Cristian Ferreyra, leader of the Lule Vilela Indigenous community of San Antonio, Santiago del Estero province, was shot dead. He was involved in defending the community's traditional land from deforestation and the expansion of soya plantations.

■ In August a court in Tucumán province ordered the suspension of attempts to evict the Quilmes Indigenous community of Colalao del Valle pending the conclusion of proceedings to determine the ownership of the property where the community was living. The community had faced continual threats of eviction.

Justice and impunity

Significant progress was made in securing the conviction of those responsible for grave human rights violations under military rule (1976-1983).

■ In October, former navy captain Alfredo Astíz and 15 others were given prison sentences of between 18 years and life for their role in 86 crimes against humanity committed at a secret detention centre in a Buenos Aires naval school (Escuela Superior de Mecánica de la Armada, ESMA). Under military rule, hundreds of people were held in the ESMA after being abducted; some were killed under torture while others were flung to their deaths from aeroplanes.

■ In April, former military general Reynaldo Bignone and politician and former police officer Luis Abelardo Patti were sentenced to life imprisonment for several cases of murder, abduction and torture in the town of Escobar during the 1970s.

■ In May, eight former soldiers were sentenced to life imprisonment for the 1976 Margarita Belén massacre in Chaco province in which 22 political prisoners were tortured and executed.

■ In May, former generals Luciano Benjamín Menéndez and Antonio Domingo Bussi, as senior commanders, were judged to have been direct participants in gender-based violence against women held at the Villa Urquiza secret detention centre, Tucumán province, in the

1970s, and in the aggravated and repeated rape of a 19-year-old woman. Antonio Domingo Bussi died in November while under house arrest.

Torture and other ill-treatment

In February, mobile phone images of the torture in 2010 of two prisoners by prison guards in San Felipe prison, Mendoza province, came to light. Prisoners Matías Tello and Andrés Yacante, who were suspected by prison officers of involvement in circulating the images, received threats and were transferred to Almafuerte prison where they alleged that they were tortured. By the end of the year nobody had been brought to justice.

Sexual and reproductive rights

Women continued to face difficulties in accessing legal abortions.

■ In April, the UN Human Rights Committee ruled against Argentina for impeding access to a legal abortion for a 19-year-old woman with a mental disability who was raped by her uncle in 2006. The Committee found that the state's failure to guarantee her right to terminate her pregnancy caused her physical and moral pain and ordered Argentina to pay damages and to take measures to prevent similar violations in the future.

Excessive use of force

Police used excessive force during the removal in July of 700 families from a private estate in Libertador San Martín, Jujuy province. Four people, including a policeman, were killed and at least 30 injured. The police officer in charge was removed from his post and the provincial government Minister of Security and Justice resigned.

ARMENIA

REPUBLIC OF ARMENIA

Head of state:	Serzh Sargsyan
Head of government:	Tigran Sargsyan
Death penalty:	abolitionist for all crimes
Population:	3.1 million
Life expectancy:	74.2 years
Under-5 mortality:	21.6 per 1,000
Adult literacy:	99.5 per cent

The ban on public assemblies in the central square of the capital was lifted and an improved Law on Assemblies was adopted. However, concerns remained regarding the implementation in practice of the right to freedom of peaceful assembly. Torture and other ill-treatment in police stations also remained a concern.

Background

Large-scale protests led by the opposition Armenian National Congress started in February. They called for democratic reforms, the release of all opposition activists detained following the 2008 post-election protests and a new inquiry into clashes between police and protesters that left 10 people dead and more than 250 wounded. On 26 May, a general amnesty was declared for all the people imprisoned in connection with the 2008 protests. On 20 April, the President ordered a renewed investigation into the deaths of 10 people during the events, but at the end of the year no one had been brought to justice in connection with the deaths.

Freedom of assembly

There were a number of improvements regarding freedom of assembly. The ban on public assemblies in Yerevan's Freedom Square was lifted. The square had been closed to demonstrations since the March 2008 clashes.

However, concerns continued. The Council of Europe Commissioner for Human Rights reported in May about the "unlawful and disproportionate impediments to the right of peaceful assembly, such as intimidation and arrest of participants, disruption of transportation means and blanket prohibitions against assemblies in certain places".

The new Law on Assemblies was assessed by the Council of Europe's Venice Commission to be largely in accordance with international standards, but concerns remained. In this respect, the Commission highlighted the Law's blanket prohibition against assemblies organized within a certain distance from the presidential residence, the national assembly and courts; the seven-day notice period before a protest was allowed to take place as being unusually long; and the articles prohibiting assemblies which aimed at forcibly overthrowing the constitutional order, inciting racial, ethnic and religious hatred or violence as being too broad.

Torture and other ill-treatment

Torture and other ill-treatment remained a concern. In a report published in February, the UN Working Group on Arbitrary Detention stated that many of the detainees and prisoners they interviewed had been subjected to ill-treatment and beatings in police stations. Police and investigators used ill-treatment to obtain confessions, and prosecutors and judges frequently refused to admit evidence of ill-treatment during court proceedings.

In August, the European Committee for the Prevention of Torture reported that it had received a significant number of credible allegations of ill-treatment, some amounting to torture, by police during initial interviews.

Steps were taken during the year to establish a National Preventive Mechanism (NPM) – an independent body to monitor places of detention – in line with Armenia's obligations under the Optional Protocol to the UN Convention against Torture. A Torture Prevention Expert Council was set up within the Human Rights Defender's Office to act as the NPM, and the composition and guidelines for the NPM were discussed with NGOs and experts and approved. Recruitment for the NPM began in October.

■ On 9 August, seven young opposition activists detained following a clash with police alleged that they were beaten and ill-treated while in police custody. The activists were reportedly beaten up and detained after they tried to intervene as police officers were searching another man. The activists circulated internet images described as being taken by themselves on their mobile phones, showing some of them with visible injuries on their faces and backs. All seven were charged with hooliganism and assault on state officials, but six were later released on bail. There had been no investigation into the allegations of police ill-treatment by the end of the year.

Prisoners of conscience

In December, 60 men were serving prison sentences for refusing to perform military service on grounds of conscience. The alternative service remained under military control.

AUSTRALIA

AUSTRALIA

Head of state:	Queen Elizabeth II, represented by Quentin Bryce
Head of government:	Julia Gillard
Death penalty:	abolitionist for all crimes
Population:	22.6 million
Life expectancy:	81.9 years
Under-5 mortality:	5.1 per 1,000

Australia continued to violate the rights of Indigenous Peoples, stripping essential services from Aboriginal homelands. Refugee policy favoured deterrence, with mandatory, indefinite and remote detention for asylum-seekers arriving by boat.

Indigenous Peoples' rights

The government continued to limit funding for housing and municipal services such as water and sanitation to Aboriginal peoples living on traditional homelands in the Northern Territory. As a result, people were effectively forced to abandon their traditional homelands to access essential services.

An expert panel on the constitutional recognition of Indigenous Australians was due to provide recommendations to the Federal Parliament by December.

Justice system

Indigenous Peoples, while accounting for roughly 2.5 per cent of Australia's population, comprised 26 per cent of the adult prison population. Half of all juveniles in detention were Aboriginal. A parliamentary committee report on Aboriginal youth and justice published in June showed a jump of 66 per cent in Aboriginal imprisonment rates between 2000 and 2009.

■ In September and October, security firm employees were fined for failing to prevent the death of Aboriginal elder Mr Ward, who collapsed from heatstroke in a prison van in 2008.

Refugees and asylum-seekers

In July, the Australian and Malaysian governments agreed to swap 800 asylum-seekers who arrived by boat in Australia with 4,000 refugees (predominantly from Myanmar) who were in Malaysia awaiting resettlement.

■ 42 asylum-seekers (predominantly Afghans), including six unaccompanied boys, challenged their removal to Malaysia. In a landmark decision, the High Court ruled in August that the swap was invalid under Australia's Migration Act. The Act prohibits Australia from deporting asylum-seekers to countries that do not have sufficient legal guarantees for refugee protection (see Malaysia entry).

As of November 5,733 people were in immigration detention, including 441 children. Thirty-eight per cent of the 5,733 had been detained for over 12 months. Increasing rates of suicide and self-harm, including by children as young as nine, were reported in nearly all detention centres. In July, the Commonwealth Ombudsman launched an investigation; the findings remained pending.

In September, the government introduced Complementary Protection laws that strengthened protection for people fleeing abuses – such as female genital mutilation, honour killings and the death penalty – which are not covered by the UN Refugee Convention.

Violence against women and children

In February, the National Plan to Reduce Violence against Women and their Children was endorsed by federal, state and territory governments.

International scrutiny

In January, Australia's human rights record was assessed for the first time under the UN Universal Periodic Review. Australia agreed to ratify the Optional Protocol to the UN Convention against Torture and to consider ratifying ILO No. 169 Indigenous and Tribal Peoples Convention. However, it rejected: introducing a Human Rights Act; ending mandatory detention of asylum-seekers; allowing same-sex marriage; and compensating Indigenous People who were forcibly removed from their families when they were children.

Amnesty International visits/reports

🚐 Amnesty International's Secretary General visited Australia in October.

📱 The land holds us: Aboriginal Peoples' right to traditional homelands in the Northern Territory (ASA 12/002/2011)

AUSTRIA

REPUBLIC OF AUSTRIA

Head of state:	Heinz Fischer
Head of government:	Werner Faymann
Death penalty:	abolitionist for all crimes
Population:	8.4 million
Life expectancy:	80.9 years
Under-5-mortality:	4.1 per 1,000

Austria failed to introduce the crime of torture into domestic legislation. Children were at higher risk of detention pending deportation.

International scrutiny

In January, Austria's human rights record was assessed under the UN Universal Periodic Review (UPR). The government accepted 131 of the 161 recommendations received and committed to implement them in consultation with civil society.

Legal, constitutional and institutional developments

In November, following consultations with civil society, Austria adopted a law establishing a National Preventive Mechanism (NPM) within the Ombudsman's Board, as required under the Optional Protocol to the UN Convention against Torture. There were concerns among civil society organizations about the full independence of the NPM.

Amendments to the Security Police Law allowing police surveillance of individuals without judicial control were pending adoption at the end of the year.

Torture and other ill-treatment

Austria failed to introduce the crime of torture into its criminal code despite repeated recommendations by the UN Committee against Torture.

■ Gambian citizen Bakary J., who was tortured by four police officers in 2006 following an unsuccessful deportation, had still not received reparation and was at risk of deportation. His complaint before the European Court of Human Rights was still pending.

■ In January, the police officer who in February 2009 injured US citizen Mike B., an African-American teacher, during a plain-clothes police operation in Vienna, was sentenced to a fine for grievous bodily harm by the Vienna Regional Criminal Court. In

September, the fine was reduced by the Austrian Supreme Court.

Police and security forces

In June, the Vienna Regional Criminal Court sentenced three individuals respectively to life, 19 and 16 years' imprisonment for the killing of Chechen refugee Umar Israilov on 13 January 2009. In March, the Independent Administrative Tribunal in Vienna rejected a complaint alleging that the police had failed to provide the victim with protection. Complaints against this decision were pending before the Constitutional Court and the Administrative Court.

Racism

Reports of racially motivated police misconduct towards foreign nationals and ethnic minorities continued. Structural shortcomings within the criminal justice system when responding to discrimination, including the lack of a comprehensive data collection system that would make it possible to record and evaluate these incidents, were not addressed.

Migrants' and asylum-seekers' rights

Although the government did not officially suspend transfers of asylum-seekers to Greece under the Dublin II Regulation, no such transfers took place following the verdict of the European Court of Human Rights in the case of *M.S.S. v. Belgium and Greece* (see Belgium and Greece entries).

In July, an amendment to the Austrian Aliens Law came into force that placed foreign children aged 16 to 18 at higher risk of detention pending deportation.
■ Following the death in July 2010 of Reza H. while in police detention in Vienna, the Ministry of Interior carried out an internal evaluation. Reza H., an Afghan asylum-seeker who had alleged that he was 16 years old, died from injuries sustained following a suicide attempt some months earlier. The Ministry subsequently adopted measures to improve the information exchange between asylum and foreign police authorities. Inquiries by the Ombudsman's Board were still pending at the end of the year.

AZERBAIJAN

REPUBLIC OF AZERBAIJAN

Head of state:	Ilham Aliyev
Head of government:	Artur Rasizade
Death penalty:	abolitionist for all crimes
Population:	9.3 million
Life expectancy:	70.7 years
Under-5 mortality:	33.5 per 1,000
Adult literacy:	99.5 per cent

Peaceful protests were banned and violently dispersed. Opposition activists were imprisoned. Protests and expression of dissent were repressed and freedom of expression, assembly and association were restricted.

Background

Increasing frustration with authoritarian rule, and tight controls over those expressing critical views, led to a series of protests in March and April. Hundreds of people gathered in the capital Baku to demand democratic reform and greater respect for human rights. These nascent signs of popular protest were repressed by the government with a new wave of repression and intimidation. The authorities imprisoned youth activists and opposition supporters behind the protests and stepped up the harassment of the civil society groups and media who could speak on their behalf.

Prisoners of conscience

On 26 May, following significant international pressure, Eynulla Fatullayev, halfway through serving an eight-and-a-half-year prison sentence on trumped-up charges, was released by a presidential pardon. On 26 December, opposition youth activist Jabbar Savalan was released following a presidential pardon. He had been arrested on 5 February, a day after calling for protests online and re-posting an article critical of the government. He was allegedly beaten while in police custody to force him to sign a false confession and was sentenced to over two years in prison on fabricated charges of drug possession.

However, 16 activists and opposition supporters remained imprisoned as prisoners of conscience in connection with the protests in March and April.
■ Following the protests, 13 activists and members

of opposition political parties were convicted of "organizing and participating in public disorder" and sentenced to up to three years in prison following unfair trials. No evidence was presented to show that any of those imprisoned was engaged in anything more than the legitimate exercise of their rights. Four of the 13 were additionally convicted of specific acts of violence allegedly committed during the protests.

■ On 31 March, Shahin Hasanli, one of the protest organizers, was arrested and charged with illegal possession of pistol bullets. On 22 July he was convicted and sentenced to two years' imprisonment. The prosecutors at his trial failed to present evidence that he was in possession of any firearms at the time of his arrest.

■ On 18 May, Bakhtiyar Hajiyev, an opposition activist who called for an online protest on 11 March, was convicted of evading military service and sentenced to two years in prison. He had been arrested three times since he had stood in parliamentary elections in 2010, although he had only received a valid draft card at the time of his second arrest.

■ On 27 August, human rights defender and former parliamentary candidate Vidadi Isgandarov was sentenced to three years in prison for allegedly interfering with the 2010 parliamentary elections. Charges, previously dropped due to lack of evidence, were reinstated on 2 May, immediately after his detention for participating in the April protests had ended.

Freedom of expression – journalists

Independent and opposition journalists faced increased violence during the protests and were prevented from carrying out their work. By the end of the year, there had been no effective investigation into violent attacks on journalists and no one had been brought to justice.

■ On 2 April, several journalists covering the anti-government protests were detained. They reported that law enforcement officials prevented them from photographing and interviewing protest participants.

■ On 26 March, Seymur Haziyev, a journalist with opposition newspaper *Azadlıq*, was reportedly abducted and beaten by six masked assailants. He reported that his abductors warned him against writing critical articles about the President.

■ On 3 April, another *Azadlıq* journalist, Ramin Deko, was reportedly abducted, warned not to write critical articles about the President and physically assaulted.

Freedom of assembly

A ban on demonstrations effectively criminalized the protests in March and April, and led to imprisonment for many of those who organized and took part in them.

■ On 11 March, police dispersed about 100 people attempting to rally in Baku and arrested 43 people. The police also detained and harassed individuals who tried to disseminate information about the protests before the event.

■ On 12 March, police broke up peaceful protests by 300 people in the centre of Baku. Some 100 protesters were detained and 30 were sentenced to between five and eight days in prison in summary trials lasting 10 to 15 minutes.

■ On 2 April, another opposition protest in central Baku of some 1,000 participants was violently broken up by the police using shields, truncheons and rifles to beat and arrest protesters. The peaceful protest turned violent as several protesters resisted arrest. Some 174 people were detained both before and after the protest; 60 people received from five to 10 days administrative detention and four organizers were jailed for up to three years.

Freedom of association

NGOs working on democratic reform and human rights issues faced increased pressure and harassment.

■ On 4 March, three local NGOs located in Ganja, the Election Monitoring and Democracy Studies Centre, Demos Public Association and the Ganja Regional Information Centre, were evicted from their premises by the authorities without any formal explanation or apparent legal grounds.

■ The branches of two international organizations, the National Democratic Institute and the Human Rights House, in Baku were shut down on 7 March and 10 March respectively on the grounds that they had failed to comply with registration requirements.

■ On 11 August the office of Leyla Yunus, director of the Institute for Peace and Democracy, was destroyed, days after she had spoken against the government-endorsed forced evictions and the demolition of buildings in central Baku as part of a reconstruction project. The demolition began without any prior notice and despite a court order banning any demolition attempts on the property before 13 September 2011.

Torture and other ill-treatment

Several activists detained at and after the protests in March and April complained of ill-treatment at the moment of their arrest and subsequently while in police custody. By the end of the year none of these allegations had been effectively investigated.

■ Bakhtiyar Hajiyev alleged that he had been ill-treated and threatened with rape while in police custody in March, but his allegations were dismissed without effective investigation.

■ Tural Abbasli, leader of the youth wing of the opposition Musavat Party, maintained that he had been beaten when arrested on 2 April and again while in custody in Yasamal district police station in Baku.

■ Tazakhan Miralamli, of the opposition Popular Front Party, was allegedly beaten with batons by the police while being taken into custody on 2 April. His left eye was badly injured. He maintained that he was beaten again in the Sabail district police department before being taken to hospital, where, in addition to the injury to his eye, he was diagnosed with a broken finger, kidney problems and extensive soft tissue damage.

Amnesty International visits/reports

🚍 Amnesty International delegates visited Azerbaijan in March and November.

📄 "Don't let them be silenced": Azerbaijani activists imprisoned for speaking out (EUR 55/010/2011)

📄 The spring that never blossomed: Freedoms suppressed in Azerbaijan (EUR 55/011/2011)

BAHAMAS

COMMONWEALTH OF THE BAHAMAS

Head of state:	Queen Elizabeth II, represented by Sir Arthur Alexander Foulkes
Head of government:	Hubert Alexander Ingraham
Death penalty:	retentionist
Population:	0.3 million
Life expectancy:	75.6 years
Under-5 mortality:	12.4 per 1,000

There were concerns about the treatment of Haitian migrants. Cases of ill-treatment by the police were reported. A new law regulating the death penalty was passed; no executions were carried out.

Background

The Bahamas faced a continuing rise in violent crime in 2011, with a record 127 killings reported during the year, a 35 per cent increase compared with 2010. In November, Parliament approved new laws with the stated purpose of improving the criminal justice system. An official study showed that only 5 per cent of killings committed between 2005 and 2009 resulted in a conviction for either murder or manslaughter.

In June, the authorities publicly supported the UN Human Rights Council's resolution condemning discrimination based on sexual orientation.

Police and security forces

At least one person was killed during the year by the police in disputed circumstances.

There were reports of ill-treatment and excessive use of force by the police during arrests and detentions.

■ On 12 October, Samuel Darling was beaten by several police officers in front of his house and arbitrarily detained. When his wife, who witnessed the beating and arrest, went with her eight-year-old son to report the abuse at the nearest police station, she was arrested and charged with disorder. The family filed a formal complaint and were awaiting the conclusions of a police investigation at the end of the year.

Death penalty

At least five people remained under sentence of death. Four had spent more than five years on death row. Their sentences were eligible for commutation under a 1993 ruling by the UK-based Judicial Committee of the Privy Council, the highest court of appeal, which deemed that execution after five years on death row would constitute inhuman and degrading punishment.

In the context of an ongoing debate on public security, the authorities presented the retention of the death penalty as a measure to deter crime. In November, a law was passed that provided for mandatory death sentences and "imprisonment for the whole of the remaining years of a convicted person's life" for certain categories of murder.

Violence against women

A bill introduced into Parliament in 2009 to criminalize rape within marriage had still not been voted on by the end of 2011. In October, the Minister of State for Social Development publicly stated that the

B

government "has no intention of reintroducing" the bill before general elections which were due by May 2012.

According to police statistics, 13 women were murdered between January and August. The highest figure recorded previously was in 2009 when 10 women were murdered during the year.

Refugees and migrants

The Bahamas failed to implement calls from two UN agencies to stop all involuntary returns of Haitian nationals on humanitarian grounds following the 2010 earthquake in Haiti.

Statistics from the Department of Immigration reported that 2,392 Haitians were repatriated during 2011, representing 72 per cent of all the repatriations carried out in the Bahamas during the year. There were reports of the use of violence during arrests of irregular migrants.

BAHRAIN

KINGDOM OF BAHRAIN

Head of state:	King Hamad bin 'Issa Al Khalifa
Head of government:	Shaikh Khalifa bin Salman Al Khalifa
Death penalty:	retentionist
Population:	1.3 million
Life expectancy:	75.1 years
Under-5 mortality:	12.1 per 1,000
Adult literacy:	91.4 per cent

Bahrain experienced an acute human rights crisis in which at least 47 people were killed, including five members of the security forces and five people who died in custody as a result of torture. Security forces used excessive force against peaceful protesters and detained hundreds of people, including prisoners of conscience. Many detainees were tortured and otherwise ill-treated. Hundreds of civilian detainees received unfair trials before military courts; leading opposition activists were sentenced to up to life imprisonment. People who demonstrated against the government, including students, were dismissed from their jobs and from university. An independent inquiry by international experts appointed by the King confirmed the serious human rights violations and called for independent investigations, accountability and other reforms. Five people were sentenced to death; two had their sentences reduced at appeal. There were no executions.

Background

Mass pro-reform protests began on 14 February. Most demonstrators were from the majority Shi'a community, who believe they are discriminated against by the ruling Sunni minority. The protests centred on Pearl Roundabout in the capital, Manama, where a protest camp was established. Police and other security forces dispersed the protesters on 17 February using excessive force. Two days later, protesters re-established the camp and became more vociferous in their calls for change. On 23 February, the King pardoned 23 leading opposition activists, detained since August 2010, and more than 200 other prisoners and detainees.

On 13 March, a small group of anti-government protesters were reported to have attacked Asian migrant workers in Manama, causing two deaths and injuries to others. On 15 March, as demonstrations and strikes continued, the King declared a three-month state of emergency. This came a day after around 1,200 Saudi Arabian troops in armoured vehicles had arrived in the country to buttress Bahrain's security forces. By the end of March, the main protests had been crushed, although sporadic protests in predominantly Shi'a villages continued for the rest of the year. The King lifted the state of emergency on 1 June.

In late June, the King appointed the Bahrain Independent Commission of Inquiry (BICI), comprising five international legal and human rights experts, to investigate alleged human rights violations committed in connection with the protests. It reported to the King on 23 November. The government also initiated a "national dialogue" with the parliamentary opposition, businesses, NGO representatives and others; however, the largest Shi'a political opposition association, al-Wefaq, whose 18 members of parliament had resigned in February in protest at police brutality, withdrew after two weeks complaining that unacceptable conditions had been imposed.

Excessive use of force

The resort to unwarranted violence by security forces in response to the peaceful protest on 14 and 15 February resulted in the deaths of two people. On

17 February, riot police and other security forces destroyed the protest camp established at Pearl Roundabout. They used tear gas, beat people with batons and fired shotguns and rubber bullets at protesters at close range; five people were killed and many others were injured. The security forces also impeded and assaulted medical workers who sought to assist the wounded.

On 16 March, the security forces launched a concerted crackdown. Backed by helicopters and tanks, they stormed the Pearl Roundabout and Financial Harbour areas. They evicted the protesters using shotguns, rubber bullets and tear gas, causing deaths and injuries to protesters. They also took control of Manama's main Salmaniya Medical Complex, detaining doctors and other medical workers they accused of supporting the protesters. In response to the continuing protests in predominantly Shi'a villages, the security forces sometimes responded with excessive force. By the end of the year, at least 47 people had died in all the protests, including five police officers.

■ 'Ali 'Abdulhadi Mushaima' died after being shot several times at a demonstration on 14 February in al-Daih village, west of Manama. Some 10,000 people who attended his funeral procession the next day were attacked without warning by riot police using tear gas and shotguns; Fadhel 'Ali Matrook was shot dead.

■ 'Isa 'Abdulhassan, aged 60, died on 17 February when he was shot in the head at close range as the security forces stormed the protest camp at Pearl Roundabout.

■ Ahmed al-Jaber al-Qatan, aged 16, died in hospital on 6 October after being hit by shotgun pellets during a protest in the village of Abu-Saeiba'. Riot police used shotguns and sound bombs to disperse the protesters. The government said that it was investigating his death, but the outcome had not been made public by the end of 2011.

Arbitrary arrests and detentions

More than 1,000 people were arrested in connection with the protests; some were Sunni Muslims but the vast majority were Shi'a Muslims. Most were arrested in March and April, many in pre-dawn raids at their homes, often by armed, masked security officers who did not produce arrest warrants and often assaulted those they arrested and, sometimes, their relatives. Detainees were usually taken to undisclosed locations and held incommunicado for up to several weeks,

during which they were interrogated and, in many cases, allegedly tortured and otherwise ill-treated. Their whereabouts frequently remained unknown until they were brought to trial.

■ Ebrahim Sharif, Secretary General of the National Democratic Action Society (Wa'ad), a secular political opposition association, was taken from his home in Manama on 17 March by armed masked security men who refused to produce an arrest warrant when asked to do so. They took him to an undisclosed location and his family and lawyer were denied access to him for weeks.

Unfair trials

Hundreds of people were prosecuted for offences allegedly committed in connection with the protests, including political opposition activists, medical professionals, teachers, students and human rights activists. Many faced grossly unfair trials before a special military court – the National Safety Court (NSC) – set up under the state of emergency. Those convicted and sentenced to imprisonment included prisoners of conscience. The BICI reported that an estimated 300 people were convicted on charges relating to their exercise of freedom of expression. Others were convicted even though they repudiated "confessions" they said had been extracted under torture; the court did not investigate these allegations. In some cases, the NSC refused defence requests to call witnesses; in many, defence lawyers were denied access to their clients until the trial began and so had inadequate time to prepare their defence. Initially, appeals against NSC judgements were heard by a similarly deficient NSC appeal court.

Following wide criticism of the NSC, on 29 June the King decreed that all ongoing cases being examined by the NSC and linked to the February-March protests would be transferred to civilian courts, but on 18 August he decreed that the NSC would continue to try the most serious – felony – cases. However, all NSC judgements were made subject to appeal before a civilian court, including those already upheld by the NSC appeal court. In September, a military court sentenced 20 health professionals to up to 15 years in prison on charges that included occupying a government hospital, possession of weapons and stealing medicine. The cases were sent for appeal before a civilian court before the end of the year.

By early October, all cases had been transferred to civilian courts and the NSC was no longer functioning.

■ Abdel Jalil al-Singace, Hassan Mshaima and 19 other leading opposition activists, including seven tried in their absence, were convicted on charges that included "setting up terror groups to topple the royal regime and change the constitution" after an unfair trial before the NSC that concluded on 22 June. Eight, including Abdel Jalil al-Singace and Hassan Mshaima, were sentenced to life imprisonment, the others to lesser prison terms. Most had been detained in pre-dawn raids, held incommunicado for long periods during which they alleged they were tortured and forced to sign "confessions", and allowed only minimal access to lawyers before they were brought to trial. They were convicted despite the reported failure of the prosecution to provide strong evidence against them. Most of them appeared to have been prosecuted for calling for the end of the monarchy and the establishment of a republic. There was no evidence that they used or called for violence; they therefore appeared to be prisoners of conscience. The NSC appeal court confirmed the sentences imposed on all 21 defendants on 28 September; they remained in prison awaiting the Court of Cassation's ruling on their appeal.

Torture and other ill-treatment

Many of the people detained in March and April were taken to police stations and to the Criminal Investigations Department in Manama, where they were held incommunicado and interrogated by members of the National Security Agency and other security forces. Many alleged that they were beaten, made to stand for long periods, given electric shocks, deprived of sleep and threatened with rape. Many said they were held incommunicado for weeks after their interrogation ended.

The authorities failed to conduct independent investigations into most of these allegations. The NSC also failed to adequately investigate defendants' allegations of torture in pre-trial detention and accepted contested "confessions" as evidence of guilt. However, in November, shortly before the BICI presented its report and in anticipation of its findings, the government said it would amend the Penal Code to criminalize torture and that 20 members of the security forces were on trial in connection with allegations of torture of detainees, deaths in custody as a result of mistreatment, and unlawful killings of civilians. Full details of these prosecutions had not been disclosed by the end of the year.

■ Aayat Alqormozi, a student who had read out poems during the February protests, was arrested when she presented herself to the authorities on 30 March after masked members of the security forces twice raided her parents' house and threatened to kill her brothers if she did not surrender. She was held incommunicado for the first 15 days, during which she said that she was punched and kicked, given electric shocks to the face, forced to stand for hours, verbally abused and threatened with rape. On 12 June, the NSC sentenced her to one year in prison after convicting her of participating in illegal protests, disrupting public security and inciting hatred towards the regime. She was conditionally released on 13 July after she pledged not to participate in protests or criticize the government. Her case was referred to the High Criminal Court of Appeal, which ruled on 21 November that the case was suspended but without clarifying her legal status. She was at liberty at the end of the year, but was prevented from resuming her studies at Bahrain University.

Deaths in custody

Five people detained in connection with the protests died in custody as a result of torture. Those responsible for their torture were said to be among the 20 security officers facing prosecution at the end of the year.
■ Hassan Jassem Mohammad Mekki was arrested at his home in the early hours of 28 March. Six days later, his relatives were called to a morgue to identify his body, which they said bore marks and bruises on the head, neck and legs that appeared to have been caused by beatings. The cause of death was officially attributed to heart failure, but no autopsy was known to have been conducted. The BICI concluded that his death was caused by mistreatment in custody.
■ 'Ali 'Issa Ibrahim al-Saqer died in custody on 9 April, a few days after police called him in for questioning about the killing of a police officer during the March protests. The Interior Ministry said he died while being restrained by police. No autopsy was known to have been conducted. His body was said to have borne marks suggesting that he had been tortured. The BICI concluded that his death was due to mistreatment in custody.

Dismissals of protesters

More than 2,000 workers from the public sector and more than 2,400 from the private sector were dismissed from their jobs for participating in or supporting the protests. They included university lecturers, school teachers, medical doctors and nurses. Almost all were Shi'a Muslims. In late November, the BICI reported that 1,682 dismissed public sector employees had been reinstated.

Death penalty

The NSC sentenced five people to death after convicting them of killings committed during the protests. The NSC appeal court confirmed two of the sentences and commuted two others; the fifth case was awaiting appeal. The five were the first Bahraini nationals to be sentenced to death for more than 10 years. One foreign national sentenced to death in 2010 was still awaiting execution. There were no executions.

■ 'Ali 'Abdullah Hassan al-Sankis and 'Abdulaziz 'Abdulridha Ibrahim Hussain were sentenced to death on 28 April after the NSC convicted them of killing two police officers during the protests in March. The NSC appeal court upheld their sentences on 22 May. The Court of Cassation was due to rule on their cases in January 2012. Their lawyer sought a retrial on the grounds that the trial court had failed to investigate their allegations of torture and their sentences had been confirmed by an unfair military appeal court.

Bahrain Independent Commission of Inquiry

In its substantial report published on 23 November, the BICI said it had examined more than 8,000 complaints; interviewed more than 5,000 individuals, including male and female detainees; and visited various prisons, detention centres and the Salmaniya Medical Complex in Manama. It confirmed that many detainees had been tortured by security officials who believed they could act with impunity; that police and other security forces had repeatedly used excessive force against protesters, resulting in unlawful killings; and that legal proceedings before the NSC had been seriously defective. Among its recommendations, the BICI called for all allegations of torture to be independently investigated, for those responsible for abuses to be held criminally liable whatever their rank, and for the release of all those imprisoned on account of their legitimate exercise of freedom of expression. The King and government undertook to implement the BICI's recommendations.

Rights of lesbian, gay, bisexual and transgender people

At least 200 men were arrested on 2 February when police raided a party in al-Muharraq believed to involve gay men after neighbours complained about noise. Most were released without charge but 50 were prosecuted, 30 on charges of prostitution and other illicit acts. They were sentenced in March to prison terms of up to six months. The High Criminal Court of Appeal confirmed the sentences in December; by then all had already been released.

Amnesty International visits/reports

🚍 Amnesty International delegates visited Bahrain for research and government meetings in February, April and November. A medical expert participated in the February visit and a policing expert took part in the April visit. In November, Amnesty International delegates were among those present when the BICI presented its report to the King.

📄 Crackdown in Bahrain: Human rights at the crossroads (MDE 11/001/2011)

📄 Bloodied but unbowed: Unwarranted state violence against Bahraini protesters (MDE 11/009/2011)

📄 Bahrain: A human rights crisis (MDE 11/019/2011)

📄 Bahrain: Protecting human rights after the protests – Amnesty International submission to the UN Universal Periodic Review, May-June 2012 (MDE 11/066/2011)

BANGLADESH

PEOPLE'S REPUBLIC OF BANGLADESH

Head of state:	Zillur Rahman
Head of government:	Sheikh Hasina
Death penalty:	retentionist
Population:	150.5 million
Life expectancy:	68.9 years
Under-5 mortality:	52 per 1,000
Adult literacy:	55.9 per cent

Extrajudicial executions continued despite a government pledge to end them. Rapid Action Battalion (RAB) personnel, suspected of more than 54 unlawful killings during the year, were neither investigated independently nor brought to justice. The government failed to enforce its new policy to support women victims of violence. Amendments to the rules

governing the Bangladeshi International Crimes Tribunal reduced, but did not eliminate, the possibility of unfair trials for those accused of 1971 war crimes. The government failed to secure the right to livelihood and land of Indigenous People in the Chittagong Hill Tracts. More than 49 people were sentenced to death and at least five men were executed.

Background

In June, Parliament passed the 15th amendment to the Constitution, which removed provisions allowing for elections to be organized by a non-party caretaker government. It also banned the military from assuming state power. Also in June, the World Bank announced that Bangladesh had reduced poverty levels and improved living standards. However, more than 35 per cent of the rural population and 21 per cent of the urban population lived below the poverty line. In November, Parliament passed the Vested Property Return (Amendment) Act. The new law ended legally sanctioned violations of the economic and social rights of Hindus by allowing them to reclaim property that had been taken away under the decades old Vested Property Act.

Extrajudicial executions

RAB allegedly killed at least 54 people in 2011, bringing the total number of people killed since 2004 – when RAB was formed – to more than 700. RAB injured or tortured scores more. In many cases, family members told Amnesty International that victims died after being arrested by RAB and not in an encounter as RAB claimed. The authorities failed to investigate these incidents credibly.

■ Limon Hossain, aged 16, was shot in the leg by RAB officers in Jhalakathi on 23 March. RAB officials alleged that he was a member of a criminal gang and that he was injured when RAB officers returned fire after the gang shot at them. Limon Hossain said he was alone, bringing cattle home, when RAB personnel arrested and shot him. The conclusions of a separate government inquiry – never made public – reportedly confirmed his claim. The police charged Limon Hossain with trying to kill RAB officers.

Violence against women

Under a new National Women Development Policy, published in March, the Ministry of Women and Children's Affairs announced a plan to, among other things, "eradicate violence against, and oppression of, women and children by providing medical treatment, legal assistance and counselling to abused women and children". Human rights organizations said the authorities had failed to implement the plan and many women and children subjected to sexual and other violence were receiving no support from state institutions.

■ Human rights defender Shampa Goswami was abducted for several hours by a gang of men in Satkhira in October after she encouraged a female survivor of gang rape to report the incident to the police. The abductors threatened to harm Shampa Goswami if she did not stop supporting the victim. Shampa Goswami told Amnesty International delegates visiting her in Satkhira in November that initially police ignored her request for protection. The authorities subsequently promised to protect her following a vocal campaign by national and international human rights organizations.

International justice

In May, the International Crimes Tribunal, a Bangladeshi court set up in 2010 to try people accused of large-scale human rights abuses during the 1971 war of independence, began to address procedural shortcomings that were rendering its trials unfair. Its amended Rules of Procedure provided for bail, presumption of innocence before guilt is proven, and measures to ensure the protection of witnesses and victims. However, a constitutional ban on the right to challenge the jurisdiction of the Tribunal remained in force.

■ Motiur Rahman Nizami, Ali Ahsan Muhammad Mojahid, Muhammad Kamaruzzaman, Abdul Quader Molla and Delwar Hossain Sayeedi from Jamaat-e-Islami, and Salauddin Quader Chowdhury and Abdul Alim from the Bangladesh Nationalist Party, were indicted for war crimes. All but Abdul Alim, who was released on bail, remained detained. Five of the detainees were in custody for more than 18 months without charge. Delwar Hossain Sayeedi was formally charged in October for allegedly assisting the Pakistani army to commit genocide; kill, torture and rape unarmed civilians; torch houses of local Hindus; and force Hindus to convert to Islam. No one was indicted for crimes committed immediately after the victory of independence forces in late 1971.

Indigenous Peoples' rights

The government failed to prevent confiscation of Indigenous Peoples' land by Bengali settlers in the

Chittagong Hill Tracts. This led to violent clashes between the two communities, ending in loss of property and, at times, loss of lives. Bengali settlers usually entered Indigenous Peoples' land and appropriated it for agricultural use. Indigenous People told Amnesty International delegates visiting the area in March that Bengali settlers, emboldened by the army's tolerance of their actions, had frequently set fire to Indigenous homes, usually in clear sight of soldiers or other law enforcement personnel, without being stopped.

■ In March, Indigenous People from Langadu, in Rangamati hill district, told Amnesty International that local officials and soldiers from the local Border Guard Bangladesh unit failed to prevent an imminent attack by Bengali settlers against them in Rangipara village. They said that soldiers stood by while the settlers torched their homes on 17 February.

Torture and other ill-treatment

At least three people died in police custody, allegedly after being tortured. The government announced that criminal charges would be brought against any police personnel found responsible for these deaths. However, no one was charged or prosecuted by the end of the year. The government did not commit to bringing to justice police, RAB or other security personnel who allegedly tortured thousands of individuals in their custody throughout the year.

■ Newspaper editor Mahmudur Rahman told Amnesty International after his release in March that he was beaten severely on his back over the course of a night at a police station inside the army cantonment. He was detained in mid-2010 after publishing articles exposing alleged government corruption. The beating was so severe that he lost consciousness for several hours. He said he saw no point in complaining as he knew the authorities would not bother to act.

Death penalty

At least five men were executed, and more than 49 people were sentenced to death.

Amnesty International visits/reports

🚌 Amnesty International delegates visited Bangladesh in March, June and November.

📓 Crimes unseen: Extrajudicial executions in Bangladesh (ASA 13/005/2011)

BELARUS

REPUBLIC OF BELARUS

Head of state:	Alyaksandr Lukashenka
Head of government:	Mikhail Myasnikovich
Death penalty:	retentionist
Population:	9.6 million
Life expectancy:	70.3 years
Under-5 mortality:	12.1 per 1000
Adult literacy:	99.7 per cent

B

Restrictions on freedom of expression, association and assembly increased during the year. The government continued to carry out executions. Prisoners of conscience remained in detention and were subjected to torture and other ill-treatment. The right to a fair trial was restricted.

Background

Social unrest increased due to a worsening economic situation, and the government responded with restrictions on freedom of assembly and association.

On 17 June, the UN Human Rights Council expressed concerns at the situation in Belarus. It condemned the human rights violations following the December 2010 elections; it urged the government to co-operate fully with UN human rights mechanisms and to allow international monitors to carry out their work, and not to detain or expel them. Relations with the EU worsened. On 10 October the EU Council announced that it would extend until 31 October 2012 its travel ban on those responsible for violations of international electoral standards and for the crackdown on civil society.

Death penalty

The government executed two men during the year and passed two death sentences.

■ Andrei Burdyka and one other man were executed between 14 and 19 July. Andrei Burdyka's mother received official confirmation of his death three months later. The other family had not been notified by the end of the year. The executions were carried out despite a formal request sent on 17 December 2010 by the UN Human Rights Committee to the government of Belarus not to execute the two men until the case had been considered by the Committee.

Torture and other ill-treatment

There was no independent system of monitoring places of detention. Complaints against law enforcement officers were usually rejected by prosecutors, and those who complained faced reprisals from police.

■ On 28 February, after being released on bail, Alyaksei Mihalevich, a presidential candidate charged with organizing a demonstration in Minsk on 19 December 2010, held a press conference. He alleged that he and other detainees had been subjected to torture and other ill-treatment, including being strip-searched up to six times a day, and being forced to stand in stress positions.

■ Zmitser Dashkevich, who was sentenced to two years' hard labour on 24 March in connection with the demonstration in December 2010, was placed in solitary confinement eight times during the year. Conditions in solitary confinement include being denied exercise, refused bedding and deprived of sleep. Prisoners are also prevented from lying or sitting on bunks during the day.

Freedom of expression

In March, journalist Andrzej Poczobut, was charged with "insulting the President" and "libelling the President" for articles that he had written for the Polish newspaper *Gazeta Wyborcza*. On 5 June, he received a three-year suspended prison sentence.

Freedom of association

Registered and unregistered human rights groups faced prosecution and harassment throughout the year. The Law on Public Associations changed on 3 October to prohibit Belarusian NGOs from holding funds or bank accounts abroad. The Council of Europe's Venice Commission commented that the Criminal Code, which makes participation in the activities of non-registered political parties, or other public associations, a crime, "was incompatible with a democratic society."

■ On 4 August, the Chair of the NGO Viasna Human Rights Centre (Viasna), Ales Bialiatski, was arrested. He was charged on 12 August with "concealment of income on a large scale", which carries a sentence of up to seven years. The charges related to the use of a personal bank account in Lithuania to support Viasna's human rights work. Viasna was derecognized by the Belarusian authorities in 2003 and as such was barred from opening a bank account in Belarus. The trial began on 2 November. and on 24 November Ales Bialiatski was sentenced to four and a half years' imprisonment. Amnesty International considered him to be a prisoner of conscience and demanded his unconditional release.

■ On 12 January, the Ministry of Justice formally censured the Belarusian Helsinki Committee for sending a report to the UN Special Rapporteur on the independence of judges and lawyers, concerning restrictions faced by lawyers. The Ministry complained that the report was an "attempt to discredit the Republic of Belarus in the eyes of the world." In June, the organization was issued with a back-dated tax bill, relating to European Commission funds received in 2002 (which had originally been exempt from tax). The tax bill was accompanied by a second warning from the Ministry of Justice for breaching NGO regulations. In December, the Ministry for Taxes and Duties applied to the Ministry of Justice for the closure of the Belarusian Helsinki Committee.

Freedom of assembly

Restrictions on all forms of public gatherings increased during the year. On 3 October Parliament approved amendments to the Law on Public Assemblies. Any kind of pre-planned public gathering requires official permission: organizers are required to report "financial sources" used for the event; and they are not allowed to publicize the event until official permission is granted, which might not be until five days prior to the event. Law enforcement officers also have wider powers to make audio and video recordings, limit participants' access to the event and carry out body searches.

■ Throughout May, June and July, there were regular weekly "silent protests". Groups of people throughout the country would stroll wordlessly, applaud or use their mobile phone alarms simultaneously. Viasna reported that the authorities detained more than 2,000 people involved in "silent protests", and some of them were beaten and subjected to other forms of disproportionate force. Up to 80 per cent of those initially detained were subsequently sentenced to between five and 15 days' administrative detention or fined. On 29 July, the government introduced a draconian new law. It required government permission for any gatherings carrying out "action or inaction intended as a form of public expression of socio-political attitude or as a protest".

■ Human rights lawyer Roman Kislyak was detained on 16 October after walking alone down the main street of Brest with a megaphone asking for the release of Ales Bialiatski. He was charged with simultaneously picketing and marching. He was brought before an administrative court the following morning, and the judge returned the case to the police for further investigation. On 28 October the Lenin District Court in Brest imposed a fine equivalent to €3, and the appeal court upheld the judgement.

Prisoners of conscience

Between January and June, trials continued against leading political activists in connection with their participation in, or organization of, the mainly peaceful demonstration in Minsk on 19 December 2010. At the end of the year six remained in detention in connection with these events, all of them prisoners of conscience. Zmitser Bandarenka was sentenced to two years' hard labour on 26 March. Andrei Sannikau was sentenced to five years on 14 May. Pavel Sevyarynets was sentenced to three years on 16 May. Mykalaj Statkevich was sentenced to six years on 26 May. On 24 March, Zmitser Dashkevich and Eduard Lobau were sentenced to two and four years respectively for hooliganism. Others, including Andrei Sannikau's wife Iryna Khalip, were given suspended sentences. Six other prisoners of conscience were released during the year: three were informed that their cases had been closed, and one was released on bail and sought asylum abroad.

Unfair trials

Despite legislative guarantees, people who were charged following the demonstration on 19 December 2010 had infrequent access to their lawyers and were not able to meet them in private. Some lawyers reported that they were often refused access to their clients on the grounds that no meeting rooms were available. The government reported that there were only two rooms available for lawyers at the KGB detention centre in Minsk and for that reason meetings had been restricted.

Some lawyers who defended opposition leaders accused of organizing mass disorder in December 2010 were disbarred. In March 2011, Pavel Sapelko, who had defended Andrei Sannikau, was disbarred. On 7 August, Tamara Sidorenko, Alyaksei Mihalevich's lawyer, lost her licence.

Amnesty international visits/reports

🚌 An Amnesty International delegate visited Belarus in December.

📑 Clemency status of Belarusian men probably still pending (EUR 49/010/2011)

📑 Belarus: Six months after the Presidential elections clampdown on dissenting voices continues unabated (EUR 49/015/2011)

📑 The human rights situation in Belarus: Written statement to the 18th session of the United Nations Human Rights Council (EUR 49/017/2011)

BELGIUM

B

KINGDOM OF BELGIUM

Head of state:	King Albert II
Head of government:	Elio Di Rupo (replaced Yves Leterme's interim government in December)
Death penalty:	abolitionist for all crimes
Population:	10.8 million
Life expectancy:	80.0 years
Under-5 mortality:	4.6 per 1,000

The authorities continued to leave many asylum-seekers destitute and homeless. The European Court of Human Rights ruled that Belgium had violated the prohibition of removing anyone to a country where they would be exposed to a real risk of torture (*non-refoulement*), and the right to an effective remedy. The government attempted to rely on diplomatic assurances to remove foreign nationals to countries where they might face torture and other ill-treatment. A law prohibiting and penalizing concealing the face entered into force.

Refugees and asylum-seekers

The "reception crisis" that started in 2008 worsened by the end of 2011. According to NGOs, over 12,000 asylum-seekers, including children, were refused access to the official reception system between October 2009 and the end of 2011. They were left without shelter or medical, social or legal assistance. Over the year, despite some positive government measures, the number of people left out in the streets grew to over 4,000. Legislation adopted in November limited the right to reception for some groups of asylum-seekers and introduced a list of "safe countries of origin". Asylum-seekers from these "safe countries" would receive a decision within 15 days, and they could be forcibly removed from Belgium before an appeal had been heard.

■ On 21 January, the European Court of Human Rights ruled in the case of *M.S.S. v. Belgium and Greece* that both Belgium and Greece had violated the European Convention on Human Rights (see Greece entry).

■ On 1 July, M.L., a Moroccan national, was granted asylum in Belgium after spending over one year in administrative detention. After serving a six-year prison sentence for terrorism-related offences in Belgium, he applied for asylum on 16 March 2010. The Commissioner for Refugees and Stateless Persons stated in May that M.L. could be deported, if the government obtained diplomatic assurances from the Moroccan authorities that they would not torture and ill-treat M.L. there. The Council for Alien Law Litigation quashed this decision and M.L. was granted asylum. At the end of the year the government's appeal was pending.

■ On 13 December, the European Court of Human Rights ruled in *Kanagaratnam and others v. Belgium* that, by detaining three children and their mother in a secure detention centre for four months in 2009, Belgium had violated the prohibition of torture and other ill-treatment in respect of the three children, and the right to liberty of the children and their mother.

Torture and other ill-treatment

On at least two occasions the authorities attempted to rely on diplomatic assurances to remove foreign nationals to countries where they could be at risk of torture and other ill-treatment.

■ A.A., a Dagestani national in detention since September 2010, faced extradition to the Russian Federation on charges of participating in the activities of illegal armed groups. The charges against him were based on testimony allegedly obtained through torture, which was later retracted by the witness. The Belgian courts rejected A.A.'s appeals against extradition, based in part on diplomatic assurances that he would not be tortured in the Russian Federation. The Minister of Justice's decision on the extradition was pending at the end of the year.

■ In March, the Minister of Justice decided to allow the extradition of Arbi Zarmaev, an ethnic Chechen, to the Russian Federation, despite the Court of Appeal advising against it. The Court suggested that there was a lack of adequate guarantees that Arbi Zarmaev's

human rights would be respected in Russia. The Minister of Justice's decision was in part based on diplomatic assurances from the Russian authorities that he would not be tortured. At the end of the year his appeal against that decision was pending before the Council of State.

Discrimination

Discrimination on the grounds of religion continued. Individuals wearing symbols or dress perceived to be Muslim were particularly affected by discrimination when trying to access employment.

■ On 23 July, a law prohibiting and penalizing the concealing of the face in public entered into force. Although neutrally formulated, the law appeared to target the wearing of full face veils. The legality of the law was challenged before the Constitutional Court and the case was pending at the end of the year.

Legal, constitutional or institutional developments

Following the UN Universal Periodic Review in May, the authorities agreed to establish a National Human Rights Institution and to ratify both the Optional Protocol to the UN Convention against Torture and the Optional Protocol to the International Covenant on Economic, Social and Cultural Rights.

In June, Belgium ratified the International Convention for the Protection of All Persons from Enforced Disappearance.

Amnesty International visits/reports

🚍 An Amnesty International delegate visited Belgium in March and June.

▨ The European Court of Human Rights vindicates the rights of asylum-seekers in the EU (EUR 03/001/2011)

▨ Belgium: A fundamental step forward on human rights, the ratification of the Enforced Disappearance Convention (EUR 14/001/2011)

▨ Belgium: Amnesty International welcomes commitment to establish a National Human Rights Institution (EUR 14/002/2011)

▨ Suggested recommendations to States considered in the 11th round of the Universal Periodic Review, 2-13 May 2011 (IOR 41/008/2011)

BENIN

REPUBLIC OF BENIN

Head of state and government:	Thomas Boni Yayi
Death penalty:	abolitionist in practice
Population:	9.1 million
Life expectancy:	56.1 years
Under-5 mortality:	118 per 1,000
Adult literacy:	41.7 per cent

President Boni Yayi was re-elected in March, amid protests by opposition parties that compilation of the electoral lists meant that a significant proportion of the electorate was excluded. The rising prices of basic commodities led to some social unrest. In May and June civil servants went on strike over salary claims.

Repression of dissent

In March, security forces dispersed demonstrations by opposition supporters contesting the re-election of President Boni Yayi. Some demonstrators, including member of parliament Raphaël Akotègnon, were briefly held in police custody.

Death penalty

In August, Benin took an important step towards abolishing the death penalty after the National Assembly voted in favour of ratifying the Second Optional Protocol to the International Covenant on Civil and Political Rights. The ratification process was not completed by the end of the year.

Prison conditions

Prisons remained overcrowded. The prison in the city of Cotonou held six times its capacity, resulting in harsh conditions. Official detention figures showed that of the 2,300 inmates held, 99 per cent were in pre-trial detention.

BOLIVIA

PLURINATIONAL STATE OF BOLIVIA

Head of state and government:	Evo Morales Ayma
Death penalty:	abolitionist for ordinary crimes
Population:	10.1 million
Life expectancy:	66.6 years
Under-5 mortality:	51.2 per 1,000
Adult literacy:	90.7 per cent

Scores of people were injured when police violently dispersed a camp set up by Indigenous protesters during a march to La Paz over plans to construct a road through protected Indigenous territory. There were convictions in the 2003 "Black October" case.

Background

Social tensions increased during the year amid recurring protests over economic issues and Indigenous rights.

In March, the UN Committee on the Elimination of Racial Discrimination welcomed legislation passed by Congress in January to combat racial discrimination. However, it expressed concern about its implementation, the under-representation of Indigenous Peoples in decision-making bodies, access to justice and lack of clarity over mechanisms to ensure co-ordination and co-operation with the ordinary justice system in the new Law of Jurisdictional Delimitation.

Indigenous Peoples' rights

On 25 September scores of people were injured when police used tear gas and truncheons to break up a makeshift camp set up near Yucumo, Beni Department, by Indigenous protesters. The protesters were taking part in a 360-mile march from Trinidad, Beni Department, to La Paz in protest at government plans to build a road through the Isiboro-Sécure Indigenous Territory and National Park (Territorio Indígena y Parque Nacional Isiboro-Sécure, TIPNIS), in breach of constitutional guarantees on prior consultation with Indigenous Peoples, and of environmental preservation laws. Police arrested hundreds of Indigenous protesters and took them to the towns of San Borja and Rurrenabaque to be flown home by the military.

The government stated that the road would bring economic development. However, Indigenous

B

protesters said it would open up the area to extractive industries and encourage deforestation and coca production. The police crackdown led to the resignation of the Defence and Interior Ministers and nationwide protests.

In October, President Morales cancelled the project. In November a judge ordered the house arrest of the deputy police commander for allegedly ordering the police operation in Yucumo. Criminal investigations into the actions of the police were continuing at the end of the year.

Impunity

Those responsible for serious human rights violations, including enforced disappearance and extrajudicial executions, carried out before democracy was re-established in 1982, continued to evade justice.

By the end of the year, the armed forces had not handed over to prosecutors information relating to past human rights violations, despite Supreme Court orders in April 2010 requiring them to declassify the information. The government did not press for the information to be disclosed.

■ In August, the Supreme Court convicted seven former high-ranking officials for their part in the events known as "Black October", which left 67 people dead and more than 400 injured during protests in El Alto, near La Paz, in late 2003. This was the first time that a trial of military officials accused of human rights violations had reached a conclusion in a civilian court. Five former military officers received prison sentences ranging from 10 to 15 years, while two former ministers were sentenced to three years' imprisonment. Former President Gonzálo Sánchez de Lozada and two of his ministers, who had fled to the USA soon after the violence, were facing extradition proceedings at the end of the year. Other ministers subsequently fled to Peru and Spain.

■ Four military officers under investigation for the torture in 2009 of an army conscript in Challapata, Oruro Department, were released in April after a judge quashed the charges against them. In July, the Oruro Appeals Court overturned the judge's decision and ordered judicial proceedings to continue under civilian jurisdiction. The trial had not started by the end of the year. Video footage showing the army conscript being repeatedly submerged in water in 2009 by officers had come to light in 2010.

■ In September, a judge revoked the charges against five members of the National Police accused of involvement in the dispersal of protesters who mounted a roadblock in Caranavi Province in May 2010 in which two people died and at least 30 were injured. At the end of the year, prosecutors were considering whether to bring further charges.

■ Trial proceedings connected to the 2008 Pando massacre, in which 19 people, mostly *campesinos*, were killed and 53 others injured, continued but were subject to delays.

Torture and other ill-treatment

In February, Gróver Beto Poma Guanto died in hospital two days after being beaten by training instructors at the Condors of Bolivia Military Training School in Sanandita, Tarija Department. Three military personnel remained under investigation in connection with the case at the end of the year. However, despite repeated calls for the case to be transferred to civilian jurisdiction, it remained under investigation in the military justice system, which lacked independence and impartiality.

BOSNIA AND HERZEGOVINA

BOSNIA AND HERZEGOVINA
Head of state: rotating presidency – Željko Komšić, Nebojša Radmanović, Bakir Izetbegović
Head of government: Nikola Špirić
Death penalty: abolitionist for all crimes
Population: 3.8 million
Life expectancy: 75.7 years
Under-5 mortality: 14.4 per 1,000
Adult literacy: 97.8 per cent

Nationalistic and divisive rhetoric increased and an agreement to form a coalition government was reached at the end of December, 15 months after the general election. Institutions at the state level, including the judiciary, were weakened throughout the year. The trial of Ratko Mladić began. Prosecution of crimes under international law continued, but progress remained slow and impunity persisted. Civilian victims of war were still denied access to justice and reparations.

Background

Divisive and nationalist rhetoric weakened institutions at the state level, including the judiciary. Unwillingness of the leading political parties to reach a consensus following the general election held in October 2010 resulted in political paralysis. At the end of December, composition of the Council of Ministers was agreed, 15 months after the elections, but a budget was not yet adopted. The state was under temporary financing.

Ratko Mladić, former commander of the main staff of the Army of Republika Srpska was arrested in Serbia in May (see Serbia entry) and transferred to the International Criminal Tribunal for the Former Yugoslavia (Tribunal).

The international community maintained its presence in Bosnia and Herzegovina (BiH). The EU kept its peacekeeping force with approximately 1,300 troops. In June, a decision was made to end the EU Police Mission to BiH by the end of June 2012. The pre-accession negotiations with the EU continued and the EU-BiH Structured Dialogue on Justice, a formal consultative process on justice matters, began in June. In September, Peter Sørensen formally assumed office as the EU Special Representative to BiH, consolidating the EU presence in BiH.

The separate role of the UN High Representative in BiH, still held by Valentin Inzko, as the "final authority in theatre regarding the interpretation of civilian implementation of the Peace Agreement" was reaffirmed by the UN Security Council in a resolution adopted in November.

International justice

At the end of 2011, six war crimes cases concerning BiH were pending before the Trial Chamber of the Tribunal. In addition, three cases were on appeal.

■ In September, after a trial lasting over two years, the Tribunal found former chief of the general staff of the Yugoslav Army, Momčilo Perišić, guilty of committing crimes against humanity and violations of the laws or customs of war by aiding and abetting murders, inhumane acts, persecutions on political, racial or religious grounds, and attacks on civilians in Sarajevo and Srebrenica. He was sentenced to 27 years' imprisonment. In November, Momčilo Perišić appealed on 17 grounds.

■ Proceedings against former Bosnian leader Radovan Karadžić continued. In 2011, the Tribunal examined evidence around crimes in north-west BiH, including "Manjača" and "Trnopolje" camps and unlawful killings at the Korićanske cliffs, as well as many other crimes committed during the 1992-5 conflict.

■ On 31 May, Ratko Mladić, former commander of the main staff of the Army of Republika Srpska was transferred to the Tribunal. An amended indictment against him, containing charges of genocide, crimes against humanity and war crimes, was filed in October. Originally charged in a single indictment, both Radovan Karadžić and Ratko Mladić had been indicted for genocide, as well as extermination, murder, persecution, deportation, inhumane acts, acts of violence, terror, unlawful attack on civilians and taking of hostages amounting to crimes against humanity and war crimes. In December, the Tribunal agreed with the Prosecution proposal to reduce the indictment against Ratko Mladić from 196 to 106 crimes, and to limit the number of municipalities concerned from 23 to 15.

Justice system – crimes under international law

The domestic justice system continued to work on the large backlog of open war crimes cases. The implementation of the National Strategy for War Crimes Processing was delayed, primarily due to a lack of political and financial support. Progress in resolving war crimes cases was also hampered by political obstacles to improving regional co-operation, including failure to dismantle legal barriers to extradition of war crimes suspects between BiH, Croatia, Serbia and Montenegro. A proposed bilateral agreement between Serbia and BiH to resolve parallel investigations in war crimes cases reached a stalemate in June.

Six cases relating to 10 mid- and low-level defendants transferred by the Tribunal to the BiH State Court, known as 11bis cases, were completed. However, generally, prosecution of crimes under international law continued before the domestic judiciary in BiH at a slow pace. The continued practice of non-harmonized application of criminal law in war crimes cases, due to the use of the 1976 Criminal Code in cases tried in courts in the different entities, resulted in serious obstacles to the fair and efficient delivery of justice. These included: inability to charge acts as crimes against humanity; failure to prosecute command responsibility; and inequality before the law owing to the low mandatory minimum and maximum sentences for war crimes.

B

The War Crimes Chamber of the BiH State Court continued to play the central role in war crimes prosecutions in BiH. However, verbal attacks on this and other judicial institutions dedicated to investigating and prosecuting war crimes, along with the denial of war crimes – including the genocide in Srebrenica in July 1995 – by high-ranking politicians, undermined the country's efforts to prosecute war crimes cases. In addition, the authorities failed to collect data on the total number of investigations and prosecutions at all levels of crimes under international law.

Witness support services at the state level were extended to cover the period prior to trial in January. However, witness support and protection measures in cases tried at the lower levels, identified in the National Strategy for War Crimes Processing as being necessary, continued to be absent. This situation deterred victims from seeking justice. A proposal to amend the law to allow the entity-level prosecution services to call upon the BiH Witness Protection Programme moved forward but required widespread parliamentary support to be adopted.

The authorities failed to provide a comprehensive programme of reparations for victims of crimes under international law during the conflict.

Women's rights
Survivors of war crimes of sexual violence
The UN Committee against Torture in January recommended that the legislation criminalizing war crimes of rape and other forms of sexual violence be brought in line with international standards but the government failed to introduce the necessary changes. The BiH 2003 Criminal Code required that the victim be subjected to force or threat of immediate attack on his or her life or body. This arguably did not take into account the circumstances of armed conflict, which may be considered coercive and therefore vitiate consent to sexual intercourse.

Despite the increase in the number of prosecutions and investigations involving war crimes of rape and other forms of sexual violence committed during the war since 2010, the number remained low in contrast to the overall high rate of occurrence of crimes of rape and sexual violence during the conflict.

The Prosecutor's Office reported to Amnesty International in June that there were 100 cases with charges of rape and other forms of sexual violence cases currently being investigated by the Prosecutor's Office, and six indictments had been confirmed by the State Court. A final verdict had been delivered in only 21 cases since 2005. The authorities failed to establish the total number of such cases investigated and prosecuted at the entity level.

In most parts of the country, especially in rural areas, survivors were unable to enjoy their right to reparation, and were stigmatized as rape victims. In particular, female survivors were denied access to adequate health care services even if they suffered from medical conditions developed as a result of rape. Only a few of those who suffered from post-traumatic stress disorders were able to seek psychological assistance. Many survivors lived in poverty. Most could not get help to find employment or continue with their education.

Additionally, survivors, like all other civilian victims of war, were discriminated against in access to social benefits in comparison to war combatants. The Ministry for Human Rights and Refugees prepared a draft Law on the Rights of Victims of Torture and Civilian War Victims and established a working group responsible for drafting a Programme for Victims of Sexual Violence in Conflict and beyond, but these measures had yet to be further developed and adopted.

Enforced disappearances
Despite problems with budget allocations for exhumations caused by the absence of the government, exhumations continued. In January, the State Prosecutor's Office assumed control of exhumations previously conducted by local prosecutors, which had a positive impact in expediting the recovery of the remains of missing people from mass and clandestine graves. Around 10,000 people were still unaccounted for. Unwillingness of insider witnesses to provide information on mass graves remained the biggest obstacle in the process.

In February, the Central Record of Missing Persons was created as a permanent database in BiH. It gathered around 34,000 names from various existing databases and conducted verification of those names. It was expected that the database would help the state-level Missing Persons Institute to strategically address the remaining cases.

Despite the accurate DNA-led identifications made by the International Commission on Missing Persons

B

over the past years, the identification process began to slow down. The Commission reported that around 8,000 bodies had already been identified through the classical methods of identification. However, due to the existence of hundreds of secondary, tertiary and quaternary mass grave sites, the recovery of body parts of already identified and buried people could continue for years.

Despite progress made in the recovery and identification of disappeared people and the prosecution of perpetrators, victims' families were still denied the rights to justice and reparation.

The non-implementation of the 2004 Law on Missing Persons led to problems for the families of the disappeared, including the lack of independent functioning of the Missing Persons Institute and the non-existence of the Fund for Providing Assistance to the Families of Missing Persons. In addition, many judgements of the Constitutional Court of BiH in cases involving enforced disappearances remained unimplemented.

Refugees and internally displaced people

The official figures from the UN of over one million returnees across BiH did not reflect the number of refugees and internally displaced people who actually returned to their pre-war homes. The sustainability of return remained an issue for those who wanted to return, as they would face discrimination in accessing their rights to health care, pensions, social protection and employment.

According to UNHCR, the UN refugee agency, almost 8,600 people still lived in 159 collective centres or other temporary accommodation 16 years after the war. Basic facilities, including running water, heating and electricity, were lacking in the collective centres. Durable solutions were not yet found for particularly vulnerable people living in the collective centres.

Discrimination
Minority rights
The authorities failed to implement the December 2009 judgement of the European Court of Human Rights in the case brought by Dervo Sejdić (a Romani man) and Jakob Finci (a Jewish man).

The applicants had complained that, as they did not belong to any of the main ethnic groups, they were denied the right to be elected to the state institutions

(as under the current legal framework this right was restricted to Bosniaks, Croats and Serbs). The Court had ruled that the constitutional framework and the electoral system discriminated against the applicants and the authorities were obliged to amend it.

At the end of 2011, the Parliament established another temporary commission to draft the amendments to the relevant legislation.

Rights of lesbian, gay, bisexual and transgender people
In its 2011 Progress Report, the European Commission reported widespread discrimination against lesbians, gay men, bisexual and transgender people, threats and harassment of lesbian, gay, bisexual and transgender activists, and hate speech and intolerance towards the community by media and politicians. No progress was made by the end of 2011.

Counter-terror and security
The state authorities continued to violate the rights of some people who had settled in BiH during or after the war and who had subsequently been granted BiH citizenship. As a result of decisions by the State Commission for the Revision of Decisions on Naturalization of Foreign Citizens, some of them lost their citizenship and deportation procedures were initiated against them. The recommendations by the UN Committee against Torture relating to forcible return had not been implemented.

Amnesty International visits/reports
🚌 Amnesty International delegates visited Bosnia and Herzegovina in June and November.

📗 Key international court ruling delivers victory to victims of crimes committed during the war in the former Yugoslavia (EUR 70/017/2011)

BRAZIL

FEDERATIVE REPUBLIC OF BRAZIL

Head of state and government:	**Dilma Rousseff**
	(replaced Luiz Inácio Lula da Silva in January)
Death penalty:	**abolitionist for ordinary crimes**
Population:	**196.7 million**
Life expectancy:	**73.5 years**
Under-5 mortality:	**20.6 per 1,000**
Adult literacy:	**90 per cent**

Despite some important advances in public security policy, law enforcement officers continued to use excessive force and carry out extrajudicial executions and torture. Death squads and militias remained a concern. Severe overcrowding, degrading conditions and torture and other ill-treatment were reported in the prison and juvenile detention systems and in police cells. In rural areas conflict over land resulted in numerous killings of land and environmental activists. Gunmen hired by landowners continued to attack Indigenous and *Quilombola* (Afro-descendent) communities with impunity. Thousands were forcibly evicted to make way for large development projects.

Background

Brazil's first female president, Dilma Rousseff, took office on 1 January promising to promote development and eradicate extreme poverty. Despite strong economic growth and improvements across most social and economic indicators over the last decade, more than 16.2 million Brazilians continued to live on less than R$70 (approximately US$40) per month, according to census data. In June, the federal government launched a national plan to eradicate extreme poverty within four years. During the year, seven ministers were forced to resign amid allegations of corruption involving misuse of public funds.

The new government pledged to pursue a human rights agenda in its foreign policy. In March, Brazil supported the creation of a UN Special Rapporteur on the situation of human rights in Iran, but in November was criticized for abstaining on a UN Security Council resolution condemning human rights abuses in Syria. In contravention of promises made on its election to the UN Human Rights Council, Brazil refused to accept the precautionary measures issued by the Inter-American Commission on Human Rights on the Belo Monte hydroelectric project.

Large-scale development projects under the Growth Acceleration Programme continued to pose risks for Indigenous Peoples, fishing communities, small-scale farmers and marginalized urban communities.

In January, flooding and mudslides swept through a mountainous region (Região Serrana) near the city of Rio de Janeiro. More than 800 people were killed – the majority in the towns of Nova Friburgo and Teresópolis – and more than 30,000 were made homeless. The floods were followed by widespread allegations of corruption involving misuse of public funds earmarked for relief. Some residents made homeless from the previous flooding that hit Rio de Janeiro and Niterói in 2010 were still living in precarious conditions awaiting the provision of adequate housing.

In May, the Supreme Federal Court unanimously recognized the rights of same-sex couples in a stable partnership as equivalent to those of heterosexual couples.

Past human rights violations

On 18 November, President Rousseff ratified laws limiting to 50 years the period state secrets can be held, and creating a Truth Commission to investigate human rights violations committed between 1946 and 1988. The Commission, made up of a seven-member panel appointed by the President, will hear evidence for two years, before issuing a report. These reforms were important advances in tackling impunity. Nevertheless, there were concerns about conditions that could potentially prejudice the outcome of the Commission, most notably whether the 1979 Amnesty Law, previously interpreted to include those responsible for crimes against humanity, would preclude the prosecution of those found responsible for such crimes through this process.

Public security

In the face of high levels of violent crime, law enforcement practices continued to be characterized by discrimination, human rights abuses, corruption and military-style policing operations. Promised public security reforms were undermined by severe budget cuts and a lack of political will.

Some states invested in targeted security projects, such as the Pacifying Police Units (Unidades de

Polícia Pacificadora, UPPs) in Rio de Janeiro, the Stay Alive (Fica Vivo) project in Minas Gerais and the Pact for Life (Pacto Pela Vida) in Pernambuco. By the end of 2011, 18 UPPs had been installed across the city of Rio de Janeiro. In November, a major police and military operation in the southern zone of the city cleared Rocinha and Vidigal of criminal gangs in preparation for the installation of further units. While the UPPs represented important progress in moving away from policing based on violent confrontation, more comprehensive investment in social services for communities living in poverty was still lacking. In addition, overall reform of the security system, including police training, intelligence and external control, was still needed. Reports of excessive use of force and corruption in some units indicated the absence of effective oversight mechanisms to monitor the UPPs' presence in the communities.

Socially excluded communities continued to face violence by criminal gangs and abusive policing that often resulted in residents being treated as criminal suspects. This in turn increased social deprivation and distanced communities from broader state services such as access to schools, health care and sanitation.

Between January and September, 804 people were killed in situations defined as "acts of resistance" in Rio de Janeiro and São Paulo. While in Rio de Janeiro this reflected a decline of 177 from the previous year, the number of reported violent deaths recorded by police as "undetermined" rose.

■ In July, 11-year-old Juan Moraes disappeared during an operation in the Danon community in Nova Iguaçu, Rio de Janeiro state. His body was later found in Rio Botas, Belford Roxo, in the municipality of Nova Iguaçu. A civil police inquiry concluded that he had been killed by the military police and his body removed by police officers. Between them, the four police officers implicated had previously been involved in at least 37 killings registered as "acts of resistance". Following the killing, the civil police introduced new measures, including mandatory crime scene, forensic and ballistic investigations, in cases registered as "acts of resistance".

Similar measures were introduced in São Paulo. From April, all cases of police killings in greater São Paulo were referred to a specialized homicide unit.

Death squads and militias

Police officers were believed to be involved in death squads and *milícias* (militias) engaged in social cleansing, extortion, as well as in trafficking in arms and drugs.

■ In February, the federal police's Operation Guillotine uncovered a web of corruption extending to senior officials in Rio de Janeiro's civil police. Forty-seven serving or former police officers were accused of forming armed gangs, embezzlement, arms trafficking and extortion.

■ In February in the state of Goiás, 19 military police officers, including the sub-commander of the military police, were arrested and charged with involvement in death squads. In June, a special commission investigating police involvement in death squads in the state released a report examining 37 cases of enforced disappearance where police involvement was suspected. Following the release of the report, members of the commission themselves received death threats.

In São Paulo a report by the civil police attributed 150 deaths between 2006 and 2010 to death squads in the north and east of the city.

In Rio de Janeiro, militias continued to dominate large swathes of the city, extorting protection money from the poorest residents and illegally providing services such as transport, telecommunications and gas. This placed vulnerable communities at risk through the imposition of illegal or unregulated services. Those who opposed them were subjected to threats, intimidation and violence.

■ In August, Judge Patrícia Acioli was shot 21 times outside her home in Niterói, in the metropolitan region of Rio de Janeiro. She had received a series of death threats related to her uncompromising stand against the militias and police criminality. Ten police officers, along with the commander of the São Gonçalo Battalion, were arrested in connection with the killing and were detained awaiting trial at the end of the year.

■ Between October and December, the President of the Rio de Janeiro State Human Rights Commission, State Deputy Marcelo Freixo, who had headed an inquiry into the militias, received 10 death threats.

Torture and other ill-treatment

Torture was prevalent at the point of arrest and during interrogation and detention in police stations and prisons.

Prison conditions

The prison population reached around 500,000 in 2011, with 44 per cent of all prisoners held in pre-trial detention. Severe overcrowding, degrading conditions, torture, and prisoner-on-prisoner violence were commonplace.

In October, a long-awaited bill was sent to Congress for the creation of a National Preventative Mechanism and a National Committee for the Prevention and Eradication of Torture, in line with requirements under the Optional Protocol to the UN Convention against Torture. By the end of the year, three states – Rio de Janeiro, Alagoas and Paraíba – had passed legislation for the creation of state preventative mechanisms and one, Rio de Janeiro, had started implementation.

■ In September, a 14-year-old girl was lured to the Heleno Fragoso semi-open prison in Belém's metropolitan region, where she was drugged and raped over a period of four days. She later escaped and told police that two other adolescents were being used as prostitutes within the unit. Thirty staff members, including the Superintendent of the prison system, were suspended pending an inquiry. After receiving death threats, the girl, along with another girl who was raped in the unit, was forced to enter the Programme for the Protection of Children and Adolescents.

In most states, many prisons and police cells were effectively under the control of criminal gangs.

■ In February, in the state of Maranhão, six inmates were killed – four of whom were decapitated – when riots broke out in protest at overcrowding in the Pinheiro Regional Police Station where 90 inmates were crowded into a cell designed for 30. According to the state bar association, the deaths brought the total number of people killed in detention in the state since 2007 to 94.

Land conflicts
Indigenous Peoples and *Quilombola* communities

Indigenous communities continued to be subjected to discrimination, threats and violence in the context of land disputes. In October, concerns were raised when President Rousseff presented a decree to facilitate the provision of environmental licences for major development projects, especially those affecting the lands of Indigenous or *Quilombola* communites.

The situation in Mato Grosso do Sul remained acute. According to the Missionary Council for Indigenous Peoples (Conselho Indigenista Missionário, CIMI), 1,200 families were living in extremely precarious conditions, encamped by the side

of highways, awaiting restitution of their lands. Delays in the demarcation process exposed communities to heightened risk of human rights violations.

■ A group of armed men repeatedly threatened and attacked 125 families of the Guarani-Kaiowá community of Pyelito Kue after they reoccupied traditional lands in the municipality of Iguatemi, Mato Grosso do Sul state. In September, armed men arrived in two trucks and fired rubber bullets, set fire to shacks, beat individuals and shouted threats as the community fled in panic. Several people, including children and the elderly, were seriously injured in an attack described by federal prosecutors as genocide and the formation of a rural militia.

■ In November, 40 gunmen, many hooded, attacked the Guaiviry encampment near the Brazil-Paraguay border, shooting Indigenous leader Nísio Gomes dead and taking his body away in a truck. His fate was not known at the end of the year.

In February, three men accused of killing Guarani-Kaiowá leader Marcus Veron were convicted of kidnapping, the formation of a criminal gang and torture, but were acquitted of homicide. At the end of the year, the three were at liberty pending an appeal against their sentences. Marcus Veron was beaten to death on traditional lands in February 2003.

■ In February, the Brazilian Institute of the Environment and Renewable Natural Resources issued the environmental licence for work to begin on the Belo Monte hydroelectric project in Pará state. Indigenous Peoples and local communities protested at the plans, arguing that the project would affect their livelihoods and that the licence had been issued without a fair consultation process with those affected. In April, the Inter-American Commission on Human Rights called on Brazil to suspend the licensing process pending free, prior and informed consultations with affected groups and the implementation of measures to safeguard their health and physical integrity. The federal authorities responded by withdrawing their representative to the OAS and stopping contributions to the Commission, among other measures.

Rural killings

Land activists continued to be threatened and killed in their struggle for access to land and for speaking out against illegal logging and ranching in the Amazon region.

■ In May, environmental activists José Cláudio Ribeiro da Silva and his wife, Maria do Espírito Santo, were shot dead by gunmen in the municipality of Ipixuna, in Pará state. They had exposed the activities of illegal loggers, ranchers and charcoal producers in the region. Three men were subsequently arrested in September in connection with the killings. However, threats against the victims' relatives and community continued.

■ In May, rural leader and survivor of the Corumbiara massacre in 1995, Adelino Ramos, was shot dead in Vista Alegre do Abunã, in the municipality of Porto Velho, Rondônia state. He had previously highlighted the activities of illegal loggers operating along the borders of Acre, Amazônia and Rondônia states.

In the wake of the killings, the NGO Pastoral Land Commission presented the Federal Human Rights Secretary with the names of a further 1,855 people under threat because of land conflicts nationwide.

Violent land conflicts were reported in many other states in the north and north-east of the country.

■ In June, 40 families in the settlements of Assentamento Santo Antônio Bom Sossego and Acampamento Vitória, in the municipality of Palmeirante, Tocantins state, were attacked by gunmen who fired shots over the encampment and threatened to kill land activists.

■ In Maranhão state, residents of the Salgado *Quilombola* community complained of a sustained campaign of harassment and intimidation by local farmers, who destroyed crops, killed livestock, fenced off water sources and issued death threats against community leaders.

Housing rights

In Brazil's urban centres, large-scale development projects – including preparations for the 2014 World Cup and the 2016 Olympic Games – left communities living in poverty at risk of intimidation and forced eviction. In April, the UN Special Rapporteur on adequate housing as a component of the right to an adequate standard of living, and on the right to non-discrimination said that she had received reports of evictions involving human rights violations in cities across Brazil, including São Paulo, Rio de Janeiro, Belo Horizonte, Curitiba, Porto Alegre, Recife, Natal and Fortaleza.

■ In February, council workers with bulldozers, accompanied by municipal guards, arrived without warning at the community of Vila Harmonia in Recreio dos Bandeirantes, Rio de Janeiro, one of several communities threatened with eviction because of the construction of the Transoeste bus corridor. Residents reported that municipal workers ordered them to leave

immediately, without sufficient time to clear belongings from their houses before they were demolished.

In São Paulo, thousands of families were threatened with eviction to make way for urban infrastructure developments, including the construction of a ring road; the widening of highways running along the Tietê River; and the building of parklands along the banks of streams and rivers, where up to 40 per cent of the city's favelas are situated. Residents affected by the evictions complained of lack of consultation and inadequate compensation.

Human rights defenders

The National Programme for the Protection of Human Rights Defenders was fully operational in five states – Pará, Pernambuco, Espírito Santo, Minas Gerais and Bahia – and in the process of being implemented in a further two – Ceará and Rio de Janeiro. However, in many instances, bureaucratic problems hampered its effectiveness and some defenders in the programme complained that they had not received adequate protection.

Local NGOs faced intimidation and threats.

■ In Maranhão state, activists working for the Pastoral Land Commission were threatened with death outside a court in the town of Cantanhede. They were attending a hearing related to a land dispute.

■ In Rio de Janeiro, members of the Network of Communities and Movements against Violence were subjected to threatening phone calls and intimidation by police officers.

Sexual and reproductive rights

In the five years since the Maria da Penha Law on domestic violence was passed, more than 100,000 people had been sentenced under the Law.

In August, in a landmark decision, the CEDAW Committee concluded that Brazil had failed to fulfil its obligation to "ensure to women appropriate services in connection with pregnancy, confinement and the post-natal period, granting free services where necessary". The decision was handed down in the case of Alyne da Silva Pimentel, a 28-year-old woman of African descent and resident of one of Rio de Janeiro's poorest districts. She was six months pregnant with her second child in 2002 when she died of complications resulting from pregnancy after her local health centre misdiagnosed her symptoms and delayed providing her with emergency care.

BULGARIA

REPUBLIC OF BULGARIA

Head of state:	Georgi Parvanov
Head of government:	Boyko Borissov
Death penalty:	abolitionist for all crimes
Population:	7.4 million
Life expectancy:	73.4 years
Under-5 mortality:	10 per 1,000
Adult literacy:	98.3 per cent

The authorities were criticized for failing to prevent anti-Roma violence, which spread throughout the country in September. A demonstration by supporters of a "far-right" political party resulted in a violent assault against Muslims in Sofia. Asylum-seekers were reported to be routinely detained in violation of domestic and EU legislation.

Discrimination

In July, the UN Human Rights Committee expressed concerns over the ongoing widespread discrimination suffered by Roma in accessing justice, employment, and services such as housing and education. The Committee reminded the authorities of their obligation to prevent, investigate and punish acts of hate crime and harassment against minorities and religious communities, especially Roma and Muslims.

Violent attacks against Roma

Anti-Roma violence spread throughout Bulgaria after a non-Romani man was hit by a minibus with a Romani driver in Katunitza on 24 September. The incident triggered demonstrations with strong anti-Roma sentiments. In Katunitza, several houses belonging to Roma were set on fire. NGOs, including the Bulgarian Helsinki Committee, criticized the authorities for their failure to take the necessary steps sooner to stem the violence. It was reportedly only in the subsequent days that the police guarded entrances to some Roma neighbourhoods and arrested more than 350 people. According to media reports, the Prosecutor General responded to the protests by sending instructions to regional prosecutors, reminding them of the need to respond to acts that may amount to violence on racial, religious and ethnic grounds.

A number of criminal proceedings against individuals arrested during and after the protests were reportedly concluded.

Violent attacks against Muslims

On 20 May, Muslims were assaulted while praying in front of the Banya Bashi Mosque in Sofia when a demonstration organized by supporters of the nationalist political party National Union Attack (Ataka) turned violent. Four Muslim men and a member of parliament from Ataka were reportedly injured. An investigation was opened, but the Bulgarian Helsinki Committee reported that the assaults were prosecuted as "hooliganism" rather than acts of discriminatory violence. The assault was noted with concern by the UN Human Rights Committee, which criticized the authorities for their poor enforcement of existing anti-discrimination legislation.

Violent attacks against lesbian, gay, bisexual and transgender people

On 18 June, following the Sofia Pride march, five Pride volunteers were attacked by a group of unknown individuals. The rights activists, three of whom suffered minor injuries, suspected that their attackers had followed them as they were leaving the march. They expressed their concern that the incident would be treated by the authorities as "hooliganism" rather than a hate crime because the Bulgarian Criminal Code does not recognize sexual orientation as a possible motive for such crimes. According to the Minister of Interior, the police investigation into the case was closed without the perpetrators being identified.

Justice system

In November, the UN Committee against Torture noted with concern the lack of transparency regarding the selection and appointment of judges and members of the Supreme Judicial Council. It held that the principle of an independent judiciary had not been respected by high-ranking government officials, and was not fully applied within the judiciary.

■ In two cases, *Kanchev v. Bulgaria* and *Dimitrov and Hamanov v. Bulgaria*, the European Court of Human Rights held that Bulgaria had violated the rights to a hearing within a reasonable time and to effective remedy. In February, the Court found that the first requirement was not met in the case of a man who had to wait 12 years and four months for the criminal proceedings against him to finish. In May, the Court reached the same judgement in a case involving two individuals, whose proceedings took 10 years and eight months, and five years and three months respectively.

Torture and other ill-treatment

In November, the UN Committee against Torture expressed concerns over excessive use of force and of firearms by law enforcement officers. It called on Bulgaria to take measures to eradicate all forms of harassment and ill-treatment by police during investigations.

Mental health institutions

■ In February, the European Court of Human Rights heard the case of a man who was placed under guardianship and subsequently consigned to a social care home in Pastra for people with psychiatric disorders. The man had complained that living conditions there amounted to ill-treatment and that his deprivation of liberty was unlawful and arbitrary.

Refugees and asylum-seekers

In November, the Bulgarian Helsinki Committee alleged that asylum-seekers had been held in detention by the authorities, contravening domestic legislation and the EU Asylum Procedure Directive. Reportedly, up to 1,000 asylum-seekers were being detained in Liubimets and Busmansti detention centres. The director of the State Agency for Refugees stated that limited capacity in open reception centres had resulted in the practice. The draft National Strategy on Asylum, Migration and Integration also acknowledged that Bulgaria lacked the institutional capacity to fulfil the basic requirements for receiving asylum-seekers.

■ In July, the Court in Plovdiv ruled against extradition of an ethnic Chechen man, Ahmed Razhapovich Chataev, to Russia. Ahmed Chataev had been granted refugee status in Austria in 2003. He was reportedly arrested on 19 May when he attempted to cross the border between Bulgaria and Turkey. The basis for his arrest was an extradition request by the Prosecutor General's Office of the Russian Federation, alleging that he faced charges of incitement to terrorism and financing of terrorism activities. The Plovdiv Court ruled that Ahmed Chataev's refugee status was valid in Bulgaria. Concerns were expressed by NGOs that, if

extradited to Russia, Ahmed Chataev would be at real risk of serious harm, including torture and other ill-treatment.

Amnesty International visits/reports

🚌 Amnesty International delegates visited Bulgaria in June.

📄 Bulgaria: Authorities must urgently act to stop the escalation of violence targeting the Roma community (EUR 15/002/2011)

BURKINA FASO

BURKINA FASO	
Head of state:	Blaise Compaoré
Head of government:	Luc-Adolphe Tiao (replaced Tertius Zongo in April)
Death penalty:	abolitionist in practice
Population:	17 million
Life expectancy:	55.4 years
Under-5 mortality:	166.4 per 1,000
Adult literacy:	28.7 per cent

Serious unrest took place between February and July, and the President dissolved the government. Some 300 soldiers were charged and detained following the riots.

Background

From February to July, Burkina Faso faced one of the most serious waves of unrest since President Blaise Compaoré took power in 1987. Soldiers took to the streets on several occasions in protest against prison sentences imposed on five military officers for attacking a civilian over unpaid allowances. The President reacted by dissolving the government and firing the Chief of Staff. In September some 300 soldiers were charged and detained, many of whom were tried for rebellion, rape, robbery and looting.

Thousands of people demonstrated in the capital Ouagadougou and in other cities in March and April against food prices and the rising cost of living. They called for the resignation of President Compaoré and an end to impunity.

Excessive use of force

Anti-government protests throughout the country were triggered in February when Justin Zongo, a student, died after being beaten by police officers in Koudougou, 100 km west of Ouagadougou. Official statements that the death was due to meningitis were contradicted by later reports that it was a result of physical abuse.

During subsequent clashes between protesters and the authorities, hundreds of people were wounded and five people were killed, including a police officer, after security forces used live ammunition against the demonstrators. In August, three police officers were convicted of manslaughter in the case of Justin Zongo and received sentences ranging from eight to 10 years' imprisonment.

Death penalty

■ In January Issoufou Savadogo was sentenced to death by the Criminal Chamber of the Appeal Court of Ouagadougou after being convicted of murder.
■ In December, two people were sentenced to death, one in his absence, by the Criminal Chamber of the Appeal Court of Bobo-Dioulasso after being convicted of murder.

Right to health – maternal mortality

Although maternal health had been identified as a priority for the government, by the end of the year no real improvement had been achieved either in the quality of maternal health services or increased access to family planning and contraception. Some progress was reported regarding accountability of medical personnel.
■ In September, two health officials were dismissed for "serious professional misconduct" in Bobo-Dioulasso following the death of a pregnant woman who had been locked in a maternity ward without any supervision. In October they were sentenced to prison terms and reparations were awarded to the family.

BURUNDI

REPUBLIC OF BURUNDI

Head of state and government:	Pierre Nkurunziza
Death penalty:	abolitionist for all crimes
Population:	8.6 million
Life expectancy:	50.4 years
Under-5 mortality:	166.3 per 1,000
Adult literacy:	66.6 per cent

Impunity remained widespread and became further entrenched. Extrajudicial executions and political killings increased. The justice system remained politicized. Human rights defenders and journalists faced increased repression. The government committed itself to establishing a Truth and Reconciliation Commission in 2012, but no progress was made in setting up a Special Tribunal.

Background

The ruling party, the National Council for Defence of Democracy-Forces for Defence of Democracy, consolidated its hold on power after most opposition parties withdrew from the 2010 elections. Security forces unlawfully killed, harassed and arrested opposition members from the National Liberation Forces (FNL).

Around 40 people were killed in a massacre in Gatumba on 18 September. An Italian doctor and Croatian nun were killed in an attack on a hospital in Ngozi in November, the first attack on international humanitarian workers since 2007.

Key opposition leaders, including Agathon Rwasa of the FNL and Alexis Sinduhije of the Movement for Solidarity and Democracy (MSD), remained in exile. Two new armed opposition groups announced their existence towards the end of the year. Several former FNL members became involved in armed opposition inside Burundi and in the neighbouring Democratic Republic of the Congo.

Justice system

The justice system remained politicized and poorly resourced. Burundians lacked confidence in conventional justice and often resorted to "mob justice".

A string of politically motivated arrests and summonses of lawyers, journalists and human rights defenders demonstrated the judiciary's limited independence. Members of the Burundian Bar Association went on strike in July in support of lawyers detained for several days for exercising their right to freedom of expression.

■ François Nyamoya was arrested on 28 July and charged with influencing witnesses in a trial concluded several years before. He had also been detained in 2010 on politicized charges related to his role as spokesperson for the MSD party. He remained in detention at the end of the year.

Delays continued in commissions investigating allegations of human rights violations by security forces. This contrasted with the prompt work of a commission investigating the 18 September massacre in Gatumba. Twenty-one individuals were arrested and charged and the case was opened in November. However, it was adjourned after defence lawyers claimed the police had failed to follow proper procedures during their investigations and had denied them access to their clients' files.

Extrajudicial executions and impunity

Extrajudicial executions increased. The UN documented 57 unlawful killings by security forces. In another 42 murders, believed to be politically motivated, the perpetrators' identities remained unclear. Cases implicating state security agents mainly involved killings of former and current members of the FNL and of other opposition parties. The government continued to deny that security forces were involved in unlawful killings.

■ Audace Vianney Habonarugira, a demobilized FNL colonel, was found dead on 15 July. He had `escaped an attempted assassination in Kamenge in March, when he was shot by an individual identified as an intelligence agent. In the months before his murder, he had refused to become an intelligence informant and was persistently followed. A commission of inquiry examined the failed assassination attempt, but there were no prosecutions.

Commissions of inquiry were used to delay prosecutions of security forces allegedly implicated in unlawful killings and attempted assassinations. Two commissions of inquiry began investigating extrajudicial executions and violence linked to the 2010 elections in April and May respectively. Neither commission published its findings or led to successful prosecutions being brought during the year.

Failure to identify bodies before burial denied

victims' family members the right to truth and justice. Despite an order by the Interior Minister in November for such identification to take place, bodies continued to be hastily buried by local officials.

■ Léandre Bukuru was kidnapped from his home in Gitega by men wearing police uniforms on 13 November . His decapitated body was found in Giheta the next day and buried on a local administrator's orders, without the presence of his family or a police investigation. His head was found in Gitega two days later. The prosecution opened a case file, but failed to exhume the body for examination.

Freedom of association and assembly

The authorities continued to restrict peaceful assembly by civil society, despite positive steps taken to reinstate the legal status of the Forum for the Strengthening of Civil Society on 28 January.

■ On 8 April, the second anniversary of the murder of human rights defender and leading anti-corruption activist Ernest Manirumva, the police broke up a peaceful march for justice. Gabriel Rufyiri, President of the Observatory for the Fight against Corruption and Economic Embezzlement, and his colleague, Claver Irambona, were detained, interrogated and released several hours later without charge.

Torture and other ill-treatment

A commission of inquiry into allegations of torture in 2010 by the National Intelligence Service (SNR) failed to report publicly. No judicial investigations or prosecutions were initiated into the allegations.

Freedom of expression
Human rights defenders

The continued failure to deliver justice for Ernest Manirumva's murder left human rights defenders at risk, especially those working on the Justice for Ernest Manirumva campaign. They were subjected to repeated summonses, threats and surveillance. Two staff members at OLUCOME, the NGO where Ernest Manirumva worked, experienced security incidents in July, including a break-in by armed men.

A decision by the Higher Instance Court of Bujumbura on 22 June to call for further investigations into the Manirumva case appeared positive. However, questions put to human rights activists during interviews with judicial authorities indicated attempts to falsely implicate civil society in the murder. Judicial authorities had previously disregarded recommendations by the US Federal Bureau of Investigations (FBI) to question and DNA test high-ranking police and intelligence officers implicated by witnesses. The court set no time frame for investigations to be completed, giving rise to concerns that the trial could stall once more.

Journalists

Journalists faced increased repression. Independent journalists were repeatedly summoned before judicial authorities to respond to questions about their work. There was an increasing trend of magistrates equating criticism of the government with inciting ethnic hatred. Summonses rarely resulted in prosecutions, but were intimidating and time-consuming. Intelligence agents regularly threatened journalists and human rights defenders by telephone.

The government imposed sweeping restrictions on the media after the 18 September massacre in Gatumba. On 20 September, the National Security Council ordered journalists not to publish, comment on, or analyse information about the massacre or any other cases under investigation.

Staff of Radio Publique Africaine (RPA) were consistently harassed and threatened by the authorities. On 14 November, RPA received a letter from the Interior Minister saying the radio station was being used "to discredit institutions, undermine the legitimacy of the judiciary and accuse individuals gratuitously, inciting the population to hatred and disobedience and promoting a culture of lies". They were ordered to provide financial documentation and activity reports within 10 days.

■ Netpress editor, Jean-Claude Kavumbagu, was released in May after 10 months in prison. He had been accused of treason, which carries a life sentence, for an article questioning the security forces' ability to protect the country from terrorist attacks. He was acquitted of treason, but found guilty of harming the economy.
■ Several RPA staff were repeatedly summoned by the judicial authorities. Bob Rugurika, RPA's editor, was questioned by the judicial authorities multiple times.

Prison conditions

Prisons were overcrowded, with the majority of prisoners awaiting trial.

Some individuals accused of serious crimes were transferred from the capital Bujumbura to prisons in remote provinces. The authorities failed to justify this decision, which isolated those accused during pre-trial

proceedings. Two suspects in the Gatumba massacre were moved to the towns of Rumonge and Rutana. A journalist charged with alleged participation in terrorist activities was taken by the SNR to Cankuzo town.

Transitional justice

A committee established to amend the 2004 Truth and Reconciliation Commission (TRC) Law presented President Nkurunziza with a draft law in October. If passed by parliament, the draft law would exclude civil society and religious groups from the TRC, thereby compromising its independence. It could prevent the Special Tribunal, a judicial body set up to follow the TRC, from prosecuting cases independently. The draft law does not explicitly prohibit the granting of amnesties, including for genocide, war crimes and crimes against humanity.

Independent National Human Rights Commission

In June, Burundi's Independent National Human Rights Commission was sworn in. Limited resources prevented it from investigating human rights violations effectively. On the request of the Burundian government, the UN Human Rights Council prematurely terminated the mandate of the Independent Expert on Burundi's human rights situation. In his June report, the Independent Expert had highlighted the country's lack of judicial independence, violations of freedom of expression, and failure to prosecute torture.

Amnesty International visits/reports

🚗 Amnesty International delegates visited Burundi in March, July, November and December.

▥ Burundi: Commission must investigate conduct of security forces (AFR 16/004/2011)

▥ Burundi: Submission to the Technical Committee revising the law for a Truth and Reconciliation Commission (AFR 16/008/2011)

▥ Burundi: Strengthen support for National Human Rights Commission (AFR 16/009/2011)

▥ Burundi: Release prominent lawyers jailed on spurious charges (PRE01/369/2011)

CAMBODIA

KINGDOM OF CAMBODIA

Head of state:	King Norodom Sihamoni
Head of government:	Hun Sen
Death penalty:	abolitionist for all crimes
Population:	14.3 million
Life expectancy:	63.1 years
Under-5 mortality:	87.5 per 1,000
Adult literacy:	77.6 per cent

Forced evictions, land disputes and land grabbing continued on a large scale, with thousands of people affected. An increase in the number of economic land concessions granted to business interests by the government exacerbated the situation. Impunity for perpetrators of human rights abuses and lack of an independent judiciary remained serious problems. The authorities continued to restrict the rights to freedom of expression, association and peaceful assembly by threatening, harassing and taking legal action against human rights defenders in an effort to silence them. Grassroots communities and land and housing rights activists were particularly at risk. A controversial proposed law to regulate NGOs and associations met with widespread opposition from civil society and was postponed. Critical developments at the Extraordinary Chambers in the Courts of Cambodia threatened to derail proceedings and deny justice to the victims of Khmer Rouge atrocities.

Background

An ongoing border dispute with Thailand over ownership of the area surrounding Preah Vihear temple, a World Heritage Site, resulted in armed clashes between the two countries in early 2011. The International Court of Justice ruled in July that both sides should withdraw their troops from the area, but this was only partially adhered to.

In August, the World Bank stated that since December 2010 it had stopped granting new loans to Cambodia until an agreement could be reached with the remaining residents of Boeung Kak Lake in the capital, Phnom Penh. Almost 4,000 families have been forcibly evicted from the area since 2008.

In October, the government temporarily banned sending domestic workers to Malaysia, after a series of incidents involving the reported abuse of Cambodian women and girls recruited to work as maids. Recruitment agencies in Cambodia were also accused of unlawfully detaining women and girls for training prior to sending them abroad.

Cambodia formally assumed the chair of ASEAN in November, to begin in January 2012. The government announced its intention to seek a non-permanent seat on the UN Security Council in 2013-14.

Forced evictions

Thousands of people remained affected by forced evictions, land disputes and land grabs, often because of economic land concessions for agro-industrial and urban development, or mining concessions. Estimates by local NGOs indicated that 420,000 people had been affected in areas covering approximately half of the country monitored since 2003. In another estimate, 10 per cent of the population of Phnom Penh had either been forcibly evicted or, in some cases, evicted through voluntary planned resettlement since 2001.

■ Hoy Mai told Amnesty International how her family and 118 other households in Bos village, Oddar Meanchey province, were forcibly evicted in October 2009 by a group of security forces, officials and others believed to be company workers, as part of an economic land concession granted to Angkor Sugar Company. Their homes were burnt down and they lost all of their belongings and farmland. Hoy Mai, five months pregnant, was jailed for eight months after trying to appeal to the authorities. Despite promises that she would receive another plot of land, she received neither land nor compensation, leaving her and her children homeless and destitute.

■ In September, eight Boeung Kak Lake families were forcibly evicted, reportedly by company workers with bulldozers, while police officials looked on. They were left homeless after their houses were demolished, despite a government order in August granting 12.44 hectares of land for onsite housing development for all the remaining families. Sam Rainsy Party youth activist Soung Sophorn was severely beaten by police when protesting at the demolition site.

International justice

Flawed proceedings and allegations of government interference with the Extraordinary Chambers in the Courts of Cambodia cast a shadow over its credibility.

C

The Co-Investigating Judges announced the closure of Case 003 in April, apparently without having undertaken full investigations. Case 004 remained with the Co-Investigating Judges. In October, the Pre-Trial Chamber rejected an appeal by a victim to be recognized as a civil party in Cases 003 and 004. The two international judges who supported the appeal revealed that there had been several errors, including alleged manipulation of documents, which denied the rights of both victims and suspects. The international Co-Investigating Judge resigned a few days before these findings were made public, citing political interference. His replacement by Reserve Judge Laurent Kasper-Ansermet was delayed after the Cambodian government failed to agree to the appointment.

■ The trial of Nuon Chea, Ieng Sary and Khieu Samphan began in November. All three, aged between 79 and 85, were alleged senior leaders during the Khmer Rouge period and defendants in Case 002. They were charged with crimes against humanity, war crimes and genocide. With ongoing concerns about the health of the accused, the Trial Chamber found defendant Ieng Thirith, aged 79, unfit to stand trial, stayed proceedings against her, and ordered her release. In December, the Supreme Court Chamber overturned this decision and ordered her continued detention in hospital or in another appropriate facility, pending a medical examination and another fitness assessment.

Human rights defenders

The authorities continued to threaten, harass, physically attack and use legal action against trade unionists, land and housing rights activists, NGO workers and other human rights defenders, to prevent them from carrying out peaceful activities. Strikes and protests by trade union activists and workers were broken up with unnecessary or excessive force. Women were at the forefront of peaceful resistance to evictions at Boeung Kak Lake. On several occasions, some were injured when security officials violently intervened in peaceful protests.

■ In November, Kong Chantha, Bo Chhorvy, Heng Mom and Tep Vanny were arrested, detained and charged with "insult" and "obstructing officials" after taking part in a peaceful protest at Boeung Kak Lake. They were released under court supervision, and if found guilty, could face a large fine and up to one year's imprisonment.

■ Verbal and written threats as well as physical harassment against Venerable Loun Savath, a Buddhist monk and human rights defender, increased. Venerable Loun Savath supported and spoke out on behalf of communities at risk of losing their land or homes. In April, the Phnom Penh Monk's office banned him from staying at any monasteries in Phnom Penh. The ban was later extended elsewhere throughout the country.

■ Union leader Sous Chantha was convicted in June of distributing drugs and sentenced to 10 months' imprisonment. Two months of the sentence were suspended, and as he had already spent nine months in pre-trial detention, he was released. The charges against him were believed to be unfounded and intended to deter him and other union leaders from advocating for labour rights.

Freedom of expression, association and assembly

As grassroots communities and activists increasingly mobilized to hold meetings and protests on human rights-related issues, the authorities attempted to stop gatherings and limit protests. Threats against some human rights NGOs critical of the impact of a railway redevelopment project on communities who had to resettle, led to the first ever official suspension of a local NGO, Samakhum Teang Tnaut.

■ Indigenous Kuy people living on the edges of Prey Lang forest gathered to protest several times during the year against the destruction of their traditional land and restrictions on their access to the forest because of mining and agro-industrial concessions to companies. In August, around 300 mostly Indigenous people travelled to Phnom Penh; more than 100 were arrested and briefly detained without charge for distributing leaflets about Prey Lang which police claimed could "disrupt social order".

■ In September, armed police disrupted attempts by local NGOs the Cambodian Center for Human Rights and the Natural Resource Protection Group to hold private training meetings in Sandan district, Kompong Thom province. Conditions were placed on future human rights meetings in the province.

■ In January, Sam Chankea, a staff member of a local human rights NGO, the Cambodian Human Rights and Development Association (ADHOC), was convicted of defamation for an interview he gave on a land dispute between a community and KDC International Company in Kompong Chhnang province. He was ordered to pay a heavy fine and compensation to the company.

Legal developments

The Law on Prisons, approved by the National Assembly in November, contained provisions enabling the potentially exploitative use of prison labour by private companies. The fourth draft Trade Union Law was amended following criticism of earlier drafts by Cambodian and international unions and garment buyers. They were critical of provisions which criminalized the failure to comply with some aspects of the law. Concerns remained about vague provisions for suspension, cancellation and dissolution of unions.

Throughout the year the government attempted to finalize the draft Law on Associations and Non-Governmental Organizations, despite adequate provisions on the regulation of organizations in the Civil Code. The first three drafts met with widespread criticism from Cambodian civil society, international organizations and other governments. After the fourth draft met with similar criticism, the Prime Minister announced in December that it would be delayed until 2014 if necessary in order to find a consensus.

Amnesty International visits/reports

🚗 Amnesty International delegates visited Cambodia in February and November/December.

📕 UN-Cambodia Court: Excessive secrecy, exclusion and fears of inappropriate interference (ASA 23/004/2011)

📕 Eviction and resistance in Cambodia: Five women tell their stories (ASA 23/006/2011)

📕 Eviction and resistance in Cambodia: Five women tell their stories – recommendations (ASA 23/007/2011)

📕 Cambodia: Proposed law on associations and non-governmental organizations – a watershed moment? (ASA 23/012/2011)

CAMEROON

REPUBLIC OF CAMEROON

Head of state:	Paul Biya
Head of government:	Philémon Yang
Death penalty:	abolitionist in practice
Population:	20 million
Life expectancy:	51.6 years
Under-5 mortality:	154.3 per 1,000
Adult literacy:	70.7 per cent

The government continued to restrict the activities of political opponents and journalists. People suspected of same-sex relations were detained and some sentenced to lengthy prison terms. The government reduced some prison sentences and commuted death sentences, but did not reveal how many.

C

Background

President Biya was re-elected with 75 per cent of the vote following presidential elections on 9 October. Of the 22 opposition presidential candidates, his closest rival, John Fru Ndi of the Social Democratic Front, won just over 10 per cent. Opposition political parties claimed that the election was unfair. Election observers from the AU, International Organization of La Francophonie and the Commonwealth stated that the election was generally fair, while the US Ambassador to Cameroon said that US government observers noted widespread irregularities at every level.

Before starting a new term in November, President Biya issued a decree commuting sentences imposed by the courts. According to the decree, people serving prison sentences of one year or less were to be released and those serving life imprisonment would have their sentences reduced to 20 years. Death sentences were commuted to life imprisonment. Prisoners convicted of economic crimes, aggravated robbery or murder were excluded from the presidential pardon.

There were several attacks by armed groups on the Bakassi Peninsula, which reverted to Cameroon from Nigeria following a 2002 International Court of Justice decision. In one such attack in February, two Cameroonian soldiers were killed and at least 13 civilians abducted.

Corruption charges

Several dozen former government officials accused of corruption remained in custody, many awaiting trial or serving prison sentences. The trial of Titus Edzoa and Thierry Atangana on new corruption charges had not concluded by the end of the year, although they were close to completing their 15-year prison term imposed in 1997 following an unfair trial.

Impunity

Members of the security forces who committed or ordered serious human rights violations, including unlawful killings, during demonstrations and riots in February 2008 continued to enjoy impunity. The judiciary failed to investigate the violations and bring the perpetrators to justice.　.

Freedom of expression

Several journalists and government critics were detained and some released during the year.
■ Bertrand Zepherin Teyou, a writer arrested in November 2010 while trying to launch his book about the wife of the President, was released on 29 April. He had been found guilty of "contempt of a personality" by the High Court in Douala and sentenced to a fine of 2,030,150 CFA francs (approximately US$4,425) or two years' imprisonment.
■ Human rights defenders and lawyers continued to call for the release of former mayor Paul Eric Kingué, serving a prison sentence in connection with the February 2008 riots, on the grounds that he was victimized for criticizing abuses by government forces. He was also on trial for alleged corruption.
■ Pierre Roger Lambo Sandjo, a musician, completed his three-year prison term and was released in April without being required to pay the fine of 330 million CFA francs imposed in 2008. Human rights defenders believed that he was imprisoned because he composed a song criticizing the amendment of the Constitution that allowed the President to stand for re-election.
■ Agence France Presse correspondent Reinnier Kazé was arrested on 23 February by gendarmes while covering an opposition demonstration in Douala. Officers deleted recordings on his dictaphone before releasing him the following day.
■ In May, police prevented the public showing of a documentary on alleged human rights abuses linked to commercial banana production. The documentary reportedly claimed that small-scale banana growers were removed from their land without compensation and that plantation workers were poorly paid.
■ Gueimé Djimé, a member of OS-Civil Droits de l'Homme human rights group based in Kousséri, Extreme North province, was shot dead as he slept on the night of 10 June. Members of OS-Civil had reportedly received anonymous death threats relating to the group's opposition to the appointment of two local chiefs. Although four men suspected of killing Gueimé Djimé were arrested, no one had been brought to justice by the end of the year.

Freedom of association and assembly

Political and human rights groups were frequently denied the right to organize peaceful activities or demonstrations.
■ At least eight political activists, including former members of a students' association, were arrested in February by members of the Directorate of Territorial Surveillance security service in Yaoundé; they had met to organize a demonstration to commemorate victims of human rights violations during demonstrations in February 2008. The detainees were denied access to lawyers and charged with endangering the security of the state. They were provisionally released but had not been brought to trial by the end of the year.
■ In April, police in Douala detained political activist Mboua Massock while he tried to organize a meeting to protest against the October presidential elections. He was taken 35km from Douala and abandoned.
■ In May, riot police in Yaoundé arrested 37 farmers and dispersed more than 100 others for trying to demonstrate against bad roads and inadequate government support for agriculture. Those arrested were released on 1 June without charge.

The security forces continued to arrest members of the Southern Cameroons National Council (SCNC) and disrupt or prevent their meetings. The SCNC advocates secession of anglophone Cameroonian provinces from largely francophone Cameroon.
■ In February, members of the security forces arrested SCNC national chairman Chief Ayamba Ette Otun and several other people who were travelling with him to Bamenda, capital of North West province. Ayamba Ette Otun was reportedly returning from Buea in South West province where he had handed an SCNC memorandum to a visiting delegation from the African Commission on Human and Peoples' Rights. All were released several days later without charge.

■ On 1 October, members of the security forces disrupted a meeting of the SCNC in Buea and arrested 50 people, claiming that the SCNC had not obtained prior permission to hold the meeting. They were released without charge several days later.

Rights of lesbian, gay, bisexual and transgender people

The government proposed to amend the Penal Code to allow sentences of up to 15 years' imprisonment and large fines to be imposed on people found guilty of same-sex relations. Men convicted of same-sex relations continued to be sentenced to prison terms of up to five years.

■ Jean-Claude Roger Mbede was sentenced to three years' imprisonment on 28 April after being convicted of same-sex relations. In November, the Yaoundé Court of Appeal adjourned his appeal to February 2012.

■ Frankie Ndome Ndome, Jonas Nsinga Kimie and Hilaire Nguiffo were sentenced to five years' imprisonment in November for same-sex relations.

■ Joseph Magloire Ombwa, Nicolas Ntamack, Sylvain Séraphin Ntsama and Emma Loutsi Tiomela were still awaiting trial at the end of the year after being arrested in August. Stéphane Nounga and one other known as Eric O., who were arrested in August, were provisionally released.

■ Others arrested and released for alleged same-sex relations included Jean Jules Moussongo, Steve O., Depadou N. and Pierre Arno. Some of them had been lured into a trap by members of the security forces or their agents who claimed to be gay men seeking relationships.

Death penalty

The government informed Amnesty International in March that 17 people had been sentenced to death during 2010. The authorities said that all had appealed against their sentences but gave no further information about death sentences during 2011.

A presidential decree issued on 3 November commuted death penalty sentences to life imprisonment. However, the decree excluded those who had been convicted of murder or aggravated robbery and did not specify how many had had their sentences commuted.

CANADA

CANADA
Head of state: Queen Elizabeth II, represented by
                              Governor General David Johnston
Head of government: Stephen Harper
Death penalty: abolitionist for all crimes
Population: 34.3 million
Life expectancy: 81 years
Under-5 mortality: 6.1 per 1,000

There were continuing systematic violations of the rights of Indigenous Peoples. Limited progress was made in addressing concerns about human rights violations associated with counter-terror and policing operations.

Indigenous Peoples' rights

In March, the Canadian Human Rights Tribunal dismissed a discrimination complaint alleging that the amount spent by the federal government on child protection in First Nation communities was substantially less than that provided by provincial governments in predominantly non-Indigenous communities. The Tribunal ruled that the federal and provincial governments could not be compared to each other for the purposes of a discrimination complaint. An appeal was pending at the end of the year.

In April, a leaking pipeline spilled an estimated 4.5 million litres of crude oil onto the traditional territory of the Lubicon Cree in northern Alberta, the largest spill in the province since 1975. In August, the province allowed the pipeline to resume operation without meaningful consultation with the Lubicon People. International human rights bodies have long expressed concern over the failure to respect Lubicon land rights.

In August, a federal audit concluded that 39 per cent of water systems in First Nation communities have major deficiencies, with 73 per cent of drinking water systems and 65 per cent of waste water systems constituting medium or high risk to health. An earlier government study had linked the breakdown of First Nation water systems to inadequate government resources.

In October, the Inter-American Commission on Human Rights held a hearing into a complaint brought by the Hul'qumi'num Treaty Group, alleging violations of Indigenous land rights on Vancouver Island in the province of British Columbia. A ruling was expected in 2012.

C

There was little progress in implementing the findings of the Ipperwash Inquiry, set up to examine the fatal police shooting in 1995 of an unarmed Indigenous man during a protest in Ontario. Incidents at the Tyendinaga Mohawk community in Ontario in 2008, in which provincial police pointed high-powered rifles at unarmed protesters and bystanders, and the failure to conduct an impartial review of these incidents, underscored the urgent need for implementation of the Ipperwash findings.

A Truth and Reconciliation Commission, mandated to document and raise awareness of the abuses against First Nations, Métis and Inuit children, and broader harms caused by Canada's historic residential school system, held sessions throughout the year.

Women's rights

In July, the federal Minister responsible for the Status of Women stated publicly that the government did not intend to establish a national action plan to address the high levels of violence faced by Indigenous women.

In October, in British Columbia a provincial inquiry was opened into the police response to the cases of missing and murdered women, many of whom were Indigenous, in Vancouver. Before the inquiry began, 17 of the 20 organizations granted intervener status withdrew because of concerns over fairness.

Counter-terror and security

Hearings by the Military Police Complaints Commission into concerns that Canadian soldiers transferred prisoners in Afghanistan to the custody of Afghan officials, despite a serious risk they would be tortured, concluded in February. The Commission's report had not been issued by the end of the year.

In October, information was made public indicating that Royal Canadian Mounted Police (RCMP) officers had no information implicating Abdullah Almalki in criminal activities and viewed him only to be an "Arab running around" in October 2001 when they sent information to Syrian authorities linking him to terrorism. He was imprisoned and tortured in Syria between May 2002 and March 2004. A public inquiry concluded in 2008 that the actions of Canadian officials in his and two other men's cases contributed to the human rights violations they experienced. The government failed to apologize or provide them with compensation. A lawsuit brought by the three men in 2008 was pending at the end of 2011.

Omar Khadr, a Canadian citizen apprehended by US forces in Afghanistan in 2002 when he was 15 years old and detained at Guantánamo Bay since October 2002, became eligible to be transferred to serve the remainder of his sentence in Canada on 1 November. He had been sentenced to an eight-year prison term in October 2010 following a plea agreement. The Canadian government had not reached a decision on his transfer application by the end of 2011.

Refugees and asylum-seekers

In June, the government reintroduced proposed legislation that would penalize asylum-seekers arriving in Canada in an irregular manner, such as when a human smuggler arranges their travel in a group by sea. The proposals include lengthy mandatory detention without timely review of the grounds of detention and other measures that violate international norms.

Police and security forces

In April, RCMP officers in Prince George, British Columbia, used a Taser against an 11-year-old boy. The RCMP announced in September that the officers involved would not be disciplined or charged.

In June, the Toronto Police Services released an internal review of policing of the G8 and G20 Summits in 2010, during which more than 1,000 people were arrested. The Toronto Police Services Board's independent civilian review of some aspects of the policing operation was continuing at the end of 2011. The provincial and federal governments rejected calls for a public inquiry.

International justice

In October, the government failed to arrest former US President George W. Bush when he travelled to British Columbia, despite clear evidence that he was responsible for crimes under international law, including torture.

Amnesty International visits/reports

▥ Canada/USA: Visit to Canada of former US President George W. Bush and Canadian obligations under international law – Amnesty International memorandum to the Canadian authorities (AMR 51/080/2011)

▥ *Amicus Curiae* Case of the *Hul'Qumi'Num Treaty Group v. Canada*: Submitted before the Inter-American Commission on Human Rights (AMR 20/001/2011)

C

CENTRAL AFRICAN REPUBLIC

CENTRAL AFRICAN REPUBLIC
Head of state:	François Bozizé
Head of government:	Faustin Archange Touadéra
Death penalty:	abolitionist in practice
Population:	4.5 million
Life expectancy:	48.4 years
Under-5 mortality:	170.8 per 1,000
Adult literacy:	55.2 per cent

The human rights situation remained dire as the Central African Republic (CAR) continued to be ravaged by conflict involving numerous armed groups. The civilian population was subjected to widespread human rights abuses, including unlawful killings, abductions, torture and sexual violence, including rape.

Background

President Bozizé was re-elected in January, beating his nearest rival, former President Ange-Félix Patassé, with more than 60 per cent of the vote. The provisional results issued by the Independent Electoral Commission were confirmed by the Constitutional Court in February.

A significant proportion of the CAR was beyond the control of the government. At least 200,000 people were internally displaced, having been forced to flee their homes because of attacks, while about 200,000 refugees lived in neighbouring countries.

The north-west of the CAR was under the effective control of the Popular Army for the Restoration of Democracy (APRD), an armed group which had signed a peace agreement with the government. In the south-east and east, the Lord's Resistance Army (LRA) increased the number and severity of its attacks.

In mid-July, members of the Union of Democratic Forces for the Rally (UFDR) attacked and occupied the north-eastern town of Sam Ouandja. The UFDR, an armed group based in Haute-Kotto province, claimed that it was in retaliation for attacks on its positions by the Convention of Patriots for Justice and Peace (CPJP). Hundreds of people were displaced by fighting between CPJP and UFDR armed groups in September.

Between June and August, three CPJP factions signed peace agreements with the government, although their fighters continued to be armed.

Peacekeeping

US President Barack Obama announced in October that he had sent about 100 US troops to central Africa, including the CAR, to help and advise government forces battling the LRA.

As many as 200 French government soldiers continued to be deployed in the CAR, helping to restructure and train the government's armed forces.

Under the responsibility of the Economic Community of Central African States (ECCAS), the Mission for the Consolidation of Peace in the Central African Republic (MICOPAX) established a presence in Ndélé, in the north-east, in February. The contingent was composed of soldiers from Chad, Gabon, Cameroon, the Republic of Congo and the Democratic Republic of the Congo.

The Ugandan army continued to deploy thousands of troops in the east of the CAR. A Ugandan field court-martial found a Ugandan soldier guilty of murdering a civilian in Obo and sentenced him to death in August.

Disarmament, demobilization and reintegration

In January, President Bozizé appointed six leaders of various armed groups as his advisers on Disarmament, Demobilization and Reintegration (DDR), although it was unclear whether they took up their positions. At the end of July, the government minister responsible for DDR said that demobilization of members of the APRD was taking place in Ouham-Pendé province. He reportedly added that a similar operation would soon start in the north-east. CPJP factions signed peace agreements with the government during the year.

International justice

The trial of Jean-Pierre Bemba, former Vice-President of the Democratic Republic of the Congo, continued before the International Criminal Court in The Hague. He faced two counts of crimes against humanity and three counts of war crimes, accused of leading militias in the CAR in 2002 and 2003 that killed and raped civilians.

No other government or armed group leaders who may have committed war crimes and crimes against

C

humanity in the CAR were issued with an arrest warrant by the ICC or prosecuted by the national justice system.

Abuses by armed groups

Armed groups abused civilians with impunity in large parts of the CAR affected by armed conflict. Civilians were killed and injured, women and girls were raped, and homes, granaries and shops were looted and destroyed. The levels of insecurity made it very difficult for human rights and humanitarian organizations to establish details of these incidents.

The APRD maintained effective control in the north-west of the country. In January, the Representative of the UN Secretary-General on the human rights of internally displaced persons expressed concern that the APRD had been responsible for summary justice and that trials were carried out in an arbitrary manner. He reported that in May 2010 the APRD had executed five people convicted of witchcraft by people's tribunals – informal courts operated and run by the APRD.

■ On 30 January, suspected members of the APRD abducted eight workers with the Spanish section of Médecins Sans Frontières who were travelling in a vehicle close to the CAR/Chad border. Six were found and released two days later, but two Spanish nationals were held until 10 February.

The LRA carried out hundreds of attacks in the CAR, abducting people, including girls, looting and pillaging, and killing hundreds of civilians.

■ In March, members of the LRA reportedly killed at least two civilians and four government soldiers, and abducted as many as 50 people, in the area of Nzako in Mbomou province. LRA fighters also reportedly looted private property and burned many houses. The previous month, LRA fighters had reportedly attacked and occupied Nzako for several hours before leaving the area with at least 10 abducted civilians and looted property.

■ In June, LRA fighters reportedly killed a doctor and his driver during an ambush on a vehicle carrying polio vaccines. The attack took place on the road between Zémio and Rafaï in Haut-Mbomou province. According to Radio Ndeke Luka, the attackers burned the vehicle and all its contents.

The CPJP was accused of rapes, killings, looting and extortion in north-eastern CAR.

■ In September, CPJP fighters killed seven people, including a government official, near Bria.

Child soldiers

In a report issued in April, the UN Secretary-General expressed grave concern about the recruitment and use of children as fighters by armed groups between June 2008 and December 2010.

The report identified several armed groups that continued to use children. They included the UFDR, CPJP, the Central African People's Democratic Front (FDPC), the Movement of Central African Liberators for Justice (MLCJ) and local self-defence militias associated with the government. The report also highlighted the abduction and forced recruitment of children by the LRA in the CAR and neighbouring countries, and their use in the CAR; the LRA was known to use children as fighters, spies, servants, sex slaves and carriers.

The UN Secretary-General welcomed the removal of 1,300 children from within the ranks of the APRD between 2008 and 2010. The Special Representative of the UN Secretary-General for Children and Armed Conflict visited the CAR in November.

Prisoners of conscience

Suspected critics of the government, and their associates and relatives, were imprisoned on false charges.

■ Eleven people remained in detention, despite a court order for their release in July. They were arrested in June 2010 because they had links to a lawyer and a businessman sought by the authorities. Symphorien Balemby, President of the CAR Bar Association, and businessman Jean-Daniel Ndengou fled the country in June 2010. The 11 detainees included Albertine Kalayen Balemby, wife of and secretary to Symphorien Balemby, and Gabin Ndengou, brother of Jean-Daniel Ndengou and a driver for the World Health Organization. The detainees were reported to have been charged with arson, incitement to hatred and criminal association. Amnesty International considered them prisoners of conscience.

Freedom of expression – journalists

A climate of self-censorship was prevalent in the news media.

■ In July, Faustin Bambou, editor of the weekly *Les Collines de l'Oubangui*, and Cyrus Emmanuel Sandy, editor of the daily *Médias,* were fined and released from custody after being held for weeks in connection with their coverage of public protests by retired military officers claiming the government had deprived them of EU funds. The prosecution had sought three-year prison terms and higher fines on charges of "inciting hatred" and "endangering the security of the state".

Several members of the opposition and at least one journalist were barred without explanation from travelling out of the country.

Torture and other ill-treatment

Members of the security forces were accused of torture; the government took no action against those accused of torture in previous years.
■ In August, a supermarket worker in the capital, Bangui, who had been accused of theft, was severely beaten and had his right arm broken by members of the Central African Office for the Repression of Banditry in Bangui.

Amnesty International visits/reports

Central African Republic: Action needed to end decades of abuse (AFR 19/001/2011)

CHAD

REPUBLIC OF CHAD

Head of state:	Idriss Déby Itno
Head of government:	Emmanuel Djelassem Nadingar
Death penalty:	retentionist
Population:	11.5 million
Life expectancy:	49.6 years
Under-5 mortality:	209 per 1,000
Adult literacy:	33.6 per cent

Arbitrary arrests and illegal detentions, as well as torture, attacks against human rights defenders, journalists and trade unionists increased. Rape and other violence against women and girls were widespread. Forced evictions continued in the capital N'Djamena. Members of the Chadian security forces and armed groups responsible for human rights abuses were not held to account, while victims were left without assistance.

Background

Legislative and presidential elections were organized in February and April respectively. The presidential elections were boycotted by the opposition. President Déby was re-elected and appointed a new government in August.

Thousands of Chadians returned from Libya following the escalation of violence there. More than 280,000 refugees from Darfur, Sudan, and around 130,000 internally displaced Chadians were still living in camps in eastern Chad. UNHCR, the UN refugee agency, discussed with Chad and Sudan the possibility of a voluntary return of refugees to Sudan. At least 68,000 refugees, mostly from the Central African Republic, continued to live in refugee camps in southern Chad.

Thousands of Chadian soldiers remained deployed near the town of Goré on the border with the Central African Republic, where they had been since December 2010.

Violence against women and girls

Rape and other violence against women and girls continued to be widespread in various parts of Chad. Internally displaced Chadians, as well as refugees and local women and some children, were among the victims. Not all cases were reported, for reasons including fear of reprisals from perpetrators who were often members of their communities, armed groups or security forces. Those responsible mostly acted with impunity.
■ A 15-year-old girl was abducted from the house of a humanitarian worker and raped several times by at least three men in military uniform on the night of 4/5 March during a search for arms in the town of Goz Beida, eastern Chad. Although the family lodged a complaint, the authorities had not responded by the end of the year.
■ In July, a woman and her daughter aged 13 were raped by men in military uniform in the town of Goré, southern Chad. The girl died from her injuries in September. At the end of the year, no investigation was known to have begun.
■ On 25 December, three girls and a woman from Darfur, all refugees, were raped near Gaga refugee camp in eastern Chad by four armed men as they were collecting firewood. Humanitarian workers were informed that three suspects had been detained by the police.

Child soldiers

On 15 June, Chad and the UN signed an Action Plan on children associated with armed forces and groups in Chad, to end the recruitment and use of child soldiers. At the end of the year, it was not clear whether implementation of the Action Plan had started.

Prison conditions

Prison conditions were harsh and amounted to cruel, inhuman and degrading treatment or punishment. Detention facilities were overcrowded and prisoners often had no access to adequate health services and other basic facilities. Many of the prisoners were sick and malnourished.

Deaths in custody

■ On 17 September, nine men died of asphyxiation four hours after being detained at the National Gendarmerie in the town of Léré in the Mayo-Kebbi West region of southern Chad. Some were subjected to ill-treatment during their arrest. After the deaths, the remaining detainees at the Gendarmerie were transferred to N'Djamena central prison where another man, Bouba Hamane, later died. No investigation into the 10 deaths was known to have been initiated by the end of the year.

Torture and other ill-treatment

The police, the gendarmerie and members of the National Security Agency (Agence Nationale de Sécurité, ANS) regularly tortured suspects, sometimes with the involvement of local administrative authorities.
■ On 20 September Guintar Abel, a civil servant at the Ngondong sub-division in the Lac Wey department in southern Chad, died in hospital three weeks after being beaten by a local district chief and his bodyguards. At the end of the year, no action was known to have been taken.

Arbitrary arrests and detentions

People continued to be arrested and detained without charge by ANS members, and in some cases were prevented from receiving visits from family members, doctors or lawyers. Others were detained by the police and gendarmerie for civil matters, contrary to provisions of the Chadian Constitution and laws.
■ Two students, Bebkika Passoua Alexis and Nedoumbayel Nekaou, were arrested on 7 May at a bus station in N'Djamena for allegedly carrying documents calling for Chadians to organize demonstrations. The two men were first detained incommunicado by the ANS before being transferred to N'Djamena central prison. They received a suspended sentence of eight months' imprisonment and were released on 22 September.

Human rights defenders

Human rights defenders continued to face intimidation and harassment by government officials, particularly those in remote areas in eastern and southern Chad.
■ Kedigui Taroun Grace, a local president of the national women's organization Cellule de Liaison et d'Information des Associations Féminines, was arrested by police with five other women on 19 September in the town of Sarh, southern Chad, following a demonstration in protest against the sacking of a local district chief. The six women were released the same day but Kedigui Taroun Grace was re-arrested on 29 September. She was again released later that day. She was not charged with any criminal offence but the local authorities warned her that she was "politicized".
■ On 19 December, Daniel Deuzoumbe Passalet, President of the Chadian organization Human Rights without Borders, was arrested in N'Djamena. While being interviewed by Radio France Internationale the previous day, he had expressed concern about impunity for the deaths of 10 men who had been in the custody of the Chadian National Gendarmerie in Léré in September. Daniel Deuzoumbe Passalet was released on 30 December after the N'Djamena High Court sitting in Moussoro ruled that there was insufficient evidence to charge him.

Freedom of association and assembly

Thousands of demonstrators, including magistrates, teachers and health workers, protested peacefully in N'Djamena in October and November against low salaries and increasing prices of food and fuel. People were arrested and beaten and others detained following the demonstrations.

Freedom of expression – trade unionists

Trade unionists were subjected to harassment and arbitrary arrest.
■ Boukar Barka, aged 61, secretary general of the Chadian Trade Union Confederation (Confédération Syndicale du Tchad, CST), was arrested on 4 November at his home in N'Djamena by members of the security services. The authorities stated that the arrest was in relation to Boukar Barka's previous conviction for embezzlement. He was released on 11 November but re-arrested on 13 November and held at the police station in Moursal before being transferred to N'Djamena central prison on 14 November. He was later charged with "provocation directly linked to an

unarmed demonstration." Boukar Barka's arrest and detention followed the support which he and his trade union had given to the former workers of the Tchad Cameroon Contractor, a sub-contractor of Esso involved in the Chad-Cameroon pipeline project.

Forced evictions

Forced evictions which had begun in 2008 continued in N'Djamena, affecting hundreds of people whose homes were destroyed. Evictions were conducted without due process, adequate notice or consultation. Those who lost their homes did not receive alternative housing or other form of compensation despite some court orders. Most of the sites from which residents were forcibly evicted remained unoccupied at the end of the year. The N'Djamena municipal authorities announced further eviction plans, particularly affecting those living in the Sabangali and Gassi 3 and 4 areas of the capital.

International justice – Hissène Habré

Although the AU had stated since 2006 that former Chadian President Hissène Habré should be tried in Senegal "on behalf of Africa", this failed to take place. In July the Commission of the AU identified Rwanda as "the country most suitable to be entrusted with the Hissène Habré trial". This followed the meeting of the Assembly of Heads of States and Governments of the AU that urged Senegal to expedite the trial of Hissène Habré or extradite him to another country willing to do so. Human rights organizations, Chadian victims and their lawyers stated their preference for the trial to take place in Belgium, which had investigated the case and charged Hissène Habré with serious violations of international human rights and humanitarian law, and made an extradition request to Senegal in 2005, reiterated in November. The Chadian government publicly supported this option. In November, the UN Committee against Torture called on Senegal to comply with its obligation to prosecute or extradite Hissène Habré.

Impunity

Chadian officials and members of armed groups responsible for serious human rights violations, including unlawful killings, rape and other torture, continued to act with impunity.
■ On 10 January, the President passed an ordinance granting amnesty for crimes committed by members

of armed groups. Some of those who benefited were suspected of committing crimes under international law.
■ Important recommendations of the commission of inquiry into the events in Chad between 28 January and 8 February 2008 had not been implemented by the end of the year, despite a presidential decree of 23 May installing a follow-up committee. The recommendations included investigations into the fate of opposition leader Ibni Oumar Mahamat Saleh, who was subjected to enforced disappearance following his arrest at his home in N'Djamena by members of the security services on 3 February 2008.

Amnesty International visits/reports

🚌 Amnesty International delegates visited Chad in March, May, June, September and November.

📕 Chad: A compromised future – children recruited by armed forces and groups in eastern Chad (AFR 20/001/2011)

📕 Chad: Government must immediately repeal amnesty ordinance (AFR 20/002/2011)

📕 Chad: No homes, no justice, no dignity – victims of forced evictions in Chad (AFR 20/004/2011)

📕 Chad: Briefing to the UN Committee on the Elimination of Discrimination against Women, 50th session, October 2011 (AFR 20/009/2011)

📕 Chadian students to face trial over protest pamphlets, 12 September 2011

CHILE

REPUBLIC OF CHILE

Head of state and government:	**Sebastián Piñera Echenique**
Death penalty:	**abolitionist for ordinary crimes**
Population:	**17.3 million**
Life expectancy:	**79.1 years**
Under-5 mortality:	**8.5 per 1,000**
Adult literacy:	**98.6 per cent**

There were widespread protests during the year over education and environmental and other government policies. The number of criminal complaints for grave human rights violations committed during military rule (1973-1990) continued to rise but less than a third of those convicted were serving prison sentences. The inappropriate use of anti-terrorism legislation against Indigenous Peoples persisted.

Background

Tens of thousands of students, teachers, trade unionists and others took part in demonstrations, demanding fundamental changes to the public education system. Although largely peaceful, some demonstrations ended in confrontations with police.

In June, following widespread opposition and protests, an appeals court issued an order suspending the controversial HidroAysén hydroelectric dam project in Patagonia. However, in October, the court lifted the suspension order. The Supreme Court rejected two further appeals against the project.

The remains of former President Salvador Allende were exhumed in May as part of a new judicial investigation into his death. In July international forensic experts confirmed that his death during the 1973 military coup led by General Augusto Pinochet was not the result of third parties.

A proposed law on anti-discrimination and one recognizing same-sex civil partnerships were before Congress at the end of the year.

Indigenous Peoples' rights

In September, the government bowed to demands to suspend a nationwide consultation process with Indigenous Peoples and agreed to consider repealing Decree 124, which regulates consultation with Indigenous Peoples. The move followed widespread criticism that Decree 124 fails to comply with ILO Convention No. 169 on Indigenous and Tribal Peoples which sets out the right of Indigenous Peoples to participate in decision-making processes that affect them.

There were continuing concerns about the inappropriate use of anti-terrorism legislation in cases involving Mapuche activists, including minors. In August, the Inter-American Commission on Human Rights filed a case with the Inter-American Court of Human Rights concerning the selective application of the anti-terrorism law against Mapuche Indigenous people in a way that was unjustified and discriminatory.

■ Five Mapuche minors continued to face prosecution under the anti-terrorism law at the end of the year, despite amendments to the law in June excluding under-18s.

■ In June, the Supreme Court partially upheld an appeal in the case of four Mapuche activists convicted in March of common crimes by a civilian court in Cañete. The Cañete court had rejected the terrorism charges against them brought by the Public Ministry. However, the proceedings had been conducted under anti-terrorism legislation which permits the use of anonymous witnesses. The Supreme Court reduced their sentences but failed to order a new trial, allowing the convictions, based on the testimony of an anonymous witness, to stand. The four men staged an 87-day hunger strike in protest at the use of anti-terrorism legislation and at violations of due process. The strike ended with the formation of an independent Commission on the Rights of the Mapuche.

■ In February, the Inter-American Commission on Human Rights granted precautionary measures for the Indigenous Peoples of Rapa Nui (Easter Island). The Commission called on the government to guarantee that actions taken by its officials during protests and evictions did not jeopardize the lives or physical integrity of Indigenous people. This followed violent clashes in December 2010. Criminal proceedings were initiated against some clan members and investigations into the actions of the police were continuing at the end of the year.

Impunity

In August, the Valech II Commission issued a report confirming five additional cases of enforced disappearance, 25 political killings and 9,795 cases of torture. The commission had been established in 2010 to assess cases of enforced disappearance, political killings, political imprisonment and torture that had not been presented to the Rettig and Valech Commissions. By the end of the year, the total number of people officially recognized as disappeared or killed between 1973 and 1990 stood at 3,216 and survivors of political imprisonment and/or torture at 38,254.

The number of cases of human rights violations under investigation by the courts rose to its highest level yet following the submission in January by a court prosecutor of 726 new criminal complaints and more than 1,000 complaints filed over the years by relatives of those executed on political grounds.

According to the Interior Ministry Human Rights Programme, as of May there were 1,446 ongoing investigations. Between 2000 and the end of May 2011, 773 former members of the security forces had been charged or sentenced for human rights violations and 245 had had final sentences confirmed. However, only 66 were in prison, the rest having benefited from non-custodial sentences or sentences that were later reduced or commuted.

Police and security forces

There were several reports of torture and other ill-treatment, including beatings and threats of sexual violence, against students arbitrarily detained by police during student demonstrations.

■ In August, 16-year-old Manuel Gutiérrez Reinoso died after being shot by a police officer during student demonstrations in the capital Santiago. Five police officers were subsequently dismissed and a police general resigned. In November, the military appeals court ordered the release on bail of the policeman accused of the shooting.

There were renewed reports of excessive use of force during police operations against Mapuche communities.

Sexual and reproductive rights

Abortion remained a criminal offence in all circumstances. In September the Senate Health Commission agreed to debate proposals to decriminalize abortion in certain cases, but President Piñera said he would veto any bill that came before him.

CHINA

PEOPLE'S REPUBLIC OF CHINA

Head of state:	Hu Jintao
Head of government:	Wen Jiabao
Death penalty:	retentionist
Population:	1,347.6 million
Life expectancy:	73.5 years
Under-5 mortality:	19.1 per 1,000

Fearful of a protest movement inspired by events in the Middle East and North Africa, in February the authorities unleashed one of the harshest crackdowns on political activists, human rights defenders and online activists since the 1989 Tiananmen Square demonstrations. Harassment, intimidation, arbitrary and illegal detention, and enforced disappearances intensified against government critics. Ethnic minority regions were under heightened security as local residents protested against discrimination, repression and other violations of their rights. The authorities

increased ongoing efforts to bring all religious practice within the control of the state; this included harsh persecution of some religious practitioners. China's economic strength during the global financial crisis increased the country's leverage in the domain of global human rights – mostly for the worse.

Background

China's economy remained relatively resilient despite the global financial crisis, raising fears that international actors would be reluctant to criticize China's human rights record, a trend already evident in the recent past. China was increasingly successful in using its growing financial and political clout to pressure other countries to forcibly return increasing numbers of Chinese nationals of certain backgrounds, such as Uighurs, back to China, where they risked unfair trials, torture and other ill-treatment in detention, and other human rights violations.

Freedom of expression

The authorities continued to abuse criminal law to suppress freedom of expression. They detained or arrested close to 50 people and harassed and intimidated dozens more during the crackdown on "Jasmine" protests that began in February in response to the popular movements in the Middle East and North Africa. An initially anonymous call for peaceful Sunday strolls spread across a growing number of cities as a form of protest against corruption, the suppression of rights, and the lack of political reform.

Amendments in March to the Regulations on the Administration of Publications added a new requirement that those who distributed publications over the internet or information networks must be licensed, or risk criminal penalties. The authorities shut down or took direct control of a number of publications that had published investigative journalism pieces on sensitive issues. They reportedly banned hundreds of words from mobile phone text messages, including "democracy" and "human rights".

■ Two veteran activists detained during the "Jasmine" protests were sentenced to long prison terms for their political writings. On 23 December, Chen Wei was charged with "inciting subversion of state power" and sentenced to nine years for 11 articles he had written in support of democracy and political reform. On

26 December, Chen Xi was sentenced to 10 years on the same charge, for 36 articles he published overseas. Ding Mao in Sichuan province, and Liang Haiyi in Guangdong province, remained in detention for their involvement in the "Jasmine" protests.

Human rights defenders

The authorities continued to harass, intimidate, persecute and criminalize pro-democracy and human rights activists. Activists supporting the China Democracy Party were sentenced to long prison terms.
■ In March, Liu Xianbin was charged with "inciting subversion of state power" and sentenced to 10 years in prison for his pro-democracy activism, his support of the Charter 08 petition movement, and his writings on political reform.
■ Human rights activist Chen Guangcheng remained under illegal house arrest along with his wife, Yuan Weijing, and daughter, since his release from prison in September 2010. A grass-roots movement in support of Chen Guangcheng, who is blind, gained momentum across the nation, with many activists posting photos of themselves online wearing his signature dark glasses. Supporters travelled from different parts of China to his home town in an effort to see him, and were beaten and robbed by plain-clothes police stationed in the area.

Enforced disappearances

The number of people subjected to enforced disappearances grew. Many were held in secret detention, including Hada, a Mongolian political activist. Many others remained or were placed under illegal house arrest. They included Liu Xia, wife of Nobel Peace Prize winner Liu Xiaobo, and Zheng Enchong, a housing rights lawyer from Shanghai.

On 30 August, the authorities released draft revisions of China's Criminal Procedure Law, the first proposed changes since 1997. Notwithstanding some positive amendments, the revisions proposed to legalize detention of individuals for up to six months without notification of their family or friends. Many legal commentators regarded this as a legalization of enforced disappearances. Prohibitions against the use of illegal evidence, including coerced confessions and other evidence obtained through torture and other ill-treatment, were incorporated into the draft revisions. However, torture remained pervasive in places of detention, as government policies, such as ones requiring prison and detention centre staff to

"transform" religious dissidents to renounce their faith, fostered a climate conducive to torture.
■ On 16 December, Gao Zhisheng, a well-known human rights lawyer who had been subjected to enforced disappearance on and off for nearly three years, was sent to prison to serve his three-year sentence for "repeatedly violating his probation", just days before his five-year probation was due to end. During his disappearance he was believed to have been in official custody.

Forced evictions

The forced eviction of citizens from their homes and farms, without adequate due process or compensation, accelerated and was increasingly marked by violence. On 21 January, the State Council issued new regulations on the expropriation of houses in urban areas. While a step in the right direction, the regulations only covered city dwellers and not tenants or other non-owners, leaving the majority of Chinese people unprotected against forced evictions.
■ On 29 December, former lawyer Ni Yulan was tried on charges of "picking quarrels" and "fraud" and faced a possible lengthy prison sentence. Ni Yulan was herself forcibly evicted from her home in 2008, before the Beijing Olympics, and was paralysed from the waist down as a result of beatings in detention.

Death penalty

In February, the National People's Congress passed the eighth revision of China's Criminal Law which removed the death penalty as punishment for 13 crimes. At the same time, it added a number of new capital crimes and expanded the scope of others. China continued to use the death penalty extensively, including for non-violent crimes, and to impose it after unfair trials. Executions were estimated to number in the thousands. However, statistics on death sentences and executions remained classified.

Freedom of religion or belief

The authorities pursued their goal of bringing all religious practice under state control, including state oversight over religious doctrine, appointment of religious leaders, the registration of religious groups and construction of sites of worship. People practising religions banned by the state, or without state sanction, risked harassment, detention, imprisonment, and in some cases, violent persecution. Banned religions included underground Protestant house churches and Catholics who accept the authority of the Holy See. Around 40 Catholic bishops remained unaccounted for, and were presumed to be held by the authorities.

■ Between 10 April and the end of the year, members of the underground Shouwang Church in Beijing were detained on a weekly basis as they attempted to hold an outdoor Sunday service in north-west Beijing. Most detainees were held in police stations or under house arrest to prevent the service from taking place. The Church had been repeatedly expelled from rented locations and prevented from taking possession of a building it had purchased years ago.

Falun Gong

The authorities continued to pursue a systematic, nationwide, often violent campaign against the Falun Gong, a spiritual group banned since 1999 as a "heretical cult". The government was in the second year of a three-year campaign to increase the "transformation" rates of Falun Gong practitioners, a process through which individuals were pressured, often through mental and physical torture, to renounce their belief in and practice of Falun Gong. Practitioners who refused to renounce their faith were at risk of escalating levels of torture and other ill-treatment. The authorities operated illegal detention centres, informally referred to as "brainwashing centres", for this process. Falun Gong sources reported that one practitioner died every three days while in official custody or shortly after release, and said that thousands remained unaccounted for.

■ On 5 March, Zhou Xiangyang, a Falun Gong practitioner, was arrested at his home in Tangshan, Hebei province and taken to Binhai Prison in Tianjin city. He immediately went on hunger strike. He had previously spent over nine years in detention and was subjected to forced labour and torture, including sleep deprivation, electric shocks, beatings, and being stretched over a low table with his limbs anchored to the floor. The authorities continued to refuse him a lawyer. In response to an appeal written by his wife, Li Shanshan, more than 2,500 residents in and around his home town signed a petition calling for his release. She was subsequently detained in September, along with Zhou Xiangyang's older brother and at least four others.

Inner Mongolian Autonomous Region

The murder on 10 May of Mergen, an ethnic Mongolian herder, by a Han Chinese coal truck driver sparked widespread protests across the region. Relations were already tense due to grievances on the part of local herders who felt their livelihood was being threatened by land grabbing and environmental damage to livestock grazing from mining companies, many of which were Han Chinese.

■ From 23 to 31 May, hundreds of herders and students took part in largely peaceful, daily protests across the region. While responding to some of the grievances raised, the authorities widely deployed armed security and military forces, and detained dozens of protesters. They blocked off internet sites that mentioned the protests, restricted mobile phone access and shut down most Mongolian-language websites.

Xinjiang Uighur Autonomous Region (XUAR)

The authorities escalated security measures through a succession of "strike hard" campaigns which increased around-the-clock street patrols and involved "mobilizing society to wage battle" against acts the authorities claimed harmed state security. In Urumqi, whole neighbourhoods were reported to have been sealed off by security checkpoints.

Extreme restrictions on the flow of information within and from the XUAR left uncertain the fate of many hundreds detained in the aftermath of the 2009 crackdown on protests in Urumqi. In January, the head of the XUAR High People's Court referred to ongoing cases connected to the 2009 protests, but the authorities provided no information on the trials. Family members of detained individuals were often not informed of the fate or whereabouts of their loved ones and were often too afraid to communicate with those outside China, for fear of retribution by the authorities.

Freedom of expression in the XUAR continued to be severely restricted, including by vaguely defined crimes of "ethnic separatism" and "terrorism", which included distributing materials or literary works with "separatist content".

■ Noor-Ul-Islam Sherbaz died on 13 November, allegedly as a result of torture in prison. He was serving a life sentence on charges of "murder" and "provoking an incident" after an unfair trial. He was alleged to have thrown stones during the July 2009 protests, and was

C

aged 17 at the time of his detention. According to a family friend with access to information from the jail, Noor Ul-Islam had been regularly beaten with electric batons in prison. His family were not allowed access to his body and the authorities buried him before an autopsy was done. The authorities failed to provide adequate evidence at his trial, except for his "confession", which may have been extracted through torture. During his trial, he was represented by a lawyer appointed by the court.

The Chinese government used economic and diplomatic pressure on other countries, including Kazakhstan, Malaysia, Pakistan and Thailand, to forcibly expel or hand over more than a dozen Uighurs to the Chinese authorities. Uighurs forcibly returned to China were at high risk of torture, arbitrary detention and unfair trials, and were often held incommunicado.

Tibet Autonomous Region

From 16 March to the end of the year, 10 monks or former monks and two nuns in the Tibetan areas of China set themselves on fire. Six were believed to have died as a result. These protests appeared to be in response to increasingly punitive security measures imposed on religious institutions and lay communities in the region, following the March 2008 protests. The first self-immolation, by Phuntsok Jarutsang, was followed by protests, mass arrests (including of 300 Kirti Monastery monks), enforced disappearances and possible killings by security forces. Two elderly Tibetans (a man and a woman) died after local residents clashed with security forces while trying to stop the arrests. A third man died from injuries sustained following a police crackdown on demonstrators outside a police station. Individuals connected to protests around the immolations were sentenced to prison terms ranging from three to 13 years. Despite the rash of self-immolations, there was no indication that the Chinese authorities intended to address the underlying causes of the protests or acknowledge the grievances of the Tibetan community.

Hong Kong Special Administrative Region

Freedom of expression, association and assembly

Security forces and police used excessive force against peaceful protesters.

■ During a peaceful demonstration on 15 May, the International Day Against Homophobia and Transphobia, police threatened to arrest protesters unless they stopped dancing. Police argued that organizers – including Amnesty International Hong Kong – had not obtained a "temporary public entertainment license". Critics considered this harassment, having no legal basis.

■ On 2 July, police arrested 228 participants in the annual 1 July pro-democracy march, for causing an obstruction in a public place and unlawful assembly. The Hong Kong Journalists Association said that 19 journalists were attacked with pepper spray and one journalist was arrested during the 10,000-strong march. Police also attempted to arrest Law Yuk Kai, Director of Hong Kong Human Rights Monitor, while he observed them removing and arresting protesters who were blocking traffic. All those arrested were released later the same day. Several were subsequently charged with disturbing public order.

During Chinese Vice Premier Li Keqiang's three-day visit to Hong Kong in August, police set up "core security areas" keeping protesters and press away from him. Legislative Councillors and others criticized these tactics as heavy-handed, undermining freedom of expression. Police dragged away one resident wearing a t-shirt commemorating the 1989 Tiananmen massacre.

Legal developments

■ In June, the government introduced controversial proposals which in some circumstances would end by-elections as the means for replacing Legislative Council members whose terms ended early.

■ Also in June, the Law Reform Committee issued a consultation paper on setting up a Charity Law and a Charity Commission. Amnesty International and other rights-based groups criticized the proposals' definition of charity, which excluded human rights activities while recognizing 13 other sectors, including animal rights.

Discrimination

■ On 30 September, the High Court ruled in favour of a Filipina domestic helper, determining that immigration provisions prohibiting foreign domestic helpers from applying for right of abode were unconstitutional. The government appealed against the ruling. Critics of the government's stance believed the exclusion amounted to ethnic discrimination.

■ On 25 November, a post-operative transsexual woman lost her second appeal against a judgement

C

denying her the right to marry her boyfriend in her reassigned sex. The Court of Appeal stated that any potential changes to law were a matter for the legislature and not the courts. The appellant said she would take the case to the Court of Final Appeal.

Refugees and asylum-seekers
In July, the government introduced the Immigration (Amendment) Bill 2011, as a step towards creating a statutory framework to handle claims made under the UN Convention against Torture.

COLOMBIA

REPUBLIC OF COLOMBIA
Head of state and government: **Juan Manuel Santos Calderón**
Death penalty: **abolitionist for all crimes**
Population: **46.9 million**
Life expectancy: **73.7 years**
Under-5 mortality: **18.9 per 1,000**
Adult literacy: **93.2 per cent**

The government continued to express a commitment to human rights. Despite this, there were few tangible improvements in the overall human rights situation. Civilians – especially Indigenous Peoples, Afro-descendent and peasant farmer communities, human rights defenders, community leaders and trade unionists – continued to bear the brunt of the human rights consequences of the long-running internal armed conflict.

The Victims and Land Restitution Law, signed by President Juan Manuel Santos in June, was an important step in acknowledging the rights of many victims of the conflict and returning some of the millions of hectares of land stolen, often through violence, to the rightful owners. However, continuing threats and killings of those campaigning for land restitution risked undermining implementation of the law.

The government made commitments to end impunity for human rights abuses, and progress was made in some emblematic cases. However, the authorities failed to ensure that most of those responsible, especially for sexual crimes against women and girls, were brought to justice. There were concerns that government plans to broaden the scope of military jurisdiction could reverse what little progress had been made in the fight against impunity.

More than 40 candidates were killed during local and regional elections in October, considerably more than during the 2007 elections. Several candidates with alleged close ties to politicians convicted or under criminal investigation for illegal links with paramilitaries were elected to office, including as departmental governors.

Internal armed conflict
Guerrilla groups, paramilitaries and the security forces continued to be responsible for crimes under international law, including unlawful killings, abductions or enforced disappearances, and forced displacement. Those living in rural areas, particularly Indigenous Peoples and Afro-descendent and peasant farmer communities, were most at risk, as were those living in poverty in urban areas, human rights defenders and trade unionists.

According to the National Indigenous Organization of Colombia, 111 Indigenous people were killed in the first 11 months of 2011.
■ In June, paramilitaries killed five leaders from the Zenú Indigenous People in Zaragoza Municipality, Antioquia Department.
■ The body of Indigenous Katío youth leader Crisanto Tequia Queragama was found on 26 February in Bagadó Municipality, Chocó Department. Indigenous leaders blamed the guerrilla group the Revolutionary Armed Forces of Colombia (Fuerzas Armadas Revolucionarias de Colombia, FARC) for the killing.

Around 308,000 people were forcibly displaced in 2011, compared to 280,000 in 2010.
■ In October, some 400 Indigenous people from Pradera Municipality, Valle del Cauca Department, fled their homes following combat between the security forces and the FARC.
■ In March, more than 800 Afro-descendants from rural Buenaventura, Valle del Cauca, were forcibly displaced during fighting between the security forces and the FARC.
■ In January, some 5,000 people, including some 2,300 children, were forced to flee their homes in Anorí Municipality, Antioquia Department, after threats from the FARC.

On 2 November, the government issued Decree 4100, which created the National Human Rights and

C

International Humanitarian Law System. The government claimed this body would improve the co-ordination and implementation of the state's human rights policies.

Victims and Land Restitution Law

The Victims and Land Restitution Law acknowledges the existence of an armed conflict and the rights of victims. It provides for reparations for some survivors of human rights abuses, including those perpetrated by state agents. However, there were concerns that many victims would be excluded from making claims for reparation, while significant tracts of stolen land might still not be returned to their rightful owners. There were also concerns that some returnees may be forced to cede control over their land to those who had forcibly displaced them.

Leaders of displaced communities and those seeking the return of stolen lands continued to be killed and threatened.

■ On 30 June, Antonio Mendoza Morales, leader of the San Onofre and Montes de María Association of Displaced Peoples, was killed by unidentified gunmen in San Onofre, Sucre Department.

Security forces

At least 17 extrajudicial executions by security force personnel in which the victim was falsely presented as a "guerrilla killed in combat" were reported in the first half of 2011. Although this marked an increase on 2010, the figures were still significantly lower than those recorded in 2008, when some 200 such killings were reported.

■ In July, a judge sentenced eight members of the army to between 28 and 55 years' imprisonment for the 2008 killing of two young men in Cimitarra Municipality, Santander Department. This was the first conviction of soldiers implicated in the killing of more than a dozen young men from Soacha, near Bogotá, falsely presented by the army as "guerrillas killed in combat".

Most of the thousands of extrajudicial executions carried out over the course of the conflict, including those being investigated by the Office of the Attorney General, remained unresolved.

At the end of the year, measures remained before Congress to extend the military justice system's role in investigating human rights violations in which the security forces were implicated. The military justice system regularly has closed such investigations without a serious attempt to hold those responsible to account. If passed, this measure would be contrary to international human rights standards which state that human rights violations should be investigated exclusively by civilian courts.

Congress was also debating measures which could allow human rights abusers, including members of the security forces, to benefit from de facto amnesties.

The guerrilla

The FARC and the smaller National Liberation Army (Ejército de Liberación Nacional, ELN) committed serious human rights abuses and violations of international humanitarian law, including unlawful killings, hostage-taking, forced displacement and the recruitment of children.

■ On 22 May, FARC guerrillas reportedly attacked a boat in Medio Atrato Municipality, Chocó Department, killing three civilians and injuring a further two.

■ On 19 March, ELN guerrillas killed a young Indigenous man in Tame Municipality, Arauca Department, after members of the Indigenous *resguardo* (reservation) where he lived refused to be forcibly recruited into the guerrilla group.

■ On 9 July, FARC guerrillas detonated a car bomb in the urban centre of Toribío Municipality, Cauca Department, an area inhabited predominantly by Indigenous Peoples. The explosion and fighting between the FARC and the security forces left at least three civilians and a police officer dead and 120 civilians and two police officers injured.

According to government figures, in the first 10 months of the year, 49 members of the security forces and 20 civilians were killed and hundreds more injured by anti-personnel mines deployed predominantly by the FARC.

According to official statistics, there were 305 kidnappings in 2011 compared to 282 in 2010. Most were attributed to criminal gangs, but guerrilla groups were responsible for the vast majority of conflict-related kidnappings.

■ On 26 November, FARC guerrillas reportedly executed four members of the security forces they had been holding captive for at least 12 years.

On 4 November, FARC commander Guillermo León Sáenz Vargas (alias "Alfonso Cano") was killed by the security forces during a military operation.

Paramilitaries

Despite their supposed demobilization, paramilitary groups, labelled "criminal gangs" (Bacrim) by the government, continued to expand their territorial presence and influence. In February, the then Minister of the Interior and Justice, Germán Vargas Lleras, acknowledged that Bacrim had territorial control in many parts of the country, both in urban and rural areas. Reports were received that increasing numbers of paramilitaries were operating in areas with a significant security force presence.

Paramilitaries, sometimes with the collusion or acquiescence of the security forces, continued to commit serious human rights violations, including killings and enforced disappearances, as well as social cleansing operations in poor urban neighbourhoods. Their victims were mainly trade unionists, human rights defenders and community leaders, as well as members or representatives of Indigenous Peoples and Afro-descendent and peasant farmer communities.

■ On 12 September, at least 30 armed and uniformed members of the paramilitary group Los Rastrojos arrived at the hamlet of Pesquería, Cumbitara Municipality, Nariño Department. They threatened and ransacked the community and accused them of collaborating with the guerrilla. The paramilitaries reportedly dismembered two civilians while they were still alive in front of the whole community. They also kidnapped 13 people, at least two of whom were killed.

The Justice and Peace process

The Justice and Peace process made little progress. Under this process, introduced in 2005, some 10 per cent of the more than 30,000 paramilitaries who supposedly demobilized can qualify for reduced prison sentences in return for confessing to human rights violations. The remaining 90 per cent received de facto amnesties. By the end of the year only 10 paramilitaries had been convicted under the process; most had appeals against their convictions pending at the end of the year.

In February, the Constitutional Court ruled that Law 1424, which sought to grant de facto amnesties to tens of thousands of supposedly demobilized rank-and-file paramilitaries if they signed a so-called Agreement to Contribute to the Historic Truth and to Reparation, was constitutional.

The civilian intelligence service

On 31 October, the government disbanded the civilian intelligence service (Departamento Administrativo de Seguridad, DAS). This had operated under the direct authority of the President and had been mired in an illegal "dirty tricks" scandal, which included threats, killings, illegal surveillance and wire-tapping, targeting human rights activists, politicians, judges and journalists, mainly during the government of President Álvaro Uribe Vélez (2002-2010). It was replaced by the National Intelligence Directorate.

Several senior DAS officials were still under investigation for their involvement in the scandal; others had already been sentenced. However, another former DAS director, María del Pilar Hurtado, continued to evade justice; she was granted asylum in Panama in 2010.

■ On 14 September, former DAS Director Jorge Noguera was sentenced to 25 years' imprisonment for the killing of academic Alfredo Correa de Andreis and for links to paramilitary groups.

■ In November, the Procurator General called on the congressional committee investigating the role played in the scandal by former President Uribe to examine whether he had ordered illegal wire-tapping by the DAS.

Human rights defenders

The work of human rights activists continued to be undermined by killings, threats, judicial persecution and the theft of sensitive case information.

■ On 23 August, Walter Agredo Muñoz, a member of the Valle del Cauca Branch of the Political Prisoners Solidarity Committee, and Martha Giraldo, a member of the Movement of Victims of State-Sponsored Crimes, received a death threat via text message, accusing them of being communists and members of the FARC. The message listed several human rights NGOs, trade unions, and Afro-descendent and Indigenous organizations.

More than 45 human rights defenders and community leaders, including many working on land issues, and at least 29 trade union members, were killed in 2011.

■ On 23 March, human rights activists Orlando Enrique Verbel Rocha and Eder Verbel Rocha and his son were on their way home in San Onofre Municipality, Sucre Department, when two paramilitaries shot at them and beat them. Eder Verbel Rocha was fatally wounded.

■ On 17 March, Gabriela, a member of the Transgender Foundation of the South, was killed by gunmen in Pasto Municipality, Nariño Department. The killing came shortly after fliers were circulated in Pasto calling for the "social cleansing" of members of the LGBT community, among others.

In response to the spate of killings of human rights defenders, the Office in Colombia of the UN High Commissioner for Human Rights called on the government in March to fundamentally revise its physical protection programmes. On 31 October, the government issued Decree 4065 which unified all the Ministry of the Interior's protection programmes under a single new agency, the National Protection Unit.

Impunity

Progress was made in a limited number of key human rights cases.

■ On 28 April, a judge sentenced retired General Jesús Armando Arias Cabrales to 35 years' imprisonment for his role in the enforced disappearance of 11 people in November 1985 after the army stormed the Palace of Justice where people were being held hostage by members of the M-19 guerrilla group. The government and the military high command both made statements criticizing his conviction and that of retired Colonel Luis Alfonso Plazas Vega, sentenced in 2010 to 30 years' imprisonment in the same case. Retired General Iván Ramírez Quintero, who was charged with one of the disappearances, was acquitted in December.

Impunity persisted in the vast majority of cases, exacerbated by threats against and killings of witnesses, lawyers, prosecutors and judges.

■ On 22 March, the judge presiding over the case against an army officer accused of the rape of one girl, the rape and killing of another, and the killing of her two brothers, was shot dead in Saravena, Arauca Department. The NGO assisting the victims' families received a telephone death threat soon after the killing, as did the family of the three siblings.

Violence against women and girls

Women human rights defenders and community leaders, especially those working on land issues, were threatened and killed.

■ On 7 June, Ana Fabricia Córdoba, an Afro-descendent leader who campaigned on behalf of displaced communities, was killed in Medellín, Antioquia Department.

■ On 5 May, 11 paramilitaries surrounded Sixta Tulia Pérez and Blanca Rebolledo, two women leaders of the Afro-descendent community in Caracolí, Chocó Department. The paramilitaries tried to rip their clothes off and grabbed a child who was with them. One of them hit Sixta Tulia Pérez with a whip. Later that day, the paramilitaries threatened the women in front of soldiers, who did not react when asked to help.

Women human rights organizations, especially those working with displaced women and survivors of sexual violence, were also threatened.

■ On 19 June, a number of NGOs, including many women's organizations, received a death threat by email from the paramilitary Black Eagles Capital Bloc. The email read: "Death penalty to the guerrilla bitches of the FARC who are opposing the policies of our government".

The government made commitments to combat conflict-related sexual violence against women and girls, but the problem remained widespread and systematic. Government compliance with Constitutional Court rulings on the issue, especially Judicial Decision 092 of 2008, remained poor. Impunity for such crimes continued to be significantly higher than for other types of human rights abuse. However, in December, a paramilitary was found guilty of conflict-related sexual crimes, the first such conviction in the Justice and Peace process.

US assistance

US assistance to Colombia continued to fall. In 2011, the USA allocated some US$562 million in military and non-military assistance to Colombia. This included US$345 million for the security forces, of which US$50 million was designated for the armed forces, 30 per cent of which was conditional on the Colombian authorities meeting certain human rights requirements. In September 2011, some US$20 million in security assistance funds from 2010 was released after the US authorities determined that the Colombian government had made significant progress in improving the human rights situation.

In October 2011 the US government ratified the US-Colombia Free Trade Agreement (FTA), despite opposition from human rights and labour organizations which expressed concerns about the safety of labour leaders and activists in Colombia and the impact the FTA might have on small-scale farmers, Indigenous Peoples and Afro-descendent communities.

International scrutiny

The report on Colombia of the UN High Commissioner for Human Rights, published in February, recognized "the commitment to human rights expressed by the Santos administration". However, the report stated that all parties to the conflict continued to violate international humanitarian law, and expressed particular concern "about the continuing homicides, threats, attacks, information theft, illegal surveillance and intimidation targeting human rights defenders and their organizations".

Amnesty international visits/reports

🚍 Amnesty International delegates visited Colombia in February, March, September and November.

📑 Colombia: Authorities must ensure safety of judge in key human rights case (AMR 23/014/2011)

📑 "This is what we demand, justice!" – Impunity for sexual violence against women in Colombia's armed conflict (AMR 23/018/2011)

📑 Colombia: Amnesty International condemns guerrilla attack which results in civilian casualties (AMR 23/023/2011)

📑 Colombia: Victims law an important step forward but questions remain (PRE01/285/2011)

CONGO (REPUBLIC OF)

REPUBLIC OF CONGO

Head of state and government:	**Denis Sassou-Nguesso**
Death penalty:	**abolitionist in practice**
Population:	**4.1 million**
Life expectancy:	**57.4 years**
Under-5 mortality:	**128.2 per 1,000**

Torture and other ill-treatment by members of the security forces were reported, in some cases leading to deaths. Three asylum-seekers from the Democratic Republic of the Congo (DRC) remained in detention without charge or trial after almost eight years. Government critics were arbitrarily arrested or ill-treated by security forces. The expected termination of refugee status for most Rwandan and Angolan refugees gathered momentum. At least three prisoners were sentenced to death.

Background

In February, President Sassou-Nguesso promulgated a law to protect the rights of Indigenous People and to make it an offence to identify them as Pygmies.

The government of the DRC accused the Republic of Congo of supporting an armed group that reportedly attacked the residence of DRC President Joseph Kabila in February. Former DRC army general Faustin Munene, the alleged leader of the armed group who had fled to the Republic of Congo, sought asylum in Poland. He had been sentenced in his absence to life imprisonment on 4 March by a DRC military court, which found him guilty of fomenting rebellion.

In July, the government of Gabon proceeded to cease the refugee status of 9,500 Congolese, most of whom had fled the armed conflict in the Republic of Congo during the 1990s. Those who wished to remain in Gabon were given the option to apply either for a residence permit under Gabonese law and remain in the country as migrants, or for exemption from termination of their refugee status. UNHCR, the UN refugee agency, assisted 685 Congolese to return home and 900 others to obtain Gabonese residence permits.

President Sassou-Nguesso visited Rwanda in November and his delegation reportedly discussed with the Rwandese authorities the termination of refugee status of Rwandan refugees in the Republic of Congo.

Torture and other ill-treatment

Members of the security forces tortured or otherwise ill-treated detainees with impunity, in some cases resulting in deaths. The judiciary failed to respond to complaints by relatives of detainees who died in custody in previous years.

■ Anicet Elion Kouvandila died on 2 June after he was detained for eight days and severely beaten at Lumumba police station in the capital, Brazzaville. Relatives found his body at a mortuary, registered under a different name.

■ A pregnant woman, Blanche Kongo, was arrested on 17 October with her child by police seeking her husband regarding an alleged theft. Blanche Kongo was severely beaten at Mbota police station and suffered a miscarriage.

■ On 28 August, an army colonel severely beat Jean Karat Koulounkoulou and Rock Inzonzi in a land dispute. The colonel buried the men up to their necks, threatening to bury them alive. A local government official and police officers stopped the ill-treatment but no action was taken against the colonel.

Refugees and asylum-seekers

At the end of November, Germain Ndabamenya Etikilime, Médard Mabwaka Egbonde and Bosch Ndala Umba, asylum-seekers from the DRC detained for almost eight years without charge or trial in Brazzaville, were transferred from military custody to the General Directorate for the Surveillance of the Territory. Government officials told Amnesty International delegates in December that their situation would soon be resolved but gave no further details. The delegates were refused access to the detainees.

At the end of the year, the Congolese government announced that in 2012 the refugee status of nearly 8,000 Rwandan refugees and 800 Angolan refugees would change, on the grounds that in both countries there had been a fundamental, durable and stable change of circumstances. Congolese officials stated that no refugees would be forced to return, but failed to clarify what would be the status of those choosing to stay in the Republic of Congo.

Freedom of expression and association

The authorities broke up demonstrations by government opponents. A government critic was briefly detained.

■ Eric Mampouya, a blogger and government critic, was arbitrarily arrested on 7 August after he arrived at Brazzaville airport from France, where he was resident. Members of the security forces held him unlawfully for 10 hours before releasing him with a warning to end his criticism of the government.

■ The co-ordinator of the Rally for Young Patriots, Jean-Marie Mpouele, and several members of the organization were beaten on 1 September by armed men in civilian clothes, believed to be members of the security services. The group had been attempting to hold a demonstration in Brazzaville.

Enforced disappearances

A delegation of the UN Working Group on Enforced or Involuntary Disappearances visited the Republic of Congo from 24 September to 3 October to gather information on efforts to investigate and prevent enforced disappearances. Discussions focused on the

1999 disappearance of some 350 refugees returning from the DRC, and the 2005 trial of 16 security and government officials which failed to establish individual criminal responsibility. The UN Working Group made several recommendations to the government, including enactment of a law criminalizing enforced disappearances.

Death penalty

Three people were sentenced to death in July after a court convicted them of trafficking human bones. The authorities had not revealed how many people were on death row by the end of the year.

Amnesty International visits/reports

🚗 Amnesty International delegates visited the Republic of Congo in December.

CÔTE D'IVOIRE

REPUBLIC OF CÔTE D'IVOIRE

Head of state :	Alassane Ouattara
Head of government :	Guillaume Soro
Death penalty:	abolitionist for all crimes
Population:	20.2 million
Life expectancy:	55.4 years
Under-5 mortality:	118.5 per 1,000
Adult literacy:	55.3 per cent

The violence that followed the disputed presidential election in November 2010 caused the most serious humanitarian and human rights crisis in Côte d'Ivoire since the de facto partition of the country in September 2002. Hundreds of people were unlawfully killed, often only on the grounds of their ethnicity or presumed political affiliation. Women and adolescents were victims of sexual violence, including rape, and hundreds of thousands of people were forced to flee their homes to seek refuge in other regions of Côte d'Ivoire or in neighbouring countries, especially Liberia. Both sides committed war crimes and crimes against humanity, and in October the International Criminal Court opened an investigation into some of these crimes.

Background

The November 2010 presidential elections led to a political stalemate after outgoing President Laurent Gbagbo refused to recognize the victory of Alassane Ouattara. After three months of sporadic fighting, at the end of March forces loyal to Alassane Ouattara launched an offensive and occupied almost all the areas held by forces loyal to Laurent Gbagbo. In April, soldiers with the UN Operation in Côte d'Ivoire (UNOCI) and the French Force Licorne bombed the artillery deployed by troops loyal to Laurent Gbagbo, who was eventually arrested.

Human rights violations and abuses continued to be committed after April, and in the economic capital Abidjan real or perceived supporters of former President Gbagbo were targeted. In Abidjan and the west of the country, thousands of people fled their homes and went to neighbouring countries, including Ghana. By the end of the year, more than 250,000 refugees and displaced people had not returned home for fear of attacks or reprisals.

In December, legislative elections that were boycotted by the Ivorian Popular Front (FPI), the party of former President Gbagbo, led to a decisive victory for the coalition supporting President Ouattara.

In September, a national Truth, Reconciliation and Dialogue Commission was officially inaugurated by President Ouattara but had not begun its work by the end of the year.

Abuses by armed groups

Pro-Gbagbo security forces

During the first four months of the year, pro-Gbagbo security forces extrajudicially executed and arrested people during demonstrations, in the streets or in their homes. Some were victims of enforced disappearance and most were Dioulas, a generic term designating those with a Muslim name or from the north of Côte d'Ivoire or other countries in the sub-region.

■ In January, Bamba Mamadou, nicknamed Solo, a football player, was beaten to the ground and shot dead by security forces patrolling in the Banfora Adjamé neighbourhood of Abidjan.

■ In February, security forces loyal to Laurent Gbagbo shelled densely populated areas of Abobo, a district of Abidjan, killing many people, including women and children.

Republican Forces of Côte d'Ivoire (FRCI)

The Republican Forces of Côte d'Ivoire (FRCI),

created in March by Alassane Ouattara, killed and tortured real or presumed supporters of Laurent Gbagbo, notably in the west of the country.

■ In April, Basile Mahan Gahé, Secretary General of the trade union organization Confédération Dignité, was tortured after being arrested by the FRCI. He was reportedly made to face a mock execution and was pounded on his back with the flat side of a machete blade.

■ In May, three military officers were arrested by the FRCI in Yopougon. Two were released but the third, Mathurin Tapé, who was a Bété (the ethnic group to which Laurent Gbagbo belongs), remained unaccounted for by the end of the year.

■ After the arrest of Laurent Gbagbo, dozens of his real or presumed supporters were arrested and detained arbitrarily. A number of military and police personnel were held in a Korhogo military camp, in reportedly life-threatening conditions. By the end of the year, some of these detainees had been released but others, including Simone Gbagbo, wife of the former President, had been charged with offences against state security and economic offences and were still held without trial.

Abuses by militias

Young patriots and other pro-Gbagbo militias and Liberian mercenaries killed scores of people in Abidjan as part of a pattern of reprisals and retribution against real or perceived supporters of Alassane Ouattara.

■ In May, Liberian mercenaries entered the village of Gobroko, near the town of Sassandra, and reportedly killed at least 23 Dioulas. Most were from neighbouring countries, including four from Nigeria, five from Mali, one from Benin and 10 from Burkina Faso.

Militias composed especially of Dozos (traditional hunters) that supported Alassane Ouattara killed and tortured real or presumed supporters of Laurent Gbagbo, notably members of specific ethnic groups in the west of the country.

■ In May, a group of Dozos attacked an encampment outside the village of Bédi-Goazon, 450 km west of Abidjan, killing four men and injuring many others.

Duékoué massacre

At the end of March and beginning of April, several hundred civilians were unlawfully killed by forces of both sides to the conflict in the town of Duékoué and surrounding villages.

Liberian mercenaries and militias loyal to Laurent Gbagbo killed a number of Dioulas while entering compounds often inhabited by several families. After taking control of Duékoué, the FRCI, supported by Dozos and armed elements in plain clothes, led a manhunt in the Quartier Carrefour area, where the population was mainly Guérés. They entered the compounds, demanded money and looted houses. Women and girls were made to leave and hundreds of men and boys were summarily executed.

Violence against women and girls

Pro-Gbagbo militia members raped women accused of supporting Alassane Ouattara, in some cases with the involvement of security forces loyal to the former President. FRCI members were also responsible for rape and other crimes of sexual violence against women and girls.

■ In May, Laurence Banjneron, aged 27, was killed while resisting rape by FRCI soldiers in the village of Toulepleu, near the Liberian border. After killing her, a soldier reportedly later shot and killed her husband, Jean-Pierre Péhé, when he arrived to inquire about his wife.

Freedom of expression – journalists

A number of journalists were arrested for their links with the former regime of Laurent Gbagbo or for criticizing the new authorities.

■ In July, Herman Aboa, a journalist from Radio Télévision Ivoirienne, was arrested and charged with endangering state security and incitement to racial hatred. He was released in December after the prosecution dropped all charges against him.

■ In November, three journalists with the FPI newspaper *Notre Voie,* including the editor César Etou, were arrested and charged with incitement to theft, looting and destruction of the property of others through the press. They were released in December after a court dismissed the charges.

Refugees and asylum-seekers

As a result of the post-electoral violence and human rights violations and abuses, hundreds of thousands of people fled their homes either to other parts of the country or to neighbouring countries, notably Liberia. At the height of the crisis there were more than one million refugees and internally displaced people. People attempting to return home were often victims of violence and many found their homes occupied by others. By the end of the year, more than 250,000

had not returned home for fear of harassment or retaliation.

International justice

In October, the Pre-Trial Chamber of the International Criminal Court (ICC) authorized an investigation into crimes against humanity and war crimes perpetrated by both sides in Côte d'Ivoire, limited to the post-electoral crisis since 28 November 2010. However, the Pre-Trial Chamber also asked the Prosecutor to present information on potentially relevant crimes committed between 2002 and November 2010, when some of the most serious crimes took place. In response, the Prosecutor detailed specific incidents that may also amount to crimes falling under the jurisdiction of the ICC, including the use of child soldiers.

In October, during a visit to Côte d'Ivoire, the ICC Prosecutor stated that between three and six people carrying the greatest responsibility for crimes under international law committed in Côte d'Ivoire would be investigated. In November, former President Gbagbo was transferred to the ICC in The Hague, Netherlands, following the issuing of an arrest warrant.

Corporate accountability

Five years after the dumping of toxic waste that affected thousands of people, many of the victims had not received compensation from the oil-trading corporate group Trafigura. At the end of the year, victims still did not have access to information relating to possible health consequences, and a number of sites where the toxic waste was dumped had not been fully decontaminated.

Amnesty International visits/reports

Côte d'Ivoire: Mission report (AFR 31/001/2011)

Côte d'Ivoire: Arbitrary detention of actual or perceived supporters of Laurent Gbagbo (AFR 31/006/2011)

Côte d'Ivoire: "We want to go home, but we can't" – continuing crisis of displacement and insecurity (AFR 31/007/2011)

Côte d'Ivoire: The ICC Prosecutor should investigate the most serious crimes committed since 2002 (AFR 31/010/2011)

Côte d'Ivoire: Missing millions must reach Trafigura toxic waste victims (PRE01/408/2011)

CROATIA

REPUBLIC OF CROATIA

Head of state:	Ivo Josipović
Head of government:	Zoran Milanović (replaced Jadranka Kosor in December)
Death penalty:	abolitionist for all crimes
Population:	4.4 million
Life expectancy:	76.6 years
Under-5 mortality:	5.4 per 1,000
Adult literacy:	98.8 per cent

Progress in prosecution of crimes under international law committed during the 1991-1995 war was slow. Many crimes allegedly committed by members of the Croatian Army and police forces against Croatian Serbs remained unaddressed. Some efforts were undertaken by the President and the judicial authorities to deal with the wartime past, but there was little action by the government. Instead, key political figures engaged in attacks on judgements made by international courts. Discrimination against Roma, Croatian Serbs and lesbians, gay men, bisexuals and transgender people continued.

Background

In December, Croatia signed the EU Accession Treaty and was expected to join the EU on 1 July 2013. The EU continued monitoring, among other things, the implementation of Croatia's commitments to tackle impunity for crimes under international law committed during the 1991-1995 war.

Justice system

Progress in prosecution of crimes under international law committed during the war continued to be slow.

In April, the State Prosecutor's office started to develop plans for the implementation of the Strategy for the Investigation and Prosecution of War Crimes adopted by the government in February. In May, specialized courts in Osijek, Rijeka and Split were made operational, in addition to the existing court in Zagreb, in order to prosecute the most significant cases.

However, capacity to prosecute crimes under international law remained low, with only five final judgements delivered in the year. Investigations of around 370 alleged perpetrators were ongoing. There

were around 540 cases at a pre-investigative stage, in which the perpetrators had not yet been identified.

The 1993 Criminal Code continued to be applied in these cases, although it did not accord with international standards. The Code lacked clear definitions of crucial criminal concepts such as the principle of command responsibility, war crimes of sexual violence and crimes against humanity. Its application resulted in impunity for many crimes.

Some progress was made in providing psychological support to witnesses, but witness protection measures continued to be inadequate. Those responsible for intimidation of witnesses were not brought to justice.

■ There was no proper investigation of the killing of Milan Levar, a potential witness at the International Criminal Tribunal for the Former Yugoslavia (Tribunal), who had also campaigned for justice for war victims. In August 2000, he was killed by an explosive device underneath his car, after making statements to the media alleging that Mirko Norac and some other high level officials were responsible for crimes committed against the Croatian Serb population in the Lika region.

The authorities failed to provide victims of crimes under international law and their families with access to reparation. Survivors of crimes of sexual violence were denied access to psychosocial assistance and other support. Many of their perpetrators enjoyed impunity.

Some progress was made by the judicial authorities in prosecuting crimes under international law committed against Croatian Serbs. Several investigations were opened, including two into the crimes committed in Sisak and Pakračka poljana.

■ In June, an investigation was opened against three men for killings of Croatian Serb civilians in Sisak between 1991 and 1992. One of them was Đuro Brodarac, the war-time Chief of Police in Sisak. All three suspects were placed in detention. Đuro Brodarac died while in custody in July.

■ In June, Tomislav Merčep, former adviser to the Interior Minister and commander of the Ministry's special reserve unit, was indicted. He had been under arrest since December 2010. The charges were that due to his orders and omissions, 43 Croatian Serb civilians in the area of Zagreb and Pakračka poljana were killed or went missing.

Also in June, the State Prosecutor charged six individuals with crimes under international law committed during "Operation Storm" in 1995, although no one had been prosecuted by the end of the year. One was charged under command responsibility. According to the Croatian Helsinki Committee for Human Rights, at least 677 people were killed in "Operation Storm".

Despite the existence of publicly available information, allegations against some high-profile military and political officials were not investigated. These included allegations against the Deputy Speaker of the Croatian Parliament, Vladimir Šeks, for holding command responsibility for crimes committed in eastern Slavonia in 1991. Allegations against him were based on information from court proceedings against Branimir Glavaš. A Croatian army general, Davor Domazet-Lošo, was also alleged to hold command responsibility for the crimes committed in 1993 in Međak Pocket. Allegations against him were based on court proceedings against General Rahim Ademi and General Mirko Norac.

In October, parliament adopted a law that would make indictments and other legal acts ineffective when issued by the authorities of Serbia, former Yugoslavia and the Yugoslav National Army (JNA) against Croatian nationals for crimes under international law committed in the territory of the Republic of Croatia. The law was passed after the Serbian judicial authorities requested co-operation from the Croatian State Prosecutor on processing indictments issued by the Military Prosecutor of the JNA in 1992. They included charges for crimes under international law committed by Croatian military and police forces in Gospić. Vladimir Šeks was among the accused.

The law breached Croatia's obligation to co-operate with the Republic of Serbia in criminal matters. It could result in impunity for crimes under international law committed by Croatian nationals if Croatia refuses to prosecute or extradite them. In October, the President announced that he would request that the Constitutional Court assess compatibility of the law with the Constitution.

The law would allow judicial authorities not to act on requests from the Republic of Serbia for legal assistance in criminal proceedings if acting on those requests was contrary to the Croatian legal order and detrimental to its sovereignty and security. The Minister of Justice, who would be authorized to decide on how to respond to such requests, might dismiss indictments issued by the Serbian juridical authorities.

■ In September, the Ministry of Justice released Mirko Norac after he had served over two-thirds of his 15-year prison term for war crimes, including murder, inhumane treatment, plunder and wanton destruction of property, against Croatian Serb civilians and prisoners of war during military operations in 1993.

■ Branimir Glavaš, convicted in 2010, continued serving his five-year sentence for crimes under international law committed against Croatian Serbs in Osijek.

International justice

Five cases related to crimes under international law committed on Croatian territory during the 1991-1995 war were pending before the Tribunal in The Hague.

■ In April, the Tribunal convicted two generals, Ante Gotovina and Mladen Markač, for crimes against humanity and war crimes. They were found guilty of having participated in a joint criminal enterprise during and after "Operation Storm" between August and November 1995, with the aim of permanently removing the ethnic Serb population from the Krajina region of Croatia.

The Tribunal found military forces and the Special Police responsible for a "large number of crimes" against the Serb population during "Operation Storm". Ante Gotovina held the rank of Colonel-General in the Croatian Army and was the Commander of the Split Military District at the time. Mladen Markač held the position of Assistant Minister of Interior in charge of special police matters. They were convicted of persecution, deportation, plunder, wanton destruction, murder, inhumane acts and cruel treatment of the civilian Serb population. They were sentenced to 24 and 18 years' imprisonment respectively.

Government representatives immediately rejected the Tribunal's judgement. The Prime Minister stated repeatedly that the Croatian government found it unacceptable, and that the Croatian nation should be proud of all people who took part in the operation and contributed to the Croatian victory. In May, both generals appealed against the judgement.

■ The trial of Vojislav Šešelj, who was accused of crimes in Bosnia and Herzegovina, Croatia and the Vojvodina province of Serbia, continued. He was indicted for crimes against humanity, including persecution on political, racial or religious grounds, deportation and inhumane acts. He was also accused of war crimes, including murder, torture, cruel treatment, wanton destruction of villages, or devastation not justified by military necessity, destruction or wilful damage done to religious or educational institutions and plunder of public or private property. In October, the Trial Chamber found him guilty of contempt for publishing confidential information on protected witnesses and sentenced him to 18 months' imprisonment.

■ In July, Goran Hadzić was arrested in Serbia on charges of crimes against humanity and war crimes in eastern Slavonia in Croatia. He was transferred to the Tribunal where he awaited trial at the end of the year. Goran Hadzić had been President of the self-declared Republic of Serbian Krajina. His charges included, among others, extermination, murder, torture, imprisonment and persecutions on political, racial or religious grounds.

Discrimination
Ethnic minorities
Roma continued to face discrimination in access to economic and social rights, including education, employment and housing, while measures undertaken by the authorities remained insufficient.

The authorities failed to implement the judgement by the European Court of Human Rights in the case of *Oršuš and Others v. Croatia,* announced in 2010. The Court had concluded that the placement in 2002 of 14 Romani schoolchildren in separate classes based on their command of the Croatian language amounted to discrimination on the basis of ethnicity.

Croatian Serbs continued to face discrimination, especially in access to adequate housing. During Croatia's UN Universal Periodic Review in November 2010, several states recommended that Croatia take steps to combat discrimination against ethnic minorities. Croatia supported recommendations to strengthen its efforts to combat racial discrimination against the Serb minority, in particular in the area of housing, and to increase measures to integrate ethnic Serb and Roma minorities into the fabric of Croatian life.

Rights of lesbian, gay, bisexual and transgender people
The first attempt to hold a Pride march in Split was made in June. Lesbian, gay, bisexual and transgender

(LGBT) rights activists had organized the march to call for the equal rights of same-sex couples and an end to the widespread discrimination the LGBT community suffers in Croatia. However, it was interrupted by violence. At least five Pride participants were injured when counter-demonstrators from far-right groups threw rocks and other missiles. One was hospitalized with a head injury.

The police failed to adequately protect the participants from attacks and the Pride march had to be stopped; 44 individuals were prosecuted by the authorities in Split for crimes committed against the Pride participants.

A week after the violent events in Split, the annual Pride march in Zagreb was held successfully without major incident.

C

Amnesty International visits/reports
▥ Submission to the Committee of Ministers of the Council of Europe on Oršuš and Others v. Croatia (EUR 64/007/2011)

▥ Briefing to the European Commission on the progress made by the Republic of Croatia on prosecution of war crimes (EUR 64/008/2011)

▥ Croatia: The state must ensure the right to free assembly and expression (EUR 64/009/2011)

▥ Croatia: Praise for "Operation Storm" creates climate of impunity (EUR 64/010/2011)

▥ Briefing to the European Commission on the ongoing concerns over impunity for war crimes in Croatia (EUR 64/011/2011)

CUBA

REPUBLIC OF CUBA

Head of state and government:	Raúl Castro Ruz
Death penalty:	retentionist
Population:	11.3 million
Life expectancy:	79.1 years
Under-5 mortality:	5.8 per 1,000
Adult literacy:	99.8 per cent

The last 11 prisoners of conscience detained during the March 2003 crackdown were released in March, along with 62 other political prisoners. However, government repression continued, resulting in hundreds of short-term arrests and detentions. Journalists and political dissidents faced harassment

and intimidation by security officials and government supporters acting with government acquiescence.

Background

The Cuban authorities continued to stifle freedom of expression, association and assembly, in spite of the much publicized releases of prominent dissidents. Hundreds of pro-democracy activists and dissidents suffered harassment, intimidation and arbitrary arrest.

In April, the Cuban Communist Party held its first congress since 1997 and adopted a package of more than 300 economic reforms that were due to be introduced gradually. However, no resolutions were adopted granting Cubans greater enjoyment of civil and political rights or proposing legislative reforms to allow greater political freedom on the island. During the year, the Cuban government introduced minor economic reforms authorizing the sale of cars and houses, and permitting some income-generating activities outside its direct control.

Alan Gross, a US citizen arrested in December 2009 for distributing telecommunications material in Cuba, was sentenced by a Cuban tribunal to 15 years in prison for crimes against the security of the state. US officials and personalities attempted to secure his release on humanitarian grounds but were unsuccessful.

Freedom of expression, assembly and association

The authorities continued to severely restrict the freedom of expression, assembly, and association of political dissidents, journalists and human rights activists. They were subjected to arbitrary house arrest and other restrictions on their movements by the authorities and government supporters which prevented them from carrying out legitimate and peaceful activities. All media remained under the control of the Cuban government.

Repression of dissent

In February, the authorities detained more than 100 people in a single day and placed over 50 people under house arrest in a pre-emptive strike designed to stop activists marking the death of activist Orlando Zapata Tamayo, who died in 2010 following a prolonged hunger strike while in detention.
■ Reina Luisa Tamayo, Orlando Zapata's mother; her husband, José Ortiz; and Daniel Mesa, a human rights activist, were arrested on 22 February by about 15 state security agents as they left their home in Banes, Holguín province. The arrests were intended to prevent them from undertaking any activities in memory of Orlando Zapata on the first anniversary of his death on 23 February. All three were released 12 hours later. In June, Reina Luisa Tamayo went into exile in the USA with her family.

Prisoners of conscience

In March, the Cuban authorities completed the release of the prisoners of conscience detained during the March 2003 crackdown, as well as political prisoners, some of whom had been imprisoned since the 1990s. The release of the last 52 prisoners of conscience started in July 2010 following an agreement with the Spanish government and dialogue with the Catholic Church. Most of the former prisoners and their relatives were forced into exile and only a few were allowed to remain in Cuba.
■ Nestor Rodríguez Lobaina, president and co-founder of the Cuban Youth Movement for Democracy, was forced into exile in Spain; he was a prisoner of conscience. He had been arrested in December 2010 and spent four months in detention without trial in connection with a meeting he organized at his home and anti-government banners he displayed outside his home in August 2010. Nestor Rodríguez Lobaina had served a six-year prison term between 2000 and 2005 for contempt for the authorities.

Arbitrary detention

The authorities continued to use arbitrary detention in an attempt to silence critics of government policy.
■ The Ladies in White, relatives of former prisoners of conscience from the 2003 crackdown, and their supporters repeatedly faced arbitrary arrest and physical attacks as they staged protests in several towns in Cuba. In August, five Ladies in White living in the city of Santiago de Cuba were arrested before they could reach the cathedral from where they planned to begin their march. Nineteen members of the group were rearrested a few days later and 49 Ladies in White and their supporters were prevented from carrying out a protest in central Havana in support of their members in Santiago de Cuba and other eastern provinces. On several occasions, the Ladies in White reported that they were subjected to physical and verbal aggression from government supporters during peaceful marches. In October, 26 members of the Ladies in White were briefly detained by the authorities to prevent them from

C

participating in a meeting following the death of their leader Laura Pollán in October. In July, more than 20 members of the Support Group of the Ladies in White were detained the day before a march called by the Ladies in White at Our Lady of the Rosary Church in Palma Soriano, Santiago de Cuba province. Dissidents on their way to the church were also detained and prevented from taking part in the peaceful march.

The US embargo against Cuba

In January, the US government announced minor changes to the embargo, allowing greater travel to Cuba for educational, cultural, religious and journalistic activities. In October, for the 20th consecutive year, the UN General Assembly adopted a resolution calling on the USA to lift its economic and trade embargo against Cuba, in place since 1961.

UN agencies working in Cuba, such as the WHO, UNICEF and UNFPA, continued to report the negative effects of the US embargo on the health of the population, particularly members of marginalized groups. Access to specific commodities, equipment, medicines and laboratory materials remained scarce as a result of restrictions imposed on the importation of items manufactured by US companies and their subsidiaries or produced under US patents.

Amnesty International visits/reports

🚗 The Cuban authorities have not granted Amnesty International access to the country since 1990.

CYPRUS

REPUBLIC OF CYPRUS

Head of state and government:	Demetris Christofias
Death penalty:	abolitionist for all crimes
Population:	1.1 million
Life expectancy:	79.6 years
Under-5 mortality:	3.5 per 1,000
Adult literacy:	97.9 per cent

Hundreds of irregular migrants, including rejected asylum-seekers, were detained for prolonged periods in poor conditions solely due to their immigration status.

Background

Negotiations between Greek Cypriot and Turkish Cypriot leaders continued on issues such as power-sharing.

In November, new legislation seeking to transpose the EU Returns Directive into domestic law came into force amid concern that people were languishing in immigration detention. It set six months as the maximum length of pre-removal immigration detention, with extensions of up to 18 months under certain circumstances.

In December, Parliament enacted legislation giving powers to the Office of the Commissioner for Administration (Ombudsperson) to act as the national human rights institution.

Refugees, asylum-seekers and migrants

Migrants, including asylum-seekers whose claims had been rejected, were detained in extremely poor conditions solely due to their immigration status. The use of unsuitable facilities, such as short-stay police cells and two wings in Nikosia Central Prison, also gave rise to concern. Detainees reported limited or no access to legal assistance and health care.

In December, about 200 migrants languished in immigration detention. Many of them had no immediate prospects of being removed from Cyprus. As a result, their detention appeared arbitrary, unnecessary and therefore unlawful. The Supreme Court ordered the release of some detainees on the grounds that their detention had been unlawfully prolonged. However, they were immediately re-detained, following their release, on the same grounds as before.

C

A new immigration detention facility in Mennoia, with capacity for 276 people, was due to begin operation early in 2012. The EU had financed 30 per cent of its construction.

■ In December, a Tamil asylum-seeker was forcibly returned to Sri Lanka following a negative decision by the Reviewing Authority on his appeal against the initial rejection of his claim. The circumstances of his forced return gave rise to concerns that he had been denied the opportunity to apply both for a judicial review of the decision before the Supreme Court and for the suspension of his deportation.

Police and security forces

There were several allegations of ill-treatment of migrants and asylum-seekers by police.

■ In July, according to reports, about 35 police officers severely beat, threatened and verbally abused a group of asylum-seekers detained in Larnaca police station. One of the asylum-seekers reportedly suffered injuries to one leg and was denied medical assistance for several days. Investigations into the incident by the Ombudsperson and police complaints authority were pending at the end of the year.

Human rights defenders

Concerns were expressed by international refugee and migrant NGOs over the prosecution of the executive director of pro-equality NGO, KISA, after the authorities brought criminal charges against him "for rioting and participating in an illegal assembly". The charges related to events at the anti-racism Rainbow Festival in Larnaca in November 2010, in which participants were reportedly attacked by members of an anti-migrant demonstration. The December hearing was postponed until February 2012.

Amnesty International visits/reports

🚌 Amnesty International delegates visited Cyprus in November.

CZECH REPUBLIC

CZECH REPUBLIC

Head of state:	Václav Klaus
Head of government:	Petr Nečas
Death penalty:	abolitionist for all crimes
Population:	10.5 million
Life expectancy:	77.7 years
Under-5 mortality:	3.5 per 1,000

Anti-Roma demonstrations organized by "far-right" political groups in the north led to clashes with police. The government failed again to address discrimination against Roma in education, despite a European Court of Human Rights judgement.

Discrimination – Roma

In March, the Council of Europe Commissioner for Human Rights noted that racist and anti-Roma discourse was still common among mainstream politicians at both national and local levels. Both the Commissioner and the UN Committee on the Rights of the Child expressed concerns over the perpetuation of systemic and unlawful segregation of Romani children from mainstream education.

Racism and violent attacks

Following tensions between Roma and non-Roma in Nový Bydžov in the Hradec Králové region, the town's mayor stated in November 2010 that "citizens... want the Roma to disappear. But... [t]he hands of the local government are tied by the legislation".

Representatives of the Workers' Social Justice Party welcomed the mayor's statement and announced their readiness to help the municipality. On 12 March, the Party organized a march in Nový Bydžov. Three Roma were attacked by the demonstrators. NGOs expressed concerns about reports of excessive use of force by the police against peaceful counter-demonstrators, who attempted to create a blockade to prevent the marchers from passing through the predominantly Roma neighbourhood.

■ In March, the High Court upheld the decision of the Regional Court in Ostrava, which found four men guilty of racially motivated attempted homicide and property damage in an arson attack against a Romani family in Vítkov in 2009. The perpetrators appealed against the High Court decision at the Supreme Court in July. In December, the Supreme Court rejected their appeal.

■ On 11 July, an arson attack was reported in Býchory, central Bohemia. No one was injured. A police spokesperson told the media that the perpetrators had passed through the neighbourhood shouting racist slogans. Within several hours, the police arrested four individuals. The regional prosecutor pressed charges of attempted racially motivated serious bodily harm against one of the suspects. The remaining three were charged with violence against a group of people and against individuals.

■ In August, following two incidents between Roma and non-Roma, "far-right" political groups including the Workers' Social Justice Party staged several anti-Roma protests in the towns of Nový Bor, Rumburk, Varnsdorf and Šluknov in northern Bohemia. The protests, marked by violent clashes between protesters and police, continued until late September. Special police units were deployed to ensure public order. High-level officials including the President condemned the anti-Roma violence and the police spokesperson expressed readiness to prevent racially motivated abuses.

In response to increased tensions between Roma and non-Roma in the Šluknov area, the Minister of Interior met with the mayors of the region on 8 November. He announced the establishment of a special public order police unit. The Prime Minister reportedly said that the tensions were the result of excessively generous welfare policies and that the state should not assist "slackers and delinquents" who abuse benefits.

Education

Approximately 50 experts from NGOs, academia and government agencies resigned from their Ministry of Education working groups in May. The resignations were in protest against the government's failure to allocate sufficient resources to implement the National Action Plan for Inclusive Education, and its retrograde action on implementing necessary reforms. The group stated that remaining would amount to participation in a "window-dressing" exercise to mask the lack of action by the authorities.

The government continued to be criticized also for its failure to implement the European Court of Human Rights judgement in the case of *D.H. and Others v. Czech Republic*, in which the Court held that the state had discriminated against Romani pupils in access to education. The judgement required the Czech Republic to adopt measures to prevent discrimination and redress its effects. In May, the government adopted amendments to the decrees on the provision of counselling services in schools and on the education of children, pupils and students with special educational needs. These entered into force on 1 September. However, local NGOs expressed concerns that the amendments had not introduced the strong framework necessary to implement the judgement. Moreover, the CERD Committee had stated in August that the amended decrees may in fact reinforce discrimination.

Following a review in June, the Committee of Ministers of the Council of Europe called on the government to speed up its implementation of the National Action Plan and provide precise information on its current state. The Committee also noted with concern that much remained to be done to ensure that Romani children were not discriminated against within the education system.

Housing

■ In August, the Regional Court in Prague rejected two complaints of ethnic discrimination and segregation of Roma in access to housing. The complaints involved Romani families in Kladno who had been evicted by the municipality and relocated to inadequate housing in a former slaughterhouse complex that was segregated from the town. The Court held that the families' relocation did not amount to segregation and discrimination and failed to call on the municipality to justify why only Romani tenants had been relocated to the site. An NGO, Z§vůle práva, representing the Romani applicants, appealed against the decision at the High Court.

Enforced sterilization of Romani women

■ In June, the Supreme Court ruled that the High Court in Olomouc, Moravia, had to review the case of a Romani woman who was allegedly sterilized without her informed consent. The Supreme Court disagreed with the lower court's decision that a victim of sterilization was not entitled to compensation because the statute of limitations had expired.

Migrants' rights

In January, legislation came into force extending the maximum period of immigration detention to 18 months, giving rise to profound concern that it would lead to foreign nationals languishing in detention solely for immigration purposes. In July, the Ministry of Interior presented a draft of the new Act on the Stay of Foreigners. The draft maintained the extended maximum period of immigration detention. Moreover, the human rights Ombudsperson expressed concern that the draft, if adopted and implemented, would sanction a discriminatory two-tier system for Czech nationals and their non-EU family members.

■ Credible allegations emerged concerning trafficking in foreign migrant workers and fraud in the forestry industry, where people were forced to work for up to 12 hours per day without being paid their salary. In some cases no wages had been paid at all, often for several months. A police investigation into those reports was ongoing at the end of the year, but its pace and effectiveness gave rise to concern. Czech forestry companies continued to recruit new workers for the 2011 season.

Amnesty International visits/reports

🚌 An Amnesty International delegate visited the Czech Republic in July.

📁 Czech Republic: Police fails to protect the Roma of Nový Bydžov (EUR 71/002/2011)

📁 Czech Republic: Submission to the Committee of Ministers of the Council of Europe on *D.H. and Others v. the Czech Republic* (EUR 71/005/2011)

📁 Czech Republic: Joint statement – Committee of Ministers fails Romani children in Czech Republic (EUR 71/006/2011)

DEMOCRATIC REPUBLIC OF THE CONGO

DEMOCRATIC REPUBLIC OF THE CONGO

Head of state:	Joseph Kabila
Head of government:	Adolphe Muzito
Death penalty:	retentionist
Population:	67.8 million
Life expectancy:	48.4 years
Under-5 mortality:	198.6 per 1,000
Adult literacy:	66.8 per cent

Impunity for crimes under international law continued in the Democratic Republic of the Congo (DRC), despite some limited progress. Government security forces and armed groups committed scores of human rights violations in eastern DRC. Nine soldiers from the Congolese armed forces, including a lieutenant colonel, were convicted of crimes against humanity, notably rape, committed on 1 January in the town of Fizi, South Kivu. They were sentenced to jail in February in a rare example of perpetrators being promptly brought to justice. However, investigations stalled into other cases of mass rapes committed by the national army and armed groups. The general elections were marred by many human rights violations, including unlawful killings and arbitrary arrests by security forces. Human rights defenders and journalists faced intimidation and restrictions on the freedoms of expression and association.

Background

The presidential residence and a military camp in Kinshasa were attacked on 27 February in what the government called a "coup d'état". A wave of arbitrary arrests followed, mainly targeting people from Equateur province.

The DRC's second presidential and legislative elections since independence took place on 28 November. On 5 January, a constitutional amendment changed the presidential electoral system from a two-round voting system to a single round, first-past-the-post vote. This amendment, and logistical problems including delays in the electoral calendar, and controversy over the revised electoral register, increased tensions between the presidential majority coalition and the opposition.

The national army, Forces Armées de la République Démocratique du Congo (FARDC), continued its military operations against foreign armed groups in eastern and northern DRC, including the Democratic Liberation Forces of Rwanda (FDLR), the Lord's Resistance Army (LRA) and the Allied Democratic Forces/National Army for the Liberation of Uganda (ADF/NALU), causing further displacement of civilians. In January, the national army started withdrawing troops for training and redeployment as part of its reconfiguration. This led to armed groups resuming control of former FARDC areas and the desertion of armed groups recently integrated into the army. A deteriorating security situation in North and South Kivu ensued, with increased activity by the FDLR, Mayi-Mayi Yakutumba and the Burundian Forces Nationales de Libération (FNL). The army's reconfiguration plan and the 31 December 2010 presidential decree to redistribute ranks within the FARDC created additional difficulties for the already failing process of integrating former armed groups into the FARDC.

On 28 June, UN Security Council Resolution 1991 (2011) extended the mandate of the UN Organization Stabilization Mission in the DRC (MONUSCO) until 30 June 2012. It reiterated that future MONUSCO configurations should be determined based on the evolving security situation on the ground and on meeting objectives, such as improved government capacity to protect the population. The mandate included technical and logistical support for the elections and continued support for a limited number of FARDC military operations.

Abuses by armed groups

Armed groups, including the LRA, the FDLR, FNL, the ADF/NALU and various Mayi-Mayi groups, reportedly committed numerous human rights abuses against civilians. These included rapes, killings, looting and abduction, notably in Orientale, North and South Kivu provinces. Mayi-Mayi armed groups targeted civilians in protest against the government, despite the government policy of integrating national armed groups into the army as an incentive to stop fighting.

The former armed group National Congress for the Defence of the People (CNDP), which was integrated into the national army in 2009 while retaining its autonomy, allegedly committed human rights violations including unlawful killings and arbitrary arrests. Disputes between the army and armed groups about control over mining areas also worsened the security situation and prompted more abuses.

In May, FDLR fighters reportedly abducted 48 people and looted many houses in Mwenga territory, South Kivu.

The LRA abducted civilians and forced them to carry looted goods in Orientale province throughout the year. The LRA remained a significant threat to the civilian population, forcing thousands to flee. Armed groups also attacked humanitarian workers on several occasions.

Unlawful killings

The periods before and after the elections were marked by unlawful killings and dozens of arbitrary arrests by security forces, including the Republican Guard.

■ On 4 October, Mayi-Mayi Yakutumba reportedly ambushed a vehicle belonging to Eben Ezer Ministry International, a Congolese NGO, killing seven people, including four staff members, in Kalongwe, Fizi territory, South Kivu.

■ From December 2010, FARDC soldiers and agents of the national police (PNC) reportedly committed summary executions, rape and lootings in the Mbororo community in Ango, Banda and Buta territories, Orientale province.

■ After President Kabila was declared the winner of the contested elections on 9 December, Congolese security forces reportedly killed at least 24 people, mostly in Kinshasa.

Violence against women and girls

Rape and other forms of sexual violence remained endemic and were committed by government security forces, including the PNC, and armed groups. Sexual violence often accompanied other human rights violations, such as looting and torture. While some prosecutions took place, impunity was still widespread and victims were often threatened. Rape survivors did not receive adequate support and assistance and continued to be stigmatized. Male victims were particularly marginalized.

■ On 31 December 2010 and 1 January 2011, FARDC soldiers reportedly committed mass rapes in Bushani and Kalambahiro villages, Masisi territory, North Kivu.

■ On 1 and 2 January, FARDC soldiers committed mass rapes in Fizi town, South Kivu.

■ On 27 April, a PNC agent allegedly raped a 16-year-old girl in Mbuji-Mayi, Kasai Orientale province.

■ Between November 2010 and January 2011, FDLR fighters raped at least 102 women and one girl during attacks on villages in Katanga and South Kivu provinces.

■ In June, following clashes between Mayi-Mayi Sheka and Alliance des patriotes pour un Congo libre et souverain, elements of both armed groups reportedly committed mass rapes in Mutongo and surrounding villages, Walikale territory, North Kivu.

Child soldiers

Armed groups and the FARDC continued to recruit and use children, notably in eastern DRC, despite hundreds being released. Children continued to be abducted by armed groups, particularly the LRA and the FDLR, and used as fighters, spies, sexual slaves or carriers. Although the FARDC formally stopped

D

recruiting children in 2004, no plan of action was adopted for separating children from armed forces, as required by UN Security Council Resolutions 1539 (2004) and 1612 (2005).

Internally displaced people and refugees

An estimated 1.57 million people remained displaced within the DRC, including 1 million in North and South Kivu. Living conditions remained dire both in camps and host communities.

In July, the DRC, Uganda and UNHCR, the UN refugee agency, agreed on voluntary repatriation of 32,000 Congolese refugees living in Uganda.

Congolese nationals continued to be expelled from Angola to the DRC. Some reportedly suffered human rights violations, including rape, in Angola.

Torture and other ill-treatment

Torture and other ill-treatment were committed by armed groups and government security forces, including the FARDC, the national police, the National Intelligence Agency and the Republican Guard. Security forces often committed torture and other ill-treatment in detention facilities following arbitrary arrests. NGOs and UN officials continued to be denied access to many facilities, and secret and unofficial holding cells were still in use.

In July, the DRC promulgated a law criminalizing torture. Implementing this legislation remained a key challenge as security services continued to commit torture and other ill-treatment, including in illegal detention facilities.

■ Between 27 July and 1 August, during a military operation in Rutshuru territory, North Kivu, FARDC soldiers reportedly arbitrarily arrested 27 people as a reprisal for alleged FDLR collaboration. At least eight of them were allegedly subjected to torture and other cruel, inhuman or degrading treatment, and forced labour.
■ On 13 April, in Vusamba, Lubero territory, North Kivu, a PNC detainee was whipped 40 times before being freed because he could not pay the US$40 requested for his release.

Death penalty

Military courts continued to sentence scores of people to death, including civilians. No executions were reported. On 23 June, four policemen were sentenced to death for abducting and assassinating a prominent human rights defender (see below).

Impunity

The justice system remained largely incapable of securing justice and reparations for victims. Impunity for past and current violations of human rights and international humanitarian law remained widespread, despite some prosecutions and convictions. Suspected perpetrators of crimes under international law were not removed from their posts or brought to justice. A lack of resources, corruption and political and military interference continued to paralyse courts throughout the country. Scores of civilians were tried by military courts.

The Minister of Justice and Human Rights submitted a draft law for establishing a specialized court composed of Congolese and international personnel with jurisdiction over genocide, crimes against humanity and war crimes. The Senate rejected this draft law on 22 August.

■ On 21 February, the South Kivu military court in Baraka town sentenced nine FARDC officers to between 20 and 10 years' imprisonment for crimes against humanity, including rape, committed during an attack on Fizi town on 1 and 2 January. Investigations launched into other cases proceeded slowly.
■ Investigations into the systematic rape of more than 300 women, men, boys and girls committed in July and August 2010, in Walikale territory, North Kivu, led to a trial against eight suspected perpetrators, only one of whom was in detention. The hearings were adjourned after the trial opened on 1 November, due to the court's decision to relocate the trial to Walikale.

Judicial investigations into mass rapes and other human rights violations committed by FARDC soldiers in Bushani and Kalambahiro villages in North Kivu did not progress significantly.

Prison conditions

Prisons continued to lack the resources to ensure people were detained in conditions that met international minimum standards. Several prisoners died as a result of these poor conditions. Decaying facilities prevented women from being effectively separated from men, and pre-trial detainees from convicted prisoners. Prison escapes occurred throughout the country due to limited resources and poor infrastructure.

On 7 September, 963 prisoners escaped from Kasapa prison, Lubumbashi, Katanga province,

D

following an armed attack. The escapees included the former Mayi-Mayi chief Gédéon Kyungu Mutanga, who was convicted of war crimes, crimes against humanity and terrorism in March 2009.

Human rights defenders

Government security forces and armed groups continued to attack and intimidate human rights defenders, including through death threats and arrests.

■ On 28 January, the president of a local NGO that had protested against illegal exploitation of natural resources facilitated by the provincial authorities was reportedly detained in Gemena town, Equateur province. His arrest warrant reportedly stated "incitement to rebellion" as a motive.

■ On 1 and 2 February, the President and Vice-President of the African Association for the Defence of Human Rights received death threats following a press conference criticizing the constitutional reform of the presidential electoral system.

■ On 23 June, the Kinshasa/Gombe military court sentenced five policemen to death in relation to the abduction and assassination of prominent human rights defender Floribert Chebeya and the disappearance of his driver, Fidèle Bazana, in June 2010. Other key individuals allegedly involved were not investigated.

Freedom of expression

The administrative authorities and security services placed restrictions on the freedoms of expression and association. Government security forces forcibly repressed demonstrators, and clashes occurred between supporters of various political parties.

Journalists

Many journalists were threatened, arbitrarily arrested, prosecuted, intimidated, warned by state authorities not to report on certain subjects, and sometimes killed for their work. Such violations increased in the context of the general elections.

Radio stations and TV channels were given official suspension orders and their premises targeted for politically motivated violence.

■ On 21 June in Kirumba, North Kivu, a community radio journalist was shot dead by unidentified armed men, following remarks he reportedly made about the security situation in the area.

■ On 1 September, a journalist was beaten by agents of the Congolese Rapid Response Police Unit while covering an opposition party demonstration in Kinshasa/Gombe.

International justice

The International Criminal Court (ICC) was due to deliver its judgement in January 2012 in the case of Thomas Lubanga, charged with war crimes consisting of recruiting and using children aged under 15 for the Union des Patriotes Congolais armed group in Ituri.

■ In January, Callixte Mbarushimana, Secretary of the FDLR, was transferred to the ICC after his arrest in France in October 2010. On 16 December, the ICC Pre-Trial Chamber declined to confirm the charges against him and ordered his immediate release. On 20 December, the ICC Appeals Chamber rejected the Prosecutor's appeal against this decision. Callixte Mbarushimana was released on 23 December and returned to France, where an investigation was ongoing into his alleged role in Rwanda's 1994 genocide.

■ The trial of FDLR leaders Ignace Murwanashyaka and Straton Musoni began in May in Stuttgart, Germany, where they had been living. Both were charged with crimes against humanity and war crimes.

■ In October, the President of the DRC reiterated the authorities' refusal to surrender Bosco Ntaganda to the ICC, which had sought his arrest and surrender since 2006 on charges of war crimes consisting of recruiting and using children in the armed conflict.

Amnesty International visits/reports

🚌 An Amnesty International delegation visited the DRC in March, July and November.

📰 Democratic Republic of the Congo: Human rights concerns in the run-up to presidential election campaigns (AFR 62/002/2011)

📰 The time for justice is now: New strategy needed in the Democratic Republic of the Congo (AFR 62/006/2011)

📰 Democratic Republic of the Congo: From occasional outrage to sustained response – the need for the Human Rights Council to play a role in the areas of judicial reform and the fight against impunity (AFR 62/009/2011)

📰 Democratic Republic of the Congo: Colonel's rape conviction is first step on road to justice (PRE01/078/2011)

📰 DRC: Post-election intimidation through arrests must end (PRE01/634/2011)

DENMARK

KINGDOM OF DENMARK

Head of state:	Queen Margrethe II
Head of government:	Helle Thorning-Schmidt (replaced Lars Løkke Rasmussen in October)
Death penalty:	abolitionist for all crimes
Population:	5.6 million
Life expectancy:	78.8 years
Under-5 mortality:	4 per 1,000

A new investigation into the use of Denmark's territory for rendition flights conducted by the CIA was announced, although it lacked sufficient powers and was severely limited in its scope. Immigration detention practices gave rise to concern as vulnerable people continued to be detained. Women were denied equal and effective protection against violence in law.

Counter-terror and security

In February, a hearing was conducted into the government review of counter-terrorism legislation in the previous year, following concerns that the review had been inadequate and insufficiently thorough.

On 2 November, the government announced that the Danish Institute for International Studies (DIIS) would investigate the use of its territory for rendition flights conducted by the CIA since 2001. The investigation, however, would be limited to flights involving Greenland and not all Danish territory. Furthermore, the DIIS would only be allowed to review documents from a previous Danish inquiry held in 2008, and investigators would not be allowed to compel witness testimony or request any new information. In light of these restrictions the investigation would not constitute an independent, impartial, thorough and effective investigation as required by international human rights law and standards.

Torture and other ill-treatment

In June, the High Court upheld a previous ruling that Niels Holck could not be extradited to India, because diplomatic assurances negotiated between the Danish and Indian governments did not sufficiently protect him from risk of harm.

In November, the City Court in Copenhagen ruled that Qais J. Khaled (an Iraqi national) could sue the Danish authorities for damages for transferring him to Iraqi police custody in Basra in 2004, despite allegedly knowing there was a risk that he would be subject to torture or other ill-treatment.

In December, further information emerged indicating that at least 500 Iraqi nationals may have been handed over to Iraqi authorities in similar circumstances. Concerns were also raised that information confirming that the Danish army was aware of the risk of torture that would be faced by those transferred to the Iraqi authorities was withheld from parliament.

Refugees and asylum-seekers

Policies towards refugees and asylum-seekers continued to give rise to concern.

In January, transfers of asylum-seekers to Greece under the Dublin II Regulation were halted, following a ruling by the European Court of Human Rights which found that Greece did not operate an effective asylum system (see Greece entry). No efforts were made by the authorities to locate the 20 individuals who were transferred in 2010 to Greece under the Regulation.

At least 43 Iraqi nationals were forcibly returned to Baghdad, Iraq, contrary to guidelines from UNHCR, the UN refugee agency.

Vulnerable people – including victims of torture and human trafficking – continued to be detained for immigration purposes.

At the beginning of the year it emerged that 36 stateless Palestinian youths had been refused citizenship in contravention of the UN Convention which requires signatory states to grant citizenship to stateless children born in the territory of the state. Subsequent revelations indicated that up to 500 Palestinian youths had been misinformed and refused citizenship. As a consequence of the revelations, the Minister for Refugees, Immigration and Integration stepped down from her post. An independent committee was established to investigate and some of the individuals concerned began legal proceedings against the government for compensation.

Violence against women and girls

Legislation did not provide equal and adequate protection for all victims of sexual violence. A number of crimes of sexual violence and abuse continued to be not punishable by law if the perpetrator and victim were married, such as non-consensual sex where the victim was in a helpless state due to illness or intoxication.

An expert committee, commissioned by the government in 2009 to examine existing legislation on rape, had still not submitted its findings by the end of the year. However, in May the government put forward proposals to increase prison sentences for rape committed by a stranger. Concerns were raised that these proposals would inappropriately reinforce the treatment of rape as a lesser crime where the victim and the perpetrator knew each other.

Discrimination – Roma

In March, the Supreme Court found that the expulsion of two Romani men from Romania in 2010, on the basis of staying illegally in public parks and buildings, was unlawful. The decision to expel had been criticized by a number of politicians and members of civil society as being discriminatory. As a result of the Court's decision the government annulled the expulsion orders of a further 14 Romanian Roma.

Amnesty International visits/reports

🗐 Denmark: Amnesty International welcomes commitment to observe the principle of *non-refoulement* but regrets unwillingess to reform legislation on anti-terrorism and rape (EUR 18/001/2011)

DOMINICAN REPUBLIC

DOMINICAN REPUBLIC

Head of state and government:	Leonel Antonio Fernández Reyna
Death penalty:	abolitionist for all crimes
Population:	10.1 million
Life expectancy:	73.4 years
Under-5 mortality:	31.9 per 1,000
Adult literacy:	88.2 per cent

Unlawful killings by police were reported. Many alleged human rights violations committed by the police remained unresolved. People of Haitian descent continued to be denied identity documents.

Violence against women and girls remained a major concern.

Background

Several organic laws regulating state institutions were adopted by Congress. Members of the Supreme Court and the new Constitutional Court were appointed at the end of the year. For the 10th consecutive year, Congress failed to appoint a Human Rights Ombudsman.

Police and security forces

According to statistics from the Office of the Prosecutor General, 289 people were killed by the police in 2011, compared with 260 in 2010. Evidence suggested that many of these killings may have been unlawful.

■ Luis Alfredo Domínguez Rodríguez was killed by police on 26 January in Nagua. His friend, Henry Ortiz, who was injured in the same incident, said that he had just stopped his motorbike to give Luis Alfredo Domínguez Rodríguez a lift when four officers in a patrol car approached them and, without issuing a warning, shot him five times. He said an officer then shot Luis Alfredo Domínguez Rodríguez after one of the officers said they did not want a witness to the shooting. Luis Alfredo Domínguez Rodríguez died a few hours later. Henry Ortiz remained hospitalized for 20 days. Three police officers were on trial at the end of the year in connection with the shootings.

Reports of torture during police interrogations and mass arbitrary detentions continued to be received.

■ On 13 October, Pedro Arias Roja was beaten in his house in San Cristobal by five police officers who went to arrest him for illegal possession of a firearm. In the police station, the officers placed a plastic bag over his head and beat him. He filed a complaint, but no effective investigation had been initiated by the authorities by the end of the year.

In several cases, police used unnecessary or excessive force to disperse demonstrators.

■ On 20 October, university student Claudia Espíritu was shot in the leg by the police while she was demonstrating at the Autonomous University of Santo Domingo against the newly adopted budget law. At least three other students were shot and injured by the police.

D

Impunity

Many alleged cases of abuses by the police remained unpunished, despite compelling evidence.

■ The authorities failed to clarify the enforced disappearance of Gabriel Sandi Alistar and Juan Almonte Herrera. The men were last seen in police custody in July and September 2009 respectively and their whereabouts remained unknown at the end of 2011.

Discrimination – Haitian migrants and Dominico-Haitians

A survey carried out by the Jesuit Service for Refugees and Migrants in four rural communities revealed that at least 1,584 people had been denied identity documents by the Dominican Electoral Board, mainly on the basis of a directive issued in March 2007; 96 per cent had been affected between 2005 and 2011 and the vast majority of cases occurred in 2011. Some 72 per cent of those affected were aged between 15 and 34 years. Denial of identity documents had effectively prevented them from pursuing their studies, finding employment or obtaining other official documents.

The impact of the 2007 directive on thousands of Dominicans of Haitian descent was discussed in a hearing in October of the Inter-American Commission on Human Rights. Five days before the hearing, the Dominican Electoral Board issued a decision allowing the temporary release of identity documents to descendants of foreign citizens. This temporary release was made pending the conclusion of investigations into claims that identity documents had been wrongly issued prior to 2007. However, according to migrants' rights organizations, the release of documents remained at the discretion of administrative officers, who, in many cases, continued to deny the documents to Dominico-Haitians.

Migrants' rights

In January, following an outbreak of cholera in Haiti, the Dominican authorities intensified mass deportations of Haitian migrants, claiming that the move was necessary to prevent the spread of the disease. In spite of an appeal in June from two UN agencies to suspend all involuntary returns to Haiti on humanitarian grounds, mass deportations continued throughout the year.

■ On 20 September, at 5am, at least 80 Haitian migrants living in Navarrete were deported to Haiti. According to local organizations working with migrants, during the raid some of the migrants were beaten and some children were separated from their parents. The migrants, many of whom had been living in the community for more than 10 years, did not have an opportunity to have their cases individually examined.

Violence against women and girls

According to the Office of the Prosecutor General, 127 women and girls were killed by partners or former partners in 2011, compared with 97 in 2010.

At the end of the year, Congress was examining a draft law on femicide (the killing of women and girls) and considering including this as a specific crime in the Penal Code.

Freedom of expression – journalists

According to the Dominican National Union of Press Workers, 60 journalists and other media workers were harassed or physically attacked between January and August, in many cases by police officers. In August, more than 60 journalists denounced a smear campaign by state officials against independent journalists reporting on corruption and drug trafficking.

■ On 2 August, TV journalist José Silvestre was abducted and killed in La Romana. He had been attacked and threatened earlier in the year, but the authorities had failed to provide protection, despite a call from the National Union of Press Workers that they do so.

Housing rights – forced eviction

According to local NGOs, at least 100 forced evictions were carried out between January and September. In most cases there was a lack of due process or consultation with affected communities. On several occasions, fatalities and gunshot wounds were reported during forced evictions.

■ On 15 October, some 72 families were forcibly evicted from private land in the neighbourhood of Brisas del Este in Santo Domingo Este. According to eyewitnesses, police and soldiers fired buckshot and tear gas into the families' houses to force them out. At the end of the year, dozens of families were still living in a makeshift camp on a nearby street.

Amnesty International visits/reports

Amnesty International delegates visited the Dominican Republic in March and October.

"Shut up if you don't want to be killed": Human rights violations by the police in the Dominican Republic (AMR 27/002/2011)

Urgent Action: Families evicted, threatened (AMR 27/007/2011)

ECUADOR

REPUBLIC OF ECUADOR

Head of state and government:	**Rafael Vicente Correa Delgado**
Death penalty:	**abolitionist for all crimes**
Population:	**14.7 million**
Life expectancy:	**75.6 years**
Under-5 mortality:	**24.2 per 1,000**
Adult literacy:	**84.2 per cent**

Indigenous and community leaders faced spurious criminal charges. Those responsible for human rights violations continued to evade justice.

Background

Six police officers were found guilty in July of crimes against state security following police protests over pay cuts in September 2010. In May President Correa narrowly won a 10-question referendum, which included a proposal to reform the judicial system as well as to regulate the media.

In February, an Ecuadorian court fined the oil company Chevron US$18 billion for widespread contamination of the Amazon basin. An appeal by Chevron was pending at the end of the year.

Indigenous Peoples' rights

■ In July, Ecuador appeared before the Inter-American Court of Human Rights accused of failing to respect the right of the Indigenous Kichwa community of Sarayaku to be consulted and to give free, prior and informed consent before permissions for oil exploration on traditional lands were granted in 1996. At the end of the year a decision by the Court remained pending.

■ In October, the executive issued a decree authorizing the military to intervene in Chone city, Manabí province, where Indigenous communities were protesting against the construction of a dam that could lead to the forced eviction of around 1,700 families. The following day, hundreds of police entered the area, destroying farmland with tractors. One person was injured. Protests eventually resumed and three days later, four people were injured during operations to remove the protesters.

Indigenous leaders and community members continued to face spurious charges of sabotage, terrorism, murder and illegal obstruction of roads for alleged crimes committed in the context of demonstrations against extractive industries.

■ In February, Indigenous leaders José Acacho, Pedro Mashiant and Fidel Kaniras were arrested in Sucúa, Morona Santiago province, on charges that included murder, sabotage and terrorism, in connection with the 2009 protests against a national water law during which one person was killed and 40 people, including police officers, were injured. The men were released after seven days, but the charges remained pending at the end of the year despite the absence of evidence against them.

■ In May, charges of sabotage and terrorism were brought against community leaders Carlos Pérez, Federico Guzmán and Efraín Arpi. The three men had participated in a protest against a proposed state water law in Azuay province. The charges were dismissed in August, but new charges for illegal obstruction of roads were brought against them and Carlos Pérez was sentenced to eight days in prison.

■ Marco Guatemal, President of the Indigenous and Peasant Federation of Imbabura, and two other Indigenous community members were accused of terrorism and sabotage also after participating in a protest against the water laws. The charges were later dropped due to lack of evidence. Marco Guatemal was arrested in October after new charges for obstruction of roads were brought against him, but the charges were dropped in November.

Human rights defenders

In July, human rights defender Marlon Lozano Yulán, a member of Land and Life Union which works with rural communities on land issues, died in Guayaquil after being shot by two unidentified assailants travelling on a motorbike. He had received threats prior to his murder. By the end of the year, no progress had been reported in the investigations into this attack.

On 25 November, Monica Chuji, an Indigenous leader and former minister, was sentenced to one year in prison and a fine for slander for criticizing the government in the press. However, following a public outcry, she was pardoned by the government and her case was archived, removing the opportunity for her to appeal the decision.

Impunity

In his report published in May, the UN Special Rapporteur on extrajudicial executions expressed concern about impunity in cases of killings and abuses by police, hired gunmen and rural juntas, as well as illegal armed groups and the military in the area bordering Colombia.

■ In July, 12 police officers from the disbanded National Police Group on trial for the torture in 2009 of Karina, Fabricio and Javier Pico Suárez and the enforced disappearance of Georgy Hernán Cedeño were sentenced to between two and 10 months' imprisonment. They were immediately released as they had already served their sentences.

■ In October the Attorney General announced he was replacing the team of prosecutors investigating the enforced disappearance of Colombian teenage brothers Carlos Santiago and Pedro Andrés Restrepo in 1988 because of lack of progress.

Freedom of expression

Curbs on freedom of expression included the use of criminal defamation charges against journalists critical of the government or local officials.

■ In July, a judge ordered three directors and a former columnist of the newspaper *El Universo* to pay President Correa US$40 million in damages and sentenced them to three years' imprisonment for criminal defamation. President Correa brought a criminal complaint against the four men in March, a month after an article was published referring to him as a "dictator" and suggesting that he might face criminal prosecution over the September 2010 disturbances when the armed forces rescued him from a hospital in Quito. He had sought refuge there from police officers protesting against proposed cuts in their pay and benefits. An appeal against the sentence imposed on the directors and columnist was pending in the National Court of Justice at the end of the year.

EGYPT

ARAB REPUBLIC OF EGYPT

Head of state:	Mohamed Hussein Tantawi (replaced Muhammad Hosni Mubarak in February)
Head of government:	Kamal Ganzouri (replaced Essam Sharaf in December, who replaced Ahmed Shafik in March, who replaced Ahmed Nazif in January)
Death penalty:	retentionist
Population:	82.5 million
Life expectancy:	73.2 years
Under-5 mortality:	21 per 1,000
Adult literacy:	66.4 per cent

At least 840 people were killed and 6,000 were injured mostly by police and other security forces during the "25 January Revolution" which forced President Hosni Mubarak to leave office in February. The Supreme Council of the Armed Forces (SCAF), headed by Mohamed Hussein Tantawi, replaced Hosni Mubarak, who was put on trial with his sons and other officials. However, there were continuing protests; the army and the police responded in some cases with excessive force. The SCAF released political prisoners and allowed the registration of previously banned political parties and independent trades unions, but maintained the 30-year state of emergency, criminalized strikes, tightened restrictions on the media and used military courts to try and sentence more than 12,000 civilians, many of them arrested in connection with continuing protests over what they saw as the slow pace of reform. Hosni Mubarak's notorious State Security Investigations (SSI) police force was disbanded, but torture of detainees remained common and widespread and took on a shocking new dimension when a number of women were forced by army officers to undergo "virginity tests" in detention. The army forcibly evicted residents of informal settlements (slums) in Cairo and elsewhere, as well as squatters who sought shelter in empty public housing. Women participated prominently in the protests but continued to face discrimination in both law and practice. Discrimination persisted against religious minorities, particularly Coptic Christians. At least 123 death sentences were imposed and at least one person was executed.

Border guards continued to shoot migrants, refugees and asylum-seekers seeking to cross Egypt's Sinai border into Israel. Twenty were reported killed in 2011, including at the border with Sudan; others were prosecuted or forcibly returned to countries where they were at risk of serious human rights violations. Some were reportedly victims of human trafficking.

Background

President Mubarak resigned on 11 February after 30 years in power following 18 days of mass, largely peaceful protests across Egypt to which the security forces responded with lethal and other excessive force. According to official reports, at least 840 people were killed or died in connection with the protests and more than 6,000 others were injured. Thousands were detained; many were tortured or abused. The military assumed power, in the form of the SCAF, but appointed interim civilian prime ministers and government ministers pending parliamentary elections that began in November and were to be completed in early 2012. Presidential elections were promised for mid-2012.

Immediately after Hosni Mubarak's fall, the SCAF suspended the 1971 Constitution, dissolved parliament and issued a Constitutional Declaration guaranteeing a number of rights. It also released hundreds of administrative detainees. In March, the powerful but long-banned Muslim Brotherhood and other proscribed organizations were allowed to register and operate lawfully, and subsequently contested the parliamentary elections. The Muslim Brotherhood's political party, the Freedom and Justice Party, emerged as the strongest party in early election results. Hosni Mubarak's National Democratic Party was dissolved in April.

In March, the Interior Ministry acceded to weeks of pressure from protesters and disbanded the SSI, the security police force notorious for torture and other abuses. Before the disbanding, activists broke into the SSI headquarters in Alexandria and Cairo after news spread that SSI officers were destroying evidence of human rights abuses. The SSI was replaced by the National Security Agency; it was unclear whether any vetting mechanism was established to prevent the recruitment or transfer of SSI officers implicated in torture or other human rights violations. The head of the SSI was, however, charged in connection with the killings of protesters in January and February.

The SCAF maintained the national state of emergency and in September expanded the Emergency Law to criminalize acts such as blocking roads, broadcasting rumours, and actions deemed to constitute "assault on freedom to work". Amendments to the Penal Code stiffened the penalties for "thuggery", kidnapping and rape, up to the death penalty, and Law 34 of 2011 was enacted, criminalizing strikes and any form of protest deemed to "obstruct work". After violence in October that killed 28 people, mostly Copts, the SCAF prohibited discrimination on the basis of gender, origin, language, religion or belief.

Torture and other ill-treatment

Despite the dissolution of the SSI, whose officials had committed torture with impunity, there were continuing allegations of torture and other ill-treatment by the police and armed forces, and a number of detainees died in custody in suspicious circumstances. In June, the Public Prosecutor set up a committee of three judges to examine torture complaints. While some of the torture allegations against the police were investigated, none of those against the armed forces was adequately investigated or led to prosecution.

■ Mostafa Gouda Abdel Aal was arrested in Cairo's Tahrir Square on 9 March by soldiers who beat and dragged him to the nearby Egyptian Museum. There, they blindfolded him, tied his hands behind his back and threw him to the floor, doused him with water and subjected him to electric shocks to his penis and buttocks, and beat him on his back with a cable. He was held for a night in a van with other detainees before being taken to Heikstep Military Prison where the detainees were beaten and mocked by military prosecution interrogators. Officials did not ask them about their injuries, which were visible, or why their clothes were bloodstained, and they were hit with electric shock batons before being tried before a military court held in the prison canteen. After grossly unfair trials, they were sentenced to between one and seven years in prison and transferred to Tora Prison. They were released on 23 May following a pardon by the SCAF; Mostafa Gouda Abdel Aal still had visible injuries caused by torture.

■ On 26 October, two police officers were sentenced to seven-year prison terms by an Alexandria court for the manslaughter of Khaled Said, whose death in June 2010 – he was brutally beaten in public by police – became a *cause célèbre* during the anti-Mubarak protests. The court ignored the finding of a second autopsy, which stated that he had died after a plastic roll of drugs was forced down his throat. In December, the prosecution appealed the sentence.

Unfair trials

From 28 January, when the army was deployed to police demonstrations after the police were withdrawn from the streets, people accused of protest-related offences and violence were tried before military courts rather than ordinary criminal courts, even though those accused were civilians. The military courts were neither independent nor impartial. By August, according to the military judiciary, some 12,000 people had been tried before military courts on charges such as "thuggery", curfew violations, damage to property and "insulting the army" or "obstructing work". Many were released with a suspended prison sentence or after a pardon, but thousands remained in detention at the end of the year.

■ Amr Abdallah Al-Beheiry was jailed for five years in February after a military court convicted him of breaking the curfew and assaulting a public official. He was first arrested on 26 February when soldiers and military police forcibly dispersed protesters gathered outside the parliament building in Cairo; many of those arrested were beaten and subjected to electric shocks before they were released. Amr Abdallah Al-Beheiry was rearrested, however, apparently because the injuries he sustained were filmed. The military judge at his trial, which was grossly unfair, refused to allow him to be defended by a lawyer hired by his family, insisting on a court-appointed lawyer. He was sent first to Wadi Guedid Prison, where he and other prisoners were reportedly assaulted by guards and allowed to leave their cells only once a day to use the toilet, then moved to Wadi Natroun Prison, where at the end of the year he remained waiting an appeal date.

■ Five workers who staged a sit-in protest outside the Ministry of Petroleum after they were sacked by the Egyptian General Petroleum Corporation were arrested, charged under Law 34 of 2011, tried and convicted by a military court in June; they received suspended prison sentences.

Excessive use of force

The security forces used lethal and other excessive force against demonstrators before the fall of Hosni Mubarak. Prison guards also shot and killed some sentenced prisoners. Subsequently, the army, military police and central security forces continued to use force, including excessive force, to disperse renewed protests by demonstrators angry and frustrated at the slow pace of political and human rights reform. On some occasions, demonstrators were attacked by and clashed with "thugs" – armed men in plain clothes believed to be linked to the police or supporters of the former ruling party. In many cases, the security forces fired tear gas, shotgun pellets and rubber bullets at demonstrators recklessly; they also fired live ammunition and on at least one occasion drove armoured vehicles at and over protesters.

■ On 9 October, a demonstration mostly by Copts outside the Maspero state television building in Cairo, was broken up with extreme force by the security forces, who alleged that groups of armed men in plain clothes were responsible for triggering the violence. Twenty-eight people, mostly protesters but including one soldier, were killed, and others were injured, many having been shot with live ammunition or run over at speed by soldiers driving armoured vehicles. The SCAF ordered an investigation and, following further protests and the return of protesters to Cairo's Tahrir Square, referred the case to the public prosecutor, who then appointed an investigating judge to examine the case. The trial of three soldiers charged with the manslaughter of 14 Maspero protesters opened in December, before the investigating judge submitted his report.

■ In November, the security forces used tear gas and fired shotgun pellets and live rounds against protesters in five days of clashes near the Interior Ministry building in Cairo after the army and the central security forces dispersed protesters and families of the victims of the "25 January Revolution" from Tahrir Square. Some 51 people died and more than 3,000 were injured, while others were arrested to face charges such as illegal gathering, attacking protesters with shotguns, obstructing traffic, destroying property, and attacking officials.

■ In December, military police and other security forces used excessive and disproportionate force and live ammunition to disperse protesters near the ministerial Cabinet building. At least 17 people were killed, most of them with gunfire, and a hundred others injured or arrested. Several women said they were brutally beaten and threatened with sexual assault while under arrest.

Freedom of expression and association

Before the fall of Hosni Mubarak, the authorities sought to hamper protesters' efforts to organize by ordering the cutting of telephone and internet lines. Under the SCAF, new restrictions were imposed on the media, and the security forces raided TV stations and threatened journalists and bloggers with imprisonment. The SCAF also took action targeting human rights NGOs.

■ Maikel Nabil Sanad, a blogger, was sentenced to three years in prison in April after an unfair trial before a military court because he had "insulted" the SCAF, criticized its use of excessive force against protesters in Tahrir Square, and objected to military service. He went on a protest hunger strike in August and remained in detention, although a military appeals court ordered his retrial in October. He was transferred to a psychiatric hospital at the request of a lawyer in proceedings at which neither he nor his lawyers were present. His sentence was reduced to two years after a retrial by a military court. A prisoner of conscience, he was still held at the end of the year and was being denied adequate medical treatment. On 31 December, he ended his hunger strike.

The authorities said that they were examining the legal registration and funding of some 37 human rights organizations and that the Supreme State Security prosecution was considering whether to bring "treason" or "conspiracy" charges against those deemed to be operating without being registered, to have received funding from abroad without the authorities' consent, or to have engaged in "unpermitted" political activity. The Central Bank ordered all banks to provide details of the financial transactions of NGOs and individual activists to the Ministry of Solidarity and Social Justice. In December, security forces raided some 17 human rights NGOs and seized their computers and documents.

Women's rights

Women continued to face discrimination in law and in practice, yet played a prominent role in the protests, both before and following the fall of Hosni Mubarak. Some women activists and journalists were targeted for sexual and other abuse.

■ All but one of 18 women detained when the army forcibly cleared protesters from Cairo's Tahrir Square on 9 March were strip-searched and seven of them subjected to "virginity tests", a form of torture, at Heikstep Military Prison, and threatened that those deemed "not to be virgins" would be charged with prostitution. All 18 had been taken first with other detainees to the Egyptian Museum where they were handcuffed, beaten with sticks and hoses, subjected to electric shocks to the chest and legs, and insulted by soldiers. Seventeen of them were taken before a military court, even though they are civilians, on 11 March and released two days later. Several were convicted of offences such as disorderly conduct and obstructing traffic, and were sentenced to suspended prison terms. In December, an administrative court ruled that these tests were illegal and ordered the military to suspend them.

■ Journalist Mona Eltahawy was arrested and detained for 12 hours by the security forces on 24 November amid ongoing clashes between security forces and protesters. She said that she was sexually assaulted by security officials and beaten, sustaining fractures to her left hand and right arm.

The SCAF ended the quota system in the election law that had previously reserved 64 parliamentary seats (12 per cent) for women; instead, it required that every political party include at least one woman on its list of electoral candidates but without requiring that she be high on the list.

Discrimination – Copts

There was a rise in communal violence between Muslims and Coptic Christians, who remained subject to discrimination and felt themselves inadequately protected by the authorities. Sectarian attacks on Copts and their churches by alleged Islamists appeared to increase after the SCAF assumed power, and the killings of Copts at the Maspero demonstration in October exacerbated tensions.

■ Clashes erupted in Imbaba, a working-class area of Giza, on 7 May when alleged Islamists attacked a church in the apparent belief that a woman who had converted to Islam was held against her will. Fifteen Copts and Muslims died, and many others were injured. Copts' homes and businesses were damaged and another local church was burned. At first, the army reportedly failed to intervene but then opened fire, killing several people. Many Imbaba residents, including injured people, were arrested; most were released on 26 May but the trial of 48 people, Muslims and Copts, before an (Emergency) Supreme State Security Court in Cairo was continuing at the end of the year.

E

Impunity and accountability

The authorities prosecuted some of those allegedly responsible for orchestrating the killings in January and February but otherwise failed to deliver justice to the relatives of those killed and to people injured during the "25 January Revolution". Police and other members of the security forces charged with or implicated in the killings or wounding of protesters remained in their posts or were transferred to administrative posts within the Ministry of Interior; many reportedly sought to pressurize or induce families and witnesses to withdraw complaints. Members of the armed forces and the police committed human rights abuses, including torture and unlawful killing, with impunity.

■ In April, the trial began of former Interior Minister Habib Ibrahim El Adly and six of his former aides on charges arising from the killings of protesters. The case was joined to that of Hosni Mubarak and his two sons and all then went on trial in August, charged with premeditated and attempted murder. The trial, whose first two sessions were broadcast on national television, was continuing at the end of the year.

Housing rights – forced eviction

Thousands of people continued to live in localities within informal settlements in Cairo and elsewhere that have been officially designated as "unsafe areas" for residence due to rock falls and other dangers. The residents were also at risk of forced eviction. The army forcibly evicted residents from some "unsafe areas" and also forcibly evicted squatters seeking shelter in empty state housing; those evicted were not consulted or given reasonable notice, and were often left homeless.

Official plans to rehouse residents of "unsafe areas" were devised by governorates in collaboration with the Informal Settlements Development Facility (ISDF), a fund established in 2008, but affected residents were not consulted or even given details of the plans. The Cairo 2050 plan was not published or submitted for full consultation with the communities living in informal settlements who are likely to be most affected, although in August the Housing Ministry affirmed that the plan would not lead to forced evictions.

In the aftermath of the "25 January Revolution", there was an upsurge of squatting in empty government buildings. Local authorities responded by calling in the army and riot police to forcibly evict

the squatters, which they did without warning.

■ In Zerzara, one of Port Said's designated "unsafe areas", the army demolished the shacks of over 200 families, rendering 70 families homeless, in early July. Those affected were given only one day's notice and were not consulted. Many of the families made homeless were headed by women. Weeks earlier, the local governorate had announced plans to provide 3,500 new accommodation units for residents by June 2012, partly by constructing buildings to rehouse residents on site. The demolitions led other families to fear forcible eviction despite official letters promising that they will receive alternative housing when it becomes available.

■ In July, some 200 families were made homeless when they were forcibly evicted without warning from some 20 buildings in Manshiyet Nasser, Cairo, in which they had made their homes. With the help of the local "Popular Community Committee" set up by young people during the uprising, they were rehoused at the remote 6 October City, south-west of Giza.

Refugees and migrants

Security forces continued to shoot foreign migrants, refugees and asylum-seekers who sought to cross Egypt's Sinai border into Israel, killing at least 10 people. They also killed 10 Eritreans who sought to enter Egypt from Sudan. Many others were shot and injured, some seriously, or arrested and tried before military courts for "illegal entry" and sentenced to prison terms. At least 83 refugees and asylum-seekers were deported to countries where they would be at risk of serious human rights violations; many were Eritreans. More than 100 refugees and asylum-seekers remained at risk of forcible return at the end of the year.

People-traffickers reportedly extorted, raped, tortured and killed refugees, asylum-seekers and migrants crossing the Sinai Peninsula into Israel, as well as forcibly removing their organs to sell on the black market.

Death penalty

At least 123 people were sentenced to death, including at least 17 who were sentenced after unfair trials before military courts. At least one person was executed.

■ Mohamed Ahmed Hussein, convicted of a drive-by killing of Coptic Christian worshippers as they left a church in Upper Egypt on 6 January 2010, was hanged on 10 October.

Amnesty International visits/reports

🚍 Amnesty International delegates visited Egypt from January to March, in May and June, and from August to December.

📓 "We are not dirt": Forced evictions in Egypt's informal settlements (MDE 12/001/2011)

📓 Human rights activists detained in Egypt (MDE 12/008/2011)

📓 Egypt: Human rights agenda for change (MDE 12/015/2011)

📓 Egypt: Constitution proposals faltering first step to reform (MDE 12/023/2011)

📓 Egypt rises: Killings, detentions and torture in the "25 January Revolution" (MDE 12/027/2011)

📓 Time for justice: Egypt's corrosive system of detention (MDE 12/029/2011)

📓 10 steps for human rights: Amnesty International's human rights manifesto for Egypt (MDE 12/046/2011)

📓 Women demand equality in shaping new Egypt (MDE 12/050/2011)

📓 Broken promises: Egypt's military rulers erode human rights (MDE 12/053/2011)

📓 Arms transfers to the Middle East and North Africa: Lessons for an effective Arms Trade Treaty (ACT 30/117/2011)

EL SALVADOR

REPUBLIC OF EL SALVADOR

Head of state and government:	Carlos Mauricio Funes Cartagena
Death penalty:	abolitionist for ordinary crimes
Population:	6.2 million
Life expectancy:	72.2 years
Under-5 mortality:	16.6 per 1,000
Adult literacy:	84.1 per cent

Impunity for human rights violations committed during the armed conflict (1980-1992) persisted. Violence against women and girls, including violations of their sexual and reproductive rights, remained a concern. The Ombudsperson for human rights received multiple reports of women and girls being abused by military personnel in prisons across the country.

Background

The rate of violent crime continued to soar. In response to increasing security concerns in several prisons, the government deployed the military to run 11 out of the 14 prisons in the country.

In October, storms led to several landslides in which more than 30 people died, and flooding destroyed the homes and crops of thousands of families.

Impunity

The 1993 Amnesty Law remained in place, despite repeated decisions from the Inter-American Court of Human Rights ordering the state to repeal it. The Law seeks to obstruct anyone, including the armed forces, from being held to account for human rights violations, including crimes against humanity, committed during the armed conflict.

■ In March, the case of 700 men, women and children who were tortured and killed by the armed forces over a three-day period in 1981 in El Mozote and surrounding hamlets, Morazán province, was referred to the Inter-American Court. This was one of the thousands of cases of human rights violations, including crimes against humanity committed by members of the military, where the 1993 Amnesty Law has prevented those responsible being brought to justice.

In December, during a ceremony to mark the anniversary of the massacres, the Minister of Foreign Affairs acknowledged state responsibility for the crimes against humanity perpetrated in El Mozote and surrounding hamlets. However, the Minister gave no commitment to repealing the Amnesty Law or holding perpetrators to account for their crimes.

Violence against women and girls

In February, the UN Special Rapporteur on violence against women expressed grave concern and warned that government inaction in the investigation, prosecution and reparation for such crimes had led to a situation of impunity for gender-based violence in El Salvador.

In her report, the UN Special Rapporteur urged the government to review the laws that ban abortion in all circumstances, even for survivors of rape or where the life of the woman or girl is at stake. The government stated that it was committed to addressing the issue of violence against women.

The Ombudsperson for human rights received an increasing number of reports of military personnel conducting illegal vaginal and anal searches on women and girls visiting relatives in prison.

In March the government opened the first branch of the "ciudad de la mujer" where women and girls affected by violence can go to report crimes

E

committed against them to the police in safety, as well as to receive support services and legal advice.

International justice

In August the Supreme Court decided not to fulfil a red alert from Interpol, originating from the Spanish authorities. This demanded the arrest and extradition of nine former members of the military accused of the killing in 1989 of six Spanish Jesuit priests, their housekeeper and her daughter. The Court demanded that further procedural steps be fulfilled by the Spanish authorities before they could consider the order.

Human rights defenders

Human rights activists and journalists working in Cabañas department were subjected to threats because of their human rights and anti-corruption work.

■ In January, Hector Berríos, a community activist and human rights lawyer, received a phone call saying that someone had been paid a lot of money to kill him, or a member of his family.

■ In May Pablo Ayala, Manuel Navarrete and Marixela Ramos, two journalists and a news producer respectively at Radio Victoria, received two death threats by text message. One of the messages read "Look fool, we already know where you live... stop that news bulletin that you co-ordinate. You also have a daughter".

EQUATORIAL GUINEA

REPUBLIC OF EQUATORIAL GUINEA

Head of state:	Teodoro Obiang Nguema Mbasogo
Head of government:	Ignacio Milán Tang
Death penalty:	retentionist
Population:	0.7 million
Life expectancy:	51.1 years
Under-5 mortality:	145.1 per 1,000
Adult literacy:	93.3 per cent

Political tension increased throughout the year and the authorities continued to stifle opposition by harassing, arresting and briefly detaining political activists. There was an upsurge in the number of arrests in the run-up to the AU summit in June. In November, at least 30 detainees, apparently held as hostages, were acquitted by a military court and released. They had been held since October 2010 in incommunicado detention without charge or trial. Five prisoners of conscience and 17 political prisoners were released in a presidential pardon. Freedom of expression and assembly continued to be curtailed and journalists were briefly detained or suspended from their functions. Constitutional reforms giving more power to the President were approved in a referendum in November.

Background

In January, President Teodoro Obiang Nguema Mbasogo took over the rotating presidency of the AU, and in June hosted the AU summit in the capital, Malabo. The same month, the President signed the African Charter on Democracy, Elections and Governance.

In September, French police investigating the alleged misuse of Equatorial Guinea's oil revenues by President Obiang and his family seized several luxury cars belonging to his eldest son, Teodoro Nguema Obiang, from outside his residence in Paris. Also in September, a French court acquitted the French NGO Terre Solidaire of charges of defamation brought against them by President Obiang. The charges related to a report published by Terre Solidaire in 2009 referring to "ill-gotten gains" by President Obiang and his family.

In October the US Justice Department filed a legal claim with the federal court to seize the President's son's property and other assets in the USA, alleging they were obtained by plundering Equatorial Guinea's natural resources and transferred to the USA through corruption.

Legal, constitutional or institutional developments

Following mass protests in North Africa and the Middle East, President Obiang announced in March that he would reform the Constitution to broaden the judicial framework for the exercise of fundamental freedoms and increase people's opportunities to participate in the county's political affairs. In May he set up a commission to draft the reforms and appointed its members, including representatives of political parties. The country's only two independent political parties, Convergence for Social Democracy (CPDS) and the People's Union, refused to participate in the commission on the grounds that their demands for a general amnesty and the safe return of exiles had not been met. They also objected to President Obiang appointing their representatives to the commission. In July the Chamber of People's Representatives approved the reform proposals without debate, and in October President Obiang announced a date for a referendum on the reforms. However, the text of the proposed reforms was not made available to the public, and political parties received the text just two weeks before the referendum. On 13 November the reforms were approved by referendum with 97.7 per cent of the votes. The referendum was conducted in an atmosphere of intimidation and harassment of voters, with armed police and soldiers present in polling stations. In Bata, several representatives of political parties observing the voting were expelled from polling stations; some were briefly detained and beaten. The reforms increased the President's powers further, including after he leaves office. Although it limited the presidential terms in office to two consecutive seven-year terms, it removed the age limit for presidential candidates, previously set at 75 years, created the position of vice-president who will be appointed by the President and who must be a member of the ruling Democratic Party of Equatorial Guinea, and created a Senate and Audit Court, whose members will be appointed by the President, as will the newly-created Ombudsman. The revised Constitution was not promulgated at the end of the year.

Arbitrary arrests and detentions

Political opponents and some 100 students were arrested and briefly detained prior to the AU summit in June. There were further politically motivated arrests in the run-up to a referendum on constitutional reforms in November.

■ Two members of CPDS, Juan Manuel Nguema Esono, a teacher, and Vicente Nze, a doctor, were arrested in Bata on 25 April. They were suspected of planning a demonstration on Labour Day, and of pasting posters to that effect on the walls of Bata hospital. Juan Manuel Nguema was initially taken to Bata central police station. Later that day he was put on a flight to Malabo where he was held incommunicado in the central police station until his release without

charge four days later. Vicente Nze was arrested when he went to Bata police station to inquire about Juan Manuel Nguema. He was held there incommunicado until his release on 29 April. The authorities refused to give information about the whereabouts of the two men.

■ Marcial Abaga Barril, a leading member of CPDS and its representative in the National Election Commission, was arrested at his home by two plain-clothes police officers on 1 November. The officers did not have a warrant for the arrest. He was taken to Malabo central police station where he was held until his release without charge four days later. While in prison he was told that the police were investigating the killing of one of President Obiang's cooks. However, no such killing had previously been reported.

Detention without trial

At least 30 people held incommunicado and without charge in Bata prison were released after being acquitted by a military court in November. They were arrested in October 2010, following the escape from Evinayong prison of two political prisoners, together with six prison guards who also fled. Those held were mostly relatives and friends of the escaped prisoners and people suspected of aiding their escape. They included women and a six-month-old child. In mid-November, all the detainees were unexpectedly tried by a military court in Bata, charged with assisting the prisoners' escape. All civilians and most military detainees were acquitted and released, while around six military and police officers were convicted and sentenced to prison terms that were not made public. Despite the acquittal of most of the defendants, the trial did not conform to international fair trial standards.

Freedom of expression – journalists

Freedom of expression remained curtailed, with the press firmly under state control. Reports deemed as unfavourable by the authorities were suppressed. In February the government ordered a news blackout on events in North Africa, the Middle East and Côte d'Ivoire. Journalists were briefly detained and foreign journalists were expelled from the country. The NGO Reporters Without Borders was denied visas to visit Equatorial Guinea in April for referring to President Obiang in pejorative terms.

■ In March, Juan Pedro Mendene, a radio journalist working for the state radio's French language programme, was indefinitely suspended for mentioning

Libya on air. The Secretary of State for Information went to the radio station and ordered him to leave. As he left, Juan Pedro Mendene was beaten by the Secretary of State's bodyguard. A week later, the director of the station announced that French broadcasts were temporarily suspended on the orders of a higher authority.

■ In June, police officers arrested and detained for five hours three crew members of the German television network ZDF, who were in Equatorial Guinea to film a documentary on the national women's football team. The crew had also filmed slums in Malabo and interviewed the leader of the opposition party CPDS and a human rights lawyer. The authorities deleted footage of the slums saying it showed the country in a negative light. They also said that the crew had no permission to interview political opponents and confiscated memory cards containing the interviews.

Freedom of assembly

Although guaranteed by the country's Constitution, the authorities continued to suppress freedom of assembly.

■ Following the popular uprisings in the Middle East and North Africa, in March the government banned all demonstrations, including official celebrations on women's day and religious processions, and deployed increased numbers of security personnel in the streets to enforce the ban.

■ In March the authorities turned down a request from the People's Union political party to hold a rally calling for political reforms. A request by CPDS to hold a Labour Day march on 1 May was also rejected.

■ The authorities disrupted rallies organized by CPDS and the People's Union against constitutional reforms prior to the referendum on 13 November, and dispersed participants.

Prisoners of conscience – releases

Five prisoners of conscience, Emiliano Esono Micha, Cruz Obiang Ebebere, Gumersindo Ramírez Faustino, Juan Ekomo Ndong and Gerardo Angüe, who had been serving six-year custodial sentences since 2008 for illicit association and alleged possession of arms and ammunition, were released in June following a pardon on the occasion of President Obiang's birthday. Seventeen political prisoners, who may have been prisoners of conscience, and who were serving long sentences for alleged attempts to overthrow the government, were also pardoned and released. All were made to sign a document thanking President Obiang for his benevolence and undertaking not to commit offences similar to those for which they were pardoned.

Amnesty International visits/reports

▯ Equatorial Guinea: Relatives of two escaped prisoners detained without charge or trial for a year (AFR 24/003/2011)

▯ Equatorial Guinea: Surge in arbitrary arrests ahead of AU summit (PRE01/309/2011)

ERITREA

ERITREA
Head of state and government:	Isaias Afewerki
Death penalty:	abolitionist in practice
Population:	5.4 million
Life expectancy:	61.6 years
Under-5 mortality:	55.2 per 1,000
Adult literacy:	66.6 per cent

Freedom of expression and association were severely restricted. No political opposition parties, independent media, civil society organizations or unregistered faith groups were permitted. Military conscription was compulsory, and frequently extended indefinitely. Thousands of prisoners of conscience and political prisoners continued to be held in arbitrary detention. Torture and other ill-treatment were common. Detention conditions were appalling. Large numbers of Eritreans continued to flee the country.

Background

A severe drought hit the region, leaving more than 10 million people in need of urgent assistance. Eritrea's government denied the country was affected by the drought or food shortages, and denied UN aid agencies and humanitarian organizations access to the country.

In November, the government informed the EU delegation in the capital Asmara that it intended to close all ongoing EU development programmes.

In July, a report by the UN Monitoring Group on Somalia and Eritrea stated that Eritrea had co-planned a bomb attack on an AU summit in Ethiopia in January.

In December, the UN Security Council reinforced sanctions on Eritrea for continuing to provide financial, training and other support to armed opposition groups, including al-Shabab; for failing to resolve the border dispute with Djibouti; and for planning to attack the AU summit. The Security Council demanded that Eritrea cease all efforts to destabilize states, end the use of "diaspora tax" on Eritreans abroad to fund the destabilization of the region, and stop using threats of violence and other illicit means to collect the tax. It also demanded transparency on the use of profits from the mining industry and requested that all states promote vigilance in business dealings with Eritrea to ensure no assets contributed to Eritrea's violation of Security Council resolutions.

■ Two Djiboutian prisoners of war escaped from Eritrea, despite the Eritrean government's denial that it continued to hold such prisoners since the clashes between the two countries in 2008. In December, the UN demanded that Eritrea publish information about any Djiboutian combatants held as prisoners of war.

Political prisoners and prisoners of conscience

There were thousands of prisoners of conscience in the country. These included political activists, journalists, religious practitioners and draft evaders. None were charged or tried for any offence. The families of most prisoners did not know their whereabouts.

■ The government refused to confirm reports that nine of the G15 group – 11 high-profile politicians detained arbitrarily since 2001 – had died in detention in recent years.

■ In October it was reported that Dawit Isaak, one of 10 independent journalists also detained since 2001, might have died in detention, as he was no longer in the prison where he had been held. The government did not confirm the reports.

■ In October, Senay Kifleyesus, a businessman, was arrested, reportedly after he was cited criticizing the President in a Wikileaks cable.

Freedom of religion or belief

Only members of permitted faiths – the Eritrean Orthodox, Roman Catholic and Lutheran Churches, and Islam – were allowed to practice. Members of banned faiths continued to be arrested, arbitrarily detained and ill-treated.

More than 3,000 Christians from unregistered church groups, including 51 Jehovah's Witnesses, were believed to be arbitrarily detained.

■ Jehovah's Witnesses Paulos Eyassu, Isaac Mogos and Negede Teklemariam, continued to be detained without charge in Sawa military camp, where they had been held since 1994 for conscientious objection to military service.

■ In May, 64 Christians were reportedly arrested in a village near Asmara. Six were released but the remaining 58 continued to be arbitrarily detained. In June it was reported that over 26 college students were arrested on suspicion of practising an unregistered faith, and were detained at an undisclosed location. It was believed that the majority were taken to Me'eter prison, which was regularly used to imprison religious detainees.

■ In November, Mussie Eyob, an evangelist, was returned to Eritrea after being arrested for proselytizing in Saudi Arabia. He was believed to be in incommunicado detention.

■ In July, Misghina Gebretinsae, a Jehovah's Witness, died in detention in Me'eter prison, where he had been detained without charge since July 2008.

■ In October it was reported that three Christians had died in detention. Two women, Terhase Gebremichel Andu and Ferewine Genzabu Kifly, reportedly died in Adersete Military Camp in western Eritrea because of harsh conditions and ill-treatment. They had been detained since 2009, when they were arrested during a prayer meeting in a private home. Angesom Teklom Habtemichel reportedly died of malaria, after he had been denied medical treatment, in Adi Nefase Military Camp, Asab, after two years of arbitrary detention.

Military conscription

National service was compulsory for all men and women over the age of 18. All schoolchildren were required to complete their last year of secondary education at Sawa military training camp, and children as young as 15 were reportedly caught in round-ups and taken to Sawa.

The initial national service period of 18 months was frequently extended indefinitely. Conscripts were paid minimal salaries that did not meet their families' basic needs. Penalties for desertion and draft evasion included torture and detention without trial.

National service often involved forced labour in state projects, including road building, or working for companies owned and operated by the military or

E

ruling party elites. International mining companies risked using forced labour by sub-contracting work to these companies.

Torture and other ill-treatment

Prison conditions were appalling, and in many cases amounted to cruel, inhuman or degrading treatment or punishment. Many detainees were held in underground cells or metal shipping containers, often in desert locations and therefore suffered extremes of heat and cold. Prisoners were given inadequate food and drinking water. Many prisoners were held in severely overcrowded and unhygienic conditions.

Torture and other ill-treatment of detainees were frequent. Prisoners were forced to undertake painful and degrading activities, and were tied with ropes in painful positions for long periods.

Refugees

UNHCR, the UN refugee agency, estimated that 3,000 Eritreans fled the country every month, mostly to Ethiopia or Sudan, despite a "shoot to kill" policy for anyone caught attempting to cross the border. Many of those fleeing were young people escaping indefinite national service conscription. Families of those who fled faced reprisals, including harassment, fines and imprisonment.

Eritrean asylum-seekers forcibly returned to the country faced a serious risk of arbitrary detention and torture. Despite this, large numbers were forcibly returned by a number of countries.

■ In July, one Eritrean woman died and another was seriously injured when they jumped off a truck in which they were being forcibly returned to Eritrea by the Sudanese authorities. In October, the Sudanese authorities forcibly returned more than 300 Eritrean refugees and asylum-seekers. These forcible returns coincided with a visit to Sudan by the President of Eritrea. During detention in Sudan, five of the Eritreans were reportedly taken away by Eritrean soldiers; their fate remains unknown.

■ In October, at least 83 Eritreans were deported from Egypt, without being granted access to UNHCR. In late October, a further 118 Eritreans in detention in Egypt were reportedly facing imminent deportation. Eritrean diplomatic representatives were given access to the detainees, who were asked to fill in forms to arrange for their return. Many were reportedly beaten by security forces for refusing to do so.

ETHIOPIA

FEDERAL DEMOCRATIC REPUBLIC OF ETHIOPIA

Head of state:	Girma Wolde-Giorgis
Head of government:	Meles Zenawi
Death penalty:	retentionist
Population:	84.7 million
Life expectancy:	59.3 years
Under-5 mortality:	104.4 per 1,000
Adult literacy:	29.8 per cent

A crackdown on freedom of expression saw scores of journalists and political opposition members arrested and charged with terrorism, treason and other offences. Repressive legislation effectively prevented human rights organizations from functioning. Large tracts of land were leased to foreign companies, leading to large-scale displacement of local populations. Construction continued on a dam which could affect the lives of half a million people.

Background

On 28 May the Ethiopian People's Revolutionary Democratic Front celebrated its 20th anniversary of coming to power. In the capital Addis Ababa there was a pro-government demonstration, at which attendance was mandatory for civil servants. The government took steps to ensure that planned peaceful protests against the government did not take place.

Ethiopia was affected by the drought that hit the region. Severe food shortages were reported, particularly in the Somali and Oromia regions.

Skirmishes continued between government forces and armed opposition groups in several parts of the country, including the Somali, Oromia, Afar and Tigray regions.

In February, elections took place for thousands of seats in district, local and city councils. The opposition announced they were boycotting the elections as they said the outcome was predetermined.

In November and December, the Ethiopian military made incursions into Somalia.

Freedom of expression

The authorities used criminal charges and accusations of terrorism to silence dissent. Large numbers of independent journalists and members of political opposition parties were arrested on suspicion of committing terrorist offences, many after writing articles critical of the government, calling for reform or applying for demonstration permits. Detainees were denied full and prompt access to lawyers and family members.

■ In March and April, at least 250 members and supporters of the Oromo Federalist Democratic Movement (OFDM) and the Oromo People's Congress (OPC) opposition parties were arrested across the Oromia region. Many were former members of parliament or the regional assembly. Some were reportedly subjected to enforced disappearance after their arrest.

■ In June, journalists Woubshet Taye and Reyot Alemu, and members of the opposition Ethiopian National Democratic Party, Zerihun Gebre-Egziabher and Dejene Tefera, were arrested.

■ In July, Swedish journalists Martin Schibbye and Johan Persson were arrested in the Somali region. They had entered the country illegally to report on the ongoing conflict in the region.

■ In August and September, nine more members of the OFDM and OPC were arrested. Two – Bekele Gerba and Olbana Lelisa – were arrested a few days after meeting Amnesty International delegates.

■ In September, at least seven opposition party members and two journalists were arrested, including former prisoners of conscience Eskinder Nega and Andualem Arage.

By November, 107 of the journalists and opposition members mentioned above had been charged with terrorism-related crimes. Six more journalists, two opposition members and one human rights defender – all in exile – were charged in their absence. It appears that all were prosecuted because of their peaceful and legitimate activities. In December, Martin Schibbye and Johan Persson were convicted and sentenced to 11 years' imprisonment.

In September, another journalist fled the country after he was cited in a Wikileaks cable and summoned for interrogation by government officials and federal police. In November, the independent *Awramba Times* newspaper shut down, and two more journalists fled the country after being threatened with arrest.

In May, government officials and leaders of government-controlled press unions disrupted a UNESCO event to celebrate World Press Freedom Day, excluding independent journalists and installing a moderator from the state-sponsored broadcasting corporation.

Many radio stations, satellite TV stations, news websites and human rights organizations' websites were blocked, including Al Jazeera, Voice of America, ESAT satellite TV, Addis Neger news and Amnesty International's website.

Arbitrary arrests and detentions

Hundreds of Oromos were arrested, accused of supporting the Oromo Liberation Front. The rights of detainees were often not respected. Many were held arbitrarily without charge or trial.

■ In April, many students were reportedly arrested at the universities of Jimma, Haromaya and Nekemte. Some had been protesting about other arrests in Oromia.

■ In December, 135 Oromos were arrested, including further members of the OPC and OFDM parties.

Many civilians were also reportedly arrested and arbitrarily detained in the Somali region on suspicion of supporting the Ogaden National Liberation Front (ONLF). Torture and extrajudicial executions of detainees in the region were regularly reported.

Large numbers of Oromos and Somalis, arrested in previous years, were believed to still be arbitrarily detained in their respective regions and in Addis Ababa. A lack of transparency made the numbers in detention impossible to verify.

■ A local UN employee, arrested in late 2010, continued to be detained arbitrarily in Jijiga, reportedly in an attempt to force the return of his brother, in exile in Denmark, who was accused of involvement with the ONLF.

Torture and other ill-treatment

There were regular reports of torture in detention.

A significant number of the 107 opposition members and journalists mentioned above complained of torture or other ill-treatment during interrogation in Maikelawi detention centre. Detainees reported beatings, including with pieces of wire, metal and furniture; suspension by the wrists; sleep deprivation; and being held in isolation and in complete darkness for prolonged periods. Many reported being forced to sign confessions and other documents that would be presented against them as evidence.

E

The use of unofficial places of detention was also reported during the year, where detainees were reportedly badly beaten and subjected to other forms of ill-treatment.

Human rights defenders

Human rights organizations struggled to operate within restrictions on their work put in place by the 2009 Charities and Societies Proclamation.

In February, the Board of the Charities and Societies Agency upheld an earlier decision to freeze the bank accounts of the country's two leading human rights organizations, the Human Rights Council and the Ethiopian Women Lawyers Association, who then appealed to the High Court. In October the Court upheld the Board's decision in the Human Rights Council's case.

Forced evictions

Forced evictions displaced tens of thousands of people in Southern Nations, Nationalities, and People's Region (SNNPR); Gambella; Oromia; Tigray; and Somali regions. Some people protesting against the forced evictions were arrested.

In February, the Minister of Agriculture announced that the government had set aside 3.9 million hectares of farm land for lease to foreign investors, including 800,000 hectares in Gambella region. Large tracts of land were subsequently leased in Gambella, causing major displacement and widespread deforestation.

In February, 15,000 people in Gambella were reportedly resettled to newly built villages, with an intention to move a total of 45,000 households (approximately 225,000 people) over a three-year period. The government said that the "villagization" programme was not linked to land leasing, but part of a separate project to improve access to basic amenities, and that the majority of people were resettled voluntarily. However, it was widely reported that most people were removed by force and that the new "villages" seriously lacked the promised facilities, infrastructure and livelihood opportunities.

In April, as part of promised action against corruption, 5,000 residents of Mekele in Tigray region were ordered to demolish their homes, because the land they were built on had been illegally leased by corrupt officials. In response to protests by residents, police reportedly fired tear gas and temporarily detained around 400 protesters. Most were released,

but five women who were suspected of organizing the protests were reportedly subjected to enforced disappearance after their arrest. The demolitions went ahead in May, leaving around 15,000 people homeless.

Construction continued on the Gibe III dam on the Omo river. In September, the CERD Committee requested that Ethiopia provide information on measures taken to conduct an independent assessment of the negative effects of construction on local livelihoods, and to properly consult Indigenous people. Experts say the dam could cause the displacement of around 200,000 people in the Omo valley and hundreds of thousands more in Kenya, cause serious environmental problems, threaten two world heritage sites and possibly provoke cross-border conflict. In October around 100 Indigenous people were reportedly arrested for opposing the dam.

In October, 60 people in the SNNPR were reportedly arrested after filing a complaint to the Prime Minister about land-grabbing by the regional administration.

Conflict in the Somali region

Skirmishes continued in the long-running conflict between the ONLF and government forces.

Government forces and allied local militia reportedly continued to commit human rights violations, including extrajudicial executions, mass arrests and arbitrary detentions, torture and rape. In October it was reported that the army was forcibly relocating thousands of people for the purposes of oil exploration. Many reports were impossible to verify due to the extreme restrictions on access to the region for independent journalists, human rights monitors and other observers.

In May, a UN worker was killed and two others were kidnapped in the region, reportedly by the ONLF. A UN employee who negotiated with the ONLF over the men's release was subsequently arrested and charged with terrorism offences.

Refugees

Ethiopia hosted over 250,000 refugees from neighbouring countries while demanding the forcible return of some Ethiopian refugees abroad.

Ethiopia continued to receive large numbers of refugees from neighbouring Eritrea, and Eritreans forcibly removed from other countries, including at least 212 deported from Egypt. Tens of thousands of refugees entered Ethiopia, fleeing the humanitarian crisis in Somalia and fighting in Sudan's Blue Nile state. New refugee camps were opened to accommodate the influx.

Ethiopian refugees were forcibly returned to Ethiopia from Sudan, Djibouti, and Somaliland during the year, all reportedly at the request of the Ethiopian government. Those returned were at risk of arbitrary detention and torture.

Communal violence

In March, clashes erupted between Muslims and Christians in Jimma, Oromia region, triggered by the alleged desecration of a copy of the Qur'an. One person was killed, at least 34 Christian churches and 16 private homes were burnt, and thousands of residents were temporarily displaced. The government reported that 130 suspects had been charged with instigating religious hatred and violence.

Amnesty International visits/reports

🚐 Amnesty International delegates visited but were expelled from the country in August.

📕 Justice under fire: Trials of opposition leaders, journalists and human rights defenders in Ethiopia (AFR 25/002/2011)

📕 Ethiopia: Submission to the United Nations Human Rights Committee (AFR 25/003/2011)

📕 Ethiopia: Briefing to the UN Committee on the Elimination of Discrimination against Women (AFR 25/004/2011)

📕 Dismantling dissent: Intensified crackdown on free speech in Ethiopia (AFR 25/011/2011)

FIJI

REPUBLIC OF FIJI

Head of state:	Ratu Epeli Nailatikau
Head of government:	Josaia Voreqe Bainimarama
Death penalty:	abolitionist for ordinary crimes
Population:	0.9 million
Life expectancy:	69.2 years
Under-5 mortality:	17.6 per 1,000

Freedom of expression, association and peaceful assembly were severely restricted under continuing military rule. Reports of torture and other ill-treatment were common. Government critics, trade unionists and some church leaders were briefly detained, threatened, intimidated or attacked. Domestic and sexual violence against women and children remained widespread.

Freedom of expression, association and assembly

The Public Emergency Regulations (PER), first enacted in 2009, remained in force and were used to restrict freedom of expression and peaceful assembly.

■ In July, police questioned and intimidated Virisila Buadromo, the Executive Director of the Fiji Women's Rights Movement, because she had not sought a permit under the PER to hold an internal planning meeting. The police then disbanded the meeting.

■ In early August, Fiji Trades Union Congress (FTUC) President Daniel Urai and Hotels Union staff member Dinesh Gounder were arrested. The two men were charged under the PER for holding a meeting without a permit and then released on bail.

■ In August, the police announced that Hindus would need to seek a PER permit for any religious events of more than 10 people.

Other members of civil society also experienced restrictions to their rights to freedom of association and peaceful assembly.

■ The Methodist Church Conference was banned in August after the church did not accept government demands for a number of its leaders to stand down. The government had earlier given permission for the Conference to go ahead for the first time in four years.

■ On 15 August, police revoked a permit for the FTUC National Council to hold its regular meeting in Nadi.

In November, the Rewa Provincial Council was banned from meeting after its Paramount Chief Ro Teimumu Kepa criticized the coup of December 2006.
■ In November, trade union leaders Daniel Urai and Felix Anthony were arrested. Daniel Urai was accused of defacing public buildings with anti-government graffiti in the capital. He was charged with sedition for "urging political violence" and was released on bail. Felix Anthony was released without charge.

Torture and other ill-treatment

■ In February, Felix Anthony and Maika Namudu were briefly detained and reportedly beaten by military officers at the Queen Elizabeth Barracks.
■ The military detained politician Sam Speight from 21 to 24 February and reportedly beat him until he lost consciousness. Sam Speight was a cabinet minister in the Laisenia Qarase government which was deposed in 2006. He sought medical treatment for his injuries in Australia and subsequently applied for asylum there.
■ In May, former Commander of the Third Infantry Battalion and member of the military council, Tevita Mara, was granted asylum in Tonga. He stated that Prime Minister Frank Bainimarama (as he is commonly known) and other members of the military council had severely beaten human rights activists in December 2006.
■ In September, trade unionist Kenneth Zinck sought asylum in Australia after he and a family member were harassed by members of the security forces. He reported that he had been detained and tortured three times since 2006.

Violence against women and children

The Fiji Women's Crisis Centre reported an increase in the number of cases of domestic violence in 2011 compared to 2010. The police said that there had been a sharp increase in reports of rape, attempted rape and domestic violence in the third quarter of the year compared to the same period in 2010. An increase in sexual violence against girls and boys within the home was also reported.

Workers' rights

The Essential National Industries (Employment) Decree 2011 came into force in September. It restricted collective bargaining rights, severely curtailed the right to strike, banned overtime payments and voided existing collective agreements for workers in key sectors of the economy, including the sugar industry, aviation and tourism.

FINLAND

REPUBLIC OF FINLAND
Head of state: Tarja Halonen
Head of government: Jyrki Katainen (replaced Mari Kiviniemi
                                                                                              in June)
Death penalty: abolitionist for all crimes
Population: 5.4 million
Life expectancy: 80 years
Under-5 mortality: 3.2 per 1,000

New information emerged concerning Finland's possible involvement in the US-led rendition and secret detention programmes. Asylum-seekers in accelerated determination procedures were subjected to unfair treatment and many were detained in unsuitable facilities. Services for women and girls who had been subjected to violence remained inadequate.

Refugees, migrants and asylum-seekers

Accelerated asylum determination procedures under the Aliens Act continued to provide inadequate protection for asylum-seekers, including by not requiring an in-country suspensive right of appeal.

In January, Finland stopped returning asylum-seekers to Greece under the Dublin II Regulation, following a ruling by the European Court of Human Rights which found that Greece did not operate an effective asylum system (see Greece entry).

However, forced returns to Baghdad, Iraq, resumed despite the real risk of persecution or other forms of serious harm people could face upon their return.

The Finnish authorities were unable to provide comprehensive and reliable statistics on the numbers of irregular migrants and asylum-seekers detained during the year. However, there were concerns that many of those being detained were held in police detention facilities, contrary to international standards. In these cases, many were detained in mixed-sex facilities, together with individuals suspected of crime. Children seeking asylum, including unaccompanied children, were also detained.

In June, the UN Committee against Torture expressed its concern over relevant sections of the Aliens Act, which allow for preventive detention if an alien is suspected of committing a crime.

Violence against women and girls

Services for victims of violence remained inadequate. This was partly due to the ongoing absence of legislation requiring municipalities to provide support to victims. As a result, with only two centres providing support to rape victims, and the absence of any self-referral centres, victims' needs across the country could not be met.

In addition, because shelters for victims of domestic violence were funded by child protection services, they provided shelter mainly to women with children, and did not accept women suffering from mental illness. This placed many vulnerable people at risk of further violence.

Concerns were raised about the adequacy of the proposed €14 million budget for the National Action Plan to prevent violence against women, which was agreed in 2010. Civil society organizations argued that this would be insufficient to ensure full and effective implementation of the Plan.

Counter-terror and security

New information emerged regarding a number of aircraft linked to the US-led rendition and secret detention programmes, which landed in Finland between 2001 and 2006. One aircraft was photographed at Helsinki-Vantaa airport on 20 September 2004, the same day it was reported to have landed in Lithuania. The Lithuanian government acknowledged that two CIA secret sites had been established in the country between 2002 and 2004. Finland had previously been linked to three rendition flights and to "dummy flight plans".

International justice

In September, appeal proceedings began in the Helsinki Court of Appeal in the case of François Bazaramba, who had been convicted for crimes of genocide committed in Rwanda in 1994. Some of the hearings were conducted in Rwanda and Tanzania to facilitate the hearing of witness testimony and allow the judges to visit locations relevant to the case.

Prisoners of conscience

Conscientious objectors to military service continued to be imprisoned for refusing the alternative civilian service, which remained punitive and discriminatory in length. The duration of alternative civilian service remained at 362 days, more than double the shortest military service period of 180 days.

Amnesty International visits/reports

Finland: Further investigation into USA rendition flights needed (EUR 20/001/2011)

FRANCE

FRENCH REPUBLIC

Head of state:	Nicolas Sarkozy
Head of government:	François Fillon
Death penalty:	abolitionist for all crimes
Population:	63.1 million
Life expectancy:	81.5 years
Under-5 mortality:	3.9 per 1,000

The new Defender of Rights institution started operations. Investigations into allegations of torture or other ill-treatment, including deaths in custody, remained inadequate. Roma continued to be forcibly evicted. A law banning the wearing of any form of clothing concealing one's face in public came into force. Many asylum-seekers were left homeless and destitute.

Legal, constitutional or institutional developments

In June, the new Defender of Rights was appointed, replacing the Ombudsperson, the National Commission on Ethics in Security, the Equal Opportunities and Anti-Discrimination Commission and the Defender of Children. Concerns remained that the institution would find it difficult to maintain the required levels of expertise and independence for the different roles.

On 1 June, a new law on pre-charge detention entered into force. It allowed detainees to be assisted by a lawyer at any time during their detention and during questioning, and required that detainees be informed of their right to remain silent. However, the prosecutor could postpone the presence of a lawyer for up to 12 hours for "compelling reasons"; detainees' meetings with their lawyer continued to be limited to 30 minutes; and the special regime of pre-trial detention for suspects of terrorism or organized crime, under which access to a lawyer can be postponed for up to 72 hours, remained in place.

Torture and other ill-treatment

The Criminal Code continued to lack a definition of torture in line with the UN Convention against Torture. There was a lack of prompt, independent, impartial and effective investigations into allegations of ill-treatment by law enforcement officials.

■ Arezki Kerfali's trial for insulting a police officer (a charge he denied), was set for March 2011 but postponed until March 2012. Arezki Kerfali's complaint of ill-treatment against the police officers who arrested and detained him and his friend Ali Ziri on 9 June 2009 was not investigated. Ali Ziri died the following morning (see below), and Arezki Kerfali was declared unfit for work for eight days as a result of the injuries he sustained while in police custody. At the end of the year he continued to suffer from serious psychological trauma.

■ Lamba Soukouna's complaint of ill-treatment by police officers on 8 May 2008 was heard by an investigating judge in September. Lamba Soukouna, who suffers from sickle cell anaemia, a serious genetic illness, said he was severely beaten by police near his home in Villepinte, a suburb of Paris, and had to remain in hospital for three days following the incident. An investigation was still pending.

Deaths in custody

There continued to be little progress in investigations into deaths in police custody, and concerns about the independence of those investigations remained.

■ In April, a new autopsy confirmed that Ali Ziri, a 69-year-old man, died of lack of oxygen due to the restraint techniques he was subjected to and repeated vomiting while in police custody on 9 June 2009. In December, the Prosecutor of Pontoise asked that the case be closed, although the police officers involved in Ali Ziri and Arezki Kerfali's arrest and transportation to the Argenteuil police station had not been questioned.

■ In April, a reconstruction of Abou Bakari Tandia's detention in the police station at Courbevoie on the night of 5 to 6 December 2004 took place. He fell into a coma during his detention and died in hospital on 24 January 2005. In June, a new report by the Paris Medico-Legal Institute confirmed that the pressure on Abou Bakari Tandia's chest exerted by a police officer led to the lack of oxygen which caused his death. However, in December the investigating judge requested a sixth medical report to determine the cause of Abou Bakari Tandia's death. His family's lawyer subsequently requested that the case be transferred to the jurisdiction of another tribunal. At the end of the year the police officer who restrained him had not been questioned and was still in post.

■ In April, a reconstruction of the arrest of Mohamed Boukrourou, who died during arrest in a police van on 12 November 2009 in Valentigney, took place. A previous autopsy report had concluded that heart failure was the probable cause of death and noted injuries which could have been caused by third parties, and requested further medical examinations to clarify the circumstances. The four police officers involved in his arrest had not been questioned as suspects by the end of the year. In December the Defender of Rights found that Mohamed Boukrourou had been subjected to "inhuman and degrading treatment", and called for disciplinary proceedings against the four police officers.

■ In October, the date was set in January 2012 for the trial of seven police officers involved in the arrest and transportation of Abdelhakim Ajimi, who died during his arrest in Grasse in May 2008. Two police officers were to be tried for involuntary homicide and five for non-assistance to a person in danger.

■ The investigation of Lamine Dieng's death during his arrest on 17 June 2007 in Paris made no progress. A face-to-face "confrontation" between his family and the police officers accused was due to take place in October, to help investigators decide whether to pursue the case. However, it was cancelled for the second time with no explanation and no new date was set. Lamine Dieng had been restrained by police officers in the street and then in a police vehicle, where he lost consciousness and died of mechanical asphyxia. At the end of the year the police officers were still in office.

Discrimination

Acts of discrimination against people belonging to ethnic and religious minorities continued to be documented by human rights organizations.

Discrimination against Roma continued. Camps and makeshift homes inhabited by Roma continued to be dismantled in alleged forced evictions. In June, the European Committee of Social Rights found that the evictions of Roma camps in mid-2010 "took place against a background of ethnic discrimination, involving the stigmatisation of Roma, and constraint, in the form of the threat of immediate expulsion from France", and that the expulsions of Roma to Romania and Bulgaria in 2010 were discriminatory.

■ On 1 September, between 150 and 200 Roma were forcibly evicted from makeshift homes, which were then demolished, in a camp in St Denis (Paris). Anti-riot police forced the Roma to board a tram with no indication of its destination, violating their rights to freedom of movement.

In June, the Parliament rejected a proposal to legalize same-sex marriage.

A law banning the wearing of any form of clothing concealing one's face in public came into force on 11 April. On 22 September, two women were fined by an Administrative Tribunal, as allowed for in the legislation.

Throughout 2011, several political and legislative initiatives were put forward with the aim of enforcing the principle of secularism. On 2 March, the Minister of Education stated that parents accompanying children on school outings should not wear religious symbols. The same prohibition was also applied to adult students enrolled in vocational training.

Refugees, asylum-seekers and migrants

New legislation further restricted the rights of asylum-seekers and migrants. In June, the Parliament adopted a law on migration increasing the maximum duration of detention for irregular migrants pending expulsion from 32 to 45 days. In addition, if a group of 10 or more irregular migrants or asylum-seekers were intercepted near the French border, they would be kept in a "holding area" for up to 26 days. Their applications to enter the rest of France to apply for asylum would be examined; if these were considered "manifestly unfounded" they would be returned to their country of origin. They would have only 48 hours to challenge the decision, which could prevent them from lodging an asylum application.

Around two thirds of the asylum-seekers in France did not have access to reception centres for asylum-seekers, contrary to their rights under national and EU Law. Consequently, many asylum-seekers were homeless and destitute. They were not allowed to work while their application was first being processed, and in the majority of cases they were refused permission to work during the appeal process.

In August, the Minister of the Interior stated that, if reached, the objective of expelling 30,000 irregular migrants would be the "best result historically recorded in France". In October, he announced that he would reach that objective.

In April, the Management Board of the French Office for the Protection of Refugees and Stateless Persons (OFPRA) added Albania and Kosovo to the list of "safe" countries of origin for asylum-seekers. Claims submitted by asylum-seekers from "safe" countries were examined under an accelerated procedure and they could be forcibly returned before their appeal had been examined. In November, the Minister of the Interior announced that the budget for asylum would be reduced and the list of "safe" countries of origin would be extended. He claimed that the French asylum system was "in danger" because it was used by economic migrants to enter and remain in France. In December, the Management Board of OFPRA added Armenia, Bangladesh, Montenegro and Moldova to the list of "safe" countries.

Amnesty International visits/reports

🚌 Amnesty International delegates visited France in May, June, September and October.

📄 France: Authorities must stop forcibly evicting Roma (EUR 21/001/2011)

📄 France: Authorities must act swiftly to fully investigate suspected arson attack on Roma squat in Paris (EUR 21/002/2011)

📄 France "Our lives are left hanging": Families of victims of deaths in police custody wait for justice to be done (EUR 21/003/2011)

F

GAMBIA

REPUBLIC OF THE GAMBIA

Head of state and government:	Yahya Jammeh
Death penalty:	abolitionist in practice
Population:	1.8 million
Life expectancy:	58.5 years
Under-5 mortality:	102.8 per 1,000
Adult literacy:	46.5 per cent

Gambia continued to restrict freedom of expression. Government opponents, human rights defenders and journalists were arbitrarily arrested and detained. Torture and other ill-treatment were carried out by security forces and there were unresolved cases of enforced disappearance.

Background

Presidential elections took place on 24 November. The incumbent, President Jammeh, was declared winner, continuing his 17-year rule. Political parties were given 11 days to campaign.

Arbitrary arrests and detentions

The National Intelligence Agency (NIA), the police and the army unlawfully arrested and detained people. Detainees were rarely informed of their rights or the reason for their arrest or detention and were often held for more than 72 hours without charge, in violation of the Constitution. Torture continued to be used routinely to extract confessions and as punishment.

■ In April, graduate student Mouctar Diallo was arrested by the NIA, accused of terrorism and spreading revolution from Egypt to Gambia. After months under house arrest and then several days in detention he was released in July without charge.

Repression of dissent

Human rights defenders, including lawyers and journalists, were unlawfully arrested and detained.

■ In March, two family members of exiled opposition leader Mai Fatty were arrested and detained for displaying political campaign materials.

■ On 7 June, former Minister of Information and Communication Dr Amadou Scattred Janneh was arrested and detained at Mile 2 Central Prison along with Michael C. Ucheh Thomas, Modou Keita and Ebrima Jallow. They were charged with treason, which carries the death penalty, for printing and distributing T-shirts with the slogan "End to Dictatorship Now". Their trial was ongoing at the end of the year. Human rights defender Ndey Tapha Sosseh was also charged but she was out of the country at the time.

■ On 19 September, Moses Richards, a lawyer and former High Court judge, was convicted of "giving false information to a public servant" and "sedition" and sentenced to two and a half years' imprisonment with hard labour. He was released in October under a presidential pardon.

■ Edwin Nebolisa Nwakaeme, a Nigerian human rights defender sentenced to six months in prison for giving false information to a public officer, was released on 14 January and deported after serving his sentence.

Freedom of expression

Journalists and other media workers were routinely subjected to harassment, arrests and threats of closure, making it extremely difficult for them to carry out their work.

■ In January, state security agents temporarily shut down Teranga FM, one of the last independent radio stations operating in Gambia. It was later allowed to reopen reportedly on condition that it stopped reviewing newspapers.

■ In July, Nanama Keita was detained and charged with giving "false information" after he petitioned President Jammeh over his alleged wrongful dismissal from the *Daily Observer* newspaper, where he was sports editor. He fled the country after receiving death threats he believed to be from the government. Journalist Seikou Ceesay was detained in October for acting as a guarantor for Nanama Keita. Seikou Ceesay's wife was also arrested and briefly detained.

■ No payment was made by the government in the case of Musa Saidykhan, who was awarded US$200,000 damages by the ECOWAS court in December 2010. Musa Saidykhan, former editor-in-chief of *The Independent*, was tortured after state security agents raided the newspaper's offices in 2006, shut it down and imprisoned its staff.

Enforced disappearances

In October, Justice Minister Edward Gomez stated during an interview with the *Daily News* newspaper that disappeared journalist Ebrima Manneh was still alive "somewhere". A journalist with the government-owned newspaper *Daily Observer*, Ebrima Manneh was arrested by members of the NIA at the newspaper's offices on 11 July 2006. He was last seen in hospital under police custody in July 2007. The government had yet to comply with a July 2008 ECOWAS court judgement, ordering it to immediately release Ebrima Manneh from unlawful detention and pay US$100,000 in damages to his family. The government continued to deny any involvement in his arrest and disappearance.

Death penalty

Thirteen death sentences were passed in 2011, bringing the number of people on death row to 44.

In April, the government passed the Drugs Control (amendment) Act 2011, which replaced the death penalty with life imprisonment for possession of more than 250g of cocaine or heroin. The death penalty had been in place since October 2010 for this offence, but was repealed to bring sentencing in line with the 1997 Constitution. Amendments removing the death penalty were also reportedly made to the Criminal Code Act and the Trafficking in Persons Act 2007 to make them compatible with the 1997 Constitution.

Also in April, the Court of Appeal dismissed the appeal of seven of the eight people sentenced to death in June 2010 following a grossly unfair trial for allegedly plotting to overthrow the government.

Prison conditions

Conditions in Gambia's prisons were appalling. The harsh conditions of detention in Mile 2 Central Prison – overcrowding, poor sanitary conditions and inadequate food – constituted cruel, inhuman and degrading treatment.

Amnesty International visits/reports

▤ Climate of fear continues: Enforced disappearances, killings and torture in Gambia (AFR 27/001/2011)

▤ Arrests in Gambia for distributing T-shirts (AFR 27/002/2011)

GEORGIA

GEORGIA

Head of state:	Mikheil Saakashvili
Head of government:	Nikoloz Gilauri
Death penalty:	abolitionist for all crimes
Population:	4.3 million
Life expectancy:	73.7 years
Under-5 mortality:	29.1 per 1,000
Adult literacy:	99.7 per cent

The police used excessive force in dispersing demonstrations. Evictions failed to meet international standards. The independence of the judiciary remained a concern.

Aftermath of armed conflict

The breakaway regions of Abkhazia and South Ossetia held presidential elections on 26 August and 13 November respectively. The elections were declared illegitimate by the Georgian authorities and the international community. The elections in South Ossetia were accompanied by protests, reports of increased violence and harassment of opposition candidates.

Security and freedom of movement for civilians living in the conflict-affected areas remained a concern. Some progress towards greater security was made and detainees were exchanged under the internationally mediated Incident Prevention and Response Mechanism, bringing together the Georgian and South Ossetian sides. However, incidents of shooting, injury and the detention of civilians for the alleged illegal crossing of the Administrative Boundary Line between South Ossetia and Georgia were reported throughout the year.

The right of internally displaced people to return to their original places of residence in Abkhazia and South Ossetia continued to be denied by the de facto authorities there.

Internally displaced people

The government prioritized the provision of adequate housing for some 247,000 people displaced after the armed conflicts in the 1990s and 2008. However, a government programme intended to provide them with more permanent housing led to several forced evictions, which violated domestic and international standards.

G

Hundreds of internally displaced families were affected by a series of forced evictions in Tbilisi. In most cases the evictions were carried out without adequate consultation, notice or access to legal remedies. Those evicted were offered alternative accommodation outside the capital, mainly in rural areas. Aspects of the right to adequate housing – such as access to employment and sustainable livelihoods – were not always respected.

Freedom of assembly

Several protests during the course of the year were violently dispersed.

■ On 3 January, police violently dispersed an authorized peaceful demonstration of dozens of veterans of Georgia's armed conflicts. Police officers and individuals in plain clothes beat and dragged the demonstrators into police cars. Video footage also showed a plain-clothes police officer hitting a female demonstrator in the face as she tried to back away. Police arrested 11 people on charges of petty hooliganism and disobedience. The court convicted those charged reportedly without viewing available video evidence, relying instead on the testimony of police officers. The detainees were each ordered to pay 400 lari (US$240). The police officer seen hitting the woman was dismissed and an investigation initiated. However, by the end of the year, the investigation had not produced any results.

■ On 26 May, the police used excessive force to disperse an anti-government protest of some 1,000 demonstrators calling for the resignation of President Saakashvili. Riot police moved in at midnight, immediately after the rally permit expired. The available video footage showed police officers beating unarmed demonstrators who were offering no resistance. At least 10 journalists were verbally and physically assaulted by police officers. Others were detained for questioning, and had their equipment damaged or confiscated. Four people died, including one police officer, and dozens were injured. The police officer and a civilian were killed after being hit by a speeding car, carrying an opposition leader away from the scene.

More than 105 demonstrators were arrested and later sentenced to up to two months' imprisonment for resisting police. The families of the detained only learned of their arrest two days later, following inquiries made by the Ombudsperson.

The investigation into the death of two protesters, found on the roof of a shop close to the protest, concluded that they had died after being accidentally electrocuted. This version was contested by an alleged eyewitness, who claimed that he last saw one of the victims being taken into police custody.

An internal investigation conducted by the Ministry of the Interior into the 26 May events resulted in several administrative punishments and dismissal of four police officers for excessive use of force. However, no public, independent investigation was conducted and allegations of ill-treatment by police were not investigated.

The authorities had still failed to carry out effective investigations into allegations of the excessive use of force by law enforcement officials during demonstrations in 2009 and 2007.

Justice system

After visiting Georgia in June, the UN Working Group on Arbitrary Detention raised concerns regarding aspects of the justice system, including the role of prosecutors, an extremely low acquittal rate and the excessive use of pre-trial detention.

■ On 26 April, the European Court of Human Rights ruled that Georgia had failed to carry out an effective investigation into a high-profile murder case involving government officials. The court found that the investigation into the death of Sandro Girgvliani in 2006 lacked "independence, impartiality, objectivity and thoroughness". It was particularly concerned by attempts by the Ministry of the Interior, the Prosecutor's Office, the domestic courts and the President to "prevent justice from being done". The Court ordered the government to pay €50,000 (US$74,000) to the victim's parents. Sandro Girgvliani, aged 28, was kidnapped and beaten to death by Ministry of the Interior officials in January 2006, after he argued with a group of high-ranking ministry officials in a Tbilisi café. No new investigation was opened into the case.

Amnesty International visits/reports

🚌 Amnesty International delegates visited Georgia in March.

📕 Uprooted again: Forced evictions of the internally displaced persons in Georgia (EUR 56/005/2011)

GERMANY

FEDERAL REPUBLIC OF GERMANY

Head of state:	Christian Wulff
Head of government:	Angela Merkel
Death penalty:	abolitionist for all crimes
Population:	82.2 million
Life expectancy:	80.4 years
Under-5 mortality:	4.2 per 1,000

Independent police complaints bodies were not introduced. Several federal states continued to forcibly return Roma to Kosovo despite the risk of persecution and discrimination there. Criminal proceedings for crimes against humanity and war crimes against the former President and Vice-President of the Democratic Forces for the Liberation of Rwanda were ongoing.

International scrutiny

In May, the UN Committee on Economic, Social and Cultural Rights urged Germany to sign the Optional Protocol to the Covenant, to ensure that its policies on investments by German companies abroad serve the economic, social and cultural rights in the host countries, and to ensure that asylum-seekers enjoy equal access to social assistance, health care and employment.

In November, the UN Committee against Torture recommended that to prevent torture or other ill-treatment, Germany should refrain from automatically relying on information provided by foreign intelligence services and ban all German authorities and agencies from undertaking investigations abroad where this could involve co-operation with foreign agencies suspected of coercion. The Committee was concerned about the lack of ongoing efforts to investigate German involvement in extraordinary renditions. It also recommended that all allegations of torture and ill-treatment by the police be investigated by independent bodies, and expressed concern that police officers in most federal states were not obliged to wear identification badges.

Torture and other ill-treatment

Investigations into allegations of ill-treatment were not always effective due to a lack of independent police complaints mechanisms in all federal states and to difficulties in the identification of police officers. In July, the federal state of Berlin started implementing individual identification consisting of name or number tags for all its police officers.

■ Investigations into excessive use of force during a demonstration in Stuttgart in September 2010 were ongoing. In March, the Stuttgart Local Court fined one police officer €6,000 for the use of pepper spray against a woman participating in a sit-in. The lawyer of four protesters who sustained severe eye damage from a water cannon blast requested that the chief public prosecutor be discharged from the case due to an alleged lack of impartiality.

■ On 4 August, the Frankfurt Regional Court awarded moral damages to Markus Gäfgen for having been threatened by two police officers with the infliction of intolerable pain in 2002 as he was apprehended on suspicion of having kidnapped an 11-year-old boy. The court qualified the threat as "inhuman treatment" under the European Convention on Human Rights.

Refugees and asylum-seekers

On 13 January, the Federal Ministry of the Interior ordered that transfers of asylum-seekers to Greece under the Dublin II Regulation be suspended for one year (see Greece entry). In November, the suspension was prolonged until 12 January 2013.

On 9 November, the authorities agreed to establish a permanent programme for the resettlement of vulnerable refugees with a quota of 300 each year in the next three years.

Asylum-seekers entering Germany via an airport who went through an accelerated asylum procedure were routinely detained in the airport transit area. The authorities did not consider that holding asylum-seekers there amounted to a deprivation of liberty.

Several federal states continued to forcibly return Roma, Ashkali and Egyptians to Kosovo despite the ongoing real risk of persecution and cumulative forms of discrimination there. In August, there were media reports that the Baden-Württemberg authorities had stopped returns for an interim period. In December, North Rhine-Westphalia stopped forcible returns to Kosovo of Roma considered vulnerable, such as families with minors, single women and the elderly, until 1 April 2012.

Asylum-seekers continued to be discriminated against in access to social benefits: they received benefits well below subsistence level, 31 per cent lower than those for permanent residents. The law

G

regulating social benefits for asylum-seekers was under review by the German Constitutional Court.

Migrants' rights

Social services departments remained under obligation to report a person's irregular status to the Office of Alien Affairs when handing out health vouchers for non-emergency medical treatment. This undermined the right to health of undocumented migrants. Amendments to the Residence Act were passed to exempt education staff from this obligation.

Counter-terror and security

Concerns remained about several aspects of the government's counter-terrorism policy. Regulatory rules governing the Residence Act allowed the use of "diplomatic assurances" to justify returning terrorism suspects to places where they were at risk of torture or other ill-treatment. The German government declined to state that it would rule out intelligence co-operation and information-sharing with states that have a well-known record of torture.

■ In April, the *TAZ* newspaper reported that the detained Uzbek witness A.S. had died in prison in Tashkent, allegedly of a heart attack. He had been interrogated by German investigators in June and September 2008 in Tashkent in the presence of the Uzbekistani National Security Service, despite findings of the UN Special Rapporteur on torture that torture was systematic in Uzbekistani prisons.

■ In January, German national Khaled El-Masri withdrew his appeal against the decision by Cologne Administrative Court in December 2010. The court had dismissed Khaled El-Masri's action against Germany for not pursuing the extradition of 13 US nationals suspected of transferring him illegally to Afghanistan in 2004.

Crimes under international law

In May, a criminal trial against Rwandan citizens Ignace Murwanashyaka and Straton Musoni was opened before the Higher Regional Court of Stuttgart. As the former President and Vice-President of the Democratic Forces for the Liberation of Rwanda, they were accused of having commanded 26 crimes against humanity and 39 war crimes on Congolese territory between January 2008 and November 2009 via telephone and internet. This was the first trial in Germany based on the German Code of Crimes against International Law, which came into force in 2002.

Arms trade

Although the German government supported a comprehensive Arms Trade Treaty, it repeatedly authorized arms transfers that may have contributed to human rights violations. In July, there were media reports that the German government had approved in principle the delivery of about 200 Leopard 2 Main Battle Tanks to Saudi Arabia.

Amnesty International visits/reports

Germany: Briefing to the UN Committee against Torture, October 2011 (EUR 23/002/2011)

GHANA

REPUBLIC OF GHANA

Head of state and government:	John Evans Atta Mills
Death penalty:	abolitionist in practice
Population:	25 million
Life expectancy:	64.2 years
Under-5 mortality:	68.5 per 1,000
Adult literacy:	66.6 per cent

Thousands remained under threat of forced eviction. The criminal justice system remained slow, and prisons overcrowded and poorly resourced. Four people were sentenced to death; there were no executions. High levels of violence against women and girls were reported.

Background

The Constitution Review Commission, inaugurated in January 2010 by President Mills to conduct public consultation on the 1992 Constitution, published its report in December. Its recommendations included abolition of the death penalty, and direct enforcement of decisions by the Commission on Human Rights and Administrative Justice (CHRAJ). It also recommended that the powers of the CHRAJ be increased to initiate any investigation within its mandate without formal complaint.

Police and security forces

Violence and unlawful killings by the police and security forces were reported. In June, the UN

Committee against Torture expressed concern about impunity for police brutality and excessive use of force, and about the authorities' admission that torture in detention centres was likely.

In February, the police were accused of firing indiscriminately in an attempt to restore order in the Buduburam refugee camp. One person was reportedly killed.

Justice system

There were continued long delays in police and court procedures. Access to legal aid was inadequate and many prisoners spent years awaiting trial. Prisons were overcrowded and under-resourced. The government agreed to increase the budget for food in prison, but by the end of the year this had not yet been implemented.

Death penalty

Four people, including a woman, were sentenced to be hanged for murder. At the end of the year, 138 people were on death row, including four women. No executions were carried out, and in December the Constitutional Review Commission recommended that the death penalty be abolished.

Housing rights

In January, the Accra Metropolitan Assembly announced a plan to demolish structures built next to Accra's disused railways as part of a railway refurbishment project, threatening the forcible eviction of thousands of people. By the end of the year, no forced evictions had been carried out.

In Old Fadama, Ghana's biggest informal settlement in Accra, between 55,000 and 79,000 people continued to live without security of tenure. In previous years, the Accra Metropolitan Assembly repeatedly announced plans to demolish the settlement, but the process had not begun by the end of the year. In September, President Mills publicly committed not to forcibly evict the people living in Old Fadama, and said that discussions were ongoing to relocate people.

Violence against women and girls

High levels of violence against women and girls continued to be reported throughout the country. In December, a member of parliament was arrested on suspicion of raping a 12-year-old girl.

Rights of lesbian, gay, bisexual and transgender people

Human rights abuses against individuals suspected of same-sex relations continued. On 20 July, Paul Evans Aidoo, the Western Region Minister, ordered security forces to arrest all gay men and lesbians in the west of the country, and called on landlords and tenants to report anyone they suspected of being gay or lesbian.

Amnesty International visits/reports

🚗 Amnesty International delegates visited Ghana in July and September.

📖 "When we sleep, we don't sleep": Living under the threat of forced eviction in Ghana (AFR 28/003/2011)

GREECE

HELLENIC REPUBLIC

Head of state:	Karolos Papoulias
Head of government:	Loukas Papademos (replaced George Papandreou in November)
Death penalty status:	abolitionist for all crimes
Population:	11.4 million
Life expectancy:	79.9 years
Under-5 mortality:	3.4 per 1,000
Adult literacy:	97.2 per cent

Reports continued of ill-treatment and excessive use of force by law enforcement officials. People detained for immigration purposes were held in inhuman and degrading conditions. European courts concluded that Greece did not operate an effective asylum system. There was an escalation of racially motivated attacks.

Background

The financial crisis continued and the country was driven into deeper recession.

A series of demonstrations took place in June and October ahead of the Parliament voting on a series of austerity measures. In addition, from May until August the Greek movement of "the indignant" staged peaceful sit-ins against the austerity measures in the main squares of Athens and Thessaloniki.

On 26 October, the Eurozone leaders and the International Monetary Fund reached an agreement with banks and other creditors for the latter to take a 50 per cent loss on the face value of their Greek loans. Following the decision of the Prime Minister to step down, and intense negotiations between Greece's major political parties, a transitional coalition government was formed in November.

Torture and other ill-treatment

Allegations of torture and other ill-treatment in immigration detention facilities and police stations, during arrest and/or detention, persisted.

A law was enacted in January to pave the way for a police complaints mechanism. Concerns remained, however, over the office's independence and effectiveness of mandate.

■ In December, the Mixed Jury Court of Athens found a former police officer guilty of torturing two young men on separate occasions with an electric shock device in August 2002 at the Aspropyrgos police station. The Court handed down a six-year prison sentence, suspended on appeal.

■ In December, two police officers were found guilty of causing bodily harm under the torture provision of the Criminal Code to two refugees in Aghios Panteleimon, Athens in December 2004. The officers were also found guilty for causing unprovoked bodily harm to five other Afghans. One officer was sentenced to five years and five months imprisonment and the other, five years. Both sentences were suspended on appeal. Concerns were expressed by NGOs that the Court had converted the original charge of torture in relation to the treatment of the two refugees to the lesser offence of violations against human dignity proscribed under the torture provision.

There was a large a number of allegations of ill-treatment by police during demonstrations.

In April, police withdrew from the town of Keratea where clashes between police and residents protesting against the creation of a landfill site had been ongoing since December 2010. There were reports of excessive use of tear gas and other chemicals by the police, and allegations of ill-treatment of town residents. The authorities also reported a large number of injuries to police officers.

There were mounting allegations of excessive use of force, including the use of chemicals, by police during the anti-austerity demonstrations that took place during the year. On several occasions, the otherwise peaceful demonstrations became violent

when a minority of rioters clashed with police. Video footage, pictures, press reports and witness testimonies pointed to the repeated use of excessive force by police in the demonstrations in Athens on 15, 28 and 29 June, including the extensive use of chemicals, against largely peaceful protesters. A criminal investigation was ordered by the Athens Prosecutor's Office into the allegations.

■ On 11 May, riot police reportedly used excessive force and chemicals against a large number of peaceful protesters, in Panepistimiou Street in Athens. More than 30 protesters sought hospital treatment, mainly for head injuries, including two who were seriously injured and required further hospital treatment. A criminal investigation began into the case of Yiannis Kafkas, one of the protesters seriously injured.

■ Manolis Kypraios, a journalist, suffered total loss of hearing after a riot police officer threw a stun grenade in front of him while he was covering the demonstration in Athens on 15 June. A criminal and disciplinary investigation began into his case. At the end of the year, the Athens Prosecutor's Office filed charges against as yet unidentified police officers for intentionally causing the journalist serious bodily harm.

Refugees, asylum-seekers and migrants

Inhuman and degrading detention conditions in immigration detention facilities, particularly in the Evros region, persisted. Asylum-seekers and irregular migrants, including unaccompanied minors, continued to be detained for prolonged periods.

In March, the European Committee for the Prevention of Torture took the exceptional step of publicly condemning Greece's continued failure over many years to take measures to improve very poor detention conditions.

■ In January, in a landmark ruling in the case of *M.S.S. v. Belgium and Greece* (see Belgium entry) the Grand Chamber of the European Court of Human Rights found that M.S.S., an Afghan asylum-seeker whom the Belgian authorities had returned to Greece under the Dublin II Regulation, had been denied effective determination of his asylum claim because of major structural deficiencies in the Greek asylum procedure, and concluded that Greece did not have an effective asylum system in place. The Court found that Greece had violated the applicant's right to an effective remedy, and that his detention conditions, and the destitution in which he was left in Greece upon his release, amounted to degrading and inhuman or degrading treatment respectively. In December, in two linked cases arising from the crisis of the Greek asylum system, the Court of Justice of the EU reiterated that asylum-seekers transferred to Greece under the Dublin II Regulation risked grave human rights violations there.

New legislation enacted in January provided for the creation of a new asylum-determination authority with no police involvement. It was due to start operations in 2012. Until then, however, the continued role of the police as the sole authority responsible for the first stage examination of international protection claims gave rise to concern.

The new legislation also provided for the establishment of "first reception centres" where third country nationals, arrested for "irregular entry" into Greece, could be detained for up to 25 days. However, among other things, the legislation failed to provide a remedy for those detained in such centres to challenge the lawfulness of their detention in court.

The erection of a fence along over 10km of Greece's border with Turkey in the Evros region, announced in January, gave rise to profound concern that it would physically prevent people seeking international protection from reaching safety.

In September and October, seven asylum-seekers, who had expressed their wish to apply for asylum, were reportedly forcibly returned to Turkey under the Readmission Agreement with Turkey, in violation of the principle of *non-refoulement.*

Concern remained over the long delays experienced by asylum-seekers before being able to lodge an asylum application in Athens and Thessaloniki.

In February, 300 migrants in Athens and Thessaloniki started a hunger strike prompted by their irregular status and demanded to be regularized, among other things. The strike continued for 43 days, with many migrants being hospitalized as a result. It ended after the authorities and the hunger strikers reportedly came to an agreement over, among other things, the provision of temporary six-month residence permits.

Prison conditions

Poor detention conditions and severe overcrowding continued to be reported in many prisons including Chania, Korydallos, and Thiva women's prison.

In October, the European Court of Human Rights found against Greece, regarding an application lodged in 2009 by 47 prisoners held in Ioannina prison (*Taggatidis and others v. Greece*), and that the conditions there amounted to inhuman or degrading treatment.

Racism

There were reported failures by police officers to protect third country nationals from racially motivated attacks.

In June, UNHCR, the UN refugee agency, observed a "dangerous escalation in phenomena of racist violence targeting indiscriminately aliens, based solely on their skin colour or country of origin". In particular, in May and June, after two migrants were suspected in connection with the killing of a man as he prepared to get his wife to the maternity hospital, migrants, refugees and asylum-seekers were reportedly attacked nearly every day by far-right groups in certain areas of Athens.

■ On 16 September, three Afghan asylum-seekers were subjected to a reportedly racially motivated attack outside their house in the neighbourhood of Aghios Panteleimon in Athens. One of them was hospitalized after being stabbed in the chest. Three individuals were arrested in relation to the attack and were referred for trial.

Discrimination – Roma

The living conditions in many Roma settlements in Greece continued to be a cause of concern. A community of around 800 Roma in the village of Examilia (Korinthia) reportedly lacked access to clean water, drainage and electricity and lived in appalling sanitary conditions.

The NGO Greek Helsinki Monitor reported that Romani children continued to be segregated or excluded in education in various areas of Greece. The European Court of Human Rights communicated to the authorities two applications concerning the continuing educational segregation of Romani children in schools in Aspropyrgos and Sofades, in March and October respectively. In 2008, the Court had already found that Greece had excluded and then segregated Romani children in the Aspropyrgos school. In September, the Council of Europe Committee of Ministers decided to close their examination of the execution of the case.

G

Conscientious objectors

The repeated prosecution of conscientious objectors continued.

In February, a ministerial decision set the length of alternative service at 15 months. However, the length remained effectively punitive for the vast majority of conscripts.

■ In March, the Review Military Court of Athens rejected the appeal of religious conscientious objector Nikolaos Xiarhos against the decision of the Judicial Council of the Pireus Naval Court, which referred him to trial for a second desertion charge. Nikolaos Xiarhos was a professional soldier who became a conscientious objector after his baptism as a Jehovah's Witness.

Human rights defenders

There were concerns about the criminal prosecution and trial in January of human rights defenders on charges of false accusations and aggravated defamation against Kostantinos Plevris, the author of the book *Jews – The Whole Truth*. The trial was postponed until 2012.

Amnesty International visits/reports

🚌 Amnesty International delegates visited Greece in May.

📄 The European Court of Human Rights vindicates the rights of asylum-seekers in the EU (EUR 03/001/2011)

📄 Greece: Briefing on the draft law on asylum, migration-related detention and returns of third country nationals (EUR 25/002/2011)

📄 Greece must urgently remedy deplorable detention conditions (EUR 25/006/2011)

📄 Greece: Alleged abuses in the policing of the demonstration of 11 May 2011 (EUR 25/008/2011)

📄 Greece: Briefing to the UN Committee against Torture (EUR 25/011/2011)

GUATEMALA

REPUBLIC OF GUATEMALA

Head of state and government:	Álvaro Colom Caballeros
Death penalty:	retentionist
Population:	14.8 million
Life expectancy:	71.2 years
Under-5 mortality:	39.8 per 1,000
Adult literacy:	74.5 per cent

Violations of the rights of Indigenous Peoples persisted. Some successful prosecutions were brought for human rights violations committed during the period of internal armed conflict (1960-1996). Human rights defenders were threatened, intimidated and attacked.

Background

Presidential, congressional and local government elections were held in September. Retired General Otto Pérez Molina was declared the winner in the run-off presidential election in November and was due to take office in January 2012.

High levels of violent crime, gang violence and drug-related violence persisted. The authorities recorded 5,681 homicides during the year. Conflict between drug-trafficking organizations often gave rise to torture and killings. In May, at a farm in El Naranjo, Petén Department, armed men killed and decapitated 27 labourers. The violence was attributed to a dispute between drug traffickers and the farm owner.

It was widely reported that street gangs, known as *maras*, were involved in extortion and violent crime in communities living in poverty. Efforts by the police to stem the violence were widely viewed as ineffective.

At the end of the year, 13 prisoners remained on death row. No executions had taken place since 2000 and President Colom had vetoed a number of bills proposing that executions resume. However, President-elect Molina announced he would resume executions on taking office.

Indigenous Peoples' rights

Indigenous Peoples' rights continued to be violated in the context of land disputes and development projects which were undertaken without consultation and the free, prior and informed consent of affected communities. In March, the UN Special Rapporteur on indigenous people noted the high level of instability and social conflict connected with the activities of mining companies on Indigenous lands. He called on the authorities to recognize Indigenous Peoples' territorial rights and ensure their participation in decision-making processes.

■ In March, around 2,500 Indigenous people from the Valle del Polochic, Alta Verapaz Department, were evicted in the context of a dispute over land ownership with a local company. One member of the community. Antonio Beb Ac, was killed and two were injured during the eviction. In the following months, two community members were killed and six injured. In August the state refused to fully implement the IACHR's request that it provide protection and humanitarian aid to the communities. At the end of the year, the communities still had limited access to adequate shelter, clean water, food or health care.

Impunity for past human rights violations

There was progress in some prosecutions for human rights violations committed during the internal armed conflict. The army declassified a number of documents in July. However, documents relating to the period 1980 to 1985, the years which saw the vast majority of human rights violations, were not made available.

■ In August, four former members of an elite army unit were sentenced to lengthy prison terms for their role in the 1982 Dos Erres massacre of 250 men, women and children; many of the women and girls were raped.

■ In October, the Constitutional Court ordered the Supreme Court to clarify its ruling that a civilian court should try those suspected of the 1992 enforced disappearance and torture of Efraín Bámaca Velásquez. They had already been tried and acquitted in a secret military trial in 1994.

■ Former generals Héctor López Fuentes, Oscar Mejía Victores and José Mauricio Rodríguez Sánchez were charged with planning and overseeing genocide, organized sexual violence and the forced transfers of populations between 1982 and 1983. The three were awaiting trial at the end of the year.

Women's rights

According to the authorities, 631women were the victims of homicide during the year. The 2008 Law against Femicide and Other Forms of Violence against Women which, among other things, introduced

special courts for violence against women, seemed to have had little impact on either reducing violence against women or holding those responsible to account.

Human rights defenders

Those defending human rights, including journalists and trade unionists, continued to be threatened, harassed and attacked. Local organizations documented 402 such incidents.

■ In February, Catalina Mucú Maas, Alberto Coc Cal and Sebastian Xuc Coc of the Indigenous community of Quebrada Seca, Izabal Department, were killed. All three had been actively involved in negotiations related to land disputes. Several other members of the community received death threats. By the end of the year, nobody had been held to account for the killings or the threats.

■ In August, four staff members of the Guatemalan Forensic Anthropology Foundation received death threats after four former members of the army were convicted of the Dos Erres massacre.

■ Trade unionist, Byron Arreaga, who had campaigned against corruption, was shot dead in Quetzaltenango Department in September.

Amnesty International reports/visits

🚌 Amnesty International delegates visited Guatemala in November/December.

G

GUINEA

REPUBLIC OF GUINEA

Head of state:	Alpha Condé
Head of government:	Mohamed Saïd Fofana
Death penalty:	retentionist
Population:	10.2 million
Life expectancy:	54.1 years
Under-5 mortality:	141.5 per 1,000
Adult literacy:	39.5 per cent

President Condé's residence was attacked in July. The police and gendarmerie used excessive force; at least three people were killed. Arbitrary arrests as well as torture and other abuses by security forces continued in a climate of impunity. Freedom of expression remained under threat. Sixteen people were sentenced to death. The National Commission for Human Rights was created.

Background

Ahead of parliamentary elections initially scheduled for late 2011, fears of potential instability grew after two gunfire and rocket attacks were mounted in July on President Condé's residence in the capital, Conakry. Army officers as well as civilians were arrested and accused of organizing the attacks. President Condé also blamed Senegal, Gambia and opposition leaders during an interview with a Senegalese radio station. Both countries denied these allegations, and political opponents criticized the President's stance. The independence and impartiality of the National Independent Electoral Commission were questioned after it proposed election dates without consulting the political opposition. No dates were confirmed by the end of the year.

In February, the UN High Commissioner for Human Rights published a report on Guinea. Among the concerns highlighted were human rights violations committed with impunity over decades by security and armed forces, and sexual and gender-based violence sometimes linked to traditional practices. The report recommended that Guinea implement the recommendations of the UN Universal Periodic Review of 2010, including developing close co-operation with the treaty bodies and special procedures of the UN Human Rights Council, and allowing it to visit at regular intervals. In a subsequent resolution adopted at its 16th session (A/HRC/RES/16/36), the Council supported the conclusions of the UN High Commissioner for Human Rights. The Council reiterated the need for Guinea to pursue efforts to implement the recommendations of the UN Commission of Inquiry, including taking measures to combat impunity.

In March, President Condé created by decree the National Commission for Human Rights. In July, the National Transitional Council adopted a new law relating to the organization and function of the Independent National Institution of Human Rights.

Excessive use of force

The misuse of lethal force by the police and other law enforcement officials continued. In September, live rounds, tear gas and batons were used against protesters on their way to an unauthorized demonstration against the organization of elections. At least three people were killed, including Amadou Boye Barry. In a public statement, the Minister of Communications responded to Amnesty International, stating that two people had died and a judicial inquiry had begun.

Possible prisoners of conscience

Arbitrary arrests and detention by police and army of possible prisoners of conscience were reported. Most were carried out with excessive force.

In April, supporters of the Union of Democratic Forces in Guinea (UFDG), were dispersed by security forces using excessive force at Conakry airport where they were greeting UFDG leader Cellou Dalein Diallo. At least 25 people were injured. Others were arrested, including Alpha Abdoulaye Sow and Abdoulaye Diallo, soldiers in charge of the opposition leader's security. They were sentenced to prison terms for "participating in a prohibited demonstration, acts of vandalism and violence" but were pardoned in August.

In September, more than 300 people opposing the way elections were organized were arrested for participating in a banned demonstration. Some were later released. Over 50 were sentenced to between one month and one year's imprisonment and a further 95 were given suspended prison sentences.

Torture and other ill-treatment

Soldiers and police officers continued to torture and ill-treat detainees and others with impunity.

In February, a man arrested in Mamou for setting up roadblocks was taken to the police station. He was handcuffed to a window with his feet barely touching the ground and left for more than eight hours. He was beaten while handcuffed and suspended in a squatting position with a piece of wood between his knees and elbows.

In April, a supporter of the UFDG was arrested and beaten on the way to the airport at Dixinn by armed forces. He was blindfolded and threatened at a police station in Conakry.

Freedom of expression – journalists

Daniel Loua and Théodore Lamah, journalists from Radio Liberté de Nzérékoré, were arrested in January and accused of "inciting violence and disturbing the peace" after referring to the possible return of former President Camara during a radio broadcast. They were released the following day.

In May, following a story in the newspaper L'indépendant-Le Démocrate concerning salary increases among the armed forces, soldiers attempted to arrest the publisher, Mamadou Dian Diallo, and other journalists. They left the newspaper's offices after mediation by two human rights organizations.

In July, the National Communication Council banned all local and foreign media from reporting the attack on President Condé's residence. The ban was lifted three days later.

Impunity

Impunity and lack of discipline within the armed forces continued to be of concern.

Families of more than 150 people who were killed, and over 40 women who were publicly raped, when security forces attacked a peaceful opposition rally in September 2009 against former President Camara's military junta, were still awaiting justice. A UN Commission of Inquiry stated that it was reasonable to consider the events as crimes against humanity. Despite the opening of a judicial inquiry in 2010, the perpetrators of the massacre had not been suspended from duty and none had been brought to trial by the end of the year.

Death penalty

Sixteen people were sentenced to death in September, eight in their absence, by a court in Kankan. They had been convicted of "premeditated murder, violent killings, criminal conspiracy and destruction of property" following confrontations between two ethnic groups in which at least 25 people were killed.

The sentences contradicted a statement by President Condé in July during a meeting with foreign diplomats that the death penalty did not exist in Guinea. He said that sentencing people to death was never acceptable, even for those making an attempt on the President's life, as this would not bring him back to life.

GUINEA-BISSAU

REPUBLIC OF GUINEA-BISSAU

Head of state:	Malam Bacai Sanhá
Head of government:	Carlos Gomes Júnior
Death penalty:	abolitionist for all crimes
Population:	1.5 million
Life expectancy:	48.1 years
Under-5 mortality:	192.6 per 1,000
Adult literacy:	52.2 per cent

Tension within the military remained a potential source of instability. There were reports of an attempted coup in late December. With no progress in the investigation into the killings of political and military figures in 2009, thousands of people took to the streets to demand an end to impunity. Freedom of expression came under threat as a newspaper was ordered to close after implicating a military official in the killing of the country's former President. A law prohibiting female genital mutilation (FGM) was passed in July, and in October a case was filed against two practitioners.

Background

Magistrates and other justice officials went on strike several times throughout the year to demand better salaries and working conditions.

In February, the EU partially suspended development aid. It also threatened to freeze assets and impose visa bans on several military officers and other officials suspected of involvement in drug trafficking and of threatening peace, security and stability. The EU repeated its demand for an investigation into the political killings that took place in 2009.

In March, 600 Angolan police and military officers were deployed as part of the Angolan Military Mission to Guinea-Bissau (MISSANG) to assist with training and reforming the country's security sector. The Angolan government had agreed to provide funds and training for reforming the military and police after the EU ended its Security Sector Reform Mission in September 2010.

In June, the National Assembly approved several new laws, including one banning FGM and another aimed at preventing and penalizing people-trafficking. Both were promulgated in July and came into force with immediate effect.

In July, thousands of people took part in demonstrations organized by 10 opposition political parties in the capital, Bissau, to protest against the lack of progress in investigating the 2009 political killings. They also demanded the resignation and prosecution of the Prime Minister, and others whom they accused of being responsible for the killings.

In August, the newly appointed Procurator General pledged to fight corruption, organized crime and impunity.

In late December, the Chief of Staff of the Armed Forces announced that an attempted coup had been foiled involving soldiers and civilians, including a former minister and a parliamentarian. Other reports suggested a military revolt caused by disagreements between the Chiefs of Staff of the Armed Forces and the Navy. Around 50 people, mostly soldiers, were reportedly arrested. About 10 were quickly released without charge. At least 25 people remained in prison.

Extrajudicial executions

On 27 December, the Rapid Response Police extrajudicially executed Iaia Dabó as he prepared to hand himself over to the Judiciary Police. He was suspected of involvement in an alleged coup attempt the previous day. No arrests had been made in connection with his killing by the year's end. Iaia Dabó was the brother of a politician killed by soldiers in June 2009 following accusations of involvement in another alleged coup.

Impunity

No one had been brought to justice for the killings of politicians and high-ranking military officers in 2009 and before.

In March, the former Procurator General announced that investigations into the killings of President João Bernardo Vieira and the Chief of Staff of the Armed Forces, General Tagme Na Waie, had reached a dead end because of difficulties in gathering evidence.

In May, he also announced that there was no evidence of an attempted coup in June 2009 and provisionally closed the investigation. He submitted the case of two politicians killed in the alleged coup to the Military High Court, which he said had jurisdiction over it. The Military High Court refuted this and the case was passed to the Supreme Court. No decision had been made by the end of the year on who should deal with the case.

Violence against women and girls
Female genital mutilation

In July, a new law was passed which forbids FGM and penalizes practitioners with prison terms of between one and five years. In October, two practitioners and another woman were arrested in the eastern town of Bafatá after being accused of subjecting four girls to FGM in September. The four girls, who are related and between two and five years old, were taken by their grandmother to be excised. She was among those arrested in October. After a few days in detention, the three women were conditionally released pending further investigation, and had to report daily to the local Prosecutor's office. The case had not been brought to court by the end of the year.

Freedom of expression – newspapers

In April, the government ordered the weekly newspaper *Última Hora* to close after it published an article quoting excerpts from an official, as yet unpublished report which apparently implicated the navy's then Chief of Staff in the killing of President Vieira. Following widespread condemnation by civil society groups, the government denied it had ordered the newspaper to close. However, it warned all newspapers to be prudent with their reporting or else they would lose their licences.

Amnesty International visits/reports
🚗 An Amnesty International delegation visited Guinea-Bissau in March.

GUYANA

REPUBLIC OF GUYANA
Head of state and government: **Donald Ramotar (replaced Bharrat Jagdeo in December)**
Death penalty: **retentionist**
Population: **0.8 million**
Life expectancy: **69.9 years**
Under-5 mortality: **35.3 per 1,000**

State response to violence against women remained inadequate. At least three people were sentenced to death; no executions were carried out.

Background

The People's Progressive Party won its fifth successive election in December, although it lost its parliamentary majority. A coalition of opposition parties claimed that irregularities had occurred during the elections. An investigation was ongoing at the end of the year into the police's firing on an opposition demonstration on 6 December which left several people injured.

Police and security forces

There were reports of ill-treatment of detainees in police stations and allegations that the practice of holding people without charge beyond the stipulated 72-hour time period was widespread.

Torture and other ill-treatment

In June, Guyana's High Court awarded damages against two police officers accused of torturing a 14-year-old boy in Leonora police station in October 2009, as well as against the Commissioner of Police and the Attorney General. The Court found that the boy had suffered "torture and cruel and inhuman treatment". An appeal by the state was pending at the end of the year and the accused officers remained on active duty.

Violence against women and girls

Implementation of the Sexual Offences Act, passed in April 2010, remained slow. The Act created a National Task Force for the Prevention of Sexual Violence. This was required to meet at least every three months, but by the end of 2011 it had only met once. The Task Force is charged with developing and implementing a National Plan for the Prevention of Sexual Offences. Women's rights organizations deemed the general response from the police and the courts to complaints of domestic and sexual violence to be unsatisfactory.

Rights of lesbian, gay, bisexual and transgender people

There were reports of police harassment of transgender sex workers, including through the use of arbitrary detention. A constitutional motion seeking to repeal an article from the Summary Jurisdiction (Offences) Act, which criminalizes cross-dressing and is often used by police to harass sex workers, was pending before the High Court at the end of the year. The motion was brought by four people who were charged and fined under the legislation in February 2009 and seeks its repeal on the grounds that it is discriminatory and unconstitutional.

Right to health – HIV/AIDS

Stigma and discrimination surrounding HIV/AIDS and the criminalization of sex between men continued to be a barrier to accessing HIV-related information, testing and treatment. Following consultation with civil society, a motion to criminalize wilful HIV transmission was rejected by a parliamentary select committee in September, on the grounds that it might discourage individuals from seeking tests and increase stigma and discrimination against people living with HIV/AIDS.

Death penalty

At least three people were sentenced to death and 34 people remained on death row at the end of the year. Guyana's last execution took place in 1997. At the end of the year constitutional motions were pending before the High Court to overturn the death sentences of two prisoners on the grounds that the length of time they had spent on death row – 23 and 16 years – constituted cruel, inhuman and degrading treatment. Both men remained on death row at the end of the year.

G

HAITI

REPUBLIC OF HAITI

Head of state:	**Michel Joseph Martelly**
	(replaced René García Préval in May)
Head of government:	**Garry Conille**
	(replaced Jean-Max Bellerive in October)
Death penalty:	**abolitionist for all crimes**
Population:	**10.1 million**
Life expectancy:	**62.1 years**
Under-5 mortality:	**86.7 per 1,000**
Adult literacy:	**48.7 per cent**

The number of people displaced by the January 2010 earthquake who were living in makeshift camps declined from 1.3 million to 500,000 by the end of 2011. Violence against women and girls in the camps was rife. Poor sanitary conditions and limited access to water contributed to the spread and renewed outbreaks of cholera. Haiti's justice system faced the challenge of ending impunity for grave human rights abuses and crimes against humanity committed under the government of Jean-Claude Duvalier (1971-1986).

Background

Jean-Claude Duvalier returned to Haiti in January after nearly 25 years in exile in France. The judicial authorities immediately relaunched a criminal investigation into embezzlement and theft of public funds, and an investigation into crimes against humanity started after victims filed complaints. In March, former President Jean-Bertrand Aristide, who was ousted in 2004, returned to Haiti after seven years in exile in South Africa.

Michel Martelly was elected President in March in a run-off election against Mirlande Manigat. The first round of elections in November 2010 had resulted in a stand-off between most of the presidential candidates and the electoral board which was accused of manipulating the ballot in favour of the official candidate, Jude Célestin. Criticisms were also voiced by international and national election observers.

Michel Martelly was sworn in on 14 May, but failed to form a government until October when the National Assembly accepted the nomination of Garry Conille as Prime Minister.

The mandate of the UN Stabilization Mission in Haiti (MINUSTAH) was renewed until October 2012, with a reduction of military and police personnel.

The serious cholera epidemic that began in October 2010 continued. There were renewed outbreaks in late 2011. More than 523,904 cases and 7,018 deaths had been reported by the end of 2011. The introduction of the South Asian cholera strain was widely attributed to Nepalese UN peacekeepers based in the upper Artibonite River region, the origin of the epidemic. In May, an independent panel of international experts mandated by the UN Secretary-General to determine the source of the outbreak concluded that the large-scale epidemic was caused by a combination of factors: the contamination of the Artibonite River with faeces, and deficiencies in the water, sanitation and health care systems. In November, the US-based Institute for Justice and Democracy in Haiti and its partner in Haiti, the Bureau des Avocats Internationaux, filed a petition with the Chief of the Claims Unit of MINUSTAH – in accordance with the procedures set out in the Status of Forces Agreement (SOFA) – against the UN seeking reparation for more than 5,000 victims for the negligent introduction of cholera.

Food insecurity affected nearly half the population; 800,000 people lacked regular access to staple foods. In October, Haiti's human rights record was assessed under the UN Universal Periodic Review for the first time.

Internally displaced people

The number of internally displaced people decreased throughout 2011 from 1.3 million in January to just over 500,000 in December. However, more than 900 makeshift camps were still registered in areas affected by the earthquake. Reconstruction of temporary and semi-permanent shelter gathered pace but remained insufficient to meet demand. Access to water and sanitation continued to deteriorate in camps, leading to high rates of cholera. Displaced people living in camps in the metropolitan area of Port-au-Prince had higher rates of food insecurity than the rest of the population.

Forced evictions

Local authorities and landowners forcibly evicted thousands of displaced families from public and private land without due process.

H

■ In June, police officers and local officials from the Port-au-Prince town hall forcibly evicted 514 families from the car park at Sylvio Cator stadium without due process. Only 110 families were offered relocation to another site, but this lacked adequate sanitation. In March 2010, the same families were forcibly removed from the football pitch and relocated to the car park.

Violence against women and girls

Sexual violence in the camps for internally displaced people and in marginalized communities was widespread; many of those affected were young girls. The vast majority of those responsible for these crimes were not brought to justice. Access to health care and other services for survivors of gender-based and sexual violence remained limited in the metropolitan area of Port-au-Prince and was virtually non-existent in rural areas.

Survivors of sexual violence faced multiple obstacles in getting access to justice. The police and the judicial authorities lacked the resources to investigate and prosecute perpetrators. Although an increasing number of survivors of sexual and gender-based violence did speak out, the majority remained silent because of the social stigma attached to these crimes and for fear of reprisals from their attackers.

The Minister for Women's Affairs and Women's Rights worked on a draft bill on preventing, punishing and ending violence against women. This proposed, among other things, the creation of special courts throughout the country to deal with cases of violence against women, and stronger sanctions for all forms of gender-based violence. As part of a three-year strategic plan to combat violence against women, the government created a gender and women's affairs co-ordination unit within the Haitian National Police.

Impunity – crimes under international law

Former President Jean-Claude Duvalier was under investigation for crimes against humanity and economic crimes. The investigation into crimes against humanity committed under his government progressed slowly. The investigating judge submitted his findings to the Office of the Prosecutor of Port-au-Prince in July. However, by the end of the year, a decision from the Prosecutor's Office on next steps remained pending. Supporters of Jean-Claude Duvalier repeatedly subjected victims of human rights abuses and judicial officials to verbal abuse. Witness

support and protection measures were non-existent and remained a major obstacle for victims and their families seeking justice.

Justice system

Haiti's dysfunctional justice system continued to be a source of human rights violations with thousands of people facing prolonged pre-trial detention. According to Haiti's National Human Rights Defence Network, less than 30 per cent of prisoners had been tried and convicted.

Minors were also imprisoned while awaiting trial, some for years. By the end of the year, only 23 per cent of boys and none of the 18 girls in detention had been brought to trial.

Poor infrastructure and lack of human and financial resources within the justice system resulted in a large backlog of cases and severely overcrowded prisons. More than 275 inmates died in the cholera epidemic.

■ Joseph, then aged 12, was arrested in April 2006 for rape. In October 2011, he was still in prison awaiting trial. He was first brought before an investigating judge in November 2008 and had been held in a detention facility for minors since then.

Trial of police officers for the extrajudicial execution of prisoners

Thirteen police officers and 21 men, including prison guards, were brought to trial for their involvement in the killing of at least 12 inmates in the civil prison in the city of Les Cayes in January 2010 during a prison uprising. A decision was pending at the end of the year.

Amnesty International visits/reports

🚗 Amnesty International delegates visited Haiti in January, June, September and December 2011.

▨ Aftershocks: Women speak out against sexual violence in Haiti's camps (AMR 36/001/2011)

▨ Haiti: "You cannot kill the truth" – the case against Jean-Claude Duvalier (AMR 36/007/2011)

HONDURAS

REPUBLIC OF HONDURA

Head of state and government:	**Porfirio Lobo Sosa**
Death penalty:	**abolitionist for all crimes**
Population:	**7.8 million**
Life expectancy:	**73.1 years**
Under-5 mortality:	**29.7 per 1,000**
Adult literacy:	**83.6 per cent**

Several people were killed in ongoing land disputes in the Aguan region. Forced evictions left hundreds of *campesino* (peasant farmer) families homeless. Impunity persisted for human rights violations by the military and police, including those committed during the 2009 coup d'état. Human rights defenders continued to be subjected to intimidation.

Background

In January, the Inter-American Commission on Human Rights stated it was "deeply concerned about threats, serious acts of violence against and killings of members of the transgender community".

In November, 28 Honduran mothers, whose children had gone missing in Mexico while travelling to the USA, went to Mexico to urge the authorities to establish an official search mechanism to help trace their loved ones and to enhance the protection of the tens of thousands of Central American migrants who travel through Mexico each year (see Mexico entry).

Impunity – consequences of the coup d'état

In April, the government established a Truth and Reconciliation Commission to analyse the events leading up to and during the coup d'état. In its report issued in July, the Commission acknowledged that the events of 2009 did constitute a coup d'état and that multiple human rights violations occurred, including acts of excessive use of force by the military and police. By the end of the year, no one had been brought to justice or held to account for these human rights violations.

In June, Honduras was readmitted to the OAS; it had been expelled following the 2009 coup d'état.

Members of the judiciary who were dismissed in unfair proceedings under the de facto government had not been returned to their posts by the end of the year.

Human rights defenders

Human rights defenders were threatened and harassed as they carried out their work.

■ In January and June, Alex David Sánchez Álvarez was threatened and physically attacked by unidentified individuals in connection with his work for the Colectivo Violeta, which works for the protection of the rights of members of the LGBT community, and his work with the Centre for the Prevention, Treatment and Rehabilitation of Torture Victims and their Families. Both incidents were reported to the Public Prosecutor's Office, but those responsible had not been brought to justice by the end of the year.

■ By the end of 2011, no one had been brought to justice for the killing in 2009 of LGBT human rights activist Walter Trochez.

Sexual and reproductive rights

A decree concerning contraception that had been issued in 2009 by the de facto authorities remained in place. This criminalized the use of emergency contraception by women and girls whose contraceptive method had failed or who were at risk of pregnancy resulting from sexual coercion.

Land disputes and forced evictions

Military personnel and large numbers of police were deployed in the Aguan region, where disputes over land ownership between hundreds of *campesinos* and various companies and private landowners erupted into violence.

Also in this context, forced evictions occurred throughout the year in the Aguan region, and little effort was made to resolve the problem. Agreements drawn up between the government and *campesino* organizations were not implemented, leaving thousands of *campesino* families homeless or at constant risk of eviction.

■ In June, police forcibly evicted a community in the town of Rigores, in Colón department. The eviction order was issued in May, but the community was not informed or given any prior warning of the eviction. Families, some of whom had lived on the land for many years, were given just two hours to pack up their belongings and leave their homes. During the eviction, houses belonging to community members, as well as seven classrooms that formed part of the local school and kindergarten, and two churches were destroyed. Some 493 people were made homeless. Nobody was offered alternative housing, resettlement or access to productive land, either in advance of the eviction or after it had happened. Nor was anyone guaranteed safe access to tend their crops, many of which were destroyed during the eviction.

Abuses by police

There were further allegations of human rights abuses by police.

■ In October, two university students were found shot dead in Tegucigalpa, the capital. Four police officers were charged with the killings, which they had reportedly carried out while on duty patrolling the city. Reports indicated that up to eight police officers may have been involved. Following public outrage at the killings of the two students, the government established a cross-party committee of members of Congress and representatives from the Executive to review public security policies.

HUNGARY

REPUBLIC OF HUNGARY

Head of state:	**Pál Schmitt**
Head of government:	**Viktor Orbán**
Death penalty:	**abolitionist for all crimes**
Population:	**10 million**
Life expectancy:	**74.4 years**
Under-5 mortality:	**6.3 per 1,000**
Adult literacy:	**99.4 per cent**

The new Constitution raised concerns over human rights protection. The trial began of those accused of the attacks against Roma committed in 2008 and 2009. Roma were intimidated by vigilante groups. The Ministry of Interior made a commitment to strengthen legislation on hate crimes.

Background

In April, Parliament adopted a new Constitution. It introduced changes that may in practice restrict human rights, including protecting the life of the foetus from conception and the possibility of life imprisonment without parole. It also omitted age, sexual orientation and gender identity from the list of prohibited grounds for discrimination.

In September, the UN Human Rights Council recommended that the government strengthen hate crimes legislation and establish a plan of action to prevent racist attacks.

Racism

In March, the trial began at the Pest County Court of the suspects in the series of attacks against Roma in 2008 and 2009 during which six people, including a child, were killed. Three men were accused of the crimes of multiple homicide and armed attack against Roma houses. One further suspect faced charges of being an accomplice to these crimes.

Discrimination – Roma

Discrimination against Roma remained entrenched in many areas of life. Roma inhabitants of Gyöngyöspata suffered intimidation from several vigilante groups between March and April. The police did little to stop the abuse.

■ Following an anti-Roma march by the far-right Jobbik party in Gyöngyöspata on 6 March, three vigilante groups continued to "patrol" the area. On 18 March, the Prime Minister instructed the Interior Minister to take measures to stop the activity of paramilitary organizations. In June, Parliament set up a committee to investigate the events. The investigation focused on who had "discredited Hungary" by spreading false information. Human rights NGOs who had monitored the situation were requested to testify to the committee. They expressed concerns that the committee's mandate did not ensure a thorough investigation into the events.

■ The Hungarian Civil Liberties Union (HCLU) submitted complaints to the Prosecutor in relation to four cases of verbal abuse and the attempt of physical violence against Roma in Gyöngyöspata. The HCLU alleged that in all four cases the police failed to investigate in accordance with international human rights standards. The police allegedly failed to classify the acts as violence against a member of a community, a criminal charge under which racially motivated violence can be prosecuted. They also failed to inform both victims about the relegation of these crimes to minor offences and of the stages of investigation. The Prosecutor ordered the police to reopen investigations in those cases.

H

Justice system

In January, the Ministry of Interior started to develop a protocol for police work on hate crimes. Parliament amended the Criminal Code in May, and outlawed blatantly abusive behaviour against a community that might threaten members – real or perceived – of an ethnic, racial or other group. The amendment also criminalized unauthorized activities to maintain public order or public security, which induced fear in others.

In November, Parliament adopted a new law on the Constitutional Court, which introduced restrictions to individual petitions, as well as a penalty for those complainants who abuse the right to submit a petition.

Housing rights

Budapest City Council adopted a decree in April that made sleeping on the street an offence punishable by a fine. As a result, a number of homeless people were reportedly arrested in October. The government proposed further amendments to the Criminal Code, which would allow imprisonment of those found guilty of rough sleeping who could not afford to pay the fine. The European Federation of National Organisations Working with the Homeless described the proposal as disproportionate and said that it constituted a denial of state responsibility for structural problems leading to homelessness.

Freedom of expression

Two new media laws entered into force in January. They included content regulation and compulsory media registration, and introduced a Media Authority with powers over the registration of media. In February, the Council of Europe Commissioner for Human Rights recommended the media laws should be reviewed. Although Parliament amended the legislation in April, the UN Special Rapporteur on freedom of expression warned that it "still risks generating a climate of self-censorship". The OSCE and human rights NGOs expressed concerns over the lack of independence of the Media Authority from government, as well as its broad powers.

Freedom of religion or belief

On 12 July, a new law sparked protests from several churches, NGOs and the Council of Europe's Commissioner for Human Rights. The legislation "de-registered" numerous religious groups – including several Islamic groups and the Hungarian Methodist Church. A religious group could apply for registration only if it could prove that it had been organized in Hungary for at least 20 years and had at least 1,000 members. Several religious groups submitted a petition to the Constitutional Court to review the law. On 19 December, the Court found that the law was unconstitutional on procedural grounds. On 30 December, Parliament adopted the law again with only minor changes.

Rights of lesbian, gay, bisexual and transgender people

In February, Budapest Metropolitan Court overturned a police decision to ban the route of the Pride march in Budapest, which the police claimed would disrupt the traffic. The court did not agree that this justified a ban. The Pride march was adequately protected, but NGOs reported several cases of incitement to hatred against lesbians, gay men, bisexual and transgender people and an attack against two marchers.

Police and security forces

In March, Parliament annulled court decisions on the anti-government protests in Budapest in September and October 2006. In 2006, the courts had sentenced several demonstrators for violence and acquitted police officers involved in the incidents. The courts' decisions were alleged to be biased as they were based exclusively on police testimony. In 2006, police officers reportedly used excessive force on peaceful demonstrations that later turned violent. Rubber bullets, water cannon and tear gas were said to have been used indiscriminately and without warning.
■ In June, the European Court of Human Rights held that the police had used inhuman and degrading treatment. The court awarded more than €10,000 to the applicant represented by the Hungarian Helsinki Committee, who was ill-treated by the police while in custody.

Amnesty International visits/reports

 Freedom of expression under fire: Briefing to the Hungarian government on the new media legislation (EUR 27/004/2011)

 Hungary: Newly adopted Constitution at odds with human rights (EUR 27/006/2011)

 Amnesty International welcomes Hungary's commitment to combat discrimination and urges full and effective investigation and prosecution of racially motivated crimes (EUR 27/007/2011)

H

INDIA

REPUBLIC OF INDIA

Head of state:	Pratibha Patil
Head of government:	Manmohan Singh
Death penalty:	retentionist
Population:	1,241.5 million
Life expectancy:	65.4 years
Under-5 mortality:	65.6 per 1,000
Adult literacy:	62.8 per cent

The government maintained its focus on economic growth, at times at the cost of protecting and promoting human rights within the country and abroad. Around 250 people were killed in ongoing clashes between armed Maoists and security forces in several central and eastern states. At least 40 people were killed in bomb attacks in Mumbai and Delhi. Anna Hazare's campaign for comprehensive laws against corruption scored initial successes; however, Parliament failed to enact the proposed legislation. Adivasi (Indigenous) communities intensified their protests against corporate-led moves to acquire and mine their lands without free, prior and informed consent, resulting in suspension of some industrial projects. Authorities introduced new legal frameworks to reform land acquisition, rehabilitation and mining. Human rights defenders faced the ire of both state and non-state agencies, with sedition and other politically motivated charges levelled against some. Many were threatened, harassed and intimidated, and at least four activists were killed.

Authorities extended a standing invitation to all UN Special Procedures to visit the country. However, torture and other ill-treatment, extrajudicial executions, deaths in custody and administrative detentions remained rife in a number of states. New legal initiatives to outlaw torture had yet to yield results. Institutional mechanisms meant to protect human rights remained weak, and judicial processes were slow in ensuring justice for victims of past violations including extrajudicial executions and mass killings. This was despite new legislation introduced to ensure justice and reparations for victims of past communal violence. Past violations and abuses continued to remain outside the purview of ongoing peace initiatives on Nagaland and Assam. Courts sentenced at least 110 people to death, but, for the seventh successive year, no executions took place.

Background

Rapid economic growth in key urban sectors slowed down, in part as a result of the global downturn and rising inflation. The recent growth left large parts of rural India relatively untouched, with communities living in endemic poverty aggravated by a stagnant agricultural sector and problems of food security. According to official estimates, India's poor accounted for between 30 and 50 per cent of the country's population. At least 15 per cent of the population were leading a precarious existence in urban slums without proper access to health care, water, food and education.

India's election to the UN Security Council and the UN Human Rights Council underscored its growing international and regional status. The country took positive steps to co-operate with UN Special Procedures. In January, the UN Special Rapporteur on the situation of human rights defenders visited India on official invitation. In September, in an unprecedented move, the authorities issued a standing invitation to all thematic UN Special Procedures.

Authorities were reluctant to speak out on human rights crises in the region and elsewhere. India was silent on violations committed during the dramatic changes in the Middle East and North Africa, as well as on those committed by neighbouring Myanmar. It failed to support demands for Sri Lanka to be held accountable for the violations committed at the end of that country's war in 2009.

Violence between security forces, militia and Maoists

In Chhattisgarh state, clashes continued between armed Maoists and security forces supported by the state-sponsored Salwa Judum militia. Both sides routinely targeted civilians, mainly Adivasis, and engaged in killings, abductions and arson. In Chhattisgarh alone, more than 3,000 people, including combatants, had been killed in the clashes since 2005. Around 25,000 people remained displaced; about 5,000 were living in camps and 20,000 were dispersed in neighbouring Andhra Pradesh and Orissa.

Similar clashes between Maoists and state forces took place in Adivasi areas of Orissa, Jharkhand and West Bengal. The suspension of anti-Maoist operations in West Bengal since May was marred by political violence and arrests; peace initiatives collapsed in November after the death of Maoist leader Koteshwar "Kishenji" Rao, who was allegedly extrajudicially executed.

In July, India's Supreme Court issued a landmark judgement to disband all Chhattisgarh state-sponsored anti-Maoist militias alleged to have committed serious human rights violations. The state authorities responded by disbanding and incorporating them into a 6,000-strong auxiliary force, ignoring allegations of their involvement in such violations.

■ In January, the Orissa police and security forces claimed to have shot dead 25 Maoist suspects in six separate combat operations, but human rights activists uncovered evidence suggesting that two of the victims were anti-mining campaigners, and the others were unarmed Maoist sympathizers detained during search operations and extrajudicially executed.

■ In February, the Maoists held two district officials hostage for nine days in Malkangiri, Orissa, and exchanged them for five jailed Maoist leaders who were released on bail by the authorities.

■ In March, more than 300 police and Salwa Judum personnel involved in anti-Maoist operations attacked Morpalli, Timmapuram and Tadmetla villages in Chhattisgarh state, killing three villagers, sexually assaulting three women and burning down 295 houses. The Maoists retaliated by killing four special police officers and injuring five others. Adivasi activist Lingaram, who brought the violations to light, and another activist, Soni Sori, were arrested in October on several charges, including transferring funds from Essar Steel, a corporate firm, to the armed Maoists. Soni Sori was tortured in police custody. Both were prisoners of conscience.

■ In March, Maoists in Jharkhand state killed Niyamat Ansari and threatened his associate Bhukan Singh after they exposed corruption involving Maoists, local contractors and forest officials. In July, Maoists also issued a threat – later withdrawn – to four well-known activists, including Jean Dreze and Aruna Roy, after they criticized the Maoists for the murder.

■ In September, armed Maoists shot dead Jagabandhu Majhi, a legislator belonging to the ruling Biju Janata Dal, and his security officer in Nabrangpur district, Orissa. They justified the killing, saying that the legislator was indulging in corruption and extortion.

■ In October, security forces engaged in anti-Maoist operations sexually assaulted 29-year-old Shibani Singh of West Midnapore district, West Bengal, while attempting to rearrest her husband who was out on bail.

Corporate accountability

In several states, protests by Adivasi and other marginalized communities blocked ongoing and proposed extractive, irrigation and other corporate projects affecting their rights over their traditional lands. In response, the authorities proposed to reform outdated legal frameworks and ad hoc practices for land acquisition and mining, offering monitored rehabilitation and benefit-sharing arrangements to the communities. Nevertheless, the protests continued, with the communities complaining that recent legislation guaranteeing their rights over forest lands was not being properly implemented, and alleging that the new laws did not address the issue of their free, prior and informed consent for the projects.

■ In June, July and November, peaceful protests by farmers foiled several attempts by police to forcibly evict farmers from common lands acquired for South Korean Pohong Steel Company's (POSCO) proposed steel project in Jagatsinghpur district, Orissa, following which two leaders, Abhay Sahoo and Narayan Reddy, were detained on false charges.

■ In July, the Orissa high court upheld the Indian authorities' 2010 decision to reject Vedanta Aluminium's (a subsidiary of UK-based Vedanta Resources) bid to expand its Lanjigarh alumina refinery. The Indian authorities made the decision after concurring with Amnesty International's findings that the refinery's activities violated the communities' right to water, health and a healthy environment, and that the expansion would perpetrate further abuses against Adivasi communities. The court ordered the company to re-apply for mandatory clearances for expansion, but the company challenged this decision.

Excessive use of force

In several instances, police used excessive force to quell protests by marginalized local communities, including small farmers, Adivasis and Dalits. The authorities also failed to carry out impartial and timely inquiries into most of these incidents.

■ In September, seven Dalits were killed when police opened fire on protesters demanding the release of Dalit leader John Pandyan, who was arrested on his way to Paramakkudi town, Tamil Nadu, to commemorate anniversary of the death of another Dalit leader, Immanuel Sekaran.

■ In September, eight people, all Muslims, were killed when police and members of a Gujjar militia opened fire inside a mosque and set fire to it in Gopalgarh village near Bharatpur in Rajasthan.

■ In February, two people were killed and five wounded when police fired at those protesting against the takeover of their lands for a thermal power plant run by East Coast Energy in Vadditandra village, Andhra Pradesh.

■ In April, one person was killed and another injured when police fired at villagers protesting against the harmful effects of the proposed French Areva firm's nuclear project at Jaitapur town in Maharashtra. Subsequently, the police enforced night-time detentions for peaceful protesters on a four-day march from Mumbai.

■ In May, two protesters and two policemen were killed after police fired at farmers at Bhatta Parsaul village. The farmers had kidnapped three officials in protest against the authorities' decision to forcibly acquire their land to build an expressway near Noida on the outskirts of Delhi. The police sexually assaulted seven women and looted the village. A Noida court later charged 30 police officials with rape and robbery, and a Supreme Court order declared part of the land acquisition illegal.

■ In May, two people were shot dead by police during forced evictions at Jamshedpur town in Jharkhand. At least 100,000 people were forcibly evicted in Jamshedpur, Ranchi and Bokaro towns.

Human rights defenders

People defending the rights of Adivasis and other marginalized communities, and those using recent legislation to obtain information to protect their rights, were targeted by state and non-state agencies. Activists demanded special legislation to protect them from such attacks – a fact highlighted by the UN Special Rapporteur on human rights defenders in January.

■ In April, prisoner of conscience Dr Binayak Sen, sentenced to life by a Chhattisgarh district court in 2010 after being convicted of sedition charges and collaborating with armed Maoists, was released on bail by India's Supreme Court after a vigorous national and international campaign.

■ In June, environmental activists Ramesh Agrawal and Harihar Patel were jailed on false charges after trying to protect local communities from industrial pollution in Raigarh district, Chhattisgarh.

■ In August, environmental activist Shehla Masood was shot dead in Bhopal city. She had sought to expose environmental violations by urban infrastructure projects and had challenged mining plans in Madhya Pradesh.

■ In November, Nadeem Sayed, a witness in the Naroda Patiya massacre case, was stabbed to death after he testified at the hearing. Ninety-five people had been killed in the massacre during the Gujarat anti-Muslim riots of 2002.

■ In November, Valsa John, an activist nun who had worked to protect the rights of Adivasis, was murdered after she received death threats allegedly from illegal mining outfits in Jharkhand.

Impunity

Impunity for abuses and violations remained pervasive. Despite ongoing protests in the north-east and Jammu and Kashmir, the authorities remained unwilling to repeal the Armed Forces Special Powers Act 1958, or revoke the Disturbed Areas Act, which grant security forces in specified areas the power to shoot to kill even where they are not at imminent risk.

Perpetrators of past enforced disappearances, extrajudicial executions and other human rights violations in Punjab (in 1984 and 1994), Assam (in 1998 and 2001), Nagaland and Manipur continued to evade justice. Members of Dalit communities in several states faced attacks and discrimination. There was little political will to use existing special laws to prosecute perpetrators of such violence.

Communal violence

Almost a decade after the 2002 riots which killed about 2,000 Muslims in Gujarat, the first convictions were announced.

■ In March, a Gujarat special court sentenced 11 people to death and 20 others to life for an arson attack on the Sabarmati express train which killed 59 Hindu pilgrims and triggered the riots.

■ In November, a Gujarat special court sentenced 31 of the 73 accused of the Sardarpura massacre – which killed 33 Muslims – to life imprisonment. This was the first of 10 major cases being monitored directly by India's Supreme Court.

Those working to ensure justice for the victims of past violations in Gujarat continued to face harassment.

■ In January, Teesta Setalvad of the Centre for Justice and Peace and a team of lawyers defending the rights of victims and their families were harassed by Gujarat police, who charged them with concocting evidence about a mass grave of victims.

Jammu and Kashmir

Impunity prevailed for violations in Kashmir, including unlawful killings, torture and the disappearance of thousands of people since 1989 during the armed conflict there. A majority of the killings of more than 100 youths by the security forces during protests in 2010 also went unpunished.

■ In March, 15 years after the murder of human rights lawyer Jaleel Andrabi, the state authorities urged the federal government to extradite Major Avtar Singh, charged with the killing, from the USA to face trial in a Srinagar court. The federal authorities had yet to respond.

■ In September, the state human rights commission identified over 2,700 unmarked graves in north Kashmir. Despite the local police's claims that these contained bodies of "unidentified militants", the commission identified 574 bodies as those of disappeared locals and asked the state authorities to use DNA profiling and other forensic techniques to identify the remaining bodies. The authorities had yet to act on this recommendation.

In March, Amnesty International published a report in Srinagar, calling for an end to administrative detentions there and for the repeal of the Public Safety Act (PSA). Following this, the state authorities proposed to amend the PSA to limit the period of detention, and amend the state juvenile justice law to ban the detention of anyone below the age of 18. However, detentions under the PSA continued on a regular basis and a number of political leaders and activists remained held without charge or trial. Several children were released after Amnesty International's intervention.

■ In May, 17-year-old Murtaza Manzoor was released after being detained for the second time. Earlier in the month, he had been released on the orders of the Jammu and Kashmir high court which quashed his four-month-long detention.

Arbitrary arrests and detentions

More than 50 people were detained without charge, for periods of one week to a month, in connection with bomb attacks in Mumbai and Delhi. Security legislation, tightened after the November 2008 attacks

in Mumbai, was used to detain suspects. However, investigations and trial proceedings relating to a majority of past cases of terror attacks made little progress.

■ In November, seven Muslim men, accused of a 2006 bomb attack in Malegaon town, Maharashtra, were freed on bail after five years in jail in Mumbai. The release came after a Hindu leader, Aseemananda, confessed to the involvement of a Hindu right-wing armed group in the bomb attack.

Death penalty

At least 110 people were sentenced to death. However, for the seventh successive year, no executions took place. Nevertheless, fears grew that executions would be revived with the authorities rejecting mercy petitions of five death row inmates, including three people convicted for the assassination of former Prime Minister Rajiv Gandhi.

New laws, passed in December, provided for the death penalty for those convicted of "terrorist" attacks on oil and gas pipelines that result in death, and in Gujarat state, for those found guilty of making and selling illicit liquor.

Amnesty International visits/reports

▥ "A lawless law": Detentions under the Jammu and Kashmir Public Safety Act (ASA 20/001/2011)

▥ Open letter to India's Minister of Environment and Forests on the threat of leakage from Vedanta Aluminium's red mud pond in Orissa (ASA 20/032/2011)

▥ Generalisations, omissions, assumptions: The failings of Vedanta's Environmental Impact Assessments for its bauxite mine and alumina refinery in India's state of Orissa (ASA 20/036/2011)

▥ An open letter from Amnesty International to Members of the Jammu and Kashmir Legislative Assembly (ASA 20/046/2011)

▥ Indian executions would be blow to human rights (PRE01/274/2011)

▥ India urged to implement court ban of anti-Maoist militias (PRE01/340/2011)

INDONESIA

REPUBLIC OF INDONESIA

Head of state and government:	Susilo Bambang Yudhoyono
Death penalty:	retentionist
Population:	242.3 million
Life expectancy:	69.4 years
Under 5-mortality:	38.9 per 1,000
Adult literacy:	92.2 per cent

Indonesia assumed the chair of ASEAN and in May was elected to the UN Human Rights Council for a third consecutive term. The government strengthened the national police commission but police accountability mechanisms remained inadequate. The security forces faced persistent allegations of human rights violations, including torture and other ill-treatment and use of unnecessary and excessive force. Provincial authorities in Aceh increasingly used caning as a judicial punishment. Peaceful political activities continued to be criminalized in Papua and Maluku. Religious minorities suffered discrimination, including intimidation and physical attacks. Barriers to sexual and reproductive rights continued to affect women and girls. No executions were reported.

Torture and other ill-treatment

Security forces faced repeated allegations of torturing and otherwise ill-treating detainees, particularly peaceful political activists in areas with a history of independence movements such as Papua and Maluku. Independent investigations into such allegations were rare.

■ In January, three soldiers who had been filmed kicking and verbally abusing Papuans were sentenced by a military court to between eight and 10 months' imprisonment for disobeying orders. A senior Indonesian government official described the abuse as a "minor violation".

■ There were no investigations into allegations of torture and other ill-treatment of 21 peaceful political activists by Special Detachment-88 (Densus-88), a police counter-terrorism unit. The 21 had been tortured during arrest, detention and interrogation in Maluku in August 2010.

Caning was increasingly used as a form of judicial punishment in Aceh. At least 72 people were caned

for various offences, including drinking alcohol, being alone with someone of the opposite sex who was not a marriage partner or relative (khalwat), and for gambling. The Acehnese authorities passed a series of by-laws governing the implementation of Shari'a law after the enactment of the province's Special Autonomy Law in 2001.

Excessive use of force

The police used unnecessary and excessive force against demonstrators and protesters, especially in land dispute cases. In the rare instances where investigations took place, little progress was made in bringing perpetrators to justice.

■ In January, six palm oil farmers were seriously injured in Jambi Province after Police Mobile Brigade (Brimob) officers fired rubber bullets at them in an attempt to evict them from a plantation they were working on. The plantation was the subject of an ongoing land dispute between the farmers and a palm oil company.

■ In April, police in Papua shot Dominokus Auwe in the chest and head, killing him, and wounded two others in front of the Moanemani sub-district police station. The three men had approached the station peacefully to inquire about money the police had seized from Dominokus Auwe earlier that day.

■ In June, security forces used unnecessary and excessive force while attempting to forcibly evict a community in Langkat district, North Sumatra. The community had been involved in a land dispute with the local authorities. When the community protested against the eviction, police officers fired on the crowd without warning, injuring at least nine people. Six others were kicked and beaten.

Freedom of expression

The government continued to criminalize peaceful political expression in Maluku and Papua. At least 90 political activists were imprisoned for their peaceful political activities.

■ In August, two Papuan political activists, Melkianus Bleskadit and Daniel Yenu, were imprisoned for up to two years for their involvement in a peaceful political protest in Manokwari town in December 2010.

■ In October, over 300 people were arbitrarily arrested after participating in the Third Papuan People's Congress, a peaceful gathering held in Abepura town, Papua Province. Although most were held overnight and released the next day, five were charged with "rebellion" under Article 106 of the Criminal Code. The charge could carry a maximum life sentence. A preliminary investigation by the National Human Rights Commission (Komnas HAM) found that the security forces had committed a range of human rights violations, including opening fire on participants at the gathering, and beating and kicking them.

Some human rights defenders and journalists continued to be intimidated and attacked because of their work.

■ In March, journalist Banjir Ambarita was stabbed by unidentified persons in the province of Papua shortly after he had written about two cases of women who were reportedly raped by police officers in Papua. He survived the attack.

■ In June, military officers beat Yones Douw, a human rights defender in Papua, after he tried to monitor a protest calling for accountability for the possible unlawful killing of Papuan Derek Adii in May.

Discrimination

Attacks and intimidation against religious minorities persisted. The Ahmadiyya community was increasingly targeted and at least four provinces issued new regional regulations restricting Ahmadiyya activities. By the end of the year, at least 18 Christian churches had been attacked or forced to close down. In many cases the police failed to adequately protect religious and other minority groups from such attacks.

■ In February, three Ahmadis were killed after a 1,500-person mob attacked them in Cikeusik, Banten Province. On 28 July, 12 people were sentenced to between three and six months' imprisonment for their involvement in the incident. No one was charged with murder and local human rights groups raised concerns about the weak prosecution.

■ The Mayor of Bogor continued to defy a 2010 Supreme Court ruling ordering the authorities to reopen the Taman Yasmin Indonesian Christian Church. The congregation was forced to conduct its weekly services on the pavement outside the closed church, amid protests from radical groups.

Sexual and reproductive rights

Women and girls, especially those from poor and marginalized communities, were prevented from fully exercising their sexual and reproductive rights. Many continued to be denied the reproductive health services provided for in the 2009 Health Law, as the Ministry of Health had yet to issue the necessary implementing regulation. The government failed to challenge discriminatory attitudes and cruel, inhuman and degrading practices, including female genital mutilation and early marriages.

■ In June, the Minister of Health defended a November 2010 regulation permitting specifically defined forms of "female circumcision" when performed by doctors, nurses and midwives. The regulation legitimized the widespread practice of female genital mutilation. It also violated a number of Indonesian laws and contradicted government pledges to enhance gender equality and combat discrimination against women.

The maternal mortality ratio remained one of the highest in the region.

Domestic workers

In June, the President expressed support for the new ILO No. 189 Domestic Workers Convention. However, for a second successive year, parliament failed to debate and enact legislation providing legal protection for domestic workers. This left an estimated 2.6 million domestic workers – the vast majority of them women and girls – at continued risk of economic exploitation and physical, psychological and sexual violence.

Impunity

Perpetrators of past human rights violations in Aceh, Papua, Timor-Leste and elsewhere remained free from prosecution. The Attorney General's office failed to act on cases of serious human rights violations submitted by the National Human Rights Commission (Komnas HAM). These included crimes against humanity committed by members of the security forces.

■ A Memorandum of Understanding between Komnas HAM and the Timor-Leste Provedor (Ombudsman for Human Rights and Justice) which called for, among other things, information on people who disappeared in 1999 in Timor-Leste, lapsed in January and was renewed in November. No progress was reported (see Timor-Leste entry).

■ In September, the Attorney General reportedly declared the case of murdered prominent human rights defender Munir "closed". There remained credible allegations that, despite the conviction of three people for their involvement in his death, not all the perpetrators had been brought to justice.

■ The government had yet to implement the 2009 recommendations of parliament to investigate and prosecute those responsible for the abduction and enforced disappearance of 13 political activists in 1997-1998.

Death penalty

For a third successive year no executions were reported. However, at least 100 people remained under sentence of death.

Amnesty International visits/reports

🚗 Amnesty International delegates visited Indonesia in April, May, September, October, November and December.

📄 Making the fair choice: Key steps to improve maternal health in ASEAN – Briefing to the ASEAN Intergovernmental Commission on Human Rights (ASA 03/001/2011)

📄 Open letter to Head of National Police on failure of police accountability in Indonesia (ASA 21/005/2011)

📄 Indonesia: Open letter on human rights violations against the Ahmadiyya in West Java (ASA 21/032/2011)

IRAN

ISLAMIC REPUBLIC OF IRAN

Head of state:	**Ayatollah Sayed 'Ali Khamenei (Leader of the Islamic Republic of Iran)**
Head of government:	**Mahmoud Ahmadinejad (President)**
Death penalty:	**retentionist**
Population:	**74.8 million**
Life expectancy:	**73 years**
Under-5 mortality:	**30.9 per 1,000**
Adult literacy:	**85 per cent**

Freedom of expression, association and assembly were severely restricted. Political dissidents, women's and minority rights activists and other human rights defenders were arbitrarily arrested, detained incommunicado, imprisoned after unfair trials and banned from travelling abroad. Torture and other ill-treatment were common and committed with impunity. Women as well as religious and ethnic minorities faced discrimination in law and in practice. At least 360 people were executed; the true total was believed to be much higher. Among them were at least three juvenile offenders. Judicial floggings and amputations were carried out.

Background

The security forces, including the paramilitary Basij militia, continued to operate with near total impunity and there was virtually no accountability for the unlawful killings and other serious violations committed at the time of mass, largely peaceful protests following the 2009 presidential election and in earlier years.

In March, the UN Human Rights Council appointed a Special Rapporteur to investigate human rights in Iran; the government refused to allow him to visit the country. In October, the UN Human Rights Committee considered Iran's record on civil and political rights. In December, the UN General Assembly passed a resolution condemning human rights violations in Iran.

Iranian troops attacked bases of PJAK (Free Life Party of Kurdistan), an armed group that advocates autonomy for Iran's Kurds, in Iraqi Kurdistan; at least two civilians were killed and hundreds of families in Iraqi Kurdistan were displaced. PJAK's combatants reportedly include people recruited as child soldiers.

International tensions over Iran's nuclear programme heightened in November when the International Atomic Energy Agency reported that Iran could be secretly constructing a nuclear weapon; the government denied this. The government accused Israel and the USA of being behind several murders of Iranian scientists possibly linked to Iran's nuclear programme, including physicist Dariush Rezaienejad, killed in July by an unidentified gunman in Tehran. The government denied allegations by the US authorities implicating senior Revolutionary Guard officials in a plot to kill Saudi Arabia's ambassador to the USA.

Freedom of expression, association and assembly

The authorities maintained the tightened restrictions on freedom of expression, association and assembly imposed before, during and following the 2009 mass protests and sought to impose further restrictions. Parliament discussed draft laws that would further restrict freedom of expression, association and assembly, including the activities of NGOs and political parties.

■ Mohammad Seyfzadeh, arrested in April to serve a prison sentence, and Abdolfattah Soltani, arrested in September, both lawyers and founder members of the

Centre for Human Rights Defenders, whose offices were forcibly closed by the government in 2008, were still held at the end of 2011.

■ In December, Zhila Karamzadeh-Makvandi, a member of the group Mothers of Park Laleh, which campaigns against unlawful killings and other serious human rights violations, began serving a two-year prison sentence for "founding an illegal organization" and "acting against state security". Fellow member Leyla Seyfollahi faced implementation of a similar prison term.

The authorities refused permission for demonstrations on 14 February called in solidarity with the uprisings in Tunisia and Egypt, and conducted pre-emptive arrests. However, demonstrations went ahead in Tehran, Esfahan, Kermanshah, Shiraz and elsewhere. They were violently dispersed by security forces, who arrested scores and killed at least two people. Subsequent demonstrations were also forcibly dispersed.

■ Prisoner of conscience Haleh Sahabi, a political activist, died on 1 June while on leave from prison to attend the funeral of her father, Ezatollah Sahabi, a prominent dissident. She was reported to have been hit by security forces before collapsing.

The security forces clamped down on provincial demonstrations, reportedly using excessive force, and arrested scores, possibly hundreds, of protesters. In Khuzestan, dozens of members of the Ahwazi Arab minority were said to have been killed before and during demonstrations in April to commemorate protests in 2005. Scores of environmental protesters calling for government action to halt the degradation of Lake Oroumieh were arrested in East Azerbaijan province in April, August and September.

The government maintained close control over the media, banning newspapers, blocking websites and jamming foreign satellite television channels. Scores of journalists, political activists and their relatives, film-makers, human rights defenders, students and academics were harassed, banned from foreign travel, arbitrarily arrested, tortured or jailed for expressing views opposed to those of the government. Some arrested in previous years were executed following unfair trials.

■ Five documentary film directors, and a producer/distributor were detained in September after their films were sold to the BBC. All were released by mid-December.

■ Student activists Majid Tavakkoli, Bahareh Hedayat and Mahdieh Golrou, all serving prison terms for their peaceful student and human rights activities, were sentenced to new six-month prison terms because of a Students' Day declaration they jointly wrote from prison in 2010.

■ Women's rights activist and journalist Faranak Farid was reportedly beaten severely after her arrest on 3 September in Tabriz in connection with the Lake Oroumieh protests. She was released on bail in October.

Arbitrary arrests and detentions

Security officials continued to arrest and detain government critics and opponents arbitrarily, often holding them incommunicado and without access to their families, lawyers or medical care for long periods. Many were tortured or ill-treated. Scores were sentenced to prison terms after unfair trials, adding to the hundreds imprisoned after unfair trials in previous years.

■ In February, opposition leaders Mehdi Karroubi and Mir Hossein Mousavi, and their wives, were placed under house arrest, without a warrant, after calling for demonstrations on 14 February; they remained under house arrest at the end of the year with the exception of Mehdi Karroubi's wife Fatemeh Karroubi.

■ Mohammad Tavassoli, arrested in November, was one of at least five members of the banned Freedom Movement detained in 2011. He was held in connection with a letter sent by 143 political activists to former President Khatami in October warning that forthcoming parliamentary elections would be neither free nor fair. Five others were banned from leaving Iran.

■ Shane Bauer and Josh Fattal, two US nationals who had been detained for more than two years and accused of spying after they allegedly strayed into Iran while hiking in Iraq, were released after payment of hefty bail in September and allowed to leave Iran.

Human rights defenders

Repression intensified against human rights defenders, including lawyers. Many were arbitrarily arrested and imprisoned or harassed. Others remained in prison after unfair trials in previous years; they included women's and minority rights activists, trades unionists, lawyers and students. Many were prisoners of conscience. Independent trade unions remained banned and several union members remained in prison.

■ In September, the 11-year prison sentence imposed in April on human rights lawyer Nasrin Sotoudeh after she was convicted of "acting against national security" for her legal defence work, was reduced to six years on appeal. Her 20-year ban on practising law or leaving Iran was halved.

■ Reza Shahabi, treasurer of the independent Union of Workers of the Tehran and Suburbs Bus Company (Sherkat-e Vahed), remained held at Evin Prison in Tehran without completion of his trial. Arrested in June 2010, he was a prisoner of conscience, as was the union's leader, Mansour Ossanlu, who was conditionally released for medical treatment in June.

■ Human rights activist Kouhyar Goudarzi disappeared for several weeks after his arrest in July until discovered to be in solitary confinement at Evin Prison, where he remained at the end of 2011. Behnam Ganji Khaibari, arrested with him and apparently tortured, committed suicide after release.

■ Prominent human rights activist Emadeddin Baghi was released in June after serving two concurrent one-year prison sentences for "propaganda against the state" relating to his human rights and media activities. He remained banned from any political or media activity for five years.

Unfair trials

Political suspects continued to face grossly unfair trials often involving vaguely worded charges that did not amount to recognizably criminal offences. They were frequently convicted, sometimes in the absence of defence lawyers, on the basis of "confessions" or other information allegedly obtained under torture during pre-trial detention. Courts accepted such "confessions" as evidence without investigating how they were obtained.

■ Omid Kokabi was arrested at Tehran airport in February on his return from studying in the USA. Charged with "espionage" and other offences, he went on trial in October. He said he had been forced to "confess" in detention. His lawyer said he had been denied access to him.

■ Zahra Bahrami, a Dutch-Iranian national, was executed without warning on 29 January, only 27 days after she was sentenced to death for alleged drug-smuggling. She was arrested at the time of demonstrations in December 2009 and first charged with *moharebeh* (enmity against God) for alleged contact with a banned opposition group, but not tried on this charge. Her lawyer said there was no right of appeal against the death sentence.

Torture and other ill-treatment

Torture and other ill-treatment in pre-trial detention remained common and committed with impunity. Detainees were beaten on the soles of the feet and the body, sometimes while suspended upside-down; burned with cigarettes and hot metal objects; subjected to mock execution; raped, including by other prisoners, and threatened with rape; confined in cramped spaces; and denied adequate light, food, water and medical treatment. Up to 12 people reportedly died in custody in suspicious circumstances, including where medical care may have been denied or delayed; their deaths were not independently investigated. At least 10 others died during unrest at Ghezel Hesar Prison in Karaj near Tehran in March. No allegations of torture or ill-treatment were known to have been investigated by the authorities; those who complained of torture faced reprisals. Harsh prison conditions were exacerbated by severe overcrowding.

■ At least four Ahwazi Arabs – Reza Maghamesi, Abdol Karim Fahd Abiat, Ahmad Riassan Salami and Ejbareh Tamimi – were reported to have died in custody in Khuzestan province between March and May, possibly as a result of torture.

■ Journalist Issa Saharkhiz; Zahra Jabbari; Azerbaijani minority rights advocate Sa'id Metinpour; and dissident cleric Hossein Kazemeyni Boroujerdi were among many political prisoners, including prisoners of conscience, with serious health problems who were denied adequate health care. Political activist Hoda Saber died in prison in June after going on hunger strike in protest at Haleh Sahabi's death. Other prisoners said that prison officials had beaten him and denied him adequate medical care.

Cruel, inhuman or degrading punishments

Sentences of flogging and amputation continued to be imposed and carried out. Sentences of blinding were imposed.

■ Somayeh Tohidlou, a political activist, and Peyman Aref, a student activist, were flogged 50 and 74 times respectively in September after they were separately convicted of "insulting" President Ahmadinejad.

■ Four men convicted of theft were said to have had the four fingers of their right hands amputated on 8 October.

■ Majid Movahedi, who blinded Ameneh Bahrami in an acid attack in 2004 and was sentenced to be blinded by acid himself, was reprieved shortly before the punishment was to be carried out at a hospital on 31 July when his victim agreed to accept compensation.

Discrimination against women

Women were discriminated against in law and in practice, including by a mandatory dress code. Women's rights activists, including those involved in the One Million Signatures Campaign to demand legal equality for women, were persecuted and harassed. The draft Family Protection Bill, which would exacerbate discriminatory law against women, remained before parliament pending final approval. Some universities began segregating students by gender.

■ Fatemeh Masjedi and Maryam Bidgoli, activists in the One Million Signatures Campaign, each served six-month prison terms – the first members of the Campaign to be jailed for collecting signatures.

Rights of lesbian, gay, bisexual and transgender people

People accused of same-sex sexual activities continued to face harassment and persecution, and the judicial punishments of flogging and the death penalty.

■ On 4 September, three men identified only by their initials were reported to have been executed in Karoun Prison, Ahvaz, Khuzestan province, after they were convicted of "sodomy".

■ Siyamak Ghaderi, a former journalist for the state news agency held since August 2010, was sentenced to four years' imprisonment, flogging and a fine in January after he was convicted of "publishing lies", committing "religiously unlawful acts" and other charges for, among other things, posting interviews with people from the lesbian, gay, bisexual and transgender community on his blog.

Discrimination – ethnic minorities

Iran's ethnic minority communities, including Ahwazi Arabs, Azerbaijanis, Baluch, Kurds and Turkmen, suffered ongoing discrimination in law and in practice. The use of minority languages in government offices and for teaching in schools remained prohibited. Activists campaigning for the rights of minorities faced threats, arrest and imprisonment.

■ Prisoner of conscience Mohammad Sadiq Kabudvand continued serving a sentence of 10 and a half years for his role in founding the Human Rights

Organization of Kurdistan, and was denied adequate medical treatment.

■ Mohammad Saber Malek Raisi, a Baluch youth aged 16 from Sarbaz held since September 2009, possibly to force his elder brother to surrender to the authorities, was sentenced to five years' prison in exile – meaning that he must serve his sentence at a prison far from his home.

Freedom of religion or belief

Members of religious minorities, including Christian converts, Baha'is, dissident Shi'a clerics and members of the Ahl-e Haq and Dervish communities, faced continuing persecution following repeated calls by the Supreme Leader and other authorities to combat "false beliefs" – apparently an allusion to evangelical Christianity, Baha'ism and Sufism. Sunni Muslims continued to face restrictions on communal worship in some cities and some Sunni clerics were arrested.

■ At least seven Baha'is were jailed for between four and five years after they and over 30 others were arrested in raids targeting the Baha'i Institute for Higher Education. The Institute provides online higher education courses for Baha'i students, who are barred from universities. The seven were among over 100 Baha'is held in connection with their beliefs, including seven leaders who had 20-year prison terms reimposed in March, reversing a 2010 appeal court decision.

■ Up to 100 Gonabadi Dervishes (a Sufi religious order), three of their lawyers, as well as 12 journalists for *Majzooban-e Noor*, a Gonabadi Dervish news website, were arrested in Kavar and Tehran in September and October. At least 11 were still detained, mostly without access to lawyers or family, at the end of 2011.

■ The retrial of Yousef Nadarkhani, a Christian pastor charged with "apostasy", began in September. Born to Muslim parents, he was arrested in October 2009. He was sentenced to death in 2010 for refusing to renounce Christianity, to which he had converted, but the sentence was overturned by the Supreme Court in June.

■ Sayed Mohammad Movahed Fazeli, the Sunni prayer leader of the city of Taybad, was held between January and August following protests in Taybad against his enforced resignation as prayer leader.

Death penalty

Hundreds of people were sentenced to death. At least 360 executions were reported by official sources, although other credible information suggested over 274 other executions, with many prisoners executed secretly. Up to 80 per cent of executions were for alleged drug-related offences, often imposed on people living in poverty and marginalized communities, particularly Afghan nationals. An amended Anti-Narcotics Law came into force in January; people sentenced to death under it appeared to be denied the right to appeal.

The number of public executions quadrupled; at least 50 were reported officially and a further six were recorded from unofficial sources. At least three juvenile offenders – people sentenced for offences committed when they were under 18 – were executed; a further four cases were reported by credible sources. No stoning executions were reported, but at least 15 people sentenced to death by stoning remained on death row, including Sakineh Mohammadi Ashtiani. Thousands of other prisoners were held awaiting execution.

■ Ja'far Kazemi and Mohammad Ali Haj Aghaei were hanged on 24 January; they were convicted of moharebeh for having contact with the People's Mojahedin Organization of Iran, a banned opposition group, and "propaganda against the system" relating to the 2009 unrest.

■ On 21 September, 17-year-old Alireza Molla-Soltani, convicted of murdering a popular athlete, was publicly hanged in Karaj where the killing occurred in July. He said he had stabbed Ruhollah Dadashi in self-defence after the athlete attacked him in the dark.

■ In December, Kurdish political prisoner Zeynab Jalalian learned that her death sentence had been commuted.

Amnesty International visits/reports

🚗 Amnesty International discussed its denial of access to Iran with Iranian diplomatic officials, but it remained barred from Iran. The authorities rarely responded to communications from Amnesty International.

▤ Determined to live in dignity – Iranian trade unionists' struggle for rights (MDE 13/024/2011)

▤ Iran: Submission to the Human Rights Committee (MDE 13/081/2011)

▤ Addicted to death: Executions for drugs offences in Iran (MDE 13/090/2011)

IRAQ

REPUBLIC OF IRAQ

Head of state:	Jalal Talabani
Head of government:	Nuri al-Maliki
Death penalty:	retentionist
Population:	32.7 million
Life expectancy:	69 years
Under-5 mortality:	43.5 per 1,000
Adult literacy:	78.1 per cent

Government security forces used excessive force against peaceful and other protesters, some of whom were shot dead. Others were arrested and tortured. Thousands of people were detained; many had been arrested in previous years and held without charge or trial. Torture and other ill-treatment remained rife. Hundreds of people were sentenced to death, many after unfair trials, and dozens of prisoners were executed. US forces also committed serious human rights violations. Armed groups opposed to the government and the presence of US troops continued to commit gross human rights abuses; they carried out numerous suicide and other bomb attacks, killing hundreds of civilians.

Background

Inspired by the popular uprisings in Tunisia and Egypt, thousands of Iraqis demonstrated in Baghdad, Basra and other cities against corruption, unemployment and lack of basic services, and in favour of greater civil and political rights. The largest demonstrations, held across Iraq on 25 February, were forcibly dispersed by the security forces.

On 18 December, the last US soldiers left Iraq in accordance with the Status of Forces Agreement signed by the US and Iraqi authorities in 2008. A proposed deal, under which several thousand US troops would remain in Iraq as military trainers, fell through because of legal issues relating to immunity.

In July, Iraq became party to the UN Convention against Torture.

Abuses by armed groups

Armed groups opposed to the government and to the presence of US forces continued to commit gross human rights abuses, including indiscriminate killings of civilians and kidnapping. Many such attacks were carried out by al-Qa'ida in Iraq and its allies.

■ On 10 February, nine people were killed and at least 27 others were wounded when a car bomb exploded near a procession of Shi'a pilgrims heading towards the holy Shi'a shrines in Samarra' in Salahuddin governorate.

■ On 15 August, at least 89 people were killed across Iraq in more than 40 co-ordinated attacks. The deadliest attack was in a crowded market in Kut, south-east of Baghdad, when two explosions killed at least 35 people and injured more than 60.

■ On 29 August, at least 29 people were killed and many wounded in a suicide bomb attack in Um al-Qura mosque, Baghdad's largest Sunni mosque. Among the dead was Khalid al-Fahdawi, a member of parliament.

Detention without trial

Thousands of people remained detained without charge or trial. In July, the Chairman of the Supreme Judicial Council (SJC) said there were around 12,000 untried detainees, referring only to those held in facilities controlled by the Justice Ministry. Many other detainees were believed to be in prisons run by the Ministries of Defence and Interior. Many detainees had no access to lawyers or their families.

In July, the US authorities transferred two half brothers of former President Saddam Hussain and his former Defence Minister, all under sentence of death, to Iraqi custody together with almost 200 detainees who were alleged members of armed groups. These were the last prisoners and detainees under the control of the US military in Iraq. They all remained in al-Karkh Prison (formerly Camp Cropper), near Baghdad International Airport.

Torture and other ill-treatment

Torture and other ill-treatment were widespread in prisons and detention centres, in particular those controlled by the Ministries of Interior and Defence. Commonly reported methods were suspension by the limbs for long periods, beatings with cables and hosepipes, electric shocks, breaking of limbs, partial asphyxiation with plastic bags, and rape or threats of rape. Torture was used to extract information from detainees and "confessions" that could be used as evidence against them in courts.

■ Abdel Jabbar Shaloub Hammadi, who helped organize anti-government protests, was arrested on 24 February in a Baghdad street by 30 armed police. He was beaten, blindfolded and taken to a police building in Baghdad's al-Baladiyat district. During the first five days he was held there, he alleges that he was suspended by his wrists with his legs and arms bound together, and had icy water thrown over him. He was released without charge on 8 March.

Excessive use of force

The security forces used excessive force in response to anti-government protests in Baghdad and other cities, particularly in February and March, using live ammunition, sound bombs and other weapons to disperse peaceful protests. At least 20 people were killed in the protests that began in February.

■ On 25 February, Mu'ataz Muwafaq Waissi was one of five people shot dead by security forces at a peaceful demonstration in Mosul. He was said to have been killed by a sniper. According to witnesses, the security forces used sound bombs and fired into the air at first but then used live fire against protesters.

■ Also on 25 February, during protests in Basra, Salim Farooq was killed and scores of other protesters were injured during clashes between security forces and protesters outside the provincial council building.

Death penalty

Hundreds of people were sentenced to death; in July, the SJC Chairman said that courts had imposed 291 death sentences in the first half of the year. In September, an SJC spokesperson revealed that 735 death sentences had been referred to the Iraqi Presidency for final ratification between January 2009 and September 2011, of which 81 had been ratified. According to the Ministry of Justice, 65 men and three women were executed during the year.

Most death sentences were imposed on people convicted of belonging to or involvement in attacks by armed groups, kidnapping or other violent crimes. Trials consistently failed to meet international standards for fair trial. Defendants commonly complained that "confessions" accepted as evidence against them had been obtained under torture when they were held incommunicado and interrogated, and that they could not choose their own defence lawyers. In many cases, these "confessions" were broadcast on television, in some cases in advance of trials, undermining the right to be considered innocent until proven guilty. The government rarely disclosed information about executions, especially names of those executed and exact numbers.

■ On 16 June, the Central Criminal Court of Iraq sentenced to death 15 men after "confessions" by several of them were aired on television a few days earlier. The 15, said to be members of armed groups, were reportedly found guilty of murdering dozens of people at a wedding party and the rape of women and girls, including the bride, in a village near al-Taji, north of Baghdad, in June 2006. On 24 November, the Ministry of Justice announced that 12 people involved in this case had been executed earlier on the same day. The fate of the remaining three was not known at the end of the year.

■ On 16 November, 10 men, including a Tunisian and an Egyptian national, who had been convicted of "terrorism" and murder, were reported to have been executed in al-Kadhimiya Prison in Baghdad.

Trials of former Ba'ath and army officials

The Supreme Iraqi Criminal Tribunal (SICT) continued to try former senior Ba'ath and army officials associated with Saddam Hussain's rule who were accused of war crimes, crimes against humanity and other offences. The court, whose independence and impartiality has been undermined by political interference, imposed several death sentences. In September, the President of the SICT told Parliament that the court was no longer operating as it had completed all of the criminal cases it was due to hear.

■ On 21 April, Hadi Hassuni, 'Abd Hassan al-Majid and Farouq Hijazi, all former senior intelligence officers, were sentenced to death for the murder of Taleb al-Suhail, an opposition leader, in 1994 in Lebanon. The court's Appellate Chamber upheld the sentences, but at the end of 2011 they were still awaiting ratification by the Presidency.

■ On 6 June, 'Aziz Saleh al-Numan, a former senior Ba'ath party official, was sentenced to death after he was found guilty of crimes against humanity in connection with the suppression of the 1991 Shi'a uprising in southern Iraq.

Attacks on media workers

A new law passed in August, ostensibly to protect the rights of journalists, was criticized as inadequate by media organizations and journalists, who continued to face politically motivated threats and attacks by the security forces in what appeared to be an orchestrated clampdown on the media. Those working for independent or opposition media outlets were particularly targeted. Several journalists were arrested and tortured.

■ Prominent radio journalist Hadi al-Mahdi was shot dead in his flat in Baghdad on 8 September shortly before he was due to attend a protest. Friends said that he had received threats in the weeks before his murder. Earlier, he and three other journalists had been detained by soldiers when they attended the 25 February protest, held overnight and interrogated while being tortured, including with beatings, electric shocks and threats of rape.

Human rights violations by US forces

US forces were involved in a number of incidents in which civilians were killed in suspicious circumstances.

■ On 7 March, a joint US-Iraqi force arrived by helicopter at the village of Allazika, Kirkuk province, and raided the house of Ayad Ibrahim Mohammad 'Azzawi al-Jibbouri, a physician. They took away both him and his brother Khalil, a teacher. On 8 March, Ayad al-Jibbouri's relatives were contacted by the morgue in Tikrit and informed that they should collect his body, which had been brought there by US forces the previous day. Khalil al-Jibbouri was taken by US forces to their military camp in Tikrit. At the end of the year it was not known whether he had been handed over to Iraqi custody or released.

■ On 30 July, Shaikh Hamid Hassan, a tribal leader, and two of his relatives were killed in Rufayat village, north of Baghdad, when their house was attacked during a joint US-Iraqi security operation. At least six other relatives – four of them women – were reported to have been wounded.

Camp Ashraf

Iraqi security forces continued to tighten their grip on and use violence against residents of Camp Ashraf, some 60km north of Baghdad. Renamed Camp New Iraq, it still housed some 3,250 Iranian exiles, members and supporters of the People's Mojahedin Organization of Iran, which opposes the Iranian government. On 8 April, Iraqi troops stormed the camp using grossly excessive force, including live ammunition, against residents who tried to resist them. Some 36 residents – 28 men and eight women – were killed and more than 300 wounded. Subsequently, those injured and others who were seriously ill were prevented or obstructed from leaving the camp to obtain specialized medical treatment.

Senior Iraqi government officials insisted that the camp would be closed by the end of 2011, leading UNHCR, the UN refugee agency, to call for an extension to allow it to interview residents seeking to register as refugees. At the end of the year, the Iraqi government agreed to extend the deadline to April 2012 provided that the residents would be moved to Camp Liberty near Baghdad International Airport.

Kurdistan region of Iraq

People also staged demonstrations in the Kurdistan region, especially in Sulaimaniya, protesting against corruption and calling for political reform.

Several new laws were enacted. A new law on NGOs simplifies the legal registration process, permits NGOs to receive funds from both local and foreign sources, recognizes that NGOs have a role to monitor government institutions and access information, and allows them to open branches and form networks. A new law to combat violence against women prohibits a wide range of acts of violence within the family, requires that the identities of victims are protected and establishes a special court to try cases of violence against women.

Excessive use of force

Kurdish security forces used excessive force, including live ammunition, to quell protests in Sulaimaniya and Kalar, resulting in at least six deaths.
■ Rezhwan 'Ali, a 15-year-old boy, was shot in the head and died instantly on 17 February when thousands of people demonstrated in Sulaimaniya's Sara Square. At least 50 people were injured.
■ On 19 February, Surkew Zahid, aged 16, and Sherzad Taha, aged 28, were seriously injured when security forces opened fire on a mass protest in Sulaimaniya. Both died in hospital the following day. At least 14 other people were injured.

Torture and other ill-treatment

A number of pro-democracy activists, including members of opposition political parties, were detained and tortured and otherwise ill-treated.
■ Sharwan Azad Faqi 'Abdullah, who was arrested in Erbil during the protests on 25 February, was detained for four days and tortured. He was repeatedly punched to force him to sign a "confession", and still had visible injuries apparently caused by torture when Amnesty International delegates saw him on 11 March in Erbil.

■ In early December, scores of members of the Kurdistan Islamic Union, an authorized Islamist party, were arrested in Dohuk and Zakho by Kurdish security forces. Many were released within days, but at least 14 were held for several weeks. Some were reported to have been tortured. The arrests took place immediately after attacks by Islamist protesters on shops selling alcohol and other businesses.

Attacks on media workers

Several journalists, particularly those working for independent media, were threatened, harassed or attacked, apparently by security officials.
■ On 29 August, Asos Hardi, editor of the independent newspaper *Awene*, was beaten by an armed assailant as he left his office in Sulaimaniya.
■ On 7 September, Ahmed Mira, editor of the independent *Levin* magazine, was held for three hours by members of a special force in Sulaimaniya, during which he was kicked and hit with a rifle butt. He was freed by order of a judge.

Amnesty International visits/reports

🚗 Amnesty International delegates visited the Kurdistan region of Iraq in March for research and government meetings.

📗 Days of rage: Protests and repression in Iraq (MDE 14/013/2011)

IRELAND

REPUBLIC OF IRELAND

Head of state:	Michael D. Higgins
	(replaced Mary McAleese in November)
Head of government:	Enda Kenny
	(replaced Brian Cowen in March)
Death penalty:	abolitionist for all crimes
Population:	4.5 million
Life expectancy:	80.6 years
Under-5 mortality:	4.2 per 1,000

Criticisms were raised by the UN Committee against Torture regarding the lack of prosecutions in reported cases of violence against children in religious-run institutions. Provision of mental health services continued to be inadequate. Prison conditions fell below required standards.

Legal, constitutional or institutional developments

The 2011 Programme for Government, published in March, promised consideration of comprehensive constitutional reform, including in the areas of same-sex marriage, women's equality and removing blasphemy from the Constitution.

In September, the Council of Europe Commissioner for Human Rights published the report of his June visit to Ireland, which raised concerns about the possibly detrimental effect of existing and proposed budgetary measures on the protection of human rights, particularly in relation to vulnerable groups. In September, the government announced its intention to merge the Irish Human Rights Commission and Equality Authority into a new Human Rights and Equality Commission.

Children's rights

In June, the UN Committee against Torture expressed concern that few cases of violence against children in religious-run institutions were forwarded for prosecution, despite extensive evidence of such abuse in the 2009 Report of the Commission to Inquire into Child Abuse (the Ryan Report).

The report of the Commission of Investigation, Dublin Archdiocese, Catholic Diocese of Cloyne (the Cloyne Report) was published in July. Among other findings, it concluded that two thirds of allegations of clerical sexual violence against children in that diocese made to the Catholic Church between 1996 and 2009 had not been forwarded to the Irish police force, An Garda Síochána, as required by the Church's 1996 guidelines. The government subsequently renewed commitments regarding mandatory reporting of suspected violence against children.

Arms trade

After a significant delay, the first annual report under the Control of Exports Act 2008 on military and dual-use exports and brokering was published in September, covering the period 2008 to 2010. However, there were gaps in the information it contained; for example, the end-use of the products was not listed.

Prison conditions

Both the UN Committee against Torture and the European Committee for the Prevention of Torture raised concerns regarding prison conditions, particularly around overcrowding, lack of in-cell sanitation, health care, and violence between prisoners in some prisons.

The UN Committee against Torture further noted the lack of independent and effective investigations into allegations of ill-treatment by prison staff.

Right to health

Acknowledging delays in access to, and problems in the affordability of, health care, the government committed to introducing a system of universal health care.

In February, the European Committee for the Prevention of Torture noted the slow pace of progress in mental health reform, and highlighted concerns with the Mental Health Act 2001, including the lack of protection for so-called "voluntary patients" and provisions regarding the use of electroconvulsive therapy.

Refugees and asylum-seekers

There continued to be significant delays for asylum applicants to have their asylum or other protection needs assessed. Long-promised legislation to establish a single procedure for considering claims was still not enacted.

Violence against women and girls

The UN Committee against Torture recommended an independent investigation into all allegations of torture and other ill-treatment of women and girls placed in religious-run "Magdalene Laundries" between 1922 and 1996. In June, the government established an interdepartmental committee to "clarify any State interaction with the Magdalene Laundries". However, this was, in itself, insufficient to fulfil the Committee against Torture's recommendation.

Ireland's National Action Plan on UN Security Council Resolution 1325 on women, peace and security was launched in November.

Police and security forces

The Smithwick Tribunal began public hearings in June to examine allegations that members of An Garda Síochána or other state agents colluded in the killing of two senior Royal Ulster Constabulary police officers by the Provisional Irish Republican Army in 1989 in Northern Ireland.

Amnesty International visits/reports

📄 Ireland: Briefing to the UN Committee against Torture
(EUR 29/001/2011)

📄 Ireland: Protecting human rights on the ground – Amnesty
International submission to the UN Universal Periodic Review, October 2011
(EUR 29/003/2011)

ISRAEL AND THE OCCUPIED PALESTINIAN TERRITORIES

STATE OF ISRAEL

Head of state:	Shimon Peres
Head of government:	Benjamin Netanyahu
Death penalty:	abolitionist for ordinary crimes
Population:	7.6 million (Israel); 4.2 million (OPT)
Life expectancy:	81.6 years (Israel); 72.8 years (OPT)
Under-5 mortality:	4.4 per 1,000 (Israel); 29.5 per 1,000 (OPT)

The Israeli authorities continued to blockade the Gaza Strip, prolonging the humanitarian crisis there, and to restrict the movement of Palestinians in the Occupied Palestinian Territories (OPT). In the West Bank, including East Jerusalem, the authorities continued to construct the fence/wall, much of it on Palestinian land, and to expand settlements, breaching international law. They demolished Palestinian homes and other facilities in the West Bank, and homes of Palestinian citizens inside Israel, especially in "unrecognized" villages in the Negev. The Israeli army frequently used excessive, sometimes lethal force against demonstrators in the West Bank and civilians in border areas within the Gaza Strip. Israeli military forces killed 55 civilians in the OPT, including 11 children. Settler violence against Palestinians in the West Bank increased, and three Palestinians were killed by Israeli settlers. Israeli settlers and soldiers accused of committing abuses against Palestinians generally escaped accountability. The authorities failed to conduct independent investigations into alleged war crimes by Israeli forces during Operation "Cast Lead" in 2008-2009. The Israeli authorities arrested thousands of West Bank Palestinians. More than 307 were administrative detainees held without charge or trial; others received prison terms following military trials. Israel held more than 4,200 Palestinian prisoners at the end of 2011. Reports of torture and other ill-treatment of detainees continued.

Background

International efforts to restart negotiations between Israel and the Palestinian Authority (PA) failed. Israel opposed the PA's application for full UN membership and temporarily withheld tax revenues due to the PA after Palestine became a full member of UNESCO.

Palestinian armed groups in Gaza fired indiscriminate rockets and mortars into southern Israel, killing two Israeli civilians (see Palestinian Authority entry); Israeli forces carried out attacks targeting Palestinians they deemed responsible. An Israeli high-school student was fatally injured in April when a missile fired from Gaza struck a school bus in the Negev. Eight Israeli settlers were killed by Palestinians in the West Bank, including one by PA security forces. Seven other civilians were killed in Israel, including six by armed militants who entered Israel from Egypt in August.

In October and December, Israel released 1,027 Palestinian prisoners, including some sentenced for killing Israeli civilians, in exchange for the release of Israeli soldier Gilad Shalit on 18 October. He had been held captive in Gaza and denied access to the ICRC by Palestinian armed groups since 2006. Israel also released 25 Egyptians in October in exchange for the release of an Israeli-US national imprisoned in Egypt.

From July to October, hundreds of thousands of Israelis participated in peaceful protests calling for lower housing costs and improved health and education systems.

Gaza blockade and humanitarian crisis

Israel maintained its military blockade of Gaza, imposed in 2007, and closed the Karni crossing in March, leaving Kerem Shalom as the only entry point for goods, despite its lack of capacity. The blockade prolonged the humanitarian crisis faced by Gaza's

1.6 million residents, more than 70 per cent of whom were dependent on humanitarian aid. A near-complete ban on exports continued, stifling the economy, and severe restrictions on imports fuelled shortages and high prices. The blockade constituted collective punishment – a breach of international law – and particularly affected children and the sick. The Israeli authorities hindered or prevented hundreds of patients from leaving Gaza to obtain medical treatment.

Egypt opened the Rafah crossing to Gazans in May, but strictly controlled movement into and out of Gaza. At least 36 Palestinians were killed in accidents in or Israeli air strikes on tunnels used to smuggle goods between Egypt and Gaza.

Israel's navy blocked several international flotillas seeking to break the Gaza blockade. In September a UN Panel of Inquiry ruled that the naval blockade of Gaza was lawful but did not address the legality of the overall closure regime imposed on Gaza.

Restrictions in the West Bank

More than 500 Israeli military checkpoints and barriers continued to hinder Palestinians' access to workplaces, schools and hospitals in the West Bank, and Israel continued its construction of a 700km fence/wall, mostly on Palestinian land within the West Bank, separating thousands of Palestinian farmers from their land and water sources. West Bank Palestinians with Jerusalem entry permits were allowed to use only four of the fence/wall's 16 checkpoints.

Palestinians were denied access to areas surrounding Israeli settlements, established and maintained in breach of international law. The construction of settlements increased. Settlements in the West Bank, including East Jerusalem, had more than 500,000 residents at the end of 2011.

Movement restrictions compelled some 200,000 Palestinians from 70 villages to take detours between two to five times longer than the direct route to reach the closest city, undermining their access to basic services.

Housing rights – forced eviction

The Israeli authorities generally withheld construction permits from Palestinian residents of East Jerusalem and Area C of the West Bank, where Israel retains full authority for planning and zoning, impeding their right to adequate housing. The Israeli authorities intensified their demolition of Palestinian homes and other facilities in the West Bank that had been built without

permits, demolishing more than 620 structures during 2011. Almost 1,100 Palestinians were displaced as a result, an 80 per cent increase over 2010; more than 4,200 others were affected by demolitions of 170 animal shelters and 46 cisterns. Vulnerable Bedouin and herding communities were particularly affected, with some at risk of permanent displacement due to severe restrictions on their movement, repeated demolitions and violence by settlers.

■ In June, Israeli forces carried out repeated demolitions in Hadidiya, a herding community in the northern Jordan Valley, destroying 33 structures and making several families homeless. An appeal to the High Court of Justice resulted in a temporary injunction against further demolition orders that were issued in November.

The authorities also intensified demolitions of Palestinian homes inside Israel, particularly in officially "unrecognized" villages, where all construction is banned. In September, the cabinet approved plans to regulate "illegal" Bedouin construction in the southern Negev region; if implemented, these could lead to the forced eviction of thousands of Palestinian citizens of Israel.

■ Shacks and other structures in al-'Araqib, an "unrecognized" village in the Negev, were demolished at least 20 times in 2011, following other demolitions in 2010. In July, the Israeli authorities brought a legal claim against the village residents seeking 1.8 million NIS (approximately US$500,000) to meet the costs of the repeated demolitions and evictions.

Excessive use of force

Israeli forces used live fire and other excessive force against Palestinian demonstrators in the West Bank and protesters at the Lebanese and Syrian borders, and to enforce the "exclusion zone" within Gaza and along its coast. They killed 55 Palestinian civilians in the OPT, including 11 children. Among them were 22 civilians, including nine children, killed by Israeli fire in Gaza's land and sea restricted areas. The army initiated internal investigations into some of these incidents, but these were not independent or transparent.

■ Up to 35 people were reportedly killed and hundreds injured when Israeli soldiers fired at thousands of Palestinian refugees and others who protested on 15 May and 5 June at the Lebanese border with Israel and the Syrian border with the Israeli-occupied Golan. Some protesters threw stones and some crossed the border in the Golan Heights, but demonstrators did not have firearms and did not appear to pose a direct threat to the soldiers' lives. Israel disputed the numbers killed and the circumstances.

■ Israeli soldiers regularly used excessive force against Palestinians demonstrating against the fence/wall, and those demonstrating against settlement expansion in the West Bank village of al-Nabi Saleh. On 9 December, they fatally injured Mustafa Tamimi, aged 28, who was struck in the face with a tear gas grenade fired at close range, in violation of military regulations, after he threw a stone at a military jeep.

Impunity

In January, Israel's Turkel Commission concluded that Israeli forces had not violated international humanitarian law when they attacked a Gaza-bound aid flotilla in May 2010 and killed nine Turkish nationals, but failed to account for the nine deaths.

The authorities again took no steps to conduct credible, independent investigations into alleged war crimes and possible crimes against humanity committed by Israeli forces during Operation "Cast Lead" in 2008-2009, in which hundreds of Palestinian civilians were killed, although a few military police investigations into specific incidents continued.

Israeli settlers and security forces accused of abuses against Palestinians generally escaped accountability. The Israeli authorities routinely opened investigations, but these rarely resulted in prosecutions. Yesh Din, an Israeli NGO, reported that almost 90 per cent of official investigations into alleged settler violence that it had monitored since 2005 were closed, apparently because of investigatory failures, and that only 3.5 per cent of complaints to Israeli military authorities made by Palestinians alleging rights violations by Israeli soldiers between 2000 and 2010 had resulted in indictments.

Detention without trial

The Israeli authorities held at least 307 Palestinians from the OPT without charge or trial during 2011, under renewable administrative detention orders based on secret information withheld from the detainees and their lawyers. Three women administrative detainees were among the Palestinians released in exchange for the release of Gilad Shalit by Hamas.

■ Writer and academic Ahmad Qatamesh was arrested in April and held under a six-month administrative detention order which was renewed in September; he was still detained at the end of 2011. He was a prisoner of conscience.

Prison conditions – denial of family visits

The Israeli authorities continued to bar families from visiting Palestinian prisoners from Gaza held in Israeli prisons, maintaining a policy in force since June 2007. Although more than 200 prisoners from Gaza were released during 2011, some 440 remained in Israeli prisons at the end of the year. Relatives of West Bank prisoners were also frequently denied visitor permits by the Israeli authorities on unspecified "security" grounds.

Unfair trials

Palestinians in the OPT continued to be tried before military courts and routinely denied access to lawyers during pre-trial interrogation. On 27 September, Military Order 1676 raised the age of majority for Palestinians being tried before Israeli military courts from 16 to 18. Previously, 16 and 17 year olds had been tried by these courts on the same basis as adults. The new order failed to require that child detainees be provided with access to legal counsel during interrogation or that children over 16 be held separately from adults.

Torture and other ill-treatment

Allegations of torture and other ill-treatment, including of children, continued to be reported. Among the most commonly cited methods were beatings, threats to the detainee or their family, sleep deprivation, and being shackled in painful positions for long periods. Confessions allegedly obtained under duress were accepted as evidence in Israeli military courts.

■ Islam Dar Ayyoub, aged 14, was arrested at his home in the West Bank village of al-Nabi Saleh at around 2am on 23 January. Blindfolded and handcuffed, he was transferred by military jeep via the nearby settlement of Halamish to the police station in the settlement of Ma'ale Adumim, where he was interrogated for hours without the presence of a lawyer; he was not allowed to rest, eat, or go to the toilet. Information obtained from him during interrogation was used to incriminate al-Nabi Saleh protest organizer Bassem Tamimi (see below).

■ In February, Gazan engineer Dirar Abu Sisi was forcibly transferred to Israel from Ukraine and held at Shikma Prison, near Ashkelon, where he was denied access to a lawyer for 25 days. In April, he was charged with developing rockets for Hamas' military wing; the Israeli authorities said he had confessed but his lawyers alleged that his confession had been obtained under torture. He was still held, reportedly in solitary confinement, at the end of the year.

Freedom of expression and association

The Knesset, Israel's parliament, passed laws restricting freedom of expression and association, including one which made it an offence to advocate a boycott of Israeli individuals or institutions in Israel or Israeli settlements in the West Bank. Another penalized commemoration by institutions or municipalities of the Nakba (catastrophe), a term used by Palestinians to describe their dispossession in 1948. The Knesset also discussed, but by the end of 2011 had not passed, proposed legislation to limit or prevent the receipt of funds from foreign governments by Israeli human rights NGOs, particularly those that provided information to the 2009 UN Fact-Finding Mission on the Gaza Conflict.

Palestinian activists in the West Bank who mounted protests, some peaceful, against the fence/wall and the presence of illegal Israeli settlements continued to face arrest and trial before Israeli military courts. The Israeli authorities arrested at least 14 Palestinian journalists, two of whom were held as administrative detainees.

■ In January, a military appeals court extended the sentence of Abdallah Abu Rahma, a non-violent activist against the fence/wall from the village of Bil'in, from one year to 16 months. He had been convicted of incitement and organizing illegal demonstrations on the basis of statements made by children under duress. He was a prisoner of conscience. He was released in March after serving his full sentence.

■ Bassem Tamimi, a long-standing activist and peaceful critic of Israeli policies, was arrested on 24 March and later charged with organizing protests in the village of al-Nabi Saleh. He remained in custody as his military trial continued at the end of 2011. He was a prisoner of conscience.

Refugees and asylum-seekers

The Israeli authorities continued to deny access to refugee-determination procedures to Eritrean and Sudanese asylum-seekers, who comprised about 80 per cent of the approximately 45,000 asylum-

seekers in Israel. They were provided only with temporary documents and were not allowed to work or access public health and welfare services. Only a small number of asylum-seekers from other countries were granted refugee status.

Tough new measures to deter future asylum-seekers progressed through parliament. In March, the Knesset approved the first reading of an Anti-Infiltration Bill under which undocumented migrants and asylum-seekers would be liable to imprisonment for three or more years. In September, the National Council for Building and Planning published plans for a 10,000-bed detention centre for asylum-seekers near Israel's border with Egypt. Despite an Israeli army decision in March to suspend the practice of "hot returns" of asylum-seekers entering Israel from Egypt without first checking their asylum claims, NGOs documented further cases of forced returns to Egypt until July.

Prisoners of conscience – Israeli conscientious objectors

At least three Israeli conscientious objectors were imprisoned during 2011 for refusing military service because they opposed Israel's occupation of the Palestinian territories.

Amnesty International visits/reports

🚗 Amnesty International delegates visited Israel and the OPT in May and November.

📄 Amnesty International's updated assessment of Israeli and Palestinian investigations into the Gaza conflict (MDE 15/018/2011)

📄 Gaza blockade must be lifted following UN panel finding on flotilla raid (MDE 15/030/2011)

ITALY

REPUBLIC OF ITALY

Head of state:	Giorgio Napolitano
Head of government:	Mario Monti (replaced Silvio Berlusconi in November)
Death penalty:	abolitionist for all crimes
Population:	60.8 million
Life expectancy:	81.9 years
Under-5 mortality:	4 per 1,000
Adult literacy:	98.9 per cent

Forced evictions of Romani communities and discrimination against them continued. The "Nomad Emergency" (a state of emergency declared in 2008 in relation to the settlements of nomad communities in several Italian regions) was declared unlawful by the Council of State in November. The authorities' failure to respond adequately to increased arrivals by sea from North Africa resulted in violations of the human rights of migrants, asylum-seekers and refugees. Racism and discrimination towards minorities such as Roma and migrants continued. Italy failed to establish effective mechanisms to prevent and prosecute torture and other ill-treatment.

Background

In the wake of the economic crisis in parts of Europe, a new government led by Mario Monti replaced the government of Silvio Berlusconi in November. Significant austerity measures were passed by the end of the year.

International scrutiny

International bodies criticized Italy's treatment of Roma, Muslims, migrants, asylum-seekers and refugees. The Council of Europe Commissioner for Human Rights highlighted in his report in September that the declaration of the "Nomad Emergency" in 2008 provided the bedrock for widespread evictions from Roma settlements, often in violation of human rights standards. The declaration authorized "delegated commissioners" in several regions to derogate from a number of laws when dealing with people living in "nomad settlements". The report also highlighted the sharp increase in arrivals by sea from North Africa since the beginning of the year, and that the reception system for migrants, asylum-seekers

and refugees had been put under considerable strain. The Commissioner urged the authorities to strengthen Italy's reception capacity as well as the integration system for refugees and other beneficiaries of international protection. He also called on the authorities to ensure that when confronted with boats in distress at sea, the safety and rescue of those on board should enjoy absolute priority over all other considerations.

The Advisory Committee on the Council of Europe Framework Convention for the Protection of National Minorities published its third opinion on Italy in May. It noted an increase in racist and xenophobic attitudes towards groups such as Roma, Muslims, migrants, refugees and asylum-seekers. The Committee also expressed concern that living conditions of Romani communities had deteriorated further.

The CEDAW Committee issued concluding observations in July urging Italy, among other things, to introduce a policy to overcome the portrayal of women as sexual objects and challenge stereotypes regarding the role of men and women in society and in the family.

Discrimination

Serious episodes of racial violence were reported. People were discriminated against on the basis of their sexual orientation, ethnicity and religion.

A draft law banning the wearing of full veils in public spaces was discussed in Parliament. If implemented the ban would have a disproportionate effect on women who chose to wear a burqa or niqab as an expression of their identity or beliefs.

Racial violence

In December in Turin, a Roma settlement was set on fire by some local residents. The attack occurred after a protest allegedly organized in solidarity with a 16-year-old girl who had accused two Romani men of raping her. She later admitted to having lied about the violence against her.

Roma

Under the "Nomad Emergency", authorities in five regions continued to be able to derogate from legislation that protects human rights, including several provisions of the law on administrative procedure. This facilitated the continuation of forced evictions of Romani communities, enabled impunity for these human rights violations and aggravated discrimination against them. In November, the Council of State declared the "Nomad Emergency" unlawful.

Reports of forced evictions continued in other regions not covered by the "Nomad Emergency".

■ In Rome the authorities continued to implement the "Nomad Plan", designed after the declaration of the "Nomad Emergency", which proposed the closure of all unauthorized camps, and the relocation of up to 6,000 Roma to 13 new or refurbished camps. The authorities carried out forced evictions of Roma settlements throughout the year, each time making people homeless. Evictions took place without adequate notice and due process, and in most cases only temporary shelter for women and small children was offered. Local NGOs reported that conditions and facilities in new camps fell short of international standards on adequate housing.

■ Although the Milanese authorities elected in May did not publicly celebrate evictions from Roma camps in the media like their predecessors, evictions continued in a manner that was inconsistent with human rights standards. In April, the authorities declared that since 2007 more than 500 evictions from irregular settlements had taken place. As in Rome, evictions did not follow administrative procedures and those affected did not have access to effective remedies; there was neither genuine consultation nor reasonable notice. Only temporary shelter was offered and only to women with small children. The authorities started closing down several authorized camps, sometimes linked to building projects for "EXPO 2015", a world fair that is held every five years in a different location around the world. Inhabitants of the via Triboniano and via Barzaghi authorized camps were evicted over several months without being provided with long-term adequate alternative housing. They were not consulted beforehand on alternatives to the eviction and on the resettlement options.

■ In August, new legal provisions came into force which allowed for the forcible removal from Italy of EU citizens who did not fulfil the requirements set by the EU Directive on Free Movement and who failed to comply with an order to leave the country within a certain time frame. There were concerns that these provisions might be applied in a discriminatory manner and pave the way for the selective deportation of people belonging to specific ethnic minorities, in particular, Roma.

Rights of lesbian, gay, bisexual and transgender people

Italian authorities failed to fill the gaps in legislation punishing hate crimes. As a result, victims of crimes based on their sexual orientation and gender identity and expression were not given the same protection as victims of crimes motivated by other sorts of discrimination.

■ In July, the Parliament rejected a draft bill on homophobic and transphobic crimes, considering it incompatible with the Italian Constitution.

Refugees, asylum-seekers and migrants

By the end of the year, over 52,000 people had arrived by sea from North Africa, in particular on the island of Lampedusa, considerably more than in previous years. The authorities' response was flawed and resulted in violations of the human rights of asylum-seekers, migrants and refugees. Actions included collective summary expulsions, violations of the prohibition of *non-refoulement* and unlawful detention. There were profound concerns that the implementation of agreements on migration control signed with several North African countries such as Libya, Tunisia and Egypt were resulting in asylum-seekers being denied access to international protection and in people being subjected to summary removals. Conditions in reception and detention centres fell short of international standards, and asylum-seekers and refugees were left destitute.

■ In March, a humanitarian crisis unfolded on the island of Lampedusa as a result of the failure of the authorities to ensure timely transfers of enough people to Sicily or to other regions of Italy. Thousands of migrants, asylum-seekers and refugees were left stranded on Lampedusa in appalling conditions, with many of them having to sleep rough with limited or no access to sanitary and washing facilities.

■ In April, the government reached an agreement with the Tunisian authorities allowing for the summary removal of Tunisian citizens. Like other agreements on migration control, its content was not fully disclosed to the public.

■ In June, the government signed a memorandum of understanding on migration control with the Libyan Transitional Council, in which both parties agreed to implement existing arrangements. There were concerns that, as in previous years, this would lead to asylum-seekers being denied access to procedures to claim international protection, and to violations of the prohibition of *non-refoulement*.

■ On 21 August, the authorities carried out a "push-back" operation after Italian vessels intercepted a boat travelling from North Africa towards Lampedusa. There were reports that this was not an isolated episode and that such operations were taking place on a regular basis.

■ In September, a fire was started by people held in the overcrowded first aid and reception centre of Lampedusa, in protest at their detention there and the threat of forcible repatriation by the Italian authorities. The fire destroyed most of the facilities in the centre. Afterwards, some of those evacuated protested on the streets of Lampedusa. Clashes with the Italian police and some inhabitants of the island broke out and resulted in several people sustaining injuries. In response to these events, the Italian authorities resumed transferring people to other locations in Italy.

Legislation adopted in August to transpose the EU Returns Directive into domestic law violated migrants' right to liberty. It extended the maximum period of detention of individuals solely for immigration purposes from six to 18 months. It also failed to reflect key safeguards included in the Returns Directive, thus undermining the promotion of voluntary returns, and favouring instead detention and enforced removals.

Following the decision of the European Court of Justice on the El Dridi case in April, the sanction of imprisonment of between one and four years for failure to comply with an order to leave the country was replaced by fines in August. The Court had been requested to assess the compliance of the Italian law with the EU Returns Directive.

In October, several organizations including UNHCR, the UN refugee agency, and the International Organization for Migration, denounced the fact that they were denied access to 150 individuals in Bari who had been intercepted at sea. Of those, more than 70 were immediately repatriated. All the organizations were partners of the government in the implementation of the "Presidium project", which aimed to improve the capacity and quality of the reception of people potentially in need of international protection.

Counter-terror and security

The government's record on the use of counter-terror legislation continued to be a cause of concern.

■ In April, the European Court of Human Rights ruled in *Toumi v. Italy* that Italy had violated the ban on torture and other ill-treatment during the deportation of a man to Tunisia in 2009. The Court ruled that Ali Ben Sassi Toumi, a Tunisian national who had been convicted of terrorism-related offences, had been forcibly returned from Italy to Tunisia in violation of its order requesting a halt to his transfer. It held that diplomatic assurances of humane treatment that had been given by the Tunisian government, in advance of the deportation, did not eliminate the risk of torture and other ill-treatment.

Guantánamo detainees

In April, the media reported that Adel Ben Mabrouk, a Tunisian national transferred from detention in Guantánamo Bay to Italy in 2009, was deported from Italy to Tunisia. He had been convicted in February of terrorism-related offences but was released after having been in pre-trial detention, as the court counted his years of detention at Guantánamo as time served.

Renditions

Appeals before the Court of Cassation were still pending in the case relating to the rendition of Egyptian national Abu Omar in 2003. In December 2010, the Milan Court of Appeal had confirmed the convictions of 25 US and Italian officials involved in the abduction of Abu Omar from a Milan street, and sentenced them to up to nine years' imprisonment. The Court confirmed the dismissal of charges against five high-level officials of the Italian intelligence agency for reasons of state secrecy. The 23 convicted US officials were tried in their absence. After his kidnapping, Abu Omar was unlawfully transferred by the CIA from Italy to Egypt where he was held in secret and allegedly tortured.

Torture and other ill-treatment

Reports of ill-treatment by law enforcement officials continued. There were no effective mechanisms established to prevent ill-treatment by police. Nor were concrete measures taken to ensure proper investigations and, where appropriate, prosecution of all law enforcement agents involved in human rights violations. The authorities failed to ratify the Optional Protocol to the Convention against Torture and to establish an independent National Preventive Mechanism for the prevention of torture and other ill-treatment at the domestic level. Torture was also not incorporated as a specific offence in ordinary criminal legislation.

Genoa G8 trials

Appeals against the second instance verdicts, issued by the Genoa Court of Appeal in the trials of law enforcement officials, medical personnel and prison officers for the ill-treatment of protesters at the 2001 Genoa G8 summit, were still pending before the Court of Cassation.

■ In March, the European Court of Human Rights ruled that there was no violation of the right to life in relation to the death of protester Carlo Giuliani on the streets of Genoa on 20 July 2001. In May 2003, the inquiry into his fatal shooting by a law enforcement officer had ended with the judge of the preliminary investigation ruling that the officer had acted in self-defence and should not be charged.

Deaths in custody

■ In June, the Bologna Court of Appeal confirmed the first instance guilty verdict against four police officers for the unlawful killing of 18-year-old Federico Aldrovandi. Owing to the application of a law on pardon, the initial sentence of three years and six months was commuted to six months only. Federico Aldrovandi died in 2005 after being stopped by police officers in Ferrara. Appeals were filed before the Court of Cassation. In May, one of three police officers who had been sentenced in 2010 to prison terms of eight, 10 and 12 months respectively for helping to throw the inquiry off track, was also given a suspended sentence of a further three months. In January, a fourth police officer was acquitted of charges of involvement in deflecting the investigations.

■ In March, the trial against a prison guard for failing to assist Aldo Bianzino and other criminal offences, began. Aldo Bianzino died in prison in Perugia in 2007 two days after his arrest. Proceedings for homicide against unidentified perpetrators were closed in 2009.

■ The trial in relation to the death of Stefano Cucchi was ongoing. Six doctors, three nurses and three prison officers stood accused of various criminal offences, including abuse of authority and abuse of office, bodily harm and failure to offer assistance. In January, a high-level official in the prison service was sentenced to two years' imprisonment for falsifying official documents and for abuse of office. Stefano Cucchi died in October 2009 in a hospital's prison wing in Rome several days after his arrest.

■ Investigations were still ongoing into allegations of ill-treatment suffered by Giuseppe Uva while in police custody hours before his death. He died in June 2008 in a hospital in Varese. The trial against a doctor for his manslaughter, allegedly due to wrong medical treatment, was ongoing. In December, the body of Giuseppe Uva was exhumed to undergo further forensic examination.

Amnesty International visits/reports

🚄 Amnesty International delegates visited Italy in March, April, July and November.

📃 Current evidence: European complicity in the CIA rendition and secret detention programmes (EUR 01/001/2011)

📃 Italy: Amnesty International findings and recommendations to the Italian authorities following the research visit to Lampedusa and Mineo (EUR 30/007/2011)

📃 Italy: "Zero tolerance for Roma": Forced evictions and discrimination against Roma in Milan (EUR 30/020/2011)

JAMAICA

JAMAICA

Head of state:	Queen Elizabeth II, represented by Patrick Linton Allen
Head of government:	Andrew Holness (replaced Bruce Golding in October)
Death penalty:	retentionist
Population:	2.8 million
Life expectancy:	73.1 years
Under-5 mortality:	30.9 per 1,000
Adult literacy:	86.4 per cent

Hundreds of people in inner-city communities were the victims of gang murders or police killings. Nobody was held accountable for alleged human rights violations under the 2010 state of emergency. Attacks and harassment of lesbians, gay men and bisexual and transgender people were reported. No death sentences were passed and there were no executions.

Background

High levels of armed gang violence, mainly in marginalized inner-city communities, remained a concern. However, the number of killings recorded fell by 15 per cent compared with 2010.

An independent commission of inquiry appointed to investigate the handling of the US extradition request for suspect drug-dealer Christopher Coke reported in June. It found that Prime Minister Golding's involvement in the decision to extradite had been "inappropriate". In September, Prime Minister Golding announced he was stepping down as Prime Minister and as leader of the Jamaica Labour Party.

In April, the Charter of Fundamental Rights and Freedoms was adopted, replacing Chapter III of the Constitution.

In July, the Supreme Court ruled that the 2010 Bail (Interim Provisions for Specified Offences) Act was unconstitutional. Another temporary act, granting extra powers of detention and arrest to the police, was extended in July for another year.

In November, the UN Human Rights Committee considered Jamaica's third periodic report and made several recommendations on issues including investigations of allegations of extrajudicial executions; protection of lesbians, gay men and bisexual and transgender people; and combating gender-based violence.

The People's National Party, led by former Prime Minister Portia Simpson Miller, won the general elections which were held on 29 December.

Police and security forces

The number of people killed by the police between January and June fell by 32 per cent compared to the same period in 2010. However, several people were killed in circumstances suggesting that they may have been extrajudicially executed.

Nobody was held accountable for alleged unlawful killings and enforced disappearances carried out under the 2010 state of emergency. The Public Defender, whose office conducted an independent investigation into alleged human rights violations during the state of emergency, had not submitted his report to Parliament by the end of the year. A commitment to appoint an independent commission of inquiry to establish the truth about what happened was not forthcoming from the government, despite calls for such an inquiry from the Public Defender and Jamaican human rights organizations.

The Independent Commission of Investigations (INDECOM), established in August 2010 to investigate abuses by the security forces, received resources to recruit and train additional investigators. However, debate continued over whether INDECOM has the power to charge police officers, highlighting the need to clarify and strengthen its powers in law.

The implementation of police reform continued. In April, the police stated that, of the 124 recommendations for reform proposed by a panel of independent experts in June 2008, 53 had been implemented and 65 were in advanced stages of delivery.

Justice system

In October, the Minister of Justice stated that a significant number of recommendations for the reform of the justice system had been implemented. However, he also acknowledged that significant delays in the delivery of justice persisted.

A Special Coroner charged with examining cases of fatal shootings by the police was appointed in February. However, because of the very limited resources assigned to his office, he lacked the capacity to deal effectively both with the backlog of cases and with the high number of new cases.

Children's rights

Following criticism over the holding of children together with adults in police lockups, the government opened the Metcalfe Street Juvenile Remand Center for boys in July and ordered the transfer of all detained boys to the Center. However, according to local human rights organizations, as of 3 September, 28 children remained in police lockups. Girls continued to be held together with adults.

Violence against women and girls

Police statistics revealed a decrease in complaints of sexual crime against women and girls. However, in May, the police stated that sexual attacks against children aged between 11 and 15 had increased compared with the same period in 2010.

A National Policy for Gender Equality was adopted in March.

Rights of lesbian, gay, bisexual and transgender people

LGBT organizations reported scores of cases of attacks, harassment and threats against lesbians, gay men and bisexual and transgender people, which in many cases were not fully and promptly investigated.

The Charter of Fundamental Rights and Freedoms failed to include the right to non-discrimination on grounds of sexual orientation and gender identity.

A petition was filed with the Inter-American Commission on Human Rights on behalf of two gay men to challenge the articles of the Offences Against the Person Act (commonly known as the "buggery" law). A UN Human Rights Committee recommendation called on the state to amend the law and to provide protection for lesbians, gay men and bisexual and transgender people, and for human rights defenders working on their behalf.

Death penalty

No death sentences were handed down. There were seven people on death row at the end of the year.

The Charter of Fundamental Rights and Freedoms included a provision intended to reverse the effects of a landmark 1993 ruling by the UK-based Judicial Committee of the Privy Council, Jamaica's highest court of appeal. This had found that execution after five years on death row would constitute inhuman and degrading punishment.

Amnesty International visits/reports

🚋 Amnesty International delegates visited Jamaica in March.

📰 Jamaica: A long road to justice? – Human rights violations under the state of emergency (AMR 38/002/2011)

📰 Jamaica: Submission to the UN Human Rights Committee for the 103rd Session of the Human Rights Committee (AMR 38/004/2011)

JAPAN

JAPAN

Head of government:	Yoshihiko Noda (replaced Naoto Kan in September)
Death penalty:	retentionist
Population:	126.5 million
Life expectancy:	83.4 years
Under-5 mortality:	3.3 per 1,000

A magnitude 9 earthquake off the eastern coast of Japan on 11 March caused a massive tsunami with catastrophic results, including the world's worst nuclear disaster in 25 years. Abusive interrogations by police continued to take place under the *daiyo kangoku* system. The government failed to apologize and provide reparations in line with international standards for survivors of Japan's military sexual slavery system. The Minister of Justice came under heavy pressure to carry out executions. Despite increases in the number of asylum-seekers arriving in Japan, very few were granted refugee status.

Background

On 11 March, an earthquake followed by a tsunami devastated the Tohoku area of eastern Japan. An estimated 20,000 people died or were reported missing. The Fukushima Daiichi Nuclear Power Plant suffered severe damage. Radiation emissions exceeding safe levels raised serious concerns about the lasting impact on health and food safety. A 20km compulsory evacuation zone – considered by many to be too narrow – was established. Tens of thousands, including those from the evacuation zone, were displaced in temporary shelters and houses in Fukushima prefecture. The Japanese government and Tokyo Electric Power Company were heavily criticized for their handling of the crisis, including their failure to provide timely information about risks, resulting in serious concerns about negative impacts on the affected population's right to health.

Justice system

In April, the Minister of Justice instructed the Public Prosecutor's Office to monitor on a trial basis all recorded interrogations conducted by the Special Investigation Department and the Special Criminal Affairs Department, as well as interrogations of suspects with learning disabilities or mental illness. A review of the Criminal Detention Centers and Treatment of Detainees Act was discussed by the Ministry of Justice and the Police Agency. However, this did not result in any amendments to the law or to the *daiyo kangoku* system, which allows police to detain suspects for up to 23 days.

■ Shoji Sakurai and Takao Sugiyama were acquitted of murder and robbery in May after spending 29 years in prison. During their retrial, the court found that tape recordings of the interrogations, including the confession, were doctored, and lacked credibility due to doubts over whether the confession had been obtained voluntarily.

Violence against women and girls

On 30 August, the Constitutional Court of South Korea ruled it unconstitutional for the South Korean government to make no tangible effort to settle disputes with Japan over reparations for survivors of Japan's military sexual slavery system. Japan continued to refuse to compensate Korean women mobilized as sex slaves before and during World War II. The Constitutional Court noted that South Korea violated the basic rights of the former "comfort women" with its inaction. In October, the South Korean government raised the issue of Japan's military sexual slavery system at the UN, saying that "this systematic rape and sexual slavery constitute war crimes and also, under defined circumstances, crimes against humanity". The Japanese government responded that all issues had been settled under treaties. On 14 December, activists and survivors in Seoul, South Korea, demonstrated for the 1,000th time in front of the Japanese embassy, in a weekly protest that began in 1992.

Death penalty

There were no executions; 130 prisoners, including several prisoners with mental illness, remained on death row. In October, Minister of Justice Hideo Hiraoka stated that he would not end capital punishment, but would consider cases on an individual basis. He was under pressure from within government to resume executions. On 31 October, the Osaka District Court ruled hanging constitutional.

Refugees and asylum-seekers

An estimated 1,800 individuals applied for asylum in Japan. On 17 November, the Japanese parliament passed a resolution pledging its commitment to the UN Refugee Convention on the 30th anniversary of Japan's ratification. Under a resettlement programme established in 2010, Japan accepted 18 refugees in 2011 from Myanmar who had been processed in Thailand. Some refugees from Myanmar, accepted under the programme in 2010, complained publicly that they were forced to work 10 hours a day, that they were given insufficient support by the government, and were deliberately misinformed by authorities prior to arriving in Japan.

JORDAN

HASHEMITE KINGDOM OF JORDAN

Head of state:	King Abdullah II bin al-Hussein
Head of government:	Awn al-Khasawneh (who replaced Marouf al-Bakhit in October, who replaced Samir Rifai in February)
Death penalty:	retentionist
Population:	6.3 million
Life expectancy:	73.4 years
Under-5 mortality:	25.3 per 1,000
Adult literacy:	92.2 per cent

Peaceful protesters calling for reform were forcibly dispersed and reportedly beaten by the security forces and pro-government supporters, causing injuries and possibly the death of one man. Freedom of expression and association remained restricted. The Constitution was amended to specifically prohibit torture. Trials continued before the State Security Court (SSC), whose procedures did not satisfy international standards for fair trial. Among those tried were around 100 alleged Islamists, many of whom said they were tortured or otherwise ill-treated while held incommunicado in April. Thousands of people were held without charge or prospect of trial on the authority of provincial governors. Women faced legal and other discrimination and at least 10 people were reported to have been victims of so-called honour killings. Migrant domestic workers continued to be exploited and abused. According to media reports, at least 15 people were sentenced to death. No executions were carried out.

Background

Demonstrations were held at various points throughout the year by people calling for political, economic and social reform, prompting the King to promise change. In February, he appointed a new Prime Minister tasked with expediting reforms and later suggested that these would see a transfer of power from the monarchy to parliament and that future governments would be democratically elected and based on representative political parties. In September, amendments to the Constitution were ratified which, if implemented, would improve protection of civil and political rights. However, public criticism continued over the slow pace of reform.

In October, the King appointed a new government by decree and another new Prime Minister. The same month, the head of the feared General Intelligence Department, a military security agency, resigned and was replaced by royal decree.

Excessive use of force

Peaceful protesters and journalists were injured apparently as a result of the use of excessive force by the security forces; some members of the security forces were also reported to have been injured when demonstrations became violent. Most protests were peaceful, but some became violent after government supporters attacked peaceful demonstrators. In at least one case, the security forces refused to intervene and may have facilitated and been involved in such attacks.

■ Khayri Sa'id Jamil died on 25 March after apparently peaceful pro-reform demonstrators were attacked and stoned by government supporters and security forces on 24 and 25 March in Amman. The first attack occurred in the presence of the security forces who failed to intervene. The next day, members of the gendarmerie and other security forces reportedly joined with government supporters in attacking pro-reform demonstrators, using stones and beating them with sticks and batons, after blocking escape routes. An official autopsy was said to have found no evidence that Khayri Sa'id Jamil was beaten prior to his death, which it attributed to heart failure; unofficial sources alleged that his teeth had been broken, his body was bruised and he had wounds to his head, ears, legs and genitals. The authorities said a full official investigation would be held into the events on 24 and 25 March, but provided no further details and any outcome was not made public.

Freedom of expression, association and assembly

Freedom of expression and association remained restricted under several laws. Journalists and others who criticized the government, monarchy or state institutions were liable to arrest and prosecution, or attack by government supporters.

A draft Anti-Corruption Commission law would further restrict media freedom if enacted, imposing substantial fines against individuals for the dissemination or publication of information about any person accused of corruption that "leads to defamation, impacts on his dignity or targets his personality". The proposed law was still being considered at the end of 2011.

A new amendment to the Public Gatherings Law required that the authorities be notified in advance of planned "public gatherings", replacing the requirement that prior official authorization be obtained. However, the amendment failed to define the term "public gathering".

Torture and other ill-treatment

The government amended Article 8 of the Constitution to explicitly provide that detainees are not to be "tortured… or harmed physically or emotionally" and are only to be held in places "sanctioned by law", and to invalidate "confessions" or other statements obtained under duress. Despite these important new safeguards, reports of torture and other ill-treatment persisted.

Unfair trials

Over 100 people, most of them alleged Islamists, faced unfair trials before the SSC in 2011 for alleged offences against state security. Constitutional amendments included the stipulation that civilians should not be tried before a panel comprising only military judges except in cases involving treason, espionage, terrorism, drugs offences and counterfeiting. Local and international human rights organizations, including Amnesty International, have called for the SSC to be abolished.

■ In August, some 150 people went on trial before the SSC, around 50 of them in their absence, in connection with their alleged participation in a demonstration at Zarqa in April to demand the release of hundreds of Islamist prisoners; the demonstration had been followed by violence between demonstrators, pro-government supporters and security forces. The demonstrators faced charges of "plotting terrorist acts" and "inciting riots and sectarianism". Detained in mass arrests on 15 and 16 April, many were reported to have been held incommunicado and tortured and otherwise ill-treated to the extent that some still had visible injuries when their families first gained access to them up to five days later. In May, the Director of the Public Security Directorate denied that they had been tortured or abused but it was unclear whether any independent investigation was carried out.

Detention without trial

According to the official Jordan National Centre for Human Rights, around 11,300 people were held under the 1954 Law on Crime Prevention. This gives provincial governors the power to detain people indefinitely without charge if they are suspected of committing a crime or deemed a "danger to society".

Violence and discrimination against women

Women continued to face discrimination in law and in practice, and gender-based violence. According to media reports, at least nine women were killed by male relatives and one man was killed in cases where the perpetrator claimed to have acted in the name of family "honour".

Women's rights activists called for reform of the Citizenship and Nationality Law to enable Jordanian women married to a foreign spouse to pass on their nationality to their children and husband, as Jordanian men married to a foreign spouse can do. The law had not been amended by the end of 2011. In June, the King spoke in favour of abolishing all forms of legal discrimination against women, but when the Constitution was ratified its Article 6(i), which prohibits discrimination on grounds of "race, language or religion", was not amended to prohibit discrimination on grounds of gender.

At the end of her 14-day visit to Jordan in November, the UN Special Rapporteur on violence against women pointed out that constitutional prohibition of gender discrimination was necessary to ensure that women can properly challenge inequality. She also said that any steps towards eradicating violence against women must be preceded by improved equality for women.

Migrants' rights – domestic workers

Thousands of migrant domestic workers continued to be inadequately protected against exploitation and abuse, including sexual violence, by their employers despite legislation and official regulations introduced since 2008. During her visit in November, the Special Rapporteur on violence against women encouraged the government to strengthen measures to prevent abuses against women migrant domestic workers. Tens of women who fled employers for reasons ranging from non-payment of wages to physical abuse were unable to return to their countries of origin because they could not pay fines imposed for over-staying their residence visas.

Refugees and asylum-seekers

People fleeing violence in Syria continued to arrive in Jordan. By December, at least 2,300 Syrians had registered with UNHCR, the UN refugee agency, in Amman. Jordan continued to host hundreds of thousands of refugees from other countries.

Death penalty

According to media reports, at least 15 people were sentenced to death although at least five of those sentences were commuted. The last execution took place in 2006.

Amnesty International visits/reports

- "Investigation" into attacks on demonstrators in Jordan must be transparent (MDE 16/001/2011)
- Jordan: Impartial investigation into 15 July demonstration violence needed (MDE 16/002/2011)

KAZAKHSTAN

REPUBLIC OF KAZAKHSTAN

Head of state:	Nursultan Nazarbaev
Head of government:	Karim Massimov
Death penalty:	abolitionist for ordinary crimes
Population:	16.2 million
Life expectancy:	67 years
Under-5 mortality:	28.7 per 1,000
Adult literacy:	99.7 per cent

Reports of torture and other ill-treatment by security forces continued unabated, despite government claims that it was successfully addressing these violations. Security forces used excessive force to break up large-scale protest strikes by oil and gas workers and detained dozens of protesters and their supporters, as well as trade union and opposition activists. At least 16 people were killed during clashes between protesters and police in December. A trade union lawyer was sentenced to six years in prison for allegedly inciting social discord during the strikes. The authorities forcibly returned asylum-seekers and refugees to China and Uzbekistan despite international protests and interventions by the UN.

K

Background

In April, President Nursultan Nazarbaev won uncontested elections with over 95 per cent of the vote. The OSCE concluded that the vote had been marred by "serious irregularities". Shortly afterwards, the President announced his intention of creating a two-party parliament and, in November, he dissolved the one-party parliament and called early elections for January 2012.

The authorities stepped up counter-terrorism operations targeting unregistered or banned Islamic groups and Islamist parties and organizations following an unprecedented number of bomb explosions, suspected suicide bombings and violent attacks by unidentified armed groups throughout the country. At least 35 people, including security forces and civilians, were killed during these violent incidents which the authorities described as terrorist attacks by illegal Islamist groups. Human rights groups claimed that the authorities used these alleged threats to national security to tighten state control over religious groups. In October, a new law imposed strict regulations on religious organizations, making it compulsory for them to re-register with the state within 12 months or face closure. All mosques were required to come under the authority of the state-controlled Muslim Board or would be outlawed.

On 16 December, in the worst confrontation in recent history, celebrations of the 20th anniversary of Kazakhstan's independence in the south-western oil city of Zhanaozen were marred by violent clashes between protesters and police. At least 15 people were killed and more than 100 seriously injured. One protester was killed later in a separate incident. Officials reported 42 buildings burned down or destroyed, including the town hall. The President imposed a 20-day state of emergency in Zhanaozen, sent in military reinforcements and set up a special commission to investigate the violence. All communications with the town were temporarily cut off. The President, who visited the city on 22 December, blamed the violence on "young hooligans" who had taken advantage of the dissatisfaction and anger of the striking workers to destroy and loot public and private property. He said security forces had acted strictly within the law. However, the Prosecutor General's Office opened a criminal investigation into the use of force by security forces after video footage of the events was released.

It also invited the UN to join an impartial investigation into the violence.

Torture and other ill-treatment

In July, the UN Human Rights Committee discussed Kazakhstan's report on implementing the ICCPR. It regretted that Kazakhstan had not made more progress in eliminating torture and questioned the political will of the authorities to fulfil their commitments, especially in initiating effective investigations into allegations of torture or other ill-treatment. In the same month, in a retrograde move, the President signed a decree authorizing the transfer of the prison system back to the authority of the Ministry of Internal Affairs, thereby defeating years of reform efforts by government and NGOs. Access by public monitors to prisons and pre-trial detention centres had greatly improved since their transfer to the authority of the Ministry of Justice in 2004. In contrast, access to police cells and other places of detention under the authority of the Ministry of Internal Affairs remained problematic and most allegations of torture continued to be received from there.

■ Nikolai Maier, aged 21, and four of his friends were reportedly attacked by 15 police officers while they were sitting in the courtyard of his apartment block in Rudni on 25 July. Eyewitnesses stated that the police officers hit the young men with rubber batons and kicked them. Nikolai Maier lost consciousness. All five men were then detained at the police station. Nikolai Maier was charged with endangering the life and health of law enforcement officers. The following morning, Nikolai Maier was taken to hospital and diagnosed with concussion, and head, eye and thigh injuries. He was placed under house arrest. Despite medical evidence and numerous complaints from his family and their lawyer, the Prosecutor's Office made no investigation into the allegations of torture and ill-treatment by the police. The Kostanai Regional Internal Affairs Department found that the use of force by the police officers was justified. The trial started in November and no verdict had been reached at the end of December.

■ Following the violence in Zhanaozen on 16 December, released detainees and relatives of detainees reported that scores of people, including young women, had been rounded up and kept incommunicado in overcrowded cells in police custody. They claimed the detainees had been stripped naked, beaten, kicked, and doused with cold water. Journalists

K

reported hearing screams coming from interrogation rooms in police stations. However, without access, independent monitors found it difficult to verify the allegations. At least one man was alleged to have died as a result of the torture he was subjected to in police custody.

Workers' rights

Thousands of oil industry workers in south-western Kazakhstan staged a series of strikes and public protests from May onwards, following disputes over pay and working conditions. The companies took legal action: the strikes were declared illegal and hundreds of striking employees were dismissed.

The authorities used excessive force to break up the protests, including in Zhanaozen, and arrested dozens of striking workers as well as trade union and opposition political party activists. Most were sentenced to short administrative terms of detention or fined. Security forces also threatened, detained and beat relatives and supporters of the striking workers, and harassed human rights monitors. Independent journalists covering the strike were assaulted by unidentified attackers in October. The failure of the authorities to investigate such violations added to the workers' grievances and increased tensions. However, the events of 16 December in Zhanaozen took national and international scrutiny to a higher level. Following a visit to Zhanaozen on 22 December, the President dismissed senior regional and national oil and gas company executives and the regional governor for failing to adequately address the demands of the striking oil workers.

■ On 16 December in Zhanaozen, young men and oil workers on strike since May tore down festive displays in the town's central square and reportedly attacked police and local town officials with stones. Eyewitnesses claimed that some police fired warning shots into the air but that others fired directly into the large crowd in the square, which included women and children out to celebrate. Amateur video footage showed security forces aiming and shooting their weapons at protesters running away and beating those lying injured on the ground. At least 15 people were killed and more than 100 seriously injured. The Prosecutor General's Office announced that 16 people had been arrested on charges of organizing the violence while over 130 had been detained for participating in violent mass disorders.

■ On 24 May, Natalia Sokolova, a lawyer and trade union activist representing workers in the Karazhanbasmunai Oil Company, was found guilty of organizing an unsanctioned mass gathering in Aktau and sentenced to administrative detention. On the day of her release, she was charged with "inciting social discord" and remanded in custody for two months. Repeated requests from relatives to visit her were rejected. On 8 August, Aktau City Court sentenced Natalia Sokolova to six years in prison and on 26 September the Mangistau Regional Court turned down her appeal, rejecting her defence that she had only acted in her professional capacity as the trade union's legal adviser. An appeal with the Supreme Court was pending at the end of December.

Refugees and asylum-seekers

The authorities increased efforts to forcibly return asylum-seekers and refugees to China and Uzbekistan, despite international protests and interventions by the UN.

■ On 30 May, Ershidin Israil, an ethnic Uighur teacher and a Chinese national, was forcibly returned to China. On 14 June, the Chinese authorities confirmed that he was in their custody, and being treated as a "major terror suspect". Ershidin Israil fled China for Kazakhstan in September 2009, after he gave an interview to Radio Free Asia, exposing the alleged beating to death in custody of a young Uighur man involved in the July 2009 unrest in Urumqi. In March 2010, UNHCR, the UN refugee agency, had recognized Ershidin Israil as a refugee in Kazakhstan and he was accepted for resettlement in Sweden. However, on 3 April 2010 he was taken into custody by the Kazakhstani authorities. He applied for asylum in Kazakhstan five times and each application was rejected by the courts.

■ Kazakhstan extradited 28 ethnic Uzbek men to Uzbekistan on 9 June, where they were at real risk of torture. In May, the UN Committee against Torture reaffirmed its 2010 interim measures prohibiting Kazakhstan from extraditing these individuals. Four more ethnic Uzbek men who remained in detention, as well as the wives and children of all 32, continued to be at risk of forcible return at the end of December. Some of the relatives of the detained men had been campaigning for their safety. They spoke publicly about the poor conditions in which the men were kept in detention, the beatings and other ill-treatment the security forces subjected them to and the risks they faced if forcibly returned to Uzbekistan. As a result, they were intimidated and threatened by security forces.

The men originally fled Uzbekistan, fearing that they would be persecuted due to their religious beliefs, practices or affiliations with banned or unregistered Islamist organizations. They were detained in June 2010, at the request of the Uzbekistan government. Appeals had been lodged against the decision to extradite them, but they were rejected by a district court in Almaty on 15 March.

Amnesty International visits/reports

▨ Kazakhstan: Ethnic Uzbeks at risk of torture if returned (EUR 57/002/2011)

▨ Kazakhstan: Authorities urged to protect rights of protesting oil workers in the south-west of country (EUR 57/004/2011)

KENYA

REPUBLIC OF KENYA

Head of state and government:	Mwai Kibaki
Death penalty:	abolitionist in practice
Population:	41.6 million
Life expectancy:	57.1 years
Under-5 mortality:	84 per 1,000
Adult literacy:	87 per cent

Laws bringing into effect some of the provisions of the Constitution were enacted, new institutions created and public officials appointed. There were proposals for further legal and institutional reforms. However, there was continued impunity for past and current human rights violations, including unlawful killings and other violations by the police, and crimes committed during the post-election violence of 2007-8.

Background

The Commission on the Implementation of the Constitution, established to advise on and oversee the process of implementing the 2010 Constitution, started functioning on 4 January. Various laws were proposed by the government, considered by the Commission and passed in Parliament. These included the Judicial Service Act and the Vetting of Judges and Magistrates Act, which provide a legal framework for judicial reforms – including the establishment of a new Judicial Service Commission (JSC) responsible for hiring and setting the terms and conditions of judicial officers. The law on vetting established a board to investigate the integrity of current judicial officers. Following a public recruitment process led by the JSC, a new Chief Justice and Deputy Chief Justice were appointed to head the judiciary, along with five judges of the new Supreme Court – Kenya's highest judicial body. The Chief Justice, Deputy Chief Justice and Director of Public Prosecutions were sworn into office in June.

Two laws providing a new legal framework for fresh appointment of members of the Kenya National Commission on Human Rights (the state human rights institution) and the National Gender and Equality Commission were also enacted. Other laws passed during the year established a new anti-corruption commission, a commission on the administration of justice, and the Independent Electoral and Boundary Review Commission – the body tasked with running elections and reviewing electoral and administrative boundaries.

At the end of the year several bills were undergoing public debate. These included draft laws on the structure and authority of county governments established under the Constitution.

Impunity

Post-election violence

Although the government stated several times that investigations were continuing into crimes and human rights violations, including possible crimes against humanity, allegedly committed during the post-election violence, steps were not taken to bring perpetrators to justice.

The CEDAW Committee, in its Concluding Observations issued in April following a consideration of Kenya's record in implementing CEDAW, expressed concern that perpetrators of sexual and gender-based violence, including rape and gang rapes committed during the post-election violence, remained unpunished.

Police and security forces

There were incidents of unlawful killing and torture and other ill-treatment by the police and other security personnel.

K

■ In January, plain-clothes police officers shot dead three men in Nairobi after ordering them out of their car. According to eyewitnesses, the men had surrendered before being shot. After the incident the police claimed the men were armed criminals. Although the Minister of Internal Security announced that the officers involved had been suspended, the government did not specify any steps it had taken to bring them to justice.

The authorities took no steps to bring to justice police officers and other security personnel who had reportedly carried out extrajudicial executions and other unlawful killings in recent years.

■ Police halted their investigations into the 2009 killings of Oscar Kingara and Paul Oulu, two human rights activists, by unknown gunmen.

Key laws setting the framework for police reform were passed. These included the Independent Policing Oversight Authority Act (establishing an oversight authority to deal with complaints against the police), the National Police Service Act (providing a new legal framework for policing) and the National Police Service Commission Act (establishing a Police Service Commission). As of December, the process of appointing members of the Police Service Commission was ongoing.

International justice

On 8 March, the International Criminal Court (ICC) summonsed six Kenyan citizens believed to be responsible for crimes against humanity committed during the post-election violence. In April, the six men appeared before the Court in two separate cases. Confirmation hearings were conducted by the Pre-Trial Chamber in September and October to determine whether there was evidence to refer the cases to full trial. The Court's decision was pending at the end of the year.

In April, the government requested that the cases be declared inadmissible before the ICC, because amendments to Kenyan law, including the adoption of a new Constitution and the enactment of the International Crimes Act, meant that "national courts were now capable of trying crimes from the post-election violence, including the ICC cases." The Pre-Trial Chamber rejected the application, maintaining that it had no evidence of ongoing investigation and prosecution of the six suspects, and that a promise to carry these out could not be used to pre-empt the Court's jurisdiction over the cases.

In March, the government unsuccessfully sought a consideration by the UN Security Council for a deferral of the ICC cases.

The government did not act on a parliamentary motion passed in December 2010 that urged it to start Kenya's withdrawal from the Rome Statute and to repeal the International Crimes Act which incorporates the Statute into Kenyan law.

On 28 November, the High Court ruled that the government was obliged to effect the arrest of President al-Bashir of Sudan on the strength of existing ICC warrants for his arrest if he were to visit Kenya in the future. The government announced its intention to appeal against the decision.

Truth, Justice and Reconciliation Commission

The Truth, Justice and Reconciliation Commission (TJRC) conducted country-wide public hearings where individuals testified about alleged human rights violations, the impact of grand corruption, land injustices and other issues that form part of its mandate. The Commission planned to conclude these hearings by the end of January 2012, and conduct thematic hearings during February and March. The final report documenting its findings and recommendations was planned for May 2012. The Commission's work was hampered by insufficient funding.

A tribunal appointed to investigate allegations into the credibility of the Commission's Chair had not started its work by the end of the year; this was due to a pending court case filed by the Chair to stop the tribunal from investigating his alleged complicity in committing past human rights violations that are the subject of the TJRC's mandate. The Chair remained suspended throughout the year.

Violence against women and girls

In its Concluding Observations, the CEDAW Committee expressed concern at the "persistence of adverse cultural norms, practices and traditions as well as patriarchal attitudes and deep-rooted stereotypes regarding the roles, responsibilities and identities of women and men in all spheres of life." The Committee noted that such stereotypes perpetuate discrimination against women and contribute to the persistence of violence against women as well as harmful practices, including female genital mutilation, polygamy, bride price and wife inheritance. It expressed concern that despite such negative impacts on women, the government "had not taken sustained and systematic action to modify or eliminate stereotypes and negative cultural values and harmful practices."

Housing rights – forced evictions

In September, more than 100 people died after a petrol pipeline exploded in Sinai informal settlement in the industrial area of Nairobi. The resulting fire quickly spread through the settlement due to dense concentration of housing, poor building materials and lack of access roads for emergency services.

In October and November the authorities carried out mass forced evictions and house demolitions in at least five informal and formal settlements in Nairobi, mostly around Jomo Kenyatta International Airport, Wilson Airport and the Moi Air Base. The evictions rendered hundreds of families homeless. According to Kenya Airports Authority officials, the evictions were necessary to reclaim land for the airport to prevent possible air disasters. In most instances residents complained that they had not been given adequate notice of the demolitions, or an opportunity to challenge them or seek alternative housing. Thousands of residents of Kyang'ombe settlement, next to Jomo Kenyatta International Airport, were forcibly evicted from their homes by the police and other personnel acting under the instructions of the Kenya Airports Authority. This was despite an existing temporary court order, filed by a group of residents, pending the outcome of a court case regarding land ownership.

In at least three separate cases during the year, the High Court ruled that the right to adequate housing under Article 43(1) of the Constitution includes a legal prohibition against forced evictions. By the end of the year the government had not fulfilled its 2006 pledge to publish national guidelines on evictions.

Internally displaced people

Government figures released in September indicated that most people displaced as a result of the post-election violence of 2007-8 had returned to their homes, been integrated into various communities or resettled in other parts of the country. Around 158 households remained in transit displacement camps.

Local NGOs reported that the official figures excluded hundreds of internally displaced households still living in self-help makeshift camps not recognized by the government. Groups of people internally displaced as a result of the post-election violence complained that official measures to help them, such as subsidies, were inadequate. Thousands of other people remained displaced as a result of ethnic clashes before the 2007-8 violence.

Refugees and asylum-seekers

As of November, more than 152,000 Somali refugees fleeing conflict and drought had arrived in the Dadaab camps in eastern Kenya. In July, the Kenyan government opened the Ifo extension of the camp. However, there remained inadequate space and facilities for the residents of the camps.

In October, the government deployed the Kenyan army in Somalia to fight against the al-Shabab armed Islamist group. Following the intervention, the government stopped the registration of new arrivals in Dadaab by UNHCR, the UN refugee agency, and the transportation of asylum-seekers from the border to Dadaab.

In October, November and December there were a number of grenade and bomb attacks in border towns in north-eastern Kenya and an attack at a public bus park in Nairobi by suspected al-Shabab members and sympathizers. Several people were killed, including a refugee leader in Hagadera camp in Dadaab, and dozens were injured. The government announced it would investigate the attacks.

Death penalty

Courts continued to impose the death penalty. There were no executions.

Some courts ignored the July 2010 decision by the Court of Appeal that the mandatory application of the death penalty was unconstitutional.

Amnesty International visits/reports

🚌 Amnesty International delegates visited Kenya in January, March, July, October, November and December. There is an Amnesty International office in Nairobi.

📄 Examination of Kenya's state report under the Convention: Oral statement by Amnesty International to the CEDAW Committee (AFR 32/001/2011)

📄 Kenya's application before the International Criminal Court: A promise is not enough to pre-empt the Court's jurisdiction (AFR 32/003/2011)

📄 Kenya: Fire shows need for protection for slum-dwellers (AFR 32/005/2011)

📄 Kenya: Triple killing by police must be investigated (PRE01/022/2011)

📄 Kenya must comply with ICC summons on post-election violence (PRE01/126/2011)

KOREA

(DEMOCRATIC PEOPLE'S REPUBLIC OF)

DEMOCRATIC PEOPLE'S REPUBLIC OF KOREA
Head of state:	Kim Jong-un (replaced Kim Jong-il in December)
Head of government:	Choe Yong-rim
Death penalty:	retentionist
Population:	24.5 million
Life expectancy:	68.8 years
Under 5-mortality:	33.3 per 1,000

The year ended with Kim Jong-un succeeding his father as absolute ruler of the country on 17 December, but there were no indications of an improvement in the country's dismal human rights record. North Koreans continued to suffer violations of nearly the entire spectrum of their human rights. Six million North Koreans urgently needed food aid and a UN report found that the country could not feed its people in the immediate future. There were reports of the existence of numerous prison camps where arbitrary detention, forced labour, and torture and other ill-treatment were rife. Executions, including public executions, persisted. Collective punishment was common. Violations of freedom of expression and assembly were widespread.

Background

Kim Jong-il died, reportedly of a heart attack, in December, ending his 17-year tenure as state leader, a position he inherited from his father, Kim Il-sung. Kim Jong-un, Kim Jong-il's son, was appointed his successor.

In June, the UN Security Council extended for a third term the mandate of the expert body dealing with UN sanctions imposed on North Korea for nuclear arms testing.

Flooding caused by heavy rains beginning in June was compounded by a typhoon in August, causing widespread damage, especially in north and south Hwanghae provinces. A total of 68 people were reportedly killed or missing and more than 25,000 left homeless as a consequence.

Food crisis

Deaths from starvation were reported in South Pyongan province in January, and in North and South Hamkyung provinces since April 2010. In April, the World Food Programme, Food and Agricultural Organization and UNICEF launched an emergency operation to reach 3.5 million of the most vulnerable children, women and elderly.

A report, released in November by the Food and Agricultural Organization and the World Food Programme, found that much of the population suffered prolonged food deprivation from May to September as the Public Distribution System ration of cereals was reduced to 200g or less per person per day. This amounted to just one third of a person's minimum daily energy requirements. The report indicated that malnutrition affected one in four women aged 15 to 49, while just over a third of all infants suffered from stunting and nearly a fifth were underweight. The report further cited a 50 to 100 per cent increase in the admissions of malnourished children into paediatric wards compared with the previous year.

Despite the crisis, international food aid remained dependent on geopolitics. Reports in February suggested that the government had ordered its embassies to appeal to foreign governments for food aid. Following an aid-monitoring visit, the European Commission decided in June to provide €10 million in emergency food aid. The USA did not send food aid to North Korea, reflecting concerns over the monitoring of its distribution.

Arbitrary arrests and detention

In apparent preparation for a succession of power, unconfirmed reports suggested that, in January, the State Security Agency detained over 200 officials, some of whom were feared executed, while others were sent to political prison camps. Credible reports estimated that up to 200,000 prisoners were held in horrific conditions in six sprawling political prison camps, including the notorious Yodok facility. Thousands were imprisoned in at least 180 other detention facilities. Most were imprisoned without trial or following grossly unfair trials and on the basis of forced confessions.

Torture and other ill-treatment

Men, women and children in the camps were tortured and ill-treated, including by being forced to work in dangerous conditions. The combination of hazardous forced labour, inadequate food, beatings, totally inadequate medical care and unhygienic living conditions, resulted in prisoners falling ill, and a large number died in custody or soon after release. The government continued to deny the existence of political prison camps.

Death penalty

In July, there were unconfirmed reports that the authorities had either executed by firing squad or killed in staged traffic accidents 30 officials who had participated in inter-Korean talks or supervised bilateral dialogue. On 10 March, the Special Rapporteur on extrajudicial, summary or arbitrary executions wrote to the government regarding 37 reported cases of executions between 2007 and 2010 for "financial crimes".

Freedom of expression

In June, the authorities allowed the Associated Press to establish a news bureau in Pyongyang. Reuters news agency announced that it had received permission to operate a satellite dish in Pyongyang. Nevertheless, there were no independent domestic media, no known independent opposition political parties and no independent civil society. Criticism of the government and its leaders was strictly curtailed, and punishable by arrest and incarceration in a prison camp. Only a select few people had internet access, mostly through a closely monitored intranet network. Officials clamped down on users of Chinese mobile phones, and phone connections were blocked in Sinuiju, the border city near Dandong in China.

Freedom of movement

North Korean citizens faced severe restrictions on travel both within the country and abroad. Thousands of North Koreans who fled to China in search of food and employment were often forcibly repatriated to North Korea by the Chinese authorities. They were routinely beaten and detained upon return. Those suspected of being in touch with South Korean NGOs or attempting to escape to the Republic of Korea

(South Korea) were more severely punished. Reports in July suggested that North Korean authorities ordered a crackdown on people leaving the country without permission. In October, unconfirmed reports indicated that the National Security Agency had arrested at least 20 North Koreans in September in Shenyang, China. The 20 were forcibly returned to North Korea and detained at a National Security Agency facility in North Hamkyung province.

Refugees and asylum-seekers

More than 23,500 North Koreans were granted nationality in South Korea; hundreds were in Japan. According to figures released in 2011 by UNHCR, the UN refugee agency, there were 917 North Korean asylum-seekers in "refugee-like situations" in 2010 in countries including Australia, Germany, Netherlands, UK and USA.

■ In March, 27 North Koreans were handed over to the North Korean navy. They were part of a 31-member group (20 women, 11 men) whose fishing boat had drifted into South Korean waters in thick fog in February. Four of this group decided to remain in South Korea and were given nationality.

■ In June, nine North Koreans reached South Korea by boat. Following this, the North Korean authorities reportedly restricted travel of its citizens to border areas and banned small boats along its west coast.

■ In September, nine North Koreans, including three children, were discovered off the coast of Japan's Ishikawa Prefecture aboard a small wooden fishing boat. They were initially detained in Nagasaki and were later allowed to leave for South Korea.

International scrutiny

The UN Special Rapporteur on the situation of human rights in North Korea was denied permission to visit the country. In September, 40 NGOs, including Amnesty International, inaugurated an international coalition in Tokyo, calling for a Commission of Inquiry to investigate crimes against humanity committed by the North Korean government. In May, Robert King, the US Ambassador for North Korean human rights and humanitarian affairs, made an unprecedented visit to the country, leading a delegation to gauge the seriousness of the food crisis. On his departure, he was accompanied by newly released Korean-American missionary Jun Eddie Yong-su, who had been detained for six months for "inappropriate or illegal religious activity".

KOREA

(REPUBLIC OF)

REPUBLIC OF KOREA
Head of state:	Lee Myung-bak
Head of government:	Kim Hwang-Sik
Death penalty:	abolitionist in practice
Population:	48.4 million
Life expectancy:	80.6 years
Under 5-mortality:	4.9 per 1,000

The government increasingly invoked the National Security Law to restrict freedom of expression, particularly in the context of discussions pertaining to North Korea. The authorities closely monitored the internet and social networking sites such as Twitter and Facebook. There were no executions. Migrant workers remained vulnerable following the Constitutional Court's ruling against job mobility and a government crackdown against undocumented migrants.

Background

As the National Human Rights Commission of Korea celebrated its 10th anniversary, it faced a boycott from local human rights NGOs after it failed to properly consult civil society on recommendations to the Ministry of Justice which was drafting a new National Action Plan.

In August, the Constitutional Court ruled it unconstitutional for the government to make no tangible effort to settle disputes with Japan over reparations for Korean survivors of Japan's military sexual slavery system (see Japan entry).

Freedom of expression

The authorities increasingly used the National Security Law (NSL) to target individuals and organizations perceived to oppose the government's policy on North Korea. In March, Frank La Rue, UN Special Rapporteur on freedom of expression, observed that there was a "shrinking space for freedom of expression" in the Republic of Korea (South Korea). He attributed this to the rising number of prosecutions and harassment of individuals critical of the government. By the end of the year, 135 people had been investigated for violating the NSL.

■ In May, online bookseller Kim Myeong-soo was acquitted of the charge of violating Article 7(5) of the NSL. He had been accused of selling 140 books and possessing 170 others "with the intention of endangering the existence and security of the State." Prosecutors appealed against his acquittal.

Charges were levelled against those who peacefully expressed their opinions or disseminated information on the internet. By 31 October, the police had deleted 67,300 web posts they believed threatened national security by "praising North Korea and denouncing the U.S. and the government", a sharp rise from 14,430 posts in 2009.

■ In July, prosecutors charged 244 officials and teachers under provisions of the State Public Officials Act, Political Parties Act and Political Fund Act for joining the Democratic Labor Party and paying membership fees.

■ In September, police authorities investigated Park Jeonggeun for violating Article 7 of the NSL. A member of the Socialist Party and critic of North Korea, he had mockingly re-tweeted lines from a North Korean website and posted the phrase "long live Kim Jong-il".

Conscientious objectors

In March, the UN Human Rights Committee considered the cases of 100 South Korean conscientious objectors, and found that South Korea had violated the right to freedom of thought, conscience and religion, protected under Article 18 of the ICCPR. The Committee's decision obliged the state to provide an effective remedy, including compensation, to the 100, and to avoid similar violations in the future. In September, however, the Constitutional Court ruled that refusal to undertake military service was not covered by the "right to freedom of conscience" which is protected in the Constitution. At least 810 conscientious objectors remained in prison as of December.

■ In June, lawyer Baek Jong-keon was sentenced to one and a half years in prison. As of November, his appeal was pending before the Seoul Central District Court.

Freedom of assembly

Protests against the construction of a naval base in Gangjeong village, Jeju island, continued, with many residents and activists facing civil and criminal charges.

■ In August, the Supreme Prosecutors' Office labelled the protests a challenge to state power. Several demonstrators had blocked vehicles from carrying construction material to the naval base. Police arrested 133 people during the protests.

■ In November, trade unionist Kim Jin-sook ended an 11-month protest from the top of a crane in the Hanjin Shipyard, Busan. The protest, against job losses at the shipyard, attracted hundreds of supporters who rallied to her side, travelling on "Buses of Hope". Song Kyong-dong, a poet, and Jeong Jin-woo, a member of the New Progressive Party, were detained in November and later charged with, among other things, "obstruction of business", for taking part in the "Buses of Hope" campaign.

Migrants' rights

Hundreds of migrant workers were arrested and deported, following a crackdown against undocumented migrant workers which began in September.

■ In February, the Korea Immigration Service (KIS) cancelled Michel Catuira's work visa and ordered him to leave the country by March. Michel Catuira, who was President of the Migrants' Trade Union (MTU), appealed against this decision. In September, the Seoul Administration Court upheld his appeal, ruling that efforts to deport him violated South Korean and international human rights law. The KIS subsequently appealed against this decision. Since the MTU was founded in 2005, the government had arrested and deported at least five of its leaders, suggesting that the authorities were attempting to stop it from conducting its legitimate union activities.

■ In September, the Constitutional Court ruled that restricting migrant workers to three changes of workplace within a work permit issued under the Employment Permit System did not violate their freedom of occupation. The judgement weakened the 2007 Constitutional Court ruling which recognized that migrant workers had the same rights to work as South Korean nationals, under Article 32 of the Constitution.

■ In November, a Chinese migrant worker died in a police vehicle just after his arrest by immigration

authorities. Despite frantic calls from fellow detainees, officials reacted slowly and medical help arrived too late.

Death penalty

Draft legislation aimed at abolishing the death penalty was pending consideration by the National Assembly. In September, South Korea observed 5,000 days free of executions. As of December, 60 people remained on death row.

Amnesty International visits/reports

🚌 Amnesty International delegates visited the country in April and November.

KUWAIT

STATE OF KUWAIT
Head of state: al-Shaikh Sabah al-Ahmad al-Jaber al-Sabah
Head of government: al-Shaikh Jaber al-Mubarak al-Hamad al-Sabah (replaced al-Shaikh Nasser Mohammad al-Ahmad al-Sabah in November)

Death penalty:	retentionist
Population:	2.8 million
Life expectancy:	74.6 years
Under-5 mortality:	9.9 per 1,000
Adult literacy:	93.9 per cent

Freedom of expression was curtailed. Critics of the government, including those using social media, were at risk of arrest, and security forces beat some demonstrators. One man died in police custody apparently after being tortured. Women continued to face discrimination in law and in practice. Thousands of Bidun continued to be denied Kuwaiti nationality and so were denied access to health care, education and employment on the same basis as citizens. At least 17 people were sentenced to death; no executions were reported.

Background

There were a number of protests, some apparently inspired by events elsewhere in the region. Partly in response, it appeared, the government disbursed grants in February reportedly worth around US$4,000 and food rations to Kuwaiti citizens. In June, hundreds of mostly young Kuwaitis demonstrated, calling for a change of government and an end to corruption. A wave of strikes began in September by workers demanding better pay and benefits. In November, in response to escalating demands by protesters who occupied parliament and by members of the opposition, the Prime Minister resigned. Kuwait was elected to the UN Human Rights Council in May. Kuwait's record was considered by the UN Committee against Torture (CAT) in May and by the CEDAW Committee in October.

Freedom of expression and assembly

Government critics were liable to arrest. Demonstrations were generally allowed, although at least one was forcibly dispersed. Riot police occasionally beat demonstrators.

■ In January, the Supreme Court overturned the prison sentence imposed on journalist Muhammad 'Abd al-Qader al-Jasem in November 2010 after he was convicted of defamation in a case filed against him by the Prime Minister. He faced further allegations of defamation.

■ Online activist Nasser Abul was arrested on 7 June and charged with breaching "state security", "damaging the country's interests" and "severing political relationship with brotherly countries" because of messages he posted on Twitter. On 24 September, he was convicted of writing derogatory remarks about Sunni Muslims and sentenced to three months' imprisonment, but immediately released due to the time he had already been detained. He was found not guilty of insulting the ruling families of Bahrain and Saudi Arabia.

■ On 16 November, riot police beat protesters outside the Prime Minister's residence before they occupied parliament, demanding an end to corruption and the resignation of the Prime Minister.

Torture and other ill-treatment

One man died in custody apparently after being tortured by police.

■ Mohammad Ghazzai al-Maimuni al-Mutairi died after police arrested him in January for possessing alcohol. Initially, the authorities said he resisted arrest and died from a heart ailment but then launched an investigation after an opposition MP produced medical evidence indicating that he had been bound and severely beaten before he died. Some 19 police officers were charged in connection with his death; their trial was continuing.

The CAT urged the government to amend the law to make torture a crime punishable by severe penalties.

Discrimination – the Bidun

Throughout the year, hundreds of Bidun, long-term residents of Kuwait, demonstrated to protest against their continuing statelessness and to demand Kuwaiti nationality, which would allow them to access free education, free health care and employment opportunities on the same basis as Kuwaiti citizens. More than 100,000 Bidun continued to be denied nationality. The security forces used force to disperse demonstrations and arrested protesters. The government said it would address some Bidun grievances but stated that only 34,000 Bidun were eligible for citizenship.

Migrant workers

Migrant domestic workers, many from countries in south and south-east Asia, were still not protected by Kuwait's labour laws. Many faced exploitation and abuse by employers. Those who left their jobs without their employer's permission, even when fleeing abuse, were liable to arrest, detention, prosecution under immigration laws for "absconding", and deportation.

■ In October, an unnamed Indonesian domestic worker died after she hanged herself in a police cell after being arrested for fleeing her place of work and charged with "absconding".

The CAT urged the government to urgently enact labour legislation to cover domestic work and ensure that migrant domestic workers, particularly women, are protected against exploitation and abuse.

Women's rights

Women continued to face discrimination in law and in practice. In October, the CEDAW Committee urged the government to criminalize domestic and sexual violence, introduce tougher penalties for perpetrators of so-called honour crimes, and introduce legislation to promote gender equality.

Death penalty

At least 14 men and three women were sentenced to death after being convicted of murder or drug-trafficking. Most were foreign nationals. At least one death sentence was commuted to life imprisonment. No executions were reported.

The CAT urged the government to restrict the application of the death penalty to "most serious" crimes and treat death row prisoners humanely.

Amnesty International visits/reports

▤ Kuwait's candidacy for election to the UN Human Rights Council: Open letter (MDE 17/002/2011)

▤ Kuwait: Online activist sentenced for tweeting – Nasser Abul (MDE 17/004/2011)

KYRGYZSTAN

KYRGYZ REPUBLIC

Head of state:	Almaz Atambaev
	(replaced Roza Otunbaeva in December)
Head of government:	Omurbek Babanov
	(replaced Almaz Atambaev in December)
Death penalty:	abolitionist
Population:	5.4 million
Life expectancy:	67.7 years
Under-5 mortality:	36.6 per 1,000
Adult literacy:	99.2 per cent

Despite facilitating two independent commissions of inquiry, the authorities failed to fairly and effectively investigate the violence of 2010 and its aftermath. The authorities rejected the strong evidence of crimes against humanity, including rape and sexual violence, being committed against ethnic Uzbeks in Osh during the violence. Lawyers defending ethnic Uzbeks continued to be threatened and physically attacked. Despite official directives from the General Prosecutor's Office to investigate every single report of torture, prosecutors regularly failed to thoroughly and impartially investigate such allegations and bring those responsible to justice.

Background

Following the violence between ethnic Kyrgyz and ethnic Uzbeks in southern Kyrgyzstan in June 2010, which left hundreds dead, thousands injured and hundreds of thousands displaced, the authorities recognized the need to ensure an independent investigation into the events. They mandated two commissions of inquiry: one national, one international. While serious crimes were committed by members of both ethnic groups, the majority of the damage, injuries and deaths were suffered by ethnic Uzbeks.

The National Inquiry issued its report in January. It failed to address the human rights violations committed, ignored the evidence of crimes against humanity and reiterated the official narrative of co-ordinated Uzbek aggression provoking a spontaneous response on the part of ethnic Kyrgyz. In May, the International Commission of Inquiry, also known as the Kyrgyzstan Inquiry Commission (KIC), concluded differently. There was strong evidence of widespread, systematic and co-ordinated offences against ethnic Uzbeks in the southern city of Osh that would amount to crimes against humanity if proved in court. The investigations and prosecutions that had taken place were flawed and ethnically biased. The report concluded that the torture of detainees in connection with the violence had been "almost universal".

The authorities accepted the KIC's findings that torture and ill-treatment had taken place but categorically rejected that crimes against humanity had been committed, and in turn accused the KIC of ethnic bias and flawed methodology.

Torture and other ill-treatment

Reports of torture and other ill-treatment in the aftermath of the June violence continued throughout 2011. The authorities acknowledged that torture and ill-treatment in detention was a problem.

In April, a new Prosecutor General was appointed. She soon issued a directive requiring all reports and complaints of torture to be immediately investigated and all places of detention to be inspected regularly and without notice. In September, she issued detailed instructions on the methodology of investigating torture. Human rights organizations and the Ombudsman's Office co-operated with the OSCE in order to set up independent detention monitoring groups throughout the country with the right of unimpeded access to all detention facilities. The groups started operating in August.

The then President and the new Prosecutor General made repeated efforts to stop the routine use of beatings and other ill-treatment in order to extract confessions. However, at regional and local levels there appeared little commitment to effectively address and prevent these serious human rights violations. The KIC concluded that "acts of torture were committed in detention centres by the

K

authorities of Kyrgyzstan in the aftermath of the June events... [S]uch acts of torture are ongoing and … the response of the authorities to allegations of torture has been grossly inadequate."

There were serious concerns that while investigating crimes, police officers continued to disproportionately target Uzbeks and Uzbek neighbourhoods, threatening to lay charges of serious crimes, such as murder, in relation to the June violence in order to extort money from them. At least two ethnic Uzbeks died in police custody reportedly from torture.

■ Usmonzhon Kholmirzaev, an ethnic Uzbek Russian citizen, died on 9 August, reportedly as a result of torture, two days after he was arbitrarily detained in Bazar-Korgan by plain-clothes police officers and taken to the local police station. He told his wife a gas mask had been put over his face and he had been beaten. When he collapsed, one of the officers reportedly kneed him in the chest two or three times until he lost consciousness. The police threatened that if he did not pay them US$6,000, they would charge him with violent crimes in relation to the June 2010 violence. He was eventually released after his family gave the officers US$680. He was hospitalized the next morning and died of his injuries a day later. His wife said that he had told her that the officers were responsible for his injuries. His wife and her lawyer, who were present at his autopsy, reported that the forensic examination found that he had died of internal haemorrhaging. Following an official request from the Russian consulate, the prosecutor of Jalal-Abad opened a criminal case in August against four police officers with several charges, including torture.

The government renewed its invitation to the UN Special Rapporteur on torture and he visited the country in December. He concluded that the use of torture and ill-treatment was widespread for the purpose of extracting confessions. Torture methods included "being subjected to asphyxiation through plastic bags and gas masks, punched, beaten… and applied electric shocks… during arrest and first hours of informal interrogation." Conditions of detention ranged from "adequate to dreadful".

Unfair trials

Trials and appeal hearings at all levels fell short of international standards. Allegations of forced confessions were not investigated; defence witnesses were not interviewed; lawyers continued to be

threatened and physically attacked, including inside the courtroom.

■ In April, the Supreme Court indefinitely postponed the appeal hearing of prominent human rights defender Azimzhan Askarov and seven co-defendants, accused of the murder of a Kyrgyz police officer during violence in Bazar-Korgan. The presiding judge ordered a thorough and independent investigation into prison conditions in the south of the country after the defence argued that there were no facilities to house long-term prisoners or those sentenced to life and that Azimzhan Askarov and his co-defendants would be at risk of torture and cruel, inhuman and degrading conditions if returned to Jalal-Abad. The Court did not order investigations into the allegations that the defendants were tortured to force them to "confess". On 20 December the Supreme Court turned down the appeal and confirmed Azimzhan Askarov's life sentence amid international protests. He remained in a prison medical facility outside the capital city Bishkek to which he had been transferred in November 2010. He was allowed to receive visitors and was provided with adequate medical assistance. The Special Rapporteur on torture described conditions in detention facilities in Bishkek as "dreadful" and "unacceptable".

■ In August, lawyer Tatiana Tomina, an ethnic Russian who regularly represented ethnic Uzbek clients, described how she had been assaulted by four ethnic Kyrgyz women on leaving Osh city court. One of the women hit her with a bag and the others then beat, kicked and punched her, while shouting abuse. Court employees and police officers who witnessed the assault did not intervene. Before leaving the court building, the women threw stones at her and threatened her with more violence.

■ During a hearing at Kara Suu district court in September, relatives of an ethnic Kyrgyz man killed in the 2010 violence shouted threats at the defence lawyer of the accused, Makhamad Bizurkov, an ethnic Uzbek Russian citizen. They pulled the lawyer's hair, threw rocks at the defendant who was sitting in a metal cage, and attacked the police officers present in the courtroom. A human rights monitor attending the hearing reported that the judge admonished the relatives but did not order them to leave the court or sanction them for assaulting the lawyer and obstructing justice. After the judge and the prosecutor had left the courtroom, the victim's relatives continued throwing rocks and plastic bottles at the defendant's cage. The women also hit the police officers who tried to stop them, verbally abused and threatened the human rights monitor and pushed her out of courtroom.

Impunity

Impunity for law enforcement officers who perpetrated torture and other ill-treatment continued to be a serious problem in Kyrgyzstan. It became even more apparent following the June 2010 violence. Attempts by relatives to complain to police and prosecutors about this treatment continued to be obstructed. Prosecutors invariably failed to adequately investigate the allegations and bring those responsible to justice.

In February, the President reiterated her concerns about the lack of investigation into the complaints she had received of torture and other ill-treatment by security forces. The Osh Regional Prosecutor's Office then announced that it would review 995 criminal cases to check whether the proceedings complied with national legislation. However, by the end of the year, there had been only one successful prosecution for torture and other ill-treatment in police custody and the five police officers convicted of torture received only suspended sentences. Their appeals were pending at the end of the year.

Investigators and prosecutors also failed to investigate and prosecute the vast majority of crimes against ethnic Uzbeks committed during and since the June 2010 violence, including crimes against humanity committed in Osh in June 2010. In at least 200 documented cases of murders of ethnic Uzbeks during the June violence, either no criminal investigation was opened or the proceedings were suspended. However, many relatives were reluctant to follow up on the murders for fear of reprisals.

Human rights and women's organizations reported that women and girls were reluctant to report rapes and other sexual violence, given the cultural stigma attached to the victims in their traditional communities. Although some 20 incidents had been documented and independently corroborated, human rights monitors believed the real figure to be much higher.

Most of the rapes and other sexual violence were committed by groups of Kyrgyz men, against Uzbek women and girls, although there were also instances of Uzbek men raping Kyrgyz women. There were also reports of boys being raped and one report of a middle-aged Uzbek man being gang-raped by Kyrgyz attackers before being stabbed and set on fire. In most instances the rapes were accompanied by verbal ethnic abuse and severe physical violence.

Amnesty International visits/reports

🚌 Amnesty International delegates visited Kyrgyzstan in June.

📄 Still waiting for justice: One year on from the violence in southern Kyrgyzstan (EUR 58/001/2011)

LAOS

LAO PEOPLE'S DEMOCRATIC REPUBLIC

Head of state:	Choummaly Sayasone
Head of government:	Thongsing Thammavong
Death penalty:	abolitionist in practice
Population:	6.3 million
Life expectancy:	67.5 years
Under-5 mortality:	58.6 per 1,000
Adult literacy:	72.7 per cent

State control over the media and political, judicial and social affairs continued to restrict freedom of expression, association and peaceful assembly. Lack of transparency and a scarcity of information made independent monitoring of the human rights situation difficult. At least three prisoners of conscience and two political prisoners remained imprisoned. Harassment of Christians was reported. The fate and welfare of Lao Hmong asylum-seekers and refugees forcibly returned from Thailand remained largely unknown. The death penalty was retained as a mandatory punishment for some drug offences; however, no official statistics on death sentences were made public.

Background

The ruling Lao People's Revolutionary Party (LPRP) held its five-yearly Congress in March. The President was re-elected as Secretary-General, and the Central Committee and Politburo were expanded. All except four businessmen elected to the National Assembly in April were LPRP members and central or local government officials. A new government was formed in June with four new ministries. In December, Laos

L

reluctantly suspended work on the controversial Xayaburi hydropower dam following concerns of neighbouring countries and activists about its impact on fisheries and the livelihoods of people living downstream.

Refugees and asylum-seekers

Information remained scarce about the situation of some 4,500 Lao Hmong forcibly returned from Thailand in December 2009. Many of the approximately 3,500 returnees resettled to the remote village of Phonekham in Borikhamsay province were living under tight controls with no freedom of movement and little opportunity to make a living. Despite this, a small number managed to flee to Thailand and seek asylum.

■ According to credible sources, a former asylum-seeker died in custody in July after he was arrested by Lao police on suspicion of planting a bomb in Phonekham village. His body showed signs of mutilation. No investigation into his death was known to have been carried out.

Prisoners of conscience and political prisoners

■ Thongpaseuth Keuakoun, Bouavanh Chanhmanivong and Seng-Aloun Phengphanh, arrested in October 1999 for attempting to stage a peaceful protest, remained in prison beyond the expiry of their 10-year sentences. The authorities did not respond to requests for clarification and appeals for their release.

■ Ethnic Hmong Thao Moua and Pa Fue Khang continued to serve 12- and 15-year sentences respectively. They were arrested in 2003 for helping two foreign journalists gather information about Hmong groups hiding in the jungle, and were convicted after a grossly unfair trial.

Freedom of religion or belief

Reports continued to emerge of local authorities harassing Christian communities and targeting individuals who refused to recant their faith.

■ Two pastors arrested in January in Khammouan province were detained after holding a Christmas ceremony without official approval. They were still held in harsh conditions six months after their arrest.

LEBANON

LEBANESE REPUBLIC

Head of state:	Michel Suleiman
Head of government:	Najib Mikati (from June, replacing Saad Hariri who resigned in January)
Death penalty:	retentionist
Population:	4.3 million
Life expectancy:	72.6 years
Under-5 mortality:	12.4 per 1,000
Adult literacy:	89.6 per cent

People accused of security-related offences faced unfair trials and some were sentenced to death. Torture and other ill-treatment by the judicial police were reported. Human rights defenders were prosecuted for reporting allegations of torture. Palestinian refugees continued to face discrimination, impeding their rights to work, health, education and adequate housing. Other refugees and asylum-seekers were detained and some were forcibly returned to their countries of origin despite risks of serious abuses there. Women remained subject to discrimination, although a law that provided for lenient penalties for perpetrators of so-called honour crimes was repealed. Migrant workers, particularly women employed as domestic workers, were inadequately protected from exploitation and abuse. Eight people were sentenced to death but there were no executions.

Background

The coalition government of Prime Minister Saad Hariri fell in January. A political impasse followed, only ending in June when a new administration, headed by Najib Mikati and supported by Hizbullah, took office.

Tensions continued along the southern border with Israel. On 15 May, according to the UN, seven Palestinian refugees were killed and 111 people were injured when Israeli troops fired on Palestinian refugees and others who had gathered at the border to commemorate Nakba Day, some of whom attempted to cross into Israel.

At least three people were killed and others injured by Israeli cluster bomblets and landmines left in southern Lebanon in previous years.

The Special Tribunal for Lebanon, established by the UN Security Council to try those accused of assassinating former Prime Minister Rafic Hariri in

2005 and related crimes, issued its first indictments in June. It indicted four members of Hizbullah, who remained at liberty. Hizbullah denounced the indictments and vowed not to co-operate.

Unfair trials

People suspected of security-related offences were arrested and at least 50 of them were tried before military courts. Some were accused of collaborating with or spying for Israel; of these, at least nine were sentenced to death. Their trials before military courts were unfair; the court, whose judges include serving military officers, are neither independent nor impartial. Some defendants alleged that they had been tortured or otherwise ill-treated in pre-trial detention in order to force them to "confess", but the courts generally failed adequately to investigate such allegations or to reject contested "confessions".

■ Fayez Karam, a senior official of the Free Patriotic Movement political party, was convicted on 3 September of providing information to Mossad (Israel's intelligence agency) for payment and sentenced to two years' imprisonment with hard labour. He told the military court that convicted him that he had been tortured by officials of the Internal Security Forces (ISF) while detained following his arrest in August 2010 and forced to make a "confession" that he later retracted. He lodged an appeal.

■ Sheikh Hassan Mchaymech, a Shi'a cleric, was detained on 11 October when he was handed over to the ISF by Syrian security officials. He had been detained and reportedly tortured in Syria because he was suspected of supplying information to Mossad. After his release he was handed over to the Lebanese authorities. He was held incommunicado by the Lebanese authorities, first at an ISF detention prison in Beirut, then in Roumieh Prison until early December when his family were allowed to visit him for the first time.

Torture and other ill-treatment

Cases of torture and other ill-treatment by the judicial police were reported.

The government had still not established an independent monitoring body to visit prisons and detention centres, breaching a requirement of the Optional Protocol to the UN Convention against Torture, which Lebanon ratified in 2008.

■ In April, four inmates of Roumieh Prison in Beirut died in unclear circumstances when security forces quelled a protest by detainees against overcrowding and prolonged pre-trial detention. The Interior Minister appointed the head of the ISF to conduct an inquiry, but its outcome was not made public.

Human rights defenders

Several human rights activists were harassed for reporting alleged human rights violations by the security forces and political parties.

■ Saadeddine Shatila, a human rights activist working for the NGO Alkarama, was accused of "publishing information harmful to the reputation of the Lebanese Military" after he submitted information to the UN Special Rapporteur on torture and others about cases of alleged torture. The Military Investigating Judge was still considering the case at the end of the year.

■ Marie Daunay and Wadih Al-Asmar, staff members of the Lebanese Center for Human Rights, were questioned by the General Prosecutor on 22 March after the Amal political party, headed by Parliamentary Speaker Nabih Berri, filed a criminal complaint against the organization because it had reported allegations of torture by people affiliated to Amal. The case was pending at the end of the year.

Discrimination – Palestinian refugees

Some 300,000 Palestinian refugees, long-term residents of Lebanon, remained subject to discrimination and were prevented from accessing a range of rights available to Lebanese citizens. They were not permitted to work in certain professions or inherit property. An unknown number of Palestinian refugees continued to reside in Lebanon without an official ID card, leaving them with even fewer rights. They remained, for example, unable to register marriages, births and deaths.

Over 1,400 Palestinian refugees who fled fighting in Nahr al-Bared camp near Tripoli in the north of Lebanon in 2007 returned to the camp in 2011, but over 25,000 remained displaced.

Women's rights

Women continued to be discriminated against in law and practice, and to face gender-based violence, including from male relatives. However, in August the government repealed Article 562 of the Penal Code, which had allowed a person convicted of killing or injuring relatives to receive a reduction in sentence if the crime was held to have been committed to uphold family "honour". The same month, the Penal Code was amended to define the crime of trafficking of persons and to prescribe penalties for traffickers.

Lebanese women remained unable to pass their nationality on to their husbands and children, but in September the labour laws were reformed to remove employment restrictions for non-Lebanese spouses and children of Lebanese women. The impact of these reforms was not clear by the end of 2011. Parliament also discussed but did not pass a draft law criminalizing domestic violence, including marital rape.

Migrants' rights

Foreign women employed as domestic workers continued to face exploitation and abuse, including sexual abuse, by employers and were inadequately protected under the law. However, a draft law setting out the rights of domestic workers was under discussion in the Parliament.

Refugees and asylum-seekers

Dozens of refugees and asylum-seekers, mostly Iraqi and Sudanese nationals, were detained beyond the expiry of sentences imposed for irregular entry into Lebanon or after their acquittal. Many were held in poor conditions at an underground General Security facility in 'Adliyeh in Beirut or at Roumieh Prison and were forced to choose between remaining in indefinite detention or returning "voluntarily" to their countries of origin.

At least 59 asylum-seekers or recognized refugees were forcibly deported in violation of international refugee law.
■ Sudanese refugee Muhammad Babikir 'Abd al-'Aziz Muhammad Adam, who was detained in January 2010 and sentenced in March 2010 to a one-month prison sentence for violating a deportation order, remained held until January 2011, when he was taken from detention and flown to Norway for resettlement. He said that between September and November 2010 he was beaten and held for prolonged periods in solitary confinement, and that numerous attempts were made to forcibly return him to Sudan, where he would have been at risk of arbitrary arrest, torture and other ill-treatment.

Impunity – enforced disappearances and abductions

On 1 July, the government promised to seek information on the fate of "missing and detained

Lebanese" from the Syrian government and take other steps to address the legacy of past gross abuses, including by creating a national committee to follow up on enforced disappearances. However, the government took few if any steps towards addressing thousands of cases of people who remained missing since the 1975-90 civil war, including victims of enforced disappearance.

Death penalty

Eight people were sentenced to death, including five people tried in their absence, but no executions were carried out. The last execution was in 2004.
■ Radwan Khalaf Najm, a Syrian national, was sentenced to death in January by a criminal court for murder.

Amnesty International visits/reports

🚗 Amnesty International delegates visited Lebanon in April, May-June and July-August.

📘 Never forgotten: Lebanon's missing people (MDE 18/001/2011)

LIBERIA

REPUBLIC OF LIBERIA

Head of state and government:	Ellen Johnson Sirleaf
Death penalty:	abolitionist in practice
Population:	4.1 million
Life expectancy:	56.8 years
Under-5 mortality:	112 per 1,000
Adult literacy:	59.1 per cent

Long delays in the judicial system led to appalling overcrowding in prisons, as most detainees were awaiting trial, suffering inhumane conditions. Human rights abuses against women and girls, including rape and other forms of sexual violence, remained prevalent. The police used excessive force during demonstrations.

Background

Presidential and legislative elections took place on 11 October. No presidential candidate secured an outright majority, and a run-off election took place on 8 November. The main opposition party, Congress for

Democratic Change (CDC), boycotted the run-off and the incumbent, Ellen Johnson Sirleaf, was declared winner with 90.7 per cent of the vote.

More than 173,000 Ivorian refugees crossed into Liberia between November 2010 and December 2011 following post-election violence in neighboring Côte d'Ivoire. By the end of 2011 the influx of refugees had almost stopped, and some started returning to Côte d'Ivoire.

In November, President Ellen Johnson Sirleaf and human rights defender Leymah Gbowee were two of the three women awarded the Nobel Peace Prize "for their non-violent struggle for the safety of women and for women's rights to full participation in peace-building work".

Impunity

No progress was made in bringing to justice people responsible for serious human rights violations and abuses during the years of armed conflict and violence. The recommendation of the Truth and Reconciliation Commission (TRC) that a criminal tribunal be established to prosecute people identified as responsible for crimes under international law was not implemented, nor were most TRC recommendations on legal and other institutional reforms, accountability, and reparations.

In March, the Special Court for Sierra Leone, sitting in The Hague, finished hearing evidence in the trial of former Liberian President Charles Taylor, who was charged for his individual criminal responsibility in crimes against humanity and war crimes committed during the 11 years of armed conflict in Sierra Leone. He was not charged with crimes committed in Liberia, as the competence of the Court is limited to crimes committed in Sierra Leone. The judges were still deliberating at the end of the year.

Death penalty

In March, in response to recommendations made during Liberia's UN Universal Periodic Review, Liberia acknowledged its international obligations under the Second Optional Protocol to the ICCPR, which it acceded to in 2005, and stated that it was holding consultations with a view to repealing the 2008 law imposing the death penalty for armed robbery, terrorism and hijacking offences, if these resulted in death. However, no further steps were taken to abolish the death penalty.

One person was sentenced to death for murder by the Circuit Court in Voinjama, Lofa County.

Justice system

Inadequate police investigations, a shortage of public defenders, poor case management, corruption, and a judiciary that lacked the capacity to hear cases in a timely manner contributed to a backlog in the criminal justice system. Around 80 per cent of prisoners were awaiting trial; some were detained for years before their trial.

The continued detention of people awaiting trial meant that a pilot parole and probation scheme in Monrovia and Gbarnga and a magistrate sitting programme did not significantly reduce the number of pre-trial detainees.

People were often required to pay for services that are supposed to be free, for example for police to carry out investigations. Magistrates routinely denied bail. The judiciary lacked independence.

Customary courts often failed to follow due process. Trial by ordeal continued, whereby the guilt or innocence of the accused was determined in an arbitrary manner, sometimes involving torture or other ill-treatment.

Prison conditions

Prison conditions were extremely poor. In several prisons, inmates were crowded into dark, dirty cells, with grossly inadequate health services, and lack of ventilation and time outdoors. Hygiene and sanitation were poor, without adequate food and drinking water and basic necessities such as clean bedding and toiletries.

In July, President Ellen Johnson-Sirleaf launched a 10-year National Health Policy and Plan. Prison health services were incorporated as a cornerstone of the policy – the new Essential Package of Health Services. However, it had not been implemented by the end of the year.

Police and security forces

Despite some improvements, inadequate police protection led to some communities forming vigilante groups.

The police repeatedly used excessive force during public order operations.
■ On 11 March, police beat student protesters, 17 of whom needed medical treatment. The President set up an investigating committee, which submitted its report

in June. The committee found that the police had used excessive force, and recommended that the Inspector General of the Liberia National Police (LNP) be suspended and the Deputy Director for Operations dismissed. The Deputy Director for Operations was suspended for two months without pay. No action was taken against the Inspector General.

■ On 7 November, police opened fire on CDC supporters during a demonstration, killing at least one person and injuring many more. A commission of inquiry was established by the President to investigate the violence. It submitted its findings on 25 November. The commission found that the police had used excessive force, and in line with the commission's recommendations the Inspector General of the LNP was dismissed.

Freedom of expression

Journalists continued to face harassment, and at times threats and assault.

■ On 22 January, the Supreme Court sentenced Rodney Sieh, editor-in-chief of the privately owned *Front Page Africa* newspaper, to 30 days in prison for contempt of court. He had published a letter criticizing a judge of the Supreme Court. He was released two days later after President Sirleaf intervened.

■ On 7 November, following a petition by the Ministries of Justice and Information, the Circuit Court Judge of Criminal Court A issued a court order temporarily closing three media houses; this was carried out by armed police from the Emergency Response Unit. The media houses were accused of spreading hate messages in connection with the CDC rally and subsequent violence. On 15 November the managers of the media houses were found guilty. However, the court decided that "at this time" there would be no punishment and ordered that the media institutions be reopened.

Children's rights

There was only one juvenile court, located in Monrovia, and the juvenile justice system remained weak, with no rehabilitation or detention centres for children in conflict with the law. Children were regularly detained in police cells along with adults.

Female genital mutilation (FGM) remained widespread and was regularly performed on girls between the ages of eight and 18, some as young as three. FGM is not explicitly prohibited in Liberian law.

■ In July, two people accused of carrying out forced FGM were found guilty of kidnapping, felonious restraint and theft and sentenced to three years in prison.

Women's rights

Rape, other forms of sexual violence, domestic violence and forced and underage marriage remained widespread. The majority of reported rape cases involved girls under 18. Sexual and gender-based violence crimes units in police stations were understaffed and under-resourced and struggled to cope.

There were no functioning safe houses for survivors of gender-based violence. The management of two safe houses in Bong and Lofa counties, previously run by NGOs, was taken over and temporarily closed by the Ministry of Gender and Development. However, they had not reopened by the end of the year.

Maternal mortality remained high. UNFPA attributed this to an acute shortage of skilled medical staff, inadequate emergency obstetric care, weak referral systems, poor nutritional status of pregnant women, and extremely high numbers of teenage pregnancies. In March, the President launched a five-year plan to reduce maternal and newborn deaths in the country.

Amnesty International visits/reports

🚍 Amnesty International delegates visited Liberia in July, September and November.

📘 Good intentions are not enough: The struggle to reform Liberia's prisons (AFR 34/001/2011)

LIBYA

LIBYA

Head of state: Mostafa Abdeljalil (effectively replaced Mu'ammar al-Gaddafi in August)

Head of government: Abdurrahim al-Keib (replaced Mahmoud Jibril in October, who replaced al-Baghdadi Ali al-Mahmoudi in August)

Death penalty:	retentionist
Population:	6.4 million
Life expectancy:	74.8 years
Under-5 mortality:	18.5 per 1,000
Adult literacy:	88.9 per cent

Forces loyal to Libyan leader Colonel Mu'ammar al-Gaddafi unlawfully killed and injured several thousand people, including peaceful protesters and bystanders, after anti-government protests broke out in mid-February and then developed into an armed conflict that lasted around eight months. During the conflict, international forces, acting under a UN Security Council mandate to protect civilians, attacked al-Gaddafi forces from the air, helping to tip the balance in favour of opposition forces. Al-Gaddafi forces fired mortars, artillery and rockets into residential areas and used anti-personnel mines, cluster munitions and other inherently indiscriminate weapons; these indiscriminate attacks caused numerous civilian casualties, particularly in Misratah, Libya's third largest city. Al-Gaddafi forces also abducted thousands of individuals and tortured or ill-treated them, and extrajudicially executed captured fighters and other detainees. Opposition forces used rockets and other indiscriminate weapons in residential areas. Even after the National Transitional Council (NTC) – the loosely structured leadership of the opposition to Colonel al-Gaddafi established in late February – took control of most of the country in late August, it failed to get a grip on the militias formed during the conflict. War crimes and other violations of human rights and international humanitarian law committed during the conflict by both parties added to the dismal legacy of human rights violations of previous years. The conflict exacerbated pre-existing xenophobia and racial tensions against foreign nationals. Opposition militias took captive thousands of suspected al-Gaddafi loyalists, soldiers and alleged "African mercenaries", many of whom were beaten and abused in custody and remained held without trial, or any means to challenge the legality of their detention at the end of the year, months after the conflict ended. Scores of other suspected al-Gaddafi loyalists were killed upon or following capture by opposition fighters; among the victims were the ousted Libyan leader himself and one of his sons. Opposition forces also looted and burned homes and carried out revenge attacks and other reprisals against alleged al-Gaddafi supporters. The conflict saw hundreds of thousands of people fleeing, resulting in mass displacement inside and outside Libya, and prompting major evacuation efforts. Impunity for gross human rights violations of the past and ongoing abuses by militias remained entrenched. Discrimination against women continued in law and practice.

Background

Anti-government demonstrations planned for 17 February erupted two days early in Benghazi, Libya's second largest city, after security forces detained two prominent activists. The authorities quickly released them but the protests mushroomed and spread across Libya as government forces resorted to lethal and other excessive force to try and contain them. Within two weeks, the protests developed into an internal armed conflict as people overpowered and took up arms against government forces in eastern Libya, the Nafusa Mountain area and the coastal city of Misratah. When armed confrontations intensified as al-Gaddafi forces sought to regain territory lost to the opposition and the latter tried to gain new ground, the UN Security Council adopted Resolution 1973 on 17 March, authorizing the establishment of a no-fly zone over Libya and the implementation of all necessary measures, short of foreign occupation, to protect civilians. Two days later, an international alliance began aerial attacks on al-Gaddafi forces, poised on the outskirts of Benghazi, and began assisting opposition forces to drive them back. In late March, NATO took over military operations, carrying out thousands of air strikes on al-Gaddafi forces and infrastructure until 31 October. The forces opposing Colonel al-Gaddafi gained control of most of Libya, including Tripoli, by late August but fighting continued, notably in Beni Walid and in Sirte. On 23 October, NTC Chairman Mostafa Abdeljalil formally declared the "liberation of Libya".

L

The NTC committed to establishing a democratic, multi-party state based on respect for fundamental human rights. Its Constitutional Declaration issued on 3 August enshrines human rights principles, including respect for fundamental freedoms, non-discrimination and the right to fair trial.

Excessive use of force

Colonel al-Gaddafi's security and armed forces used lethal and disproportionate force to try and quell the demonstrations that broke out in February, firing live rounds from automatic assault rifles at unarmed demonstrators. Some 170 people were killed and more than 1,500 injured in Benghazi and al-Bayda between 16 and 21 February. Protests in Tripoli on 20 February and its suburbs were also met with live fire by security forces, leading to scores of deaths and injuries. Those killed included peaceful protesters and bystanders.

■ Naji Jerdano, who joined anti-government demonstrations in Benghazi, was struck with a baton and shot dead on 17 February by al-Gaddafi security forces. He and two other men were killed near al-Nasr Mosque during sunset prayers by security forces snipers firing from the Jalyana bridge.

■ On 18 February, Roqaya Fawzi Mabrouk, a girl aged eight, was shot dead through her bedroom window. The bullet was fired from the Hussein al-Jaweifi military base in Shahat, near al-Bayda, where al-Gaddafi forces were then reportedly based.

Abuses during armed conflict

Al-Gaddafi forces committed serious violations of international humanitarian law, including war crimes, in their efforts to retake cities and towns held by the opposition. They carried out indiscriminate attacks and attacks targeting civilians in areas that included Misratah, Ajdabiya, al-Zawiya and the Nafusa Mountain area. They fired artillery, mortars and rockets at residential areas. They used inherently indiscriminate weapons such as anti-personnel mines and cluster bombs, including in residential areas. These unlawful attacks killed and injured hundreds of civilians not involved in the fighting.

The toll on civilians was particularly heavy in Misratah, where residents were trapped from late February onwards as al-Gaddafi forces laid siege to the city and fired rockets into the port area – the only entry point for humanitarian aid and the only

evacuation point for wounded and sick patients. Indiscriminate attacks ceased in May but resumed in mid-June and continued sporadically until early August. According to local medical sources, more than 1,000 people were killed during the siege of the city.

■ One-year-old Rudaina Shami and her brother, Mohamed Mostafa Shami, aged three, were killed on 13 May when Grad rockets fired by al-Gaddafi forces struck homes in Misratah's Ruissat neighbourhood. Their five-year-old sister Malak was severely injured, requiring the amputation of her right leg.

Al-Gaddafi forces also fired live ammunition and heavy weapons, including tank shells and rocket-propelled grenades, at residents who were fleeing areas of fighting in Misratah, Ajdabiya, al-Zawiya and elsewhere.

■ Miftah al-Tarhouni and his adult son Mohammad were killed on 20 March near Ajdabiya's eastern gate when their car was hit by a projectile – seemingly a rocket or an artillery shell – apparently fired by al-Gaddafi forces.

Opposition fighters also launched Grad rockets from their front-line positions in eastern Libya, Misratah and Sirte; it was not known to what extent these caused civilian casualties.

Colonel al-Gaddafi's government accused NATO of targeting civilian objects and causing hundreds of civilian casualties but exaggerated and failed to provide clear evidence. However, there were credible reports that some NATO strikes killed at least tens of civilians between June and October, including in Majer, Tripoli, Surman and Sirte. No impartial and independent inquiries were known to have been conducted by NATO to ascertain whether all necessary precautions had been taken to spare civilian objects and minimize civilian casualties, as required by international humanitarian law.

■ NATO airstrikes on 8 August killed 18 men, eight women and eight children when two houses in the rural area of Majer, near Zlitan, were hit. All the victims were reported to be civilians.

Arbitrary arrests and detentions

Al-Gaddafi forces detained thousands of people across Libya; some were subjected to enforced disappearance. Arrests began before the February protests, then became more numerous and widespread as the conflict developed. Those held included real or perceived opposition supporters and fighters and others captured in or near areas of fighting. Some were seized in their homes. Others were detained on the roads or in public places in areas controlled by the opposition but into which al-Gaddafi forces made armed incursions, notably Misratah and towns in the Nafusa Mountain area. Detainees were mostly denied all contact with the outside world. Some were released by al-Gaddafi forces but the great majority were freed by opposition fighters after they won control of Tripoli in late August. The total number of people who went missing during the conflict remained unclear. Scores were killed in custody (see below).

■ Jamal al-Haji, a long-standing critic of Colonel al-Gaddafi, was arrested in Tripoli on 1 February by plain-clothes security agents after he called for protests using websites based abroad. He was held for nearly seven months in appalling conditions without contact with the outside world at the Nasr Intelligence Office and in Tripoli's Abu Salim Prison, part of the time in solitary confinement. He was freed on 24 August by pro-NTC fighters.

Opposition fighters captured and detained thousands of real or suspected al-Gaddafi supporters and soldiers, including suspected foreign mercenaries, during and after the conflict. Many were seized by groups of heavily armed men from their homes or detained on the streets or at checkpoints. Many were beaten or ill-treated upon capture, and had their homes looted and destroyed. No detainee was granted access to lawyers. Under the NTC, neither the Ministry of Justice and Human Rights nor the Public Prosecution had effective control or oversight of most detention facilities. Thousands of detainees continued to be held without trial or the opportunity to challenge the legality of their detention at the end of 2011.

Sub-Saharan Africans made up a large number of those detained. In the east and in Misratah from February onwards, some of them were arrested on suspicion of being mercenaries. Others in Tripoli and other western cities were detained from August, when these areas first came under opposition control. In eastern Libya and Misratah, most were released when no evidence of their involvement in fighting was found. Hundreds of men from Tawargha, an area seen as loyal to Colonel al-Gaddafi, were hunted down and abducted from homes, makeshift camps and checkpoints, detained and then tortured or ill-treated.

Torture and other ill-treatment

Individuals arrested and detained by al-Gaddafi forces were tortured or ill-treated, particularly upon capture and during initial interrogations. Detainees were beaten with belts, whips, metal wires and rubber hoses; suspended in contorted positions for prolonged periods; and denied medical treatment, including for injuries sustained as a result of torture or shooting. Some were tortured with electric shocks. Several were shot after being apprehended and while posing no threat. Some were left to suffocate in metal containers.

■ On 6 June, guards ignored pleas for water and air by detainees held in two metal containers in al-Khums; 19 suffocated to death.

Several male detainees were raped by their captors or guards.

■ A 50-year-old man was arrested by al-Gaddafi forces while receiving treatment at Tajoura Heart Hospital in Tripoli in late February. At Ain Zara Prison, also in Tripoli, he was kicked, hit with sticks and rifle butts, given electric shocks and tied to a tree. While in custody, he was raped twice using implements.

Allegations of rape by al-Gaddafi forces were widely reported by NTC supporters, and some women detained by pro-NTC forces in al-Zawiya, Tripoli and Misratah alleged they had been sexually abused.

■ Eman al-Obeidi told international journalists on 26 March that she had been raped by soldiers loyal to Colonel al-Gaddafi. After periods of being detained by al-Gaddafi forces, she was released and fled Libya in May. She was forcibly returned from Qatar to Benghazi in June, but was later allowed to leave NTC-controlled territory.

In areas controlled by the NTC before as well as after August, when Tripoli fell to the forces opposing Colonel al-Gaddafi, militias in control of detention centres tortured or ill-treated detainees with impunity, seemingly to punish them for alleged crimes or to extract "confessions". The most commonly reported methods included beatings all over the body with belts, sticks, rifle butts and rubber hoses; punching; kicking; and death threats. Individuals with dark skin, whether Libyan or foreign nationals, were especially vulnerable to abuse.

■ A 17-year-old migrant worker from Chad was taken from his home in August by armed men who handcuffed and slapped him and dragged him along the ground before detaining him at a school that they were using as a detention facility. There, he was punched and beaten with sticks, belts, rifles and rubber cables, mostly on the head, face and back. The torture only stopped when he agreed to "confess" to killing civilians and raping women.

Several detainees died in the custody of militias in circumstances suggesting that torture contributed to or caused their death.

■ Abdelhakim Milad Jum'a Qalhud, a school director from the town of al-Qarabuli, east of Tripoli, was detained at his home on 16 October by a local militia. In the following days he was seen twice by doctors who noticed multiple bruises on his body and urged his hospitalization. However, the militia ignored the medical advice and on 25 October the body of Abdelhakim Milad Jum'a Qalhud was delivered to the local hospital. The forensic report suggested that he had died as a result of beatings with an instrument. No effective investigation into the circumstances of his death was initiated.

Extrajudicial executions

Al-Gaddafi soldiers killed opposition fighters after capture in eastern Libya and Misratah. Bodies were found with hands tied behind the back and multiple gunshot wounds to the upper body.

■ The bodies of three opposition fighters – brothers Walid and Hassan al-Sabr al-Obeidi, and Walid Sa'ad Badr al-Obeidi – were found near Benghazi on 21 March. Relatives said that all three had their hands tied behind their backs and two of the bodies had visible injuries, suggesting that they were beaten before being killed.

Al-Gaddafi forces also extrajudicially executed dozens of detainees in western Libya between June and August. Most were shot.

■ On 23 August, guards threw five hand grenades and opened fired on around 130 detainees held in a hangar in a military camp in Khilit al-Firjan, Tripoli. About 50 charred bodies were later found.

Opposition fighters and supporters deliberately killed suspected al-Gaddafi soldiers and loyalists, and alleged "African mercenaries", when towns including al-Bayda, Benghazi, Derna and Sirte first came under their control. Some victims were beaten to death; some were hanged; others were shot dead after they surrendered or were captured.

Members of Colonel al-Gaddafi's security apparatus and other suspected loyalists were targeted for revenge attacks. Several were found dead after they

were seized by heavily armed men; some of the bodies were found with their hands tied behind their backs.

■ Hussein Gaith Bou Shiha, a former Internal Security Agency operative, was taken from his home on 8 May by armed men and the next morning was found dead near Benghazi. He was handcuffed and had been shot in the head.

■ Abdul Fatah Younes al-Obeidi, former Secretary of the General People's Committee for Public Security (equivalent to the Interior Minister) who defected to the opposition in February, and his two aides, Mohamed Khamis and Nasser Mathkur, died from gunshot wounds in late July. They had been taken by heavily armed men for questioning to a military camp in Gharyounes on 27 July and later allegedly to another location.

■ Video footage and other evidence indicated that Colonel al-Gaddafi was captured alive while trying to escape from Sirte and was then apparently extrajudicially executed on 20 October, together with his son Mu'tassim. The NTC announced an investigation but no findings had been made public by the end of the year.

■ On 23 October, the bodies of 65 men – civilians as well as possible fighters for al-Gaddafi forces – were found in Mahari Hotel in Sirte where opposition fighters had been based. Some victims had their hands bound behind their backs and many had been shot in the head. Video footage taken by the opposition fighters three days earlier shows 29 men being abused and threatened with death, almost all of whom were among the 65 later found dead. No investigation into the killings was initiated.

Forced displacement

Before the conflict, at least 2 million foreign nationals were living in or transiting through Libya, many in need of international protection. As the conflict intensified, hundreds of thousands of people, foreign nationals and Libyans alike, fled Libya, including through organized evacuations. Many among those in flight were robbed; some were arrested and detained for hours or days and beaten before being allowed to proceed. Sub-Saharan Africans were particularly targeted. The vast majority fled to Tunisia and Egypt (see Egypt and Tunisia entries and Europe regional overview).

Hundreds of thousands of people were involuntarily displaced within Libya. With the end of hostilities, some people were able to return to their homes, but residents of areas considered supportive of Colonel al-Gaddafi feared that they would face reprisals and were still internally displaced at the end of 2011. They included some 30,000 former residents of Tawargha, who fled the town as Misratah-based opposition fighters approached it in August, and members of the Mashashiya tribe in the Nafusa Mountains. In Misratah and other areas, militias prevented some alleged supporters of Colonel al-Gaddafi from returning to their homes, or looted or destroyed them with impunity.

Refugees, asylum-seekers and migrants

The NTC promised to uphold the right to seek and enjoy asylum, but did not commit to ratifying the UN Refugee Convention and its 1967 Protocol. In April, the NTC Chairman promised to "close the borders in front of these Africans", raising concern that refugees, asylum-seekers and migrants would continue to suffer discrimination and abuse in Libya, and be perceived as unwelcome guests. In a further move reminiscent of past abusive practices, including operations conducted at sea to "push back" foreign nationals to Libya where they faced arrest, torture and detention in appalling conditions, the NTC signed a memorandum of understanding in June with the Italian authorities. This committed both parties to joint management of the "migration phenomenon" through the implementation of existing co-operation agreements on "illegal migration" (see Italy entry).

At the end of the year, hundreds of sub-Saharan Africans continued to be held in indefinite detention without trial for alleged "immigration offences".

Women's rights

The NTC promised to promote women's rights and enshrined the principle of non-discrimination, including on the basis of gender, in its Constitutional Declaration. However, discrimination against women remained entrenched in law and practice.

On 23 October, the NTC Chairman promised to amend any legislation contrary to Shari'a (Islamic law), referencing Libya's marriage laws. Law 10 of 1984 on Marriage, Divorce and their Consequences allows polygamy, but stipulates that, before remarrying, a man must seek authorization from a special court to ensure that he is mentally, socially and financially fit.

Impunity

Colonel al-Gaddafi's government took no steps to investigate past gross human rights violations or bring to justice those responsible. The NTC vowed to do so, but struggled to secure key evidence, such as archived material and government records, some of which had been burned and looted.

In June, the International Criminal Court issued arrest warrants against Colonel al-Gaddafi, his son Saif al-Islam al-Gaddafi and security chief Abdallah al-Senussi for alleged crimes against humanity, including murder and persecution. Saif al-Islam was captured on 19 November. Despite statements by the NTC that it would seek to prosecute him before Libyan courts, by the end of the year no application had been made to the International Criminal Court challenging its jurisdiction.

Death penalty

The death penalty remained in force for a wide range of crimes. No information was available about death sentences or executions in 2011.

Amnesty International visits/reports

🚋 Amnesty International fact-findings teams visited Libya between late February and late May and between mid-August and late September.

🗐 Libya: Misratah – under siege and under fire (MDE 19/019/2011)

🗐 The battle for Libya: Killings, disappearances and torture (MDE 19/025/2011)

🗐 Libya: Human rights agenda for change (MDE 19/028/2011)

🗐 Detention abuses staining the new Libya (MDE 19/036/2011)

L

LITHUANIA

REPUBLIC OF LITHUANIA
Head of state: Dalia Grybauskaitė
Head of government: Andrius Kubilius
Death penalty: abolitionist for all crimes
Population: 3.3 million
Life expectancy: 72.2 years
Under-5 mortality: 6.2 per 1,000

The government failed to conduct an effective investigation into its role in US-led rendition and secret detention programmes. Discrimination against lesbians, gay men, and bisexual and transgender people was widespread.

Counter-terror and security

In January, the Lithuanian Prosecutor General closed a criminal investigation into the alleged involvement of state officials in two secret CIA detention sites. The reasons he gave were the need to protect state secrets and that the statute of limitations had expired on the investigation of the officials abusing their authority.

In May, the European Committee for the Prevention of Torture published a report on Lithuania, which included its inspection of the CIA detention sites. In September, NGOs presented new data about rendition flights to Lithuania. In October, however, in spite of the new information, the Prosecutor General refused to reopen the investigation.

■ On 27 October, lawyers of Abu Zubaydah, a Palestinian detained in Guantánamo Bay, filed a complaint in the European Court of Human Rights, alleging that he was unlawfully transferred to Lithuania in 2005, where he was tortured at a secret detention facility.

Discrimination – lesbian, gay, bisexual and transgender people

In June, following public pressure, a further amendment to the Law on Provision of Information to the Public came into force. It reversed the 2010 amendment, and banned discrimination in advertising and public broadcast on the basis of sexual orientation, as required under international law.

However, other legislation or proposals remained discriminatory. The parliamentary agenda published in September included amendments to the Code on Administrative Offences. These amendments covered fines for "denigrating constitutional moral values and the principles of family" as well as "organizing events contradicting social morality". The same agenda proposed amendments to the Civil Code to ban gender reassignment surgery.

The Law on the Protection of Minors against the Detrimental Effect of Public Information remained in force. Any information which "denigrates family values", or encourages marriage between anyone other than between a man and a woman, was banned from places accessible to children.

Amnesty International visits/reports

🚍 Amnesty International delegates visited Lithuania in September.

▨ Current evidence: European complicity in the CIA rendition and secret detention programmes (EUR 01/001/2011)

▨ Lithuania: Homophobic legislation and accountability for complicity in US-led rendition and secret detention programmes (EUR 53/001/2011)

▨ Unlock the truth in Lithuania: Investigate secret prisons now (EUR 53/002/2011)

▨ Lithuania: Re-open secret prison investigation now (PRE01/459/2011)

MACEDONIA

THE FORMER YUGOSLAV REPUBLIC OF MACEDONIA
Head of state: Gjorge Ivanov
Head of government: Nikola Gruevski
Death penalty: abolitionist for all crimes
Population: 2.1 million
Life expectancy: 74.8 years
Under-5 mortality: 10.5 per 1,000
Adult literacy: 97.1 per cent

Ten years after the 2001 armed conflict, prosecutions for war crimes cases, returned from the International Criminal Tribunal for the former Yugoslavia (the Tribunal) for prosecution, were annulled. The government curtailed freedom of the media.

Background

Respect for human rights deteriorated throughout the year. An election was called in June following a parliamentary boycott by opposition parties, partially because of alleged government interference in the media.

The VMRO-DPMNE (Internal Macedonian Revolutionary Organization – Democratic Party for Macedonian National Unity) was returned to power, in coalition with the ethnic Albanian Democratic Union for Integration (DUI). The DUI joined the coalition on several conditions, including an amnesty for war crimes cases.

The construction of nationalist monuments exacerbated inter-ethnic tensions. In February, ethnic Albanians, including DUI officials, attempted to stop the construction of a church-shaped museum inside Skopje Fortress; eight people were injured. In October, a population census was cancelled shortly after it started because of disagreement on the inclusion of ethnic Albanians who had lived outside Macedonia for over a year, in violation of EU rules on data gathering.

The European Commission in October again recommended that negotiations on EU accession should begin, but the EU Council of Ministers again deferred the commencement of talks, partially due to the continuing dispute with Greece over the name of the country.

War crimes

In July, parliament adopted a new interpretation of the 2002 Amnesty Law, which had granted amnesty to those involved in the 2001 armed conflict except in cases taken under the jurisdiction of the Tribunal. This interpretation stated that four war crimes cases returned in 2008 from the Tribunal to Macedonia for prosecution could only be prosecuted by the Tribunal and not by domestic courts – in violation of Macedonia's international obligations.

As a result, Skopje Criminal Court dismissed the "Mavrovo" road workers case at the request of the Public Prosecutor in September. In 2001 the road workers were allegedly abducted, ill-treated, sexually abused and threatened with death before release by the ethnic Albanian National Liberation Army (NLA). The court granted the victims leave to claim compensation in civil proceedings.

The remaining cases were annulled by the end of October. The "NLA Leadership" case included charges against Ali Ahmeti, leader of the DUI, then leader of the NLA. Another case, "Neprosteno", alleged the abduction of 12 ethnic Macedonians and one Bulgarian by the NLA.

Impunity continued for the enforced disappearance in 2001 of six ethnic Albanians by the Macedonian authorities.

Torture and other ill-treatment

In April, the Ombudsman's Office started functioning as a National Preventive Mechanism under the Optional Protocol to the UN Convention against Torture, but lacked the authority and resources to fulfil its mandate.

Impunity for ill-treatment by the police continued. Prosecutors failed to effectively investigate allegations. Reports of ill-treatment by the "Alpha" police unit continued.

Unlawful killings

■ Martin Neskovski was severely beaten on 6 June during post-election celebrations in Skopje, and died of head wounds. Despite initial denials, Igor Spasov, a member of the "Tigers" anti-terrorist police unit was detained on 8 June. Repeated public protests questioned delays in the investigation and called for stricter civilian oversight of the police. Criminal proceedings in connection with the death opened in November.

Counter-terror and security

Proceedings had not been initiated in a complaint to the European Court of Human Rights by Khaled el-Masri against Macedonia, relating to Macedonia's role in his abduction, unlawful detention and ill-treatment for 23 days in Skopje in 2003.

Khaled el-Masri had been subsequently transferred to the custody of US authorities and flown to Afghanistan, where he was allegedly subjected to torture and other ill-treatment. In civil proceedings in February, an expert witness provided evidence relating to alleged rendition flights transferring Khaled el-Masri from Skopje to Kabul. However, proceedings were adjourned in the absence of procedures allowing Khaled el-Masri to testify by video link from Germany.

Freedom of expression

The freedom of expression of journalists and independent media workers was increasingly limited by government interference, ranging from direct intimidation to control of advertising companies. By October, some 105 defamation cases had been brought against journalists, many by government officials. Jadranka Kostova, editor of Focus, was fined 1 million denar (€16,259) for alleged defamation.

In January, the authorities froze the bank accounts of the A1 television channel and associated

M

newspapers, *Vreme, Shpic* and *Koha e Re*, which were critical of the government. This followed the arrest and detention for alleged fraud and tax evasion of A1 TV's owner and 14 others in December 2010. The subsequent trial was highly politicized, and concerns were expressed about the length of defendants' detention.

In July, A1 TV closed and print versions of the newspapers ceased. Hundreds of journalists protested against their closure and consequent sacking of journalists; a union leader was dismissed, reportedly for participating in the protests. Later that month, amendments to the Law on Broadcasting increased government control over the Broadcasting Council, which regulates electronic media.

In October, talks began between government officials and journalists, who demanded the decriminalization of defamation. In a television interview, the Prime Minister accused journalist Borjan Jovanovski of undermining the country's accession to the EU.

Discrimination

The 2010 Anti-Discrimination Law came into force in January; the Commission for Protection against Discrimination began to receive complaints in April. NGOs questioned the Commission's competence and independence, as elected members lacked human rights expertise and three were state employees. The Law lacked provisions for the protection of lesbians, gay men, bisexual and transgender people, although the Commission ordered the withdrawal of a psychology text book with homophobic content.

Implementation of the 2001 Ohrid Agreement, addressing discrimination against Albanians, continued. Decentralization of powers to municipalities progressed slowly and the Law on Languages was partially implemented. The segregation of ethnic Albanian and Roma children in education continued.

Roma

In July, Macedonia assumed the Presidency of the Decade of Roma Inclusion, but failed to commit adequate resources for the implementation of its own action plans or the National Strategy for the Advancement of Romani Women.

Many Roma remained without the personal documentation needed to access education, health, employment and social protection. The NGO National Roma Centrum assisted 1,519 Roma in applying to legalize their property under a law adopted in March.

Informal Roma settlements lack running water, electricity, drainage and roads.

The European Roma Rights Centre reported in May that Romani children comprised 46 per cent of students attending special schools or primary-school classes for children with special needs.

Refugees and asylum-seekers

Around 1,519 asylum-seekers, including 1,100 Kosovo Roma and Ashkali, remained in Macedonia. The Ministry of Labour and Social Welfare failed to provide them with financial assistance and housing required under a 2010 local integration agreement. Some 193 Roma, Ashkali and Egyptians returned to Kosovo and 16 moved to Serbia. Another 185 were waiting to return while 726 opted to integrate locally.

Under pressure from the European Commission, the government strengthened border controls, introducing exit controls which limited the right to leave the country, often targeting Roma. The Interior Minister reported that 764 nationals had been denied the right to leave Macedonia in June alone.

Amnesty International visits/reports

🚗 Amnesty International delegates visited Macedonia in December.

MADAGASCAR

REPUBLIC OF MADAGASCAR

Head of state:	Andry Nirina Rajoelina
Head of government:	Jean Omer Beriziky (replaced Camille Albert Vital in October)
Death penalty:	abolitionist in practice
Population:	21.3 million
Life expectancy:	66.7 years
Under-5 mortality:	57.7 per 1,000
Adult literacy:	64.5 per cent

Security forces committed serious human rights violations including unlawful killings, torture, and unlawful arrests and detentions. Harassment and intimidation of journalists and lawyers as well as detention without trial of political opponents continued. Prison conditions were harsh and the rights of detainees were regularly violated.

Background

A "road map" to resolve the ongoing political crisis was signed in the capital Antananarivo on 17 September by Malagasy political leaders under the mediation of the Southern African Development Community (SADC). A new Prime Minister was appointed in October and a Government of National Unity, including opposition members, was formed in November. Former President Didier Ratsiraka returned to Madagascar in November after nine years of exile in France but went back to Paris on 12 December. A new Transitional Parliament was proclaimed on 1 December.

Unlawful killings

Criminal suspects were killed by members of the security forces with almost total impunity.

■ Three men were shot dead in Antananarivo on 8 September by police officers from the Rapid Intervention Group (GIR). The men were reportedly unarmed and did not resist the police orders to stop. Despite wide publicity around the incident, no investigation had been opened at the end of the year.

■ On 9 December, prosecutor Michel Rahavana was killed near his office and the prison in Toliara by a group of police officers attempting to release a colleague who had been arrested by the prosecutor in connection with a theft. Following a strike by members of the judiciary, the Minister of Justice announced at the end of the year that an investigation would be conducted.

Death in custody

■ On 17 July, taxi driver Hajaharimananirainy Zenon, known as Bota, died after being arrested and tortured in the 67 ha neighbourhood of Antananarivo by members of the Intervention Police Force (FIP) who dropped his body at the Antananarivo Hospital morgue the following morning. Hajaharimananirainy Zenon's family lodged a formal complaint on 30 August but it was not clear at the end of the year if any official investigation had started.

Detention without trial

Dozens of perceived or real opponents to the High Transitional Authority (Haute Autorité de la Transition, HAT) remained detained without trial, some since 2009.

■ Rakotompanahy Andry Faly, a former intern at the Malagasy Broadcasting System (MBS) radio station, remained in detention despite his serious medical condition and repeated requests to be granted bail that were turned down by the authorities. Andry Faly had been arrested with three other MBS staff in Antananarivo in June 2009 by members of the National Joint Commission of Inquiry (CNME), a security body especially created by the HAT. In July 2011, he was transferred to the clinic of the Antanimora central prison in Antananarivo where he remained at the end of the year. He was among 18 detainees who went on hunger strike in 2010 calling on the authorities to expedite their trial.

Prison conditions

Prison conditions were harsh and prisoners' rights were ignored. Detainees did not have access to adequate health care, food or sanitation. According to a June report by the authorities, 19,870 people were detained in prisons with a maximum capacity of 10,319. They included 785 women and 444 minors. The report also stated that 10,517 of the detainees were under preventive detention.

Death penalty

According to official figures, 58 detainees were on death row, where some had remained for years while waiting for their cases to come before the Supreme Court.

Children's rights

The UN Children's Fund (UNICEF) reported that children in Madagascar were adversely affected by poor nutrition, homelessness, loss of schooling, lack of basic health care and little or no access to water and sanitation. UNICEF stated that trafficking of children for domestic service and sexual exploitation continued. Such practices were carried out with impunity.

Arbitrary arrests and detentions

Arbitrary arrests and detention were common. In some cases, lawyers assisting or defending perceived or real opponents to the HAT were themselves subject to arrest and detention amounting to harassment and intimidation and denial of the right to legal counsel for their clients.

■ On 28 February, Rolland Stephenson Ranarivony, lawyer for a member of the Reformed Protestant Church of Madagascar (FJKM), was arrested and detained by officials from the Territory Security Directorate (DST) when he arrived to inquire about the situation of his client held in DST cells in Antananarivo.

M

He was released later that day after the president of the Malagasy Bar Association publicly complained about his arrest and detention.

Freedom of expression – media

Privately owned media outlets and those believed to have links with the opposition were targeted by the HAT.

■ According to the Minister of Communication, 80 media outlets were notified of suspension in August after their licences were pronounced illegal. Some media outlet owners and journalists denounced what they called the politically motivated decision. It was not clear whether the suspensions remained in place at the end of the year.

Amnesty International visits/reports

🚌 Amnesty International delegates visited Madagascar in September.

📓 Madagascar: Human rights must be at the heart of the road map to end the crisis (AFR 35/001/2011)

MALAWI

REPUBLIC OF MALAWI

Head of state and government:	Bingu wa Mutharika
Death penalty:	abolitionist in practice
Population:	15.4 million
Life expectancy:	54.2 years
Under-5 mortality:	110 per 1,000
Adult literacy:	73.7 per cent

Human rights defenders and other government critics were subjected to harassment and intimidation. Several civil society leaders were forced into hiding as attacks on government critics increased. Anti-government protests were brutally suppressed when police used live ammunition on protesters. An amendment to the Penal Code further restricted freedom of the press. Lesbians, gay men, bisexual and transgender people continued to face persecution.

Background

Tensions increased throughout the year as civil society continued to express concerns about human rights violations, the deteriorating economic situation and bad governance.

The British High Commissioner to Malawi was expelled in April following the leaking of a diplomatic cable in which he described President Mutharika's rule as increasingly "autocratic and intolerant of criticism". The UK government responded by expelling Malawi's representative to the UK and freezing aid. In July, the UK indefinitely suspended general budget support to Malawi worth £19 million, in line with other international donors who had previously suspended or ended general budget support, citing concerns about economic management, governance and human rights. Following the deaths in July of 19 people when police used live ammunition to break up protests, the USA withheld US$350 million in aid.

In breach of its legal obligations to the International Criminal Court, Malawi failed to arrest Sudan's President Omar Al Bashir during his visit in October for a regional trade summit.

Repression of dissent

Human rights defenders and other critics of the government were harassed and intimidated including through death threats, forced entry to homes and offices, petrol bombings and other attacks. There were several suspicious break-ins at NGO offices. Threats and attacks were made either by people identifying themselves as aligned with the ruling Democratic Progressive Party (DPP) or by unidentified men believed to be state security agents. Human rights defenders speaking at international forums and those involved in organizing anti-government demonstrations were publicly criticized and threatened with violence and arrest by government officials, including President Mutharika.

■ In March, the President told DPP supporters at a rally broadcast on television and radio that those who criticize the government would be "left in your hands [to] ensure discipline in Malawi".

■ Also in March, unidentified men armed with knives and machetes broke into the office of the Centre for Human Rights and Rehabilitation at night and forced the guard to take them to the home of the Director, Undule Mwakasungura. The guard was subsequently abducted, beaten and dumped in Lilongwe's Area 18.

■ In July, the President publicly threatened to "smoke out" the leaders of anti-government protests which took place across the country on 20 and 21 July.

■ Between March and September, numerous civil society leaders and academics reported receiving death threats. They included Benedicto Kondowe of the Civil Society Coalition for Quality Basic Education; Dorothy Ngoma of the National Organisation of Nurses and Midwives; and Dr Jessie Kwabila Kapasula, Acting President of the Chancellor College Academic Staff Union.

■ In September, unidentified men forcibly entered the office of the Centre for the Development of People looking for the Director, Gift Trapence. During the same month, petrol bomb attacks targeted the homes or offices of several government critics, including opposition politician Salim Bagus and activists Rafiq Hajat and Reverend Macdonald Sembereka.

Freedom of assembly and expression

In January, Section 46 of the Penal Code was amended to give the Minister of Information arbitrary exercise of power to prohibit a publication "if the minister has reasonable grounds to believe that the publication or importation of any publication would be contrary to the public interest."

On 20 and 21 July, protests over bad governance, fuel shortages and human rights abuses took place in major urban centres including Blantyre, Lilongwe, Mzuzu and Zomba. At least 19 people were killed and several people, including children, were injured after police used live ammunition to break up the protests. In the northern town of Mzuzu, nine people were killed and dozens, including children, suffered gunshot wounds. Around 500 people were arrested in connection with the protests, including several human rights activists, who were briefly detained on 20 July and released without charge.

Twenty-two journalists reported being beaten by police during the protests. At least eight sustained serious injuries from assaults with gun butts. Many journalists covering the protests had their equipment, including cameras and writing materials, seized and destroyed or discarded by police. Two journalists, Collins Mtika and Vitima Ndovi, were arrested and held for several days; both said they were beaten by police. Four independent radio stations covering the demonstrations were temporarily taken off air.

On 14 October, five activists – Billy Mayaya of the Presbyterian Nkhoma Synod and Habiba Osman, a lawyer with the NGO Norwegian Church Aid, as well as Brian Nyasulu, Ben Chiza Mkandawire and Comfort Chitseko – were arrested after participating in a demonstration urging President Mutharika to hold a referendum calling for an early election.

Rights of lesbian, gay, bisexual and transgender people

In January, Malawi enacted a law criminalizing sexual relations between women. In April, two men, Stanley Kanthunkako and Stephano Kalimbakatha, were charged with buggery and gross indecency and awaited trial at Zomba Magistrates Court. In May at a DPP rally in Lilongwe, President Mutharika described gay men as "worse than dogs".

MALAYSIA

MALAYSIA

Head of state:	King Abdul Halim Mu'adzam Shah (replaced King Mizan Zainal Abidin in December)
Head of government:	Najib Tun Razak
Death penalty:	retentionist
Population:	28.9 million
Life expectancy:	74.2 years
Under-5 mortality:	6.1 per 1,000
Adult literacy:	92.5 per cent

The authorities unleashed a brutal campaign of repression when a mass movement for fair elections swept the capital in July. More than 1,600 people were detained after a violent crackdown on the peaceful demonstration. In September, the government announced its intention to replace the Internal Security Act (ISA) with new security laws.

Background

Najib Tun Razak began his third year as Prime Minister. Although he had until March 2013 to call a general election, preparations by officials signalled plans for a poll in early 2012. Opposition leader Anwar Ibrahim faced prison and a ban from political office as his politically motivated trial on criminal sodomy charges neared its end.

Freedom of assembly and association

When the Bersih ("Clean") movement held a march in Kuala Lumpur in July, 1,667 peaceful protesters were arbitrarily arrested and temporarily detained. Police beat protesters and fired tear-gas canisters directly into the crowds, injuring protesters including

M

at least two opposition members of parliament. Before the rally, the authorities arrested dozens of people for alleged involvement in Bersih, which the government declared illegal on 2 July.

■ The government prevented Hindraf Makkal Sakthi (Hindraf), an NGO which advocates for equal rights for Malaysians of Indian origin, and the affiliated Human Rights Party, from holding an anti-racism march in Kuala Lumpur in February. In April, criminal trials began for 52 Hindraf members charged with belonging to a banned organization.

Arbitrary arrests and detentions

In a surprise announcement in September, Prime Minister Najib said his government would seek to repeal the ISA. However, repeal was deferred until March 2012, and the government planned to replace the ISA with a law which would likewise allow for indefinite detention without trial. In November, the authorities detained another 13 people under the ISA.

■ In August, the authorities released eight immigration officers detained under the ISA. Their arrest in 2010 was the country's first for human trafficking, but the eight were never charged.

■ In September, the government deported an ISA detainee to Singapore, where he was held under a similar internal security law. In May, the authorities arrested Abdul Majid Kunji Mohamad, a Singaporean national, for suspected links with the Philippine separatist Moro Islamic Liberation Front. He was also deported to ISA detention in Singapore (see Singapore entry).

■ Six activists were held in administrative detention at a secret location in July. All were officers of the Socialist Party, including Jeyakumar Devaraj, a member of parliament. They were arrested in Penang in June en route to a Bersih event, and released at the end of July.

Freedom of expression

The government suppressed criticism by requiring licences for publications and threatening critics with criminal prosecution under the Sedition Act.

■ In February, Malaysiakini, a leading independent news portal, challenged the government's rejection of its application for a permit to publish a newspaper. In September, the Home Ministry replied that permission to publish a newspaper was a "privilege" rather than a right. The day before the Bersih rally on 9 July, Malaysiakini's website was disabled by a cyber attack.

■ In October, police investigated law professor Aziz Bari under the Sedition Act for an online posting which criticized the Sultan of Selangor's support for a church raid by the state Islamic religious police. He was also investigated by the Malaysian Communications and Multimedia Commission, and suspended from his post at the International Islamic University.

Torture and other ill-treatment

People continued to be subjected to systematic torture and other ill-treatment through judicial caning, a punishment imposed for more than 60 penal offences.

■ In June, the Home Minister revealed that 29,759 foreign workers were caned for immigration offences between 2005 and 2010; 60 per cent of them were Indonesians.

Refugees and migrants

In August, the Australian High Court ruled that a bilateral agreement to swap refugees between Australia and Malaysia was invalid. Under the plan, Australia was to send to Malaysia 800 asylum-seekers who had reached Australia by sea. In exchange, Australia would have resettled 4,000 refugees from Malaysia. The ruling prohibited Australia from deporting the asylum-seekers on the basis that Malaysia, which had not ratified the UN Refugee Convention, lacked sufficient legal guarantees for refugee protection (see Australia entry).

■ In April, detained migrants rioted at the Lenggeng Detention Centre near Kuala Lumpur. A police investigation cited poor detention conditions and indefinite detention as some of the causes for the incident. Undocumented migrants in Malaysia are routinely detained and, if convicted, face prison sentences and judicial caning.

■ On 30 May, Malaysia and Indonesia signed a memorandum of understanding (MoU) on migrant domestic workers. The MoU allowed migrant Indonesian domestic workers in Malaysia to keep their passports and have a weekly rest day. However, it did not set a minimum wage or tackle debt bondage.

■ In August, Malaysia forcibly returned at least 11 Chinese nationals of Uighur ethnicity to China after arresting them in a targeted police raid. China had been pressuring various states, including those in Asia, to return Uighurs of Chinese nationality. Malaysia violated customary international law against *refoulement* by returning them to China, which has a record of torturing Uighurs.

M

Death penalty

The Malaysian government did not publish statistics on death sentences or executions. However, the authorities rejected calls to impose a moratorium on executions, and Malaysian courts regularly imposed new death sentences.

■ In response to a parliamentary question in April, Home Minister Hishammuddin Hussein said that 441 people had been executed since 1960. He said that 696 prisoners were on death row as of February 2011. The majority of death sentences were for drug offences (69 per cent), followed by murder (29 per cent). Both offences carried mandatory death sentences.

International justice

In March, Malaysia's Cabinet decided to accede to the Rome Statute of the International Criminal Court (ICC); however this remained pending.

■ In June, the government announced that Sudanese President Omar Al-Bashir would participate in an economic forum in Malaysia. Omar Al-Bashir was subject to ICC arrest warrants for genocide, crimes against humanity and war crimes in Darfur. Law Minister Nazri Aziz urged the government to rescind its invitation, citing Malaysia's decision to join the ICC. The visit was cancelled.

Amnesty International visits/reports

🚐 Amnesty International delegates visited Malaysia in March.

▤ Government reveals nearly 30,000 foreigners caned (PRE01/129/2011)

▤ Police use brutal tactics against peaceful protesters (PRE01/345/2011)

▤ New ISA detentions show U-turn on reform promises (PRE01/574/2011)

MALDIVES

REPUBLIC OF MALDIVES

Head of state and government:	Mohamed Nasheed
Death penalty:	abolitionist in practice
Population:	0.3 million
Life expectancy:	76.8 years
Under-5 mortality:	12.7 per 1,000
Adult literacy:	98.4 per cent

Progress on human rights was hampered by the ongoing political impasse between the President and the opposition-dominated parliament. The government kept flogging as a punishment in an apparent attempt to appease opposition demands to retain it in Maldivian law. An opposition campaign for strict application of Shari'a stifled public moves towards religious freedom. The government took no action to bring to justice those responsible for human rights violations during the 30-year rule of former President Maumoon Abdul Gayoom.

Cruel, inhuman or degrading punishments

The UN High Commissioner for Human Rights called for a moratorium on flogging, sparking a national debate on the punishment in November. The debate ended in late December with the opposition Adhalaat Party calling for strict application of Shari'a, and for flogging to be retained in law to "protect Islam". Other opposition politicians endorsed the call.

Statistics on the number of people flogged were not available, but human rights defenders reported that courts frequently imposed the punishment, which was then carried out behind the court premises.

Freedom of religion or belief

Calls for religious freedom and tolerance were swiftly quashed by influential Islamist groups and other opposition politicians.

■ On 14 December, police detained prisoner of conscience Ismail "Khilath" Rasheed, a Sufi, for taking part in a peaceful demonstration in the capital, Malé, calling for religious tolerance. During the protest, which was held on 10 December, he and fellow activists were attacked by a group of around 10 men. Ismail Rasheed sustained a skull fracture as a result. He was detained on grounds that his calls for religious tolerance were unconstitutional. According to a constitutional provision, all Maldivians must be Muslim. The authorities made no attempt to arrest or charge his attackers.

M

Justice system

The Maldives continued to lack a codified body of laws capable of providing justice equally to all. Some laws were too vaguely formulated to prevent miscarriages of justice. Most judges had no formal training in law, yet exercised considerable discretion – often based on their own interpretation of Islamic law – in determining an offence and its appropriate punishment. A draft penal code intended to address these shortcomings remained dormant in parliament.

Amnesty International visits/reports

Maldives' police arrest campaigner seeking religious tolerance and allow his attackers impunity (ASA 29/001/2011)

MALI

REPUBLIC OF MALI

Head of state:	Amadou Toumani Touré
Head of government:	Mariam Kaïdama Cissé Sidibé (replaced Modibo Sidibé in April)
Death penalty:	abolitionist in practice
Population:	15.8 million
Life expectancy:	51.4 years
Under-5 mortality:	191.1 per 1,000
Adult literacy:	26.2 per cent

Mali joined neighbouring countries in operations against al-Qa'ida in the Islamic Maghreb (AQIM). Of the seven hostages abducted by the group in 2010, three were released. One person was killed and five others abducted. The National Human Rights Commission recommended that the government abolish the death penalty. Ten people were sentenced to death.

Background

In May, officials from four neighbouring sub-Saharan countries, including Niger and Mauritania, met in the capital, Bamako, to strengthen co-operation against AQIM. Mali and Mauritania carried out joint military operations on the border against an alleged AQIM base; several people, including Mauritanian soldiers, were killed in June.

In October, the Special Representative of the UN for West Africa expressed concerns about the security threat posed by the return of combatants from Libya to northern Mali.

In December, the National Assembly adopted the new version of the Family Code, which perpetuates discrimination against women.

National Human Rights Commission

In March, the National Human Rights Commission published its first report. It recommended adoption of the bill supporting abolition of the death penalty, approved by the government in 2007. The report urged that the government prohibit female genital mutilation, and that prison conditions be improved and measures taken to prevent torture and other cruel, inhuman or degrading treatment.

Deaths after military exercise

In October, five trainee officers died at the Malian Armed Forces Military School in Koulikoro after a traditional endurance test. Three senior military officers and several training staff members were arrested. The Ministry of Defence ordered an investigation.

Abuses by armed groups

In January, two people were injured after a member of AQIM, a Tunisian national, exploded a gas bottle outside the French embassy in Bamako.

In January, two French nationals abducted by AQIM in Niamey, the capital of Niger, died during a failed rescue operation on the Malian border.

In February, three people abducted in Niger in September 2010 were released after payment of a ransom. Four others remained held in northern Mali by AQIM.

In March, Hamma Ould Mohamed Yahya, abducted by AQIM in 2010, was released.

In November, five people were abducted by AQIM and one other person was killed. Two French nationals were abducted from their hotel in Hombori. During the same month nationals from the Netherlands, South Africa and Sweden were abducted in Tombouctou. One German hostage was killed while trying to resist.

Death penalty

Ten people were sentenced to death. Among them were Mariam Sidibé, who was sentenced in July for the murder in 2008 of Mariam Traoré, her co-wife;

and Bachir Simoun, a Tunisian national, who was sentenced in November for causing an explosion outside the French embassy in Bamako. On 15 December, Bachir Simoun was pardoned by President Touré after Tunisian President Marzouki requested that he be returned to his country of origin.

MALTA

REPUBLIC OF MALTA

Head of state:	George Abela
Head of government:	Lawrence Gonzi
Death penalty:	abolitionist for all crimes
Population:	0.4 million
Life expectancy:	79.6 years
Under-5 mortality:	6.7 per 1,000
Adult literacy:	92.4 per cent

Migrants and asylum-seekers continued to be detained on arrival, in breach of international human rights law. Living conditions in detention and open reception centres reportedly worsened. The EU "Returns Directive" was transposed into domestic legislation, but its scope of application was restricted. Policies affecting migrants, refugees and asylum-seekers were criticized by international bodies.

Migrants, refugees and asylum-seekers
Detention
During 2011, more than 1,500 people arrived by sea from either the Middle East or North Africa, returning to the levels seen in 2009. Immigration detention continued to be mandatory for anyone whom the authorities deemed to be a "prohibited immigrant", and was often prolonged for up to 18 months. According to reports, conditions in both detention and open reception centres worsened as a consequence of the number of new arrivals, increasing the impact on detainees' mental and physical health.

In March, the EU's 2008 "Returns Directive" was transposed into domestic legislation. The Directive provided common standards and procedures in EU member states for detaining and returning people who stay in a country illegally. However, the domestic legislation excluded those who had been refused entry – or had entered Malta irregularly – from enjoying these minimum safeguards. The Directive would therefore not apply to the vast majority of those it was meant to protect.

Appeal procedures
Appeal procedures to challenge the length and legitimacy of detention, or to challenge decisions to reject an asylum claim, continued to be inadequate.
■ At the end of the year, no measures had been taken by the government to implement the 2010 judgement of the European Court of Human Rights in the case of *Louled Massoud v. Malta*, which found that "the Maltese legal system did not provide for a procedure capable of avoiding the risk of arbitrary detention pending deportation."

In November, the Constitutional Court found that the authorities had violated the human rights of two Somali men who, in 2004, had been forcibly returned to Libya, where they were tortured and subjected to unfair trials. While in Malta, the two men were denied an opportunity to apply for asylum or to be assisted by an interpreter. The two men were awarded compensation.

International scrutiny
In June, the Council of Europe's Commissioner for Human Rights reported that the policy of mandatory detention of migrants and asylum-seekers was "irreconcilable with the requirements of the European Convention on Human Rights and the case-law of the Strasbourg Court". The Commissioner also criticized living conditions in reception centres for migrants, particularly in Hal-Far tent village and hangar complex, and in Marsa, and the treatment of individuals belonging to vulnerable groups. He suggested measures to improve refugee determination procedures, called for a programme to address the social exclusion of migrants and others, and for a strategy to promote local integration and combat racism and xenophobia.

In September, the UN CERD Committee expressed concern about the detention and living conditions of irregular migrants, and their access to available legal safeguards. It also criticized the continuing discrimination in the enjoyment by migrants, refugees and asylum-seekers of their economic, social and cultural rights.

Amnesty International visits/reports
🚌 An Amnesty International delegate visited Malta in September and December.

M

MAURITANIA

ISLAMIC REPUBLIC OF MAURITANIA

Head of state:	**General Mohamed Ould Abdel Aziz**
Head of government:	**Moulaye Ould Mohamed Laghdaf**
Death penalty:	**abolitionist in practice**
Population:	**3.5 million**
Life expectancy:	**58.6 years**
Under-5 mortality:	**117.1 per 1,000**
Adult literacy:	**57.5 per cent**

Security forces used excessive and lethal force, including against protesters; one youth was killed by gunfire. Amid marches against the national census, protesters were arrested and sentenced to prison terms. The government clamped down heavily on suspected acts of terrorism. The whereabouts of 14 prisoners remained unknown after they disappeared from a prison in the capital, Nouakchott. Eight people were sentenced to death, including three minors.

Background

A census of the population, begun in April, was feared to be discriminatory by some human rights organizations. Protests took place in Nouakchott, Kaedi and Maghama. The President of the National Assembly urged that the process be suspended.

Frequent clashes between the army and al-Qa'ida in the Islamic Maghreb (AQIM) caused losses on both sides. The army also carried out operations against AQIM in Mali. In December, a member of the security forces was kidnapped by AQIM members.

In January, Mauritania's human rights record was assessed under the Universal Periodic Review. The government committed to ending the use of torture and other cruel, inhuman and degrading treatment and to end the use of excessive force by the police and security forces. It also committed to developing a national strategy for the eradication of slavery in all its forms.

There were questions surrounding the independence of the judiciary after a judge was dismissed in September.

Prisoners of conscience and other political prisoners

The authorities placed restrictions on freedom of expression, assembly and association.

- Aliyine Ould Mbareck, Biram Dah Ould Abeid and Cheikh Ould Abidine, three members of the anti-slavery organization Initiative pour la Résurgence du Mouvement Abolitionniste en Mauritanie (IRA Mauritanie), were sentenced in January to one year's imprisonment. They were arrested with six other activists in December 2010 and charged with assaulting police officers and obstructing public order after holding a rally outside a police station in Nouakchott. They were pardoned in March.
- On 23 August, four IRA Mauritanie members, including Tourad Ould Zein, were given six months' suspended imprisonment for unauthorized gathering and rebellion. They had protested against the lack of judicial action in the case of a 10-year-old girl held in slavery.
- In October, more than 50 demonstrators were arrested following protest marches against the census organized by the human rights organization "Touche pas à ma nationalité" in Nouakchott and in other parts of the country. Most were released within hours and days. Others were tried for demonstrating with the intention of theft and looting. Four demonstrators, including Brahim Diop and Mohamed Boubacar, were sentenced to three months' imprisonment and held for 13 days at Dar Naïm prison before being pardoned.
- Lemine Ould Dadde, former Commissioner for Human Rights, remained in arbitrary detention, charged with embezzlement, after his provisional detention expired in September.

Counter-terror and security

Throughout the year at least 12 people, including Mohamed Lemine Ould Mballe, were arrested on suspicion of being members of AQIM. Most spent more than 40 days in police custody.

At least 18 people were tried and sentenced to prison terms or to death. Although the detainees alleged that they had been tortured, the court did not order any inquiry.

- In March, Aderrahmane Ould Meddou, a Malian national and suspected member of AQIM, was sentenced by the Nouakchott Criminal Court to five years' imprisonment and hard labour for kidnapping an Italian couple in December 2010.
- In October, four people, including Lemrabott Ould Mohamed Mahmoud, were sentenced by the Nouakchott Criminal Court to between three and five years in prison for terrorist acts. Mohamed Lemine Ag

Maleck was acquitted but remained in detention pending an appeal by the prosecutor. He was released in December.

■ Two detainees, Assad Abdel Khader Mohamed Ali and Khalil Ould Ahmed Salem Ould N'Tahah, remained in detention although they had served their prison terms.

Enforced disappearances

In May, 14 prisoners who had been sentenced for terrorism activities were taken at night from a Nouakchott central prison to an unknown location. In June, some of their belongings were returned to their families without any explanation. The whereabouts of the 14, including Sidi Ould Sidina and Mohamed Mahmoud Ould Sebty, remained unknown at the end of the year. The authorities told an Amnesty International delegation in November that they had been transferred for security reasons.

Excessive use of force

Security forces used excessive force against peaceful demonstrators in several towns including Kaedi, Maghama and Nouakchott. The arbitrary and indiscriminate use of tear gas injured scores of protesters. One person was killed.

■ Lamine Mangane, aged 19, died on 28 September after security forces fired live ammunition during a demonstration organized by "Touche pas à ma nationalité" in Maghama. At least 10 people were injured. The authorities stated that a judicial investigation had been opened.

Discrimination – lesbian, gay, bisexual and transgender people

Individuals faced arbitrary arrest, harassment and discrimination because of their suspected homosexual activity. In November, 14 men were arrested and accused of being homosexuals; they remained held in Dar Naïm prison.

Torture and other ill-treatment

Torture and other ill-treatment continued to be widely reported in detention centres, including police stations and Dar Naïm prison. Methods included kicking, beating, suspension by the arms, shackling in painful positions and deprivation of sleep and food.

Death penalty

In November, the death sentences of seven people convicted of murder during the last decade were commuted.

Throughout the year at least eight people were sentenced to death by the Criminal Court in Nouakchott, including three aged under 18 when the crimes were committed. Following an appeal by the prosecutor, on 8 December the Court of Appeal of Nouakchott commuted the death sentences of the three aged under 18 to 12 years' imprisonment and a fine.

Slavery

Seven people, a woman and six children, escaped from slavery with the help of human rights organizations. Among the six children were Yarg and Saïd, two brothers aged 11 and 14, who escaped slavery in August. In November, the Nouakchott Criminal Court convicted six people for enslaving Yarg and Saïd and ordered that compensation be paid to their families.

Migrants' rights

At least 3,000 migrants, mostly from Senegal, Mali and Guinea, were arbitrarily arrested. They were held in detention centres in Mauritania for several days before being returned to Senegal or Mali.

In October, migrants from Mali and Senegal were arrested and charged with unauthorized assembly and threatening national security. They were each given a suspended prison sentence of one year and detained for more than 10 days at Dar Naïm prison before being sent to Senegal.

M

Amnesty International visits/reports

🚗 Amnesty International delegates visited Mauritania in November.

📄 Mauritania: Three juveniles sentenced to death in violation of national and international law (AFR 38/001/2011)

📄 Mauritania: Thirteen people convicted of terrorism subjected to enforced disappearance (AFR 38/002/2011)

📄 Amnesty International statement to African Commission on Human and Peoples' Rights on the situation of human rights in Africa (IOR 63/005/2011)

MEXICO

UNITED MEXICAN STATES
Head of state and government: **Felipe Calderón Hinojosa**
Death penalty: **abolitionist for all crimes**
Population: **114.8 million**
Life expectancy: **77 years**
Under-5 mortality: **16.8 per 1,000**
Adult literacy: **93.4 per cent**

Drug cartels and other criminal gangs, at times acting in collusion with the police or other public officials, killed and abducted thousands of people. Irregular migrants travelling in their tens of thousands through Mexico suffered grave abuses including kidnap, rape and killing, by such gangs. The government did not take effective measures to prevent or investigate widespread grave human rights violations committed by the military and police, including enforced disappearances, extrajudicial executions, torture and arbitrary arrests. The government did not provide any substantive responses to Amnesty International requests for information on investigations into such cases. The criminal justice system failed to deliver justice or security. Those responsible for the vast majority of crimes, including attacks on journalists, human rights defenders and women, were not held to account. Fair trial standards were breached. There was no action to ensure justice for the victims of gross human rights violations committed during Mexico's "dirty war" (1964-1982). There were a number of progressive constitutional human rights reforms.

Background

President Calderón's government continued to deploy 50,000 soldiers and an increasing number of navy marines to combat drug cartels. During the year, the cartels fought amongst themselves and against the security forces for territorial control in certain states, such as Chihuahua, Nuevo León, Veracruz, Coahuila, Tamaulipas and Guerrero. More than 12,000 people were killed in the ensuing violence. The vast majority of these killings were never investigated. In April the National Human Rights Commission (Comisión Nacional de Derechos Humanos, CNDH) reported that 8,898 bodies remained unidentified in morgues around the country and that 5,397 people had been reported

missing since 2006. More than 40 soldiers and more than 500 police officers were killed during 2011.

Reports indicated that an increasing number of people unconnected with the cartels were killed during the year by gangs, the military or the police. Fifty-two people died in Monterrey when a criminal gang burned down a casino with the collusion of some local police officers. More than 500 unidentified bodies were discovered in clandestine graves in Tamaulipas and Durango states. Some were believed to be Central American migrants, but the identities of fewer than 50 had been established by the end of the year. Public concern over the violence and dissatisfaction with the government's response resulted in the creation of the Movement for Peace with Justice and Dignity. The movement held protests in many parts of the country to demand an end to violence and impunity.

The US government released further security-related funding and other transfers to Mexico as part of the Merida Initiative, a three-year regional co-operation and security agreement. Although the USA temporarily withheld some funds and despite the Mexican government's continued failure to meet human rights conditions, transfers went ahead. A bungled US operation to track weapons smuggled into Mexico highlighted the absence of effective mechanisms to prevent criminal gangs from bringing weapons into the country.

Police and security forces
The army and the navy

The government ignored widespread reports of grave human rights violations, such as torture, enforced disappearances, extrajudicial executions and excessive use of force by army and, increasingly, navy personnel. It continued to assert that abuses were exceptional and perpetrators were held to account. In only one case were military personnel brought to justice during 2011: 14 soldiers were convicted in military courts of the killing of two women and three children at a roadblock in Leyva, Sinaloa state, in 2007. The government did not provide any substantive responses to Amnesty International requests for information on investigations into such cases.

The military justice system remained in control of virtually all investigations into allegations of human rights abuses by military personnel, and continued to dismiss without effective investigation the vast majority of complaints, allowing perpetrators to evade justice. This began to change in December when, for the first time, a federal court rejected military jurisdiction in a human rights case. The civilian justice system routinely refused to conduct basic investigations into alleged abuses before transferring cases to the military justice system.

A total of 1,695 complaints of abuse committed by the army and 495 committed by the navy were lodged with the CNDH, which issued 25 recommendations against the army and six against the navy. The comparatively low number of complaints resulting in CNDH recommendations was presented by the authorities as evidence that most complaints were baseless. This ignored the limitations of many CNDH investigations.

■ In June, at least six men were detained and forcibly disappeared in Nuevo Laredo, Tamaulipas state. Despite compelling evidence, including eyewitness testimony, that marines were responsible, the naval authorities would acknowledge only that there had been "contact" with the men. An investigation by the Attorney General's Office failed to establish the facts, but appeared to absolve the navy of responsibility without further investigation. The whereabouts of the men remained unknown at the end of the year. The family of one of the victims was forced to flee the area after their home was attacked in July.

■ In May, municipal police illegally detained Jethro Ramsés Sánchez Santana and a friend in Cuernavaca, Morelos state. Both men were handed over first to the Federal Police and then to the army. Soldiers tortured the two men, released the friend and forcibly disappeared Jethro Sánchez. His family filed a complaint, but the military authorities denied any involvement in the enforced disappearance, even after police testified to their participation. In the face of overwhelming evidence, the military detained two soldiers in July. The body of Jethro Sánchez was found in July. At the end of the year, two soldiers were in detention charged with homicide and at least three others were in hiding. The case remained under military jurisdiction.

Police forces

Progress in reforming federal, state and municipal police forces was extremely slow. There was evidence that some police officers acted in collusion with criminal organizations, including in the killing of suspected members of other criminal organizations.

There were widespread reports of excessive use of force, torture, arbitrary detention and enforced disappearance, most of which were not investigated effectively.

■ In December, two student protesters were shot dead by police in Chilpancingo, Guerrero, after federal and state police apparently opened fire with automatic weapons on demonstrators. Several protesters were ill-treated on arrest by Federal Police and at least one was reportedly tortured by state investigative police in order to falsely implicate him in the shootings. Several police officers were under investigation at the end of the year.

■ In April, Jesús Francisco Balderrama was arrested by state police in Mexicali, Baja California state. His family sought information on his whereabouts, but the authorities denied he had been detained. His whereabouts remained unknown at the end of the year.

■ In July, eight members of the Muñoz family were detained in Anáhuac, Chihuahua state, by heavily armed men in balaclavas; at least one apparently wore Federal Police insignia. Relatives filed a complaint, but the police authorities denied all knowledge of the detentions. At the end of the year, the whereabouts of the men remained unknown and those responsible for their detention and disappearance had not been identified.

Criminal justice system and impunity

Ongoing reforms of the criminal justice system made extremely slow progress. A number of factors contributed to unsafe convictions, including arbitrary detention, torture, fabrication of evidence, denial of due process, denial of access to an effective defence, and inadequate judicial supervision of proceedings. Eighty-day pre-charge detention (*arraigo*) continued to be used widely, facilitating torture and other ill-treatment and undermining fair trials.

Torture

Measures to prevent, investigate and punish torture remained ineffectual, and statements obtained under duress continued to be accepted in judicial proceedings.

■ In February, a woman was arbitrarily detained in Ensenada, Baja California state, and reportedly tortured by members of the army in a military barracks in Tijuana while being interrogated by a civilian federal prosecutor. She was subjected to assault, near asphyxiation, stress positions and threats to coerce her into signing a confession. She was held in pre-charge detention (*arraigo*) for 80 days before being charged and remanded in custody. The authorities initially

M

denied all knowledge of her detention. The prosecution case subsequently collapsed and she was released without charge. At the end of the year, there was no information on the investigation initiated into her torture complaint.

■ In September, a federal court ordered a partial retrial of Israel Arzate Meléndez for his alleged involvement in the Villas de Salvárcar massacre of 15 young people in Ciudad Juárez in 2010. The CNDH investigation had found that he had been tortured by the military to make a confession. However, the review court failed to rule that the defendant's rights had been violated by the trial judge's failure to order an investigation into the allegations of torture or to exclude the confession extracted under torture as evidence.

Prison conditions

More than 200 inmates died, primarily as a result of gang violence, in overcrowded and unsafe prisons.

Irregular migrants

Tens of thousands of mainly Central American irregular migrants travelling to the USA were at risk of kidnapping, rape, forced recruitment or being killed by criminal gangs, often operating in collusion of public officials. Those responsible were almost never held to account. In February, the CNDH reported that 11,000 migrants had been kidnapped over a six-month period. Federal and state government measures to prevent and punish abuses and ensure access to justice remained inadequate. There were further reports of ill-treatment by migration officials and collusion with criminal gangs, despite purges to root out corrupt officials. The authorities failed to collect sufficient data about abuses to facilitate investigations by the relatives of disappeared migrants. The families of Central American disappeared migrants carried out nationwide marches to press for action to locate their relatives and highlight the fate of many migrants.

Refugee and migration laws to improve legal protection for migrant and refugee rights were passed. However, the regulatory codes necessary to ensure their effective enforcement were drawn up without adequate consultation and remained pending at the end of the year.

Human rights defenders working at the network of shelters providing humanitarian assistance to migrants were threatened and intimidated.

■ At least 14 bodies of 72 irregular migrants killed in San Fernando, Tamaulipas state, in 2010 had still not been identified by the end of 2011. A further 193 bodies were discovered in the municipality in April; fewer than 30 had been identified by the end of the year. Relatives expressed concern that inadequate methods of collecting and preserving evidence were hampering identifications. In August, the authorities announced the detention and prosecution of more than 80 suspects linked to the Zeta cartel operating in San Fernando, including 16 police officers, among them people suspected of involvement in the killings of migrants.

Freedom of expression – journalists

According to the CNDH, at least nine journalists were killed and scores of others attacked and intimidated. Impunity remained the norm for most of these crimes, despite the existence of a Special Federal Prosecutor for crimes against journalists. Discussions continued about reforms to make crimes against journalists federal offences and improve investigations.

Coverage of crime and public security in the local press was adversely affected, and in certain places virtually non-existent, as a result of attacks and intimidation of local journalists in high-crime areas. Social media played an increasingly important role providing information about security threats to the local communities. Criminal gangs killed at least three bloggers and threatened others for posting information exposing their criminal activities.

In Veracruz, the state authorities detained two Twitter users for a month and passed legislation criminalizing the distribution by any means of false information causing social disturbance. The CNDH filed a constitutional challenge to the changes to the law on the grounds that it violated the right to freedom of expression.

■ In June, a well-known crime and political corruption journalist in Veracruz, Miguel Ángel López Velasco, his wife and son were shot and killed at their home by unidentified gunmen. He had received death threats in the past. The investigation into the killings was continuing at the end of the year.

Human rights defenders

More than 20 human rights defenders were threatened or attacked in 2011. Official investigations had not identified the perpetrators by the end of the year. The provision of protection for defenders was often slow, bureaucratic and inadequate. In July, the President signed a decree establishing a protection mechanism, but by the end of the year there was no evidence that the mechanism was active or had improved protection for journalists or human rights defenders. A bill to strengthen the mechanism was under discussion at the end of the year.

The government's commitment to respect the work of defenders was called into question in July when the Minister of the Navy publicly attacked the work of human rights organizations documenting abuses committed by the armed forces.

■ José Ramón Aniceto and Pascual Agustín Cruz continued to serve six-year prison sentences imposed in July 2010. The two Indigenous Nahua community activists were convicted on fabricated criminal charges in reprisal for their efforts to secure equitable access to water for their community in Atla, Puebla state.

Legal, constitutional or institutional developments

In July, constitutional reforms came into force that oblige the authorities at all levels to promote, respect, protect and guarantee international human rights norms which were granted constitutional status. The reforms also established that certain fundamental rights could not be suspended during states of emergency; recognized a number of social and economic rights, including the right to food and clean water, in law; and strengthened the powers of the CNDH.

In August, the National Supreme Court ruled that the state must comply with the judgements of the Inter-American Court of Human Rights on Mexico, including the ruling that military officials implicated in human rights violations must be investigated and tried by civilian courts and that the military penal code must be reformed to this effect. By the end of the year, the four military abuse cases on which the Inter-American Court had issued judgements had been transferred to civilian jurisdiction. However, compliance with other key elements of Inter-American Court rulings remained very limited, and military jurisdiction continued to be applied in other human rights cases.

Violence against women and girls

Violence against women remained widespread. Large numbers of killings of women were reported in many states and those responsible continued to evade justice in the vast majority of cases. Legislation to improve access to justice and safety for women at risk remained ineffective in many areas.

■ More than 320 women were killed in Ciudad Juárez. Those responsible for the murder of human rights defender Marisela Escobedo in December 2010 were not held to account. In December, Norma Andrade of Our Daughters Return Home was shot and seriously wounded outside her home. She and other members of the organization received death threats and were forced to flee the city for their safety during the year.

■ In October, Margarita González Carpio was seriously assaulted by her former partner, a senior Federal Police officer in Querétaro City. Federal and state officials initially refused to take action to protect her or investigate the allegations of assault. At the end of the year, she remained in hiding and no information was available on the progress of the investigation.

Sexual and reproductive rights

The National Supreme Court narrowly rejected a legal action to overturn changes to the constitutions of the states of Baja California and San Luis Potosí establishing the right to life from the moment of conception. Seven of the 11 Supreme Court judges argued that the changes were unconstitutional and restricted women's reproductive rights. However, this was an insufficient majority to overturn the changes, raising concerns that women would face additional obstacles in accessing abortion services in all 17 states that had adopted similar provisions.

Indigenous Peoples' rights

Indigenous Peoples continued to suffer routine discrimination and systemic inequality, in relation to the right to land, housing, water, health and education. Economic and development projects on Indigenous lands continued to be undertaken without the free, prior and informed consent of affected communities. A proposed bill to regulate consultation with Indigenous communities remained stalled.

■ Members of the Wixárikas Indigenous community protested against a mining concession granted to a Canadian company to exploit silver deposits in the Wirikuta Environmental and Cultural Reserve, Real de Catorce, San Luis Potosí state, without consultation or the consent of the affected communities.

■ In December, a drought in Chihuahua state resulted in increasing levels of severe malnutrition among Tarahumara Indigenous communities, in part the result of their marginalization and the neglect of their human rights over many years.

M

International scrutiny

There were a number of visits to the country by regional and international human rights mechanisms, including the UN Special Rapporteur on freedom of expression and the OAS Special Rapporteur on Freedom of Expression; the UN Working Group on Involuntary and Enforced Disappearances; and the OAS Special Rapporteur on Migrant Workers and their Families. In April, the UN Committee on the Protection of the Rights of All Migrant Workers and Members of their Families reviewed Mexico's report and compliance with the Convention. In July, the UN High Commissioner for Human Rights visited Mexico.

Amnesty International visits/reports

🚌 Amnesty International delegates visited Mexico in July.

📄 Shielding the guilty: Military justice in Mexico (AMR 41/010/2011)

📄 Mexico: Briefing to Special Rapporteur on the Rights of Migrant Workers of the Inter-American Commission of Human Rights (AMR 41/085/2011)

📄 Letter regarding forthcoming visit of the Working Group on Enforced or Involuntary Disappearances to Mexico (AMR 41/086/2011)

📄 Mexico: Letter to UN Committee on Migrant Workers (AMR 41/087/2011)

MOLDOVA

REPUBLIC OF MOLDOVA

Head of state:	Marian Lupu (acting)
Head of government:	Vladimir Filat
Death penalty:	abolitionist for all crimes
Population:	3.5 million
Life expectancy:	69.3 years
Under-5 mortality:	16.7 per 1,000
Adult literacy:	98.5 per cent

Reports continued of prison conditions amounting to inhuman and degrading treatment; impunity for torture and other ill-treatment; and unfair trials. Religious and other minorities faced discrimination, in the absence of legislation to prevent it.

Torture and other ill-treatment

Conditions in pre-trial detention and during transfer between detention centres and the courts frequently amounted to cruel, inhuman or degrading treatment.

■ Vasilii Cristioglo was detained on 19 January in Comrat, charged with burglary, and held from 21 January to the end of the year in pre-trial detention in Cahul. The cell had a toilet in full view of the other detainees, and no bedding was provided. Vasilii Cristioglo was forced to pay for blood tests when he suspected that he may have contracted hepatitis. During transfer to and from the court, Vasilii Cristioglo and other detainees were held in railway wagons for hours at a time over the summer in high temperatures, and not given any food or water during the day. In response to a complaint from his lawyer, the Cahul prosecutor admitted that hygiene regulations were ignored; there were no provisions for refrigeration and preparation of food, nor any facilities for washing dishes or for personal hygiene.

Impunity

Trials against police officers accused of torture and other ill-treatment during post-election demonstrations in April 2009 continued. On 2 March 2011, Valentin Zubic, former deputy minister of the interior, was charged with misconduct in connection with the events. A government representative told the UN Human Rights Council during the discussion of Moldova at the Universal Periodic Review that there were 100 complaints following the events, 57 of which resulted in formal investigations, 27 cases resulted in prosecutions, and only two of those led to convictions.

■ On 27 October, two policemen accused of beating Anatol Matasaru during the events in April 2009 were acquitted on appeal. They had been given suspended sentences earlier in the year. Anatol Matasaru was detained on 8 April 2009 following the demonstrations, and reported that he had been beaten by police officers at the General Police Station in Chişinău and forced to lick their boots.

Unfair trials

In its report to the UN Human Rights Council for the Universal Periodic Review, the Parliamentary Advocates for Human Rights of Moldova (the Ombudsman) stated that 25 per cent of all complaints received by the Ombudsman concerned unfair trials. The most frequent were failure to examine cases within a reasonable time, limited access to a qualified lawyer, non-enforcement of court decisions, and violations of procedural rules by courts. According to a survey conducted in May by the Institute for Public Policies, only 1 per cent of respondents had complete confidence in the justice system, and 42 per cent had no confidence at all.

On 3 November, Parliament approved an ambitious justice reform package for the court system, police and prosecutors. Measures included increasing the efficiency and independence of the judiciary; bringing the role of prosecutors into line with European standards; improving legal aid; reducing corruption; and improving respect for human rights.

Discrimination

A draft law on discrimination was submitted to Parliament in February but had not been approved by the end of the year. Opposition remained to a provision in the law banning discrimination on the basis of sexual preference. The law failed to provide for clear complaint mechanisms and adequate sanctions.

Religious minorities
In September, the UN Special Rapporteur on freedom of religion or belief reported that members of religious minorities faced intimidation and vandalism from followers of the Orthodox Church. He criticized the 2007 Law on Religious Denominations for according the Moldovan Orthodox Church "special importance and a leading role" which had led to discrimination against other faiths.

■ In March, after over a decade of being refused registration, the Islamic League of the Republic of Moldova was registered as a religious organization despite opposition from the Orthodox Church.

Transdniestrian Republic

The self-proclaimed Transdniestrian Republic remained a separate, but internationally unrecognized, entity within Moldova.

■ On 5 February, Ernest Vardanean was pardoned by the President of Transdniestria. Ernest Vardanean had been sentenced to 15 years' imprisonment for "treason in the form of espionage" in 2010 after an unfair trial.

■ Ostap Popovschii was detained by police in Tiraspol on 29 June in connection with drug crime. He was reportedly beaten by police on arrest to force him to sign a confession for an offence that he claimed he had not committed, and beaten again to force him to refuse a lawyer. He was denied medical care despite suffering from chronic bronchitis and asthma. On 29 July, the court sentenced him to 15 years' imprisonment. The pre-trial detention conditions amounted to ill-

treatment: the basement cell where he was held, designed to accommodate six people, held 19 detainees without natural light or ventilation; no bedding was provided and everyone slept on the concrete floor. Ostap Popovschii had access to a shower twice a month. During asthma attacks, he was taken into the corridor, but offered no medical assistance. At the end of the year he was in a prison hospital, but medical care remained inadequate.

International justice

The Rome Statute of the International Criminal Court entered into force for Moldova in January. However, the State failed to ratify the accompanying Agreement on Privileges and Immunities of the Court by the end of the year, and no steps had been taken to bring national legislation into line with the statute's provisions.

MONGOLIA

MONGOLIA
Head of state:	**Tsakhia Elbegdorj**
Head of government:	**Batbold Sukhbaatar**
Death penalty:	**retentionist**
Population:	**2.8 million**
Life expectancy:	**68.5 years**
Under-5 mortality:	**28.8 per 1,000**
Adult literacy:	**97.5 per cent**

Parliament continued to debate abolishing the death penalty, although a moratorium was declared in 2010. No executions had taken place since 2009. Impunity for torture and other ill-treatment remained widespread. Corruption in the justice system was reportedly commonplace.

Background

In late 2010, the Prosecution Office reopened investigations into the cases of four senior police officials, accused of authorizing the use of live ammunition to suppress the riot which broke out in Ulaanbaatar on 1 July 2008. The original investigation yielded no prosecutions.

Bat Khurts, Chief Executive of Mongolia's National Security Council, who was arrested at Heathrow Airport in London in 2010, was extradited to Germany

M

in August 2011 but was released in September after the German Federal High Court cancelled the arrest warrant. Bat Khurts was wanted in connection with the kidnapping in France of Mongolian national Enkhbat Damiran in 2003. According to the UK High Court ruling, a letter delivered to the German Public Prosecutor from the Mongolian authorities in January asserted that Bat Khurts had participated in the kidnapping. He returned in September and was later appointed Deputy Chief of the Independent Authority Against Corruption of Mongolia.

Impunity

Complaints of torture and other ill-treatment against law enforcement officials did not, according to available information, result in any convictions. As in previous years, the government did not publish information and statistics on investigations, prosecutions and convictions of law enforcement officials accused of torture and other ill-treatment.

Death penalty

There were no executions. According to the Supreme Court of Mongolia, use of the death penalty was declining. The President commuted all death sentences of those who appealed for clemency to 30-year prison terms. Parliament did not vote on ratifying the Second Optional Protocol to the ICCPR, aimed at abolishing the death penalty.

Torture and other ill-treatment

The government passed a resolution in May on the implementation of recommendations issued by UN treaty bodies. This included plans to amend the Criminal Code to define torture as a crime in line with the UN Convention against Torture. The working group, established under the Ministry of Justice and Home Affairs in 2010 to draft amendments to the Criminal Code, appeared to make little progress. The pre-trial detention facility 461, which opened in early 2011, had installed video cameras in interrogation rooms but there were insufficient safeguards or procedures in place to monitor and prevent misuse of this equipment.

■ A working group, set up in June 2010 by the Parliamentary Sub-Committee on Human Rights, continued to investigate allegations of torture and other ill-treatment of Enkhbat Damiran and his lawyer. Enkhbat Damiran was kidnapped in France in 2003

and brought to Mongolia where he was charged with the murder of Zorig Sanjaasuren, a prominent pro-democracy activist and politician. Enkhbat Damiran claimed he was tortured while in detention. He died in 2007. His lawyer, Lodoisambuu Sanjaasuren (no relation to the victim), was also arrested and convicted of exposing state secrets.

Unfair trials

Lawyers and government officials told Amnesty International that courts were corrupt and unfair trials common – including those that used confessions extracted through torture as evidence. The new pre-trial detention facility 461 and others like it lacked provisions to ensure privacy for meetings with lawyers.

Amnesty International visits/reports

🚃 An Amnesty International delegate visited Mongolia in October.

MONTENEGRO

MONTENEGRO

Head of state:	Filip Vujanović
Head of government:	Igor Lukšić
Death penalty:	abolitionist for all crimes
Population:	0.6 million
Life expectancy:	74.6 years
Under-5 mortality:	9 per 1,000

Verdicts in war crimes cases were inconsistent with international law. Defamation was decriminalized. Roma from Kosovo remained without personal documentation.

Background

In December, the European Council agreed that talks on Montenegro's accession to the European Union could begin in June 2012. They requested the European Commission to report on the implementation of measures related to the rule of law and fundamental rights, including combating corruption and organized crime.

International justice

Verdicts in war crimes cases were inconsistent with international human rights and humanitarian law. Senior officials were rarely indicted.

■ In April, the retrial began of six former Yugoslav People's Army reservists, convicted in 2010 of war crimes against prisoners of war in Morinj camp in 1991-2. This followed an appeal by the prosecution, which argued that the court had failed to consider the charges of war crimes against civilians detained in Morinj who had also been subject to torture and inhumane treatment.

■ In June, appeals were lodged against the acquittal in March of nine former police officers and government officials who allegedly participated in the enforced disappearance of 79 Bosniak refugees in May and June 1992. They were acquitted of war crimes on the basis of the Podgorica Superior Court's flawed interpretation of international humanitarian law.

■ Also in June, the December 2010 verdict acquitting seven army and police reservists of crimes against humanity in their systematic ill-treatment of Bosniak civilians in Bukovica in 1992-3 was overturned on appeal.

Torture and other ill-treatment

The Law on the Ombudsperson, adopted in July, empowered the Ombudsperson's Office to act as the National Preventive Mechanism, with authority to conduct unannounced visits to places of detention, in accordance with the Optional Protocol to the UN Convention against Torture. The Ombudsperson reported in July on overcrowding and inadequate detention conditions in almost all police stations. In November, six NGOs were authorized by the Ministry of Justice to monitor prisons and other institutions for possible violations including torture and other ill-treatment.

■ Spuž prison management disciplined only three of 15 prison officers identified in a security video showing the ill-treatment of prisoners Igor Milić and Dalibor Nikezić in 2009.

Unlawful killings

In May, police officer Zoran Bulatović fatally shot Aleksandar Pejanović, allegedly after an argument. The trial was ongoing at the end of the year.

Freedom of expression

Defamation was decriminalized in June; the Supreme Court had ruled in March that levels of non-pecuniary compensation in such cases should not exceed European Court of Human Rights standards. Journalists continued to receive threats.

■ In July and August, there were three arson attacks on four company cars belonging to the newspaper *Vijesti*.

In June, the Administrative Court annulled the Ministry of Justice's 2010 decision prohibiting the NGO Human Rights Action from accessing information on the investigation of 14 human rights cases. However, the NGO had still not received the information by December. The cases included unresolved political killings and attacks on journalists and human rights defenders.

Discrimination

The Ombudsperson's Office began to review complaints under the Anti-Discrimination Law in August but lacked experienced staff. Twenty complaints were submitted in 2011.

Lesbian, gay, bisexual and transgender people

In March, youths attacked an anti-homophobia concert with tear gas; two people were later assaulted. Organizers cancelled the Podgorica Pride planned for March; the Minister for Human and Minority Rights had refused to support the Pride and continued to make homophobic remarks. He was removed from office at the end of the year.

Roma

Based on national census data, UNHCR, the UN refugee agency, estimated that at least 4,312 people, 1,600 of whom were predominantly Roma refugees, were at risk of statelessness.

Montenegro's implementation of the Strategy to Improve the Status of the Roma, Ashkali and Egyptian Population was identified as a priority by the European Commission, but municipalities were slow to use funds allocated for Roma housing.

Refugees and asylum-seekers

Approximately 9,367 internally displaced people, including 2,994 Roma and Ashkali from Kosovo, and 3,504 displaced persons from Bosnia and Herzegovina and Croatia, remained in Montenegro. Only 54 returned to Kosovo in 2011.

By 29 December, from 3,780 internally displaced people who applied, 1,957 acquired the status of "foreigner with permanent residence". Only around 150 Kosovo Roma met the November application deadline, which was extended until December 2012;

M

few possessed personal documentation, including passports, required to obtain residency.

Under an Action Plan agreed with the European Commission to provide durable solutions for Roma and Ashkali from Kosovo, plans were developed to demolish camps at Konik in Podgorica and replace them with adequate housing.

Only three out of 235 asylum-seekers, mostly from north Africa, were granted subsidiary protection.

Amnesty International visits/reports

Amnesty International delegates visited Montenegro in December.

MOROCCO/ WESTERN SAHARA

KINGDOM OF MOROCCO

Head of state:	King Mohamed VI
Head of government:	Abdelilah Benkirane (replaced Abbas El Fassi in November)
Death penalty:	abolitionist in practice
Population:	32.3 million
Life expectancy:	72.2 years
Under-5 mortality:	37.5 per 1,000
Adult literacy:	56.1 per cent

Security forces used excessive force against protesters. Critics of the monarchy and state institutions continued to face prosecution and imprisonment, as did Sahrawi advocates of self-determination for Western Sahara. Torture and other ill-treatment of detainees persisted. Several prisoners of conscience and one victim of arbitrary detention were released under royal pardons, but charges were not withdrawn against a number of Sahrawi activists. There were no executions.

Background

Thousands of people demonstrated in Rabat, Casablanca and other cities on 20 February, calling for reforms. The demonstrations were authorized and generally peaceful. Protesters, who quickly formed the 20 February Movement, called for greater democracy, a new constitution, an end to corruption,

improved economic conditions, and better health and other services. As protests continued, on 3 March a new National Human Rights Council was created, replacing the Advisory Council on Human Rights. On 9 March, the King announced a constitutional reform process, which was boycotted by protest leaders. A proposed new Constitution was endorsed in a national referendum on 1 July. As a result, the King's powers to appoint government officials and dissolve parliament were transferred to the Prime Minister, but the King remained Morocco's commander of the armed forces, chairperson of the Council of Ministers and highest religious authority. Other constitutional changes enshrined freedom of expression and equality between women and men; and criminalized torture, arbitrary detention and enforced disappearances. In parliamentary elections held on 25 November, the Islamist Justice and Development Party won the greatest number of seats and a new government, headed by Abdelilah Benkirane, took office on 29 November.

In April, Morocco withdrew its reservations to the CEDAW; the reservations related to children's nationality and discrimination in marriage. Morocco also announced it would ratify the Optional Protocols to the Convention against Torture and CEDAW.

Negotiations between Morocco and the Polisario Front continued over the status of Western Sahara, without resolution. The Polisario Front continued to call for the independence of the territory, which Morocco annexed in 1975. On 27 April, the UN Security Council again renewed the mandate of the UN Mission for the Referendum in Western Sahara without including a human rights monitoring component.

Repression of dissent

Even though the pro-reform protests were generally peaceful, on many occasions security forces were reported to have attacked them, causing at least one death and many injuries. Hundreds of protesters were detained. Most were released, but some were tried and received prison sentences. Security forces were reported to have harassed relatives of activists in the 20 February Movement, and summonsed for questioning scores of activists advocating a boycott of parliamentary elections.

■ On 15 May, rallies and demonstrations organized by the 20 February Movement in Rabat, Fès, Tangiers and Témara were forcibly dispersed by security forces, who used truncheons and kicked and beat demonstrators.

- On 29 May, a demonstration organized in the town of Safi by the 20 February Movement was violently dispersed by the security forces. One protester, Kamel Ammari, died several days later from his injuries.
- On 20 November, security forces stormed the offices of the Moroccan Association for Human Rights in the city of Bou-Arafa and reportedly beat a number of staff and young people who were preparing to join a protest.

Freedom of expression

Journalists and others continued to face prosecution and imprisonment for publicly criticizing state officials or institutions, or for reporting on politically sensitive issues.

- On 2 March, the King pardoned retired military officer Kaddour Terhzaz, imprisoned for threatening Morocco's "external security" after he wrote to the King complaining about the treatment of former air force pilots.
- On 14 April, the King pardoned Chekib El Khiari, a human rights defender and journalist, who was serving a three-year prison sentence imposed in 2009 after he spoke out against corruption.
- On 9 June, the editor of *el-Massa* newspaper, Rachid Nini, was sentenced to one year's imprisonment for spreading "disinformation" and "threatening national security". He had been detained on 28 April following the publication of articles criticizing the counter-terrorism practices of the security services. His sentence was upheld on appeal in October.
- In a retrial in December, Zakaria Moumni, a kickboxer imprisoned for fraud after an unfair trial, was again found guilty and sentenced to 20 months in prison. He was arrested in September 2010 after he criticized sports associations in Morocco and repeatedly attempted to meet the King. His original conviction was based on a "confession" that he said was extracted using torture.
- On 9 September, rap singer Mouad Belrhouate was arrested, apparently because some of his songs were deemed offensive to the monarchy. His trial was postponed several times and he remained in detention at the end of the year.

Repression of dissent – Sahrawi activists

Sahrawis advocating self-determination for the people of Western Sahara remained subject to restrictions on their freedoms of expression, association and assembly, and leading activists continued to face prosecution.

- On 14 April, Sahrawi activists Ahmed Alnasiri, Brahim Dahane and Ali Salem Tamek were released on bail. They had been held since 8 October 2009 and still faced charges, together with four other Sahrawi activists, of threatening Morocco's "internal security" through their peaceful activities and advocacy of self-determination for Western Sahara.
- Some 23 Sahrawis continued to be detained at Salé Prison, awaiting an unfair trial before a military court for their alleged involvement in violence in late 2010 at the Gdim Izik protest camp near Laayoune. In late October, the detainees went on hunger strike to protest against prison conditions and continued detention without trial. They had not been brought to trial by the end of the year.

No impartial and independent investigation was undertaken into the events at Gdim Izik and in Laayoune in November 2010 when Moroccan security forces demolished a Sahrawi protest camp, sparking violence in which 13 people, including 11 members of the security forces, were killed.

Torture and other ill-treatment

Reports of torture and other ill-treatment of detainees, notably by the Directorate for Surveillance of the Territory, persisted, with suspected Islamists and members of the 20 February Movement particularly targeted. Detainees continued to be held incommunicado, in some cases allegedly beyond the 12 days permitted by law.

- On 16-17 May, prisoners convicted of terrorism-related offences held at Salé Prison rioted in protest against their unfair trials and the use of torture at the secret Témara detention centre. They clashed with guards, briefly holding several hostage, before the prison authorities used live ammunition to quell the riots. Several prisoners were injured.
- In late May, Moroccan/German national Mohamed Hajib serving a 10-year prison term needed hospital treatment after he was severely beaten and threatened with rape by guards at Toulal Prison in Meknes, to where he had been moved after participating in the unrest at Salé Prison.

Counter-terror and security

On 28 April, 17 people, mostly foreign tourists, were killed and others injured when a bomb exploded at a café in Marrakesh; no one claimed responsibility but the authorities attributed it to Al Qa'ida in the Maghreb (AQIM), which the group denied.

M

■ Adel Othmani was sentenced to death in October after being convicted of the Marrakesh café bombing.

■ Five men convicted of terrorism-related charges in the "Belliraj Cell" case in July 2009 were released under the general royal pardon issued on 14 April. The case had been marred by procedural irregularities, including failure to investigate defendants' allegations of torture.

Transitional justice

The authorities failed to implement key recommendations made by the Equity and Reconciliation Commission in its November 2005 report. Victims continued to be denied effective access to justice for gross violations of human rights committed between Morocco's independence in 1956 and the death of King Hassan II in 1999.

Death penalty

Moroccan courts continued to hand down the death penalty. The last execution took place in 1993. Five death row prisoners had their sentences commuted to prison terms under an amnesty issued by the King in April.

Polisario camps

The Polisario Front took no measures to end impunity for those accused of committing human rights abuses in the 1970s and 1980s at the Tindouf camps controlled by the Polisario Front in Algeria's Mhiriz region.

In October, three aid workers – an Italian woman, a Spanish woman and a Spanish man – were abducted by an armed group from a Polisario-run refugee camp. They had not been released by the end of 2011.

Amnesty International visits/reports

▤ Moroccan authorities criticized for cracking down on Témara protests (MDE 29/004/2011)

▤ Morocco: Investigate torture allegations (MDE 29/008/2011)

MOZAMBIQUE

REPUBLIC OF MOZAMBIQUE

Head of state:	Armando Guebuza
Head of government:	Aires Bonifacio Baptista Ali
Death penalty:	abolitionist for all crimes
Population:	23.9 million
Life expectancy:	50.2 years
Under-5 mortality:	141.9 per 1,000
Adult literacy:	55.1 per cent

Law enforcement officers committed human rights violations against migrants and asylum-seekers. A police officer was convicted of a murder committed in 2007, but no compensation was given to the family. Several cases were recorded of the unlawful use of force by police, some resulting in death. Torture and other ill-treatment in prisons continued to be reported.

Background

In February, Mozambique's human rights record was assessed under the UN Universal Periodic Review (UPR) and the UN Human Rights Council's final report was adopted in June. Mozambique accepted 131 recommendations made during the UPR and stated that many had already been or were in the process of being implemented. These included recommendations to investigate all cases of arbitrary detention, torture and other ill-treatment; to investigate excessive use of force by the police; and to bring perpetrators to justice.

In March, former Minister of Interior Almerino Manhenje was sentenced to two years' imprisonment by the Maputo City Court for mismanagement of funds and abuse of power. The charges related to unlawful budgetary decisions and mismanagement of expenses while he was Minister of Interior in 2004. The former Director and Deputy Director of the financial department of the Ministry were also sentenced to two years in prison in the same case.

In April, guards from the main opposition party, the Mozambique National Resistance (Resistência Nacional Moçambicana, Renamo), shot at police officers at an airport in Sofala which was being renovated for a visit by President Guebuza. They demanded that all work stop until the ruling party, the Front for the Liberation of Mozambique (Frente de Libertação de Moçambique, Frelimo) agreed to hold talks with Renamo. Afonso Dhlakama, president of Renamo, threatened to create unrest aimed at overthrowing Frelimo.

In September, 25 judges were selected for the Superior Appeal Courts, set up to relieve the Supreme Court, which was previously the only court of appeal. Systems for the functioning of the new courts had not been put in place by the end of the year.

Scores of people, mainly elderly, were killed after being accused of witchcraft. The highest reported incidence of such killings occurred in the southern province of Inhambane where at least 20 elderly people were killed between August and September.

Refugees, migrants and asylum-seekers

Border and law enforcement officials were responsible for human rights violations against undocumented migrants and asylum-seekers. Thousands of undocumented migrants and asylum-seekers – mainly Somalis and Ethiopians – entered the country through Tanzania between January and July. Many reported that border officials and police beat them, stole their property, stripped them naked and abandoned them on islands in the Rovuma River. Others said the boats they arrived in were overturned by marine police.

■ An asylum-seeker from the Horn of Africa arrived at Mocimboa de Praia, Cabo Delgado province, by boat with around 300 people. As law enforcement officials attempted to push the boat back into the sea, it overturned and at least 15 people drowned. The asylum-seeker was rescued and later deported to Tanzania, but managed to re-enter Mozambique using a different route. He was found and beaten by law enforcement officials before finally arriving at Maratane refugee camp in Nampula, having walked some 695km from the border.

■ On 29 April there were reports that at least four Somali asylum-seekers were killed by Mozambique law enforcement officials and their bodies thrown into the Rovuma River as they attempted to cross into Mozambique from Tanzania. Despite requests from UNHCR, the UN refugee agency, no investigation appeared to have been carried out.

Excessive use of force and unlawful killings

As in previous years, police used excessive force and sometimes firearms against criminal suspects. Many instances resulted in grievous bodily harm or death. A police officer was convicted for the killing of a man in November 2007. However, the majority of past cases of human rights violations by police remained unresolved, including in relation to excessive use of force during demonstrations in 2009 and 2010 when police used live ammunition.

■ On the evening of 14 January, Angelo Juiz Nhancuana was drinking in Maputo city when his uncle arrived with two police officers, demanding that he be arrested for stealing a computer. Angelo Nhancuana agreed to go with the police, but refused to be handcuffed. One of the police officers hit him over the head with his pistol and shot him through the arm when he fell. Angelo Nhancuana was in hospital for a month and was informed that the police had no case to answer as the weapon was fired accidentally. The case was reopened after intervention from Angelo Nhancuana's lawyer.

■ In the early hours of 5 March, police shot and killed Hortêncio Nia Ossufo in his home in Muatala, Nampula. Claims by police that they had attempted to immobilize Hortêncio Ossufo as he tried to escape were contradicted by an eyewitness who said he was deliberately killed in a case of mistaken identity.

■ On 22 March, a police officer was sentenced by the Inhambane Provincial Court to four years' imprisonment for killing Julião Naftal Macule in November 2007. None of the other nine police officers who took part in the operation were charged.

Torture and other ill-treatment

There were continued reports of torture and other ill-treatment of prisoners, including after attempted escapes.

■ On 24 September, two prisoners died from their injuries at the Quinta do Girassol detention centre in Zambezia province after being beaten by a prison guard with sticks, stones and bricks. The prisoners had apparently been recaptured while trying to escape.

Justice system

Access to justice continued to be a challenge for the majority of citizens due to the costs and other obstacles. Despite a law which exempts indigent people from paying court fees, many judges continued to insist on payment of such fees even from those with a certificate of poverty.

M

Amnesty International visits/reports

🚌 Amnesty International delegates visited Mozambique from 26 September to 1 November.

📖 Mozambique: Amnesty International urges investigation into cases of extrajudicial executions, arbitrary detention, torture and ill-treatment and excessive use of force (AFR 41/002/2011)

MYANMAR

REPUBLIC OF THE UNION OF MYANMAR

Head of state and government:	**Thein Sein (replaced Senior General Than Shwe, former head of state, in March)**
Death penalty:	**abolitionist in practice**
Population:	**48.3 million**
Life expectancy:	**65.2 years**
Under-5 mortality:	**71.2 per 1,000**
Adult literacy:	**92 per cent**

The government enacted limited political and economic reforms, but human rights violations and violations of international humanitarian law in ethnic minority areas increased during the year. Some of these amounted to crimes against humanity or war crimes. Forced displacement reached its highest level in a decade, and reports of forced labour their highest level in several years. Authorities maintained restrictions on freedom of religion and belief, and perpetrators of human rights violations went unpunished. Despite releasing at least 313 political prisoners during the year, authorities continued to arrest such people, further violating their rights by subjecting them to ill-treatment and poor prison conditions.

Background

Myanmar's Parliament, elected in November 2010, convened on 31 January and voted in Thein Sein as President of a government formed on 30 March. It was the first civilian government in decades. In July and August, opposition leader Daw Aung San Suu Kyi travelled outside Yangon for the first time since 2003. She met with Labour Minister Aung Gyi four times during the year and with President Thein Sein in August. Beginning that month, the government carried out a series of limited political and economic reforms. It released at least 313 political prisoners; slightly relaxed media censorship; passed an improved labour law; and established the National Human Rights Commission. In September, the government suspended construction of the controversial, China-backed Myitsone Dam in Kachin state, citing domestic opposition to the project. It also reportedly ceased demanding that ethnic minority armed groups become official Border Guard Forces. In November, the National League for Democracy re-registered as a political party, and its leader Aung San Suu Kyi announced her intention to run for Parliament in the 2012 by-elections. Parliament also passed a law that month allowing peaceful protests under certain conditions.

Internal armed conflict

The armed conflict in Kayin (Karen) state and Tanintharyi region that began in late 2010 escalated during the year. In March, conflict between the Myanmar army and various ethnic minority armed groups intensified in Shan state. In June, the army broke a 17-year ceasefire with the Kachin Independence Army (KIA) in Kachin state. Smaller conflicts continued or resumed in Kayah (Karenni) and Mon states.

In all of these conflicts, the Myanmar army launched indiscriminate attacks causing civilian casualties, at times directly attacking ethnic minority civilians. Credible accounts of the army using prison convicts as porters, human shields and mine sweepers emerged from Kayin state and adjacent areas of Bago and Tanintharyi divisions. In Kachin state, sources reported extrajudicial executions, children killed by indiscriminate shelling, forced labour, and unlawful confiscation or destruction of food and property. Shan civilians were tortured, arbitrarily detained and forcibly relocated. Soldiers reportedly sexually assaulted Kachin and Shan civilians. In August, ethnic armed groups, including some that had committed abuses, rejected the government's offer of talks between individual armed groups and the relevant regional administration rather than talks between an alliance of such groups and the federal government. However, several groups agreed to ceasefires with the army during the year. In September, the army intensified fighting in Kachin and Shan states, violating human rights law and international humanitarian law. Some of these acts amounted to crimes against humanity or war crimes.

■ On 7 June, a seven-year-old child was killed in Mae T'lar village in Kayin state's Kawkareik township, when the army shelled the village with mortars.

■ On 16 June, soldiers in Hsipaw township, Shan state, shot and killed a 35-year-old man, a 70-year-old woman and one girl, aged 13; all were civilians.

■ On 18 September, soldiers in Shan state's Kyethi township forced at least 10 local monks to act as human shields during an operation to deliver supplies to other troops in the area.

■ On 12 October, soldiers killed a 16-month-old baby in Mansi township, Bhamo district in Kachin state, while storming a village and shooting indiscriminately.

■ Beginning on 28 October and lasting several days, soldiers detained and reportedly gang-raped a 28-year-old Kachin woman in Hkai Bang village in Bhamo district, Sub-Loije township, Kachin state.

■ On 12 November, Myanmar army soldiers extrajudicially executed four captured KIA fighters and tortured four others in Nam Sang Yang village, Waingmaw township, Kachin state.

Forced displacement and refugees

Fighting in ethnic minority areas displaced approximately 30,000 people in Shan state and a similar number in or near Kachin state. The majority of them were forced out of their homes and land by the Myanmar army. Most individuals and families were unable or unwilling to leave Myanmar, and so became internally displaced. In addition, approximately 36,000 people had already been displaced in Kayin state. In a one-year period ending in July, 112,000 people were reportedly forced from their homes in Myanmar, the highest such figure in 10 years.

■ In March, the army forced approximately 200 households in Nansang township, Shan state, to move in preparation for the construction of a new regional command base.

■ In April, soldiers burned down around 70 homes in seven villages in Mong Pieng township, Shan state, accusing the residents of supporting an armed group.

■ In May, 1,200 refugees from Kyain Seikgyi township in Kayin state fled to Thailand.

In many cases, authorities prevented humanitarian agencies from entering conflict-affected areas so that they were unable to reach tens of thousands of people displaced by the fighting or the army,

especially those in camps on the Myanmar-China border. In Chin state and other ethnic minority areas, the government maintained lengthy and complex administrative procedures for obtaining travel permits both for humanitarian agencies that already have a presence and for new ones seeking permission to work in the country.

Ethnic minority Rohingyas continued to face discrimination and repression primarily in Rakhine state and remained unrecognized as citizens. As a result, many continued to leave Myanmar on their own or were smuggled out, either overland to Bangladesh or on boats during the "sailing season", in the first and final months of the year.

Forced labour

In June, the ILO noted that there had been "no substantive progress" towards compliance with the 1998 ILO Commission of Inquiry's recommendations on forced labour. On 12 August, Information Minister Kyaw Hsan stated that Myanmar was "almost free from forced labour". In November, the ILO said that forced labour complaints in Myanmar had increased to an average of 30 per month since March compared with 21 per month for the same period in 2010, 10 per month in 2009, and five per month in both 2008 and 2007. Approximately 75 per cent of these complaints related to under-age recruitment into the army, with the remainder pertaining to trafficking for forced labour and military forced labour. Labour activists and political prisoners U Thurein Aung, U Wai Lin, U Nyi Nyi Zaw, U Kyaw Kyaw, U Kyaw Win and U Myo Min remained in prison, as reportedly did 16 others.

■ In October, Myanmar border security forces in Rakhine state's Maungdaw township forced villagers to carry out construction work at a military camp.

■ In August and early September, a government official in Chin State reportedly ordered civil servants to carry out manual forced labour in the capital Hakha.

Freedom of religion or belief

Violations of the right to religious freedom affected every religious group in Myanmar. Buddhist monks who participated in the 2007 anti-government demonstrations continued to be arrested, ill-treated and harassed. Muslim Rohingyas were suppressed and forced to relocate on religious as well as ethnic grounds. Christian religious sites were relocated or destroyed.

M

■ On 9 August, soldiers set fire to the Mong Khawn monastery in Mansi township, Kachin state, apparently because they suspected that the monks had provided support to the KIA.

■ On 10 September, authorities in Htantlang village in Htantlang township, Chin state, ordered a Chin Christian preacher not to speak at a local church and to leave the area.

■ On 14 October, authorities in Hpakant township, Kachin state, ordered local Christian churches to request permission at least 15 days in advance to carry out many religious activities.

■ On 6 November, soldiers opened fire on a Christian church in Muk Chyik village, Waingmaw township in Kachin state, injuring several worshippers.

Impunity

Government officials and military personnel who committed human rights violations, including some on a widespread or systematic basis, remained free from prosecution. Article 445 of the 2008 Constitution codifies total impunity for past violations. In September, the President appointed a National Human Rights Commission whose mandate included receiving and investigating human rights complaints, but Myanmar's justice system continued to demonstrate a lack of impartiality and independence from the government. In January, the government stated that there was "no widespread occurrence of human rights violations with impunity" in Myanmar.

Political prisoners

In May, the Myanmar government released at least 72 political prisoners under a one-year reduction of all prison sentences in the country. In October, it released 241 more political prisoners. However, few of those freed were from ethnic minorities. More than 1,000 political prisoners, including prisoners of conscience, remained behind bars, but exact figures were uncertain due to Myanmar's opaque prison system, differences in definitions of what constitutes a political prisoner, and ongoing arrests.

■ In February, a court sentenced Maung Maung Zeya, a reporter with Democratic Voice of Burma – a media outlet based outside Myanmar – to 13 years in prison for peaceful activities.

■ On 26 August, Nay Myo Zin, a former military officer and member of an NLD-supported blood donation group, was sentenced to 10 years in prison for peacefully exercising his rights to freedom of expression.

■ On 14 September, Democratic Voice of Burma reporter Sithu Zeya, already serving an eight-year prison term, was sentenced to a further 10 years under the Electronic Transactions Act.

Political prisoners continued to be subjected to cruel, inhuman and degrading punishment and very poor prison conditions.

■ In February, Htet Htet Oo Wei, who was suffering from a number of health problems, was placed in solitary confinement reportedly for making too much noise. She was denied family visits and parcels.

■ In February, authorities in Yangon's Insein prison placed political prisoner Phyo Wei Aung in solitary confinement for a month, after he complained about fellow inmates bullying other prisoners.

■ In May, at least 20 political prisoners in Insein prison went on hunger strike to protest the government's limited release of such prisoners that month and to demand better prison conditions. As punishment, seven were placed in cells designed to hold dogs.

■ In July, the Monywa prison authorities in Sagaing division withdrew visitation rights to Nobel Aye (aka Hnin May Aung), after she urged high-ranking officials to withdraw recent public statements that claimed there were no political prisoners in Myanmar.

■ In October, 15 political prisoners in Insein staged a hunger strike in protest against the denial of sentence reductions for political prisoners, in contrast to criminal convicts. Some were reportedly deprived of drinking water and were otherwise ill-treated. Eight of them were placed in "dog cells".

■ In October, information emerged that U Gambira, a Buddhist monk and leader of the 2007 anti-government demonstrations, was seriously ill and being held in solitary confinement. He had been suffering from severe headaches, possibly due to torture he was subjected to in prison in 2009. Prison authorities were reported to be regularly injecting him with drugs to sedate him.

International scrutiny

In January, Myanmar's human rights record was assessed under the UN Universal Periodic Review. In March, Latvia and Denmark added their support for the creation of a UN Commission of Inquiry into international crimes in Myanmar, bringing the total number of supporting countries to 16. Despite a

M

January call by ASEAN to lift economic sanctions against Myanmar, the EU and the USA extended their sanctions. However, in April the EU eased travel restrictions on 24 officials. In May and October, the UN Secretary-General's Special Adviser on Myanmar visited the country.

President Thein Sein visited China in May and India in October. After being denied a visa in 2010 and earlier in the year, the UN Special Rapporteur on the situation of human rights in Myanmar visited in August. The US Special Representative and Policy Coordinator for Burma visited in September, October, and November. In September, the ICRC was authorized for the first time since 2005 to conduct an international staff-led engineering survey in three of Myanmar's prisons. After a year-long debate, Myanmar was named Chair of ASEAN for 2014 in November. In December, for the first time in over 50 years, the US Secretary of State visited Myanmar.

Amnesty International visits/reports

▤ No international compromise on human rights in Myanmar (ASA 16/001/2011)

▤ Amnesty International calls for the urgent establishment of an international commission of inquiry as Myanmar rejects recommendations to end violations of international human rights and humanitarian law (ASA 16/004/2011)

▤ Myanmar: Government must go further with prisoner release (PRE01/522/2011)

NAMIBIA

REPUBLIC OF NAMIBIA

Head of state and government:	Hifikepunye Pohamba
Death penalty:	abolitionist for all crimes
Population:	2.3 million
Life expectancy:	62.5 years
Under-5 mortality:	47.5 per 1,000
Adult literacy:	88.5 per cent

The dispute over the 2009 National Assembly elections remained unresolved in the Supreme Court. The long-running treason trial of Caprivi detainees continued. Human rights defenders, in particular those considered critical of the government and ruling party, were attacked by the government and by individuals linked to the government and the ruling South West Africa People's Organization (SWAPO) party.

Election dispute

The Supreme Court reserved judgement after nine political parties appealed against the ruling which dismissed their challenge to declare null and void the results of the 2009 National Assembly elections. The parties had made their challenge following inter-party violence and reports of irregularities by the Electoral Commission of Namibia. President Pohamba of SWAPO was declared the winner in 2009 and the party won 54 of the 72 National Assembly seats.

Caprivi detainees' trial

The trial of detainees arrested in connection with the 1999 attacks by a secessionist group, the Caprivi Liberation Army, continued with no sign of an end. Most of the 112 detainees had been in custody for at least 11 years. Their continued detention violated their right to a fair trial without undue delay. The death of Bevin Joshua Tubwikale in April brought the number of detainees who have died in custody since the trial began in 2003 to at least 19.

Freedom of expression, association and assembly

The police used excessive force to arrest peaceful protesters demonstrating against government policies. On 25 January, officers of the national police and the Windhoek police fired rubber bullets and live

ammunition at some 500 taxi drivers who were demonstrating against traffic fines. At least five demonstrators were injured, including Matheus Leonard.
■ In May, police officers assaulted Freddy Haixwa, President of the Wisdom Youth Organization (WIYO), who was leading about 400 WIYO demonstrators to the offices of the Ministry of Youth, National Service, Sport and Culture.

Human rights defenders

On 4 and 5 May, the national radio and television news quoted President Pohamba referring to the human rights organization NAMRIGHTS as "that diminutive human rights organization". Also in May, the Secretary General of the National Union of Namibian Workers, Evilastus Kaaronda, received death threats after his organization called for the prosecution of people accused of misappropriating monies from the Government Institutions Pension Fund, including senior government officials. A government audit had confirmed that N$660 million (approximately US$74 million) had been misappropriated.

NEPAL

FEDERAL DEMOCRATIC REPUBLIC OF NEPAL

Head of state:	Ram Baran Yadav
Head of government:	Baburam Bhattarai (replaced Jhala Nath Khanal in August, who replaced Madhav Kumar Nepal in February)
Death penalty:	abolitionist for all crimes
Population:	30.5 million
Life expectancy:	68.8 years
Under-5 mortality:	48.2 per 1,000
Adult literacy:	59.1 per cent

Nepal continued to backtrack on commitments to hold perpetrators of human rights abuses accountable before the law. Political parties in government actively subverted justice by demanding the withdrawal of criminal charges in hundreds of cases, including for serious human rights violations committed during the armed conflict. Torture and other ill-treatment in police custody remained widespread. Police increasingly suppressed Tibetan refugees' right to freedom of association and expression. Exploitation of Nepalese migrant workers abroad, including forced labour, continued. Ethnic, religious and gender discrimination and violence against women and girls went largely unchallenged.

Background

The UN Mission in Nepal, tasked with monitoring the Comprehensive Peace Agreement (CPA) of 2006, ended operations in January, but key elements of the CPA remained unfulfilled. Elected Prime Minister in February, Jhala Nath Khanal resigned on 14 August after failing to make progress on the peace process, including seeing through the drafting of a new Constitution. Baburam Bhattarai, vice chairperson of the Unified Communist Party of Nepal (Maoist) succeeded him, ultimately overseeing the extension of the mandate of the Constituent Assembly (CA) to 27 May 2012, and pledging to oversee completion of the new Constitution.

Transitional justice

Article 5 of Nepal's CPA provided for the creation of a Truth and Reconciliation Commission to investigate alleged human rights violations and crimes against humanity committed during the armed conflict. However, drafting of a bill to create the Commission had yet to be completed. The government continued to make interim payments to families of "conflict victims", but failed to fulfil victims' rights to truth and justice.

Enforced disappearances

The government had yet to set up a commission to investigate thousands of enforced disappearances by parties to the conflict between 1996 and 2006, despite promising to do so by September.

Impunity

To forge political consensus before the prime ministerial elections, the Unified Communist Party of Nepal (Maoist) signed an agreement with Terai-based parties to, among other things, withdraw criminal cases lodged against political party members, including for human rights-related offences allegedly committed during the armed conflict. On 28 August, the government announced its intention to implement withdrawals, supported by public statements from the Attorney General.

- Human rights defenders opposed the appointment in May of Agni Sapkota, accused of involvement in the 2005 abduction and murder of teacher Arjun Lama, as Minister of Information and Communications. On 21 June, the Supreme Court ordered Kavre district police to report their progress in investigating the case to the court, but stopped short of ordering Agni Sapkota's suspension.
- In July, the Supreme Court annulled an order blocking the promotion of a senior police officer accused of involvement in the 2003 "Dhanusha 5" case in which five young men, including Sanjiv Kumar Karna, were allegedly killed by security forces. Exhumations of the remains of the five victims were completed in February.
- In October, Nepal's cabinet recommended an amnesty for Maoist CA member Balkrishna Dhungel, who had been convicted of murder and sentenced to life imprisonment in January.

Torture and other ill-treatment

Torture and other ill-treatment in police custody remained widespread. In June, the Nepal-based Centre for Victims of Torture reported that since the end of the armed conflict in 2006, the majority of incidents of torture were perpetrated by the police. Of 989 prisoners interviewed, 74 per cent reported being tortured in custody.

Torture has yet to be criminalized under domestic Nepalese law. During the first assessment of its human rights record under the UN Universal Periodic Review, Nepal denied that systematic torture took place in the country, noting that a bill incorporating provisions of the Convention against Torture was "under active consideration".

Migrant workers

Poverty and high unemployment prompted at least 300,000 documented workers to migrate abroad. Some labour recruiters trafficked migrant workers for forced labour, deceiving them about pay, working conditions, and substituting contracts. High interest rate loans combined with lower pay than promised, and confiscation of identity documents meant many migrants could not refuse to work. Nepal has put in place some laws to protect migrant labourers but in some instances failed to properly monitor recruitment agencies and rarely prosecuted those who violated the Foreign Employment Act.

- 108 migrant workers stranded in Libya without pay by their employer in 2010 were awarded a partial settlement in April. In July, the Department of Foreign Employment and District Attorney General's Office in Nepal recommended the case be forwarded to the Foreign Employment Tribunal for investigation following pressure from the workers, trade unions and Amnesty International.

Freedom of assembly, association and expression

Police suppression of freedom of association and expression of Tibetan refugees increased, following pressure from China. Peaceful meetings in private buildings were disrupted by police, and people were arrested after displaying banners or slogans supporting political independence for Tibet. Tibetan activists were systematically detained before key dates.

- In March, a large group of mainly elderly Tibetan women were prevented by police from travelling by bus to a pilgrimage site.

Discrimination

Discrimination persisted on the basis of ethnicity, religion, gender, economic situation and disability. Despite promulgation on 24 May of the Caste-based Discrimination and Untouchability (Offense and Punishment) Act, Dalits continued to face social and economic exclusion. Gender discrimination continued, particularly among women from marginalized castes and ethnicities. Dalit girls and poor girls from rural areas faced discrimination in accessing education and health care, were more likely to be married as children, and experienced higher rates of child malnutrition.

Violence against women and girls

Police often refused to register complaints in cases of domestic and gender-based violence.

- In September, a woman who said she was raped by four army officers in Dailekh in 2004 attempted to lodge a complaint against her attackers, accusing them of rape and torture. But the police in Dailekh refused to comply, noting that the 35-day time limit to register a rape complaint had expired. In 2006, the Supreme Court found the time limit violated international norms and ordered parliament to change the rule; the order was not implemented.

N

🚌 Amnesty International delegates visited Nepal in May.

NETHERLANDS

KINGDOM OF THE NETHERLANDS

Head of state:	Queen Beatrix
Head of government:	Mark Rutte
Death penalty:	abolitionist for all crimes
Population:	16.7 million
Life expectancy:	80.7 years
Under-5 mortality:	4.4 per 1,000

A landmark court ruling held the government accountable for the conduct of its troops while they were serving as UN peacekeepers in Srebrenica. The detention of asylum-seekers and irregular migrants caused concern.

International justice

In July, the appeals court in The Hague ruled that the government had been responsible for the deaths of three Bosnian Muslims during the 1995 Srebrenica genocide in Bosnia and Herzegovina. The court ruled that Dutch troops had forced the three to leave a "safe area", effectively handing them over to Bosnian Serb forces, who went on to kill some 8,000 Bosnian Muslim men and boys.

Refugees, asylum-seekers and migrants

In January, the European Court of Human Rights halted the return from the Netherlands to Somalia of two asylum-seekers from south and central Somalia, by issuing interim measures. The government subsequently suspended all returns to Mogadishu, Somalia's capital. However, following a further European Court judgement in June, the government announced it would resume returns to Mogadishu of Somali nationals who did not belong to a vulnerable group and could travel to, gain admittance to and settle in areas of south and central Somalia without being at risk of ill-treatment. There were no reported deportations of Somali nationals to south and central Somalia by the end of the year.

At least 180 Iraqis were forcibly returned to Bagdad, Iraq, contrary to the advice of UNHCR, the UN Refugee Agency.

Most asylum claims were processed using the new eight-day asylum procedure. Of these, over 50 per cent received a determination of their claim within the eight days. There was concern that this procedure may impede asylum-seekers from substantiating their claims and result in the rejection of well-founded claims.

According to government figures 3,220 irregular migrants and asylum-seekers were taken into detention between January and June. They were held in detention centres under a regime designed for remand prisoners. Alternatives to detention were rarely used. In July, the Minister for Immigration and Asylum announced a small-scale pilot project to test alternatives to detention.

Discrimination

In September, the government announced it would begin drafting legislation to ban the wearing in public of clothing intended to conceal the face. A violation of the ban would be punishable with a fine of up to €380. If implemented the ban would have a disproportionate effect on women who chose to wear a burqa or niqab as an expression of their identity or beliefs.

NEW ZEALAND

NEW ZEALAND
Head of state: Queen Elizabeth II represented by Jerry
                        Mateparae (replaced Anand Satyanandin August)
Head of government: John Key
Death penalty: abolitionist for all crimes
Population: 4.4 million
Life expectancy: 80.7 years
Under-5 mortality: 6.2 per 1,000

Indigenous Peoples' property rights were partially recognized by the Marine and Coastal Area Act. The Minister of Defence admitted he could not guarantee that detainees captured during joint operations in Afghanistan had not been tortured. Levels of child poverty remained high, disproportionately affecting Māori and Pacific communities.

Legal, constitutional or institutional developments

Economic, social and cultural rights were not included in the New Zealand Bill of Rights Act. The Act did not explicitly give the judiciary the power to issue remedies for breaches of its provisions. New Zealand still had not ratified the Optional Protocol to the International Covenant on Economic, Social and Cultural Rights.

Indigenous Peoples' rights

In March, the Marine and Coastal Area (Takutai Moana) Act 2011 was passed, repealing the Foreshore and Seabed Act 2004, which had prevented Māori property claims to these areas. However, the 2011 Act did not allow Māori to apply for exclusive occupation in these areas or to claim lands in private ownership; and all claims to traditional rights had to be made within six years.

Workers' rights

In June, crew members of South Korean chartered fishing vessels *Oyang 75* and *Shin Ji* refused to reboard their vessels, docked in the ports of Lyttelton and Auckland. The government subsequently launched a ministerial inquiry in July to investigate allegations of mental, physical and sexual abuse of crew members, and that they had not received their wages.

Counter-terror and security

In October, the New Zealand Defence Force (NZDF) released a report into NZDF's potential complicity in torture in Afghanistan. The report confirmed that one person detained since September 2009 by the New Zealand Special Air Service (NZSAS) was being monitored to ensure his well-being. In contrast, the Minister of Defence admitted that the NZDF were not monitoring detainees captured during joint operations between the Afghan National Police Crisis Response Unit and the NZSAS, and could not guarantee that they had not been tortured.

Children's rights

In February, the UN Committee on the Rights of the Child expressed concern that 20 per cent of children in the country lived below the poverty line and that abuse and neglect of children within the family remained prevalent. In July, the government released a discussion paper on how the country could better protect abused, neglected and disadvantaged children. It acknowledged that child poverty afflicted Māori and Pacific communities more than other groups in New Zealand. In September, New Zealand ratified the Optional Protocol to the UN Convention on the Rights of the Child on the sale of children, child prostitution and child pornography.

N

NICARAGUA

REPUBLIC OF NICARAGUA

Head of state and government:	**Daniel Ortega Saavedra**
Death penalty:	**abolitionist for all crimes**
Population:	**5.9 million**
Life expectancy:	**74 years**
Under-5 mortality:	**25.6 per 1,000**
Adult literacy:	**78 per cent**

At least four people died and scores more were injured in post-election violence. Rape and sexual abuse were widespread. The total ban on all forms of abortion remained in force. The independence of the judiciary was called into question.

Background

In the wake of the November elections, violence erupted amid widespread allegations of electoral fraud. At least four people were killed and scores were injured in confrontations across the country between supporters and opponents of Daniel Ortega, who was re-elected for a third term as President.

Violence against women and girls

Rape and sexual abuse remained a concern. Despite this, in July the Supreme Court of Justice reduced the sentence imposed on Farinton Reyes for the rape in 2009 of his co-worker, Fátima Hernández, to four years' imprisonment. The Court sought to justify its decision on the grounds that Farinton Reyes had committed the crime while under the influence of alcohol and in a state of sexual excitement that he could not control. The judges also argued that Fátima Hernández had acted permissively and co-operated in the rape.

Sexual and reproductive rights

The total ban on all forms of abortion remained in force, giving rise to serious violations of the rights of women and girls. The revised criminal laws, which came into force in 2008, allow for no exceptions to the ban. As a result women and girls who were pregnant as a result of rape or whose lives or health were threatened by continued pregnancy were denied the right to seek safe and legal abortion services. All abortion remained a criminal offence and anyone seeking, or

assisting someone seeking, an abortion risked prosecution.

In March, the state was urged by the Inter-American Commission on Human Rights to take action to put an end to sexual violence against women and girls and to repeal the total ban on abortion.

Freedom of expression

Reports of intimidation of media workers increased in the context of a heated political debate in the run-up to the November presidential elections.

■ On 19 February, an unidentified individual telephoned journalist Luis Galeano and threatened: "You have 72 hours to change your mind about what you'll publish, otherwise your family won't see you again." The caller alluded to an investigation that Galeano and a colleague had carried out into a corruption case involving misuse of public funds by officials of the Supreme Electoral Council. The officials were alleged to have misappropriated an estimated US$20 million between 2004 and 2008. A few hours prior to the call, Luis Galeano had received a message left for him by an unidentified man at the reception desk of the offices of his newspaper, *El Nuevo Diario*. The message also contained a reference to his research on the corruption case and warned him not to publish the article.

In November, following the announcement by the Supreme Electoral Council of Daniel Ortega's victory in the presidential elections, crowds took to the streets across the country in protest.

■ On 10 November, a group of around 30 youth activists from the Nicaragua 2.0 Movement taking part in an anti-Ortega demonstration outside the University of Central America in Managua were allegedly threatened and attacked by supporters of the youth wing of the Sandinista National Liberation Front. Police officers present at the scene reportedly did not intervene to prevent the attacks. Local and international NGOs demanded that action be taken to protect the right of all Nicaraguans to demonstrate peacefully.

Amnesty International visits/reports

🚗 Amnesty International delegates visited Nicaragua in July.

📄 End the total abortion ban in Nicaragua – a film (youtube.com/watch?v=hIWQPBIb10I)

NIGER

REPUBLIC OF NIGER

Head of state:	**Mahamadou Issoufou (replaced Salou Djibo in April)**
Head of government:	**Brigi Rafini (replaced Mahamadou Danda in April)**
Death penalty:	**abolitionist in practice**
Population:	**16.1 million**
Life expectancy:	**54.7 years**
Under-5 mortality:	**160.3 per 1,000**
Adult literacy:	**28.7 per cent**

Two political leaders and 10 military officers were detained for several months without trial. Niger accepted high-ranking Libyan officials "on humanitarian grounds" while stating that it would respect its commitments to the International Criminal Court if any official named in arrest warrants entered its territory. Several foreign nationals were taken hostage or remained held by al-Qa'ida in the Islamic Maghreb (AQIM) and two were killed during a failed rescue operation.

Background

In March, Mahamadou Issoufou was elected President, ending the interim government led by a military junta which had ousted President Mamadou Tandja in 2010.

As a result of the unrest and armed conflict in Libya, more than 200,000 nationals from Niger returned home, creating a difficult humanitarian situation.

Clashes in the north of Niger were reported throughout the year between security forces and armed elements of AQIM. The Niger government stated that AQIM was obtaining arms smuggled from Libya. Niger announced in May that it would strengthen security co-operation with Mali, Mauritania and Algeria. In November, the Niger armed forces destroyed a convoy of heavy weapons on its way from Libya to Mali.

Detention without trial

Two political leaders and 10 military officers were detained for several months. At the end of the year at least three remained held without trial.

■ In January, former President Tandja, who had been under house arrest since he was ousted from power in

2010, was charged with embezzlement and imprisoned. Provisionally released in May, he had not been tried by the end of the year. The former Minister of Interior, Albadé Abouba, who had been under house arrest since February 2010, was released without charge in March.

■ In July, 10 military officers accused of plotting against the authorities were arrested and detained for several days before being released. In September, two high-ranking officials, Colonel Abdoulaye Badié and Lieutenant-Colonel Hamadou Djibo, were arrested and accused of writing and distributing a leaflet criticizing the promotion of some military officers. Both were released without charge in November.

Abuses by armed groups

Several foreign nationals were taken hostage or were still held by AQIM and two were killed during an attempted rescue operation.

■ In January, two French citizens were abducted in the capital, Niamey, and were killed the following day during a failed rescue operation on the border with Mali involving forces from France and Niger. Three gendarmes (paramilitary police) of Niger, as well as a number of alleged members of AQIM, were reportedly killed during the attack. AQIM claimed responsibility for the abductions.

■ In February, three of the seven people who were abducted by AQIM in the town of Arlit in September 2010 were released. One French national, one Togolese and one Malagasy were released while the four others – all French nationals – were still held at the end of the year.

International justice

In September, several high-ranking officials of Colonel al-Gaddafi's Libyan government, including one of his sons, Saadi Gaddafi, who was subject to sanctions imposed by the UN Security Council, entered Niger where they were accepted on "humanitarian grounds" and placed "under surveillance". At the end of the year, none had been named in arrest warrants by the International Criminal Court.

Despite requests by the Libyan National Transitional Council, Niger refused to return the men to Libya while stressing that they would abide by their international commitments towards international justice in case of an international extradition request.

NIGERIA

FEDERAL REPUBLIC OF NIGERIA

Head of state and government:	Goodluck Jonathan
Death penalty:	retentionist
Population:	162.5 million
Life expectancy:	51.9 years
Under-5 mortality:	137.9 per 1,000
Adult literacy:	60.8 per cent

Nigeria's human rights situation deteriorated. Hundreds of people were killed in politically motivated, communal and sectarian violence across the country, particularly after the April elections. Violent attacks attributed to the religious sect Boko Haram increased, killing more than 500 people. The police were responsible for hundreds of unlawful killings, most of which remained uninvestigated. The justice system remained ineffective. Around two thirds of all prison inmates were still awaiting trial. There were 982 people on death row. No executions were reported. Forced evictions continued throughout the country, and violence against women remained rife.

Background

In April, President Goodluck Jonathan was declared the winner of the country's presidential elections. Violent attacks and rioting followed, resulting in hundreds of deaths. The President signed into law several bills, including the National Human Rights Commission Act in February; the Freedom of Information Act in May; and the Legal Aid Act and the Terrorism Act in June.

The National Human Rights Commission was given power to investigate human rights violations and visit police stations and other places of detention. By the end of the year, however, funds for the Commission had not been released.

Corruption remained endemic. In November, the President dismissed the Chairperson of the Economic and Financial Crimes Commission, six months before her tenure was due to end. No explanation was given. He also approved a 12,500 naira (US$76) increase in the monthly minimum wage to 18,000 naira (US$117). 1.3 million people remained internally displaced throughout the country.

Unlawful killings and enforced disappearances

Police operations remained characterized by human rights violations. Hundreds of people were unlawfully killed, often before or during arrests on the street. Others were tortured to death in police detention. Many such unlawful killings may have constituted extrajudicial executions. Many people disappeared from police custody. Few police officers were held accountable, leaving relatives of those killed or disappeared without justice. Police increasingly wore plain clothes or uniforms without identification, making it much harder for people to complain about individual officers.

■ On 19 April, Chibuike Orduku was arrested by police at his home in Ubinini, Rivers State, and detained along with three unidentified men. Chibuike Orduku was last seen by his sister on 5 May. He reported being tortured and denied food and water. The whereabouts of all four men remained unknown.

■ On 2 November, police from the Port Harcourt Swift Operation Squad (SOS) killed three men in Abonnema Wharf and arrested four others. Two were later released while the other two were remanded in prison. Eyewitnesses said the community was peaceful before the police arrived. The police refused to release the three men's corpses to their relatives for burial. No investigation had been carried out by the end of the year.

Special task forces, including the Special Anti Robbery Squads and SOS, committed a wide range of human rights violations. In early 2011, the Bayelsa State government set up Operation Famou Tangbe – "kill and throw away" in the local language – to fight crime. Many officers linked to the operation reportedly unlawfully killed, tortured, arbitrarily arrested and detained people. Suspects in detention reportedly had no access to their lawyers or relatives.

■ On 22 February, Dietemepreye Ezonasa, a student aged 22, was arrested by Operation Famou Tangbe and taken to a police station. On 27 February, the police denied that he was in their custody. His whereabouts have since remained unknown.

■ On 11 May, Tochukwu Ozokwu, 25, was arrested by Operation Famou Tangbe. The next day the police told him to jump in a river or be shot. He could not swim and drowned. No investigation was carried out.

In September, the Federal Government stopped Operation Famou Tangbe. The human rights violations committed while it was active remained uninvestigated.

The police frequently disobeyed court orders.

■ The police refused to release Mallam Aliyu Tasheku, a suspected Boko Haram member, after a court granted him bail on 28 March. He was finally released in July.

■ The police failed to produce Chika Ibeku, who disappeared from police custody in April 2009, more than a year after a court ordered that he be brought to court.

The majority of cases remained uninvestigated and unpunished. Some relatives were threatened when they sought justice.

■ Catherine Akor continued to receive death threats after suing the police for the unlawful killing of her son, Michael Akor, and his friend, Michael Igwe, in June 2009.

Torture and other ill-treatment

There were consistent reports of police routinely torturing suspects to extract information. Confessions extracted under torture were used as evidence in court, in violation of national and international laws.

Boko Haram

Violent attacks by suspected members of the religious sect Boko Haram increased, killing more than 500 people and often targeting police officers and government officials. Since June, bars and beer gardens in northern Nigeria were targeted, killing scores of people. The situation deteriorated towards the end of the year, with weekly reports of bombings and attacks. On 31 December, the President declared a state of emergency in parts of Borno, Niger, Plateau and Yobe states.

■ On 16 June, a bomb exploded in the Nigeria Police Force headquarters car park, killing at least three people.

■ On 28 August, Boko Haram bombed the UN building in Abuja, killing 24 people and injuring at least 80.

■ On 4 November, at least 100 people were killed in bombings in Damaturu, the Yobe State capital.

■ On 25 December, at least 44 people were killed in four bombings; 37 people were also killed and more than 50 injured when Boko Haram bombed a church in Madalla, Niger State. In Jos, Plateau State, and Damaturu, a further seven people died after bombs exploded.

In response to the violence, the Federal Government set up a Special Military Task Force (JTF) in Maiduguri in June, consisting of the army, navy, air force, the Department of State Security and the Nigeria Police Force. Reports subsequently increased regarding the security forces in Borno State resorting to unlawful killings, dragnet arrests, arbitrary and unlawful detentions, extortion and intimidation. Hundreds of people were arrested. On 25 December, Nigeria's National Human Rights Commission expressed concerns about possible extrajudicial executions by security forces in northern Nigeria.

■ On 9 July, the JTF cordoned off the Kaleri Ngomari Custain area in Maiduguri after a Boko Haram bombing. Going from house to house, they reportedly shot dead at least 25 people. Many men and boys were reported missing. The JTF also burned down several houses, forcing occupants to flee. At least 45 people were reportedly injured. Women were allegedly also raped by the security forces.

■ On 20 March, Sa'adatu Umar was arrested in Bauchi and detained with her three children, all aged below six. She was not charged with any crime and was unlawfully detained for several months, reportedly because her husband was a suspected Boko Haram member. On 17 October, a court ordered the police to release her and her children and to pay 1 million naira (approximately US$6,200) in damages.

The government did not publicize the findings of a report on the July 2009 clashes between Boko Haram and security forces, in which more than 800 people died, including 24 police officers and Boko Haram's leader, Muhammad Yusuf. In July, five police officers suspected of extrajudicially executing Muhammad Yusuf were charged with his murder and detained.

A report by the Presidential Committee on Security Challenges in the North-East Zone was submitted to the President in September but was not made public. Senator Ali Ndume, representative of Borno-South and a Committee member, was arrested in November and charged under the Terrorism Act with concealing information and providing information to a terrorist group. He was released on bail in December.

■ On 17 September, Mallam Babakura Fugu, Muhammad Yusuf's brother-in-law, was killed. No investigation was carried out and no one was brought to justice.

A police appeal against the April 2010 Borno State High Court decision that they should pay compensation to the relatives of Mallam Babakura Fugu's father, Alhaji Baba Fugu – who was extrajudicially executed in police custody in 2009 – had not been heard by the end of the year.

Communal violence

Communal and sectarian violence continued in Nigeria's middle belt throughout the year. The authorities' failure to prevent violence and protect people's right to life caused violence to escalate. More than 200 people died in clashes in Plateau State alone, in relation to long-standing tensions and land conflicts between different ethnic groups. On 18 January, the Plateau State Commander of the Special Military Task Force reportedly ordered soldiers to shoot on sight.

Hundreds of people were killed in politically motivated violence across Nigeria before, during and after the national parliamentary, presidential and state elections in April. Politically motivated threats and intimidation also took place. The report of the Presidential Committee on Post-Election Violence, presented to the President in October, was not made public. The Committee Chairman highlighted Nigeria's climate of impunity as one of the main causes.

■ Hundreds of people were killed in rioting and violent attacks in northern and central Nigeria following the presidential elections. According to the Inspector General of Police, 520 people were killed in Kaduna and Niger states alone.

Impunity

Scores of people were rounded up by the police and security forces in relation to northern Nigeria's ongoing violence, but few were successfully prosecuted or convicted. Previous commissions of inquiry into the Plateau State violence reportedly named suspected perpetrators, but no criminal investigations were started during the year.

Justice system

Nigeria's criminal justice system remained under-resourced, blighted by corruption and generally distrusted. When investigations occurred, they were often cursory and not intelligence-led. The security forces often resorted to dragnet arrests instead of individual arrests based on reasonable suspicion. Suspects were regularly subjected to inhuman and degrading treatment in detention.

Court processes were slow, resulting in most detainees being kept in lengthy pre-trial detention in appalling conditions. Seventy per cent of Nigeria's 48,000 prison inmates had not been tried. Many had awaited trial for years. Few could afford a lawyer.

In August, the Federal Government set up a Committee on the Implementation of Justice Sector Reforms to draft legislation, guidelines and recommendations and implement these within 24 months.

Death penalty

Seventy-two people were sentenced to death. There were 982 people on death row, including 16 women. Fifty-five people had their sentences commuted and 11 were pardoned. No executions were reported. Many death row inmates were sentenced following blatantly unfair trials or after more than a decade in prison awaiting trial.

In June, the scope of the death penalty was expanded to include supporting terrorism resulting in death. Provisions under the Terrorism Act were imprecise, too broad and inconsistent with human rights standards for due process, lawful deprivation of liberty and fair trial.

In October, Mohammed Bello Adoke, the Attorney General of the Federation and Minister of Justice, stated that Nigeria had introduced an official moratorium on executions. However, no official gazette was issued to confirm this.

Forced evictions

Evictions continued throughout Nigeria without genuine consultation with people affected, adequate notice, compensation or alternative accommodation. More than 200,000 people continued to live at risk of forced eviction from their waterfront communities in Port Harcourt, Rivers State.

■ On 25 June, hundreds of people were forcibly evicted and at least one person killed when the Task Force on Environmental Sanitation, accompanied by armed police and soldiers, burned down structures in Panteka settlement and market in the Federal Capital Territory. Police reportedly fired shots in the air, set fire to buildings and arrested people trying to run away. Residents claimed that no prior notice had been given before the operation.

■ No investigation was carried out into the 2009 shooting of at least 12 people in Bundu waterfront, Port Harcourt, when security forces opened fire on people peacefully protesting against the proposed demolition of their homes.

Violence against women and girls

Domestic violence, rape and other forms of sexual violence against women and girls by state officials and individuals remained rife. The authorities consistently failed to prevent and address sexual violence, or to hold perpetrators to account.

Children's rights

Twelve of Nigeria's 36 states had not passed the Child Rights Act. The police frequently arrested and detained children unlawfully, including those living on the street and other vulnerable children. Children continued to be detained with adults in police and prison cells. The country's one functioning remand home remained overcrowded.

No investigation was carried out into the violent clash on 29 December 2009 in Bauchi, in which 22 children were killed. Many were reportedly shot by the police.

Freedom of expression

A pattern emerged of intimidation and attacks against human rights defenders and journalists, with several being threatened, beaten or arrested by police and security forces. Politicians increasingly used their influence to secure the arrest of people criticizing the authorities.

■ In January, Patrick Naagbanton, the Co-ordinator of CEHRD, a Nigerian human rights NGO, received multiple death threats.

■ On 9 November, Justine Ijeoma, the Director of the NGO Human Rights, Social Development and Environmental Foundation (Hursdef), was arrested after intervening to stop a police officer beating a woman. He was released after being detained for several hours. He and his staff were threatened by the police throughout the year.

■ In October, Osmond Ugwu, a human rights defender from Enugu State, and Raphael Elobuike were arrested at a peaceful trade union meeting in Enugu after campaigning for the minimum wage to be implemented. They were subsequently charged with conspiracy to murder and attempted murder. In December, the Attorney General appeared in court to personally oppose the bail application. The judge adjourned his ruling on bail until January 2012.

Niger Delta

Despite the 2009 presidential amnesty granted to members of armed groups, armed gangs continued to kidnap oil workers and attack oil installations. The security forces, including the military, continued to commit human rights violations.

■ No investigation was carried out into the JTF raid of the Ayokoromo community in 2010, in which up to 51 people were killed, including children, and at least 120 homes were burned down.

Oil industry pollution and environmental damage continued to have a serious impact on people's lives and livelihoods. However, affected communities still lacked access to vital information about the oil industry's local impact.

Environmental laws and regulations were poorly enforced, partly due to government agencies being compromised by conflicts of interest.

■ The Bodo community launched a UK High Court law suit against Shell Petroleum Development Company, requesting compensation and a clean-up after two major oil spills in 2008.

■ In August, the UN Environment Programme revealed the devastating human and environmental effects of decades of oil spills in Ogoniland. It found the contamination to be widespread and severe, and stated that people in the Niger Delta have been exposed to it for decades.

■ On 20 December, according to Shell "fewer than 40,000 barrels" of oil leaked into the Atlantic ocean at the company's off-shore Bonga oil field.

Rights of lesbian, gay, bisexual and transgender people

Human rights abuses continued against people suspected of having same-sex relationships or non-conventional gender identity. In December, the Senate approved a bill which would impose a 14-year prison sentence for same-sex marriages. Any person or groups that "witness, abet and aids the solemnization of a same sex marriage or union" or "supports" gay groups, "processions or meetings", would face a 10-year prison sentence. The same sentence would apply to a "public show of same sex amorous relationship" and anyone who registers gay clubs and organizations protecting the rights of lesbians, gay men, bisexual and transgender people.

Amnesty International visits/reports

🚗 Amnesty International delegates visited Nigeria in January/February, May, June/July, August, October, November and December.

📄 Loss of life, insecurity and impunity in the run-up to Nigeria's elections (AFR 44/005/2011)

▓ Nigeria: Human rights agenda 2011-2015 (AFR 44/014/2011)

▓ The True "Tragedy": Delays and failures in tackling oil spills in the Niger Delta (AFR 44/018/2011)

NORWAY

KINGDOM OF NORWAY

Head of state:	King Harald V
Head of government:	Jens Stoltenberg
Death penalty:	abolitionist for all crimes
Population:	4.9 million
Life expectancy:	81.1 years
Under-5 mortality:	3.3 per 1,000

Protection and access to justice for survivors of sexual violence remained inadequate. Forced returns to Iraq continued. There were concerns about the conditions in reception centres for unaccompanied children seeking asylum.

Refugees, migrants and asylum-seekers

Throughout the year the authorities carried out forced returns of Iraqi rejected asylum-seekers to Baghdad, Iraq, contrary to guidelines from UNHCR, the UN refugee agency. Some were returned on charter flights jointly organized with other European states.

In April, the CERD Committee expressed concern about the conditions in reception and detention centres for asylum-seekers and rejected asylum-seekers in the country, including in reception centres for unaccompanied children. The Committee urged the government to bring conditions in such centres into line with international human rights standards.

Violence against women and girls

Women were not adequately protected against violence in law or practice. Although the number of rapes reported to the police increased, more than 80 per cent of these cases were closed before reaching the courts. The definition of rape in the General Civil Penal Code continued to link the perpetrator's guilt to the ability to prove that the sexual act was forced by the use or threat of physical violence.

In November, the UN Human Rights Committee expressed concern about the incidence of gender-based violence, including rape, and urged the authorities to ensure that perpetrators were investigated, prosecuted and, if convicted, punished.

International justice

In April, the Supreme Court confirmed the verdict against Mirsad Repak, a naturalized Norwegian citizen who served in the Croatian Defence Forces and who had been found guilty of "deprivation of liberty" during the war in Bosnia and Herzegovina. In its decision, the Supreme Court increased his sentence to eight years' imprisonment due to the extremely serious nature of the crime.

In May, a 45-year-old Rwandan national was arrested and charged with participation in the genocide in Rwanda in April 1994. The National Criminal Investigation Service, KRIPOS, had been investigating the case since 2008, following an international arrest order issued by the Rwandan authorities. He remained in custody at the end of the year. A decision on whether to prosecute him in Norway was expected in 2012.

On 24 November, the Supreme Court ruled that a 58-year-old Rwandan national could be extradited from Norway to Rwanda to face charges of participation in the genocide there in 1994.

OMAN

SULTANATE OF OMAN

Head of state and government:	**Sultan Qaboos bin Said Al Said**
Death penalty:	**retentionist**
Population:	**2.8 million**
Life expectancy:	**73 years**
Under-5 mortality:	**12 per 1,000**
Adult literacy:	**86.6 per cent**

Police used excessive force against peaceful and other protesters; at least two people were killed and others were injured. Hundreds of protesters were arrested; at least 80 were tried, many of whom were sentenced to prison terms. The authorities tightened restrictions on freedom of expression. Women and girls continued to face severe discrimination in law and in practice.

Background

In January, people demonstrated against the cost of living and lack of job opportunities, and called for political reforms and the dismissal of government ministers and corrupt officials. Sultan Qaboos responded in February by raising the minimum wage, increasing benefits paid to the unemployed, promising to create 50,000 new jobs, and replacing several government ministers. In March, after protests spread, he dismissed more government ministers and subsequently amended the Constitution to cede some legislative powers to the Shura Council, the only elected body of the two that comprise the Majlis (Parliament). Elections were held on 15 October and those elected chose a President of the Shura Council for the first time. Oman's human rights record was assessed under the UN Universal Periodic Review in March. Oman was urged to review its legislation to combat discrimination and violence against women.

Repression of dissent

Police and security forces used excessive force to disperse peaceful and other protests, using tear gas, firing rubber bullets and beating protesters. On 27 February, one man was reported to have died when police forcibly dispersed protesters in the town of Sohar. On 29 March, the security forces carried out a pre-dawn raid on protesters camped at Globe Roundabout in Sohar, reportedly beat those who refused to leave and at the same time arrested others at their homes.

■ Abdullah al-Ghamalasi, a student, died on 27 February when police fired rubber bullets and tear gas at protesters at Globe Roundabout in Sohar. The authorities announced an investigation but its outcome was not disclosed.

Many protesters were arrested during the year and at least 80 were brought to trial. Some were convicted of offences such as insulting officials, disrupting traffic or acts of violence, and sentenced to prison terms.

■ Ahmed al-Shezawi was arrested at his home in the capital Muscat on 29 March. He was held for over a week at an undisclosed location, where he was kept in solitary confinement and allegedly subjected to constant loud music until he was transferred to the Central Prison in Samail. He was released on 10 April, together with another protester, his uncle Dr Abdul Gufar al-Shezawi, after they pledged not to destroy or damage public property. In June, both were acquitted of all charges.

■ Basma al-Kiyumi, a prominent lawyer, was the only woman among 15 people arrested on 14 May as they and others held a peaceful protest in front of the Shura Council in Muscat to call for the release of protesters detained two days earlier. She was charged with participating in an unlawful gathering and released on bail on 16 May. The other 14 were also released.

■ In June, a court in Muscat convicted seven people arrested in connection with the protests in Sohar of violence against public authorities and sentenced them to five-year prison terms.

On 20 April, Sultan Qaboos pardoned 234 people accused of committing "crimes of crowding in the streets" in the provinces of Dhank, Ibri, Sohar and Yanqul.

Freedom of expression

In October, the authorities amended Article 26 of the Press and Publications Law to prohibit the publication through any means, including the internet, of anything deemed likely to affect the safety of the state or its internal or external security or related to its military and security organs. The maximum penalty was set at two years' imprisonment and a fine.

■ Yusef al-Haj, a journalist working for *Azzamn* newspaper, and Ibrahim al-Ma'amary, the newspaper's editor-in-chief, were sentenced to five months'

O

imprisonment in September after they were convicted of "insulting" the Justice Minister in an article concerning alleged corruption within the Ministry. Haroon al-Muqaibli, a Justice Ministry employee who was their source, was similarly convicted and sentenced to five months' imprisonment. Their sentences were upheld on appeal.

Women's rights

Women and girls continued to face severe discrimination in law and in practice, particularly in relation to personal status, employment and their subordination to male guardians. Around 77 women stood for election to the Shura Council, more than triple the number in 2007, although only one was elected.

Death penalty

No information was released about the imposition of the death penalty, and no executions were reported.

Amnesty International visits/reports

Oman: Detained protesters at risk (MDE 20/003/2011)

PAKISTAN

ISLAMIC REPUBLIC OF PAKISTAN

Head of state:	Asif Ali Zardari
Head of government:	Yousuf Raza Gilani
Death penalty:	retentionist
Population:	176.7 million
Life expectancy:	65.4 years
Under-5 mortality:	87 per 1,000
Adult literacy:	55.5 per cent

Salmaan Taseer, the outspoken Governor of Punjab, and Shahbaz Bhatti, the Minister for Minorities (and sole Christian cabinet member), were assassinated in January and March, respectively, because of their criticism of the blasphemy laws. Security forces continued to be implicated in violations, including enforced disappearances, torture and extrajudicial executions, especially in Balochistan and the Northwest. In May, US forces killed al-Qa'ida leader Osama bin Laden in a raid on his hideout in the north-western city of Abbottabad. Senior US officials publicly accused Pakistan of supporting the Taleban in Afghanistan. The Pakistani Taleban and other armed groups killed civilians in targeted and indiscriminate attacks across the country. Karachi was gripped by a wave of killings sparked by rival gangs associated with different ethnic and political groups. Individuals continued to be sentenced to death, but there were no executions. A successive year of monsoonal floods led to further displacement and outbreaks of dengue fever countrywide. Chronic energy shortages caused violent protests in most major cities and stifled economic activity. Women and girls in conflict-prone areas in the Northwest and Balochistan faced severe difficulties in accessing education and health care.

Background

The human rights situation remained poor, with security and intelligence officials often complicit in violations. The authorities were frequently unwilling or unable to protect women, ethnic and religious minorities, journalists and other vulnerable groups from abuses, and bring perpetrators to justice. Promises by federal and provincial authorities aimed at improving the rule of law in violence-wracked Balochistan province – including greater oversight of police and the paramilitary Frontiers Corps, increased recruitment of ethnic Baloch into the civil service, and a rise in the province's share of the national budget – had little effect.

Nearly one million people remained displaced as a result of continued conflict between the security forces and the Pakistani Taleban, while communities returning to regions recaptured from the insurgency complained of lack of security and access to basic services. A parallel judicial system based on a narrow reading of Shari'a law was established in Malakand despite the removal of the Pakistani Taleban, creating fears that their harsh social codes might be applied. In June, President Zardari granted security forces in the Northwest retrospective immunity from prosecution and sweeping powers of arbitrary detention and punishment. On 14 August, Pakistan's Independence Day, the President approved landmark reforms, extending the Political Parties Order 2002 to the Federally Administered Tribal Areas and amending the Frontier Crimes Regulation, a British-era law that deprived residents of the region of many of their human rights and protections under

P

Pakistan's Constitution. The reforms limited state powers of arbitrary detention and collective punishment, allowed people in the region a right to judicial appeal of decisions under the Regulation, and enabled political parties to operate in the Tribal Areas.

On 9 June, Pakistan ratified the Optional Protocol to the Convention on the Rights of the Child on the sale of children, child prostitution and child pornography. In September, Pakistan removed most of its reservations to the ICCPR and the Convention against Torture, but retained other problematic reservations that prevent non-Muslims from becoming Prime Minister or President, and discriminate against women's equal right to inheritance.

Violations by security forces

Security and intelligence forces acted largely with impunity and were accused of violations, including enforced disappearances, torture and killing of civilians, journalists, activists and suspected members of armed groups in indiscriminate attacks and extrajudicial executions.

Extrajudicial executions

Reports of extrajudicial executions were most common in Balochistan province, as well as the Northwest and violence-ridden Karachi.

■ On 28 April, human rights activist Siddique Eido and his friend Yousuf Nazar Baloch were found dead in the Pargari Sarbat area of Balochistan. According to witnesses, they were abducted while travelling with police by men in plain clothes accompanied by paramilitary Frontier Corps forces on 21 December 2010. Hospital reports said their bodies had bullet wounds and bore signs of torture.

■ On 8 June, a television crew filmed the extrajudicial execution of Sarfaraz Shah by paramilitary Rangers in a Karachi park. Following the Supreme Court's intervention, the Sindh government dismissed senior law enforcement officials and, on 12 August, the Anti-Terrorism Court sentenced one of the Rangers to death for the murder. Five other Rangers and a civilian were sentenced to life in prison. All appealed against their sentences to the Sindh High Court.

■ On 17 May, police and Frontier Corps forces killed five foreigners in Quetta, including a heavily pregnant woman, whom they claimed were suicide bombers. An inquiry concluded that the victims were not armed and two police officers were suspended. A journalist who took photos of the killings went into hiding after receiving death threats, and the doctor who conducted autopsies on the victims was assaulted and later killed by a group of unknown men. Other witnesses were reportedly threatened by security personnel.

Enforced disappearances

The state failed to bring perpetrators of enforced disappearance to justice; most victims remained missing. In March, the government established a new Commission of Inquiry on Enforced Disappearances but took six months to appoint retired Supreme Court Justice Javed Iqbal to head it. Since the previous commission commenced in March 2010, over 220 of the several hundred individual cases filed had been traced. Both commissions were criticized for failing to protect witnesses and for conducting inadequate investigations, especially in cases where state security forces and intelligence agencies were implicated.

■ On 13 February, unknown men abducted Agha Zahir Shah, a lawyer representing relatives of alleged victims of enforced disappearance, in Dera Murad Jamali, Balochistan, while he was returning to Quetta. He was released in a poor state of health on 2 July.

■ Muzzaffar Bhutto, senior member of the Jeay Sindh Muttaheda Mahaz political party, was abducted on 25 February in Hyderabad, Sindh, by men in plain clothes accompanied by police. His whereabouts remained unknown.

■ In May, brothers Abdullah and Ibrahim El-Sharkawi (of Egyptian origin) went missing. Two weeks later, their family was told they were in prison charged with illegal residency, but a court confirmed they were Pakistani nationals. Ibrahim was released on bail on 27 June and Abdullah was released on 29 August. Both claimed they were tortured and ill-treated in secret detention facilities.

P

Abuses by armed groups

The Pakistani Taleban targeted civilians and carried out indiscriminate attacks using improvised explosive devices (IEDs) and suicide bombings. Several tribal elders were victims of targeted killings. The Taleban also tried to assassinate a number of politicians affiliated with the Awami National Party. According to the government, 246 schools (59 girls' schools, 187 boys' schools) were destroyed and 763 damaged (244 girls' schools, 519 boys' schools) in Khyber Pakhtunkhwa province as a result of the conflict with the Taleban, depriving thousands of children of access to education. Threats of violence from the

Pakistani Taleban imposed severe restrictions on access to health services, education and participation in public life for women and girls.

■ On 9 March, a suicide bomber attacked the funeral of an anti-Taleban leader's wife , killing 37 people in the outskirts of Peshawar. Tehrik-e-Taleban Pakistan (TTP) claimed responsibility for the bombing.

■ On 18 July, TTP released a video showing masked militants executing 16 captured policemen in response to earlier footage of Pakistani forces executing arrested insurgents.

■ TTP claimed responsibility for a suicide bombing on 19 August that killed at least 47 and injured more than 100 during Friday prayers at a mosque in Khyber tribal agency.

■ In September, Pakistani Taleban insurgents abducted 30 boys aged between 12 and 18 on the Afghanistan border in Bajaur, and attacked a school van in Peshawar, killing four children and the driver.

Nationalist groups in Balochistan assassinated members of rival factions, ethnic Punjabis and state security forces, and claimed responsibility for attacks on gas and electricity infrastructure, causing severe energy shortages in the province. Sectarian attacks by the armed group Lashkar-e-Jhangvi and others on Shi'a Muslims resulted in at least 280 deaths and injuries.

■ On 4 January, five children were injured in an IED attack on a school bus carrying more than 30 children of Frontier Corps troops in Turbat town, Balochistan. Although no one claimed responsibility, ethnic Baloch groups were blamed for the attack.

■ On 25 April, at least 15 people, including five children, were burnt to death when unidentified assailants set a Quetta-bound bus on fire in the Pirak area of Sibi district.

■ Lashkar-e-Jhangvi claimed responsibility for the execution-style killing of 26 Shi'a pilgrims in Mastung district and three of the victims' relatives as they travelled from Quetta to collect their bodies, on 20 September. A similar attack on Shi'a pilgrims on 4 October claimed 14 lives.

Karachi saw a surge of violence as rival gangs, some linked to political parties, clashed over territorial claims, killing 2,000 people. Security forces detained hundreds of suspects but the Supreme Court criticized political parties for fuelling the violence and authorities for failing to stop many known perpetrators.

Freedom of expression

At least nine journalists were killed during the year. Media workers were threatened by security forces, intelligence agencies, political parties and armed groups for reporting on them. Pakistani authorities failed to bring perpetrators to justice or provide adequate protection to journalists.

■ On 13 January, GeoNews reporter Wali Khan Babar was killed in a drive-by shooting by unidentified assailants in Karachi, hours after filing a report on a police operation against drug traffickers in the city.

■ On 29 May, Asia Times Online's Saleem Shahzad disappeared from outside his Islamabad house, minutes after leaving for a television interview. His body was found in Punjab province two days later. He had earlier filed a report on al-Qa'ida infiltration in the Pakistani Navy. In October 2010, he had privately notified colleagues that he had received death threats from the Inter-Services Intelligence agency over similar reports.

Discrimination – religious minorities

Sectarian groups continued to threaten minority Ahmadis, Christians, Hindus and Shi'as, as well as moderate Sunni practitioners, and incited violence against those calling for reform of the country's blasphemy laws. The state failed to prevent sectarian attacks against religious minorities or bring perpetrators to justice.

■ On 25 January, a suicide bomber targeting Shi'a worshippers killed at least 13 people in Lahore. Fidayeen-e-Islam claimed responsibility for the attack.

■ In June, the All Pakistan Students Khatm-e-Nubuwat Federation distributed pamphlets in the city of Faisalabad, Punjab, listing prominent members of the Ahmadiyya community and calling for their murder as an act of "jihad".

■ On 24 September, Faryal Bhatti, a 13-year-old Christian schoolgirl from Abbottabad, was expelled from school for misspelling an Urdu word, resulting in accusations of blasphemy. Her family were forced to go into hiding.

■ All suspects in the August 2009 attack on a Christian colony in Gojra, Punjab, were released on bail after witnesses failed to give evidence out of fear for their safety.

The trial judge who sentenced Salmaan Taseer's assassin to death was forced to go into hiding due to death threats while Shahbaz Bhatti's killers had yet to be brought to justice. Politician Sherry Rehman withdrew a blasphemy law reform bill from the National Assembly following death threats. Aasia Bibi, a Christian farmer sentenced to death for blasphemy in 2009, remained in detention while her case was on appeal.

Violence against women and girls

Women faced legal and de facto discrimination and violence at home and in public. The Aurat Foundation documented 8,539 cases of violence against women, including 1,575 murders, 827 rapes, 610 incidents of domestic violence, 705 honour killings and 44 acid attacks. In December, Pakistan's parliament sought to address this problem by passing the Acid Control and Acid Crime Prevention Bill 2010 and the Prevention of Anti-Women Practices (Criminal Law Amendment) Bill 2008, aimed at empowering and protecting women and increasing penalties for perpetrators of gender-based violence. This was the first time that acid attacks and practices like forced marriages were criminalized in Pakistan.

■ On 10 September, four women – all teachers – were attacked with acid by two masked perpetrators riding a motorbike, as they left a co-educational school in Quetta, capital of Balochistan province. One of the women escaped without any injuries and another two were discharged from hospital with minor burns, but the fourth sustained severe burns and required major reconstructive surgery. Federal and provincial authorities took notice of the attack, but the perpetrators had yet to be brought to justice.

■ On 15 October, a teenage girl accused 13 people, including three police officers, of abducting and gang raping her in captivity for a year in the district of Karak in Khyber Pakthunkhwa province. On 9 December, her brother was shot dead as he left the district court hearing the criminal case against the accused.

Death penalty

More than 8,000 prisoners remained on death row. According to the Human Rights Commission of Pakistan, at least 313 people were sentenced to death, over half of them for murder. Three people were sentenced to death for blasphemy. The last execution took place in 2008.

Amnesty International visits/reports

🚗 Amnesty International delegates visited Pakistan in July and November-December. Amnesty International consultants maintained a continuous presence in the country.

📰 "The bitterest of agonies": End enforced disappearances in Pakistan (ASA 33/010/2011)

PALESTINIAN AUTHORITY

PALESTINIAN AUTHORITY

Head of Palestinian Authority:	Mahmoud Abbas
Head of government:	Salam Fayyad
Death penalty:	retentionist
Population:	4.2 million
Life expectancy:	72.8 years
Under-5 mortality:	29.5 per 1,000
Adult literacy:	94.6 per cent

In the West Bank, the Fatah-controlled Palestinian Authority (PA) arbitrarily arrested and detained supporters of Hamas; in the Gaza Strip, the Hamas de facto administration arbitrarily arrested and detained supporters of Fatah. In both areas, security forces tortured and otherwise ill-treated detainees with impunity; in Gaza, four detainees died in custody. Both the PA and Hamas restricted freedom of expression and association, and their security forces used excessive force against demonstrators. In Gaza, at least eight people were sentenced to death and three people were executed. In the West Bank, there were no executions, but one man was sentenced to death. The humanitarian crisis affecting the Gaza Strip's 1.6 million residents continued due to Israel's ongoing military blockade and the sanctions imposed on the de facto Hamas authorities by other states.

Background

The West Bank, including East Jerusalem, and Gaza remained under Israeli occupation, but two separate non-state Palestinian authorities operated with limited powers – the Fatah-led PA government in the West Bank and the Hamas de facto administration in Gaza.

In September, Palestinian President Mahmoud Abbas applied to the UN to accept Palestine as a full member state; the application was still being considered at the end of 2011. Palestine was admitted as a member of UNESCO in October. Negotiations between Israel and the PA remained stalled.

Indirect negotiations between Israel and Hamas resulted in the release of Gilad Shalit, an Israeli soldier held captive in Gaza since 2006. He was freed on 18 October in exchange for the phased release of

P

1,027 Palestinian prisoners held by Israel, some of whom were sent into exile as a condition of their release.

Efforts to secure a reconciliation between the PA and Hamas and the formation of a unified Palestinian government continued, with Egypt mediating. A framework unity agreement was signed in Cairo in May but not implemented in 2011.

Despite announced ceasefires, Palestinian armed groups in Gaza fired indiscriminate rockets and mortars into Israel, and Israeli forces carried out air strikes that they said targeted Palestinians in Gaza involved in attacking Israel.

Israel continued to control Gaza's borders, coast and airspace, and maintained the military blockade in force since 2007. The blockade impacted severely on Gaza's population, particularly children and those most vulnerable, continuing the humanitarian crisis. The reopening of the Rafah crossing between Gaza and Egypt in May improved residents' access to the outside world, but did not ameliorate humanitarian conditions; Israel continued to restrict a wide range of imports to Gaza, negatively impacting food security, health and local infrastructure. Some 36 Palestinians were killed in air strikes and accidents in underground tunnels used to smuggle goods from Egypt to Gaza.

In the West Bank, Israel maintained extensive restrictions on the movement of Palestinians and continued to develop and extend Israeli settlements built on Palestinian land in breach of international law. Jewish settlers attacked and assaulted Palestinians and destroyed their property with virtual impunity. Three Palestinians, including two children, were killed in such attacks and others were wounded. Eight Israeli settlers, including five members of one family, were killed by Palestinians.

Arbitrary arrests and detentions

In the West Bank, PA security forces arbitrarily arrested and detained hundreds of suspected Hamas supporters; most were held without access to due legal process. Many were arrested when President Abbas visited the UN in New York in September.

In Gaza, Hamas security forces arbitrarily arrested and detained hundreds of suspected Fatah supporters, usually holding them without access to lawyers and often mistreating them. The Independent Commission for Human Rights (ICHR), a PA-established monitoring body, reported receiving complaints of more than 1,000 arbitrary arrests in the West Bank and more than 700 in Gaza.

Hamas continued to ban the ICHR from visiting detention centres run by Internal Security in Gaza. In the West Bank, the PA banned the ICHR from accessing General Intelligence detention centres from March until May after the ICHR criticized the security agency.

■ PA Preventive Security officials arrested Saed Yassin on 21 September and searched his home in Nablus without producing arrest or search warrants. They detained him for five days in solitary confinement before taking him before a judge. Accused of "working against the Palestinian Authority", he was acquitted and released after 22 days in custody. His interrogators told him that he was arrested for precautionary reasons in connection with President Abbas' visit to the UN.

■ After being summoned for interrogation numerous times during 2011, youth activist Mohammed Matar was detained by Internal Security officials in Gaza on 14 August and denied access to his family and lawyer until his release on 16 August. He was questioned about his travel abroad and involvement in the movement for Palestinian unity.

Torture and other ill-treatment

Detainees were tortured and otherwise ill-treated, particularly by Preventive Security and the General Intelligence Service in the West Bank, and by Internal Security in Gaza, all of which were able to abuse detainees with impunity. The ICHR reported receiving over 120 such allegations in the West Bank and over 100 in Gaza. Alleged methods included beatings, suspension by the wrists or ankles, and enforced standing or sitting in painful positions (shabeh) for long periods. The ICHR also received complaints of torture and other ill-treatment of suspects by police – over 50 in the West Bank and 100 in Gaza.

In Gaza, four people died in custody in suspicious circumstances.

■ 'Adel Razeq was reported to have died four days after he was arrested without a warrant on 14 April. The Hamas authorities said his death was due to deterioration in his medical condition; his family said he had been in good health when arrested. Hamas said his death was being investigated; the outcome was not made public.

Justice system

On 16 January, the PA said that its security agencies would abide by civil procedural law and that civilians would no longer be tried before military courts. In practice, however, PA security forces continued to ignore court orders to release detainees, and civilians continued to be tried before military courts that were neither independent nor impartial.

In Gaza, Hamas continued to try civilians before unfair military courts and to rely on prosecutors and judges who lacked adequate training, qualifications and independence rather than those who had been appointed by the PA.

Freedom of expression, association and assembly

Both the PA and the Hamas authorities maintained tight controls on freedom of expression, association and assembly. They harassed and prosecuted journalists, bloggers and other critics, and in March used excessive force against demonstrators calling for national unity; scores of people were arbitrarily arrested and detained. Both authorities prevented the Islamist organization Hizb ut-Tahrir from holding meetings, forcibly dispersing their peaceful rallies, and restricted the activities of other political parties and NGOs.

■ On 30 January, and 2 and 5 February, PA police and security forces responded with violence to people peacefully demonstrating in solidarity with protests elsewhere in the region, beating and arresting demonstrators and journalists seeking to report on the demonstrations.

■ In the West Bank, lecturer and writer Dr Abdul-Sattar Qassim, 62, was detained on 25 August after a Nablus court charged him with incitement and defamation after he accused An-Najah University of failing to implement court orders allowing the return of three students who had been expelled. He was released on bail four days later; his trial was ongoing at the end of 2011.

■ Uniformed and plainclothes Hamas police used excessive force on 15 March against thousands of demonstrators who had gathered near Gaza City to call for reconciliation between Hamas and Fatah. The attackers used sticks and clubs to beat demonstrators, including women, journalists and human rights activists. They also demolished tents put up by protesters, seized journalists' equipment, and detained scores of people.

Violence against women and girls

Women and girls continued to face discrimination in law and in practice and to face gender-based violence, including murder, committed by male relatives. Human rights groups in Gaza confirmed that a woman was a victim of a so-called honour killing in December.

■ In May, police identified the body of 20-year-old Ayat Ibrahim Barad'iyya, which had been dumped in a well near Hebron over a year earlier after she was murdered by her uncle in the name of honour. Later in May, in response to the outcry over the case, President Abbas repealed all legal provisions that had allowed men to obtain reduced sentences for murders committed in the name of honour.

Death penalty

In Gaza, military and criminal courts sentenced at least eight people to death after convicting them of "collaboration with Israel" or other offences. At least three men were executed, one by firing squad on 4 May and a father and son, who were hanged on 26 July. All had been sentenced after unfair trials.

In the West Bank, a military court sentenced one man to death for murder and other offences. There were no executions.

Abuses by armed groups

Palestinian armed groups associated with Fatah, Islamic Jihad and the Popular Front for the Liberation of Palestine fired indiscriminate rockets and mortars into southern Israel, killing two people and endangering the lives of others. The scale of rocket fire was higher than in 2010 but far less than during Israel's military Operation "Cast Lead" in 2008-09.

■ Daniel Viflic, aged 16, died after a school bus in which he was travelling was struck by a missile fired from Gaza on 7 April.

■ Vittorio Arrigoni, an Italian activist, was abducted and killed by Islamists in Gaza on 14 April. Hamas security forces killed two suspects during a raid on 19 April; four other suspects were charged and their military trial was continuing.

Impunity

The Hamas authorities failed to investigate alleged war crimes and possible crimes against humanity committed by Hamas' military wing and other Palestinian armed groups in Gaza during Operation "Cast Lead".

P

Amnesty International visits/reports

- Amnesty International delegates visited the West Bank in May and November, and Gaza in November.
- The Palestinian bid for UN membership and statehood recognition (MDE 21/003/2011)
- Amnesty International's updated assessment of Israeli and Palestinian investigations into the Gaza conflict (MDE 15/018/2011)

PANAMA

REPUBLIC OF PANAMA

Head of state and government:	**Ricardo Martinelli**
Death penalty:	**abolitionist for all crimes**
Population:	**3.6 million**
Life expectancy:	**76.1 years**
Under-5 mortality:	**22.9 per 1,000**
Adult literacy:	**93.6 per cent**

Safeguards of the human rights of Indigenous Peoples remained inadequate, especially in the context of large infrastructure projects built on Indigenous land. There were concerns about restrictions on freedom of expression.

Background

In December, France extradited former de facto head of state Manuel Noriega who was serving a prison sentence for money laundering. In 2010, Manuel Noriega had finished serving a 20-year sentence for drug trafficking, money laundering and racketeering in the USA. During this time, Panamanian courts tried and convicted him in his absence for the killing of political opponents, including Major Moisés Giroldi Vera, the leader of a failed coup attempt in October 1989, and Hugo Spadafora, former Deputy Minister for Health in 1985, as well as other offences including unlawful detention. He was due to stand trial for the enforced disappearance and execution in 1970 of Heliodoro Portugal, a trade union activist. Manuel Noriega's role in many other human rights violations committed both during and before his rule had yet to be investigated.

In March, the UN Human Rights Council urged Panama to improve the protection of women and girls and, in particular, to combat people-trafficking, domestic violence and discrimination. The Council also called for an investigation into the July 2010 violence during protests in Bocas del Toro province, when four protesters were killed, and 56 police officers and at least 700 protesters injured. No progress had been made in implementing these recommendations by the end of the year.

Indigenous Peoples' rights

Concerns were raised about lack of consultation and the failure to ensure the free, prior and informed consent of Indigenous Peoples in the context of development proposals.

Throughout the year there were protests against a mining law that facilitated new mining projects on the traditional lands of Indigenous Peoples, but did not include sufficient safeguards for the environment or ensure adequate consultation with local communities. In February the UN Special Rapporteur on indigenous people called for dialogue between the government and Indigenous Peoples and a genuine consultation process on the draft law. The law was passed in February, but repealed in March following protests in the capital. A new draft law was proposed in October amid concerns that it would negatively impact on Indigenous communities. The law had not been passed by the end of the year.

■ In May, flooding commenced in the district of Changuinola, Bocas del Toro province, in order to construct the Chan-75 dam, amid allegations that there had been a lack of consultation with the Ngöbe Indigenous Peoples living in the area affected. At the time of the flooding, some members of the Ngöbe community were still living in their homes and engaged in negotiations about their relocation.

Freedom of expression

Two journalists who had been critical of government policy were deported. The UN Human Rights Council raised concerns about reports of intimidation of the press and urged the authorities not to exert undue political pressure on the media.

■ In February, Francisco Gómez Nadal and Pilar Chato, Spanish journalists with permanent residency in Panama and active members of a human rights organization, were arrested, deported and prohibited from re-entering the country. Both had covered protests against mining policies and for labour rights and had been accused by the government of manipulating Indigenous Peoples.

P

PARAGUAY

REPUBLIC OF PARAGUAY

Head of state and government:	**Fernando Lugo Méndez**
Death penalty:	**abolitionist for all crimes**
Population:	**6.6 million**
Life expectancy:	**72.5 years**
Under-5 mortality:	**22.6 per 1,000**
Adult literacy:	**94.6 per cent**

Progress was made in resolving the land claims of the Sawhoyamaxa and Kelyenmagategma, but other Indigenous Peoples continued to be denied their right to their traditional lands. The authorities attempted to undermine and misrepresent the work of human rights defenders.

Background

A 60-day state of exception was declared in October in the northern departments of Concepción and San Pedro following two attacks attributed to the Paraguayan People's Army (Ejército del Pueblo Paraguayo, EPP), an armed opposition group.

In February, Paraguay's human rights record was assessed under the UN's Universal Periodic Review. States expressed concerns regarding Indigenous Peoples' rights, impunity, women's rights and discrimination on grounds of race, ethnicity and sexual orientation.

Following a visit in March, the UN Special Rapporteur on freedom of religion or belief expressed concern about delays in passing anti-discrimination legislation; the lack of implementation of non-discrimination mechanisms, particularly in the Chaco region; and the weak presence and capacity of state institutions.

In May, a national mechanism for the prevention of torture was approved, as required under the Optional Protocol to the UN Convention against Torture.

Indigenous Peoples' rights

Progress was made in resolving the land claims of some Indigenous communities, but other communities continued to be denied their right to their traditional lands.

■ In September, five years after a judgement by the Inter-American Court of Human Rights in their favour, the Sawhoyamaxa signed an agreement with the government and the current landowners to begin the process of restoring the community's traditional lands. Under the agreement, a government agency was due to buy a 14,404-hectare plot from two businesses based in Puerto Colón by the end of the year.

■ In August, the land claim of the Kelyenmagategma was formally recognized by the authorities and the land title on 8,700 hectares of land was officially transferred, allowing the community to recover part of their traditional territory. The community, who started the legal process to reclaim part of their land in 2000, had suffered threats and intimidation that the authorities failed to investigate.

There was no resolution to Yakye Axa or Xámok Kásek land claims and there were no significant advances in investigations into the alleged spraying of Indigenous communities in Itakyry with pesticides in 2009.

The UN Committee on the Elimination of Racial Discrimination assessed Paraguay's record in August. It recommended that Paraguay adopt reforms to ensure that the justice system protect the rights of Indigenous Peoples, including effective mechanisms for lodging complaints and claims concerning land, for bringing about the restitution of traditional lands, and for fully recognizing Indigenous land rights in a co-ordinated and systematic manner.

Human rights defenders

The authorities sought to undermine the work of human rights defenders.

■ In July, lawyers from the human rights co-ordinating body, Coordinadora de Derechos Humanos del Paraguay (CODEHUPY) lodged a legal writ requesting that the Attorney General substantiate claims he made to the press that its lawyers were in telephone contact with the EPP. The allegations were made in the context of Judge Gustavo Bonzi's decision at the end of June to release 14 people accused by the authorities of providing support to the EPP in a kidnapping case, on the grounds that prosecutors had failed to provide evidence of their involvement. CODEHUPY lawyers representing six of the accused had complained of violations of due process guarantees in these cases. The Tribunal for the Prosecution of Magistrates called for Judge Bonzi to be suspended for exceeding his authority in releasing the 14 and, in August, the Concepción Appeals Court overturned his ruling. A challenge to the constitutionality of the Appeals Court decision was pending at the end of the year.

P

■ Four members of Iniciativa Amotocodie, an NGO working to protect the rights of uncontacted Ayoreo Indigenous groups living in the Paraguayan Chaco region, faced legal proceedings on charges including breach of trust. Investigations into the organization started after they publicly declared their opposition to a scientific expedition called "Dry Chaco 2010" on the grounds that it could harm the rights of uncontacted Indigenous Peoples and were continuing at the end of the year. The expedition was subsequently cancelled.

Impunity

In July, Norberto Atilio Bianco, an army doctor at the Campo de Mayo clandestine detention centre in Argentina in the 1970s, was extradited from Paraguay for a second time to face charges of appropriating babies born to women who had been victims of unlawful detention and enforced disappearance.

In September, the authorities reported that the remains found in a grave excavated in a police station in Asunción might be those of victims of human rights violations under the military government of General Alfredo Stroessner (1954-1989). The report of the Truth and Justice Commission published in August 2008 stated that at least 59 people had been executed and another 336 detainees were the victim of enforced disappearance during the period of military rule.

Torture

Complaints of torture brought by at least four recruits at the Francisco Solano López Military Academy in Capiatá were under investigation in the military justice system.

Amnesty International visits/reports

📖 Paraguay: Briefing to the UN Committee on the Elimination of Racial Discrimination (AMR 45/001/2011)

PERU

REPUBLIC OF PERU
Head of state and government: Ollanta Humala Tasso
(replaced Alan García Pérez in July)
Death penalty: abolitionist for ordinary crimes
Population: 29.4 million
Life expectancy: 74 years
Under-5 mortality: 21.3 per 1,000
Adult literacy: 89.6 per cent

The landmark Consultation with Indigenous Peoples Law, the first in Latin America, made consultation mandatory prior to the implementation of development projects on traditional Indigenous lands. There was little progress in investigations into human rights violations committed during the internal armed conflict (1980-2000).

Background

On taking office, President Ollanta Humala said that alleviating poverty and social exclusion would be priorities for his government.

Concessions to extractive companies gave rise to protests by Indigenous Peoples. Six Indigenous people were killed and dozens injured during protests in the Puno region in May and June against mining activities and the construction of a hydroelectric dam.

In November, the Constitutional Tribunal ruled that the construction of the Majes Siguas II irrigation project could not go ahead until a hydrological impact assessment study had been carried out. The community of Espinar in the Cuzco region argued that the construction of the Angostura dam and hydroelectric power station would affect the water supply in their community and, therefore, their livelihood.

Indigenous Peoples' rights

The long-awaited Consultation with Indigenous Peoples Law came into force in September. This made consultation and agreements with Indigenous Peoples over developments on traditional lands mandatory. In cases where agreement is not reached, state agencies will have to take all necessary measures to ensure that the collective rights of Indigenous Peoples are guaranteed. However, there was concern that lack of consultation over development projects already approved might lead to further conflict.

P

In November, Indigenous communities in Cajamarca province protested when government-brokered talks between local communities and the mining company Mineria Yanacocha collapsed. The communities opposed the project as they believed it would threaten local water supplies. The regional government suspended the project pending completion of a new environmental impact assessment.

Bagua

In June, Congress approved a report that concluded no government ministers were responsible for the events in Bagua in June 2009 in which 33 people died, including 23 police officers, and at least 205 people were injured after police intervened to end Indigenous protests.

Also in June, a court dropped criminal charges against Indigenous leader Segundo Alberto Pizango Chota of the Interethnic Association for the Development of the Peruvian Jungle, and four others in connection with the clashes at Bagua.

Two generals from the National Peruvian Police and a senior army officer were convicted by a military-police court in connection with the deaths and injuries in Bagua. Court proceedings against five police officers were continuing at the end of the year.

Impunity

Investigations into past human rights violations continued at a slow pace.

■ In May, oral hearings began in the case against retired General Carlos Briceño Zevallos and six other senior military officers in connection with torture and enforced disappearances at the Cabitos barracks in Huamanga province in 1983. The trial was continuing at the end of the year.

■ In July, former military officer Telmo Hurtado was extradited from the USA to face trial in connection with the massacre of 69 villagers in Accomarca in 1985. The trial of 29 people, including members of the patrols involved in the crime and those who gave the orders, was continuing at the end of the year.

In June, the executive promulgated a decree establishing the amount of reparations to be granted to individual victims of the armed conflict registered on the official Victims' Registry and stating that the process of determining the beneficiaries would close at the end of December. Organizations representing the victims rejected the ruling on various grounds.

Excessive use of force

In April, three protesters were killed and scores injured in clashes with police during protests against the "Tía María" copper mining project in Islay province. Shortly afterwards, the authorities cancelled the project, which the community had said would contaminate the water they used for agriculture.

Trade unionists

Trade union leaders Pedro Còndori Laurente and Antonio Quispe Tamayo were released in March after two and half months in prison on unfounded charges relating to a mining accident in July 2010. At the end of the year, the charges against them remained pending.

Corporate accountability

In August, the UK-based Monterrico Metals reached an out-of-court settlement with 33 peasant farmers who alleged that security guards employed by the company had colluded in the human rights violations they suffered during protests at the Río Blanco mining project in 2005.

Sexual and reproductive rights

In October the CEDAW Committee ruled that Peru must amend its law to allow women to obtain an abortion in cases of rape; establish a mechanism to ensure the availability of those abortion services; and guarantee access to abortion services when a woman's life or health is in danger. The case, brought by the Center for Reproductive Rights and its partner organization in Peru, PROMSEX, concerned a 13-year-old who was repeatedly raped from the age of 11 and became pregnant as a result in 2007. She was left seriously disabled after a suicide attempt left her with a fractured spine on which doctors refused to operate on the grounds that the procedure could damage the foetus.

Women faced further obstacles in accessing their sexual and reproductive rights when in May the Constitutional Tribunal, clarifying an earlier ruling, banned the state from selling or freely distributing emergency contraception.

In October, the authorities announced that the Public Prosecutor had reopened an investigation into the forced sterilizations of over 200,000 women during the presidency of Alberto Fujimori in the 1990s.

P

PHILIPPINES

REPUBLIC OF THE PHILIPPINES

Head of state and government:	Benigno S. Aquino III
Death penalty:	abolitionist for all crimes
Population:	94.9 million
Life expectancy:	68.7 years
Under-5 mortality:	33.1 per 1,000
Adult literacy:	95.4 per cent

Benigno "Noynoy" Aquino III began his second year as President in June. Reports of torture, extrajudicial executions and enforced disappearance persisted, with hundreds of past cases remaining unresolved. The first ever criminal prosecution for torture was launched in September. Women and men continued to face severe restrictions on their right to reproductive health, including access to contraception. In August, the Philippines ratified the Rome Statute of the International Criminal Court.

Internal armed conflict

In February, the government began peace talks with the two main armed opposition groups, the Moro Islamic Liberation Front (MILF) and the Communist Party of the Philippines-New People's Army. Following a reduction in hostilities, clashes erupted again later in the year.

■ In the worst fighting since the 2008-2009 conflict on Mindanao island, hostilities broke out in October between the military and the MILF in the southern island of Basilan. The joint ceasefire committee was tasked with investigating the military's claim that six of the 19 government soldiers killed in the clash were captured and summarily executed by the MILF. A military incursion to apprehend members of the Abu Sayyaf armed group used aerial bombardment and ground strikes, displacing as many as 30,000 civilians. At least one civilian was reported killed.

■ In northern Mindanao, New People's Army forces attacked private mining operations in Surigao del Norte province in October, killing three security guards. In response, President Aquino approved the previous administration's policy of augmenting security at private mining operations by deploying civilian militias. Such militias, which operate without proper military discipline or accountability, have been implicated in torture, arbitrary detention, and the killing of local Indigenous leaders.

Unlawful killings

Politically motivated killings of political activists and journalists continued. In November, the USA announced it would withhold a portion of military aid until the Philippines made progress in resolving extrajudicial executions.

■ Rodel Estrellado, a member of leftist political party Bayan Muna, was abducted in February near his home in Albay province by men claiming to be members of the Philippine Drug Enforcement Agency. After two days of searching, his family found his body in a funeral parlour, registered under a fictitious name. Several hours before the abduction, the military issued a statement claiming that a person with this name had been killed in an armed encounter in another province. In May, the military confirmed that nine soldiers, including two officers, had been charged with his murder.

■ At least three journalists were killed, including Gerardo Ortega in January. A radio broadcaster in Palawan island, he had opposed mining operations on the island. Police arrested a suspected gunman and traced the weapon to a former employee of provincial Governor Joel Reyes, whom Ortega had criticized for corruption. In June, the Department of Justice dropped murder charges against the governor.

■ Two years after the Maguindanao massacre, in which an armed group killed 57 people accompanying an election caravan on Mindanao island, trials of the alleged perpetrators continued. Police had arrested at least 93 suspects, including former local officials, but no one had been convicted by the end of the year.

Enforced disappearances

Hundreds of cases of enforced disappearance remained unresolved. According to figures released in August by Families of Victims of Involuntary Disappearance, the average number of enforced disappearances per year had barely changed since the overthrow of Ferdinand Marcos in 1986. There were 875 documented cases during his 21-year rule, compared with 945 in the 25 years since.

■ In July, the Supreme Court ordered the armed forces to produce Jonas Burgos, an activist abducted from a Manila shopping mall in 2007 in a car previously impounded by the military. In its report to the Court, the Commission on Human Rights recommended that criminal charges be filed against a major who had been implicated by a witness. In June, Burgos' mother filed a criminal

P

case after the government failed to bring charges against the major.

■ The Senate passed a landmark bill to criminalize enforced disappearances in July. The bill, first filed in 1995, remained pending in the House of Representatives.

Torture and other ill-treatment

For the first time, members of the security forces were prosecuted under criminal anti-torture legislation. Yet reports of torture and other ill-treatment by the security forces continued. Prosecutions of criminal suspects remained highly dependent on individual testimony, including forced confessions.

■ In September, prosecutors filed the first criminal case under the Anti-Torture Law of 2009. The Department of Justice recommended that criminal charges be filed against a senior police inspector and six other police officers. A mobile-phone video shot in 2010 showed robbery suspect Darius Evangelista writhing in pain as the police inspector yanked Evangelista's penis with a cord; the video was broadcast on a television news programme in August that year.

■ In August, four army rangers were arrested in connection with the alleged torture of Abdul Khan Ajid in July. They were accused of dousing him with gasoline and setting him alight to force him to confess to being a member of Abu Sayyaf. The four soldiers, including one officer, were relieved of their duties in Basilan province, pending charges.

Arbitrary arrests and detentions

Peaceful activists faced the risk of harassment, arrest and detention by the military near areas where battalions were deployed.

■ In February, military officers arrested journalist Ericson Acosta in Samar province. During his interrogation at a military camp, he was threatened with death unless he confessed to being an official of the Communist Party of the Philippines – which is no longer illegal. The military then filed charges against Acosta on a non-bailable offence: illegal possession of explosives. Although the Speedy Trial Act specifies a maximum of 180 days from arraignment to trial, at the end of the year he remained in jail without trial after 10 months.

Sexual and reproductive rights

Government policies on birth control discriminated against women and violated their right to enjoy the highest attainable standard of health, by restricting access to contraception and information on family planning. Abortion remained criminalized in all circumstances, except where a medical board certifies that the pregnancy endangers the woman's life. Debate continued in Congress on the Reproductive Health Bill, which aims to remove current prohibitions and obstacles to services and information related to reproductive health.

■ In January, a local authority in Manila passed an ordinance banning sex education, condoms, contraceptive pills and other contraceptive devices. The ordinance required a doctor's prescription for buying condoms, and imposed penalties for advertising birth control methods.

■ In a speech in March, President Aquino recognized the scale of unsafe illegal abortions in the Philippines, saying there were 300,000 "induced miscarriages" each year.

■ Lesbians, gay men and bisexual and transgender people continued to be subjected to violence and discrimination, with 28 bias-related killings in the first half of 2011, according to the Philippine LGBT Hate Crime Watch. An anti-discrimination bill, introduced in 1999, remained blocked in Congress.

Amnesty International visits/reports

🚌 Amnesty International delegates visited the Philippines in April, November and December.

📄 Making the fair choice: Key steps to improve maternal health in ASEAN (ASA 03/001/2011)

📄 Progress, stagnation, regression? The state of human rights in the Philippines under Aquino (ASA 35/002/2011)

P

POLAND

REPUBLIC OF POLAND
Head of state:	Bronislaw Komorowski
Head of government:	Donald Tusk
Death penalty:	abolitionist for all crimes
Population:	38.3 million
Life expectancy:	76.1 years
Under-5 mortality:	6.7 per 1,000
Adult literacy:	99.5 per cent

The Ombudsperson expressed concerns over the growing number of racist and xenophobic attacks. The parliament rejected a proposal for a total ban on abortion. Concerns were expressed by NGOs over the detention of child asylum-seekers.

Background

The ruling political party, Civic Platform, won the parliamentary elections in October. New members of parliament included two LGBT rights activists, an expert and activist on sexual and reproductive rights and two people of African origin. For the first time in Poland, women were elected to the parliamentary roles of speaker and vice-speaker.

Counter-terror and security

In July, the Prosecutor's Office decided to extend the investigation into Poland's alleged involvement in the CIA's rendition and secret detention programmes for another six months. According to a Radio RMF FM report in September, the President rejected a request by the Prosecutor's Office to relieve former President Aleksander Kwaśniewski of his duty to keep state secrets and allow him to testify. No other information about the progress or outcomes of the investigation had been made public by the end of the year.

In October, the Council of Europe's Parliamentary Assembly adopted a resolution calling on the Polish prosecuting authorities to "persevere in seeking to establish the truth about the allegations of secret CIA detentions". The resolution also noted that the parliament had "confined [itself] to inquiries whose main purpose seems to have been to defend the official position of the national authorities."

Discrimination

The government failed to allocate the necessary resources to ensure the Ombudsperson's office could carry out its new role as an equality body. Antidiscrimination legislation adopted in December 2010 had entrusted the Ombudsperson to help victims of discrimination to pursue complaints, and to conduct independent research and issue recommendations in relation to equal treatment. The government argued that the new competences could be met without additional funding. However, the Ombudsperson stated in May that there was no specialized antidiscrimination unit in her office due to lack of funding, and that it was illegal to impose new competences on a public body without allocating sufficient resources.

Racism

In October, in a letter to the Prosecutor General, the Ombudsperson also raised concerns about the growing number of racially motivated and xenophobic attacks brought to her attention, and called on the Prosecutor to take the necessary measures to address these crimes.

Freedom of expression

Poland continued to be criticized for legislation criminalizing defamation, which was found potentially to have had an adverse effect on freedom of expression.
■ In July, in *Wizerkaniuk v. Poland*, the European Court of Human Rights found Poland in violation of the right to freedom of expression. Journalist Jerzy Wizerkaniuk had appealed against a local court judgement and fine for publishing parts of an interview with a local member of parliament without prior consent. The Court held that the provisions of the 1984 Press Act, which allow for criminal sanctions against journalists, did not adequately reflect the significance of freedom of expression in a democratic society. It concluded that criminal sanction was disproportionate in such circumstances, where civil remedies were available for protection of reputation.

Justice system

■ In May, in *Bogusław Krawczak v. Poland*, the European Court ruled that Poland had violated the right to trial within a reasonable time. Bogusław Krawczak had been in pre-trial detention for almost four years. The Court also held that arbitrary restrictions on physical contact with his family had violated his right to private and family life.

Prison conditions

In July, the European Committee for the Prevention of Torture raised concerns about prison conditions for detainees. They included overcrowding, inadequate provision of health care, ill-treatment by police officers and the lack of a developed legal aid system. The Committee called on the Polish authorities to review the regulation on living space for prisoners, and to ensure at least 4m² per inmate in multi-occupancy cells. In September, the Ministry of Justice maintained that, due to high prison population levels, it was impossible to guarantee each inmate the space defined by the Committee. According to the Helsinki Foundation for Human Rights, 4,370 claims for compensation or personal injury were brought before the courts in relation to placements in overpopulated cells.

Sexual and reproductive rights

In September, parliament rejected a proposed amendment to the 1993 Family Planning Act to ban abortion in all circumstances. It remained lawful in three strictly defined circumstances: when the pregnancy endangers a woman's life or health; in cases where prenatal or other medical tests indicate a high risk that the foetus will be severely and irreversibly damaged or suffer from an incurable life-threatening disease; and where there are strong grounds for believing that the pregnancy is a result of a criminal act.

■ Poland violated the right not to be subjected to torture and inhuman treatment and the right to private and family life of a pregnant woman, R.R., who was denied timely access to genetic tests. The European Court held that as a result of procrastination and refusal by medical professionals, R.R. had to endure weeks of painful uncertainty concerning the health of the foetus and her own and her family's future. Such treatment amounted to humiliation. The child was born with Turner syndrome and R.R.'s husband left her. The European Court emphasized that, as domestic law allowed for abortion in cases of foetal abnormality, a pregnant woman must have access to full and reliable information on the foetus' health.

■ The case of an adolescent rape victim, who was subjected to delays and harassment in accessing a legal abortion, was ruled admissible by the European Court in September.

Refugees and asylum-seekers

In July, the Helsinki Foundation for Human Rights, the Legal Intervention Association and the Halina Nieć Legal Aid Centre expressed concerns over the detention of children alongside their adult relatives, who were being held solely for immigration purposes.

Amnesty International visits/reports

🚌 An Amnesty International delegate visited Poland in May.

▤ Current evidence: European complicity in the CIA rendition and secret detention programmes (EUR 01/001/2011)

▤ Poland: Involvement in US-led rendition and secret detention programmes and women's access to sexual and reproductive rights – Amnesty International submission to the UN Universal Periodic Review, May-June 2012 (EUR 37/002/2011)

PORTUGAL

PORTUGUESE REPUBLIC

Head of state:	Aníbal António Cavaco Silva
Head of government:	Pedro Manuel Mamede Passos Coelho
	(replaced José Sócrates Carvalho Pinto de Sousa in June)
Death penalty:	abolitionist for all crimes
Population:	10.7 million
Life expectancy:	79.5 years
Under-5 mortality:	3.7 per 1,000
Adult literacy:	94.9 per cent

There was little accountability for torture and other ill-treatment. Roma were discriminated against in access to housing. Domestic violence remained a serious concern.

Torture and other ill-treatment

In February, a video showing prison guards using a dart-firing stun gun against an inmate in Paços de Ferreira prison in September 2010, allegedly to force him to clean his cell, was broadcast on the internet. The man appeared to offer no resistance. In April, the Minister of Justice issued a decree forbidding the use of stun guns in similar circumstances. An inquiry by the Audit and Inspection services of the General

P

Directorate for prisons was pending at the end of the year.

In March, the Court of Appeal of Evora confirmed an earlier ruling that Leonor Cipriano had been tortured while in police custody in 2004, but that it could not identify those responsible. Leonor Cipriano had yet to receive compensation from the state. Gonçalo de Sousa Amaral and António Fernandes Nuno Cardoso, senior officials in the judicial police, had been sentenced to 18 months' and 27 months' imprisonment respectively, for falsely claiming Leonor Cipriano had fallen down the stairs. However, both sentences were suspended on the grounds that the officers had no previous criminal convictions.

Hearings in the trial of three police officers, accused of torturing Virgolino Borges while in police custody in March 2000, took place in November and December. Virgolino Borges was asked to give his testimony again as the recording had allegedly been lost due to technical problems.

Housing rights

Roma continued to be denied the right to adequate housing. In November, the European Committee of Social Rights adopted a decision in *European Roma Rights Centre v. Portugal* that the housing situation of Roma in Portugal constituted a breach of the right to housing and to non-discrimination. The Committee found that many Roma lived in precarious housing conditions, segregated from the rest of the population, and that the government had failed to provide them with adequate housing.

■ The eviction of a settlement in Bairro da Torre in Loures, near Lisbon was due to take place on 18 October but the Loures municipality suspended it. The settlement was home to 86 families, including Roma and migrants from sub-Saharan Africa. A notice of the eviction had been sent in March, but no alternative accommodation was offered. A process granting new houses to some households, including people with disabilities, was initiated. The eviction order was still pending at the end of the year.

Violence against women and girls

Domestic violence continued to be a serious concern. In May, the government signed the Council of Europe's Convention on preventing and combating violence against women and domestic violence. According to the Domestic Violence Monitoring

Report of the Directorate General of Internal Administration, in August, 14,508 complaints of domestic violence had been received by the police and the gendarmerie in 2011. As of 11 November, the NGO UMAR had registered 23 deaths, and 39 attempted homicides as a result of domestic violence, since the beginning of the year.

PUERTO RICO

COMMONWEALTH OF PUERTO RICO

Head of state:	Barack H. Obama
Head of government:	Luis G. Fortuño
Death penalty:	abolitionist for all crimes
Population:	4 million

A federal Justice Department investigation found a pattern of ill-treatment by officers of the Puerto Rico Police Department.

Police

In September, the US Justice Department issued a report documenting a "pattern and practice" of abuses by the Puerto Rico Police Department (PRPD), including excessive force and unjustified shootings resulting in numerous injuries and deaths, and illegal searches and seizures. It found, among other things, that the police were responsible for the indiscriminate use of chemical agents, batons and other force against student demonstrators at the Sheraton Hotel, San Juan, in May 2010.

The report also noted "troubling evidence" that the PRPD failed to adequately police incidents of sexual assault and domestic violence, and routinely discriminated against people of Dominican descent.

The findings were the result of a three-year investigation by the Justice Department's Civil Rights Division and included 133 recommendations for reform, including better training, policies and supervision. These were under review at the end of the year.

Freedom of expression

The Justice Department report documented a pattern of police attacks on non-violent protesters and journalists in a manner "designed to suppress" the right to freedom of speech, guaranteed under the First Amendment of the US Constitution.

In May, Amnesty International Puerto Rico discovered that access to its website had been blocked to students using the Department of Education's computers. Although the block was subsequently lifted following protests by Amnesty International, the search term "advocacy" remained blocked by the Department at the end of the year.

QATAR

STATE OF QATAR

Head of state:	**Shaikh Hamad bin Khalifa Al Thani**
Head of government:	**Shaikh Hamad bin Jassim bin Jabr Al Thani**
Death penalty:	**retentionist**
Population:	**1.9 million**
Life expectancy:	**78.4 years**
Under-5 mortality:	**10.8 per 1,000**
Adult literacy:	**94.7 per cent**

Two people were detained, apparently as suspected government critics; one was allegedly tortured. Migrant workers were exploited, abused and inadequately protected under the law. At least six people were sentenced to flogging. At least three men were sentenced to death; there were no executions.

Background

Qatar did not experience anti-government protests similar to those in other countries in the region, despite calls for protests made on Facebook in February and March.

Municipal elections were held in May. In November, the government committed to holding the first elections to the Shura Council, postponed since 2008, in 2013.

A law prohibiting human trafficking was passed in October. Other laws reported to be under review included the 2002 Protection of Society law, which permits detention without charge for up to six months.

Freedom of expression

At least two men were arrested apparently because they were suspected of criticizing the government, and two people were jailed for blasphemy. At least 46 people, most of them foreign nationals, were convicted on charges of "illicit sexual relations" and either deported or imprisoned followed in some cases by deportation.

■ Salem al-Khawari, a civil servant, was arrested on 7 February and held without charge until 18 October. He was denied access to his family for three months, during which he was allegedly made to remain standing for up to 15 hours a day, prevented from sleeping and beaten. The authorities gave no reason for his detention and no investigation into his alleged torture was known to have been held.

■ Sultan al-Khalaifi, a blogger and founder of a local human rights organization, was arrested on 2 March by state security officials in plain clothes who also searched his home. He was detained incommunicado for a week and was released without charge on 1 April.

■ In February, a 41-year-old Qatari man was reported to have been sentenced to a five-year prison term after a court in Doha convicted him of blasphemy.

Migrants' rights

Migrant workers, who make up more than 80 per cent of Qatar's population and come mostly from south and south-east Asia, were inadequately protected under the law and continued to be exploited and abused by employers. In May, the International Trade Union Confederation criticized workers' conditions in Qatar, particularly those of women domestic workers and men employed in constructing facilities for football's 2022 World Cup, and called for major improvements.

Discrimination – denial of nationality

The authorities continued to deny Qatari nationality to some 100 people, mostly members of al-Murra, a tribe said to have supported a coup attempt in 1996. Those stripped of their nationality subsequently faced problems such as being denied employment opportunities, social security and health care, and being prevented from obtaining Qatari passports. They had no means of remedy before the courts.

Cruel, inhuman or degrading punishments

At least six men and women, all foreign nationals, were sentenced to floggings of either 40 or 100 lashes

Q

for offences related to alcohol consumption or "illicit sexual relations". Only Muslims considered medically fit were liable to have such sentences carried out. It was not known if any of the sentences were implemented.

Death penalty

At least three people were sentenced to death; at least 19 prisoners were believed to be on death row at the end of 2011, including at least six sentenced in 2001 after they were convicted of involvement in a 1996 coup attempt. No executions were reported.

ROMANIA

ROMANIA
Head of state:	Traian Băsescu
Head of government:	Emil Boc
Death penalty:	abolitionist for all crimes
Population:	21.4 million
Life expectancy:	74 years
Under-5 mortality:	11.9 per 1,000
Adult literacy:	97.7 per cent

Local authorities were found responsible for discrimination against Roma. New evidence on Romania's involvement in the CIA-led rendition programme was published by a German newspaper. The government was requested to provide information to the European Court in relation to a case of a man who allegedly died in a psychiatric hospital as a result of ill-treatment.

Background

A new labour code, introduced in response to the requirements of a loan from the International Monetary Fund and the European Commission, led to criticism from trade unions, protests across the country, and, on 16 March, a fifth attempt at a no-confidence vote in the government. The trade unions warned that the legislation stripped away labour rights protections and denied large numbers of workers the right to union representation. The austerity measures, introduced in 2009, also affected the health care system. By 1 April, 67 hospitals had been closed, which raised concerns over accessibility of health care.

Discrimination – Roma

The legislative proposal to change the name of Roma as a minority to "Ţigan" was at first endorsed by the Senate's Commission for Human Rights and Equal Opportunities in February. However, the Senate then rejected the proposal on 9 February, as did the lower chamber of the parliament on 5 April. The proposal had been criticized by NGOs for the pejorative connotations of the name "Ţigan".

Use of negative ethnic stereotyping by the President and other high-level public officials continued to be a source of concern. In June, the equality body, the National Council for Combating Discrimination (NCCD), rejected a complaint about allegedly discriminatory remarks made by the President against Roma during an official visit in Slovenia in November 2010. The NCCD held that the anti-discrimination legislation was not applicable to acts committed outside state territory. In October, the NCCD warned the President twice for making statements against Roma on television. It held that these statements violated the anti-discrimination legislation.

■ In July, the municipal authorities of Baia Mare, in north-west Romania, built a concrete wall separating blocks of houses inhabited by Roma from the rest of the residential area. NGOs protested against the construction, arguing that it amounted to discrimination and that it would lead to ghettoization. The municipality denied this, claiming that the wall was supposed to protect the inhabitants of the apartment blocks from traffic. In November, the NCCD said that the construction of the wall amounted to discrimination. The municipality was fined 6,000 Romanian new lei (€1,300). The NCCD recommended that the wall should be demolished and that the municipality take measures to improve the housing conditions for Roma.

Right to education
■ The NCCD held in August that separation of Roma and non-Roma pupils in a school in the town of Craiova amounted to both direct and indirect discrimination. The equality body had initially investigated the situation only partially. Following an appeal by the NGO Romani CRISS, the Supreme Court requested a reinvestigation of the case for another school year and as a result found direct discrimination.

Housing rights
Several municipalities reportedly attempted to evict informal Romani settlements.

■ In August, the Mayor of Baia Mare announced a plan to evict, from various areas of the city, hundreds of Roma and other socially disadvantaged people who were not registered as Baia Mare residents and to send them back to their places of origin. National and international NGOs and foreign embassies in the country immediately criticized the plan. The eviction was eventually put on hold. In September, the Mayor said that the municipality would respect national law and international human rights standards.

■ On 19 September, the Cluj-Napoca Court rejected the National Railway Company's request to remove the homes of around 450 Roma, including 200 children, in a settlement on Cantonului Street, on the outskirts of the city of Cluj-Napoca. The municipal authorities had reportedly relocated some of the families to the area in 2000. Some of the inhabitants had a verbal agreement with the municipality to construct their houses. Others had rental agreements issued by the municipality.

■ On 15 November, the NCCD stated that the relocation of Roma from Coastei Street, in the centre of Cluj-Napoca, to the outskirts near a landfill site in the area of Pata Rât, amounted to discrimination, and fined the municipality 8,000 Romanian new lei (€1,800). The authorities disagreed with the decision and argued that the eviction was not an act of discrimination. The complaint against the municipality was issued by the local Working Group of Civil Organizations (gLOC), which had been set up in response to the forced eviction from Coastei Street in December 2010.

Rights of lesbian, gay, bisexual and transgender people

The new Civil Code, which entered into force on 1 October, prohibited same-sex partnerships and marriages. It also introduced the derecognition of same-sex partnerships and marriages legally recognized in other countries.

Counter-terror and security

In November, the European Committee for the Prevention of Torture asked the Romanian authorities to provide information on why they had failed to investigate the alleged existence of secret detention centres used in the CIA-led rendition programme. The government claimed that there was no proof of the allegations of its involvement in the CIA-led rendition programme, or the existence of secret detention centres on Romanian territory.

On 8 December, the German newspaper, *Süddeutsche Zeitung,* published new evidence that the CIA had tortured and carried out renditions on "suspects of terrorism" in European states, including Romania, in the years following the attacks in the USA on 11 September 2001.

Torture and other ill-treatment
Mental health institutions
Investigations were requested into the living conditions and treatment of patients in mental health institutions.

■ In June, the European Court of Human Rights asked the Romanian government to submit information on the case of Valentin Câmpeanu, an HIV-positive Romani man with mental illness who died in 2004 at the Poiana Mare Psychiatric Hospital. The official investigation into the circumstances of his death was allegedly marked by procedural irregularities. It did not result in any charges against staff from the institutions where he was kept during the last months of his life. The case was brought to the Court by NGOs, the Centre for Legal Resources and INTERIGHTS, who asked the Court to adapt its admissibility criteria so as to allow NGOs to bring cases on behalf of a person with disabilities, even in the absence of specific authorization. The NGOs argued that inappropriate care and living conditions at the psychiatric hospital directly contributed to Valentin Câmpeanu's death.

Amnesty International visits/reports
🚌 Amnesty International delegates visited Romania in April, June, September, October and November.

📄 Mind the legal gap: Roma and the right to housing in Romania (EUR 39/004/2011)

📄 Romania must come clean over secret prisons (PRE01/611/2011)

R

RUSSIAN FEDERATION

RUSSIAN FEDERATION

Head of state:	Dmitry Medvedev
Head of government:	Vladimir Putin
Death penalty:	abolitionist in practice
Population:	142.8 million
Life expectancy:	68.8 years
Under-5 mortality:	12.4 per 1,000
Adult literacy:	99.6 per cent

Widespread demonstrations and arrests of hundreds of peaceful protesters followed disputed election results in December. Throughout the year, freedom of assembly had been frequently violated in the context of political, environmental, social and other protests. The media continued to operate in a restricted environment. Some members of religious minorities faced persecution, and concerns persisted about arbitrary use of anti-extremism legislation. Human rights defenders and journalists continued to experience pressure, and most investigations into past attacks showed no progress. Torture remained widely reported despite superficial police reforms. The security situation in the North Caucasus remained volatile and serious human rights abuses were committed by both armed groups and security officials.

Background

High oil prices and significant government stimulus spending enabled Russia to post relatively strong growth rates by the end of the year. However, the government's stated priorities in the area of continuing modernization, combating corruption and reforms of the criminal justice system showed few tangible results.

Following parliamentary elections marred by widespread allegations and numerous documented instances of vote rigging, the ruling United Russia party was returned to power in December with a significantly reduced share of the vote.

The results appeared to indicate a growing demand for civil and political freedoms and social and economic rights as opposed to the stability promised – and largely delivered – by the Putin/Medvedev "tandem".

The demonstrations that followed the elections grew to become the largest seen in the country since the collapse of the Soviet Union. The protests tapped into the growing civic engagement shown through the year by individuals, interest groups and local communities around issues such as corruption, declining welfare support, police abuses and the environment.

TV and other mass media continued to follow the official line. Harsh public criticism of the authorities was mostly confined to minor print media outlets and the internet, which continued to grow in influence.

Freedom of assembly

The authorities continued to restrict freedom of assembly of critical civil society movements, but some street rallies, banned in previous years, were allowed to go ahead. However, numerous demonstrations were banned and a number of people involved in peaceful political protest were repeatedly detained, some pre-emptively (on their way to the demonstration), and frequently sentenced to administrative arrest.

Numerous spontaneous peaceful demonstrations took place across the country in the days following the disputed parliamentary elections of 4 December. More than 1,000 protesters were arrested and more than 100 sentenced to administrative arrest in proceedings that frequently violated fair trial standards. Subsequent authorized demonstrations on 10 and 24 December brought together over 50,000 protesters in Moscow and tens of thousands elsewhere in the country and passed off peacefully.

Lesbian, gay, bisexual and transgender (LGBT) rights activists continued to face harassment and attacks. Attempted pride marches and pro-LGBT rights pickets in Moscow and Saint Petersburg were banned and promptly dispersed by police.
■ Sergei Udaltsov, leader of the Left Front movement, was detained more than a dozen times in Moscow while attempting to peacefully protest against government policies. He was repeatedly found guilty of administrative offences such as "disobeying lawful demands of police officers", and ended the year in detention following his arrest on 4 December for participating in a post-election protest.

Freedom of expression

State control over television broadcasting and other mass media remained strong. The importance of the

R

internet as an alternative source of information and a forum for exchanging comment and opinion continued to grow. Although the internet continued to be relatively free from state interference, several well-known websites and blogs reporting on electoral abuses were brought down by attacks, both before and immediately after the parliamentary elections in December.

Journalists continued to face threats and physical attacks for writing about politically sensitive issues, including corruption. Such attacks were rarely effectively investigated or prosecuted.

Anti-extremism legislation was often used arbitrarily to clamp down on those critical of the authorities. In response, the Supreme Court issued a ruling in June clarifying that criticism of government officials or politicians did not constitute incitement to hatred under anti-extremism legislation. Religious minorities such as non-traditional Muslim groups or Jehovah's Witnesses continued to face persecution. Laws banning "propaganda of homosexuality among minors" were adopted in Arkhangelsk Region. In a positive development, defamation was decriminalized at the end of the year.

■ On 15 December, prominent journalist Khadzhimurad Kamalov, founder and editor of the independent Dagestani weekly newspaper *Chernovik,* renowned for its critical reporting, was shot dead outside his office in Makhachkala in Dagestan. For years, *Chernovik*'s staff had faced intimidation and harassment by the local authorities.

■ The investigation into the violent attack on journalist Oleg Kashin in November 2010 had yielded no results at the end of the year, despite promises by the most senior Russian officials to bring the perpetrators to justice.

■ Throughout the year, several followers of the Turkish theologian Said Nursi were charged with membership of the organization Nurdzhular, which is considered to be extremist and banned in Russia. Some were sentenced to imprisonment. Those charged claimed they had never heard of the organization.

■ In December, Aleksandr Kalistratov, a Jehovah's Witness, was acquitted by the Supreme Court of the Republic of Altai of inciting hatred against other religious groups. He had been fined in October by a lower court for distributing leaflets about Jehovah's Witnesses.

Human rights defenders

Restrictive regulations imposed on NGOs in previous years were partly eased, and a Higher Court of Arbitration decision lifted some restrictions on foreign funding for NGOs. However, human rights defenders and journalists continued to face harassment and threats, including by officials whose wrongdoings they exposed. Most investigations into past cases of killings and physical attacks on human rights defenders, journalists and lawyers, continued to make little or no progress.

■ In June, a Moscow court acquitted Oleg Orlov, head of the Human Rights Centre Memorial, of criminal slander. The Head of the Chechen Republic, Ramzan Kadyrov, whom Oleg Orlov had named responsible for the murder of Natalia Estemirova, appealed against the decision, but slander was decriminalized later in the year and the charges were dropped.

■ In July, a group of human rights defenders published a report on the murder of their colleague Natalia Estemirova in July 2009. The report highlighted numerous omissions and inconsistencies in the official investigation, and concluded that leads linking her killing to Chechen law enforcement officials had not been thoroughly followed up. Following its publication, the Head of the Investigation Committee promised that all possible leads in her murder would be explored, but he had not disclosed any new information by the end of the year.

■ A new investigation into the murder of journalist Anna Politkovskaya in 2006 led in June and August to the arrest of two new suspects, one for murder. Two more named suspects, including one of those acquitted in 2009, continued to serve sentences for other crimes.

■ In May, a Moscow court sentenced two far-right activists, one to life and the other to 18 years' imprisonment, for the murder of lawyer Stanislav Markelov and journalist Anastasia Baburova in January 2009.

Torture and other ill-treatment

The new law on the police, which came into force in March, introduced the formal appraisal of all officers and reduced their numbers. However, there were no substantive new provisions for strengthening the accountability of the police or to combat impunity for violations by law enforcement officials, and the law's benefits remained elusive. Reports of torture and other ill-treatment remained widespread. Allegations

R

were seldom effectively investigated and documented injuries were often dismissed as resulting from the legitimate use of force. The successful prosecution of perpetrators was rare. The denial of adequate medical care in custody was widely reported, and was allegedly used to extract confessions. Convicted prisoners frequently reported being subjected to violence, by both prison officials and inmates, shortly after their arrival in prison.

■ The trial of two police officers on charges of abuse of power, including in relation to the unlawful detention and torture of Zelimkhan Chitigov in April 2010, began in September, the first such case ever to have reached court in Ingushetia. Reportedly, several of those who had testified against the two police officers were subjected to a campaign of pressure and intimidation.

■ Armen Sargsyan was detained by police in Orenburg on 18 November as a suspect in a theft case and died hours later, according to the police of acute heart failure. The family presented photos of his dead body showing head and other injuries. At the end of the year, two police officers were under arrest in connection with the death, a further two were under investigation, and several commanding officers were disciplined.

Unfair trials

Despite ongoing attempts to improve the efficiency and independence of the judiciary, alleged political interference, corruption and the collusion of judges, prosecutors and law enforcement officials continued to result in frequent reports of unfair trials.

■ In May, the Moscow City Court upheld the second convictions of Mikhail Khodorkovsky and Platon Lebedev. Their repeat convictions on barely distinguishable charges from their previous trials, following deeply flawed judicial proceedings, led Amnesty International to consider them prisoners of conscience. Even allowing for their extended prison sentences, both men qualified for parole towards the end of 2011 and both were denied it.

Insecurity in the North Caucasus

The security situation in the North Caucasus remained volatile and uneven. Armed groups continued to target law enforcement and other officials, with civilians caught in the crossfire and sometimes deliberately attacked. Security operations across the region were often accompanied by serious human rights violations. There were reports of

witnesses being intimidated and journalists, human rights activists and lawyers being harassed and killed.

Chechnya

The rapid post-conflict reconstruction of Chechnya continued with high levels of federal funding, though unemployment remained a problem. Activity by armed groups declined compared to other regions in the North Caucasus. Law enforcement operations continued to give rise to reports of serious human rights violations. In a letter to the human rights NGO the Interregional Committee against Torture, a senior Chechen prosecutor acknowledged that investigations into enforced disappearances in Chechnya were ineffective.

The local human rights community continued to be scarred by the unsolved killing of Natalia Estemirova in 2009 and subjected to intimidation and harassment.

■ On 9 May, car mechanic Tamerlan Suleimanov was abducted at gunpoint from his workplace in Grozny by several men believed to be police officials. Eyewitnesses reportedly gave a full account of the incident to the authorities. A criminal investigation was opened on 18 May, but the case remained unsolved.

■ In June, Supian Baskhanov and Magomed Alamov, both from the Interregional Committee against Torture, were detained following an officially authorized picket against torture in Grozny. They received repeated informal threats from police officials against their legitimate human rights work.

■ The investigation continued into the secret detention and alleged torture of Islam Umarpashaev by police officials for four months from December 2009. His family and the official federal investigation team reportedly received direct threats from a senior Chechen police official. Local police systematically refused to co-operate with the investigation, and the suspects continued to perform police duties.

■ During the course of the year, the Chechen authorities evicted over 100 families, displaced during the conflict, from temporary shelters in Grozny. Many of those evicted were given only 48 hours' notice and offered no alternative accommodation. Some were allegedly forced by armed men to sign statements that they were moving out voluntarily.

The resurgence of "Chechen traditions", actively promoted by the Head of the Chechen Republic Ramzan Kadyrov, resulted in growing gender inequalities and increased the vulnerability of women and girls to domestic and sexual violence.

R

■ Zarema (name changed) told Amnesty International that she had been systematically subjected to sexual violence by a close male relative over several years. She married in 2010 and moved to Grozny, but her husband beat her. In June 2011, she tried to move in with her grandmother, but her brothers returned her to her husband. Zarema sought help from the Muftiyat (Muslim spiritual authority) and the government commission for resolving family conflict, but was told by both to obey her husband. In late 2011, she left home, heavily pregnant and went into hiding outside Chechnya, for fear that after the birth the husband would return her to her brothers who had promised to kill her.

Dagestan

Armed groups continued to attack security officials, members of local administrations and prominent members of the public, including mullahs preaching traditional Islam. Law enforcement operations gave rise to numerous allegations of enforced disappearances, extrajudicial executions and torture. Past violations in which state security officials were allegedly implicated were neither promptly investigated nor effectively prosecuted.

■ On 26 August, brothers Zaur and Kamilpasha Gasanov and their father Murad were detained while working in the neighbouring territory of Stavropol. The father was released and Kamilpasha allegedly beaten and then dumped outside the city the same day. Zaur Gasanov remained in custody, suspected of being involved in an attack on the police, and was transferred to Dagestan, where he was allegedly beaten and subjected to electric shocks. He was initially prevented from meeting with his lawyer, reportedly on the pretext that the latter had a beard and therefore could be suspected of membership of an armed group.

■ In May, three police officials, charged with the torture of 14-year-old Makhmud Akhmedov in July 2010, were given suspended prison sentences. The family complained in court that they had been harassed and intimidated during the investigation and court hearing, and regarded the sentences as too lenient. Following a judicial review the case was returned for additional investigation.

Ingushetia

The security situation in Ingushetia appeared to improve significantly in the early part of the year. However, attacks by armed groups and reports of serious human rights violations by security officials,

particularly enforced disappearances, increased in later months.

■ Ilez Gorchkhanov disappeared on 21 March during a car journey. Eyewitnesses reported seeing his abduction by some 15 armed and masked men in the centre of Nazran. The Ingushetian authorities denied any involvement in the abduction. Ilez Gorchkhanov's body was found on 19 April.

■ On 23 March, some 80 protesters blocked a road in Nazran demanding the truth about Ilez Gorchkhanov's fate, and an end to enforced disappearances; they were dispersed by police. Later that day, civil society activist Magomed Khazbiev and his two brothers were arrested at their home in Nazran for "disobeying police orders" during the protest in Nazran. Magomed Khazbiev said he had been beaten; CCTV footage showed him being locked inside a car boot by masked police officers during his arrest.

Kabardino-Balkaria

In February, two attacks by armed groups on civilian targets in a tourist resort in the Elbrus area resulted in three deaths. Dozens of suspected armed group members were killed in the ensuing security operations, and many were arrested. There were repeated allegations of enforced disappearances and torture by law enforcement officials.

■ Murat Bedzhiev's family reported his disappearance in Tyrnyauz on 25 June. The authorities initially denied his arrest but confirmed it two days later. A report from the local hospital confirmed that an ambulance was called three times to the detention centre to see him between 27 and 28 June and documented bruising and serious head injuries.

North Ossetia

There were sporadic incidents of violence. Local and federal law enforcement forces based in North Ossetia launched security operations in the republic and neighbouring Ingushetia, reportedly resulting in numerous human rights violations.

■ On 18 March, in the village of Chermen, teenage boys Ruslan Timurziev and Imeir Dzaurov were reportedly beaten with rifle butts by some 15 military officials in front of several witnesses. The officials had been driving through the village in two minivans; they got out and urinated near a private house. The boys had remonstrated with them, and the officials beat them so badly that they needed hospital treatment. Their parents repeatedly complained to the authorities, but to no avail.

R

Amnesty International visits/reports

🚌 Amnesty International delegates visited the Russian Federation in May and June 2011.

📄 Briefing to the Human Rights Committee on follow-up to the concluding observations on Russia's sixth periodic report under the International Covenant for Civil and Political Rights (EUR 46/007/2011)

📄 Beaten up for speaking out: attacks on human rights defenders in the Russian Federation (EUR 46/038/2011)

RWANDA

REPUBLIC OF RWANDA

Head of state:	Paul Kagame
Head of government:	Pierre Damien Habumuremyi (replaced Bernard Makuza in October)
Death penalty:	abolitionist for all crimes
Population:	10.9 million
Life expectancy:	55.4 years
Under-5 mortality:	110.8 per 1,000
Adult literacy:	70.7 per cent

The authorities increasingly prosecuted individuals for criticizing government policies and there was a rise in unlawful detentions. Restrictions on freedom of expression persisted despite plans to reform laws. Opposition politicians and journalists arrested during the 2010 elections were unfairly convicted on politically motivated charges.

Background

Rwanda's human rights record was assessed under the UN Universal Periodic Review in January. The government accepted the majority of the recommendations, including those to revise existing legislation to protect freedom of expression. The government rejected recommendations to investigate cases of arbitrary arrest and detention, including those which may constitute enforced disappearances, arguing that irregular arrests were few and that officials responsible had been held accountable.

Security concerns intensified in 2011 following events including grenade attacks in 2010, divisions in the ruling Rwandan Patriotic Front (RPF) party, and disaffected supporters of Laurent Nkunda, the former leader of the National Congress for the Defence of the People.

The government co-organized a meeting in the capital Kigali to encourage other countries in Africa to follow Rwanda's example in abolishing the death penalty.

Donors remained supportive of the government, citing economic development, but privately voiced concerns about human rights violations.

Freedom of expression

Freedom of expression remained severely restricted despite pending legislative changes. A growing number of people were convicted for perceived threats to national security, such as criticizing government policies.

Laws on 'genocide ideology' and 'sectarianism'

Commitments to revise the "genocide ideology" law ran counter to the government's continued misuse of broad and ill-defined laws on "genocide ideology" and "sectarianism", more commonly known as "divisionism". The laws prohibit hate speech, but also criminalize criticism of the government. At the end of the year the government had not discussed the promised revisions to the "genocide ideology" law, first announced in April 2010.

■ Bernard Ntaganda, President of the Ideal Social Party (PS-Imberakuri), was sentenced to four years' imprisonment in February. He was found guilty of "divisionism" for making public speeches criticizing government policies ahead of the 2010 elections, breaching state security and attempting to plan an "unauthorized demonstration". His prosecution for threatening state security and divisionism was solely based on speeches criticizing government policies.

■ The trial of Victoire Ingabire, leader of the United Democratic Forces (FDU-Inkingi), opened in September. She was charged with terrorism, creating an armed group, "genocide ideology", "sectarianism" and willingly disseminating rumours aimed at inciting the public against the existing leadership. The "genocide ideology" charges were partly based on her public call for the prosecution of war crimes by the RPF (see Justice system). There were concerns about violations of fair trial standards, including by allowing the prosecution to present evidence which pre-dated the laws under which she was charged.

Journalists

A raft of legislation to enhance media freedom was before parliament at the end of the year. Human rights organizations hoped that proposed revisions to the media law, the Media High Council law and a new access to information bill would reduce state control of the media. Defamation was set to remain a criminal offence; the law against defamation had been used in previous years to silence journalists and close media outlets.

Private media outlets, shut down in 2010, remained closed and their editors and other independent journalists remained exiled.

■ Agnes Nkusi Uwimana, editor of the private Kinyarwanda tabloid newspaper *Umurabyo*, and her deputy editor Saidati Mukakibibi, were sentenced on 5 February to 17 and seven years in prison respectively for opinion pieces critical of government policies published before the 2010 presidential elections. Agnes Nkusi Uwimana was found guilty of threatening state security, "genocide ideology", "divisionism" and defamation. Saidati Mukakibibi was found guilty of threatening state security. Their appeal was adjourned to 2012.

■ The prosecution did not reopen the investigation into the June 2010 killing of journalist Jean-Leonard Rugambage, despite deficiencies in the original investigation. In September, one of the convicted killers was acquitted on appeal and the other had his sentence reduced from life imprisonment to 10 years.

Human rights defenders

Human rights defenders continued to be intimidated and harassed by officials, including through detention, threats, administrative obstacles and allegations of financial misconduct.

■ Joseph Sanane and Epimack Kwokwo, President and Acting Executive Secretary of the Human Rights League in the Great Lakes Region (LDGL), were detained on 19 August, accused of having helped LDGL's Executive Secretary, Pascal Nyilibakwe, to leave Rwanda in 2010 after repeated threats to his safety. Joseph Sanane was detained overnight and Epimack Kwokwo was released after several hours.

Freedom of association

Opposition politicians were convicted for attempting to plan or participate in "unauthorized" demonstrations. Some lower-ranking opposition party members were detained. Rwandan authorities threatened and intimidated opposition politicians in neighbouring countries, as well as in South Africa and some countries in Europe.

■ In May, police in the UK warned two Rwandan opposition activists that the Rwandan government posed an imminent threat to their lives.

Prisoners of conscience

Charles Ntakiruntinka, a former government minister, continued to serve a 10-year prison sentence in Kigali Central Prison. After an unfair trial, he was convicted of inciting civil disobedience and association with criminal elements.

Justice system

As part of continued attempts to secure transfers and extraditions of people suspected of genocide, the government amended legislation to ensure that those convicted would not be sentenced to "life imprisonment with special provisions". This sentence could constitute prolonged solitary confinement for those whose family members were unwilling or unable to visit. Such prisoners would only have the right to communicate with a lawyer in the presence of a prison guard, violating defence rights during appeal hearings. The sentence was not applied due to a lack of individual cells.

Despite requests, no independent NGO was granted access to monitor prison conditions or interview detainees in private.

Gacaca trials of genocide cases – which did not meet international fair trial standards – were set to close in late 2011 following several delays. At the end of the year, some applications for review remained pending. A new law determining how further allegations of involvement in the 1994 genocide would be investigated and prosecuted before ordinary courts was yet to be brought to parliament.

Unlawful detention and enforced disappearances

Scores of young men arrested in 2010 and 2011 were unlawfully held in military detention facilities, including Camp Kami, and in illegal detention facilities including Chez Gacinya and Gikondo, often for several months. They were denied access to lawyers, medical care and the opportunity to challenge their cases before a court. In some cases, family members officially requested information from the police which was not forthcoming. Some detainees were transferred to ordinary prisons after being charged with threatening national security. Others were released on condition that they remained silent.

R

The authorities failed to shed light on the enforced disappearance of Robert Ndengeye Urayeneza. Last seen in March 2010, he was believed to be in military custody.

International justice

International Criminal Tribunal for Rwanda

Numerous judgements were handed down by the International Criminal Tribunal for Rwanda (ICTR) during the year, although nine indictees remained at large. The ICTR was due to close in 2012.

In December, the ICTR Appeals Chamber upheld the decision to transfer the case of Jean Uwinkindi to Rwanda. The ruling cited Rwanda's expressed intention to introduce legislation that would allow foreign judges to sit on transferred cases. It would be the first genocide case to be transferred or extradited to Rwanda.

Universal jurisdiction

Judicial proceedings against genocide suspects took place in Finland, Germany and Spain. The extradition requested by France and Spain of Kayumba Nyamwasa, a Rwandese national allegedly responsible for crimes against humanity committed in Rwanda, was still pending in South Africa, where he was granted asylum in 2010. Rwanda's request for extradition was turned down by the South African authorities.

■ The European Court of Human Rights ruled in October that Sylvere Ahorugeze could be extradited from Sweden to Rwanda. Sweden had previously released Sylvere Ahorugeze due to the length of his pre-trial detention. Failure to impose effective safeguards for his appearance at trial meant that the rights to justice of Rwandan genocide victims could not be guaranteed.

■ Norway ruled to extradite Charles Bandora. The case was subject to an appeal.

Impunity for war crimes and crimes against humanity

There were no investigations or prosecutions for allegations of war crimes and crimes against humanity committed by the Rwandan Patriotic Army in 1994 in Rwanda, and gross human rights violations by Rwandan armed forces in the Democratic Republic of the Congo, as documented in the UN mapping report.

Refugees and asylum-seekers

A cessation clause for Rwandan refugees was invoked on 31 December by UNHCR, the UN refugee agency, meaning that refugees would lose their status. By the end of the year, Rwandan refugees in various countries had no access to exemption interviews to demonstrate individual grounds for continued fear of persecution. The clause was due to take effect on 1 July 2012.

Amnesty International visits/reports

🚌 Amnesty International delegates visited Rwanda in February, July, October and November. An Amnesty International observer monitored the trial of Victoire Ingabire in September, October and November.

▤ Rwanda: Reveal whereabouts of disappeared businessman (AFR 47/001/2011)

▤ Rwanda: Unsafe to speak out – Restrictions on freedom of expression (AFR 47/002/2011)

▤ Rwanda: Respect freedom of expression and end arbitrary detentions and enforced disappearances (AFR 47/005/2011)

▤ Rwanda: Opposition politician jailed for exercising rights (PRE01/059/2011)

SAUDI ARABIA

KINGDOM OF SAUDI ARABIA

Head of state and government:	King Abdullah bin Abdul Aziz Al Saud
Death penalty:	retentionist
Population:	28.1 million
Life expectancy:	73.9 years
Under-5 mortality:	21 per 1,000
Adult literacy:	86.1 per cent

Planned protests inspired by events elsewhere in the region were ruthlessly suppressed and hundreds of people who protested or dared to call for reform were arrested; some were prosecuted on security-related and political charges. Thousands of people suspected of security-related offences remained in prison. The justice system and information about detainees, including prisoners of conscience, remained shrouded in secrecy, although it was clear that torture and grossly unfair trials continued. Cruel, inhuman and degrading punishments, particularly flogging, continued to be imposed and carried out. Women and girls faced severe discrimination in law and practice, as well as violence; increased campaigning

S

for women's rights resulted in arrests as well as some small improvements. Foreign migrant workers continued to be exploited and abused by their employers, generally with impunity. At least 82 prisoners were executed, a sharp rise over the previous two years.

Background

The government responded to planned pro-reform protests in early 2011 by extending additional benefits to citizens reported to be worth around US$127bn. However, sporadic protests continued, particularly by Shi'a Muslims in Eastern Province who alleged discrimination and called for the release of political prisoners. On 5 March, the Interior Ministry reaffirmed the total ban on public demonstrations, and a large mobilization by security forces combined with threats forestalled a planned "Day of Rage" by advocates of reform called on 11 March. Even so, hundreds of people were arrested in connection with protests in 2011, mainly members of the Shi'a Muslim minority, pro-reform activists and women's rights activists. Many were released without charge.

On 15 March, the government sent 1,200 Saudi Arabian troops in tanks and other armoured vehicles across the causeway to Bahrain to help crush pro-reform protests there, apparently at the invitation of Bahrain's ruling family.

Counter-terror and security

A new draft anti-terror law was discussed in the Shura council, the body that advises the King, but it had not been enacted by the end of the year. The version of the draft law leaked to Amnesty International proposed to add sweeping new powers to those already possessed by the Interior Ministry and mandate jail sentences for anyone deemed to have criticized the King or expressed opposition to the government. It would allow for suspects to be detained without charge or trial potentially indefinitely, while the trials and appeals of those prosecuted could constitute unfair trials, even though some offences could incur the death penalty. The draft would also empower the Interior Minister to order phone tapping and house searches without judicial authorization. The overly broad definition of terrorism in the draft raised concern that it could be used to penalize or suppress legitimate expression of dissent.

Thousands of security suspects continued to be held, many for long periods without charge despite the six-month legal limit on detention without trial. Among them were government opponents who had been detained for months or years without trial. Many security detainees had been held for years without being tried and convicted or had been convicted of acts that are not recognized internationally as constituting a crime.

Security suspects are generally held incommunicado after arrest and while under interrogation, often for months, before they are permitted family visits. Many are tortured or otherwise ill-treated. They are usually held until the authorities decide they are not a security threat or they undertake not to engage in opposition activities. Some are released but then quickly re-arrested; many are detained without charge or trial.

It remained impossible independently to determine the number of people imprisoned on security grounds or for suspected involvement in terrorism; however, some indication of the scale was evident from government statements in recent years. In February, the Justice Minister announced that the Specialized Criminal Court in Riyadh had issued preliminary verdicts in 442 cases, involving 765 security suspects. In April, the Interior Ministry said that 5,831 security detainees had been released in recent years, including 184 since the start of 2011; that 5,080 security detainees had been questioned and referred for trial while 616 were still being questioned; that 1,931 others had been questioned and could be referred to the Specialized Criminal Court; and that 1,612 people had been convicted of "terrorism offences". In addition, 486 people convicted of security-related offences were said by the Interior Ministry to have been compensated for being detained beyond the expiry of their sentence.

Freedom of expression

The Press and Publications Law was extended to cover web publishing in January and further amended in April, tightening restrictions on freedom of expression. Human rights defenders, peaceful advocates of political change, members of religious minorities and others who called for reforms were among those detained without charge or trial or convicted after unfair trials in which they had no legal representation.

■ Abdul Aziz al-Wuhaibi and six other men were arrested on 16 February, a week after they and others asked for the Islamic Umma Party to be granted legal recognition; it would have become Saudi Arabia's first political party. They were held virtually incommunicado at al-Ha'ir prison and pressed to renounce their political activities; five were later released but Abdul Aziz al-Wuhaibi, who refused to make such an undertaking, was charged and sentenced to seven years' imprisonment in September after a grossly unfair trial. Among other charges, he was accused of "disobeying the ruler" of Saudi Arabia.

■ Sheikh Tawfiq Jaber Ibrahim al-Amer, a Shi'a cleric, was arrested in February after he called for political reforms in a sermon. He was held incommunicado for a week, then released. He was re-arrested on 3 August and charged with "inciting public opinion" after persisting in his call for reform.

■ Prisoner of conscience Mohammed Saleh al-Bajady, a businessman and co-founder of the Saudi Civil and Political Rights Association (ACPRA), a human rights NGO, was arrested the day after attending a protest outside the Interior Ministry in Riyadh on 20 March. He was said to have been charged in connection with the formation of ACPRA, harming the reputation of the state and possessing banned books. He was on trial but his defence lawyers had not been permitted access to him or the trial.

■ Fadhel Maki al-Manasif, a human rights activist and advocate of the rights of the Shi'a Muslim minority, was arrested on 1 May and detained incommunicado until 22 August, when he was released. He was re-arrested on 2 October after he intervened as police arrested two elderly men. He was allowed to telephone his family on 10 October but was subsequently not permitted to see or call his family or lawyer, arousing fears that he could be subject to torture.

■ In November, 16 men, including nine prominent reformists who had tried to set up a human rights association, were given sentences ranging from five to 30 years in prison by the Specialized Criminal Court, which was set up to deal with terrorism-related cases, following a grossly unfair trial. They were convicted of charges that included forming a secret organization, attempting to seize power, incitement against the King, financing terrorism, and money laundering. Several of them had already been detained for three and a half years without charge and interrogated without the presence of their lawyers. Many had been held in prolonged solitary confinement. Lawyers and families were denied details of the charges against the men for

months and were denied access to many of the court proceedings, which reportedly began in May.

■ Firas Buqna and his colleagues Hussam al-Darwish and Khaled al-Rashid were arrested on 16 October in connection with publishing an episode of their online show, "We Are Being Tricked", concerning the incidence of poverty in Riyadh. They were released two weeks later.

Repression of dissent

The authorities suppressed attempts to organize protests and those who sought to protest were arrested and faced other forms of repression.

■ Muhammad al-Wad'ani, a teacher, was arrested at a pro-reform rally in Riyadh on 4 March. He was believed to be still held incommunicado, probably in al-Ha'ir prison, at the end of the year.

■ Khaled al-Johani, the only person to turn up to a planned "Day of Rage" protest in Riyadh on 11 March, was arrested. He remained held at the end of the year, charged with supporting a protest and communicating with foreign media. For the first two months he was held incommunicado in solitary confinement in 'Ulaysha prison; he may have been tortured. He was then transferred to al-Ha'ir prison in Riyadh, where he was allowed access to his family.

■ Rima bint Abdul Rahman al-Jareesh, a member of ACPRA, and Sharifa al-Saqa'abi were arrested along with more than a dozen others while protesting outside the Interior Ministry on 3 July. They were among a group of almost 50 men, women and children calling for the fair trial or release of male relatives held in detention without charge or trial – some had been held for up to 10 years. Those arrested were released after signing pledges not to protest again, but Rima bint Abdul Rahman al-Jareesh and Sharifa al-Saqa'abi were held for two days at a prison in Qasim, north of Riyadh. They had supported earlier petitions calling for reform.

Hundreds of Shi'a Muslims were arrested following protests in Eastern Province. Most were released but some remained in detention.

■ Hussain al-Yousef and Hussain al-'Alq, regular contributors to a Shi'a website which mostly discusses problems faced by members of Saudi Arabia's Shi'a minority, were among 24 people detained on 3 and 4 March following protests in the city of al-Qatif against the prolonged detention of Shi'a prisoners. Police kicked and beat at least three of the protesters. They were released uncharged on 8 March after they signed pledges not to protest again. Hussain al-Yousef was re-arrested on 27 March and held until 18 July, when he was said to be suffering from severe back pain and barely able to move.

Women's rights

Women continued to face severe discrimination both in law and in practice. They must obtain the permission of a male guardian before they can travel, take paid work, engage in higher education or marry, and their evidence carries less weight in a court of law than that of men. Domestic violence against women was believed to remain rife.

Women joined the calls for reform and organized in support of women's rights. One group launched an online campaign "Women2Drive" and urged Saudi Arabian women possessing international driving licences to start driving vehicles on Saudi Arabian roads from 17 June. Scores of women reportedly did so; some were arrested and made to sign pledges to desist. At least two were facing trial. The campaign subsequently became part of a new, wider campaign for women's rights entitled "My right, my dignity".

In September, the King announced that from 2015 women will have the right to vote and run in municipal elections, the country's only public poll, and to be appointed to the Shura council.
■ Manal al-Sharif, a computer security consultant, was arrested on 22 May, the day after police stopped her while she was driving, accompanied by her brother, in al-Khobar city. She had also uploaded a video of herself driving on the "Women2Drive" website on 19 May. She was released 10 days later.
■ On 27 September, Shaimaa Jastaniyah was sentenced to 10 lashes in Jeddah after she drove a car. The sentence was confirmed by the court that imposed it, and was being appealed at the end of the year.

Migrants' rights

Migrant workers continued to face exploitation and abuse by private and state employers, and victims had little or no redress. Typical abuses included long working hours, non-payment of salaries and violence, particularly against women domestic workers. Women domestic workers who fled abusive sponsors often ended up facing worse conditions in the illegal labour market.
■ In a rare case, the female employer of Sumiati binti Salan Mustapa, an Indonesian domestic worker who required hospital treatment in 2010 after allegedly being cut, burned and beaten by her employer, was sentenced four months' imprisonment in October, but then released on account of time served in detention.

Torture and other ill-treatment

New reports were received of torture and other ill-treatment, a pattern of abuse that was believed to remain common with interrogators seeking to extract "confessions" from suspects.
■ A Shi'a detainee, whose identity is being withheld because of fears for his safety, told Amnesty International that he was tortured for 10 days until he agreed to sign a "confession" by being made to stand for prolonged periods with his arms raised; beaten with an electric cable; struck in the face, back and stomach; and threatened that he would be raped by other prisoners.

Cruel, inhuman or degrading punishments

Flogging was routinely imposed as a sentence by the courts and carried out as the main or as an additional punishment. More than 100 men and women were sentenced to flogging.
■ In December, the Supreme Court upheld the sentences of six Bedouin men to "cross amputation" of their right hands and left feet for "highway robbery". All six were tried before a court in Riyadh in March 2011 with no legal assistance or representation. A court of appeal was reported to have upheld the verdict in October.
■ In Riyadh on 23 December, Abdul Samad Ismail Abdullah Husawy, a Nigerian man, had his right hand amputated for theft.

Death penalty

The recorded number of executions rose sharply, with at least 82 people executed, over triple the number recorded in 2010. Those executed included at least five women and at least 28 foreign nationals. At least 250 prisoners remained under sentence of death, including some sentenced for offences not involving violence, such as apostasy and sorcery. Many were foreign nationals, sentenced for drug-related offences after grossly unfair trials.
■ Ruwayti Beth Sabutti Sarona, an Indonesian woman, was reported to have been beheaded on 18 June after being convicted of the murder of her employer. Neither her family nor the Indonesian government were said to have been notified in advance of her execution.

■ Two Saudi Arabian brothers, Muhammad Jaber Shahbah al-Ja'id and Sa'ud Jaber Shahbah al-Ja'id, were executed on 30 July. They were sentenced to death in 1998 for murder. They did not have access to a lawyer at the original trial and Sa'ud Jaber Shahbah al-Ja'id was reported to have confessed under duress when the authorities arrested his elderly father to put pressure on him. Their families were reportedly not notified of the impending executions.

■ Abdul Hamid bin Hussain bin Moustafa al-Fakki, a Sudanese man, was beheaded in Medina on 19 September. He had been arrested in 2005 then charged and convicted of sorcery after he allegedly agreed to cast a spell at the behest of a man working for the religious police. He is alleged to have been beaten in detention and forced to "confess" to sorcery. His family were reportedly not notified in advance of his execution and were not allowed to repatriate his body to Sudan.

Amnesty International visits/reports

🚌 The government continued to bar visits by Amnesty International. Officials of the Saudi Arabia Embassy to the UK met Amnesty International representatives in July to complain about the organization's publication of the draft anti-terror law.

📕 Saudi Arabia: Repression in the name of security (MDE 23/016/2011)

📕 Surge in executions in Saudi Arabia (MDE 23/025/2011)

📕 Proposed Saudi Arabian anti-terror law would strangle peaceful protest (PRE01/357/2011)

📕 Amnesty International website "blocked in Saudi Arabia" (PRE01/364/2011)

📕 Saudi Arabia executes man convicted of "sorcery" (PRE01/466/2011)

📕 Flogging sentence for Saudi Arabian woman after driving "beggars belief" (PRE01/486/2011)

SENEGAL

REPUBLIC OF SENEGAL

Head of state:	Abdoulaye Wade
Head of government:	Souleymane Ndéné Ndiaye
Death penalty:	abolitionist for all crimes
Population:	12.8 million
Life expectancy:	59.3 years
Under-5 mortality:	92.8 per 1,000
Adult literacy:	49.7 per cent

The authorities used excessive force to suppress a number of demonstrations and people were arrested for expressing dissident political opinions. Torture of suspects was routine; one detainee reportedly died as a result. In southern Casamance, clashes between the army and an armed group intensified at the end of the year, leading to civilian casualties. Despite Senegal's legal obligations and repeated calls from the African Union, the Senegalese authorities expressed unwillingness to try former Chadian President Hissène Habré.

Background

Conflict between the army and the Democratic Forces of Casamance Movement (Mouvement des forces démocratiques de Casamance, MFDC) intensified at the end of the year, leading to several civilian and military casualties.

Throughout the year, President Abdoulaye Wade's candidacy for a third term in the 2012 elections provoked large demonstrations, particularly in the capital Dakar.

In June, violent clashes took place in Dakar between riot police and those protesting against a bill proposing changes to the regulation of the presidential election. The bill was withdrawn as a result.

In June, the implementing decree of a law creating a National Inspector of Places of Deprivation of Liberty was adopted but by the end of the year no appointment had been made.

Human rights violations and abuses in Casamance

Several civilians were killed or wounded in clashes between the MFDC and the army.

■ In November, 10 civilians collecting wood in Diagnon, 30km from Ziguinchor, the main city of

Casamance, were shot dead by alleged members of the MFDC.

Repression of dissent

Demonstrations against the political and economic situation were met with government force throughout the year.

■ In May, Malick Bâ was killed by gendarmes (paramilitary police) who used live ammunition against marchers protesting against the setting up of new local authorities in the community of Sangalkam.

Freedom of expression

Several people were arrested and one was sentenced to prison for publicly expressing opposition to the government.

■ In June, Alioune Tine, Secretary General of the African Assembly for the Defence of Human Rights (Rencontre Africaine pour la Défense des Droits de l'Homme, RADDHO) and Oumar Diallo were attacked by people allegedly close to the ruling party when attempting to protest against the contested constitutional reform.

■ In October, Malick Noël Seck, leader of a movement affiliated to the Socialist Party, was sentenced to two years' imprisonment for urging members of the Constitutional Council to reject President Wade's candidacy for a third term.

Torture and other ill-treatment

The police regularly tortured suspects; one reportedly died as a result.

■ In April, the naked and handcuffed body of Aladji Konaté, bearing signs of torture, was found by a river in Bakel town. Security forces said he had jumped into the river to escape arrest for alleged drug trafficking.

■ In September, three young men were ill-treated and wounded by gendarmes in the area of Thiaroye in Dakar after being arrested following a complaint from a neighbour. An investigation was opened and two gendarmes were confined to their quarters. By the end of the year, the alleged perpetrators had not yet been tried and the victims had received no compensation.

International justice – Hissène Habré

The African Union stated in March that former Chadian President Hissène Habré should be tried by a Special Court in Senegal. In June, a coalition of NGOs and victims of Hissène Habré's government brought a case against Senegal before the International Court of Justice for failing to try or extradite him. The government announced its decision in July to return Hissène Habré to Chad, where he has been sentenced to death in his absence, but this was suspended after protests by UN bodies and human rights organizations.

Amnesty International visits/reports

▣ Senegal: The sentence of a political opponent must be quashed (AFR 49/002/2011)

▣ Senegal: Authorities must not return former Chadian President to Chad (PRE01/343/2011)

SERBIA

REPUBLIC OF SERBIA, INCLUDING KOSOVO

Head of state:	Boris Tadić
Head of government:	Mirko Cvetković
Death penalty:	abolitionist for all crimes
Population:	9.9 million
Life expectancy:	74.5 years
Under-5 mortality:	7.1 per 1,000
Adult literacy:	97.8 per cent

Ratko Mladić and Goran Hadžić were arrested in Serbia and transferred to the International Criminal Tribunal for the former Yugoslavia (Tribunal). Forced evictions of Roma from informal settlements in Belgrade continued.

Background

Following the transfer of Ratko Mladić and Goran Hadžić to the Tribunal, the European Commission (EC) in October recommended that Serbia be granted EU candidate status.

EU-mediated talks between Serbia and Kosovo opened in March, aiming to resolve technical issues relating to regional co-operation, including customs agreements. Talks broke down in September after the Kosovo authorities in July opened customs posts at the boundary with Serbia. The subsequent violence triggered a political crisis; an agreement was reached in December on joint border management. In December, the European Council deferred their

S

decision on Serbia's candidacy to February 2012, conditional on Serbia reaching an agreement on co-operation with Kosovo.

International justice

In February, former Assistant Interior Minister Vlastimir Đorđević was convicted of crimes against humanity and war crimes in Kosovo in 1999 for persecutions on political, racial or religious grounds, murder, deportation and forcible transfer. He was sentenced to 27 years' imprisonment. The Trial Chamber found that Vlastimir Đorđević was "instrumental" in efforts to "conceal the murders of Kosovo Albanians", and "gave instructions for the clandestine transportation of bodies".

Former Bosnian Serb General Ratko Mladić was arrested in Vojvodina on 26 May, and transferred to the custody of the Tribunal on 31 May (see Bosnia and Herzegovina (BiH) entry).

On 20 July, Croatian Serb Goran Hadžić, the last suspect to be surrendered to the Tribunal, was arrested in a national park in Vojvodina, where he was apparently in hiding, and transferred to the custody of the Tribunal on 22 July (see Croatia entry).

The partial retrial for war crimes of Ramush Haradinaj, former commander of the Kosovo Liberation Army (KLA), and later Prime Minister of Kosovo, along with Idriz Balaj and Lahi Brahimaj, opened in August. The retrial was ordered because of the threat that witness intimidation had posed to the trial's integrity, but once again, a key prosecution witness refused to testify.

Serbia
Crimes under international law
Proceedings continued at Belgrade Special War Crimes Chamber in relation to war crimes in BiH, Croatia and Kosovo.

In January, nine members of the KLA "Gnjilane/Gjilan group" were convicted of war crimes against Serbs and non-Albanians and sentenced to a total of 101 years' imprisonment. In 1999, they unlawfully imprisoned more than 153 people and subjected them to inhumane treatment, torture and rape. At least 80 people were murdered, and 34 remained missing; eight members of the group remained at large. The verdict was appealed.

Zoran Alić and others were indicted in February for torture, rape, sexual slavery and the murder of 23

Roma, including minors and a pregnant woman, in Zvornik municipality, BiH in 1992. In June, three Serbs were indicted for criminal acts against civilians in Bijelina, BiH, in 1992, including murder and rape. Serbia's extradition request for Bosnian Army General Jovan Divjak, for war crimes in BiH, was rejected by an Austrian court in July on the basis that he was unlikely to receive a fair trial.

Nine members of the "Jackals" paramilitary unit, including Ranko Momić, extradited from Montenegro in April, were indicted by the Office of the War Crimes Prosecutor in May for the murders of 11 Albanian civilians in the village of Ćuška/Qyshk in 1999. Another member of the group, Siniša Mišić, was arrested for the same crime in November.

Enforced disappearances
No progress was made in the identification of further grave sites in Serbia.

In March, the UN Human Rights Committee urged the authorities to "urgently take action to establish the exact circumstances, which led to the burial of hundreds of people in Batajnica region [in 1999]", to ensure that all those responsible were prosecuted, and that relatives received adequate compensation.

Torture and other ill-treatment
Detainees and prisoners remained at risk of torture and ill-treatment due to the lack of effective oversight mechanisms and a National Preventive Mechanism, required under the Optional Protocol to the UN Convention against Torture. Prisons remained under-funded, overcrowded, understaffed and with insufficient medical personnel.

In July, a 2007 video of police officers in Vrsac police station repeatedly kicking 17-year-old Roma Daniel Stojanović appeared on YouTube. The Minister of Interior agreed to re-open an internal investigation, but charges against the officers were dropped when Daniel Stojanović was arrested for stealing in the same month.

Racism
In January, 14 Partizan football club supporters received sentences totalling 240 years' imprisonment for the murder of French citizen Brice Taton in September 2009. In June, the Constitutional Court banned the extreme right-wing organization Nacionalni stroj (National Order).

Attacks on Roma continued. In November, 120 Roma were made homeless when their settlement in Zvečanska Street was burned down. There was reasonable suspicion that the fire had been started by football supporters.

In March, a Romani minor was convicted of murdering a non-Roma, D.S., in the village of Jabuka in 2010 and sentenced to four years' juvenile detention. Also in March, six young men from Jabuka, who had been prominent in several days of attacks on the Romani community which followed the murder, were convicted of instigating ethnic, racial and religious hatred and given suspended sentences.

Discrimination

In September, the Bosniak Minority Council, unrecognized by the authorities, called on the government to end discrimination against the Bosniak minority, and in particular, economic discrimination in the Sandžak region. Albanians in southern Serbia continued to experience discrimination, including in education.

The Commissioner for Equality received 349 complaints from individuals and NGOs, under provisions of the 2009 Anti-Discrimination Law (ADL).

In June, the High Court ruled that the newspaper *Press* had violated the ADL by publishing homophobic comments on its internet site, which the court considered represented hate speech against the LGBT population. In November, member of parliament Dragan Marković Palma was convicted of discrimination on the basis of sexual orientation.

The government cancelled Belgrade Pride in October in violation of their obligation to guarantee freedom of expression and assembly, following threats by right-wing groups. Homophobic attacks continued: in Belgrade in October, a lesbian was attacked with a knife and severely injured and a gay man was attacked and left bruised and concussed in Novi Sad.

Forced evictions

Forced evictions continued across Belgrade.
■ In August, 20 Roma, including 10 children, were forcibly evicted from a building in Skadarska Street, and left in the street with all their possessions.
■ Two local activists were arrested in October for trying to peacefully prevent the forced eviction of a Kosovo Roma woman and her children from her home.
■ In November, the forced eviction of 33 Roma families, including 20 families displaced from Kosovo, was postponed after interventions by local and international organizations. The Ministry of Human Rights agreed to draft procedures for the conduct of evictions.

Roma living at the Belvil settlement, who had been informed in April that they would be resettled in prefabricated houses, in advance of the construction of an access road funded by the European Investment Bank, remained at risk of forced eviction at the end of the year, pending the city's approval of an action plan.

Refugees and migrants

Under pressure from the EU, the government introduced border exit controls in order to prevent "abuse of the visa-free regime". This violated the right to freedom of movement of Serbian citizens, mainly Roma and Albanians, seeking to leave the country.

In May, the Interior Minister warned Roma that seeking asylum in the EU would damage Serbia's national interest. By 31 October, the numbers of Serbians claiming asylum had dropped to 3,000 from 17,000 in 2010.

Serbia received 2,700 applications for asylum; none were granted. In November, police allegedly beat Afghan and Pakistani migrants, and burned down their camp near Subotica, close to the border with Hungary.

Kosovo

A coalition government led by prime minister Hashim Thaçi took office in February. In April, Atifete Jahjaga, former Deputy Director of the Kosovo Police, was elected president, after the Constitutional Court annulled the February election of Behgjet Pacolli.

In October, the EC expressed concerns about the rule of law, corruption, the weakness of the judiciary and public administration, and economic sustainability. Despite the government's failure to implement a Reintegration Strategy for forced returnees – a condition for visa liberalization – in December the EC announced that a visa dialogue would start in January 2012.

The UN Secretary-General in October reported a 24 per cent increase in incidents affecting minority communities throughout Kosovo, including in the predominantly Serbian northern municipalities.

The situation in the north

In July, the Kosovo government retaliated against Belgrade's 2008 embargo on goods from Kosovo by banning Serb products, even in the north. The Kosovo authorities, in a clandestine operation led by the Kosovo Police (KP), took control of two border posts in the northern municipalities of Leposavić/q and Zubin

S

Potok. Kosovo Serbs responded by setting up roadblocks which aimed to prevent the NATO-led Kosovo force (KFOR) and the EU-led police and justice mission (EULEX) from transporting government customs officials to the posts.

On 26 July, Enver Zymberi, a KP officer, was shot in the head and killed and another officer severely injured in a Serb attack on one border post. Another border post was set alight. The following day, a KFOR helicopter carrying KP officers was fired on.

In August, Kosovo Serbs refused to remove their barricade at the Jarinje/Jarinja border post, despite an agreement between both governments and KFOR, that Serbian KP officers should staff the border posts.

In September, seven Kosovo Serbs were seriously injured at Jarinje/Jarinja, after KFOR used tear gas and rubber bullets to disperse a crowd, some of whom had thrown stones. Four KFOR personnel were injured by a home-made bomb, one seriously. On 23 November, another 21 KFOR soldiers were injured when KFOR attempted to remove the barricade.

On 28 November, 25 KFOR soldiers were injured at Jagnjenica when they were attacked when attempting to remove another barricade; they responded with water cannon, tear gas and pepper spray. Between 30 and 50 Serbs were reportedly injured.

Crimes under international law

EULEX prioritized the investigation of organized crime and corruption leading to continuing impunity for outstanding war crimes cases. Few cases were conducted by local prosecutors. The lack of effective witness protection persisted.

EULEX established a Brussels-based Task Force, headed by the former Head of the UN Interim Administration Mission in Kosovo (UNMIK)'s Department of Justice. It aimed to investigate allegations in a report adopted by the Parliamentary Assembly of the Council of Europe in January, including that in 1999, Prime Minister Hashim Thaçi and other KLA members were responsible for the abduction, torture, ill-treatment and murder of Serb and Albanian civilians transferred to prison camps in Albania, some of whom were killed and their organs removed for trafficking.

■ In August, former KLA commander Sabit Geçi was convicted of war crimes, and sentenced to 15 years' imprisonment. With three others, he was found guilty of the torture and ill-treatment of Albanians at a prison camp near Kukës, in Albania.

■ The trial of former Minister of Transport and ex-KLA leader Fatmir Limaj and nine others opened in November. They were charged with war crimes, including ordering the torture and killing of at least eight prisoners, mostly Serbs, at Klečka/Kleçkë prison camp in Drenica/Drenicë in 1999. An arrest warrant issued in March against Fatmir Limaj, a parliamentary deputy, was not enforced until the Constitutional Court ruled in September that deputies did not enjoy parliamentary immunity for actions outside their official responsibilities.

In September, Agim Zogaj, a witness in the Klečka/Kleçkë case, committed suicide in Duisburg, Germany. He left a letter which accused EULEX of psychological torture. EULEX declined to confirm whether he had been a protected witness.

Enforced disappearances

The Law on Missing Persons, promulgated in August, applied to all persons reported missing up to December 2000, including Serbs and Roma abducted after the war. The law provided for the right of relatives to know the fate of their family members and for a database of missing persons. The Law on the Status and Rights of the Heroes, Invalids, Veterans and Members of the KLA, Families of Civilian Victims of War, adopted in December, discriminated against the relatives of missing civilians, who received less than half the monthly compensation payable to the relatives of military victims. Some 1,799 missing people were still unaccounted for in November.

The Department of Forensic Medicine (DFM) was run by EULEX and the Ministry of Justice. In September, the DFM and the Serbian Commissioner for Missing Persons visited potential mass graves at Rudnica in Serbia and exhumations at the Belaćevac mine in Kosovo, where at least 25 Kosovo Serbs were reportedly buried. The DFM exhumed the bodies of 42 individuals; 51 missing persons were identified and 79 bodies were returned to families for burial. Fourteen mis-identified bodies were exhumed, most of which were re-identified, and returned to their relatives.

EULEX war crimes police investigated enforced disappearances, but lacked resources to effectively address the backlog of outstanding cases.

Torture and other ill-treatment

The European Committee for the Prevention of Torture reported in October that in June 2010 it had received "numerous and consistent allegations of physical ill-treatment by KP officers from persons who were or had recently been taken into custody", and highlighted the ill-treatment of activists from the NGO Vetëvendosje! during and after arrest.

The Kosovo Rehabilitation Centre for Torture Victims in February reported on inadequate conditions and a lack of professional staff in mental health institutions and that women detained in Pristina Psychiatric Clinic were kept tied to their beds.

Lack of accountability

In August, the UN Under Secretary-General for Legal Affairs rejected a compensation claim by 155 Roma and Ashkali who had suffered lead poisoning after UN agencies including UNMIK had moved them in 1999 to camps on lead-contaminated land in north Mitrovica/ë.

Over the year, the Human Rights Advisory Panel ruled admissible over 40 complaints, mainly by Serbs from Kosovo, that UNMIK had failed to effectively investigate the abduction of their relatives during or after the conflict.

Discrimination

Roma, Ashkali and Egyptians experienced cumulative discrimination including in access to education, health care and employment; few enjoyed the right to adequate housing. In May, the OSCE reported that "Kosovo institutions fall short of fulfilling their commitments to create appropriate conditions for the integration of Roma, Ashkali and Egyptian communities".

Refugees and migrants

According to UNHCR, the UN refugee agency, 1,143 people from minority communities voluntarily returned to Kosovo; 25 Kosovo Albanians, 64 Kosovo Serbs and 430 Roma, Ashkali and Egyptians, considered by UNHCR to be in need of continued international protection, were forcibly returned from western Europe, while 166 minority returnees were subject to "induced return".

While registration improved, returnees without documentation remained effectively stateless. In the absence of a case-management system for forcibly repatriated people, only a small percentage of €2.4 million "re-integration fund" was spent. Many returnees were denied basic rights and remained at risk of cumulative discrimination amounting to persecution. Returned children continued to be denied access to education.

Violence against women

The law relating to civilian victims of war did not include provisions, proposed by NGOs, for women raped during the war to be afforded civilian victim status and appropriate compensation.

Amnesty International visits/reports

🚍 Amnesty International delegates visited Serbia in April, July and October, and Kosovo in October.

📄 Serbia: Home is more than a roof over your head (EUR 70/001/2011)

📄 Serbia: Time for a law against forced evictions (EUR 70/025/2011)

SIERRA LEONE

REPUBLIC OF SIERRA LEONE

Head of state and government:	Ernest Bai Koroma
Death penalty:	abolitionist in practice
Population:	6 million
Life expectancy:	47.8 years
Under-5 mortality:	192.3 per 1,000
Adult literacy:	40.9 per cent

The government confirmed an official moratorium on executions. Women, particularly in rural areas, faced difficulties accessing maternal health care services. There were lengthy delays in the criminal justice system. Prisons were overcrowded and conditions poor. Violence against women and girls was widespread. There was violence between rival political parties ahead of elections in 2012.

Background

In March, the Special Court for Sierra Leone, sitting in The Hague, finished hearing evidence in the trial of former Liberian President Charles Taylor, who is charged for his individual criminal responsibility in crimes against humanity and war crimes committed during the 11-year armed conflict in Sierra Leone, including murder, rape, conscripting or enlisting children under the age of 15 into armed forces and other inhuman acts. The judges were still deliberating at the end of the year.

The peace accord included an amnesty measure, meaning that only 13 people were indicted on charges of gross human rights violations.

The Persons with Disabilities Act was passed on 5 May, with the aim of establishing the National Commission for Persons with Disabilities and

S

prohibiting discrimination against people with disabilities. However, the Commission had not been established by the end of the year.

No progress was made in the constitutional review, which was not expected to resume until after the 2012 national elections.

In May, Sierra Leone's human rights record was considered under the UN Universal Periodic Review. Sierra Leone accepted all of the recommendations except those on the rights of lesbian, gay, bisexual and transgender people.

Death penalty

There were three people on death row at the end of the year. Two men were sentenced to death for murder on 19 and 26 May respectively.

In March, the Court of Appeal overturned the death sentence of a woman who had been convicted of murdering her child in 2005.

In April, the authorities pardoned three death row prisoners, including one woman, and commuted all other death sentences to life imprisonment, except that of Baby Allieu, who remained on death row after being sentenced to death for murder in November 2010.

In December, the conviction of a woman formerly on death row was overturned on appeal by the High Court. She had been on bail since 2010.

In September, the government confirmed an official moratorium on executions.

Justice system

Magistrates were overworked and under-trained. Constant adjournments, missing case files, lack of transport for prisoners to and from court, and a shortage of magistrates created lengthy delays.

A pilot legal aid scheme saw some successes, but was only operational in Freetown. A bill to expand the provision of legal aid had not been introduced to parliament by the end of the year.

Chiefs' courts continued to exceed their jurisdiction, often issuing large fines and arbitrarily imprisoning people. A new Local Courts Act was passed in September; however it had not been implemented by the end of the year.

Corporate accountability

Land use agreements between corporations, the government and communities were characterized by inadequate consultation, lack of information, lack of

transparency and intimidation. Some human rights defenders faced intimidation and threats over their work on corporate accountability.

■ In October, 40 people were arrested in Sahn Malen Chiefdom, Pujehun district after protests against the agreement for the lease of their land to the oil palm and rubber company, Socfin. Fifteen were charged with "riotous behaviour" and "unlawful assembly" under the 1965 Public Order Act and remanded in prison custody for seven days before being released on bail. The case was ongoing at the end of the year.

Forced evictions

On 11 May, over 100 people – disabled residents, their family members and carers – were forcibly evicted by the police from a home and training centre in Freetown. A seven-day eviction notice was posted on the door before the eviction. Police fired tear gas into the building and threw out their belongings.

Freedom of expression

Journalists faced harassment, threats and assault. The Public Order Act of 1965, whose provisions on seditious libel restrict freedom of expression, was not repealed. The Right to Access Information Bill, introduced to parliament in 2010, had not been passed by the end of the year.

■ In September, Mohamed Fajah Barrie, a BBC sports journalist, and three other journalists were beaten up by presidential guards after a football match. Mohamed Fajah Barrie was beaten to a coma. President Koroma publicly stated his commitment to investigate, but by the end of the year no one had been prosecuted.

Maternal health

Pregnant women and girls continued to face serious challenges accessing drugs and medical care crucial to ensuring safe pregnancy and childbirth despite the launch of a major government initiative in April 2010 to provide free care to pregnant women and girls. The quality of care was frequently substandard, and many women continued to pay for essential drugs, despite the free care policy. As a result, many women and girls living in poverty continued to have limited or no access to essential care in pregnancy and childbirth. A critical shortcoming within the health care system was the absence of any effective monitoring and accountability systems. Maternal health services were particularly poor in rural areas.

Police and security forces

Poor conditions in police detention cells and unlawfully prolonged detention without charge were commonplace. Investigations into sexual and gender-based violence were often inadequate.

■ In June, nine people, including two aged 15 and 16 and four people with disabilities, were detained in Kissi police station for 17 days following a land dispute in Grafton. They were eventually released without charge.

Prison conditions

There was severe overcrowding in several of Sierra Leone's prisons. Most prisons had extremely poor sanitation and used buckets for toilets.

There were three juvenile detention centres in the country, two in Freetown and one in Bo. Children were routinely detained with adults in police and prison cells in other parts of the country. Police regularly exaggerated the age of children before transferring them to prison.

Only Pademba Road prison had a hospital, but inmates often had to pay to receive treatment.

Violence against women and girls

Domestic violence, rape and other forms of sexual violence remained widespread. Few cases were reported to the authorities and these were often poorly investigated, with few successful prosecutions. Medical facilities routinely charge victims of sexual violence for medical reports, without which successful prosecution is virtually impossible. Social stigma, expensive and intimidating court processes and intervention by family members and traditional leaders meant that out-of-court settlements were common. Family support units, tasked with investigating sexual and gender-based violence, were understaffed and under-resourced and struggled to cope.

Harmful and discriminatory traditional practices continued, such as female genital mutilation (FGM) and forced or early marriage, although FGM of girls under 18 decreased slightly. Some human rights defenders faced harassment and threats over their work on FGM. National law does not expressly criminalize the practice.

Little progress was made in addressing legislative loopholes in the "Three Gender Acts" and the Child Rights Act 2007, undermining the legislative protection of women and children's rights. Although NGOs raised awareness of these acts, by the end of the year implementation remained poor.

No efforts were made to amend Section 27(4)(d) of the Constitution, which permits discrimination on the basis of adoption, marriage, divorce, burial and inheritance.

Political violence

Political tension between supporters of the two main political parties, the Sierra Leone People's Party (SLPP) and the All People's Congress (APC), grew ahead of elections in 2012.

The findings and recommendations of the Shears Moses Independent Review Panel, established in April 2009 to investigate incidents of political violence in March 2009, had not been made public by the end of the year.

■ On 9 September, a clash between APC and SLPP supporters left one person dead and 23 injured when the police used tear gas and live ammunition to disperse the crowd. Stones were thrown at SLPP supporters. The APC's Bo headquarters were burnt down and an APC chairperson was stabbed. The President set up an investigative panel, but the recommendations were yet to be implemented at the end of the year.

Amnesty International visits/reports

🚗 Amnesty International delegates visited Sierra Leone in September and November.

▨ At a crossroads: Sierra Leone's free health care policy (AFR 51/001/2011)

S

SINGAPORE

REPUBLIC OF SINGAPORE

Head of state:	Tony Tan Keng Yam (replaced S.R. Nathan in September)
Head of government:	Lee Hsien Loong
Death penalty:	retentionist
Population:	5.2 million
Life expectancy:	81.1 years
Under-5 mortality:	2.8 per 1,000
Adult literacy:	94.7 per cent

Opposition candidates made small but unprecedented gains in the May parliamentary elections, winning six out of 87 seats. The government used restrictive laws to silence its critics, bringing criminal defamation cases against them and censoring the media. The death penalty, administrative detention and judicial caning were retained in law and practice.

Freedom of expression

The authorities continued to threaten and punish government critics, using sweeping criminal and civil defamation laws.

During the parliamentary election, the government eased some restrictions on the use of new media (such as blogs and Facebook) for political campaigning.

■ British author Alan Shadrake was imprisoned on 1 June, charged with contempt of court for his book which criticized the Singapore judiciary's use of the death penalty. He was released and deported on 9 July.

■ Opposition leader Chee Soon Juan, declared bankrupt after a defamation lawsuit by the country's two former prime ministers, was denied government permission, required as a bankrupt, to travel to Dubai to address an International Bar Association conference in October.

Detention without trial

In September, the Home Minister rejected a call by former political detainees to repeal the Internal Security Act (ISA).

The government alleged that two ISA detainees, Jumari bin Kamdi and Samad bin Subari, were members of Jemaah Islamiyah, and that a third,

Abdul Majid Kunji Mohamad, was a member of the Moro Islamic Liberation Front. All three were arrested in neighbouring countries and transferred to Singapore.

■ On 1 September, the authorities released one ISA detainee, Mohamed Khalim bin Jaffar, an alleged Jemaah Islamiyah member detained in 2002.

Death penalty

At least five people were sentenced to death. In early 2011, Singapore posted some of its death penalty statistics on the internet. According to the Singapore Prison Service, there were six judicial executions in 2008, five in 2009 and none in 2010. No official information was available on executions carried out in 2011.

■ Yong Vui Kong, a 23-year-old Malaysian national, exhausted his judicial appeals and remained on death row, pending a decision on clemency from the President. He was sentenced to death in 2009 for drug trafficking, a crime which carries a mandatory death sentence.

Torture and other ill-treatment

Judicial caning was imposed for some 30 offences, including immigration violations.

■ Ho Beng Hing, aged 21, was convicted in September of running away from a reform centre for offenders. He was sentenced to three strokes of the cane, more than three years in prison and a fine.

International scrutiny

In May, Singapore's human rights record was assessed under the UN Universal Periodic Review. The government rejected recommendations to end its use of mandatory death sentences and impose a moratorium on the death penalty. Singapore supported some recommendations to protect the rights of migrant workers.

Amnesty International visits/reports

▢ Singapore rejects calls to end death penalty and caning (ASA 36/003/2011)

▢ Singapore: Suggested recommendations to states considered in the 11th round of Universal Periodic Review (IOR 41/008/2011)

SLOVAKIA

SLOVAK REPUBLIC

Head of state:	Ivan Gašparovič
Head of government:	Iveta Radičová
Death penalty:	abolitionist for all crimes
Population:	5.5 million
Life expectancy:	75.4 years
Under-5 mortality:	6.9 per 1,000

Roma continued to experience discrimination in access to education, health care and housing. The government was found to have violated the human rights of a woman who alleged an enforced sterilization.

Background

Following a vote of no confidence in October, early elections were scheduled for March 2012. The Prime Minister and her cabinet had limited powers to act on crucial social and economic policy measures.

At the end of November, after negotiations failed between the government and the trade unions over hospital privatization and working conditions for doctors, over 1,200 doctors in public hospitals resigned from their jobs, and a number of hospitals were reportedly unable to provide adequate health care services. The government declared a state of emergency which obliged the doctors to come to work. A failure to comply risked criminal charges. A compromise was reached between the government and the doctors and the state of emergency ended on 8 December.

Discrimination – Roma

Slovakia was criticized by international human rights monitoring bodies and NGOs for continued discrimination against Roma. In April, the UN Human Rights Committee stated that Roma were excluded from political participation, and faced discrimination in access to education, health care and housing.

In June, the Minister of the Interior responded to existing tensions between non-Roma and Roma in the village of Žehra, eastern Slovakia. He proposed an amendment to the Act on Municipalities, allowing a municipality to separate into two parts. NGOs and the Government Plenipotentiary for Roma Communities (Plenipotentiary) criticized the initiative, as it could lead to municipalities dividing on ethnic lines.

■ In September, the municipality of Vrútky constructed a concrete wall to separate a kindergarten, retirement homes and apartment buildings from an area mostly inhabited by Roma.

Right to education

In April, the UN Human Rights Committee noted that reports of de facto segregation of Romani children in schools continued, and that Romani children were placed too often in classes for pupils with "mild mental disability". The Committee urged the government to eradicate segregation in the educational system.

In May, the European Commission held a meeting on Roma inclusion in Slovakia, where participants recognized the continuation of segregation in education. The meeting concluded with a call on the government to adopt a clear strategy for desegregation. In December, the Council of Europe's Commissioner for Human Rights recommended that the Slovak authorities introduce a duty on all schools to desegregate.

■ In September, Romani parents learned that the elementary school in the town of Levoča was to have separate first grade classes for Romani children. The school established the classes allegedly due to a petition submitted by non-Roma parents calling for a restriction on the number of children coming from "anti-social" communities. The school's director stated that the classes were intended to create a suitable education environment for the Romani children. The Plenipotentiary expressed concerns that the establishment of separate classes may amount to segregation based on ethnicity and said that a complaint would be filed to the State School Inspectorate if the practice continued.

■ Prešov County Court in eastern Slovakia ruled in December that the primary school in the town of Šarišské Michaľany had violated the anti-discrimination legislation by placing Romani children into separate classes.

Housing rights

Inhabitants of informal Romani settlements faced the threat of, and experienced, forced evictions, and lacked access to basic services. In September, the Parliament proposed an amendment to building regulations, to oblige municipalities to demolish unauthorized constructions without legal title to the land. The proposal suggested penalties for those municipalities which failed to carry out the demolition within a period required by law. The Plenipotentiary's office expressed concerns that the proposal

S

contravened anti-discrimination legislation and that it would severely affect Romani informal settlements. The Ministry of Construction and Regional Development announced in November that it would work on this proposal and submit a new draft amendment in 2012.

■ On 16 May, Demeter, an informal Romani settlement of approximately 80 people in Košice, was demolished by the municipality, which argued that the settlement and a nearby landfill site were a hazard to health and safety. Residents who asked for emergency housing were accommodated in tents. The Plenipotentiary expressed concerns that the municipal action amounted to a forced eviction, contrary to both Slovak and international law.

■ In May, the mayor of the town of Žiar nad Hronom called on the central government to "address the Roma problem", in particular that of informal settlements. The initiative – reportedly supported by more than 300 mayors – called for strict rules and control of "anti-social inhabitants". In June, the municipality of Žiar nad Hronom announced the relocation of Roma from an informal settlement to a site providing accommodation in metal containers. The eviction was carried out in November. The local authorities reportedly did not provide any help to the affected individuals arguing that none of them had asked, and 13 Roma were effectively made homeless.

■ Nearly 90 Romani families in the village of Plavecký Štvrtok, north of Bratislava, continued to be threatened with forced eviction. Previous demolition notices issued in 2010 were stopped by the prosecutor's office due to procedural shortcomings. However, the mayor of the village announced that the municipality planned to issue new demolition notices to the owners of the illegally constructed houses. In October, the houses were cut off from running water. The municipality installed a water tank for the settlement to use on a pay-as-you-go basis.

Enforced sterilization of Romani women

In April, Slovakia was criticized by the UN Human Rights Committee for the narrow focus of the investigation into past allegations of enforced sterilizations. The Committee also expressed concerns over the lack of information on the elimination of forced sterilizations, which, allegedly, continued to take place.

■ On 8 November, the European Court of Human Rights, in its first judgement on enforced sterilization, ruled that the government had violated human rights of V.C., a Romani woman. The sterilization – without her full and informed consent – amounted to a major interference in her reproductive health status. Her right not to be subjected to ill-treatment and her right to respect for private and family life had been violated. The Court also noted that in her records, medical staff would refer to V.C.'s ethnic origin, which indicated a certain mindset in the way the health of a Roma should be managed. A legal representative from the NGO Centre for Civil and Human Rights (Poradňa pre občianske a ľudské práva) said that V.C.'s case was just the tip of the iceberg. She called again on the government to stop denying its responsibility for the practice, apologize to all its victims and fully compensate them.

Torture and other ill-treatment

Slovakia was repeatedly reminded by the UN Human Rights Committee that it should strengthen its efforts to combat racist attacks committed by law enforcement personnel, particularly against Roma.

■ In September, the District Court in Košice opened a hearing in the case of alleged ill-treatment of six Romani boys by police officers in April 2009. The accused police officers and the parents of the Romani boys gave testimonies. The case was pending at the end of the year.

Guantánamo detainees

Two out of the three men formerly held in US custody in Guantánamo Bay, accepted by Slovakia in 2010, left for their native Tunisia and Egypt. One of them was reportedly arrested upon his arrival in Egypt in June and charged with terrorism. The Minister of the Interior stated that the departure of both men from Slovakia was their choice. All three former Guantánamo detainees had received residence permits in Slovakia in 2010. While waiting for these permits, they had been detained in a centre for illegal migrants where they went on hunger strike to protest against their detention and the living conditions.

Rights of lesbian, gay, bisexual and transgender people

In April, an amendment of the Labour Code came into force, extending the protected grounds against discrimination to include sexual orientation.

In June, the second annual Bratislava Pride march included more than 1,000 participants. The organizers acknowledged good co-operation with the police and therefore progress from the previous year (when the police had announced they would not be able to protect the participants, and the organizers had therefore changed the march's route). Minor incidents were reported, and the police arrested a few counter-demonstrators. The Pride march was attended by the mayor of Bratislava, as well as some members of the parliament.

Amnesty International visits/reports

🚍 Amnesty International delegates visited Slovakia in February, May, June and November.

📄 Right to education without discrimination: Policy brief to the Slovak government (EUR 72/003/2011)

SLOVENIA

REPUBLIC OF SLOVENIA

Head of state:	Danilo Türk
Head of government:	Borut Pahor
Death penalty:	abolitionist for all crimes
Population:	2.0 million
Life expectancy:	79.3 years
Under-5 mortality:	3.0 per 1,000
Adult literacy:	99.7 per cent

Despite some positive measures, the authorities failed to restore the rights of people (known as the "erased") whose permanent residency status was unlawfully revoked in 1992. Discrimination against Roma continued.

Discrimination

The "erased"

Despite some positive measures, the authorities failed to guarantee the rights of former permanent residents of Slovenia originating from other former Yugoslav republics, whose legal status was unlawfully revoked in 1992. It resulted in violations of their economic and social rights. Some of them were also forcibly removed from the country.

In March, the Parliament adopted a law which allowed for restoration of permanent residency status to the majority of the "erased". The introduction of the law was an important first step towards full restoration of their rights. However, it failed to provide them with

reparation for the human rights violations they suffered. Access to economic, social and cultural rights was not guaranteed by the law. The authorities failed to present further plans for full restoration of the rights of the "erased", and a large number of people were excluded from provisions of the law.

The case *Kuric v. Slovenia* was referred to the Grand Chamber of the European Court of Human Rights in February 2011 at the request of the government. In July, the Grand Chamber held a hearing in the case. A decision was pending at the end of the year. In July 2010 the Court had ruled that the "erasure" of applicants' identity had violated their right to remedy, and their right to family and private life.

Roma

The government failed to put in place adequate monitoring mechanisms on discrimination against Roma. There were no effective remedies for acts of discrimination committed by private and public actors.

Rights to adequate housing, water and sanitation

Despite some positive steps taken by the authorities, the majority of Roma were still denied access to adequate housing.

Many Roma lived in isolated and segregated Roma-only settlements or slums in rural areas, where they lacked security of tenure. In the informal settlements, they were denied protection from forced evictions and had no access to public services, including sanitation. In some municipalities Roma had to fetch water – for drinking, cooking and personal hygiene – from polluted streams, and public taps at petrol stations and cemeteries.

In October, following pressure by civil society organizations, the authorities of Škocjan municipality took steps to provide the Roma settlement there with access to water.

In May, the Governmental Commission for Roma Protection recommended that all municipalities make water available to informal Roma settlements. However, government funding was not provided to implement the recommendation.

In September, the UN Special Rapporteur on the human right to safe drinking water and sanitation called on the authorities to immediately ensure access to water and sanitation for the Roma and to provide them with security of tenure, including by regularizing the informal settlements.

S

Amnesty International visits/reports

🚌 Amnesty International delegates visited Slovenia in March.

📰 Parallel lives: Roma denied rights to housing and water in Slovenia
(EUR 68/005/2011)

SOMALIA

SOMALI REPUBLIC

Head of state of Transitional Federal Government:	**Sheikh Sharif Sheikh Ahmed**
Head of government of Transitional Federal Government:	**Abdiweli Mohamed Ali (replaced Mohamed Abdullahi Mohamed Farmajo in June)**
Head of Somaliland Republic:	**Ahmed Mohamed Mahamoud Silanyo**
Death penalty:	**retentionist**
Population:	**9.6 million**
Life expectancy:	**51.2 years**

Armed conflict between pro-government forces and the Islamist armed group al-Shabab continued in southern and central Somalia. Thousands of civilians were killed or injured as a result of armed conflict and generalized violence, and hundreds of thousands were displaced. In July and August, the UN declared famine in six areas of southern Somalia. Access by aid agencies to civilians remained constrained by fighting, insecurity and restrictions by parties to the conflict. Humanitarian workers, journalists and human rights activists remained targeted for abuses. The Transitional Federal Government (TFG) and allied militias extended their control over the capital Mogadishu and some areas in southern Somalia. In October, Kenya's armed forces intervened in Somalia against al-Shabab. Armed groups increasingly carried out forced recruitment, including of children, and continued abducting, torturing and unlawfully killing people in areas under their control. Serious human rights abuses, including war crimes, remained unpunished. In semi-autonomous Puntland, security deteriorated with attacks against officials, judges and journalists and local clashes in Galkayo. In Somaliland, refugees and migrants faced increased hostility.

Background

In February, the TFG and the AU Mission in Somalia (AMISOM) launched a military offensive against al-Shabab in Mogadishu. In August, al-Shabab announced its withdrawal from the capital, leaving the TFG and AMISOM in control of most of Mogadishu at the end of the year, although clashes continued on the outskirts of the capital.

In southern Somalia, TFG-aligned militia supported by Kenya and Ethiopia took control of territory previously held by al-Shabab, including Dobley, a town on the Kenyan border. In October, following kidnappings in border areas, Kenya intervened militarily on the side of the TFG in southern Somalia, stating it was taking action against al-Shabab. In December, Kenya decided that its troops in Somalia would join AMISOM. On 31 December, pro-TFG and Ethiopian forces captured the border town of Beletweyne.

In June, the Kampala Accord – brokered by Uganda and the UN to resolve tensions between the TFG President and the Speaker of Parliament – resulted in Prime Minister Farmajo resigning. A road map was adopted to end the transitional period in August 2012. Agreed by the TFG, the Puntland and Galmudug regional authorities and the Alhu Sunna Waal Jama militia in September, the road map prioritized restoring security, adopting a constitution, holding elections, political outreach and good governance.

AMISOM, mandated to protect TFG institutions with an authorized strength of 12,000 troops, increased its troops to some 9,800 Ugandan and Burundian soldiers, joined by 100 Djiboutian soldiers in December. AMISOM addressed accusations of indiscriminate shelling and shooting by its troops. In March, three Ugandan soldiers were found guilty of carelessness by a disciplinary court in two incidents during which civilians were shot at. AMISOM also endorsed an "indirect fire policy" to better control the use of mortars and artillery.

In July, the UN declared that more than 750,000 people were at risk of starvation, mainly in southern and central Somalia. In November, the UN stated that three out of six areas in these regions were no longer in a state of famine; however, 250,000 people remained at risk of starvation and 4 million in need of assistance.

International support continued for TFG security forces and allied militia, despite their lack of accountability for ongoing, serious human rights abuses. The UN Monitoring Group highlighted continuous violations of Somalia's arms embargo. In July, the UN Security Council expanded the sanctions regime to include individuals responsible for recruiting and using child soldiers, and for violations of international law. However, the UN Monitoring Group was not given additional resources to carry out this expanded mandate.

The human rights situation was mentioned by the UN Secretary-General, the UN Independent Expert on Somalia and during Somalia's Universal Periodic Review at the Human Rights Council. However, no mechanism was established to investigate crimes committed under international law and address long-standing impunity.

The UN Security Council continued to strengthen anti-piracy measures. It called on states to participate in the fight against piracy, investigate and prosecute suspected pirates and strengthen the Somali authorities' capacity to bring pirates to justice.

Indiscriminate attacks

Thousands of civilians were killed or injured in the fighting, including in unlawful attacks. Parties to the conflict continued to use mortars and artillery in areas densely populated or frequented by civilians in Mogadishu, killing or injuring thousands of people in what were often indiscriminate attacks. Civilians were also killed and injured in shooting incidents between different TFG units in Mogadishu, and by improvised explosive devices and grenades increasingly set off by al-Shabab or their sympathizers since August. Al-Shabab claimed responsibility for suicide attacks which killed or injured hundreds of people. Civilians were killed or injured in fighting between TFG allies and al-Shabab in or near towns and in air strikes, some conducted by Kenya, in southern and central Somalia.

■ In May, 1,590 people were treated for weapons-related injuries in three Mogadishu hospitals according to the WHO. Of these, 735 were children aged below five who had burns, chest injuries and internal haemorrhage caused by blasts, shrapnel and bullets. This coincided with intense fighting, including with heavy weapons, between AMISOM and the TFG against al-Shabab around Bakara market, despite a high concentration of civilians in that area.

■ On 4 October, a truck exploded at Km4, a busy road intersection by a TFG compound in Mogadishu, killing more than 70 people and injuring more than 100. Among those killed were some 50 students and their parents, who were checking the results of scholarship applications to study abroad at the Ministry of Education. Al-Shabab claimed responsibility for the attack.

■ On 30 October, an air strike hit a camp for internally displaced people (IDPs) in Jilib, Lower Juba, killing at least five people, including three children. At least 52 others were injured, including 31 children. The Kenyan army stated that it had targeted an al-Shabab military camp in an air raid on that day in the same area, but denied killing civilians. No results of a Kenyan government investigation were available by the end of the year.

Internally displaced people, refugees and migrants

Fighting, insecurity and acute malnutrition displaced hundreds of thousands of people. Some 1.36 million Somalis were internally displaced at the end of 2011, mostly in southern and central Somalia, according to UNHCR, the UN refugee agency.

In July, around 35,000 people fleeing drought in southern Somalia arrived in Mogadishu. Reports of sexual violence against women and girls in IDP camps in the capital increased from July onwards.

In October, some 41,000 people were displaced within and around Mogadishu and Lower Juba due to fighting or fear of fighting.

In August, the Puntland authorities forcibly returned some internally displaced men back to southern and central Somalia and detained others.

The flow of civilians to neighbouring countries increased. During 2011, 164,375 Somalis fled to Kenya and 101,333 to Ethiopia. Some countries, including Saudi Arabia, deported Somalis back to southern and central Somalia despite the risks they would face there.

In June, the European Court of Human Rights ruled in the lead-case of *Sufi and Elmi v. the United Kingdom* that enforcing removals to southern and central Somalia would be lawful only in exceptional circumstances, in light of the dire human rights and humanitarian situation there (see UK entry and Europe and Central Asia overview).

Restrictions on humanitarian aid

Some 4 million people needed humanitarian support by the end of 2011 because of armed conflict and

S

drought. International assistance increased after famine was declared in July. Humanitarian operations remained impeded by fighting, insecurity, restrictions on access and intimidation of aid workers. Humanitarian workers were abducted and at least six were killed. Concerns about aid being diverted continued.

■ On 20 October, Médecins Sans Frontières (MSF) was forced to suspend a measles vaccination campaign for 35,000 children in Daynile outside Mogadishu after fighting broke out between AMISOM and the TFG against al-Shabab.

■ In July, an al-Shabab spokesman stated that aid organizations could assist people affected by drought in southern Somalia, but later clarified that agencies banned by the group in January 2010 would not be allowed back. On 28 November, six UN agencies and 10 aid organizations were banned by al-Shabab from operating in areas under its control. Al-Shabab groups closed some of these agencies' compounds and looted some humanitarian equipment.

■ Humanitarian assistance in IDP camps in Mogadishu was impeded by shooting incidents between TFG units and people looting food aid. On 5 August, at least five people were reportedly killed in the Badhabo IDP camp, as trucks transporting food aid were looted by TFG militias. The TFG warned that looters would be punished. However, in November, the Karan District Commissioner was reportedly pardoned after being sentenced to 15 years' imprisonment by a military court for looting aid.

■ On 25 October, three Danish Refugee Council workers were kidnapped in Galkayo South. Two of them remained held at the end of the year.

■ On 18 November, Ahmed Jama Mohamed, a Norwegian Refugee Council worker, was shot dead by unidentified gunmen in Galkayo.

■ On 23 December, Muhyedin Yarrow and Mohamed Salad, two World Food Programme workers, and Abdulahi Ali, a Somali NGO worker, were killed in Mataban town, Hiran province.

■ On 30 December, Philippe Havet and Andrias Karel Keiluhu, two MSF workers, were shot and killed in Mogadishu.

Child soldiers

Al-Shabab continued to forcibly recruit boys, some as young as eight, into their forces before and during military operations. Many were sent to the front line. Girls were also recruited to cook and clean for al-Shabab forces or forced to marry its members.

The TFG reaffirmed its commitment to prevent the use of child soldiers. However, at least 46 TFG recruits aged below 18 were selected for military training abroad. The TFG detained ex-child combatants with adults in poor conditions and failed to provide effective reintegration opportunities after their release.

Abuses by armed groups

Al-Shabab factions continued to torture and unlawfully kill people they accused of spying or not conforming to their own interpretation of Islamic law. They killed people in public, including by stoning them to death, and carried out amputations and floggings. They also imposed restrictive dress codes on women and men.

■ On 4 January, a man named as Nur Mohamed Nur, aged about 19, had his foot and hand amputated in Baidoa after al-Shabab accused him of theft. Al-Shabab reportedly forced Baidoa residents to watch the amputation.

■ On 6 March, two men, named as Abdullahi Hajji Mohammed and Abdinasir Hussein Ali, were shot and killed in public by al-Shabab members in the Maslah military camp in Mogadishu. The first man was reportedly accused of spying for the TFG, the second of killing al-Shabab members.

■ On 16 June, Shamarke Abdullahi Mohamoud, reportedly aged 18 and accused of raping a girl, was stoned to death in the Hiran region by al-Shabab members.

■ In late August, the decapitated bodies of two young men were found in northern Mogadishu. Several other decapitated bodies were found in the same period, during which al-Shabab had reportedly warned that those co-operating with the TFG and AMISOM would be beheaded.

Freedom of expression

Somali journalists and civil society organizations continued to be intimidated by parties to the conflict. At least three media workers were killed. In Puntland, the authorities arbitrarily arrested journalists and restricted media freedom.

■ On 4 August, Farah Hassan Sahal, a Radio Simba worker, was shot in Bakara market, Mogadishu during a TFG and AMISOM offensive against al-Shabab, and later died.

■ On 2 September, Noramfaizul Mohd, a Malaysian cameraman for Bernama TV, was killed by gunfire and

S

his colleague Aji Saregar injured while covering a relief mission in Mogadishu. On 26 September, AMISOM announced that four Burundian soldiers were responsible and should be tried in their own country.

■ On 18 December, Abdisalan Sheikh Hassan, a journalist for Horn Cable TV and Radio Hamar, was shot in the head by a man in military uniform while being driven through Mogadishu, according to witnesses. He died shortly after. The TFG promised to investigate.

■ On 2 July, Faysal Mohamed Hassan, a journalist for Hiiraan Online, was sentenced to one year's imprisonment by a court in Puntland for "publishing false news". He was pardoned on 31 July.

In November, the Puntland authorities banned the Universal TV and Somali Channel TV stations, accusing them of working against peace and security. The ban on Universal TV was lifted on 3 December.

Death penalty

In Mogadishu, at least 32 death sentences and six executions were reported following TFG military court trials which lacked basic guarantees for fairness. A presidential decree in August gave the TFG military court jurisdiction over civilians in some Mogadishu areas vacated by al-Shabab. The TFG later gave assurances that civilians tried by the military court would not be executed, and that civilians would be tried by ordinary courts in future.

TFG-allied militia in southern Somalia reportedly executed at least two soldiers. In Puntland, at least four men were sentenced to death and three were executed. The Galmudug authorities executed one man for murder in Galkayo town.

■ On 22 August, two men were executed by firing squad in Mogadishu after being convicted of murder by the TFG military court.

Somaliland

Thousands of people were reportedly displaced by clashes between the Somaliland security forces and an armed group in the disputed Sool and Sanag regions. In June, a peace activist was shot and wounded in the Sool region.

Journalists were reportedly harassed by the Somaliland authorities.

In May, a new law was passed to regulate civil society organizations. There were concerns that it could increase government control over international and national organizations in Somaliland and restrict their work.

Refugees, asylum-seekers and migrants faced increasing hostility. In September, all "illegal immigrants" were given one month to leave the country by the authorities. Around 80,000 people were affected by this declaration, most of them Ethiopians.

■ In June, Abdusalam Haji Mukhtar, an Ethiopian refugee, was forcibly returned to Ethiopia, where he risked torture.

Amnesty International visits/reports

▨ In the line of fire: Somalia's children under attack (AFR 52/001/2011)

▨ Somalia: A humanitarian and human rights catastrophe (AFR 52/012/2011)

▨ Suggested recommendations to States considered in the 11th round of Universal Periodic Review, 2-13 May 2011, Somalia (IOR 41/008/2011)

SOUTH AFRICA

REPUBLIC OF SOUTH AFRICA

Head of state and government:	Jacob G. Zuma
Death penalty:	abolitionist for all crimes
Population:	50.5 million
Life expectancy:	52.8 years
Under-5 mortality:	61.9 per 1,000
Adult literacy:	88.7 per cent

There were substantial improvements in access to treatment and care for people living with HIV. However, discriminatory factors still limited their access to HIV health services, particularly in rural areas. Discrimination and targeted violence against asylum-seekers and refugees occurred and policy changes reduced their access to the asylum system. Police used excessive force against protesters, and their misuse of lethal force remained a concern. Systematic hate-motivated violence against lesbians, gay men, bisexual and transgender people began to be officially addressed. The National Assembly passed the Protection of State Information Bill, which threatened freedom of expression.

Background

High levels of poverty, inequality and unemployment continued to fuel protests in poor urban communities.

S

Local government authorities were often the targets of these protests because of corrupt practices or slow delivery of basic services. Some members of President Zuma's government and senior police officials were dismissed or suspended pending investigations into alleged corruption. There was increasing concern that the conduct of state business was being affected by political tensions within the ruling African National Congress party linked to its 2012 national conference, in which the party's new leadership will be elected. Significant rulings by the higher courts compelled the government to amend or reverse decisions affecting the independence and integrity of prosecution and investigation bodies. There was widespread opposition to proposed legislation curbing access to state information.

Right to health – people living with HIV

An estimated 5.38 million people were living with HIV. The number of AIDS patients receiving antiretroviral treatment had increased to 1.4 million people by the end of June. This resulted from progress in implementing new policies and guidelines, including people being able to access treatment at an earlier stage of the disease and expanding access to treatment at the primary health clinic level.

Despite these improvements, discrimination still prevented many from accessing HIV-related health services, particularly people living in poor rural households. Their access to treatment or their ability to remain on treatment continued to be affected by the cost and unreliability of local transport systems and poor road infrastructure in rural communities. Food insecurity, as well as arbitrary processes and decision-making regarding people's eligibility for support grants, were also important factors. Persistent patriarchal attitudes continued to affect rural women's access to services and their autonomy in making decisions about their own sexual and reproductive health.

In October, the Ministry of Health launched a new Human Resources for Health Strategy. Its aims included solving the country's critical shortage of public health care professionals, particularly in rural areas, which are home to 44 per cent of the population but served by less than 20 per cent of the country's nurses and doctors.

On World AIDS Day on 1 December, following a national consultation led by the South African National AIDS Council (SANAC), the government launched a new five-year National Strategic Plan for HIV and AIDS, sexually transmitted infections and tuberculosis. The document was intended to guide the efforts of provincial governments and other institutions to achieve five main goals. These included ensuring access to antiretroviral treatment for at least 80 per cent of those needing it, reducing HIV-related social stigma and protecting the rights of people living with HIV.

In December, civil society organizations launched the National Health Insurance Coalition to campaign for adopting a scheme to reduce inequalities in access to health services.

Refugees and asylum-seekers

The government initiated potentially far-reaching changes to the asylum system, including access to asylum determination procedures. In May, the Department of Home Affairs closed the Johannesburg Refugee Reception Office following successful litigation for closure by local businesses. No alternative office was opened. All applicants for asylum or recognized refugees needing to renew their documents were directed to two existing and over-burdened refugee reception offices in Pretoria. In the following months, new or "transferred" applicants struggled to gain access to Home Affairs officials there. Some queued repeatedly from the early morning and were subjected to verbal abuse or beatings with *sjamboks* (whips) and batons by security personnel, according to evidence submitted in the North Gauteng High Court. Their inability to lodge applications or renew their documents left them at risk of fines, detention and direct or constructive *refoulement*.

On 14 December, the High Court found unlawful the decision not to open a new refugee reception office in Johannesburg, and ordered the Director General of Home Affairs to reconsider it and consult those most affected. Evidence had emerged during the court proceedings that the refusal to open a new office was linked to a government decision to move all asylum services to ports of entry. The case was brought by the Consortium for Refugees and Migrants in South Africa and the Coordinating Body of the Refugee Communities, with the assistance of Lawyers for Human Rights. At the end of the year legal proceedings challenging the closure of the Port Elizabeth Refugee Reception Office were postponed until February 2012.

In August, the Department of Home Affairs stated that only Zimbabweans without valid immigration or asylum permits would be deported when the 2009 moratorium against deportations of Zimbabweans was lifted in September. However, when the moratorium ended, human rights organizations and the International Organization of Migration recorded incidents of *refoulement* and unaccompanied minors being deported without proper measures to protect them.

Violence and property destruction targeted against refugees and migrants occurred in many areas throughout the year. Local business forums appeared to be linked to many of the attacks. During May, over 60 foreign-owned shops were forcibly closed, looted or destroyed completely in different areas of Gauteng province and in the Motherwell area of Port Elizabeth. Police officers in the Ramaphosa informal settlement area near Johannesburg condoned or actively participated in the Greater Gauteng Business Forum's action, including threatening non-nationals with violence and forcibly closing or removing property from their shops.

In many of these attacks, local police stations failed to call in reinforcements to stop the violence from spreading. However, despite the efforts of humanitarian and civil society organizations, by the end of the year the police authorities had still not set up a systematic and effective national strategy for preventing or reducing violence against refugees and migrants.

In October, police allegedly used excessive force during mass arrests of "suspected illegal foreign nationals" in Nyanga township, Cape Town, and verbally abused them as unwanted foreigners. Those affected included recognized refugees who had shown their documents to the police. One refugee from the Democratic Republic of the Congo, who required medical treatment for his injuries, was actively obstructed from lodging a formal complaint against the police.

Death penalty

On 22 September, the High Court ruled in a case involving two Botswanan nationals that the government must not extradite individuals at risk of the death penalty, without first receiving written assurances from the requesting state that the accused will not face the death penalty under any circumstances. The state lodged an appeal against the ruling, which had not been heard by the end of the year.

On 15 December, at a ceremony to honour the memory of 134 political prisoners executed at Pretoria Central prison by the apartheid state, President Zuma reconfirmed his government's commitment to abolition of the death penalty.

Deaths in custody and extrajudicial executions

The police oversight body, the Independent Complaints Directorate (ICD), reported a 7 per cent decline between April 2010 and March 2011 in recorded deaths in custody and resulting from "police action". However, KwaZulu-Natal province continued to have a high rate of such incidents, with more than one third of the recorded national total of 797 deaths.

Members of police special units, particularly Organized Crime, were implicated in incidents of suspicious deaths allegedly resulting from torture or extrajudicial executions. Victims' families faced obstacles in accessing justice because of poor official investigations, lack of legal aid funds or intimidation. In December, media exposure of information about alleged assassinations by members of the Cato Manor Organized Crime Unit led the ICD to establish an investigation team to review the evidence.

■ No charges had been brought by the end of the year against police officers responsible for the death of 15-year-old Kwazi Ndlovu in April 2010. Forensic and other evidence indicated that the boy was lying on a couch in his home when he was shot and killed with high velocity rifles by police from the Durban Organized Crime Unit.

Excessive use of force

Police used excessive force against demonstrators protesting against corruption and the failure of local authorities to provide access to adequate housing and other basic services, including in Ermelo in March and in Ficksburg in April. ICD-led investigations and pre-trial proceedings against police officers charged with murder, assault and other offences were continuing at the end of the year.

In December, police officials announced restrictions on the police use of rubber bullets against protesters due to increased reports of serious injuries.

■ In April, Andries Tatane died after he was beaten with batons and shot with rubber bullets at close range by police in Ficksburg.

S

Torture and other ill-treatment

In May, the Independent Police Investigative Directorate (IPID) Act became law, but it was not operational by the end of the year. Under the Act, the ICD's original mandatory investigation obligations were expanded to include incidents of torture and rape by police. Police failure to report suspected incidents or obstruction of ICD/IPID investigations were made criminal offences.

In July, the National Commissioner of correctional services ordered an internal inquiry into the alleged torture of a prisoner by six prison officers using an electric shock stun device. A police investigation was also instituted, but no progress had been reported by the end of the year.

A draft law to make torture a criminal offence had not been presented in Parliament by the end of the year.

Rights of lesbian, gay, bisexual and transgender people

Hate-motivated violence, in particular against lesbian women, caused increasing public concern.

■ On 24 April, 24-year-old Noxolo Nogwaza was brutally murdered in KwaThema township. An active member of the Ekurhuleni Pride Organizing Committee (EPOC), she was raped, repeatedly stabbed and beaten to death. The police responsible for the investigation into her murder had made no progress by the end of the year, and no suspects had been arrested. EPOC began a campaign to have the case transferred to another police station.

In May, the Ministry of Justice announced the establishment of a government and civil society "Task Team" to seek solutions to preventing further such incidents. The Task Team was still meeting in November, but without clear results. There was also slow progress in the development of a draft law to prosecute hate crimes.

In December, a lesbian, gay, bisexual and transgender (LGBT) rights organization, OUT Well-Being, gave expert evidence about the impact of hate crimes on victims and the wider community during the sentencing phase of a trial in the Germiston magistrate's court. The defendants had been found guilty of assaulting a gay man and the court noted that the accused had been motivated by hatred and disrespect for gay people.

Human rights defenders

Harassment of human rights defenders and criminalization of their work continued. Those affected included journalists, staff from the Public Protector's office, anti-corruption investigators and community-based organizations promoting economic and social rights.

■ In July, 12 supporters of the housing rights movement, Abahlali baseMjondolo, were acquitted of all charges in the state's case against them. These included murder, attempted murder and assault relating to violence in the Kennedy Road informal settlement in September 2009. In its ruling the court noted "numerous contradictions and discrepancies in the state's case" and the lack of any reliable evidence to identify the accused. The court also found that police had directed some witnesses to point out members of Abahlali-linked organizations at the identification parade. At the end of the year, Abahlali supporters who were displaced after their homes were looted and destroyed in 2009 were still unable to return safely and rebuild their homes. In October, at a meeting with the Executive Mayor of the Ethekwini Metropolitan Municipality about this issue, a senior official allegedly threatened Abahlali's president, S'bu Zikode, with violence. A police investigation into his criminal complaint against the official had made no progress by the end of the year.

Freedom of expression

In November, the Protection of State Information Bill was passed by the National Assembly and referred to the upper house of Parliament for consideration. The bill was opposed by a campaign involving hundreds of civil society organizations, including media. The bill's provisions included minimum prescribed terms of imprisonment of from three to 25 years for a range of offences, including collecting or communicating or receiving classified state information or "harbouring" someone with such information. The bill did not include an explicit defence on the grounds of public interest, although a court could impose a lesser sentence if "substantial and compelling circumstances" existed. In response to the campaign, some changes were made to the bill before it was passed by the National Assembly, including making punishable the classification of state information deliberately to conceal unlawful acts by officials. Other concerns remained unaddressed.

Amnesty International visits/reports

🚌 Amnesty International delegates visited South Africa in May, June and November.

📱 South Africa: Police failure to protect human rights activist Jean-Pierre Lukamba is symptomatic of wider failure to respect the rights of refugees and migrants (AFR 53/002/2011)

📱 Hidden from view: Community carers and HIV in rural South Africa: Background information (AFR 53/005/2011)

📱 South Africa: Call for South Africa to fulfil its international and domestic obligations in the protection of the rights of refugees and asylum-seekers (AFR 53/007/2011)

📱 South Africa: Controversial secrecy bill could 'smother free speech' (PRE01/584/2011)

SOUTH SUDAN

REPUBLIC OF SOUTH SUDAN

Head of state and government:	**Salva Kiir Mayardit**
Death penalty:	**retentionist**
Country data covers South Sudan and Sudan:	
Population:	**44.6 million**
Life expectancy:	**61.5 years**
Under-5 mortality:	**108.2 per 1,000**
Adult literacy:	**70.2 per cent**

South Sudan became an independent state on 9 July, six months after a referendum under the 2005 Comprehensive Peace Agreement (CPA). Negotiations with Sudan continued on the sharing of oil, citizenship and border demarcation. Armed conflict and inter-communal violence led to mass displacement, killings and destruction of property. Security forces arbitrarily arrested and detained journalists, members of opposition groups and demonstrators. A large influx of South Sudanese returnees and refugees from Sudan continued.

Background

The Transitional Constitution of the Republic of South Sudan (Transitional Constitution) was adopted by the South Sudan Legislative Assembly and came into force on 9 July for an undefined interim period. A provision within the Transitional Constitution allowed for southern members of the Sudan Parliament to be integrated into the South Sudan Legislative Assembly.

The UN Mission in South Sudan (UNMISS) came into effect on 9 July for an initial period of one year. South Sudan became a member of both the UN and the AU later that month.

Leaders of armed opposition groups signed ceasefire agreements with the government, and over 1,500 of their fighters awaited integration into the Sudan People's Liberation Army (SPLA). On 23 July, armed opposition leader Gatluak Gai was killed in disputed circumstances, three days after signing an agreement brokered by the local authorities in Unity State. In early August, Peter Gadet, the former leader of the South Sudan Liberation Movement/Army (SSLM/A), signed an agreement with the government although breakaway factions from his group remained active under the SSLM/A. Armed opposition leader Gabriel Tanginye and his two deputies remained under house arrest in the capital, Juba, where they had been placed in April following fighting between his forces and the SPLA in Upper Nile and Jonglei. No charges were brought against them by the end of the year.

■ On 4 November Peter Abdul Rahaman Sule, leader of the opposition group United Democratic Front, was arrested in Western Equatoria State for allegedly recruiting young people. At the end of the year he remained in detention without charge.

■ On 19 December, George Athor, leader of the armed opposition group the Sudan Democratic Movement and its military wing, the South Sudan Army, was killed by the SPLA in Morobo County, South Sudan.

Armed conflict

Fighting between the SPLA and armed opposition groups resulted in human rights abuses by all parties, including unlawful killings of civilians and the destruction and looting of property. Armed opposition groups used antitank mines along main roads, resulting in civilian deaths and injuries.

■ On 8 October, 18 civilians, including four children, were killed when a bus ran over an antitank mine on the road between Mayom and Mankien. On 29 October the breakaway armed opposition group of the SSLM/A and the SPLA clashed in Mayom, Unity State. The SPLA reported 15 civilians killed and 18 injured.

■ On 16 November, an armed opposition group believed to be loyal to George Athor attacked three villages in Pigi County, Jonglei State, and burned and looted property. Four civilians were reportedly killed and many more fled.

S

Communal violence

A series of retaliatory attacks took place between the Lou Nuer and Murle, two ethnic groups in Jonglei. On 15 June the Lou Nuer attacked the Murle in Pibor County; several villages were looted and burned and over 400 people were killed. On 18 August the Murle launched an attack against the Lou Nuer in Uror County, where more than 600 people were reported killed and over 200 missing. Seven villages were destroyed. The UN estimated that around 26,000 people were displaced as a result of the fighting. One Médecins Sans Frontières (MSF) staff member was killed and the MSF compound and clinic were looted and burned; the World Food Programme warehouse was looted in the same incident. From 31 December, armed Lou Nuer attacked the Murle in Pibor town, looted the MSF clinic and burned civilian homes. Tens of thousands of people were displaced and hundreds killed by the attack.

Fighting between communities in Mayiandit County in Unity State, on the border with Warrap State, on 17 September led to 46 people being killed and 5,000 displaced.

Freedom of expression, association and assembly

Security forces harassed and arbitrarily detained journalists, members of opposition groups and demonstrators for criticizing the government.

■ On 23 August in Kuacjok, Warrap State, member of parliament Dominic Deng Mayom Akeen was arrested and assaulted by armed security personnel. He was detained for one day in relation to a media statement regarding food shortages.

■ On 30 September, Nhial Bol, editor-in-chief of *Citizen* newspaper, was arrested and briefly held by the police following an article alleging corruption by a Warrap State minister after the closure of the offices of a Chinese oil company and the arrest of its general manager.

■ On 4 October, secondary school students from Wau in Western Bahr el-Ghazal State peacefully protested against rising food prices and low salaries for teachers. Security forces responded with gunfire and tear gas. At least seven people, including students, were arrested and remained in detention at the end of the year in Wau prison; two people died from gunshot wounds by security forces.

■ Ngor Garang and Dengdit Ayok, chief editor and journalist respectively with *The Destiny* newspaper, were arrested separately in early November by members of the National Security Services. Ngor Garang was reportedly beaten in detention and both were released on 18 November. It was believed their arrest related to an article criticizing the President.

Torture, other ill-treatment and enforced disappearances

Security forces including the South Sudan Police Service (SSPS) harassed, arrested, tortured or otherwise ill-treated people, including UN and NGO staff. A number of individuals were subjected to enforced disappearance. On 26 July, the President ordered the dissolution of South Sudan's national security and intelligence special branch, and its public security branch. The former director of public security and criminal investigation, General Marial Nour Jok, was arrested and detained on 30 July following allegations of his involvement in the creation of illegal detention centres, as well as torture and corruption.

■ The whereabouts of John Louis Silvino, an architect at the Ministry of Housing, remained unknown following his disappearance on 25 March.

■ In October, four police officers were arrested and faced trial after Jackline Wani, aged 17, was tortured by police from the Criminal Investigation Department following allegations of theft on 13 June.

Refugees and internally displaced people

South Sudanese who had lived in Sudan prior to independence continued to return as they were no longer eligible for citizenship rights in Sudan. By the end of the year, over 10,000 people remained in camps for internally displaced people at Kosti way station in Sudan awaiting return to South Sudan.

From June, there was a large influx of refugees from Sudan after conflict erupted between the Sudan Armed Forces (SAF) and the armed opposition group Sudan People's Liberation Army-North (SPLA-N).

Death penalty

More than 150 prisoners were on death row. At least five people were executed: one in August in Juba Prison, as well as two on 11 November and two on 21 November in Wau Prison.

Amnesty International visits/reports

🚌 Amnesty International delegates visited South Sudan in February/March, April, August/September and November/December.

📄 South Sudan: A human rights agenda (AFR 65/001/2011)

📄 South Sudan: Two journalists arrested (AFR 65/003/2011)

📄 Sudan-South Sudan: Destruction and desolation in Abyei (AFR 54/041/2011)

SPAIN

KINGDOM OF SPAIN

Head of state:	**King Juan Carlos I de Borbón**
Head of government:	**Mariano Rajoy (replaced José Luis Rodríguez Zapatero in December)**
Death penalty:	**abolitionist for all crimes**
Population:	**46.5 million**
Life expectancy:	**81.4 years**
Under-5 mortality:	**4.1 per 1,000**
Adult literacy:	**97.7 per cent**

There were reports of the police using excessive force during demonstrations. Spain maintained the regime of incommunicado detention for those suspected of terrorism-related offences. People belonging to ethnic minorities were targeted for identity checks. The armed group Euskadi Ta Askatasuna announced the end of the armed struggle.

Background

On 10 January, the armed Basque group Euskadi Ta Askatasuna (ETA) unilaterally declared a permanent and general ceasefire. On 20 October, ETA announced the end of its armed struggle.

Demonstrations by the so-called 15M or "Indignados" movement took place in cities all over Spain starting on 15 May. Demonstrators demanded changes in the political and economic systems, and in social policies including employment, education and health.

On 20 November, the conservative Popular Party won the general elections by an absolute majority, and in December Mariano Rajoy was elected Prime Minister.

Torture and other ill-treatment

There were allegations of excessive use of force by law enforcement officials during demonstrations by the 15M movement across Spain between May and August.

■ On 27 May, riot police officers of the autonomous Catalan police force intervened to disperse demonstrators from Catalonia Square in Barcelona. Medical evidence and video footage corroborated reports that riot police hit apparently peaceful demonstrators with their batons and fired rubber bullets at them. The police officers did not appear to wear identification numbers on their uniform. On 8 June, the Catalan government stated that no inquiry into the allegations of excessive use of force was necessary.

■ Angela Jaramillo reported that while she stood alone, close to the demonstration in Calle Castellana in Madrid on 4 August, a riot police officer hit her in the face and on the legs. Another woman who assisted Angela Jaramillo said she was also repeatedly hit with batons by riot police and suffered injuries on her neck, hip and legs. Both filed complaints against the police the following day.

■ On 17 October, the High Court of Barcelona sentenced two municipal police officers to 27 months' imprisonment for the torture of a student from Trinidad and Tobago in September 2006. The same two police officers had been involved in another incident earlier in 2006, and three other men had filed complaints of ill-treatment against them, but investigations into those allegations had been closed in July 2007.

In January, the Catalan government abolished the Code of Police Ethics, which had implemented the European Code of Police Ethics. The Police Ethics Committee, which was mandated to receive and examine complaints from individuals about police conduct and to assess police compliance with the Code of Police Ethics, was suspended after most of its members resigned.

■ At the end of the year, two police officers, charged with killing Osamuyia Akpitaye while he was being forcibly deported from Spain in June 2007, had not been put on trial.

■ In November, the Supreme Court acquitted four civil guards convicted by the Criminal Court of Guipúzcoa in December 2010 for torturing Igor Portu and Mattin Sarasola while they were in police custody on 6 January 2008.

S

- Ali Aarrass, a Moroccan/Belgian national suspected of terrorism-related offences in Morocco, was sentenced to 15 years' imprisonment in Rabat in November. He had been extradited from Spain to Morocco in December 2010 in breach of interim measures ordered by the UN Human Rights Committee, after which his lawyers in Belgium repeatedly alleged that the Moroccan security services tortured him during interrogation and that he did not receive a fair trial. A complaint before the Human Rights Committee against Spain was still pending at the end of the year.
- Mohamed Zaher Asade and Hasan Alhusein, two Syrian nationals released from prison in September 2010 after completing eight-year sentences for terrorism-related offences, remained under threat of expulsion to Syria despite facing a real risk of torture or other ill-treatment there. Mohamed Zaher Asade had lodged an appeal against his expulsion, but his request to suspend the enforcement of his expulsion pending a final decision was dismissed. An expulsion order issued against Hasan Alhusein in August was pending at the end of the year.

Counter-terror and security – incommunicado detention

Spain continued to disregard calls by international human rights bodies to abolish the use of incommunicado detention for those suspected of terrorism-related offences. The regime allowed detainees to be held for up to 13 days, during which time they did not have access to a lawyer of their choice, could not consult their state-appointed lawyer in private, did not have access to a doctor of their choice and could not have their family informed of their whereabouts.
- In March, the European Court of Human Rights ruled in *Beristain Ukar v. Spain* that Spain had violated the European Convention on Human Rights. It had failed to conduct an effective investigation into the allegations of ill-treatment by Aritz Beristain Ukar while he was held in incommunicado detention in September 2002.
- On 15 February, the Supreme Court acquitted Mohamed Fahsi of belonging to a terrorist organization and ordered an investigation into his allegations that he was tortured while detained incommunicado for four days in January 2006.
- On 25 January, the Madrid district court ordered a court investigation into the complaint by Maria

Mercedes Alcocer of torture during her incommunicado detention in December 2008. On 30 May 2011, the Supreme Court overturned Maria Mercedes Alcocer's conviction of collaborating with an armed group, as the only evidence against her had been a statement she made while held incommunicado.

Racism and discrimination

People belonging to ethnic minorities continued to be targeted for discriminatory identity checks, and civil society activists observing those checks faced judicial proceedings for obstructing the work of the police. In March, the UN CERD Committee urged Spain to stop the practice of identity checks based on ethnic or racial profiling, but at the end of the year the authorities continued to deny the practice and no steps had been taken to eradicate it.

In November, the government approved a Strategy to Combat Racism, Discrimination and other related forms of intolerance. However, a government-sponsored anti-discrimination bill failed to be adopted before the parliamentary elections in November.
- Two municipalities in Catalonia, Lleida and El Vendrell, modified their regulations to ban the wearing of full-face veils in municipal buildings and spaces. Thirteen other municipalities in the region had initiated the process to introduce a similar ban. In June, the High Court of Justice of Catalonia endorsed the ban in Lleida, finding that concealing the face was at odds with the principle of equality between women and men.
- In September, the Catalan government presented a bill to amend legislation on the establishment of places of worship. The bill aimed to drop the requirement for municipalities to provide available space to build new places of worship. The lack of availability of places of worship was particularly severe for religious minorities including Muslims and Evangelical Christians.

Violence against women

According to the Ministry of Health, Social Policy and Equality, 60 women were killed by their partners or former partners during 2011.
- Susana Galeote was murdered by her former partner in February. She had filed a complaint and a restraining order against him in 2010. She had applied for the telephone assistance service provided by the government for victims of gender violence. Her request was turned down as she was considered to be at a low risk of being attacked.

An amendment to the Aliens Law in July provided that expulsion proceedings would not be opened against women in an irregular situation who report gender-based violence, until the criminal case against the alleged perpetrator had been resolved. If expulsion proceedings had already been initiated, they would be suspended pending the outcome of the complaint.

Refugees, asylum-seekers and migrants

According to figures issued by the Ministry of the Interior there was an increase in the number of irregular migrants arriving by sea.

According to UNHCR, the UN refugee agency, 3,414 people claimed asylum during the year. Only 326 applicants received refugee recognition and 595 were granted subsidiary protection.

Notwithstanding at least four rulings by the Andalusia High Court of Justice recognizing the right of asylum-seekers to move freely throughout Spanish territory, the Ministry of the Interior continued to prevent asylum-seekers in Ceuta and Melilla from moving to the mainland.

Enforced disappearances

The definition of enforced disappearance as a crime against humanity in domestic legislation continued to fall short of obligations under international law, despite Spain's ratification of the International Convention against enforced disappearance.

The accusation against Judge Baltasar Garzón for violating the 1977 Amnesty Law was still pending. In 2008, Baltasar Garzón had launched an investigation into crimes committed during the Civil War and under the Franco regime, which involved the enforced disappearance of more than 114,000 people between 1936 and 1951.

■ On 13 April 2010, relatives of two victims of enforced disappearance under the Franco regime launched a complaint in Argentina based on universal jurisdiction. A federal judge in Argentina asked the Spanish government whether the authorities were actively investigating the allegations of "physical elimination and the 'legalized' disappearance of children with loss of identity", conducted in the period between 17 July 1936 and 15 June 1977. In June, the government replied to the Argentine judiciary that investigations were being conducted in Spain. The case was pending at the end of the year.

International justice

Investigations into 13 cases of alleged crimes under international law committed outside Spain against Spanish citizens, or based on the principle of universal jurisdiction, were pending before the National High Court. However, progress in the investigation was very slow and faced major challenges such as lack of co-operation by other states.

■ In July, Central Investigating Court No. 1 included charges of gender-based crimes in the investigations into the crimes of genocide, terrorism and torture which were perpetrated in Guatemala during the internal conflict between 1960 and 1996.

■ In October, Central Investigating Court No. 1 issued an indictment against three US soldiers charged with the death of José Couso, a Spanish television cameraman, in Baghdad in 2003. None of the suspects was brought to trial by the end of the year.

Housing rights

Spanish law did not provide ways to access suitable and effective legal remedies to enforce economic, social and cultural rights. There was no law on transparency and access to information in relation to such rights.

■ In September, a Moroccan family with a valid residence permit was forcibly evicted from their home in Cañada Real, Madrid. The eviction took place at night, in contravention of international standards. Although the family had received notice of the eviction and filed an appeal, they were not consulted on alternative adequate accommodation nor offered any.

Children's rights

In October, the Ombudsperson reported his concerns regarding tests used to determine the age of unaccompanied minors entering Spain. Even in the presence of passports, the test results were used to decide whether the unaccompanied minors would be given access to protection and services.

There was still no legislation in line with international standards to regulate the placement of children in centres for minors with behavioural or social disorders. In September, a special committee in the Senate stated that it was necessary to provide the highest guarantees, and to clarify, define and co-ordinate the respective responsibilities of the different authorities.

S

Amnesty International visits/reports

🚌 Amnesty International delegates visited Spain in March, April and November.

📄 Spain: Briefing to the UN Committee on the Elimination of Racial Discrimination, 78th Session February 2011 (EUR 41/003/2011)

📄 Spain: Amnesty International concerned by reports of excessive use of force by police against demonstrators (EUR 41/008/2011)

📄 Spain: New reports of excessive use of force by police against demonstrators (EUR 41/010/2011)

📄 Stop racism, not people: Racial profiling and immigration control in Spain (EUR 41/011/2011)

SRI LANKA

DEMOCRATIC SOCIALIST REPUBLIC OF SRI LANKA

Head of state and government:	Mahinda Rajapaksa
Death penalty:	abolitionist in practice
Population:	21 million
Life expectancy:	74.9 years
Under-5 mortality:	14.7 per 1,000
Adult literacy:	90.6 per cent

The government continued to arbitrarily detain, torture or ill-treat people and subject people to enforced disappearance. It failed to address most instances of impunity for violations of human rights and humanitarian law. The government rejected repeated allegations of war crimes committed by both sides of the conflict that ended in 2009, prompting Amnesty International to reiterate calls for an independent international investigation.

Background

Sri Lanka continued to rely on security laws and a military apparatus that perpetuated human rights violations. It resisted efforts to increase official transparency when it blocked an opposition-sponsored Right to Information Bill in June. The country remained prone to political violence, and efforts at ethnic reconciliation made little progress. On 30 August, Sri Lanka lifted the State of Emergency, in place almost continuously for decades, but retained the repressive Prevention of Terrorism Act (PTA). It introduced new regulations under the PTA to: maintain the ban on the Liberation Tigers of Tamil Eelam (LTTE); continue detention of LTTE suspects without charge or trial; and retain High Security Zones under military control. The army was deployed for civil policing, and the Special Task Force (an elite police commando unit with a history of abuse) was active island-wide. The army restricted freedom of association and assembly in the north and east, requiring prior permission even for family celebrations. Security forces required Tamil residents in these areas to register household members despite a court judgement declaring the practice discriminatory.

Internally displaced people

Almost 400,000 conflict displaced people returned to the north by the end of 2011, but many of them continued to live in insecure conditions with poor housing and poor access to health care and education. Some 16,000 people remained in government-run camps. The authorities planned to close remaining displacement camps and relocate about 5,500 individuals from areas that remained under military control in Mullaitivu to a jungle location in Kombavil. Advocates for the displaced voiced concerns that relocation would not be voluntary.

Violations by government-allied armed groups

Gangs linked to the security forces and government-aligned political parties, including the Eelam People's Democratic Party, Tamil People's Liberation Tigers and the Sri Lanka Freedom Party, were blamed for robberies, abductions, rapes, assaults and murders in Jaffna, eastern Sri Lanka, and increasingly in other parts of the country. Political activists, returning displaced people, and former LTTE members were targets.

Enforced disappearances

Enforced disappearances continued to be reported, and thousands of cases from earlier years remained unresolved. The government failed to ratify the International Convention against enforced disappearance.

In January, witnesses appeared before Sri Lanka's Lessons Learnt and Reconciliation Commission (LLRC) in Mannar and Madhu, trying to find loved ones seen surrendering to the army in May 2009.

■ On 30 June, hundreds of demonstrators in the capital, Colombo, demanded to know the fate and whereabouts of missing family members they believed were abducted by government squads. Similarly, over 1,300 people approached newly opened Terrorist Investigation Department information centres in June, seeking information on missing relatives believed to be in government custody; few found answers.

The Sri Lankan Police Department reported in July that 1,700 people had been abducted since 2009, most of them for ransom.

Arbitrary arrests and detentions

The government acknowledged in November that 876 adults remained in administrative detention under the PTA; 845 were Tamil men and 18 were Tamil women. These detainees were among nearly 12,000 alleged LTTE members who surrendered or were captured by the army and then detained for months or years without charge in the aftermath of the conflict. People detained for "rehabilitation" were gradually released in batches (about 1,000 were held at year's end); those released remained under military surveillance, and were reportedly subjected to harassment by the authorities.

■ On 23 August, soldiers assaulted and detained scores of young men from Navanthurai, in Jaffna district. Earlier, the villagers had protested against military protection of "grease devils" (mysterious strangers, sometimes described as being smeared with grease or face paint, widely believed to be attacking civilians, especially women). More than 50 petitions were filed with the Jaffna Court by residents claiming their rights had been violated by security force reprisals in "grease devil" incidents.

Torture and other ill-treatment

Torture and other ill-treatment of criminal suspects and those detained on suspicion of links to the LTTE remained widespread, despite laws prohibiting torture. Rape and other gender-based violence amounting to torture were not taken seriously by the authorities. Sexual violence went largely under-reported and, where reported, was poorly investigated.

Excessive use of force

On 30 May, police fired tear gas and live ammunition at demonstrating workers and trade unionists in the country's largest export processing zone. Hundreds of demonstrators and police were reported injured; 21-year-old Roshan Chanaka was killed. President

Rajapaksa ordered an inquiry. The Inspector General of Police resigned following the incident; several other high-ranking police officers were transferred.

Deaths in custody

Deaths in police custody persisted, many of them under suspicious circumstances. Police often claimed that victims were killed trying to escape.

■ Police said Asanka Botheju drowned in the Kelaniya river, Colombo, on 30 August while identifying a weapons cache. He had been illegally detained for 19 days.

■ Gayan Saranga from the town of Dompe died on 29 September. Police claimed he fell from a police vehicle while being taken to identify stolen property. Witnesses said he was tortured at the police station.

■ Four Angulana policemen received death sentences in August for the custodial murder of two young men in 2009.

Lack of accountability

The government failed to adequately investigate or prosecute most alleged violations of human rights and humanitarian law, including those committed in the final phase of the armed conflict, and rejected the findings of the UN Secretary-General's Panel of Experts on Accountability in Sri Lanka.

The Panel concluded that there were credible allegations that war crimes and crimes against humanity had been committed by both sides. It found that the LLRC, touted by officials as a sufficient accountability mechanism to address wartime events, was "deeply flawed" and was not adequately independent or impartial. It recommended that the Secretary-General establish an independent investigation into the allegations and order a review of UN actions on Sri Lanka. The UN Human Rights Council failed to act on its recommendations.

The LLRC's final report, made public on 16 December, acknowledged serious human rights problems in Sri Lanka, but fell short of fully addressing allegations of war crimes and crimes against humanity committed during the final phases of the conflict. It took the government's responses uncritically, reinforcing the need for an independent international investigation.

Sri Lankan officials, including the country's President and senior diplomats, faced complaints in Swiss, German and US courts that they were responsible for murder, torture and military attacks on civilians.

S

In October, Australian police were urged to investigate war crimes allegations against Sri Lanka's High Commissioner in Canberra. In the Netherlands, five alleged LTTE members were convicted of illegal fundraising for the LTTE but acquitted of membership of a terrorist organization and, by extension, responsibility for recruitment of child soldiers and murder, as alleged by prosecutors.

■ Former Army Commander Sarath Fonseka was sentenced to three years in prison in November for inciting communal hatred. He alleged that Sri Lanka's Defence Secretary had ordered the killing of surrendering LTTE cadres at the end of the war.

■ In a rare prosecution of military personnel for human rights violations, three soldiers accused of raping and killing a young woman in northern Sri Lanka in 1996 were sentenced to death in a Sri Lankan court on 30 March; they immediately appealed against the convictions.

Human rights defenders

Suppression of peaceful dissent remained common. Human rights defenders who engaged in international advocacy or interacted with international NGOs or diplomats were portrayed in the state media as traitors and subjected to anonymous threats and smear campaigns.

■ On 22 August, Perumal Sivakumara of Puttalam district died after being beaten by police Special Task Force personnel; there was no investigation.

■ A body believed to be that of human rights defender Pattani Razeek, missing since February 2010, was exhumed in July 2011 from a partially constructed house in eastern Sri Lanka. Two suspects with ties to a government minister were arrested after months of official inaction.

■ Political activists Lalith Kumar Weeraraj and Kugan Muruganathan disappeared on 9 December in Jaffna while organizing a demonstration calling for the release of detainees held without charge since the end of the war. Colleagues alleged they were abducted by the military.

Freedom of expression – journalists

The authorities attacked and censored media workers and outlets, and failed to provide accountability for attacks on journalists. On 7 November, the government blocked websites whose content was deemed "injurious" to Sri Lanka's image, and announced that any website featuring information about

Sri Lanka should register with the Ministry of Mass Media and Information or face potential legal action.

■ Bennet Rupasinghe, news editor of the Lanka E News website, was arrested on 31 March and accused of threatening a suspect linked to an arson attack against the website's office. He was released on bail in April. The website was blocked in Sri Lanka in October after it reported that ruling party politician Baratha Lakshman Premachandra was shot and killed along with four others in an altercation with another ruling party politician.

■ In late July, Gnanasundaram Kuhanathan, news editor of the Jaffna-based *Uthayan* newspaper, was attacked by unidentified men wielding iron bars and left in a critical condition.

SUDAN

REPUBLIC OF THE SUDAN

Head of state and government:	Omar Hassan Ahmed al-Bashir
Death penalty:	retentionist
Country data covers South Sudan and Sudan:	
Population:	44.6 million
Life expectancy:	61.5 years
Under-5 mortality:	108.2 per 1,000
Adult literacy:	70.2 per cent

Major transformations were faced in Sudan as South Sudan seceded on 9 July, following a referendum on its self-determination. Post-independence agreements on the sharing of oil, citizenship and border demarcation continued to be negotiated at the end of the year. Conflict further intensified in Darfur and erupted in Abyei, Southern Kordofan and Blue Nile which led to hundreds of thousands of civilians fleeing those areas. The National Intelligence and Security Service (NISS) and other government agents continued to commit human rights violations against perceived critics of the government for exercising their rights to freedom of expression, association and assembly.

Background

A referendum on the self-determination of South Sudan was held on 9 January as part of the 2005

S

Comprehensive Peace Agreement, signed between Sudan's ruling National Congress Party (NCP) and the former southern armed opposition group, the Sudan People's Liberation Movement (SPLM). Results showed that 98.83 per cent of South Sudanese voted in favour of independence.

A referendum to determine whether Abyei would be part of Sudan or South Sudan, also scheduled for 9 January, was delayed indefinitely due to disagreements on voter eligibility of the two main ethnic groups: the northern semi-nomadic Misseryia, and southern ethnic Dinka Ngok.

Popular consultations were also scheduled in Southern Kordofan and Blue Nile, which could determine a level of autonomy for the two states within Sudan. On 17 May, NCP candidate Ahmed Mohammed Haroun was elected governor in Southern Kordofan, despite allegations by the SPLM of vote-rigging. Ahmed Haroun was wanted by the International Criminal Court (ICC) for war crimes and crimes against humanity in Darfur. Following the independence of South Sudan, the SPLM in Sudan became known as the SPLM-North (SPLM-N).

No substantive progress had been made with regard to the Darfur peace process by the end of the year. Ongoing insecurity in the region prevented consultations with stakeholders in Darfur.

The mandate of the UN Mission in Sudan (UNMIS) ended on 9 July. On 29 July the mandate of the joint UN/AU Mission in Darfur (UNAMID) was extended for a further year. On 23 September, the UN Human Rights Council adopted the outcome of the Universal Periodic Review on Sudan during its 18th session. The mandate of the Independent Expert on the situation of human rights in Sudan was renewed at the Council for one year on 29 September.

On 7 August, the Justice and Equality Movement (JEM), Sudan Liberation Army-Minni Minawi faction (SLA-M), SLA-Abdul Wahid faction and the Sudan People's Liberation Movement-North (SPLM-N) announced the formation of an alliance against the ruling NCP. On 24 December, JEM leader Khalil Ibrahim was killed by the Sudan Armed Forces (SAF) during an offensive in North Kordofan State.

International justice
The government remained unco-operative with the ICC regarding arrest warrants issued against President al-Bashir in 2009 and 2010, as well as against Ahmed Haroun, governor of Southern Kordofan, and Ali Mohammed Ali Abdelrahman (known as Ali Kushayb), a former Janjaweed militia leader, in 2007. A further arrest warrant was requested on 2 December by the ICC Chief Prosecutor for the Minister of Defence, Abdelrahim Mohamed Hussein.

In January the AU reaffirmed its decision not to co-operate with the ICC in the arrest of President al-Bashir, but it did not obtain sufficient support for its call that the UN Security Council defer the case for 12 months by invoking Article 16 of the Rome Statute. In July the AU reiterated its support for countries that had not arrested President al-Bashir. In December, the Pre-Trial Chamber of the ICC referred the fact that Malawi and Chad did not arrest President al-Bashir to the UN Security Council and the Assembly of States Parties to the Rome Statute.

Armed conflict – Darfur
Human rights abuses remained widespread during the year throughout Darfur. Attacks including aerial bombardments were carried out by government forces, including the Central Reserve Police and Popular Defense Force (PDF) and government allied militia, as well as ground attacks by armed opposition groups in and around towns and villages including camps for internally displaced people (IDPs). There were civilian deaths and injuries, and looting and destruction of property. On 27 May the UN Humanitarian Coordinator announced that over 70,000 people been displaced by the fighting since December 2010.

Between December 2010 and June 2011, fighting between government and armed opposition groups erupted in North Darfur, including in areas between Khor Abeche, Abu Zerega and Tabit. More than eight villages were reportedly destroyed and tens of thousands of people fled the fighting.

The government severely restricted access to UNAMID and humanitarian organizations, preventing them from carrying out monitoring and from providing essential services to civilians.

In February, the government suspended the relief organization Catholic Relief Services from operating in west Darfur for one month. Also in February, the medical humanitarian organization Médecins du Monde was expelled from South Darfur, reportedly accused of "spying". National and international staff of humanitarian organizations and UNAMID were arrested and detained.

S

Security forces conducted cordon and search operations in IDP camps in areas populated by members of the Zaghawa ethnic group, who were perceived to be supporters of the SLA-M. On 23 January, government forces raided Zamzam IDP camp where they arrested over 80 people, including three women, and looted property from homes. No prior notice was given to UNAMID, in violation of the Status of Forces Agreement stipulating consultation between the government and UNAMID on actions regarding IDP camps.

Rape and other sexual violence by government forces and allied militia against displaced women and girls continued. On 13 January, six internally displaced girls and women were raped near Tawilla, North Darfur, by two men believed to be government-allied militia. On 22 March, armed police abducted four women from their home near Shangil Tobaya, raping one of them and beating all four. On 1 October, in separate incidents, government-allied militia abducted and repeatedly raped two girls, aged 12 and 14, in the Kabkabiya region of North Darfur.

■ Three UNAMID staff were arrested by NISS agents. On 27 April, civil affairs officer Idris Yousef Abdelrahman was arrested in Nyala, South Darfur. He was released on 20 July and all charges against him were dropped. On 6 May, Hawa Abdallah Mohamed, a community activist and translator for UNAMID, was arrested in Abu Shouk IDP camp in North Darfur, accused of "Christianizing" children in the camp and having links to an armed opposition group. She was released on 13 July. On 3 September a staff member was arrested in El Fasher, North Darfur, and released without charge on 8 October.

Armed conflict – transitional areas

On 21 May, the SAF overran Abyei town. Attacks by SAF, PDF and SAF-backed militia forcibly displaced the entire population of the town and surrounding villages, over 100,000 people, to South Sudan. The attack followed a series of armed clashes between the SAF and the Sudan People's Liberation Army (SPLA) between January and May. Homes and NGO premises were looted and burned by the SAF-allied militia. UNMIS was denied access to Abyei town by the SAF for several days and took limited action to protect the civilian population. On 27 June, a UN Interim Security Force for Abyei (UNISFA), under UN Security Council resolution 1990, was established

following an agreement reached between the NCP and SPLM in Ethiopia, to demilitarize Abyei and allow up to 4,200 Ethiopian troops to monitor the area. At the end of the year, the SAF and the SPLA had not fully withdrawn their troops and the populations of Abyei town and most surrounding villages remained displaced in South Sudan with inadequate access to shelter, food and other essential services. The mandate for UNISFA was extended on 27 December.

Conflict erupted in Southern Kordofan on 5 June between the SAF and the armed opposition group SPLM-N. The Sudanese government repeatedly carried out indiscriminate aerial bombardments, killing and wounding civilians. A report published in August by the Office of the High Commissioner for Human Rights detailed unlawful killings, mass destruction and looting of civilian property, and other allegations which could amount to war crimes and crimes against humanity.

On 1 September conflict spread to Blue Nile State. President al-Bashir declared a state of emergency the following day, replacing SPLM-N governor Malik Aggar with a military governor.

People displaced by the fighting – over 300,000 from Southern Kordofan and over 55,000 from Blue Nile – were forced to seek refuge in other areas, including western Ethiopia, Yida in South Sudan's Unity State, and Upper Nile State. On 8 and 10 November, SAF forces bombed Upper Nile and Yida areas.

The Sudanese government denied access to international human rights and humanitarian organizations throughout the year.

Armed conflict – southern Sudan

Inter-communal violence continued in southern Sudan. The high prevalence of small arms exacerbated clashes and human rights abuses against civilians by armed opposition groups and government forces.

■ On 9 and 10 February, fighting erupted between the SPLA and forces loyal to the armed opposition leader General George Athor Deng in Fangak County, Jonglei State. At least 154 civilians were killed and 20,000 people displaced. Further clashes occurred on 12 March in Malakal, Upper Nile.

■ On 23 April, the SPLA and forces loyal to armed opposition leader Gabriel Tanginye clashed in Kaldak village in Jonglei State. The destruction of homes forced some 15,000 people to seek relocation.

S

Refugees and migrants

Over 300 Eritrean asylum-seekers and refugees were forcibly returned on 17 October, despite an agreement between UNHCR, the UN refugee agency, and the Sudanese authorities that they would be allowed to lodge asylum claims in Sudan and that some had refugee status.

■ On 25 July, one asylum-seeker, aged 23, died and another, aged 17, was seriously injured after jumping from a truck forcibly returning them to the border with Eritrea.

Freedom of association and assembly

Between January and April and in October, thousands of people throughout north Sudan demonstrated against the high cost of living and for democracy. The police and the NISS arrested hundreds of activists and opposition party members and supporters. Some were held in incommunicado detention and subjected to torture or other forms of ill-treatment. In September, the SPLM-N was banned, its offices closed and over 200 of its members reportedly arrested.

■ Over 70 people were arrested on 30 January in Khartoum to prevent them from joining protests. Mohamed Abdelrahman was reportedly ill-treated while in police custody and unconfirmed reports were received that he died in hospital the following day. No investigation was carried out.

■ Around 100 people were arrested on 20 April following protests at Nyala University in South Darfur. All had been released by September.

■ On 25 June, Bushra Gamar Hussein Rahma, a human rights activist and member of the SPLM-N, was arrested in Omdurman. A judge ordered his release on 14 August but he was immediately re-arrested by the NISS. At the end of the year he remained in detention without charge or access to a lawyer.

■ On 2 September, Abdelmoniem Rahama, an activist, poet and member of the SPLM-N, was arrested in Ed Damazin. At the end of the year he remained in detention without charge or access to a lawyer.

Freedom of expression

Newspapers continued to be subjected to closure and censorship, and journalists were harassed and in some cases arrested, where they were at risk of torture or other ill-treatment.

■ On 31 January, the opposition newspaper *Ajrass al-Hurriya* was banned by the NISS, and the newspapers

Al Sahafa and *Al Midan* were prevented from distributing all or some of their editions. Similar media clampdowns occurred in August and September.

■ The bi-weekly newspaper *Juba Post* was temporarily shut down by security agents in southern Sudan on 30 March following an article stating that forces loyal to armed opposition group leader George Athor would attack Juba before July. The newspaper's distribution officer was briefly detained at Juba airport on 31 March.

■ On 9 July, the National Council for Press and Publications withdrew the licences of six newspapers partly owned by south Sudanese.

■ Ten journalists faced charges for reporting on the case of Safia Ishag Mohamed, a woman who was sexually assaulted by NISS officers in January. On 5 July, Fatima Ghazali was sentenced to one month's detention and her editor, Saad-al Din Ibrahim, to a fine. On 25 July, Amal Habani was sentenced to one month's imprisonment.

■ Abuzar Al Ameen, deputy editor of the newspaper *Rai al Shaab,* was released on bail on 22 August. He had been arrested by NISS agents on 15 May 2010 and sentenced to five years' imprisonment for "undermining the Constitution" and "publishing false news", in relation to articles published about the April 2010 presidential and parliamentary elections and allegations of an Iranian weapons factory being built in Sudan.

Death penalty

Death sentences continued to be passed in north and southern Sudan, including against juveniles, and at least seven executions were carried out.

Amnesty International visits/reports

▥ Sudan: Southern Kordofan civilians tell of air strike horror (AFR 54/028/2011)

▥ Sudan: Activist remains in detention without trial (AFR 54/035/2011)

▥ Sudan: Government crackdown on activists and political opponents (AFR 54/036/2011)

▥ Sudan: Death sentences upheld (AFR 54/037/2011)

▥ Sudan: Poet remains in incommunicado detention (AFR 54/039/2011)

▥ Sudan-South Sudan: Destruction and desolation in Abyei (AFR 54/041/2011)

S

SWAZILAND

KINGDOM OF SWAZILAND

Head of state:	King Mswati III
Head of government:	Barnabas Sibusiso Dlamini
Death penalty:	abolitionist in practice
Population:	1.2 million
Life expectancy:	48.7 years
Under-5 mortality:	73 per 1,000
Adult literacy:	86.9 per cent

A crisis in the rule of law and the unfair dismissal of a judge undermined the independence of the judiciary. Arbitrary and secret detentions, political prosecutions and excessive force were used to crush political protests. A parliamentary committee report highlighted the risks to the right to life from anti-poaching legislation. There was slow progress in repealing laws that discriminated against women. Access to treatment for HIV/AIDS was increasingly threatened by the deteriorating financial situation in the country.

Background

The government's financial situation deteriorated dramatically. Its efforts to secure loans from various sources were not successful, partly due to its failure to implement fiscal reforms, and its unwillingness to accept conditions, including instituting political reforms, within agreed time frames. The government ignored renewed efforts by civil society organizations to open a dialogue on steps towards multi-party democracy. At the UN Universal Periodic Review hearing on Swaziland in October, the government rejected recommendations to allow political parties to participate in elections.

Justice system

Access to fair and impartial tribunals, including for victims of human rights violations, was increasingly restricted by a developing crisis in the rule of law. Restrictions, in the form of a "practice directive", implemented in the higher courts under the authority of the Chief Justice, made access to the courts difficult or impossible for civil litigants in cases in which the King was indirectly affected as a defendant. Another directive placed control over the daily allocation of cases for hearings, including urgent

ones, exclusively in the hands of the Chief Justice, whose appointment on a temporary contract was authorized by the King. The restrictions created a bias in the administration of justice, leaving some litigants or defendants in criminal proceedings without access to the courts or to a fair hearing. In August, the Law Society of Swaziland launched a boycott of the courts in protest at these developments and the authorities' failure to institute a proper hearing into its complaints regarding the running of the courts and the conduct of the Chief Justice. In the following weeks it delivered a petition to the Minister of Justice appealing for action. Lawyers' protests near the High Court building were dispersed on several occasions by armed police. In November, the Law Society temporarily suspended its boycott following discussions with the Judicial Service Commission (JSC). However, the majority of the Law Society's complaints remained unresolved.

■ In September a senior High Court judge, Thomas Masuku, was summarily dismissed from judicial office by order of the King, following unfair "removal proceedings". These were apparently triggered by allegations lodged against him by the Chief Justice, including that Justice Masuku had criticized the King in one of his rulings. In a closed hearing on the allegations by the JSC, chaired by the Chief Justice, the main complainant, no independent evidence was produced to substantiate the allegations. The JSC did not present their findings to Justice Masuku before they reported them to the King, who subsequently issued his decree on 27 September ordering his dismissal. The Minister of Justice, David Matse, was also dismissed for refusing to sign a document supporting the dismissal of Justice Masuku.

Constitutional or institutional developments

The Commission on Human Rights and Public Administration completed its second year without enabling legislation. It still lacked sufficient staff and accessible premises.

Repression of dissent

In April, the government banned protest marches planned for 12 to 14 April by trade unions and other organizations. Arbitrary and secret detentions, unlawful house arrests and other state of emergency-style measures were used to crush peaceful anti-government protests over several days. Officials from the Swaziland National Union of Students and from banned organizations were among those detained.

The police used excessive force to disperse demonstrators.

■ On 12 April, 66-year-old Ntombi Nkosi, an activist with the Ngwane National Liberatory Congress (NNLC), was on her way home, having received medical treatment after tear gas was thrown at her, when she was confronted by three armed police officers. They questioned her about wording relating to the NNLC on her T-shirt and headscarf and then allegedly grabbed her, pulled off her T-shirt and headscarf and assaulted her. They throttled her, banged her head against a wall, sexually molested her, bent her arms behind her back, kicked her and then threw her against a police truck. A passing taxi driver helped her to get away. She needed hospital treatment for her injuries.

■ In September, police used excessive force to break up a rally in the eastern town of Siteki, and assaulted S'pasha Dlamini, an executive member of the Swaziland National Association of Teachers. She had been trying to stop the police pulling a South African trade unionist speaker off the stage, when they threw her to the ground, kicked her in the head and dragged her by her arms for about 100m. She needed hospital treatment for her injuries.

Counter-terror and security

■ Maxwell Dlamini, President of the Swaziland National Union of Students, was detained between 10 and 12 April and held incommunicado without access to a lawyer or contact with his family. The day after his release he was rearrested, along with Musa Ngubeni, a political activist and former student activist leader. They were denied legal access while in police custody and during their hearing at the magistrate's court, and were charged with offences under the Explosives Act. They were denied bail on the grounds that their release would undermine public peace and security. On 20 December, the High Court overturned the decision but ordered their release on bail of 50,000 emalangeni (US$6,135) each. They were still in custody at the end of the year.

■ In December, the High Court dismissed an application for the release of Zonke Dlamini and Bhekumusa Dlamini, both charged under the Suppression of Terrorism Act in 2010 and then denied bail. The application had been brought on the grounds

that the state had failed to bring them to trial within the period required by law.

Unlawful killings

In August a parliamentary committee, appointed to investigate alleged brutality by game rangers against suspected poachers, submitted its conclusions and recommendations to parliament. The committee had investigated violent incidents resulting in the deaths and injuries of suspected poachers and of game rangers. The report listed nine incidents against game rangers and 33 against suspected poachers. The majority of cases were either still under police investigation, or with the prosecutor's office or pending in court. Some suspected poachers injured by game rangers were then prosecuted under the Game Act (as amended). No game rangers were prosecuted for fatal or non-fatal shootings. The committee recommended urgent reform of clauses in the Game Act (as amended), which could be interpreted to "condone brutality towards suspect poachers".

Deaths in custody

The coroner, Nondumiso Simelane, appointed to investigate the May 2010 death in custody of political activist Sipho Jele, presented her report to the Prime Minister in March. The report had not been made public by the end of the year.

■ On 5 December, 26-year-old Phumelela Mhkweli died shortly after police forcibly removed him from a taxi in Siteki, demanding he pay a fine for a traffic offence and insisting that he needed to be "disciplined", according to witnesses. Medical evidence showed injuries to his head and face, and indicated that the aggressive conduct of the police triggered an underlying medical condition leading to his death.

Women's rights

The Sexual Offences and Domestic Violence Bill was debated in parliament but had not been enacted by the end of the year.

In June, the government tabled the Deeds Registry (Amendment) Bill in parliament, in response to a Supreme Court order in May 2010 to amend an unconstitutional provision in the law preventing most women married under civil law from legally registering homes or other immovable property in their own name. The bill, which did not contain sufficient safeguards, had not been enacted by the end of the year.

S

The Citizenship Bill presented to parliament contained provisions that discriminated against women, denying them the right to pass on their Swazi citizenship to their children or to their non-Swazi spouses.

Rights of lesbian, gay, bisexual and transgender people

At the October Universal Periodic Review hearing, the government rejected recommendations that it decriminalize same-sex relations and prevent discrimination based on sexual orientation.

Right to health – the HIV epidemic

HIV prevalence remained "exceedingly high" but appeared to be "levelling off", according to UNAIDS. According to the government's report submitted in July for the Universal Periodic Review, 85 per cent of facilities offering antenatal services also offered treatment to prevent HIV transmission from mother to child. The government also announced it had adopted the WHO guidelines for initiation on antiretroviral treatment at an earlier stage in the disease. Some 65,000 people were receiving treatment by November.

However, access to and remaining on treatment was still difficult for some patients due to poverty, lack of transport in rural areas, food insecurity, poor drug procurement procedures and lack of funding because of the country's poor financial management.

Death penalty

Although the 2006 Constitution permits the use of capital punishment, no executions had been carried out since 1983.

■ In April, a decade after his arrest, David Simelane was sentenced to death by the High Court after being convicted of the murders of 34 women. He lodged an appeal.

Two other people remained under sentence of death. In October, at the country's Universal Periodic Review hearing, the government described Swaziland as "abolitionist in practice", but stated that a "national debate" was necessary before the death penalty could be abolished in law.

Amnesty International visits/reports

🚌 Amnesty International delegates visited Swaziland in June and November.

📓 Swaziland: Blatant unfairness of removal proceedings against leading High Court judge threatens judicial independence (AFR 55/004/2011)

📓 I want safety and equality for Swazi women (AFR 55/005/2011)

📓 Key human rights concerns highlighted by Amnesty International in advance of Swaziland's Universal Periodic Review hearing in October 2011 (AFR 55/006/2011)

📓 Swaziland activists detained ahead of banned protests (PRE01/203/2011)

📓 Swaziland authorities must end their violent crackdown (PRE01/213/2011)

SWEDEN

KINGDOM OF SWEDEN

Head of state:	King Carl XVI Gustaf
Head of government:	Fredrik Reinfeldt
Death penalty:	abolitionist for all crimes
Population:	9.4 million
Life expectancy:	81.4 years
Under-5 mortality:	2.8 per 1,000

Ahmed Agiza, who had been subject to rendition, was released from prison in Egypt. Concerns were raised that many Romani asylum-seekers from Serbia were being denied access to a fair asylum procedure. Forced returns to Eritrea and Iraq continued.

Torture and other ill-treatment

Sweden failed again to introduce torture as a crime in its Penal Code.

■ On 2 August, Ahmed Agiza was released from prison in Cairo, Egypt, having been held for over nine years following an unfair trial before a military court. Ahmed Agiza and Mohammed al-Zari, both Egyptian asylum-seekers, were detained in Sweden in December 2001 and subjected to rendition from Sweden to Egypt on a CIA-leased plane. Both men subsequently reported that they had been tortured and ill-treated while being held incommunicado in Egypt. In 2008, the Swedish government awarded both men financial compensation for the human rights violations they had suffered. However, an effective, impartial, thorough and independent investigation into these violations remained outstanding.

S

Following his release, Ahmed Agiza applied for a residence permit in Sweden in order to be reunited with his family who still lived there. Awarding him a residence permit would help to ensure that he received full and effective redress for the violations he had suffered.

Refugees, asylum-seekers and migrants

The Swedish authorities continued to consider a large number of asylum applications to be "manifestly unfounded", just under half of which were made by Roma from Serbia. In addition, the accelerated asylum determination procedures through which such cases were processed did not meet international standards; applicants were denied a proper individual determination of their protection needs and access to legal aid.

In April, the Justice Ombudsman heavily criticized the Stockholm County Police Authority's decision to deport 26 Romanian Roma as being unlawful; the deportees had been denied entry clearance on the grounds that they were "spending their time as vagrants/beggars".

Forced returns to Iraq and Eritrea continued despite the real risk of persecution or other forms of serious harm people could face upon their return.

International justice

In April, the Stockholm District Court handed down a conviction for war crimes to a former member of the Croatian Defence Forces. The convicted man was found to have participated directly and indirectly in acts of torture and other ill-treatment against Serbian prisoners between May and August 1992 while working as a guard at Dretelj detention camp during the war in Bosnia and Herzegovina. The Court found him guilty of aggravated crimes against international law, sentenced him to five years' imprisonment and ordered him to pay compensation to 22 of the victims.

Amnesty International visits/reports

- Current evidence: European complicity in the CIA rendition and secret detention programmes (EUR 01/001/2011)
- Sweden must stop forced returns to Iraq (EUR 42/001/2011)

SWITZERLAND

SWISS CONFEDERATION

Head of state and government:	Micheline Calmy-Rey
Death penalty:	abolitionist for all crimes
Population:	7.7 million
Life expectancy:	82.3 years
Under-5 mortality:	4.4 per 1,000

Discriminatory legislation against Muslims remained in place or was proposed at federal and cantonal levels. Excessive use of force during forced deportations and inadequate assistance provided to rejected asylum-seekers caused serious concerns.

Background

The Criminal Code continued to lack a definition of torture fully consistent with international law. The Swiss Centre of Expertise for Human Rights, the national human rights institution, began its work. The International Convention against enforced disappearance was signed but not ratified. In December, the National Council decided to ratify the Council of Europe Convention on Action against Trafficking in Human Beings.

Discrimination

Legislation failed to prevent discrimination, and in some cases promoted it. In May, the UN Human Rights Committee raised concerns about under-representation of ethnic minorities in the police force, inadequate racism prevention measures and lack of legal protections for victims of discrimination.

In October, the Federal Commission against Racism criticized a parliamentary proposal in Zug "to create an asylum-seeker-free zone".

In May, cantonal authorities in Ticino began examining a popular initiative seeking to amend their constitution to prohibit the wearing of full-face veils.

The ban on minarets remained in force during 2011.

Refugees, asylum-seekers and migrants

NGOs continued to raise concerns about the treatment of asylum-seekers, including the use of force and restraints during forced deportations.

- One man was ill-treated at Zurich airport during a forced deportation of 19 Nigerians in July. No independent inquiry was conducted.

S

■ A criminal investigation into the death of Joseph Ndukaku Chiakwa, a Nigerian national who died at Zurich airport during a mass deportation in March 2010, was ongoing.

■ The family of Samson Chukwu, who died during deportation in 2001, were still awaiting compensation.

"Emergency assistance" remained inadequate and often left rejected asylum-seekers destitute or vulnerable. Reception facilities continued to be inadequate.

In December, an external investigation, announced in August by the Federal Department of Justice and Police, into the apparent failure to process between 7,000 and 10,000 asylum claims made between 2006 and 2008 by Iraqi nationals at Swiss embassies in Egypt and Syria, concluded that the Federal Office for Migration's actions had been unlawful. However, the investigation did not consider disciplinary sanctions or criminal proceedings to be viable actions.

In December, the Council of States approved legislation which would accelerate the asylum procedure and remove the right to claim asylum at Swiss embassies. The legislation also called for conscientious objectors seeking protection to be refused asylum and given temporary residence permits instead. It remained subject to approval by the National Council.

In December, the National Commission for the Prevention of Torture, the national preventive mechanism, raised concerns about disproportionate use of force and restraint techniques during forced deportations.

At the end of the year, the referendum known as the "Deportation Initiative", passed in 2010, had not been implemented. It had called for a constitutional amendment to allow the automatic deportation of foreign nationals convicted of specified criminal offences.

Violence against women and girls

In September, Parliament introduced a law to allow up to 10 years' imprisonment for female genital mutilation, even when the act was perpetrated in another country where the practice of female genital mutilation was legal.

In September, the National Council refused to modify immigration legislation which had been criticized by two UN committees for failing to protect migrant women who remained in abusive relationships for fear of losing their residence permits.

Amnesty International visits/reports

🚌 An Amnesty International delegate visited Switzerland in September.

SYRIA

SYRIAN ARAB REPUBLIC

Head of state:	Bashar al-Assad
Head of government:	Muhammad Naji al-'Otri
Death penalty:	retentionist
Population:	20.8 million
Life expectancy:	75.9 years
Under-5 mortality:	16.2 per 1,000
Adult literacy:	84.2 per cent

Government forces used lethal and other excessive force against peaceful protesters who took to the streets in unprecedented numbers to demand political reform and the fall of the regime. The pattern and scale of state abuses may have constituted crimes against humanity. More than 4,300 people reportedly died during or in connection with the protests and during funerals of demonstrators, most apparently shot by members of the security forces, including snipers. Tanks were used in military operations in civilian residential areas. Some members of the security forces were also killed, some allegedly for refusing to fire on protesters and others in attacks by defecting soldiers and other individuals who joined in opposition to the government. Some prisoners were released in amnesties but thousands of people were detained in connection with the protests, with many held incommunicado and tortured. At least 200 detainees reportedly died in custody in suspicious circumstances; many appeared to have been tortured. The authorities failed to conduct independent investigations into alleged unlawful killings, torture and other serious human rights violations, which the security forces committed with impunity. Thousands of Syrians were forcibly displaced by the repression; many fled to neighbouring countries. Death sentences continued to be imposed and executions reportedly carried out.

S

Background

Small pro-reform demonstrations in February developed into mass protests in mid-March after the security forces used grossly excessive force in Dera'a against people calling for the release of children who had been detained. The protests spread rapidly as government forces tried to quell the protests by brute force, including by using snipers to shoot into peaceful crowds while claiming that shadowy "armed gangs" opposed to the government were responsible for the violence.

President Bashar al-Assad announced various reforms in response to the protests. In April, he lifted the national state of emergency that had been in force continuously since 1963, abolished the notoriously unfair Supreme State Security Court that had jailed thousands of critics and opponents of the government, and decreed that some members of the Kurdish minority should receive Syrian citizenship, although excluding others who remained stateless. At the same time, however, he issued a decree allowing detention without charge or trial for up to two months. A new Peaceful Assembly Law was introduced under which only demonstrations "properly licensed" in advance by the authorities are considered lawful. In March, June and November, the President granted five separate amnesties for different categories of prisoners; among those freed were prisoners of conscience and people detained during the protests, although the vast majority of such detainees remained behind bars. Laws covering new Parties, elections and the media were passed in August. While representing a degree of liberalization, all three reforms failed to provide effective guarantees for freedom of expression and association.

In March, the UN Human Rights Council established a fact-finding mission which in August concluded that crimes against humanity may have been committed in Syria. In August the Council established an Independent International Commission of Inquiry; on 23 November the Commission expressed grave concern that Syria's military and security forces had committed crimes against humanity, including "killings, torture, rape and other forms of sexual violence, imprisonment, or other forms of severe deprivation of liberty and enforced disappearances." The Syrian authorities refused both the Council and the Commission entry to the country, as well as most international media and independent human rights organizations.

At the UN Security Council, the Russian Federation, China and other states blocked a proposed resolution condemning the crimes and other abuses in Syria but the USA, the EU and the League of Arab States (Arab League) all imposed sanctions; from April, the US government extended sanctions against Syria in place since 2004; in May, the EU imposed targeted sanctions on Syria's leaders and later expanded them; in November the Arab League first suspended Syria and then imposed economic sanctions when the government reneged on its pledge to the Arab League to withdraw its armed forces from Syria's cities, halt the violence and release people imprisoned in connection with the protests. In late December the Arab League sent observers to monitor the Syrian government's implementation of these pledges.

Excessive use of force and extrajudicial executions

Government forces repeatedly used lethal and other excessive force against peaceful and other protesters. Many people were shot apparently by snipers while participating in mass protests or attending funerals of people killed on preceding days. Tanks and other armoured vehicles were sent into Dera'a, Homs and other places, firing into residential areas. A "scorched earth"-type policy was used in the north-western governorate of Idleb. The government sought to justify this brutal crackdown by claiming that it was under attack by armed gangs, but failed to produce any convincing evidence for this until late in the year when concerted armed resistance began in response to the continuing repression, some of it by soldiers who had defected from the army and turned against the government. By the end of the year, more than 4,300 people – the UN put the figure at over 5,000 – were reported to have been killed in connection with the protests and unrest, many of them unarmed demonstrators and bystanders who posed no threat to the security forces or others. Many more had been injured.

■ In Dera'a city, security forces were reported to have shot dead at least four people on 18 March as they protested against the detention of some children accused of writing anti-government slogans on a wall. At least seven other people were reported killed on 23 March when security forces attacked the city's 'Omari mosque where protesters had taken shelter. One,

S

Ashraf 'Abd al-'Aziz al-Masri, was wounded in the leg then reportedly shot in the head at point blank range by a member of the security forces to whom he had pleaded for help.

■ In Jisr al-Shughur, security forces snipers were reported to have killed up to 25 mourners attending the 4 June funeral of Basel al-Masri and wounded many others, including a Red Crescent paramedic who was attending to an injured man.

■ In Homs, some 15 people were reportedly shot dead on 19 July while attending the funerals of 10 protesters killed the previous day, including Rabee' Joorya. His mother and brother were among the slain mourners.

■ In Hama, Khaled al-Haamedh died after soldiers reportedly shot him in the back on 31 July while he was walking to a hospital, and then an army tank reportedly drove over him.

■ In Dayr al-Zor, 14-year-old Muhammad al-Mulaa 'Esa was reportedly shot dead by a member of the security forces on 13 November when he refused an order that he and his classmates participate in a pro-government march.

Targeting the wounded and health workers

Wounded protesters seeking medical attention at health centres risked arrest and abuse, including denial of treatment. Hospital doctors and staff also faced arrest and persecution if they participated in or supported the protests or treated wounded protesters without reporting them to the authorities; several health workers were said to have been killed possibly for treating wounded protesters.

■ Dr Sakher Hallak, who ran an eating disorders clinic, was arrested on 25 May and reportedly died two days later while held at the Criminal Security Department in Aleppo. His body was returned with broken ribs, arms and fingers, gouged eyes and mutilated genitals. He may have been targeted because he signed a petition calling for doctors to be able to treat all injured people, including protesters, and for having recently travelled to the USA.

■ The body of Ma'az al-Fares, administrative director of the National Hospital of Taldo in Homs governorate, was returned to his family on 24 November after he died in custody as an apparent result of torture.

Repression of dissent

Freedoms of expression, association and assembly remained severely restricted despite the lifting of the state of emergency and the enactment of laws purportedly to allow peaceful protests and the registration of political parties. The security forces arrested thousands of people in connection with the protests, some during demonstrations and others in raids on homes or house-to-house searches or other sweeps. Hundreds, possibly thousands, of people were victims of enforced disappearance and were held incommunicado at undisclosed official and makeshift detention centres such as sports grounds. In all these centres, torture and other abuses were rife.

Those detained included political activists and dissidents, journalists, bloggers, imams, soldiers who refused to fire on protesters, and human rights activists, some of whom went into hiding to escape arrest. Hundreds of those arrested were released following trials before military or criminal courts or under the amnesties issued by President al-Assad, but thousands of others were still held at the end of the year.

■ Human rights activist Mohammed Najati Tayyara, aged 65, was arrested by Political Security officials in Homs on 12 May and accused of disseminating "false news that could debilitate the morale of the nation" after he gave media interviews about abuses against protesters by the security forces. A judge ordered his release on bail in August but Air Force Intelligence officials then detained him incommunicado for 11 days during which he was beaten. He was still held at the end of 2011 in cramped conditions at Homs Central Prison.

■ Women's rights activist Hanadi Zahlout was detained incommunicado for two months after her arrest in Damascus on 4 August, then moved to 'Adra prison to face trial with six others on charges that included "incitement to protest". She was released on 4 December.

■ Journalist 'Adel Walid Kharsa was arrested by State Security officials on 17 August for reporting anonymously on state repression of the protests. He was held incommunicado for five weeks then released uncharged, but was re-detained by Military Intelligence on 31 October. He was still being detained incommunicado at the end of 2011, a victim of enforced disappearance.

■ Human rights activist Mohamed Iyyad Tayyara was taken from his home in Homs by soldiers on 28 August, apparently because he reported on human rights violations, and held in secret detention until early December when he was moved to Homs Central Prison.

■ Kurdish writer Hussein 'Essou remained held at the end of the year following his arrest in al-Hasakah on 3 September having declared his support for pro-reform protests.

Many dissidents and former prisoners continued to be prevented from travelling abroad under administrative bans that they had no means to challenge. Syrians abroad who demonstrated in solidarity with the protesters were monitored and harassed by Syrian embassy officials and others; some of their relatives in Syria were also targeted for abuse apparently in reprisal for their activities.

■ Mustafa Kheder Osso, President of the unauthorized Kurdish Organization for the Defence of Human Rights and Public Freedoms in Syria, was facing disciplinary measures from the Syrian Bar Association after he joined a protest calling for the release of political prisoners in July and spoke to the media. The disciplinary action threatened his ability to continue to work as a lawyer.

■ Human rights lawyer Anwar al-Bunni was prevented from travelling abroad throughout 2011.

■ The parents of US-based pianist and composer Malek Jandali were beaten in their home in Homs by armed men four days after their son demonstrated in the USA in solidarity with Syrian protesters in July. His father was told: "This is what happens when your son mocks the government."

Prisoner releases

In face of the protests and international expression of concern, President al-Assad issued five separate amnesties in which those released included prisoners of conscience, people detained in connection with the protests and members of the banned Muslim Brotherhood. According to Syrian state media but otherwise unconfirmed, under the last two amnesties, both issued in November, more than 1,700 people detained during the protests were released.

■ Veteran human rights lawyer Haytham al-Maleh, aged 80, was released in the first amnesty in March. He was serving a three-year prison term imposed after an unfair trial in 2010.

■ Human rights lawyer Muhannad al-Hassani was released in the June amnesty. Arrested in July 2009, he was sentenced to three years' imprisonment after an unfair trial in June 2010.

■ Political activist Kamal al-Labwani, founder of the Liberal Democratic Union, an unauthorized political party, was released on 15 November after completing six years of a 12-year prison term that was halved in the amnesty issued on 31 May.

Torture and other ill-treatment

Torture and other ill-treatment of detainees were widespread and committed with impunity by the security forces with the aims of obtaining information, coercing "confessions" and punishing and terrorizing those suspected of opposing the government. Some victims feared that they would face reprisals if their identities were disclosed.

■ A man detained in April in Banias said that he was held for three days without food or clean drinking water and that security forces beat him and others with rifle butts on the neck and shoulders, stripped and beat him with sticks and cables, and made him lick his own blood off the floor.

■ A man said that he was beaten until he lost consciousness, tortured with electric shocks and threatened that his penis would be severed when he was detained by Military Intelligence in Homs in May. He then agreed to thumb print while blindfolded documents he had not read.

■ A man from Damascus was whipped, suspended, deprived of sleep and had cold water repeatedly poured over him while naked following his arrest in May when he was held by State Security officials in Damascus. He became ill but was denied medical treatment.

Deaths in custody

The rising incidence of torture was reflected by an upsurge in deaths in detention, with at least 200 people reported to have died in custody after being detained in connection with the protests. In many cases, the available evidence pointed to torture or other ill-treatment as the likely cause of death. No perpetrators were brought to justice. Some of the victims were children.

■ The body of Tariq Ziad Abd al-Qadr, who was arrested on 29 April, was returned to his family in Homs in June bearing numerous injuries, according to video film taken at the time. There were apparent electricity burns on his neck and penis, other burns on his body, marks apparently caused by whipping, and stab wounds in his side. Some of his hair had been pulled

S

out. A document apparently issued by the National Hospital attributed his death to a "shot in the chest" although no bullet wounds were evident.

■ Thamer Mohamed al-Shar'i, aged 15, went missing on 29 April as the security forces were carrying out mass arrests and shooting at protesters near Dera'a. Subsequently, a released detainee reported seeing him being bludgeoned by interrogators at an Air Force Intelligence detention centre in Damascus even though he had sustained a bullet wound in the chest. His body was reportedly returned to his family on 6 June.

■ In September, a couple identified a mutilated and disfigured body as their missing daughter, Zaynab al-Hosni, and held a funeral. On 4 October, Zaynab al-Hosni appeared on state television and the authorities sought to use the case to undermine the credibility of international reporting on human rights violations in Syria. However, the fate and whereabouts of Zaynab al-Hosni remained unknown, as did the identity of the woman whose mutilated body was buried and the circumstances of her death.

The authorities announced investigations into only two alleged deaths in custody, those of Hamza 'Ali al-Khateeb, aged 13, and Dr Sakher Hallak (see above) after well-publicized allegations that they had been tortured. In both cases, the investigations, which appeared to have been neither independent nor impartial, were said to have exonerated the security forces.

Impunity

Apart from the flawed investigations into two alleged deaths in custody, the authorities failed to investigate the many unlawful killings, torture and other serious abuses committed by the security forces, and to hold those responsible to account. Nor did they take any steps to investigate and hold to account those responsible for gross violations committed in previous years, including thousands of enforced disappearances and killings of prisoners at Saydnaya Military Prison in July 2008.

■ Tahsin Mammo's family learned by chance in 2011 that he was among the Saydnaya prison inmates killed in July 2008. A prisoner of conscience, he had been arrested with four other members of the Yezidi Kurdish minority in January 2007. His family had received no word of him since July 2008.

Discrimination – Kurds

Members of the Kurdish minority, comprising an estimated 10 per cent of the population, continued to face identity-based discrimination, including legal restrictions on use of their language and culture. They were also effectively stateless until President al-Assad issued Legislative Decree No. 49 on 7 April granting Syrian nationality to Ajanib ("foreign") Kurds but not to those known as Maktoumeen ("concealed", effectively meaning unregistered) who live mostly in al-Hasakah governorate. Kurdish rights activists continued to face arrest and imprisonment.

■ Kurdish language poets Omar 'Abdi Isma'il, 'Abdussamad Husayn Mahmud and Ahmad Fatah Isma'il were each sentenced to four-month prison terms in February after a judge convicted them of "inciting racial and sectarian strife" by organizing a Kurdish poetry festival in 2010.

Women's rights

Women continued to be discriminated against in both law and practice, and to face gender-based violence, including murder and other serious crimes committed against them often by male relatives ostensibly to uphold family "honour". On 3 January, President al-Assad amended the Penal Code by decree to increase the minimum penalty for murder and other violent crimes committed against women in the name of family "honour" from at least two years to between five and seven years. The decree also imposed a penalty of at least two years' imprisonment for rape or other sexual assault; formerly, perpetrators were exempt from prosecution or punishment if they married their victim.

Death penalty

Death sentences continued to be imposed. There were unconfirmed reports of executions, but no information on this was disclosed by the Syrian authorities.

Amnesty International visits/reports

🚌 The government did not permit Amnesty International access to Syria in 2011.

📄 End human rights violations in Syria: Amnesty International Submission to the UN Universal Periodic Review, October 2011 (MDE 24/034/2011)

📄 Deadly detention: Deaths in custody amid popular protest in Syria (MDE 24/035/2011)

📄 The long reach of the *Mukhabaraat*: violence and harassment against Syrians abroad and their relatives back home (MDE 24/057/2011)

▣ Health crisis: Syrian government targets the wounded and health workers (MDE 24/059/2011)

▣ UN General Assembly should condemn the violence in Syria (MDE 24/082/2011)

TAIWAN

TAIWAN
Head of state: **Ma Ying-jeou**
Head of government: **Wu Den-yih**
Death penalty: **retentionist**

Taiwan handed down more death sentences in 2011 than in any year in the past decade, despite stating that its long-term goal was abolition of the death penalty. Restrictions on freedom of assembly remained, with no progress made towards a relaxation of existing, stringent laws. The authorities did little to protect the housing rights of farmers across the island, at times colluding in their eviction.

Background

In 2009, Taiwan ratified the ICCPR and the International Covenant on Economic, Social and Cultural Rights. Despite passing an Implementation Act, which required the government to bring all laws, regulations, ordinances and administrative measures in line with the covenants before 10 December 2011, Taiwan had yet to amend or abolish the majority of those not in compliance.

Death penalty

Five people were executed on 4 March – just one month after President Ma apologized for the 1997 execution of an innocent man. As of November, there were 55 inmates with confirmed death sentences.

■ On 28 July, the Supreme Court rejected Chiou-Ho-shun's final appeal against his death sentence. On 25 August, the Prosecutor General rejected a request to seek an extraordinary appeal for a retrial. Chiou Ho-shun had been sentenced to death for robbery, kidnapping, blackmail and murder in 1989. With no material evidence, his conviction was based on confessions he and co-defendants alleged were extracted through torture. His case had bounced

between the High Court and the Supreme Court for more than two decades.

Justice system

As a step towards ensuring judicial independence and transparency, the Legislative Yuan passed the Judges Act in June to make it easier to remove judges found to be incompetent or corrupt.

Freedom of expression and assembly

Despite continued public demand, there was no progress on the government's proposal to amend the Assembly and Parade Law. The law allows police to forcibly disperse peaceful protesters, and places other restrictions on peaceful demonstrations.

Housing rights

Government officials allowed – and sometimes helped – developers to evict farmers across the country without due process including by failing to provide alternative accommodation or adequate compensation.

Migrants' rights

Migrant workers were unable to freely change employer. Domestic migrant workers and care-givers were often forced to work without adequate rest. The media exposed abuse and exploitation of migrant workers by government officials and celebrities.

T

TAJIKISTAN

REPUBLIC OF TAJIKISTAN
Head of state: **Emomali Rahmon**
Head of government: **Okil Okilov**
Death penalty: **abolitionist in practice**
Population: **7 million**
Life expectancy: **67.5 years**
Under-5 mortality: **61.2 per 1,000**
Adult literacy: **99.7 per cent**

Safeguards against torture enshrined in domestic law were not always adhered to. Freedom of expression remained restricted. The authorities failed to effectively prevent and prosecute violence against women and to protect survivors.

Torture and other ill-treatment

Police and security forces continued to use torture and other ill-treatment with almost total impunity, despite changes to the law in 2010. The European Court of Human Rights issued emergency measures to prevent the extradition of a man to Tajikistan, due to the prevalence of torture in the country. At the end of the year the government announced its intention to amend the Criminal Code with a definition of torture, in line with international law.

■ Safarali Sangov died on 5 March, four days after being arrested by police officers of the Sino District in Dushanbe. During the arrest, police reportedly beat him and other family members, including children and a woman who was four months pregnant. Following a public outcry and allegations that Safarali Sangov died as a result of torture at the police station, two policemen were charged in March with "negligence" and one with "exceeding authority". However, the prosecution subsequently dropped the latter charge, stating that testimonies of Safarali Sangov's relatives were not acceptable as evidence. After a legal battle, the case was transferred to the General Prosecutor's office for review.

■ The trial against Ilhom Ismonov and 52 co-defendants began on 11 July at Soghd Regional Court in northern Tajikistan. All were accused of membership of the Islamic Movement of Uzbekistan and of participating in organized crime. On 19 July, he and several others told the judge that they had been tortured in pre-trial detention. On 16 September, Ilhom Ismonov told the judge that he had been pressurized by

officials to retract his earlier allegations of torture and other ill-treatment. He had not dared speak out earlier, fearing retaliation from law enforcement agencies. The judge ignored his statement. His confession, allegedly obtained under torture, was used as evidence against him. The Prosecutor requested a 12-year prison sentence. The case was ongoing at the end of the year.

Freedom of expression – journalists

Tajikistani and international human rights groups reported that independent media outlets and journalists continued to face criminal and civil law suits for criticizing the government or government officials.

■ On 14 October, a court in Khujand in northern Tajikistan found BBC journalist Urunboy Usmonov guilty of complicity in the activities of a banned religious organization. He was sentenced to three years' imprisonment but released immediately under an amnesty. The Supreme Court dismissed his appeal on 30 November. Amnesty International believes that Urunboy Usmonov was targeted for his legitimate work as a journalist investigating the banned Islamic organization Hizb-ut-Tahrir. He had no access to a lawyer for a week after his arrest and there were allegations that he was tortured or ill-treated.

■ Also on 14 October, another court in Khujand found journalist Makhmadyusuf Ismoilov guilty of libel, insult and inciting hatred. A writer for *Nuri Zindagi* (Ray of Starlight), he was arrested on 23 November 2010 in the Soghd region. Fellow journalists believed that the charges related to an article he wrote about the local authorities in Asht district, which accused some officials of corruption and criticized local law enforcement agencies. Makhmadyusuf Ismoilov was fined approximately US$7,000 and banned from journalistic work for three years. In December, the conviction was upheld on appeal but the penalties were lifted.

Violence against women and girls

Violence against women remained a serious problem. A major factor contributing to the high rate of domestic violence was the failure of the state to take adequate measures to prevent illegal, early marriages. On 1 January, the minimum marriageable age was raised from 17 to 18 years by presidential decree. However, services to protect the survivors of domestic violence, such as shelters and adequate and safe alternative housing, remained insufficient. A draft law, "Social and Legal Protection against Domestic

T

Violence" – which had been in preparation for several years – was presented to parliament in the autumn. It had not been discussed or voted on by the end of the year.

Amnesty International visits/reports

🚋 Amnesty International delegates visited Tajikistan in April.

📑 Tajikistan: A coalition of non-governmental organizations is calling on the government to end torture and fulfil its international obligations (EUR 60/003/2011)

📑 Tajikistan: Amnesty International submission to the UN Universal Periodic Review, October 2011 (EUR 60/006/2011)

TANZANIA

UNITED REPUBLIC OF TANZANIA

Head of state:	Jakaya Kikwete
Head of government:	Mizengo Peter Pinda
Head of Zanzibar government:	Ali Mohamed Shein
Death penalty:	abolitionist in practice
Population:	46.2 million
Life expectancy:	58.2 years
Under-5 mortality:	107.9 per 1,000
Adult literacy:	72.9 per cent

Burundian refugees continued to live under threat of forced repatriation. Police and other law enforcement officials accused of committing human rights violations, including unlawful killings, were not brought to justice. Impunity continued for perpetrators of sexual and other forms of gender-based violence.

Background

The Constitution Review Act 2011, which set up a Commission to lead the constitutional review process, was passed in November amid protests by the minority opposition members of Parliament that the public consultation on the new law was inadequate. Representatives of the opposition party Chama Cha Demokrasia na Maendeleo (CHADEMA) continued to call for a review of the law, particularly provisions giving the President exclusive powers to appoint the Commission.

Refugees and migrants

Following a meeting in May between representatives of the governments of Tanzania and Burundi, and UNHCR, the UN refugee agency, the government of Tanzania announced its intention to close down Mtabila camp – home to about 38,000 Burundian refugees – by the end of December 2011. Tanzania also announced its intention to remove refugee protection by invoking the ceased circumstances clause of the UN Refugee Convention. Although the government expected that some 20,000 refugees would voluntarily return to Burundi, the affected refugees remained reluctant to return. The government announced in September that it was holding interviews with affected refugees regarding their ongoing protection needs; however, there remained no procedures in place to assess whether repatriation was a valid option. Affected refugees remained fearful of being forced to return to Burundi.

Impunity

There were reports of unlawful killings and torture and other ill-treatment by the police and other law enforcement officials during security operations in some parts of the country. More than 20 people reportedly died from gunshot wounds during the year, after the police used lethal force to quell demonstrations or to prevent illegal access to mining areas.

■ In January, at least three people died in Arusha town after police used live ammunition to disperse opposition party supporters who were protesting the election of a ruling party Chama Cha Mapinduzi candidate to the local mayoral seat. By the end of the year, no adequate investigations into these killings had been carried out and those responsible had not been brought to justice.

Violence against women and girls

Sexual and other forms of gender-based violence remained widespread, particularly domestic violence. Few perpetrators were brought to justice. The practice of female genital mutilation remained prevalent in some areas of the country.

Freedom of expression

Legislation such as the Newspapers Act, the National Security Act and the Broadcasting Services Act remained in place. These laws empower the authorities to restrict media work on the basis of

T

broad, undefined provisions such as "public interest", "the interests of peace and good order" and "national security interests". By the end of the year the government had failed to formally adopt two proposed draft laws – the Freedom of Information Bill 2006 and the Media Services Bill 2007 – and failed to incorporate the concerns expressed by civil society representatives into the Freedom of Information Bill. If enacted, the two laws would recognize the right to access information and repeal laws that allow illegitimate restrictions on press freedom.

Discrimination – attacks on albino people

There were no new reports of albino people being killed for their body parts during the year, although there were at least five attempted killings. The government's efforts to prevent human rights abuses against albino people continued to be inadequate.

Prison conditions

There were continued reports of overcrowding and unsanitary and poor living conditions in prisons. The Legal and Human Rights Centre, a local human rights NGO, reported that there were over 38,000 inmates in Tanzania's mainland prisons, despite a capacity of about 27,653. The organization attributed the problem of overcrowding and poor living conditions to the ineffectiveness of the judicial system, the lack of proper physical infrastructure and inadequate staffing in the country's prisons.

Death penalty

Courts continued to hand down the death penalty for capital offences; however, there were no executions carried out during the year. A court petition filed by three local civil society organizations in 2008 challenging the constitutionality of the death penalty remained pending in the High Court.

Amnesty International visits/reports

🚌 An Amnesty International delegate visited mainland Tanzania in November.

THAILAND

KINGDOM OF THAILAND

Head of state:	King Bhumibol Adulyadej
Head of government:	Yingluck Shinawatra (replaced Abhisit Vejjajiva in August)
Death penalty:	retentionist
Population:	69.5 million
Life expectancy:	74.1 years
Under-5 mortality:	13.5 per 1,000
Adult literacy:	93.5 per cent

Violence intensified in the internal armed conflict in southern Thailand, with insurgents increasingly targeting civilians and staging indiscriminate attacks in which civilians were killed. Security forces continued to torture and ill-treat detainees in the South. For the eighth consecutive year, no official was convicted of perpetrating human rights violations in the South, and none was prosecuted for deaths that occurred during the 2010 anti-government demonstrations. Authorities continued to persecute those peacefully expressing their opinion, primarily through the use of the lèse majesté law and Computer-related Crimes Act. Authorities tightened restrictions on asylum-seekers and refugees from Myanmar, particularly during massive flooding, and exploited migrant workers from neighbouring countries.

Background

National elections in July resulted in Yingluck Shinawatra, sister of deposed Prime Minister Thaksin Shinawatra, becoming Prime Minister, and her Puea Thai party winning an absolute majority in parliament. However, the party won no parliamentary seats from the country's three southern insurgency-wracked provinces, which experienced a spike in attacks and saw the death toll for the past eight years reach 5,000. The six-year-long political crisis continued, with election-related violence, and tension between the new government and the army later in the year. The Truth for Reconciliation Commission, set up in the aftermath of the April-May 2010 demonstrations, released its first two reports with recommendations.

In August, the UN Special Rapporteur on trafficking in persons visited Thailand. In October, Thailand's human rights record was assessed under the UN Universal Periodic Review.

Internal armed conflict

In keeping with past trends, the majority of those killed in the internal armed conflict in southern Thailand were civilians; more than half were Muslims. Insurgents increasingly used bombs and improvised explosive devices that targeted civilians or harmed them in indiscriminate attacks. Such attacks were partly designed to spread terror among the civilian population.

■ On 3 February, two insurgents slashed the throat of Abdullah Kaboh, a married Muslim man with six children, while he tapped rubber late at night in Pattani's Yarang district.

■ On 4 February, also in Yarang, two insurgents on a motorcycle shot and killed Ruem Meesrisawad, aged 79, a Buddhist who was retired from his job as a state-supported practitioner of traditional medicine. The attack occurred mid-morning, within 100m of two groups of security force personnel.

■ On 16 September in Sungai Kolok district, Narathiwat province, five Malaysian civilians including a child were killed, and at least 118 people were injured, when three bombs were detonated in a nightlife entertainment area within the course of 45 minutes.

■ On 25 October, at least 11 bombs exploded in the central district of Yala province around the same time just after sunset, killing three people and wounding at least 65 others.

Security forces also continued to commit human rights violations in their counter-insurgency efforts.

■ In the wake of a January insurgent attack on a military installation in Narathiwat, authorities reportedly tortured or ill-treated at least nine suspects.

Impunity

For the eighth consecutive year, no official or member of the Thai security forces in Thailand's three southernmost provinces was convicted of committing any offences involving human rights violations. This was due in part to Section 17 of the Emergency Decree, which remained in effect there (excepting one district) since July 2005. The decree provided immunity from prosecution to officials who commit such acts in the course of their duty. No one was brought to justice for the death of 85 Muslims at the hands of authorities in the Tak Bai district of Narathiwat province in October 2004; or the death in custody through torture of imam Yapha Kaseng in March 2008 in Narathiwat.

■ On 10 August, a court in Narathiwat sentenced Sudi-Rueman Mah-Leh to two years in prison for providing false information to officials inquiring into a case he had filed against a police officer who had allegedly tortured him. His conviction was based on the fact that the police officer and five of his colleagues were acquitted.

The Department of Special Investigation concluded that security forces were responsible for at least 16 deaths during the April-May 2010 anti-government demonstrations. Their cases were sent to the Office of the Attorney General to consider a submission to a court for inquest. No one was charged with those or any of the other 76 deaths.

Freedom of expression

Freedom of expression continued to be suppressed, primarily through the lèse majesté law (Article 112 of the Criminal Code), the Computer-related Crimes Act, and intimidation of the media. Most of those detained, charged, and/or sentenced under the laws were prisoners of conscience. On 1 December, the government inaugurated the Cyber Security Operation Centre to suppress cyber crimes, particularly offences against the monarchy committed on social media websites.

■ On 10 March, Ekkachai Hongkangvarn was charged under the lèse majesté law for selling DVDs of an Australian documentary about Thailand's monarchy and translated copies of Wikileaks cables on Thailand. He was released on bail.

■ On 15 March, Thanthawuthi Thaweewarodom, designer of norporchorusa.com, was sentenced to 10 years in prison under the lèse majesté law and three more years under the Computer-related Crimes Act, for comments on the website deemed critical of the monarchy that he had either posted or not removed. He remained in custody.

■ On 8 December, Joe Gordon (aka Lerpong Wichaikhammat), a dual US-Thai national, was sentenced to five years in prison (later reduced by half) on lèse majesté charges for allegedly owning a blog that linked to a Thai-language version of a book banned in Thailand. He committed the alleged offence while in the USA.

■ In July, the Constitutional Court ruled that the closed trial of lèse majesté defendant Darunee Charnchaoengsilpakul, held in 2009, "did not in any way restrict the rights of the defendant in a criminal case". Sentenced to 18 years in 2009, she was re-sentenced to 15 years in December.

T

■ On 23 November, a criminal court sentenced Ampon Tangnoppakul, a 61-year-old man with throat cancer, to 20 years in prison under the lèse majesté law and Computer-related Crimes Act. Although he claimed that he did not know how to send SMS messages, he was found guilty of sending four deemed insulting to a member of the royal family.

Refugees and migrants

Following statements earlier in the year by the National Security Council's Secretary-General and the governor of Tak province, indicating that refugees from Myanmar would be repatriated, the Thai government pledged during its Universal Periodic Review to uphold its international obligation not to return people to countries where they faced persecution.

Thailand's refugee population grew, and third-country resettlement continued. By the end of the year, nearly 150,000 refugees lived in nine camps on the Myanmar border. However, for the fifth consecutive year, the government did not activate its procedure for screening asylum-seekers, so nearly half the camp-based population was unregistered. Authorities discouraged aid organizations from providing food and other humanitarian assistance to this population. Asylum-seekers continued to be arrested, detained indefinitely, and deported or repatriated to countries where they were at risk of persecution.

■ In June, immigration authorities for the first time allowed the release on bail of 96 refugees, all Ahmadis from Pakistan; from Bangkok's Immigration Detention Centre.

■ In July, migrant workers in the fishing industry were given until August to register their names and employers with the authorities. Migrants in other industries had to register by July. The registration programme was launched in a bid to fight exploitation by human traffickers and employers.

■ In December, authorities forcibly handed over a UNHCR-registered refugee, Ka Yang, and his family to Laotian officials at the Thai-Lao border in Ubon Ratchathani province. He had been accepted by the USA for resettlement on 24 December 2009, but was among the 158 refugees Thailand forced back to Laos that same day. Ka Yang subsequently fled Laos and returned to Thailand.

During extensive flooding in Thailand beginning in August, immigration authorities and police arrested, deported, and extorted money from many migrants who lost their documentation in the floods or whose employers had withheld it. Migrant workers who returned to the borders without passports were often intercepted at immigration checkpoints, and in the case of workers from Myanmar especially, arrested and detained. Deportation – sometimes at night – generally followed, during which some were extorted of funds either directly by Thai authorities or with their knowledge.

■ In November, the government set up at least one shelter for migrants in response to reports that they were being turned away from general shelters.

Death penalty

There were no known executions. However, Thai courts handed down 40 death sentences in 2011, a modest drop from the average of approximately one per week over the past several years. Death row prisoners continued to be shackled in leg irons throughout their detention, despite a 2009 court decision, still under appeal, declaring it illegal.

■ Ikeda Kengo, a Japanese national who was sentenced to death in March 2009, remained on death row, despite either not having a lawyer or not being aware that he had one. Thai law requires a court-appointed lawyer in capital cases for those who are without legal representation.

Amnesty International visits/reports

🚌 Amnesty International delegates visited Thailand in September.

📄 "They took nothing but his life": Unlawful killings in Thailand's southern insurgency (ASA 39/002/2011)

T

TIMOR-LESTE

DEMOCRATIC REPUBLIC OF TIMOR-LESTE

Head of state:	José Manuel Ramos-Horta
Head of government:	Kay Rala Xanana Gusmão
Death penalty:	abolitionist for all crimes
Population:	1.2 million
Life expectancy:	62.5 years
Under-5 mortality:	56.4 per 1,000
Adult literacy:	50.6 per cent

Perpetrators of gross human rights violations committed during the Indonesian occupation of East Timor (1975-1999) remained at large. There were reports of human rights violations, including ill-treatment, by security forces. Levels of domestic violence remained high.

Background

In February, the UN Security Council extended the mandate of the UN Integrated Mission in Timor-Leste by another year. That same month, the UN Working Group on Enforced or Involuntary Disappearances visited Timor-Leste. In October, the country's human rights record was assessed under the UN Universal Periodic Review. Several states noted that perpetrators of human rights violations had gone unpunished. Timor-Leste agreed to consider calls from five states to implement recommendations made by the Commission for Reception, Truth and Reconciliation (CAVR).

Impunity

Impunity for human rights violations persisted despite ongoing investigations by the Serious Crimes Investigation Team. Victims, their families and Timorese NGOs continued to call for justice for human rights violations committed by Indonesian security forces between 1975 and 1999. Nevertheless, the government continued to promote reconciliation with Indonesia at the expense of justice. The majority of those accused of human rights violations were believed to be at large in Indonesia.

■ In July, Valentim Lavio, a former Besi Merah Putih militia member, was sentenced to nine years' imprisonment by the Dili District Court. He was charged with murder as a crime against humanity committed in the aftermath of the 1999 independence referendum.

His appeal was rejected on 26 September. However, by the end of the year the authorities confirmed that he was still free and had fled to Indonesia.

A Memorandum of Understanding between the Provedor (Ombudsman for Human Rights and Justice) and the Indonesian Human Rights Commission on the implementation of recommendations of the CAVR and the joint Indonesia-Timor-Leste Commission of Truth and Friendship (CTF) lapsed in January and was renewed in November. No progress was reported (see Indonesia entry).

A debate on two draft laws establishing a National Reparations Programme and an "Institute for Memory", mandated to implement recommendations of the CAVR and CTF, had yet to take place by the end of the year after parliament postponed it in February.

Police and security forces

In March, the UN handed full responsibility for police operations in the country to the Timor-Leste National Police Force. There were reports of human rights violations, including ill-treatment, committed by police and military officers.

Violence against women and girls

Domestic violence cases were prosecuted in the courts, as per the 2010 Law Against Domestic Violence. However, levels of such violence remained high, and some cases continued to be resolved through traditional justice mechanisms which restricted access to justice for victims.

Amnesty International visits/reports

🚌 Amnesty International delegates visited Timor-Leste in February and November.

📄 Timor-Leste: Justice delayed, justice denied – Amnesty International submission to the UN Universal Periodic Review, October 2011 (ASA 57/003/2011)

TOGO

TOGOLESE REPUBLIC

Head of state:	**Faure Gnassingbé**
Head of government:	**Gilbert Fossoun Houngbo**
Death penalty:	**abolitionist for all crimes**
Population:	**6.2 million**
Life expectancy:	**57.1 years**
Under-5 mortality:	**97.5 per 1,000**
Adult literacy:	**56.9 per cent**

Peaceful demonstrations by political parties and students were dispersed by security authorities using excessive force, including tear gas and rubber bullets. Some 30 political and military officials were sentenced to prison terms on the basis of confessions extracted under torture. The Truth, Justice and Reconciliation Commission (TJRC) held hearings from September to November; impunity remained the rule among the security forces, who attempted to disrupt the process.

Background

In March a draft law, stipulating that prior notification must be given before any public demonstration, sparked political criticism and public protest marches. The law was adopted in May.

In October, the Court of Justice of ECOWAS criticized the government's handling of the case against nine parliamentarians with the opposition party National Alliance for Change (ANC) who had been dismissed from the National Assembly. The Court asked the government to "rectify this prejudice" and to give them financial compensation. Although the authorities agreed to pay compensation, by the end of the year they were still refusing to reintegrate the nine men into the National Assembly.

In October, Togo accepted some of the recommendations made by the Universal Periodic Review Working Group, including guaranteeing the independence and impartiality of the TJRC. The government refused to accept recommendations regarding the ratification of the Rome Statute of the International Criminal Court.

Excessive use of force

The security forces repeatedly dispersed demonstrators with tear gas and used excessive force against several protest marches organized by political parties and students.

■ In March, demonstrators protesting against the draft law limiting freedom of assembly were dispersed by security forces using tear gas. Jean-Pierre Fabre, President of the ANC, was put under house arrest on several occasions to prevent him from joining protest marches.

■ In June, the security forces used force against the student organization Mouvement pour l'épanouissement des étudiants togolais (Movement for the development of Togolese students, MEET), who were demanding improvements to the university system. The clashes occurred after seven students, including MEET leader Abou Seydou, were arrested and ill-treated. Several students were wounded by rubber bullets, some severely.

Torture and other ill-treatment

Torture in pre-trial detention was widespread in order to extract confessions or implicate defendants.

■ In March, Sow Bertin Agba was arrested for fraud and tortured while held in handcuffs for five days in a garage at the National Intelligence Agency premises. He suffered a fractured arm and wounds all over his body. By the end of the year, he was still detained without trial at the civil prison in Tsévié.

■ In September, 33 people accused of plotting against the State, including Kpatcha Gnassingbé, half-brother of the President, were sentenced to prison terms of up to 20 years by the Supreme Court. Immediately after the trial, the Minister of Justice asked the National Commission on Human Rights to investigate the torture allegations. It had not published its conclusions by the end of the year.

Impunity

The TJRC, set up to shed light on human rights violations committed between 1958 and 2005, held hearings from September to November. A total of 508 people were heard, selected from some 20,000 statements received. The initial hearings, in the capital Lomé and other towns, dealt primarily with the 1991 attack on the Primature (Prime Minister's office) and some of the human rights violations committed during the 2005 presidential elections. One of the sessions in September was disrupted by the security forces in a clear attempt to intimidate members of the Commission and witnesses.

No progress was made in the investigation of 72 complaints lodged by victims of political repression in 2005.

Amnesty International visits/reports

Togo: Procès Kpatcha Gnassingbé – les aveux extorqués sous la torture ne doivent pas être retenus (AFR 57/001/2011)

TRINIDAD AND TOBAGO

REPUBLIC OF TRINIDAD AND TOBAGO

Head of state:	George Maxwell Richards
Head of government:	Kamla Persad-Bissessar
Death penalty:	retentionist
Population:	1.3 million
Life expectancy:	70.1 years
Under-5 mortality:	35.3 per 1,000
Adult literacy:	98.7 per cent

A state of emergency was declared in response to rising crime levels. There were continued reports of killings by police, some in circumstances suggesting that they may have been unlawful.

Background

The government introduced a state of emergency on 21 August to address an unspecified "threat to national security" related to organized crime. This granted the security forces powers of search and arrest without a warrant, prohibited public marches or meetings without the permission of the Commissioner of Police and introduced a night-time curfew. The state of emergency was lifted on 5 December.

The Prime Minister announced that there had been a dramatic fall in violent crime during the state of emergency. However, there were frequent reports that police abused their powers and that residents of alleged crime "hotspots" were being indiscriminately targeted. More than half of the 449 people arrested under anti-gang legislation under the state of emergency were released due to lack of evidence, which the Director of Public Prosecutions blamed on poor evidence gathering by the police.

Police and security forces

Dozens of people were killed by the police. Police claims that they had fired in self-defence were frequently challenged by eyewitness testimony.

■ At 9pm on 22 July, Abigail Johnson, Allana Duncan and Kerron Eccles were shot dead by police as they were driving through the village of Barrackpore. Police claimed that they were shot at by passengers in the car and had to return fire. However, eyewitnesses reportedly stated that the three were unarmed and had been shot deliberately. The deaths led to a week of protests by local residents. Seven police officers were charged with murder in October and a trial was continuing at the end of the year.

There were reports of arbitrary detentions and ill-treatment by police during the state of emergency.

■ Arthur Lewis was arrested at his home in Williamsville on 5 September. He claimed he was beaten with batons while detained at Morvant Police Station. He was released without charge on 9 September.

Justice system

In September the Justice Minister announced that there was a backlog of over 100,000 criminal cases in the courts. A bill to expedite the judicial process by removing preliminary inquiries was enacted in December.

Violence against women and girls

There was a 30 per cent drop in reports of sexual violence between January and September 2011 compared to the same period in 2010. However, gender-based violence continued to be under-reported. This was linked to inadequate police training and the slowness of the justice system. Two and a half years after it was drafted, the National Policy on Gender and Development had yet to be adopted.

Death penalty

Two people were sentenced to death, and there were 31 people on death row at the end of the year. The government introduced a bill in January to facilitate the resumption of executions. The bill was rejected by Parliament in February.

Amnesty International reports/visits

Amnesty International delegates visited Trinidad and Tobago in November/December.

Trinidad and Tobago: New bill would make the Constitution inconsistent with human rights and pave the way to executions (AMR 49/001/2011).

T

TUNISIA

REPUBLIC OF TUNISIA

Head of state:	Moncef Marzouqi (replaced Fouad Mbezaa in December, who replaced Zine El 'Abidine Ben 'Ali in January)
Head of government:	Hamadi Jebali (replaced Beji Caid Essebsi in December, who replaced Mohamed Ghannouchi in February)
Death penalty:	abolitionist in practice
Population:	10.6 million
Life expectancy:	74.5 years
Under-5 mortality:	20.7 per 1,000
Adult literacy:	77.6 per cent

Some 300 people died and hundreds were injured by the security forces during mass protests in the weeks prior to 14 January, when President Zine El 'Abidine Ben 'Ali was toppled from power and fled the country. Many peaceful protesters were shot dead by security forces using live ammunition. A wholesale process of reform was then begun: political prisoners, including prisoners of conscience, were released; legal restrictions on political parties and NGOs were eased; the Department of State Security (DSS), notorious for torturing detainees with impunity, was dissolved; Tunisia became party to additional international human rights treaties; and a new National Constituent Assembly was elected with a mandate to draft and agree a new Constitution. However, there were continuing human rights violations, with further instances of excessive force by security forces against protesters demonstrating against what they saw as the slow pace of change; some protesters were beaten or otherwise ill-treated during arrest and in detention. Despite some improvements, women continued to face discrimination in law and practice. The death penalty remained in force but no new death sentences were reported and there were no executions.

Background

After 23 years in power, President Ben 'Ali fled Tunisia on 14 January, obtaining refuge in Saudi Arabia, following weeks of countrywide protests against his repressive rule. Over 230 protesters were killed and 700 injured during the protests, and over 70 prisoners died in prison in incidents related to the protests. Prime Minister Mohamed Ghannouchi appointed himself acting President; within hours he was replaced by Fouad Mbezaa and reverted to his position as Prime Minister. He declared a state of emergency on 15 January, which was renewed in August, November and again in December until the end of March 2012, and appointed a caretaker government. In February, he was forced to resign in the face of popular protests and was replaced as Prime Minister by Beji Caid Essebsi. Following elections to the National Constituent Assembly in October, Moncef Marzouqi was appointed President and Hamadi Jebali became Prime Minister in December.

In February, the interim government declared an amnesty, releasing prisoners of conscience and other political prisoners, and set up three commissions as part of the process of reform: the High Commission for achieving the aims of the revolution, political reform and democratic transition; the National Committee for investigating cases of bribery and corruption; and the Fact-Finding Commission on Abuses Committed in the Last Period, which was mandated to investigate killings of protesters and other abuses by the security forces during the protests that toppled President Ben 'Ali. This last Commission had still to report at the end of the year, but two former Interior Ministers, Rafik Haj Kacem and Ahmed Friaa, were among a group of 139 former officials, including the former President, referred for trial on charges arising from the killing and injuring of protesters in the weeks up to 14 January. Their trial began in November and was continuing at the end of the year. Former President Ben 'Ali and members of his family were also tried in their absence and convicted on corruption and drugs-related charges.

In March, the interim government dissolved the widely hated DSS, the security police notorious for torture and other serious human rights violations under President Ben 'Ali.

The interim government also amended the highly restrictive Law on Associations to allow the legal registration of formerly banned political parties, including Ennahda (Renaissance) Islamist party and the Tunisian Workers' Communist Party, and human rights and other NGOs; the Interior Ministry said that 1,366 associations and 111 political parties had been officially authorized by September. The former ruling party under Ben 'Ali, the Constitutional Democratic Party, was disbanded in March.

The government ratified key international human rights treaties, including the Optional Protocol to the ICCPR; the Optional Protocol to the UN Convention against Torture; the International Convention against enforced disappearance; and the Rome Statute of the International Criminal Court. It also withdrew Tunisia's reservations to CEDAW.

The first elections since the uprising were held on 23 October for a 217-seat National Constituent Assembly tasked with drafting a new Constitution and appointing a new government. Ennahda won the greatest number of seats but not an overall majority. The Assembly met for the first time on 22 November and appointed a new President, Prime Minister and Speaker drawn from the three political parties with the most seats. The appointees took up their posts in December.

The UN Special Rapporteur on torture and the UN Special Rapporteur on the promotion and protection of human rights and fundamental freedoms while countering terrorism both visited Tunisia in May.

Legal and constitutional developments

The Constitution was suspended in March. Other laws remained in effect, but some were significantly amended to ease restrictions on the exercise of human rights. These included the Press Law and the law relating to audiovisual communications, which continue to criminalize "defamation" but no longer make it punishable with imprisonment. The Law on Associations was amended to remove restrictions on forming or belonging to an association and to decriminalize providing services to an "unrecognized association". The law on torture was amended to bring the definition of torture in the Penal Code into closer conformity with the definition under international law, although prosecutions for torture are subject to a statute of limitation of 15 years, contrary to the right to remedy and reparation under international law. Other laws, such as those on Counter-terrorism, on the Regulation of Meetings, Processions and Parades, and on the Organization of the Judiciary, remained in need of reform.

The Interior Ministry set out a "road map" for reform of the police, but this included no provision for investigating and ensuring accountability for past violations of human rights by the police and the

disbanded DSS. It was unclear whether any vetting system was established to prevent former DSS or other security or police officials responsible for past human rights violations being appointed to or remaining in positions in which they could commit further abuses.

Excessive use of force

After the appointment of the interim government, renewed demonstrations protesting among other things about the perceived slow pace of reform were met with excessive force by security forces.

■ In February, three people were reported to have died when security forces violently dispersed a peaceful sit-in in Kasbah, Tunis.

■ In May, security forces beat journalists and allegedly prevented them from filming the forcible dispersal of renewed protests in Kasbah. The Interior Minister apologized but the security officers used violence again on 15 July when protesters attempted to join a sit-in in Kasbah. Many of at least 47 people reported to have been arrested alleged that they were beaten at the time of their arrest, including Ahmed Ben Nacib, a human rights activist with the NGO Liberty and Equity, who was chased by police on motorcycles, beaten with truncheons, kicked and slapped on arrest and then further assaulted in police custody before being released.

■ Thabet el Hejlaoui, aged 13, died on 17 July when he was hit apparently by a stray bullet while watching the security forces fire on anti-government protesters in front of an army compound in Sidi Bouzid.

Freedom of expression

Security forces were accused of failing to respond effectively on several occasions when members of some militant religious groups sought to prevent other people from exercising their right to freedom of expression.

■ In October, police were accused of failing to intervene effectively when religious militants attacked the headquarters of Nesma TV after it aired the animated film *Persepolis*, which they considered blasphemous. Later, the TV station's owner was attacked. The police arrested some suspects but released them without bail. The station owner faced charges of "moral corruption" – a crime punishable with imprisonment and a fine – and "disrupting public order" in a case filed against him by a group of lawyers.

T

Torture and other ill-treatment

There were new reports of torture and other ill-treatment but on a far reduced scale compared to previous years. In most cases, complainants alleged that they had been beaten by police when they were arrested during protests or while being taken to or detained at police stations.

■ Fouad Badrouci, a student aged 17, was arrested by masked police officers in Tunis on 6 May after a protest. They punched, kicked and beat him with batons before taking him with several other young protesters to Bouchoucha Prison. There, the detainees were forced to stand with their arms and one leg raised for a prolonged period, beaten and denied food and water. They were made to sign blank papers and were then released early the next day. Fouad Badrouci's injuries included a broken nose, right arm and rib.

■ Mohamed Sidki Hlimi alleged that he was raped and otherwise tortured by police officers who summoned him to an army camp in Kasserine in March after he blamed a senior police officer for deaths during the protests against President Ben 'Ali. He said that he was handcuffed and shackled throughout his seven days of detention, and kept naked after the first night when he was stripped, suspended from a pole, beaten and raped. He was beaten again when he refused to sign a statement incriminating people he did not know in the burning of police stations. He was then released.

Following his visit to Tunisia in May, the UN Special Rapporteur on torture urged the government to instruct all police and other law enforcement officials that torture and other ill-treatment are prohibited and to ensure that those who commit such abuses are held criminally liable.

Impunity

Although charges were brought against several former officials in relation to killings of protesters and other abuses during the uprising, no steps were taken to ensure accountability for the gross human rights violations committed during President Ben 'Ali's 23 years in power. Families of victims complained that they were denied justice and that police, DSS and other officials responsible for previous human rights violations remained in their positions or had been transferred to new ones and even promoted. Some families tried to initiate investigations of alleged perpetrators but investigating judges appeared generally reluctant or unable to take action against officials, compounded by the apparent unwillingness of the Interior Ministry to co-operate. From May, all cases relating to human rights violations committed during the uprising were referred to military courts.

The Fact-Finding Commission appointed in February to investigate alleged violations committed during the uprising had still not completed its work by the end of the year. The Commission said it would not refer evidence unrequested to the judiciary, prompting questions as to its effectiveness. It said it had met all the victims of violations during the uprising but many people injured in the protests refuted this. The Commission was expected to report its findings and recommendations in early 2012.

Women's rights

The interim government withdrew Tunisia's reservations to CEDAW and there were other improvements. In particular, the government adopted the principle of parity between women and men in elections, although in practice men still predominated in party candidates' lists, and women were allowed to use pictures showing them wearing a *hijab* (headscarf) in their national identity cards. However, women still faced discrimination in law and in practice; for example, the Personal Status Code still discriminated against women in matters such as inheritance and custody of children, and some women's rights activists complained that they were targeted in smear campaigns.

■ Journalist Salma Jlassi, a leading member of the National Journalists' Syndicate, reported that she was subjected to anonymous death threats and degrading comments in the media and through the internet, apparently because of her public position and opinions.

Refugees and migrants

From January on, many Tunisians sought to escape the country in small boats. Some were lost at sea; others reached the Italian island of Lampedusa. In April, the Tunisian and Italian governments agreed that some 20,000 Tunisians would be returned to Tunisia and that the Tunisian authorities would tighten controls along the coast.

Large numbers of migrants and refugees entered Tunisia from Libya following the outbreak of conflict there. Many migrants were assisted to return to their home countries but some 3,800 refugees and asylum-seekers were still stranded at the end of the year at Choucha camp, one of three camps established near the Ras Jdir border crossing with Libya. Most were from countries to which they could not return for fear of persecution, including Eritrea, Somalia and Sudan.

Death penalty

The death penalty remained in force but no death sentences were known to have been imposed and there were no executions. Tunisia has maintained a moratorium on executions since 1991.
■ Saber Ragoubi, convicted of security-related charges and sentenced to death in 2007, was released in February.

Amnesty International visits/reports

🚌 Amnesty International delegates visited Tunisia in January, February/March, April and October.

📓 Tunisia: Human rights agenda for change (MDE 30/008/2011)

📓 Tunisia in revolt: State violence during anti-government protests (MDE 30/011/2011)

📓 Amnesty International's human rights manifesto for Tunisia (MDE 30/017/2011)

TURKEY

REPUBLIC OF TURKEY

Head of state:	Abdullah Gül
Head of government:	Recep Tayyip Erdoğan
Death penalty:	abolitionist for all crimes
Population:	73.6 million
Life expectancy:	74 years
Under-5 mortality:	20.3 per 1,000
Adult literacy:	90.8 per cent

Promised constitutional and other legal reforms did not occur. Instead, the right to freedom of expression was threatened and protesters faced increased police violence. Thousands of prosecutions brought under flawed anti-terrorism laws routinely failed fair trial standards. Bomb attacks claimed the lives of civilians. No progress was made in recognizing the right to conscientious objection or in protecting the rights of children in the judicial system. The rights of refugees and asylum-seekers and lesbian,

gay, bisexual and transgender people remained unsecured in law. Preventive mechanisms to combat violence against women remained inadequate.

Background

In June the Justice and Development Party (AKP) won parliamentary elections and were re-elected to government. Nine elected opposition candidates were unable to take up their seats in Parliament due to cases against them under anti-terrorism laws: eight were being prosecuted and remained in detention, and one was barred from holding office due to a conviction.

In July, the head of the armed forces and his three most senior generals resigned, demonstrating the continuing tensions between the government and the armed forces. The resignations followed a wave of arrests of serving and retired military officials accused of plotting to overthrow the government.

In September Turkey ratified the Optional Protocol to the Convention against Torture, paving the way for independent monitoring of places of detention. However, by the end of the year, it had not introduced legislation to establish the necessary domestic implementing mechanism, or other promised preventive mechanisms such as an independent police complaints procedure and an ombudsman's office.

At the end of the year, the promised draft constitution had not been made available for discussion. Constitutional amendments adopted by a referendum during the previous parliament aimed at bringing trade union laws closer to international standards were not implemented.

Armed clashes between the Kurdistan Workers' Party (PKK) and the armed forces increased. In October, a major military intervention was launched into northern Iraq, targeting PKK bases and displacing hundreds of civilians from their villages. In December, 35 civilians were killed, the majority of them children, when a Turkish warplane bombed a group of civilians in the district of Uludere near the border with Iraq.

In October earthquakes struck the eastern province of Van resulting in more than 600 deaths. The authorities were criticized for the slowness of the response to the crisis which left thousands homeless in freezing conditions.

Turkish authorities spoke out against human rights violations across the eastern Mediterranean. In

T

September, the government announced it would challenge the legality of the naval blockade of Gaza at the International Court of Justice. A UN report into the May 2010 boarding of the Turkish ship, the *Mavi Marmara,* had concluded that Israeli defence forces had used excessive force in the operation which resulted in the deaths of nine Turkish nationals. In November, the Foreign Minister announced the imposition of sanctions against Syria due to the continued killings of peaceful protesters.

Freedom of expression

A large number of prosecutions were brought which threatened individuals' right to freedom of expression. In particular, critical journalists, Kurdish political activists, and others risked unfair prosecution when speaking out on the situation of Kurds in Turkey, or criticizing the armed forces. In addition to prosecutions brought under various articles of the Penal Code, a vast number of cases threatening freedom of expression were brought under anti-terrorism legislation (see Unfair trials). Threats of violence against prominent outspoken individuals continued. In November new regulations came into force raising further concerns regarding the arbitrary restriction of websites.
■ In February, human rights defender Halil Savda received confirmation of his conviction for "alienating the public from the institution of military service". He was sentenced to 100 days' imprisonment for voicing his support for the right to conscientious objection from military service. At the end of the year, two further prosecutions on the same charge were continuing and another conviction was pending at the Supreme Court of Appeals.
■ In March, Ahmet Şık and Nedim Şener, both journalists who investigate alleged human rights abuses by state officials, were charged with membership of a terrorist organization. Their arrests and those of six other journalists were part of a police operation against Ergenekon, an alleged criminal network with links to the military and other state institutions charged with plotting to overthrow the government. Written works by them were central to the evidence presented as part of the prosecution. They remained in pre-trial detention at the end of the year.
■ In November, 44 people, including publisher Ragıp Zarakolu and Professor Büşra Ersanlı were arrested on the grounds of their alleged membership of the PKK-linked Kurdistan Communities Union (KCK). Ragıp Zarakolu and Büşra Ersanlı were both questioned about their participation in events held by the Politics Academy of the Peace and Democracy Party, a recognized political party, and their respective publishing and academic work. Further waves of arrests in November and December saw 37 lawyers and 36 journalists detained on suspicion of KCK membership. They remained in detention at the end of the year.
■ In June, death threats were made against Baskın Oran and Etyen Mahçupyan, both journalists at the bilingual Armenian/Turkish *Agos* newspaper. Similar threats had been made since 2004 for which no one had been brought to justice.

Torture and other ill-treatment

Allegations of torture and other ill-treatment in and during transfer to police stations and prisons persisted. Police routinely used excessive force during demonstrations, notably during protests before and after the June elections. In many cases, demonstrations became violent following police intervention and the use of pepper gas, water cannon and plastic bullets. In many instances, media documented law enforcement officials beating demonstrators with batons.
■ In May and June, demonstrations in the city of Hopa in the north-eastern Artvin province of Turkey led to clashes between police and protesters, where one demonstrator died and others were injured. Metin Lokumcu died of a heart attack after being overcome by pepper gas fired by police. Demonstrators in Ankara protesting the policing of the Hopa demonstrations were also subjected to police violence. According to her lawyer, demonstrator Dilşat Aktaş was beaten by around 10 police officers, leaving her with a broken hip and unable to walk for six months. A criminal investigation into the incident had not concluded at the end of the year. The alleged assault by police officers was the second involving Dilşat Aktaş. In March, television cameras showed her being punched by a police officer, during a protest, yet the Ankara prosecutor decided not to pursue the case.
■ In October, army conscript Uğur Kantar died in hospital, reportedly as a result of torture inflicted by soldiers while he was in military custody within his garrison in northern Cyprus. Five officials, including the

T

military prison director, were indicted for causing his death. The prosecution was continuing at the end of the year.

Impunity

Investigations into alleged human rights abuses by state officials remained ineffective. In cases where criminal cases were opened, the chances of bringing those responsible to justice remained remote. Counter charges continued to be used as a tactic against those who alleged the abuse.

■ In June, Colonel Ali Öz and seven other military personnel were convicted of negligence for their failure to relay information regarding the plot to kill journalist and human rights defender Hrant Dink, which could have prevented his murder in 2007. Although a Children's Court in July convicted Ogün Samast of shooting Hrant Dink, doubt remained whether the full circumstances around the killing, including the issue of collusion by state officials, would be investigated.

■ No public investigation was carried out following the death of a family of seven in the Kurdistan region of northern Iraq in August, reportedly as a result of bombing by a Turkish warplane. Attacks by the air force on PKK bases in the area had been taking place at the time.

■ In September, the groundbreaking decision issued in 2010, convicting prison guards and other state officials following the October 2008 death in custody of Engin Çeber, was overturned by the Supreme Court of Appeals on procedural grounds. The communication of the written judgement was delayed for more than two months, further complicating efforts to ensure justice for Engin Çeber.

■ In December a police officer was convicted of "negligent killing" following the 2007 shooting in custody of Nigerian asylum-seeker Festus Okey. The court rejected an application by relatives to intervene in the case as an "injured party" in accordance with Turkish law. The judge also made criminal complaints against activists who had criticized the prosecution and sought to intervene in the case.

■ In December, a local court failed to issue a custodial sentence to a police officer who was filmed in 2009 catching and then repeatedly striking a child demonstrator in the head with the butt of his rifle. S.T., aged 14, suffered a fractured skull and remained in intensive care for six days following the attack. The court reduced the punishment on the grounds that the injury was accidental and due to the "conditions in the area". The officer was issued with a six-month suspended sentence and allowed to continue with his police duties.

Unfair trials

Thousands of prosecutions were brought during the year under overly broad and vague anti-terrorism laws, the vast majority for membership of a terrorist organization, provisions which have led to additional abuses. Many of those prosecuted were political activists, among them students, journalists, writers, lawyers and academics. Prosecutors routinely interrogated suspects regarding conduct protected by the right to freedom of expression or other internationally guaranteed rights. Other flaws included the use of extended pre-trial detention, during which time defence lawyers were prevented from examining the evidence against their clients or effectively challenging the legality of their detention due to secrecy orders preventing their access to the file.

■ At the end of the year university student Cihan Kırmızıgül had been held in pre-trial detention for 22 months, accused of damaging property and membership of a terrorist organization. The prosecution was based on his wearing of a traditional scarf, matching those worn by people alleged to have taken part in a demonstration where Molotov cocktails were thrown. One police officer also identified him as having been at the scene, contradicting the statements of other officers. Despite the prosecutor requesting Cihan Kırmızıgül's acquittal due to lack of evidence, the judge ruled that his detention and prosecution should continue.

Children's rights

Prosecutions continued of children under anti-terrorism laws, including for participation in demonstrations, despite 2010 legislative amendments which were intended to prevent child demonstrators being prosecuted under these laws. While the number of children prosecuted had gone down, many were still held in adult police custody before transfer to the children's department. Pre-charge detention periods of up to the maximum of four days were recorded and children continued to be held in extended pre-trial detention. The absence of Children's Courts in many provinces was not addressed.

T

■ By the end of the year, 17-year-old L.K. had been held in pre-trial detention for eight months awaiting the decision of the Supreme Court of Appeals regarding which court had the jurisdiction to try him.

Abuses by armed groups

Attacks·by armed groups caused civilian death and injury.

■ On 20 September three civilians were killed and 34 injured in a bomb attack targeting a busy shopping district of the capital, Ankara. The Kurdistan Freedom Falcons (TAK) claimed responsibility for the attack.

■ On the same day, four civilians were killed in a PKK attack apparently targeting police in the south-eastern province of Siirt.

Housing rights

Forced evictions violated the rights of tenants to consultation, compensation and provision of alternative housing. Many of those affected in the context of urban regeneration projects were among the poorest and most at-risk groups, including people previously forcibly displaced from villages in south-eastern Turkey. In May, the UN Committee on Economic, Social and Cultural Rights published their concerns regarding such projects.

■ In the Tarlabaşı district of Istanbul, dozens of families were forcibly evicted as part of the urban regeneration project carried out by the Beyoğlu municipality. Individuals reported that they had been made effectively homeless.

Prisoners of conscience – conscientious objectors

No progress was made in recognizing the right to conscientious objection to military service in domestic law or to end the repeated prosecution of conscientious objectors for their refusal to perform military service. In November, the European Court of Human Rights found that Turkey's refusal to grant a civilian alternative to military service violated the right to freedom of thought, conscience and religion in the case of *Erçep v. Turkey*. People who publicly supported the right to conscientious objection continued to be prosecuted (see freedom of expression).

■ Conscientious objector İnan Süver remained in prison due to multiple convictions for his refusal to perform military service until December, when he was conditionally released.

Refugees and asylum-seekers

Access to the asylum procedure was arbitrarily denied, resulting in people being forcibly returned to places where they may face persecution. The authorities failed to introduce planned legislation guaranteeing basic rights for refugees and asylum-seekers. From May onwards, thousands of Syrian nationals fled to Turkey seeking protection from violence and human rights abuses in the country. Many of them were accommodated in camps but not provided with access to UNHCR, the UN refugee agency, or to the asylum procedure. Their access to the outside world was severely restricted, including the ability to report on the human rights situation in Syria. There were reports of a number of Syrians being abducted from within Turkey and transferred to face persecution in Syria.

Rights of lesbian, gay, bisexual and transgender people

Discrimination on the grounds of sexual orientation and gender identity was not addressed. Lesbian, gay, bisexual and transgender (LGBT) rights activists continued to face harassment by the authorities. During 2011, LGBT rights groups recorded eight murders alleged to be on the grounds of the victims' sexual orientation or gender identity.

■ In November, three transgender women, all members of the Ankara-based LGBT rights group Pembe Hayat (Pink Life), were convicted of "insulting police officers" and "resisting the police". The charges were brought after they alleged that they were arbitrarily arrested and ill-treated by police officers. No police officers were prosecuted in relation to the incident.

Violence against women and girls

Turkey ratified the Council of Europe Convention on preventing and combating violence against women and domestic violence. However, domestic preventive mechanisms remained woefully inadequate and the number of shelters was far below that required by domestic law.

■ In October the Supreme Court of Appeals confirmed the reduction in sentences for 26 men convicted of raping a girl sold into prostitution at the age of 12 on the grounds that she had "consented" to sex.

Amnesty International visits/reports

🚌 Amnesty International delegates visited Turkey in January, March, April, May, June, August, September, October and December.

TURKMENISTAN

TURKMENISTAN

Head of state and government:	**Gurbanguly Berdymukhamedov**
Death penalty:	**abolitionist for all crimes**
Population:	**5.1 million**
Life expectancy:	**65 years**
Under-5 mortality:	**45.3 per 1,000**
Adult literacy:	**99.6 per cent**

The UN Committee against Torture found torture to be "widespread" in Turkmenistan. The government continued to clamp down on journalists and human rights defenders.

Torture and other ill-treatment

There were continued reports of torture or other ill-treatment of human rights defenders, journalists, and certain religious minorities by police, officers of the Ministry of National Security and prison personnel. The authorities failed to carry out effective investigations into such allegations.

In June the Committee against Torture published its Concluding Observations on Turkmenistan. The Committee expressed concern at the "numerous and consistent allegations about the widespread practice of torture and ill-treatment of detainees".

Repression of dissent

The authorities continued to suppress dissent. Journalists working with foreign media outlets known to publish criticism of the authorities faced harassment and intimidation. Independent civil society activists were unable to operate openly. The Committee against Torture urged the government to "ensure that human rights defenders and journalists, in Turkmenistan and abroad, are protected from intimidation or violence as a result of their activities". The authorities continued to use confinement in psychiatric hospitals to silence dissent.

■ Prisoners of conscience Annakurban Amanklychev and Sapardurdy Khadzhiev, associated with the NGO Turkmenistan Helsinki Foundation, continued to serve prison terms for "illegal acquisition, possession or sale of ammunition or firearms", following an unfair trial in 2006. The Committee against Torture urged the government to comply with the 2010 request from the UN Working Group on Arbitrary Detention to promptly release them and award them appropriate financial compensation.

■ Dovletmyrat Yazkuliev, a reporter for Radio Free Europe/Radio Liberty, was pardoned on 26 October as part of a presidential amnesty. After a brief trial earlier in October, he was found guilty of encouraging a relative to commit suicide and sentenced to five years' imprisonment. His supporters claim that he was targeted because of his outspoken reporting of a deadly explosion at an arms depot near Ashgabat in July. Earlier in the year, he had reported on the revolutions sweeping the Middle East and made comparisons with the situation in Turkmenistan.

■ Amangelen Shapudakov, an 80-year-old activist, was detained on 7 March and confined for 40 days in a psychiatric hospital after conducting an interview for Radio Azatlyq (the Turkmen language service of Radio Free Europe/Radio Liberty) in which he accused a local government official of corruption.

■ The independent émigré news site Chronicles of Turkmenistan was hacked into and disabled on 18 July, days after it had published material on the arms depot explosion near Ashgabat. The hackers reportedly published information about users of the site, including those in Turkmenistan, putting them at risk of harassment by the authorities. Local officials visited the home of the editor's mother, reportedly asking intimidating questions. She subsequently reported that she was under surveillance.

Freedom of religion or belief

Religious activity in Turkmenistan remained strictly controlled. Many minority religious groups continued

T

to face obstruction in registering, leaving them more susceptible to harassment by the authorities.

Refusal to serve in the army remained a criminal offence and there was no alternative civilian service for conscientious objectors. Eight Jehovah's Witnesses were serving prison terms for conscientious objection, and one was serving a suspended sentence.

The Protestant Pastor, Ilmurad Nurliev, remained in prison.

Enforced disappearances

The authorities continued to withhold information about the whereabouts of dozens of people arrested and convicted in connection with the alleged 2002 assassination attempt on former President Saparmurad Niyazov. The Committee against Torture urged the government to ensure prompt, impartial and thorough investigations into all outstanding cases of alleged disappearance, and to notify the victims' relatives of the outcomes.

Freedom of movement

On 1 August, Turkmenistani students studying in Tajikistan who had come home for the holidays were banned from returning to resume their studies. In October, the ban was lifted, but some students were still prevented from returning to their universities. The Turkmenistani authorities did not explain the reason for this.

UGANDA

REPUBLIC OF UGANDA

Head of state and government:	Yoweri Kaguta Museveni
Death penalty:	retentionist
Population:	34.5 million
Life expectancy:	54.1 years
Under-5 mortality:	127.5 per 1,000
Adult literacy:	73.2 per cent

Restrictions increased on freedom of expression. Authorities clamped down on peaceful protests, including by using excessive force which led to deaths. Law enforcement officials continued to commit human rights violations, including unlawful killings and torture. Perpetrators were not held to account. Lesbian, gay, bisexual and transgender (LGBT) people continued to face discrimination and violence.

Background

Presidential and parliamentary elections were held in February. President Museveni was re-elected with 68 per cent of the vote for a new five-year term. Opposition parties disputed the results, citing fraud and electoral irregularities. The ruling National Resistance Movement party won a majority of seats in Parliament. There were some violent clashes between political supporters, the police and other security personnel before, during and after the elections.

In October, three government ministers were charged with alleged embezzlement of public funds intended for the Commonwealth Heads of Government Meeting in 2007. Uganda also presented its report under the Universal Periodic Review to the UN Human Rights Council.

Freedom of assembly

In February, the government imposed a general ban on all public protests, which mainly affected political activity. In April, the lobby group Activists for Change called on people to walk to work in protest at the rising cost of fuel and other essential commodities. Several weeks of public demonstrations followed in the capital, Kampala, and elsewhere. The police declared the protests unlawful and intervened to disrupt a number of initially peaceful events. Some protesters subsequently hurled objects at law enforcement officials, who responded with excessive force. Leaders of political opposition parties and hundreds of their supporters were arrested.

The authorities claimed that the protest organizers intended to organize violence and "overthrow the government", without providing evidence to support this. In October, four political activists were charged with treason – which carries the death penalty – for their participation in organizing the protests. The opposition leader, Dr Kizza Besigye, was prevented from leaving his Kampala home under the measure of "preventive arrest". This appeared to be specifically designed to stop him exercising his right to freedom of assembly.

Dozens of political supporters remained in pre-trial detention and faced various criminal charges for participating in the protests.

Unlawful killings

The police and military personnel used excessive force during public demonstrations on at least six different occasions in April and May. Live ammunition was fired into crowds of protesters, killing at least nine people – including a two-year-old girl – and injuring dozens of others. The shooting of the child on 21 April was highly publicized and led to a criminal investigation and a government commitment to try the police officer involved. No action was taken to hold law enforcement officials responsible for the other killings and related human rights violations, or to grant victims and their families the right to an effective remedy.

Torture and other ill-treatment

A number of political leaders and their supporters were ill-treated during their arrest by police and other security personnel.
■ On 28 April, Dr Kizza Besigye (see above) suffered serious injuries during his arrest by police and unidentified law enforcement personnel. Government officials stated that the level of force used against him was justified.

In June, the Uganda Human Rights Commission reported that torture and other ill-treatment by the police, other law enforcement officials and the military remained widespread.

Freedom of expression

Journalists, opposition politicians and activists faced arbitrary arrest, intimidation, threats and politically motivated criminal charges for expressing views deemed critical of the authorities. Up to 30 Ugandan journalists faced criminal charges in connection with their media work.

During the April/May protests, the authorities attempted to block social networking sites and banned live television broadcasts, based on unverified claims of threats to national security and public safety. Many journalists were harassed, intimidated and beaten by the police and other law enforcement officials, particularly while covering the protests.

The proposed Press and Journalists (Amendment) Bill remained pending for cabinet discussion. If enacted, it could give the authorities the power to refuse print media licences on vaguely defined grounds such as "national security".

In October, the Public Order Management Bill was submitted for debate in Parliament. If the bill became law, it could unduly restrict the freedoms of assembly and expression.

Violence against women and girls

Violence against women and girls – particularly sexual and other forms of gender-based violence – remained widespread. The government made some positive efforts to address this, including by developing a manual for health workers on managing cases of gender-based violence. However, female victims of rape and other forms of sexual and gender-based violence continued to face economic and social obstacles to justice. Survivors of such violence committed during the northern Uganda conflict continued to urge for official reparations to address the resulting physical and emotional trauma.

International justice

International Criminal Court arrest warrants issued in 2005 remained in force for Joseph Kony, the Lord's Resistance Army (LRA) leader, and three LRA commanders. The men were still at large.
■ In July, former LRA commander Thomas Kwoyelo appeared before the International Crimes Division of the High Court to answer charges of murder, wilful killing, kidnap with intent to kill, aggravated robbery, destruction of property and other offences committed as part of attacks that he had allegedly commanded during the conflict in northern Uganda. He denied the charges and applied to the Constitutional Court for an amnesty under the Amnesty Act of 2000. In

U

September, the Court ruled that he was entitled to an amnesty, consistent with those granted to thousands of other fighters who had later renounced conflict. The government appealed against the decision to the Supreme Court. The appeal hearing was pending at the end of 2011. However, the government did not repeal legal provisions which provide for amnesties for crimes under international law.

Bomb attacks

In September, the trial of 19 people of different nationalities charged with terrorism, murder and attempted murder during the 2010 bomb attacks began at the High Court in Kampala. Two defendants pleaded guilty to terrorism and conspiracy to commit terrorism and were sentenced to prison terms of 25 and 5 years respectively.

Charges were dropped due to a lack of evidence against five suspects, including Kenyan human rights activist Al-Amin Kimathi, who had spent a year in pre-trial custody. It appeared that he had been arrested, charged and detained solely for carrying out his legitimate work. The hearing of the prosecution's evidence in the trial against the remaining 12 defendants had not begun by the end of 2011.

In April, four Kenyan human rights defenders were arbitrarily excluded from entering Uganda by immigration authorities, forced to sign deportation papers and ordered to return to Kenya. They had travelled alongside others to attend a scheduled meeting with the Ugandan authorities to discuss Al-Amin Kimathi's case (see above).

Refugees and asylum-seekers

The possible cessation of international refugee protection of Rwandan refugees and asylum-seekers in Uganda left thousands living in fear of being forcibly returned. There was no guarantee that refugees could access a fair and satisfactory procedure for the consideration of any fears regarding a return.

A 2009 ban on food cultivation by Rwandan refugees living in refugee settlements continued to greatly reduce their access to food compared with other refugee communities.

Rights of lesbian, gay, bisexual and transgender people

In January, the activist David Kato was murdered in his Kampala home. He had called for the Ugandan authorities to end discrimination, particularly in tabloid newspapers that had published names, pictures and personal details of people believed to be lesbian, gay, bisexual or transgender. In November, the person accused of David Kato's murder was sentenced to 30 years in prison after pleading guilty.

The government remained conspicuously silent about discriminatory rhetoric against lesbians, gay men, bisexual and transgender people. In January, the High Court delivered a landmark ruling banning the media from publishing their names.

The Anti-Homosexuality Bill, 2009 which would further entrench discrimination and lead to other human rights violations, was still pending in Parliament at the end of the year. It was presented for legislative debate in May, but Parliament did not debate it, nor a number of other bills. Following a vote in October in favour of a motion by the new Parliament to retain bills that had not been considered in the previous Parliament, it was listed for consideration.

Death penalty

Civilian and military courts continued to impose the death penalty for capital offences. According to official statistics from September, around 505 people – 35 of them women – were held on death row. There were no executions.

A Ugandan army soldier was found guilty of murder and sentenced to death by a Ugandan field court martial in eastern Central African Republic in August.

Amnesty International visits/reports

Amnesty International delegates visited Uganda in April, July, August and November.

Uganda: Human rights concerns in the run-up to the February 2011 general elections (AFR 59/0047/2011)

Uganda: Teargas and bullets used against peaceful protesters (AFR 59/008/2011)

Uganda: A nine point human rights agenda (AFR 59/009/2011)

Uganda: Investigate use of force against protesters (AFR 59/012/2011)

Uganda: Court's decision a setback for accountability for crimes committed in northern Uganda conflict (AFR 59/015/2011)

Stifling dissent: Restrictions on the rights to freedom of expression and peaceful assembly in Uganda (AFR 59/016/2011)

U

UKRAINE

UKRAINE

Head of state:	Viktor Yanukovych
Head of government:	Mykola Azarov
Death penalty:	abolitionist for all crimes
Population:	45.2 million
Life expectancy:	68.5 years
Under-5 mortality:	15.1 per 1,000
Adult literacy:	99.7 per cent

There was continuing impunity for torture and other ill-treatment. Reforms of the justice system failed to increase independence of the judiciary, and the rule of law was undermined by the use of the criminal justice system for political ends. Asylum-seekers risked being forcibly returned and were unable to access a fair asylum procedure. Human rights defenders were at risk of prosecution and physical attack for their work.

Torture and other ill-treatment

There were continuing reports of torture and other ill-treatment in police custody. The European Court of Human Rights ruled in nine cases against Ukraine, finding that Article 3 of the European Convention on Human Rights, which prohibits torture, had been violated.

■ Firdovsi Safarov, a Ukrainian citizen of Azeri ethnic origin, told Amnesty International that, on 26 March, he had been beaten by six police officers from Mohiliov Podilsky police station. He had been stopped by police officers while taking an old car to a scrap yard. He was punched in the head and racially abused. At the station, the Director and other police officers beat him intermittently until 1am, when he was released. Firdovsi Safarov said that he had been asked to pay US$3,000 to be released. He was later charged with resisting police officers, but was acquitted on 25 June. Firdovsi Safarov lodged a complaint about the ill-treatment and, after two refusals, the Prosecutor's Office opened an investigation in July. Although the investigation was ongoing, the Director of the police station remained in post at the end of the year. In October, Firdovsi Safarov was rehospitalized due to the injuries he had received, but his treatment was stopped early, reportedly because police officers pressurized the doctors treating him.

Impunity

A culture of impunity for the police continued. Structural shortcomings, corruption, non-existent or flawed investigations into criminal acts committed by the police (even in the face of medical or other credible evidence), harassment and intimidation of complainants, and the subsequent low level of prosecutions, all fuelled this lack of accountability. A high number of complaints about the police were rejected at the first instance. In July, the Prosecutor General's Office stated that out of the 6,817 complaints made against police officers in 2010, only 167 had resulted in criminal investigations, of which 21 were subsequently closed for lack of evidence.

■ On 17 August, three Kyiv Court of Appeal judges decided that no further investigation was required into the death in police custody of 19-year-old student Ihor Indilo in 2010. In doing so, the court effectively accepted the police explanation that his fatal head injury had been caused by falling 50cm from a bench in the cell in which he was detained. In October, the Prosecutor General announced that he had ordered a further investigation into the death.

■ On 24 October, the Kyiv Prosecutor announced that an investigation had been opened into Alexander Rafalsky's continuing and persistent claims that he had been tortured in June 2001 to force him to confess to murder. He was sentenced to life imprisonment in 2004. Prosecutors had consistently refused to open an investigation into his allegations.

Justice system

The process of reform of the justice system continued. In July a new draft Criminal Procedural Code was presented to parliament, but was not passed by the end of the year.

The independence of judges was threatened by pressure from the Prosecutor General's Office, which retained the power to prosecute judges. On 7 June, the Deputy Prosecutor General requested the dismissal of three judges from the Kyiv Court of Appeal because they refused a prosecutor's request to detain a suspect, on the basis that there were no grounds to hold him.

In October, amendments to the Law on the Judiciary and the Status of Judges were passed. The amendments responded to criticism of the Law passed in 2010, which had, among other reforms, seriously reduced the role of the Supreme Court.

U

The amendments only partially reinstated the Supreme Court's role.

In October, the Council of Europe criticized the role of parliament in the appointment and dismissal of judges. Appointing judges initially for five years before confirming their appointment for life threatened their independence. It recommended that such judges should not be appointed to deal with "major cases with strong political implications".

■ On 11 October, Yuliya Tymoshenko, who had been Prime Minister from January to September 2005 and again from December 2007 to March 2010, was sentenced to seven years' imprisonment and barred from holding public office for three years by a Kyiv court for signing a multi-million dollar energy contract with Russia in January 2009. The charges against her were not recognized criminal offences and were politically motivated. The judge in her case was on a temporary contract.

Refugees and asylum-seekers

On 8 July, Ukraine adopted a new law "on refugees and persons in need of complementary protection". It improved the status of refugees, simplified documentation for asylum-seekers, and introduced the concept of complementary protection for those who did not fall strictly within the definition of the Refugee Convention. However, it fell short of international standards by not offering complementary protection for reasons of international or internal armed conflict. UNHCR, the UN refugee agency, criticized the new law for failing to provide it with access to people of concern, or with an advisory role in refugee status determination.

A new State Migration Service of Ukraine, co-ordinated by the Ministry of Internal Affairs, had been established in December 2010. Regional migration offices stopped working in October: the new system was operational at the end of the year. Asylum-seekers risked return to countries where they could face serious human rights violations.

■ In March, a group of 10 Afghan citizens including one child were returned to Afghanistan. The asylum applications by some of the group had been refused. They were not given the opportunity to appeal against this refusal, or their deportation. The group claimed they had not been provided with interpreters while applying for asylum or during the deportation process and that they were required to sign documents in a language they did not understand. On 17 March, the State Border Guard Service told regional media that force had been used against the men because they had tried to resist their deportation.

Human rights defenders

Human rights defenders, who exposed corruption and human rights violations by local officials and police, faced physical attacks and prosecution in an attempt to silence them.

■ On 12 January, Dmytro Groysman, Chair of the Vinnytsya Human Rights Group, was charged with insulting the national flag of Ukraine and with distributing pornography for posting a sexually explicit satirical video and images on his blog. At the end of the year, the trial was still ongoing and Dmytro Groysman was on bail. The use of such images in this context fell within the limits of permissible public expression under international law. Dmytro Groysman was the only person prosecuted for posting the video, despite it having already been widely circulated within the public domain on various internet sites, which suggested that he may have been targeted because of his human rights work.

■ On 28 August, Andrei Fedosov, the head of Yuzer, an organization defending the rights of psychiatric patients, was allegedly subjected to a brutal attack because of his work to expose corruption and human rights violations in psychiatric hospitals. He had been invited to the village of Mirny in the Crimea by an unidentified man on the pretext that a psychiatric patient needed his assistance. He was taken to a flat in the village where he was tortured. When he was released, he immediately phoned the police. He saw his attacker walking down the village street and pointed him out. The police drove both Andrei Fedosov and the attacker to the police station in the village. The attacker and the police appeared to be on familiar terms. Andrei Fedosov reported the crime, gave his passport details and then left. Outside the station, he paused to phone a friend, but was then detained again by the police, who claimed that he was displaying "inadequate behaviour". The police took him to a psychiatric hospital for a test, and struck him on the head when he questioned the why he was being taken there. Once he arrived the doctors there released him. The authorities failed to investigate the attack and Andrei Fedosov had great difficulty in documenting his injuries. Despite attempts to document his injuries, doctors in the nearby city of Yevpatoriya and in Kyiv did not take his injuries seriously.

U

Amnesty International visits/reports

- Amnesty International delegates visited Ukraine in March, April and October.
- "No evidence of a crime": paying the price for police impunity in Ukraine (EUR 50/009/2011)
- Blunt force: torture and police impunity in Ukraine (EUR 50/010/2011)

UNITED ARAB EMIRATES

UNITED ARAB EMIRATES

Head of state:	**Shaikh Khalifa bin Zayed Al Nahyan**
Head of government:	**Shaikh Mohammed bin Rashid Al Maktoum**
Death penalty:	**retentionist**
Population:	**7.9 million**
Life expectancy:	**76.5 years**
Under-5 mortality:	**7.4 per 1,000**
Adult literacy:	**90 per cent**

Five men were arbitrarily detained and subsequently sentenced to prison terms in connection with criticism of the government and for calling for reforms, then released under a presidential pardon. The authorities replaced the executive boards of four NGOs who joined in a call for direct elections. Women continued to face discrimination in law and in practice. Foreign migrant workers, particularly women domestic workers, were inadequately protected against exploitation and abuse by their employers. The government refused to co-operate with UN human rights bodies. Death sentences continued to be imposed and there was at least one execution.

Background

The government acted to head off possible protests prompted by uprisings elsewhere in the region, pledging to provide "dignified living conditions" and announcing large increases in pensions for former members of the armed forces as well as rice and bread subsidies. In February, the government increased the number of people eligible to vote in the second national election for the 20 seats of the 40-member Federal National Council that are elected; the other 20 seats are appointed. In March, over 130 people co-signed a petition to the President and ruling council calling for free elections based on universal suffrage and for the Federal National Council to be given legislative powers. In November, the President promised greater rights to citizens.

Freedom of expression and association

People who criticized the government or friendly states were liable to arrest.

- Hassan Mohammed Hassan al-Hammadi, a board member of the Teachers' Association, was arrested on 4 February and reportedly charged with "disturbing public security" for publicly supporting pro-reform demonstrators in Egypt. He was held at the State Security headquarters in Abu Dhabi, then released on 17 February to await trial, which began in November.
- Six people associated with the UAE Hewar online discussion forum, which was blocked by the UAE authorities, were arrested in April. One was released after a week, but the others – known as the "UAE 5" – were brought to trial in June on criminal defamation charges relating to articles posted on UAE Hewar. The five – Ahmed Mansoor, a human rights activist and blogger; Nasser bin Ghaith, a university lecturer and advocate of political reform; and online activists Fahad Salim Dalk, Ahmed Abdul-Khaleq and Hassan Ali al-Khamis – were prisoners of conscience. Initially, their trial was held behind closed doors. Subsequently, international observers, including a lawyer who went to the UAE on behalf of Amnesty International and other international NGOs, were allowed to observe the trial. On 22 November, the UN Working Group on Arbitrary Detention found that Ahmed Mansoor had been arbitrarily detained because of his "peaceful exercise of the right to freedom of opinion and expression" and that he faced an unfair trial. It called on the government to release him and provide adequate reparation. On 27 November, however, Ahmed Mansoor was sentenced to three years in prison and the other four to two years. All were released the following day under a presidential pardon, although their criminal records remained.

In April, the Ministry of Social Affairs took action against four NGOs that had signed a joint letter earlier that month calling for reforms. The Ministry replaced with government appointees the executive boards of the Jurists' Association, the Teachers' Association and two other organizations.

In December, the government stripped six men of their UAE citizenship, citing security concerns and their alleged links to an Islamist group. Some of them had signed the March petition to the President. Another man had reportedly been stripped of his UAE citizenship 10 months earlier for similar reasons.

Women's rights

Women continued to face discrimination in law and in practice, and to face gender-based violence, including within the family. The government made little or no progress in implementing the CEDAW Committee's recommendation in early 2010 that it take comprehensive measures to protect women from domestic violence.

Migrants' rights

Foreign migrant workers were inadequately protected against exploitation and abuse by their employers. In February, it was reported that migrants who had lost their jobs in the construction industry were stranded in the UAE because their employer had not paid them or still held their passports. Many were living in abject conditions in labour camps.

Foreign women employed as domestic workers were particularly vulnerable; many were reported to work long hours for little pay and to be abused by employers or their sponsors in the UAE. A government report issued in September stated that at least 900 domestic workers who had fled the residences of their sponsors had been detained by the authorities in Dubai in the previous eight months.

In December, the International Trade Union Confederation criticized the UAE's Labour Law for not permitting trade unions to exist or to function freely; for denying the right to collective bargaining and to strike; and for giving the Labour Minister the power to unilaterally end strikes and force people back to work.

Death penalty

Death sentences continued to be passed. One execution was known to have been carried out; in February, a man convicted of the rape and murder of a child was executed by firing squad in Dubai. This was believed to be the first execution since 2008.

The death sentences imposed on 17 Indian nationals after they were convicted of murder in 2010 were set aside when they agreed to pay *diyah* (blood

money) to the victim, although failure to agree the amount to be paid meant that they were not released.

Amnesty International visits/reports

Amnesty International delegates visited the UAE in June to conduct research and in September to observe the trial of the "UAE 5".

UAE: Free activists before elections, Amnesty International joint statement (MDE 25/005/2011)

United Arab Emirates: Summary trial observation briefing paper on the UAE5 case (MDE 25/008/2011)

UNITED KINGDOM

UNITED KINGDOM OF GREAT BRITAIN AND NORTHERN IRELAND

Head of state:	Queen Elizabeth II
Head of government:	David Cameron
Death penalty:	abolitionist for all crimes
Population:	62.4 million
Life expectancy:	80.2 years
Under-5 mortality:	5.5 per 1,000

The protocol for the Detainee Inquiry was published and fell far short of human rights standards. The government confirmed its intention to expand its deportations with assurances programme to facilitate the return of individuals to countries where they face a real risk of torture. The Baha Mousa Inquiry criticized UK armed forces for serious human rights violations against detainees. The Rosemary Nelson Inquiry heavily criticized state agencies for numerous omissions that may have been able to prevent her killing. A Commission to investigate the creation of a UK Bill of Rights was established in March.

Counter-terror and security
Torture and other ill-treatment

In July, the terms of reference and protocol for the Detainee Inquiry were published. It had been established in 2010 to examine allegations of UK involvement in human rights violations of individuals detained abroad in the context of counter-terrorism operations. Concerns were raised that the protocol did not follow international human rights standards, notably because the government would retain the final say over disclosure of material, undermining the Inquiry's independence and effectiveness. Solicitors representing individuals who expected their cases to be examined by the Inquiry confirmed they had advised their clients not to participate. Ten NGOs announced that if the Inquiry proceeded as proposed they would not co-operate with it.

The formal launch of the Inquiry was delayed pending the completion of criminal investigations into alleged wrongdoing by UK intelligence agents.

In September, documents discovered in Tripoli, Libya, indicated that the UK had been involved in the unlawful transfers of Sami Mustafa al-Saadi and Abdel Hakim Belhaj to Libya in 2004, despite the real risk of torture and other ill-treatment they would have faced there. Both men subsequently initiated civil claims for damages against UK authorities for alleged involvement in the human rights violations they had suffered, including torture and other ill-treatment.

On 3 October, the High Court of England and Wales gave judgement on the lawfulness of guidance to intelligence officers on detention and interrogation operations overseas and intelligence sharing. The Court ruled that the guidance should be amended to reflect the absolute prohibition on hooding of detainees. However, it rejected arguments that the threshold of risk used to assess whether a detainee would be subjected to torture or other ill-treatment relied on in the guidance was unlawful.

In December, the government wrote to the US authorities asking them to transfer Yunus Rahmatullah to UK custody, after the Court of Appeal ordered that a writ of habeas corpus be issued in his case. Yunus Rahmatullah was captured by British forces in Iraq in February 2004 and handed over to US forces who transferred him to Afghanistan and had kept him since then detained without charge in Bagram.

Legal and policy developments

In January, the Home Office published its review of six counter-terrorism and security powers. Later that month, the maximum period of pre-charge detention in terrorism cases was reduced from 28 to 14 days. However, in February the government published draft legislation which would allow the maximum period to be raised back to 28 days in response to an unspecified future urgent situation.

■ On 13 July, in the case of *Al Rawi and others v. The Security Services and others*, the Supreme Court ruled

that courts could not order a "closed material procedure" – which would allow the government to rely on secret material in closed sessions of the court – in a civil trial for damages without the statutory power to do so.

In October, the government put forward new legislative proposals in the *Justice and Security Green Paper*. Some of these gave rise to concern. They included expansion of the use of closed material procedures in civil proceedings, including in civil trials for damages, and measures which would restrict the ability of victims of human rights violations from seeking disclosure before domestic courts of material related to those violations on national security grounds. The Green Paper did, however, include some limited proposals to improve oversight of the security and intelligence services.

Control orders

As of 14 December, nine individuals, all British nationals, were under control orders.

The Prevention of Terrorism Act 2005, which provided for the control order regime, was repealed in December. It was replaced by the Terrorism Prevention and Investigation Measures Act, which provided for a new regime of administratively-ordered restrictions (TPIMs) which can be placed on an individual who is suspected of involvement in terrorism-related activities. Although slightly narrower than those applied under the control order regime, the restrictions could still amount to deprivation of liberty or constitute restrictions on the rights to privacy, expression, association and movement. Following a transition period, TPIMs were expected to fully replace the control orders regime in early 2012. The government also provided for an "enhanced" version of TPIMs, which could be introduced in future undefined exceptional circumstances, where the most severe restrictions currently available under the control orders regime may be re-imposed.

Deportations

U

The government reaffirmed its intention to develop and extend its deportations with assurances programme in order to facilitate the return of individuals alleged to pose a threat to national security to countries where they would be at risk of torture and other ill-treatment.

Proceedings by which these deportations could be challenged before the Special Immigration Appeals

Commission (SIAC) remained unfair due to the heavy reliance on secret material undisclosed to the individual concerned, or to their lawyer of choice.

■ In March, the Court of Appeal upheld a decision by the SIAC that M.S., an Algerian national, could be deported to Algeria as diplomatic assurances negotiated between the UK and Algeria were sufficient to mitigate any risk he would face upon his return. In 2007 the SIAC had found that M.S. was not a threat to national security. However, the government continued to seek his deportation on alternative grounds, relying on diplomatic assurances to facilitate the return.

■ In July, the Court of Appeal gave permission to appeal in the case of X.X., an Ethiopian national alleged to pose a threat to national security. X.X. had challenged the government's decision to deport him on the grounds that he would be at risk of torture and other ill-treatment and subjected to a flagrantly unfair trial if returned. One of the grounds granted for appeal was that information relied upon in X.X.'s case had allegedly arisen from the unlawful prolonged incommunicado detention of individuals in unofficial detention centres in Ethiopia. X.X.'s lawyers argued that material obtained in these circumstances should not be admissible.

Armed forces in Iraq

On 7 July, the Grand Chamber of the European Court of Human Rights gave judgement in the case of *Al-Skeini and others v. the United Kingdom*, which concerned the killing of six civilians during security operations carried out by UK soldiers in Iraq in 2003. The Court found that the European Convention on Human Rights did apply to the UK's operations in Iraq during that time because it was an occupying force. Therefore the UK was required to conduct independent and effective investigations into the killings. The Court found that the UK had failed to do so in five out of six cases.

Also on 7 July, the Grand Chamber ruled in the case of *Al-Jedda v. the United Kingdom* that the prolonged internment of Hilal Abdul-Razzaq Ali Al-Jedda, for more than three years in a detention centre run by UK armed forces in Basra, Iraq, violated his right to liberty and security. The Court rejected the UK's argument that the UN Security Council resolution 1546 displaced the applicant's right to the protections of the European Convention on Human Rights.

■ On 8 September, the Baha Mousa Inquiry published its report into the death of Baha Mousa at a UK-run detention facility in Basra, Iraq and the treatment of nine other Iraqi nationals who were detained alongside him. The Inquiry reached the unequivocal conclusion that Baha Mousa died following an "appalling episode of serious gratuitous violence", and that it was "beyond doubt that most, if not all, of the [d]etainees were the victims of serious abuse and mistreatment". The report also found a corporate failure by the Ministry of Defence to provide clear and consistent guidelines about the proper treatment of detainees, which led to interrogation techniques banned by the UK government in 1972 being used by soldiers in Iraq. The Ministry of Defence accepted all but one of the recommendations made by the Inquiry and stated it would take relevant measures to ensure that such violations were not repeated. However, lawyers acting for the men and human rights organizations called for further action to be taken against those found to be responsible, including through criminal proceedings.

On 22 November, the Court of Appeal gave judgement in the case of Ali Zaki Mousa. The Court ruled that the Iraq Historical Allegations Team, established to investigate allegations of torture and other ill-treatment of Iraqi citizens by UK armed forces in Iraq, was not sufficiently independent to satisfy its investigatory obligation under the European Convention on Human Rights.

Police and security forces

On 3 May, a jury returned a verdict of unlawful killing at the inquest into the death of Ian Tomlinson, during the G-20 demonstrations in London in April 2009. The jury found that Ian Tomlinson had died of internal bleeding after being struck with a baton and pushed to the ground by a police officer. Consequently the Crown Prosecution Service reversed a decision not to bring manslaughter charges against the police officer involved. The trial was expected to begin in 2012.

The inquiry into the death of Azelle Rodney, shot by Metropolitan police officers on 30 April 2005, remained ongoing.

Discrimination

In September, the CERD Committee raised concerns about widespread discrimination against and marginalization of Gypsies and Travellers, and urged the government to take concrete measures to improve their access to education, health care and services, and employment and adequate accommodation.

■ In October, between 300 and 400 Irish Travellers were forcibly evicted from Dale Farm, Essex, despite calls from a range of UN and Council of Europe bodies and experts, NGOs and civil society and religious leaders to halt the eviction.

Corporate accountability

In September, the CERD Committee expressed concern that operations abroad by transnational corporations registered in the UK were adversely affecting the human rights of Indigenous Peoples and urged the government to adopt measures to ensure that UK companies respected human rights when operating abroad.

The Committee also criticized the Legal Aid, Sentencing and Punishment of Offenders Bill, which, if passed, would restrict the ability of foreign claimants to gain access to justice in the UK courts against transnational corporations.

Northern Ireland

Incidents of paramilitary violence in Northern Ireland continued. On 2 April, Police Constable Ronan Kerr was killed by a bomb attached under his car. Dissident republicans were blamed for the killing.

The Police Ombudsman was severely criticized over his lack of independence during investigations into historical cases of police misconduct in unlawful killings. He announced that he would step down from his post in early 2012.

In May, the Supreme Court ruled in the case of McCaughey & Anor. It found that an inquest into the death of Martin McCaughey and Dessie Grew, who were shot and killed by members of the UK armed forces in 1990, must comply with the procedural obligations of the right to life as protected by the Human Rights Act 1998.

■ In February it was announced that the Robert Hamill Inquiry had completed its final report. However, it would not be published until legal proceedings against three individuals in connection with the case on charges of perverting the course of justice had been concluded.

■ In May, the findings of an inquiry were published into the death of Rosemary Nelson, a lawyer killed on 15 March 1999 by a bomb attached to her car in Lurgan, Northern Ireland. The report heavily criticized state agencies for numerous omissions that might have prevented her killing, but did not find any evidence of any act by a state agency that directly facilitated her murder.

■ In October, the government announced that it had appointed a senior lawyer to review all available documentation relating to the killing of Patrick Finucane, a lawyer killed by loyalist paramilitaries on 12 February 1989 with the collusion of UK state agents. The decision reneged on past promises to establish a full public inquiry into the killing and was severely criticized by human rights organizations on the grounds that it would not constitute an effective, independent, impartial and thorough investigation in conformity with international human rights law. The family of Patrick Finucane commenced judicial review proceedings challenging the decision.

In September, the Northern Ireland Executive announced proposals for the establishment of an inquiry to investigate historical institutional child abuse. There could, however, be a delay in providing the inquiry with a statutory basis, which might initially leave it without the necessary powers to compel the attendance of witnesses and the production of documents.

Violence against women and girls

In March the government introduced a cross-departmental action plan on violence against women and girls. In the same month the Home Secretary announced that a pilot project, supporting victims of domestic violence who lack access to public funds because of their insecure immigration status, would be made permanent. However, the pilot project only covered women on spousal visas; women on other visas or temporary work permits continue to be denied access to essential services.

Concerns were raised that plans to abolish the migrant domestic worker visa, which allows domestic workers to change employer once in the UK, may increase the vulnerability of migrant domestic workers to exploitation and, in some cases, human trafficking.

Refugees and asylum-seekers

Proposed cuts to publicly funded legal representation (legal aid) gave rise to concerns that the lack of funds for asylum and immigration legal advice, already absent in some parts of the country, would be exacerbated.

Forced returns of rejected asylum-seekers to Afghanistan and Iraq continued despite a real risk of human rights abuses.

■ The criminal investigation into the death of Jimmy Mubenga, an Angolan national who died during an

U

attempted forcible removal in 2010, remained ongoing at the end of the year. His death triggered calls for changes to the enforced removals system due to concerns about dangerous control and restraint techniques being used by private security companies during enforced removals.

■ In June, the European Court of Human Rights ruled in the case of *Sufi and Elmi v. The United Kingdom* that the return of two Somali nationals to Mogadishu, Somalia would be a violation of Article 3 of the European Convention on Human Rights, due to the real risk of ill-treatment they would face on return (see Somalia entry).

Amnesty International visits/reports

⬛ Current evidence: European complicity in the CIA rendition and secret detention programmes (EUR 01/001/2011)

⬛ The United Kingdom fails on diplomatic assurances: Amnesty International's preliminary response to the UK counter-terrorism review (EUR 45/001/2011)

⬛ United Kingdom: Joint NGO submission to chair of the Detainee Inquiry (EUR 45/002/2011)

⬛ United Kingdom: Submission to the Joint Committee on the draft Detention of Terrorist Suspects (Temporary Extension) Bills (EUR 45/004/2011)

⬛ United Kingdom/Northern Ireland: Inquiry into the killing of human rights defender and lawyer Rosemary Nelson finds serious omissions by state agencies (EUR 45/006/2011)

⬛ United Kingdom: Terrorism Prevention and Investigation Measures Bill: Control orders redux (EUR 45/007/2011)

⬛ United Kingdom: European Court criticizes UK for violating human rights in Iraq (EUR 45/009/2011)

⬛ United Kingdom: Detainee Inquiry terms of reference and protocol fall far short of human rights standards (EUR 45/011/2011)

⬛ United Kingdom: Dale Farm Travellers face forced eviction (EUR 45/013/2011)

⬛ United Kingdom/Northern Ireland: Deplorable government decision to renege on promise of public inquiry into Finucane killing (EUR 45/017/2011)

UNITED STATES OF AMERICA

UNITED STATES OF AMERICA

Head of state and government:	Barack H. Obama
Death penalty:	retentionist
Population:	313.1 million
Life expectancy:	78.5 years
Under-5 mortality:	7.8 per 1,000

Forty-three men were executed during the year, and concerns about cruel prison conditions continued. Scores of detainees remained in indefinite military detention at Guantánamo. The administration announced its intention to pursue the death penalty against six of these detainees in trials by military commission. Some 3,000 people were held in the US detention facility on the Bagram air base in Afghanistan by the end of the year. Use of lethal force in the counter-terrorism context raised serious concerns, as did continuing reports of the use of excessive force in the domestic law enforcement context.

Counter-terror and security
Detentions at Guantánamo
At the end of 2011, nearly two years after President Obama's deadline to close the Guantánamo detention facility, 171 men were still held at the base, including four who had been convicted by military commission.

One detainee was transferred from the base during the year. Two detainees died, both Afghan nationals, one as a result of natural causes, the other reportedly by suicide. Their deaths brought to eight the number of detainees known to have died at the camp.

On 31 December, President Obama signed into law the National Defense Authorization Act, which, among other things, provided for the indefinite detention without charge or trial of individuals in the counter-terrorism context.

Trials of Guantánamo detainees
On 4 April, the US Attorney General announced that five Guantánamo detainees accused of involvement in the attacks of 11 September 2001 – Khalid Sheikh Mohammed, Walid bin Attash, Ramzi bin al-Shibh, 'Ali 'Abd al-'Aziz and Mustafa al Hawsawi – would be tried by military commission. This reversed his

announcement made in November 2009 that the five would be tried in ordinary federal court in the USA. The Attorney General blamed the U-turn on members of Congress who had "imposed restrictions blocking the administration from bringing any Guantánamo detainees to trial in the United States, regardless of the venue." Prosecutors recommended that, if convicted, the five should face the death penalty. The trials had not begun by the end of the year. The five detainees had been held incommunicado for up to four years in secret US custody before being transferred to Guantánamo in 2006.

In September, the Convening Authority for the military commissions referred the charges against Saudi Arabian national 'Abd al Rahim al-Nashiri for trial; if convicted he could face the death penalty. The government asserted that 'Abd al-Nashiri could be returned to indefinite detention if acquitted at his military commission trial, which was still pending at the end of the year.

In February, Sudanese national Noor Uthman Muhammed pleaded guilty in a military commission to providing material support to terrorism and was sentenced to 14 years' imprisonment. All but 34 months of his sentence were suspended in exchange for his agreement to testify for the USA at future military commission or federal court proceedings.

Noor Uthman Muhammed's case brought to six the number of people convicted by military commission since 2001, four of whom had pleaded guilty.

Canadian national Omar Khadr, who was 15 when he was apprehended by US forces in 2002, remained at Guantánamo at the end of 2011. He was sentenced in 2010 to 40 years' imprisonment by a military commission after pleading guilty to five "war crime" charges. His sentence was subsequently limited to eight years. The Canadian and US authorities agreed to support his transfer to Canada after he had served one year in US custody. This first year was completed in October.

The Court of Military Commissions Review issued opinions in the cases of two Yemeni nationals, Salim Ahmed Hamdan and Ali Hamza Ahmad Suliman Al Bahlul, convicted by military commissions. In both cases the court upheld the convictions and sentences.

Tanzanian national Ahmed Khalfan Ghailani, who had been convicted by a US District Court in November 2010 in connection with the bombings of the US embassies in east Africa in 1998, was sentenced to life imprisonment in January. He had been held in secret CIA custody for two years and in US military custody at Guantánamo for nearly three years before being transferred to New York in 2009. By the end of 2011, he remained the only former Guantánamo detainee to have been transferred for prosecution in federal court in the USA.

US detentions in Afghanistan

Hundreds of detainees were held in the US Detention Facility in Parwan (DFIP) on the Bagram air base in Afghanistan. Some 3,100 detainees remained held in the DFIP, about three times as many as were being held there a year earlier. Most were Afghan nationals taken into custody by coalition forces in southern and eastern Afghanistan, according to the ICRC. In January, according to the Pentagon, the process of "transitioning detention operations" at the DFIP to Afghan authorities began, with a detainee housing unit being turned over to the Afghan Ministry of Defence. (See Afghanistan entry.)

Litigation continued in US District Court on the question of whether detainees held at Bagram should have access to the US courts in order to challenge the lawfulness of their detention. In May 2010, the US Court of Appeals had overturned a 2009 ruling by a District Court judge that three Bagram detainees – who were not Afghan nationals and were taken into custody outside Afghanistan – could file habeas corpus petitions in his court.

Other detentions and trials

Ahmed Abdulkadir Warsame, a Somali national, was detained by US forces in the Gulf of Aden in April and brought to the USA in early July and charged with terrorism-related offences. Ahmed Warsame was apparently held incommunicado for at least six weeks and in secret detention for at least two weeks prior to his transfer to the USA. The authorities responded to Amnesty International's concern about his pre-transfer treatment by saying that "the US Government has consistently asserted that it is at war with al Qaida and its associated forces, and that it may take all lawful measures, including detention, to defeat the enemy".

Impunity

There was no accountability for human rights violations committed under the administration of President George W. Bush as part of the CIA's programme of secret detention and rendition (transfer of individuals from the custody of one state to another by means that bypass judicial and administrative due process).

U

On 16 May, the US Supreme Court refused to hear the *Mohamed v. Jeppesen* rendition case, leaving in place a 2010 lower court ruling dismissing a lawsuit brought by five men who claimed they were subjected to enforced disappearance, and torture or other cruel, inhuman or degrading treatment at the hands of US personnel and agents of other governments as part of the USA's secret detention and rendition programme. In November, the men took their case to the Inter-American Commission on Human Rights.

On 30 June, the US Attorney General announced that the "preliminary review" conducted into interrogations in the CIA programme was at an end. He said that he had accepted the prosecutor's recommendation that there should be a "full criminal investigation" in relation to two deaths in custody, but further investigation in other cases was not warranted.

In an opinion issued in October, a federal judge refused to hold the CIA in contempt of court for destroying videotapes of interrogations of detainees held in the secret detention programme. The tapes – which included recordings of the use of "enhanced interrogation techniques", including "waterboarding" – had been destroyed in 2005, more than a year *after* the court had ordered the government to produce or identify materials relating to the treatment of detainees.

Use of lethal force

Osama bin Laden and several others were killed on 1 May in a compound in Abbottabad, Pakistan, during an operation conducted by US special forces. The US administration made clear that the operation had been conducted under the USA's theory of a global armed conflict between the USA and al-Qa'ida in which the USA does not recognize the applicability of international human rights law. In the absence of further clarification from the US authorities, the killing of Osama bin Laden would appear to have been unlawful.

Anwar al-Awlaki, Samir Khan and at least two others were killed in Yemen on 30 September in a US drone strike on their vehicle convoy. By the end of the year, Amnesty International had not received any reply from the US authorities on the organization's concerns that these killings appeared to have amounted to extrajudicial executions.

Excessive use of force

At least 43 people died after being struck by police Tasers, bringing the number of such deaths since 2001 to 497. While coroners have attributed most of these deaths to other causes, such as underlying health problems, Tasers are listed as a cause or contributory factor in more than 60 cases. Most of those who died were unarmed and many did not appear to pose a serious threat when they were electro-shocked.

In May, the National Institute of Justice published its report into deaths following the use of conducted energy devices (CEDs) such as Tasers. This stated that there was "no conclusive medical evidence" to indicate a high risk of death or serious injury from CED exposure in normal, healthy adults. However, the report noted that many deaths attributed to Tasers involved multiple or prolonged exposure, and recommended that such usage be avoided. The study also noted that safety margins may not be applicable in the case of small children, those with diseased hearts, the elderly, pregnant women and other "potentially at-risk individuals".

Amnesty International continued to call on law enforcement agencies to suspend use of such weapons or strictly limit their use to cases involving an immediate threat of death or serious injury.

There were complaints of police use of excessive force against demonstrators participating in the Occupy Wall Street movement. In Oakland, California, police attempting to disperse protesters in October and November were accused of firing tear gas, bean-bag rounds and flash-bang grenades indiscriminately into largely peaceful crowds, and using batons, causing serious injury to at least two individuals. A civil lawsuit in the case was pending at the end of the year. In Tulsa, Oklahoma, and Seattle, Washington, police used pepper spray against non-violent protesters.

Three people, including two teenagers, were shot and killed in separate incidents by US Border Patrol police for allegedly throwing rocks at officers along the US border with Mexico. Two were reportedly on the Mexican side and were shot across the border. An investigation by the US Justice Department into the shooting of 15-year-old Sergio Adrián Hernández Güereca in similar circumstances in 2010 was still pending at the end of the year.

Prison conditions

Thousands of prisoners in California went on hunger strike in July and October to protest about cruel conditions of isolation in the state's Security Housing

Units (SHUs). In the SHU at Pelican Bay State Prison more than 1,000 prisoners were confined to windowless cells for 22.5 hours a day, in conditions a court stated in 1995 "may press the outer bounds of what most humans can psychologically tolerate". At the time of the hunger strike, more than 500 prisoners in Pelican Bay had spent at least 10 years in these conditions, and 78 had spent 20 years or more in the SHU. A number of reforms, including modifying procedures for assigning alleged gang members to indefinite SHU confinement, were under review at the end of the year. Amnesty International joined others in condemning disciplinary action taken against hunger strikers and urging an end to inhumane conditions. Thousands of prisoners remained in isolation in similar conditions in other states, including Arizona and Texas.

Bradley Manning, a US soldier accused of leaking documents to Wikileaks, spent the first 11 months of his detention confined to an isolation cell in a marine brig at Quantico, Virginia. His conditions improved after he was moved in April to a medium security military facility, where he was allowed to associate with other pre-trial inmates. A preliminary hearing on the criminal charges against him started on 16 December.

Children's rights

In March, the USA told the UN Human Rights Council that it supported the goals of the UN Convention on the Rights of the Child and recommendations made by other governments during the Universal Periodic Review process that the USA ratify the Convention. At the end of the year, the USA remained one of only two countries not to have ratified this treaty, the other being Somalia.

In August, Jordan Brown was transferred to juvenile court for trial in Pennsylvania. For the previous two and a half years he had been facing the prospect of being tried as an adult and sentenced to life imprisonment without the possibility of parole for a crime committed when he was 11 years old.

In November, the US Supreme Court agreed to consider prohibiting the imposition of life imprisonment without parole for homicide crimes committed by people under 18 years old; a ruling was not expected until mid-2012. In 2010, the Court prohibited life imprisonment without parole for non-homicide crimes by under-18s.

Migrants' rights

In September, a federal judge temporarily blocked portions of an Alabama law on undocumented migrants. Other sections were upheld, including a provision requiring state and local police to check a person's immigration status during routine traffic stops on "reasonable suspicion" that they were irregular migrants. The law, which was the strictest of its kind to be upheld in the country to date, faced challenges from the US Justice Department and church and civil liberties groups at the end of the year. Similar anti-immigrant legislation in Georgia, South Carolina, Indiana and Utah also faced legal challenges in federal court.

Right to health – maternal mortality

Hundreds of women continued to suffer preventable pregnancy-related deaths. There was no progress towards meeting targets set by the government to reduce maternal deaths, and disparities based on race, ethnicity, place of residence, and income persisted. Several bills were introduced into Congress during the year that would address health disparities, provide grants to states to form mortality review boards and expand best practices. At the end of the year, none had yet been passed into law.

Legal challenges to the 2010 health care reform law continued.

Death penalty

Forty-three prisoners – all of them men – were executed in the USA during the year, all by lethal injection. This brought to 1,277 the total number of executions carried out since the US Supreme Court lifted a moratorium on the death penalty in 1976.

In March, Illinois became the 16th abolitionist state in the USA. In November, the Governor of Oregon imposed a moratorium on executions in the state and called for "a long overdue reevaluation" of the system of capital punishment.

In November, the state of Idaho carried out its first execution for 17 years.

■ Eddie Powell was executed in Alabama on 16 June despite evidence that he had a degree of "mental retardation" which would render his execution unconstitutional.

■ Mexican national Humberto Leal García was executed in Texas on 7 July. Denied his consular rights after arrest, his execution violated international

U

law and a binding order from the International Court of Justice.

■ Troy Davis was executed in Georgia on 21 September despite serious doubts about the reliability of his conviction. The execution went ahead despite hundreds of thousands of appeals for clemency.

■ Manuel Valle was executed in Florida on 28 September after three decades on death row.

Amnesty International visits/reports

🚌 Amnesty International delegates observed military commission proceedings at Guantánamo in November, and visited the USA in February, July and November, when they visited isolation prison facilities in California, including Pelican Bay.

📑 USA: See no evil – government turns the other way as judges make findings about torture and other abuse (AMR 51/005/2011)

📑 USA: Digging a deeper hole – administration and Congress entrenching human rights failure on Guantánamo detentions (AMR 51/016/2011)

📑 Cruel conditions for pre-trial detainees in US federal custody (AMR 51/030/2011)

📑 USA: 100 years in solitary – the "Angola 3" and their fight for justice (AMR 51/041/2011)

📑 USA: Remedy blocked again – Injustice continues as Supreme Court dismisses rendition case (AMR 51/044/2011)

📑 USA: An embarrassment of hitches – reflections on the death penalty, 35 years after *Gregg v. Georgia*, as states scramble for lethal injection drugs (AMR 51/058/2011)

📑 "This is where I'm going to be when I die": Children facing life imprisonment without the possibility of release in the USA (AMR 51/081/2011)

📑 USA: Amnesty International calls for urgent reforms to California security housing units as prison hunger strike resumes (AMR 51/085/2011)

📑 USA: Guantánamo – a decade of damage to human rights (AMR 51/103/2011)

📑 Deadly delivery: The maternal health care crisis in the USA - one year update, spring 2011 (AMR 51/108/2011)

URUGUAY

EASTERN REPUBLIC OF URUGUAY

Head of state and government:	José Alberto Mujica Cordano
Death penalty:	abolitionist for all crimes
Population:	3.4 million
Life expectancy:	77 years
Under-5 mortality:	13.4 per 1,000
Adult literacy:	98.3 per cent

In October, Congress adopted a landmark law to tackle impunity for human rights violations committed during the period of civilian and military rule (1973-1985).

Background

A bill to legalize same-sex marriage was pending before Congress at the end of the year.

In September, five Uruguayan marines serving with the UN mission in Haiti were accused of sexually abusing an 18-year-old Haitian man, after video footage of the alleged incident appeared on the internet. Investigations in military and civilian jurisdictions were continuing at the end of the year.

Impunity

In February, the Inter-American Court of Human Rights ordered Uruguay to remove the obstacles blocking investigations and prosecutions for human rights violations committed during the years of civilian and military rule (1973-1985). The Court held Uruguay responsible for the enforced disappearance in 1976 of María Claudia García Iruretagoyena de Gelman, and for abducting her baby daughter María Macarena Gelman García. It ordered the state to pursue investigations to clarify María Claudia García Iruretagoyena de Gelman's whereabouts and bring those responsible to justice. In October, a court ruled that five former military officers, already serving prison sentences, should be prosecuted for the aggravated murder of María Claudia García Iruretagoyena de Gelman.

In May, the Supreme Court concluded that two former military officers could not be charged with enforced disappearance because the crime was not incorporated into domestic law until 2006 and could not be applied retroactively. Instead, they were convicted of aggravated murder in connection with the deaths of 28 people and sentenced to 25 years' imprisonment. There were concerns that this ruling could mean that grave human rights violations would be subject to a statute of limitations. This led Congress to pass a law in October that in practice annulled the effects of the 1986 Law on the Expiration of Punitive Claims of the State (Expiry Law) and repealed statutes of limitations that would have prevented victims from filing criminal complaints.

In June, President Mujica issued a decree revoking the decisions of former presidents about which cases of alleged human rights violations could be investigated. These decisions had been made using powers granted under the Expiry Law which protected police and military personnel from prosecution for human rights violations. The June decree raised hopes that some 80 cases could be reopened.

In October, legal complaints were presented on behalf of more than 150 torture survivors.

Prison conditions

In May, the government announced that prisoners would no longer be held in steel boxes known as "Las Latas" in Libertad Penitentiary. Following his visit to Uruguay in 2009, the UN Special Rapporteur on torture had condemned conditions in these steel modules as cruel and inhuman.

In July the Inter-American Commission on Human Rights expressed concern about serious shortcomings in the prison system including overcrowding, inadequate infrastructure and the widespread use of pre-trial detention.

By the end of the year the National Human Rights Institute and Ombudsman's Office, one of whose roles is to implement the national preventive mechanism under the Optional Protocol to the UN Convention against Torture, had yet to be established.

Amnesty International visits/reports

🚗 Amnesty International delegates visited Uruguay in September and October.

📄 Uruguay: Los crímenes de derecho internacional no están sujetos a prescripción (AMR 52/001/2011)

UZBEKISTAN

REPUBLIC OF UZBEKISTAN
Head of state:	Islam Karimov
Head of government:	Shavkat Mirzioiev
Death penalty:	abolitionist for all crimes
Population:	27.8 million
Life expectancy:	68.3 years
Under-5 mortality:	36.1 per 1,000
Adult literacy:	99.3 per cent

Two human rights defenders were released early from detention on humanitarian grounds but other prisoners of conscience continued to serve long prison sentences in conditions that amounted to cruel, inhuman and degrading treatment. Despite the introduction of new legislation to improve the treatment of detainees, dozens of reports of torture and other ill-treatment of detainees and prisoners continued to emerge. Freedom of expression and association contracted ever further.

Freedom of expression – human rights defenders and journalists

The authorities continued to restrict freedom of expression and association.

In April, journalists were told that they were no longer allowed to meet with representatives of foreign organizations and foreign diplomats, or attend press conferences and seminars without prior written permission from the authorities. In July, a court in Tashkent sentenced the UK Embassy press secretary and Uzbekistani national, Leonid Kudryavtsev, to a large fine for "contravening the laws on organizations holding meetings, street protests and demonstrations". The prosecution had accused him of fostering extremism during training seminars for independent human rights activists on UK Embassy premises. An appeal court rejected Leonid Kudryavtsev's appeal against the verdict in August.

As in previous years, human rights defenders and independent journalists were subjected to harassment, beatings, detention and unfair trials. They were summoned for police questioning, placed under house arrest and routinely monitored by uniformed or plain-clothes officers. Some reported being beaten by police officers or by people suspected of working for the security forces.

U

The authorities released two human rights defenders early, but at least 10 others continued to serve long prison sentences in conditions that amounted to cruel, inhuman and degrading treatment. Many of those detained were critically ill without access to the necessary medical treatment; several continued to be subjected to torture as punishment for lodging complaints about their treatment or that of their fellow prisoners.

■ On 14 October, human rights defender and prisoner of conscience Norboi Kholzhigitov, aged 61, was released early from prison on humanitarian grounds, just days before an official visit by US Secretary of State Hillary Clinton. His health had seriously deteriorated in the months before his release and his family feared he would die in prison. Norboi Kholzhigitov's colleague and co-defendant, Khabibulla Akpulatov, remained in prison. Following a visit in November, his son Yuldosh reported that his father's health and well-being had deteriorated since his last visit in July. Khabibulla Akpulatov's weight had dropped to below 50kg, he had lost sensation in both his legs and moved with difficulty. He only had six teeth left but was denied dental treatment. He appeared distressed and reluctant to speak about his treatment.

In June, the authorities closed the office of Human Rights Watch, the last international human rights organization remaining in the country. The Supreme Court granted a petition by the Ministry of Justice to close the office for the alleged repeated failure to comply with regulations, thereby forcing Human Rights Watch to stop its operations in the country.

Torture and other ill-treatment

Despite assertions by the authorities that the practice of torture had significantly decreased, and the introduction of new legislation to improve the treatment of detainees, dozens of reports of torture and other ill-treatment of detainees and prisoners emerged throughout the year. In most cases, the authorities failed to conduct prompt, thorough and impartial investigations into these allegations.

In September, the President approved a new law on the treatment of individuals in pre-charge and pre-trial detention. The new legislation allowed, among other things, for an unrestricted number of visits of undefined length by detainees' relatives and lawyers and abolished the need to obtain prior permission from the investigating security officers. However, by

the end of December there was scant evidence that the law was being implemented consistently and effectively.

Despite a handful of well-publicized releases, several thousand people convicted of involvement with banned Islamist parties or Islamic movements, as well as government critics, political opponents and human rights activists, continued to serve long prison terms under conditions that amounted to cruel, inhuman and degrading treatment. Many had their prison terms extended for allegedly violating prison rules of conduct following summary and closed trials held inside detention facilities.

■ On 19 May, the poet and government critic Yusuf Juma was unexpectedly released from Yaslik prison after serving three years of a five-year sentence for resisting arrest and injuring police officers, charges he claimed were politically motivated. He was secretly taken to Tashkent Airport and put on a plane to the USA. Yusuf Juma said that he was forced to renounce his Uzbekistani citizenship in exchange for joining his family in the USA where they had been given political asylum. In an interview with Radio Ozodlyk (the Uzbek Service of Radio Free Europe/Radio Liberty) he maintained that he had been tortured and otherwise ill-treated throughout his imprisonment, regularly spending 15 days in solitary confinement in punishment cells. He said that prison personnel and law enforcement officers used torture routinely to extract confessions from detainees or punish prisoners.

Counter-terror and security

The authorities continued to seek the extradition of members or suspected members of Islamic movements and Islamist groups and parties banned in Uzbekistan in the name of national and regional security and the fight against terrorism. Those forcibly returned to Uzbekistan were at serious risk of torture and other ill-treatment and long prison sentences in cruel, inhuman and degrading conditions following unfair trials.

At least 12 of the 28 Uzbekistani men extradited from Kazakhstan in June (see Kazakhstan entry) were reported to have been put on trial on charges of religious extremism and alleged membership of the Jihadchilar (Jihadists) Islamist organization. All of the men were held incommunicado following their extradition. Human rights monitors believed they were detained in Tashkent prison and were at grave risk of

U

torture. They also reported that relatives were intimidated by security forces and prevented from discovering the whereabouts of the men.

Three of those returned were sentenced to imprisonment in separate trials in August and September. Akhmad Boltaev and Faizullakhon Akbarov were given sentences of 15 and five years respectively by Sirdaria Regional Court on 21 August. The sentences were reduced on appeal to 13 and four years. They were found guilty of membership of Jihadchilar, distributing materials which threatened public order and planning to overthrow the constitutional order of Uzbekistan. Both had been held incommunicado for two months and were only allowed to meet their relatives after the trial. They were not given permission to hire their own lawyers and had only limited access to their state-appointed lawyers. On 13 September, Kibraisk District Criminal Court sentenced Kobidzhon Kurbanov to four years in prison for organizing illegal religious gatherings.

International scrutiny

The international community, in particular the EU and the US, took steps to increase economic and security co-operation with Uzbekistan, despite the continuing blatant human rights violations in the country.

President Karimov visited Brussels on 24 January for discussions on regional security and economic co-operation with the EU and NATO amid vocal protests by human rights organizations. It was his first official visit to Brussels since the May 2005 mass killings in Andizhan and the subsequent imposition of sanctions by the EU. European Council President Herman Van Rompuy declined to meet President Karimov for "ideological reasons". European Commission President José Manuel Barroso released a press statement which underlined that he had raised human rights issues with President Karimov during their meeting. Nevertheless, the EU continued to fail to take action to hold Uzbekistan to its human rights commitments.

Following further pledges by the President in September on economic, political and democratic reforms, the US Congress lifted its seven-year-old human rights restrictions on military assistance to Uzbekistan, to facilitate co-operation on transiting supplies to US and NATO troops in neighbouring Afghanistan.

VENEZUELA

BOLIVARIAN REPUBLIC OF VENEZUELA

Head of state and government:	Hugo Chávez Frías
Death penalty:	abolitionist for all crimes
Population:	29.4 million
Life expectancy:	74.4 years
Under-5 mortality:	17.5 per 1,000
Adult literacy:	95.2 per cent

Human rights defenders were threatened and politically motivated charges continued to be used against government critics. Accountability mechanisms to ensure justice or to act as an effective deterrent against police abuses remained weak. There were serious episodes of violence in the grossly overcrowded prison system leading to a number of deaths.

Background

Criminal and police violence remained a serious problem in Venezuela's cities. In May, the government created the Presidential Commission for the Control of Arms, Munitions and Disarmament to tackle the proliferation of small arms fuelling the violence. In November President Chávez ordered National Guard troops onto the streets to tackle widespread violent crime.

There were ongoing social protests. The Venezuelan Social Conflict Observatory registered 497 protests in September alone on a range of issues including labour rights and public security.

In October, Venezuela's human rights record was assessed under the UN's Universal Periodic Review. States raised concerns about a number of issues including the independence of the judiciary, threats to and harassment of human rights defenders, prison conditions, freedom of expression and impunity.

In October, the Supreme Court breached legally binding international obligations by disregarding a ruling by the Inter-American Court of Human Rights that the ban be lifted on opposition politician Leopoldo López running for office.

Human rights defenders

Human rights defenders were threatened and subjected to unfounded accusations by government officials and the state media. Human rights

V

organizations were concerned that the lack of definition of "political rights" in the Law for the Defence of Political Sovereignty and National Self Determination, passed by the National Assembly in December 2010, could impede their work. The Law bans organizations considered to work for the defence of political rights from receiving international funding.

■ In June, Humberto Prado Sifontes, Director of the Venezuelan Observatory of Prisons, was subjected to a campaign of intimidation and death threats after he called on the government to peacefully address a riot at El Rodeo Prison. Following accusations by government ministers and official media against him, a blog published his contact details with a note that said: "Family information to come soon… so that the people can try him. Capital punishment." His wife received an anonymous call stating that he "would be the next one to fall".

Police and security forces

There were continuing reports of human rights violations by the police, including unlawful killings and torture. Most of these abuses were not properly investigated and little, if any, judicial action was taken.

■ In May, Juan José Barrios was assassinated by two hooded men in Guanayén, Aragua state. He was the seventh member of the Barrios family to be killed in circumstances that suggested members of the Aragua State Police were involved. In January, Néstor Caudi Barrios, who had witnessed the extrajudicial execution of Narciso Barrios in 2003, was left with permanent injuries after being shot by two men on motorbikes. No progress had been reported in the investigations into these attacks by the end of the year.

■ In January, Daniel Antonio Núñez and his 16-year-old daughter Francis Daniela Núñez Martínez were beaten and threatened by police officers from the Caracas Investigative Police in an apparent attempt to intimidate them into testifying as witnesses to a shooting near their home.

■ In February, the former wife and young daughters of police officer Jonny Montoya received death threats. Jonny Montoya had complained about rising corruption under the former Chief Superintendent of the Municipal Police of Caracas.

Repression of dissent

Politically motivated charges continued to be used against government critics.

■ In February Rubén González, Secretary General of the Orinoco Iron Miners' Union, was convicted of crimes including incitement and conspiracy for organizing a strike in 2009 and was sentenced to seven years' imprisonment. Three days later, the Supreme Court ordered his conditional release.

■ In July, Oswaldo Álvarez Paz, member of an opposition party and a former governor of Zulia state, was convicted by a criminal court in Caracas of disseminating "false information" following his criticism of the government which was broadcast on Globovisión in March 2010. He was sentenced to two years' imprisonment; the judge subsequently allowed him to serve his sentence on conditional release.

Independence of the judiciary

There were continuing concerns about the independence and impartiality of the judiciary.

■ In February, Judge María Lourdes Afiuni, arbitrarily detained in December 2009 after granting conditional release to banker Eligio Cedeño, was put under house arrest. She had been held in prison for more than a year where she was threatened and denied adequate medical attention. Judge Afiuni refused to enter the court house in protest against violations of due process. Her house arrest was extended by two more years in December.

Prison conditions

Violence remained endemic in the chronically overcrowded prisons. In June, clashes between rival gangs in El Rodeo prison led to the deaths of some 27 prisoners.

In July, the Minister of Prison Services announced plans to release 40 per cent of the prison population to ease overcrowding. In November, she publicly threatened to dismiss judges who blocked her plans to speed up the trials of prisoners charged with minor offences. The Venezuelan Observatory of Prisons reported that in 2010 only a quarter of the prison population had been sentenced; the rest were on trial, awaiting a preliminary hearing or under investigation.

Freedom of expression

There were further restrictions on freedom of expression. In October, the National Telecommunications Commission, the state media regulator, imposed a large fine on Globovisión for violating the Law on Social Accountability in Radio,

Television and Electronic Media. The television station was accused of "justifying crime" and promoting "hatred for political reasons" for its coverage of the prison riot at El Rodeo. Globovisión, whose journalists have previously been threatened and attacked and which faced other administrative investigations, appealed against this latest action in November. The appeal was pending at the end of the year.

■ Leocenis García, editor of the weekly publication *Sexto Poder*, was arrested in August on charges of insulting public officials and offences based on gender in connection with the publication in August of a satirical article containing a photomontage of senior female government officials. He was conditionally released in November.

Violence against women and girls

Violence against women remained pervasive. In spite of measures taken in recent years, the authorities had yet to issue an action plan to address violence against women or regulations on implementing the 2007 Organic law on the right of women to a life free of violence.

Amnesty International visits/reports

📖 Venezuela: Human rights guarantees must be respected – a summary of human rights concerns (AMR 53/007/2011)

VIET NAM

SOCIALIST REPUBLIC OF VIET NAM

Head of state:	Truong Tan Sang (replaced Nguyen Minh Triet in July)
Head of government:	Nguyen Tan Dung
Death penalty:	retentionist
Population:	88.8 million
Life expectancy:	75.2 years
Under-5 mortality:	23.6 per 1,000
Adult literacy:	92.8 per cent

Harsh repression of dissidents continued, with severe restrictions on freedom of expression, association and peaceful assembly. Critics of government policies were targeted, including social and political activists. At least nine dissident trials took place, with 20 defendants. Vaguely worded provisions of the 1999 Penal Code were used to, in effect, criminalize peaceful political and social dissent. The government continued to censor the internet, although use of social networking sites reportedly increased as people used circumvention tools to bypass restrictions. Dozens of prisoners of conscience remained in prison. Religious and ethnic groups perceived to be opposing the government continued to face human rights violations. According to media reports, 23 people were sentenced to death and five executed; the true numbers are believed to be higher. Official statistics on the death penalty remained classified.

Background

A new government was formed in July, with the Prime Minister elected for a second five-year term.

Between June and August, the authorities allowed a series of anti-China protests in the capital, Ha Noi, as tensions increased over disputed ownership of the Paracel and Spratly islands in the South China Sea.

The UN Special Rapporteur on the right of everyone to the enjoyment of the highest attainable standard of physical and mental health visited in December. He called for the immediate closure of rehabilitation centres for drug users and sex workers, citing concerns over compulsory admittance and treatment administered without consent.

In December, donor countries attending a consultative group meeting in Ha Noi called on the

V

government to improve its human rights record, warning that the ongoing crackdown on dissidents was threatening Viet Nam's international credibility.

Repression of dissent

Severe restrictions on freedom of expression and association continued, with dissidents critical of government policies harshly repressed. Individuals most at risk included pro-democracy activists, and those calling for reform or protesting about environmental issues, land and labour rights, and the rights of ethnic and religious minorities. The authorities used vaguely worded provisions of the national security section of the 1999 Penal Code, in particular Article 79 (aiming to "overthrow" the state) and Article 88 ("conducting propaganda" against the state), to punish peaceful dissent.

At least nine dissident trials of 20 defendants took place. More than 18 individuals were arrested and in pre-trial detention at the end of the year, including at least 13 Catholic activists supporting dissident Cu Huy Ha Vu.

■ Human rights defender, legal scholar and environmental activist Cu Huy Ha Vu was sentenced to seven years' imprisonment in April under Article 88 of the Penal Code. He had twice submitted criminal complaints against the Prime Minister, once in an attempt to stop a controversial bauxite mining project, and the other challenging the legality of a ban on class-action complaints.

■ Tran Thi Thuy, Pastor Duong Kim Khai and five other land activists were sentenced to between two and eight years' imprisonment in May by a court in Ben Tre province. They were charged with aiming to "overthrow" the government. Thuy had campaigned for social justice for farmers in the province. Pastor Khai led the "Cattle Shed" Mennonite Church and had helped farmers whose land had been confiscated to petition the authorities.

Prisoners of conscience

Dozens of prisoners of conscience arrested in previous years remained held after receiving long sentences in unfair trials. Many of them were connected with the online pro-democracy movement Bloc 8406.

A small number of prisoners of conscience were released. Dissident writer Tran Khai Thanh Thuy was released in July before the end of her prison term after agreeing to go into exile overseas. Truong Quoc

Huy, a mobile phone technician, was released in December, eight months before the end of his six-year prison sentence. Human rights lawyer Nguyen Van Dai was released in March, after serving his four-year sentence. Both men were placed under house arrest for up to four years.

■ Father Nguyen Van Ly, a Catholic priest and co-founder of Bloc 8406, was rearrested by police in July and returned to Ba Sao prison in northern Viet Nam. Father Ly's eight-year prison term was temporarily suspended for 12 months in March 2010 after he had had a stroke in prison and was diagnosed with a brain tumour. The authorities claimed that he was returned to prison for distributing anti-government leaflets while on medical release.

■ Blogger and journalist Nguyen Hoang Hai, co-founder of the independent Free Vietnamese Journalists' Club and known as Dieu Cay, remained detained on reported charges of "conducting propaganda" against the state. The authorities denied repeated requests from his family and lawyer to visit him. Nor did they respond to appeals for information about his welfare after a security official stated that he had "lost his arm".

Discrimination – ethnic and religious groups

Security officials continued to harass and closely monitor members of religious and ethnic groups perceived to be opponents of the government. Disputes continued over land ownership between local authorities and the Catholic Church, in some cases involving unnecessary or excessive use of force by security officials against peaceful protesters. The Supreme Patriarch of the banned Unified Buddhist Church of Viet Nam remained under de facto house arrest. An unknown number of ethnic Montagnards remained imprisoned following protests in the Central Highlands in 2001 and 2004.

■ In November, police beat and arrested at least 30 peaceful Falun Gong demonstrators outside the Chinese embassy in Ha Noi. They had been protesting against the trial of two local Falun Gong broadcasters, Vu Duc Trung and Le Van Thanh. They were sentenced two days later to two and three years' imprisonment respectively for broadcasting illegally into China where the Falun Gong is banned.

■ Nguyen Van Lia and Tran Hoai An, members of the Hoa Hao Buddhist church, were sentenced to five and

V

three years' imprisonment respectively in December for "abusing democratic freedoms to infringe upon the interests of the state". Nguyen Van Lia, aged 72, and Tran Hoai An had briefed foreign diplomats about restrictions on freedom of religion and other human rights violations.

YEMEN

REPUBLIC OF YEMEN

Head of state:	Ali Abdullah Saleh (June-September, Vice President Abd Rabbu Mansour Hadi effectively in charge)
Head of government:	Mohammed Salim Basindwa (replaced Ali Mohammed Mujawar in November)
Death penalty:	retentionist
Population:	24.8 million
Life expectancy:	65.5 years
Under-5 mortality:	66.4 per 1,000
Adult literacy:	62.4 per cent

Government security forces and supporters of President Ali Abdullah Saleh killed more than 200 people in protests as the President faced mass demonstrations demanding reform and his departure from office. Many were killed while peacefully protesting; thousands more were injured. The protests were fuelled by popular anger over mounting poverty, unemployment, corruption and the brutally repressive response of the government. The security forces and government supporters repeatedly used live ammunition, rocket-propelled grenades and other excessive and lethal force against peaceful demonstrations and during clashes when opponents of the President also resorted to violence. The security forces carried out mass arbitrary arrests and detentions, enforced disappearances, and used torture and other ill-treatment with impunity. Media workers and outlets came under sustained attack. Women and girls continued to face severe discrimination. Many women played a key role in the protests and some were arrested, beaten or harassed as a result. New death sentences were passed and at least 41 people were executed. Government and US forces attacked and killed alleged al-Qa'ida members; some civilians were also killed in the attacks.

Background

In January, the government proposed changes to the Constitution under which President Saleh, in power since 1978, would have been able to stand for re-election on an unlimited basis. The proposals sparked widespread protests, including a large demonstration in Sana'a, the capital, on 22 January. The next day, there were further protests after Tawakkol Karman, head of the NGO Women Journalists Without Chains, was arrested; she was quickly released on bail and in October was one of three women jointly awarded the Nobel Peace Prize. The demonstrations were met with violence by the security forces but grew and spread to Aden and other cities, with some demonstrators calling for the President and his government to be replaced.

In response, on 2 February, President Saleh said he would stand down when his existing presidential term ended in 2013 and hold discussions with the Joint Meeting Parties, a coalition of six opposition parties, but this fuelled rather than halted the protests. The next day, when students and activists belonging to Youth of the Revolution demonstrated, the security forces began using lethal force against the protesters in Sana'a and elsewhere.

Several people were killed in mid-February during mass protests in various cities. Sit-in protests and protest camps of tents sprung up near Sana'a University and in Ta'izz in what were soon called al-Taghyeer (change) squares. On 23 February, nine ruling party members of parliament resigned in protest against the violence used by government forces against protesters.

On 28 February, President Saleh reportedly proposed to form a national unity government including members of the opposition. The opposition demanded that he leave office first, proposing a transition plan under which he would do so before the end of 2011. President Saleh rejected this and the crisis deepened dramatically on 18 March, when government snipers fired on the "Change Square" protest camp in Sana'a, killing at least 52 protesters; a number of government ministers and officials resigned in protest and the general commanding the army's First Brigade said he and his men would now support the protesters. President Saleh dismissed the cabinet, announced a caretaker government, and imposed a 30-day state of emergency, which the parliament approved on 23 March. This suspended

Y

the Constitution, tightened media censorship and extended security forces' powers of arrest and detention and to ban street protests.

The Gulf Cooperation Council (GCC) intervened to mediate between President Saleh and his opponents. On 23 April, President Saleh said he would accept a GCC proposal to relinquish the presidency within 30 days and allow a national unity government to be formed and under which he and his associates would be given immunity against prosecution. However, he then repeatedly refused to sign the agreement as his forces increasingly clashed with armed members of tribes who came out in opposition to him and with armed Islamists believed to be linked to al-Qa'ida in the Arabian Peninsula, who seized control of parts of Abyan province.

On 3 June, an attack on the presidential palace seriously injured President Saleh and killed and wounded others. The President was evacuated to Saudi Arabia for medical treatment, leaving the Vice President in charge. The opposition formed an alliance in August, the National Council for the Revolutionary Forces, but this quickly became divided. An uneasy stalemate developed and there were continuing armed clashes; a fact-finding team sent by the UN High Commissioner for Human Rights pointed to serious human rights violations and called for an international investigation and accountability.

President Saleh returned to Yemen on 23 September, prompting mass demonstrations by his supporters and his opponents.

On 21 October, the UN Security Council condemned the continuing violence in Yemen and urged President Saleh to hand over power in accordance with the GCC agreement. On 23 November he signed the agreement, handing power to the Vice President to appoint a new Prime Minister heading a "government of national reconciliation" and to hold presidential elections within 90 days. In return, President Saleh and his aides were to be given immunity for crimes committed during his rule. Within two weeks, a Prime Minister from the opposition was appointed and a national government was formed representing the ruling party and members of the opposition. Protests continued denouncing the reported immunity agreement.

2011 also saw armed clashes in the north and the south, leading to forcible displacement of civilians. In the north, Sa'dah province effectively came under the

control of Huthi rebels in late March and later in the year they reportedly took control of parts of other provinces. In the southern province of Abyan, government forces clashed with armed Islamist militants. Armed clashes also took place in Sana'a and Ta'izz between security forces and armed tribes and soldiers who had defected, who had announced they were seeking to protect protesters. Many were killed during the clashes, including some as a result of heavy shelling by government forces.

An already dire humanitarian situation deteriorated to crisis point as Yemenis struggled with acute shortages of water and other necessities, burgeoning unemployment and living costs, and cuts to power and oil supplies.

Excessive use of force

In the face of peaceful anti-government protests, as well as during clashes in some parts of the country, the security forces resorted to excessive and disproportionate force, including lethal force. They used live ammunition, tear gas, batons, electric stun guns and polluted water spray. Snipers on rooftops and gunmen at street level repeatedly fired at peaceful protesters. Security forces also attacked protesters when they were at their most vulnerable, late at night and during prayer. Armed men in plain clothes known as "*baltaji*" ("thugs") attacked anti-government protesters with batons and firearms, often in the presence of the security forces and with their acquiescence. They and the security forces attacked protesters with almost total impunity; the authorities announced investigations into some killings but they were not independent and their outcomes were unclear.

■ In Aden on 25 February, security forces fired on protesters from armoured vehicles and attacked houses in which they suspected protesters had taken shelter, killing some 12 people, two of them in their homes, and reportedly prevented the injured from being taken to hospital.

■ On 4 March at Harf Sufyan in the northern 'Amran governorate, soldiers at a military post fired at protesters as they sought to leave the area in cars, reportedly killing two and wounding others.

■ In central Sana'a on 18 March, snipers believed to be from the security forces fired into the protest camp from the tops of buildings after Friday prayers, and security forces at street level also opened fire in what quickly became known as "Bloody Friday". At least 52

Y

protesters were shot dead; hundreds more were wounded. The President issued a public apology but denied that the police were responsible. According to the Office of the UN High Commissioner for Human Rights, an official investigation resulted in 78 people being charged in connection with the 18 March events, but it was unclear whether these included members of the security forces. The authorities offered compensation to some of the victims' families.

■ In Ta'izz, the security forces fired into a protest camp and makeshift field hospital on 29 May, reportedly killing at least a dozen people, before bulldozing and burning the camp.

■ In Aden on 24 June, soldiers backed by tanks shot dead Dr Jiyab Ali al-Sa'adi, son of one of the leaders of the Southern Movement, when he reportedly urged them not to fire on mourners at the funeral of Ahmed al-Darwish, who had died in custody in June 2010, reportedly after torture.

■ Between 18 and 22 September in Sana'a, security forces used snipers and fired rocket-propelled grenades at protesters demanding the resignation of President Saleh, killing tens of people and injuring hundreds.

Arbitrary arrests, detentions and enforced disappearances

Hundreds of people were arbitrarily arrested and detained in connection with the protests, adding to the number of those in detention, some of whom had been held long before the protests began. In June-July, a UN delegation that gained access to a prison in Sana'a run by Political Security found both Yemenis and foreign nationals there who had been detained without charge or trial or brought before a judge for months and even years.

■ Abdul Hakim Ahmed al-Hatami, Nabil Mowqahu and Mohammed al-Zubayri were arrested in a Sana'a street on 23 November and held incommunicado for nine days before being moved to a police station. Abdul Hakim Ahmed al-Hatami was made to sign a pledge not to participate in further protests and was released on 7 December. Nabil Mowqahu and Mohammed al-Zubayri were released days later.

■ Hassan Ba'oom, aged 71 and a leading member of the Southern Movement, was arrested on 20 February while receiving treatment at a hospital in Aden. He was held incommunicado until 7 December, when he was released without charge.

Counter-terror and security

Both Yemeni government and US forces undertook security operations against suspected al-Qa'ida members, particularly in Abyan province, using air strikes and other means, some of which resulted in deaths and injuries to civilians.

■ In June, US drones and/or jets were reported to have carried out two attacks in Abyan in which several civilians were among those killed and injured.

■ On 30 September, an attack reportedly by a US drone and fighter jet in al-Jawf province killed four people, including US-born cleric Anwar al-Awlaki, an alleged al-Qa'ida member accused of responsibility for an attempt to blow up a civilian airliner over the US city of Detroit in December 2009.

Government fighter jets attacked the southern city of Zinjibar in May after it was seized by Islamist militants, who took over banks and a government compound and reportedly committed human rights abuses. On 11 September, the authorities announced that the army had regained most of the city after more than three months of fighting in which 230 soldiers and 50 members of local tribes were said to have been killed.

Freedom of expression

The government tightened controls on freedom of expression and targeted journalists and media seen as critics of President Saleh. Journalists and other media workers were killed, attacked, harassed, threatened and imprisoned during the unrest, and restrictive press laws and repressive actions by the security forces severely undermined press freedom and other expression. Several foreign journalists were attacked or expelled from Yemen. Dozens of publications were reported to have been seized and websites hacked or suspended. Several journalists employed by state-run media were sacked after they joined anti-government protests.

■ In February, BBC reporter Abdullah Ghorab and cameraman Mohammed Omran were assaulted by supporters of a government official while reporting on the protests against President Saleh.

■ One journalist was reported to have been killed when government forces attacked protesters in Sana'a on 18 March, and others were injured, arrested, threatened or had their equipment seized.

■ The authorities closed the local bureau of Al Jazeera TV station on 24 March and withdrew its reporters'

Y

permits following its coverage of the "Bloody Friday" killings of protesters.

■ In May, the Sana'a offices of both the state news agency Saba and Suhail TV, owned by a leading government opponent, were badly damaged during armed clashes between forces supporting and opposed to President Saleh. The Ministry of Communication was also reported to have disrupted some services of Sabafone, a telecommunications network belonging to the owner of Suhail TV.

■ Abdul Ilah Haydar Shayi', a freelance journalist specializing in counter-terrorism who was arrested in August 2010, remained in prison although President Saleh reportedly issued an order for his release on 1 February. He was initially detained incommunicado, during which he was said to have been severely beaten, then tried before the Specialized Criminal Court in Sana'a and sentenced to five years in prison in January 2011. He appeared to be a prisoner of conscience.

Torture and other ill-treatment

There were new reports of torture and other ill-treatment of detainees by the security forces. The most commonly reported methods were beatings, electric shocks, burning with cigarettes and suspension by the limbs, often for long periods.

■ In February, detainees at the Political Security prison in Sana'a, including alleged al-Qa'ida members or supporters, were reported to have been beaten by guards and held in solitary confinement after going on hunger strike to protest against their prolonged detention without charge or trial, ill-treatment and denial of adequate medical care. At least 10 detainees were said to have required hospital treatment as a result of the beatings.

■ Mustafa Abdu Yahya al-Nahari was reported to have been repeatedly kicked, beaten, and whipped by Central Security officials, who held him at an unknown place for a week after they arrested him at his home on 14 November. He was kept blindfolded throughout, interrogated about the protests and made to sign a document without knowing what it contained, then released by being left, still blindfolded, in a street.

Cruel, inhuman or degrading punishments

During the period that Islamist militants controlled Zinjibar, they applied a strict interpretation of Shari'a (Islamic law) there, and in September were reported to have amputated the hands of two men accused of theft, one of whom died as a result.

Women's rights

Women and girls continued to face severe discrimination in law and in practice; this was particularly pronounced in rural areas. However, women played a major and sometimes leading role in the anti-government protests, leading President Saleh on 15 April to publicly condemn as "un-Islamic" the mixing of women and men in protests; in response, thousands of women demonstrated in defiance of what they saw as an attempt by the President to curtail their rights to freedom of expression and to participate in public affairs. Women activists and journalists were targeted by the security forces and pro-government supporters, harassed, arrested and in some cases beaten for participating in the protests. Some were also threatened via their family, with male relatives being told to assert control and curtail their activism.

■ Tawakkol Karman's brother was reported to have received a phone call after her arrest in January telling him to confine her to her home or "those who weaken the whip of obedience would be killed".

■ On 9 October, government supporters attacked women, injuring dozens, as they held a march in Ta'izz to celebrate the award of the Nobel Peace Prize to Tawakkol Karman.

Refugees and asylum-seekers

Yemen continued to host more than 200,000 African refugees, mostly from Somalia, with a new influx from August sparked by drought, conflict and political insecurity. They experienced harsh conditions, exacerbated by Yemen's growing political, economic and humanitarian crisis, and many staged protests outside the offices of UNHCR, the UN refugee agency.

■ In July, UNHCR closed its offices in Sana'a for several days after hundreds of Eritrean and other refugees, who had camped outside the offices to demand resettlement because of the volatile situation in Sana'a, clashed with police.

Death penalty

At least 29 people were sentenced to death and at least 41 were executed; the real numbers may have been considerably higher. Hundreds of people remained under sentence of death.

■ Yasser Ismail and four of his male relatives, all aged in their twenties, were at risk of execution after their sentences, imposed in 2006 after they were convicted of murder, were confirmed by both the Appeal Court and the Supreme Court.

■ Ahmed Omar al-Abbadi al-Markashi was at risk of execution after his death sentence was confirmed by the Appeal Court in June. A security guard at the Sana'a home of Hisham Bashraheel, chief editor of *al-Ayyam* newspaper, he was convicted of murder in June 2010 in connection with an incident in 2008 when one of several armed men who fired shots at the editor's house was killed when his security guards returned fire. His trial was unfair.

Amnesty International visits/reports

🚌 The government did not accede to Amnesty International's requests to visit Yemen in 2011.

📄 Yemen: Human rights activist threatened, Tawakkol Karman (MDE 31/003/2011)

📄 Moment of truth for Yemen (MDE 31/007/2011)

📄 Yemen transition tainted by "immunity" deal (PRE01/591/2011)

ZIMBABWE

REPUBLIC OF ZIMBABWE

Head of state and government:	**Robert Mugabe**
Death penalty:	**retentionist**
Population:	**12.8 million**
Life expectancy:	**51.4 years**
Under-5 mortality:	**89.5 per 1,000**
Adult literacy:	**91.9 per cent**

Discord and mistrust within the Government of National Unity (GNU) continued to undermine delivery on key objectives of the Global Political Agreement. This led to severe delays in drawing up a new Constitution and implementing electoral, media and security reforms that would lead to elections. Elements within the security forces continued to exert pressure on the two Movement for Democratic Change (MDC) parties by ordering the arrest of senior party members or unlawfully disrupting their political activities. Human rights defenders were arrested, detained and tortured in police custody, especially in the aftermath of the protests in the Middle East and North Africa. The police continued

to operate in a partisan manner, failing to take action against members of President Mugabe's ZANU-PF party when they harassed, intimidated or beat up perceived political opponents.

Background

The GNU failed to complete the process towards establishing a new Constitution, which was running more than a year behind schedule. This was mainly due to inadequate funding of the Constitution process and squabbles between the parties in the unity government. ZANU-PF continued to resist security sector and media reforms that were agreed as part of the Global Political Agreement, which was signed by the three major parties in September 2008 and led to the creation of the unity government in February 2009. On 24 November, the Broadcasting Authority of Zimbabwe awarded commercial broadcasting licences to the state-controlled Zimbabwe Newspapers Group and AB Communications. Both media houses were seen as close to ZANU-PF.

The Southern African Development Community (SADC), through President Jacob Zuma of South Africa, continued to mediate between ZANU-PF and the two MDC political parties, who agreed on an election road map. However, the implementation of agreements was again hampered by suspicion and mistrust at the top levels of the government. In June, Brigadier-General Douglas Nyikayaramba caused alarm when he was quoted in the state-controlled *Herald* newspaper, saying that ZANU-PF and the security forces were one and that the Prime Minister, Morgan Tsvangirai, was a security threat.

On 31 March the SADC's Organ Troika on Politics, Defence and Security Cooperation called for an end to the violence in Zimbabwe, including arrests and intimidation of political opponents of ZANU-PF.

Talk of a possible election in 2011, mainly by President Mugabe and ZANU-PF members, increased tensions in rural and suburban communities mainly affected by the 2008 state-sponsored violence. There were reports of harassment and intimidation by ZANU-PF supporters against perceived opponents. In some areas this led to inter-party clashes. However, police appeared to only arrest opponents of ZANU-PF, leading to a perception that ZANU-PF supporters were above the law.

During the build-up to the congress of Morgan Tsvangirai's MDC party (MDC-T) in Bulawayo in April,

Z

some party members were involved in violent clashes as they competed for positions. Clashes within the MDC-T were reported in Manicaland, Masvingo, Bulawayo and Midlands provinces during provincial congresses.

Freedom of expression, association and assembly

Police used the Public Order and Security Act to undermine the political activities of the two MDC parties. Throughout the year they continued to interfere with their activities, blocking meetings or failing to act when ZANU-PF supporters attempted to disrupt meetings. In some instances police used excessive force, or threatened force, to block MDC meetings that had been sanctioned by the courts; no ZANU-PF meetings were blocked by the police. In instances of inter-party violence, police rarely arrested ZANU-PF supporters.

Chipangano, a gang linked to ZANU-PF, committed human rights abuses with total impunity in their base in Mbare and in other parts of Harare. On 23 July they invaded the Parliament building, disrupted a public hearing on the Zimbabwe Human Rights Commission Bill, and beat several people, including a member of Parliament and a journalist. No one was arrested despite the presence of the police. In October in Marondera and Mutare, groups of ZANU-PF supporters disrupted public consultations by Parliament on the Electoral Amendment Bill, causing further delays to the electoral reform process.

■ On 21 January, Amnesty International witnessed ZANU-PF supporters, demonstrating at Harare's town hall, beating members of the public in the presence of anti-riot police. They beat a high-school student for taking a photograph, and beat and stripped a young woman who was wearing an MDC-T T-shirt. The two were seriously injured and needed medical treatment. The police did not intervene to stop the violence.

■ In February, 23 villagers from Nyanga district in Manicaland province, and Douglas Mwonzora, the local MDC-T member of Parliament, were arrested and held in custody. They were accused of public violence following clashes between members of ZANU-PF and the MDC-T. No ZANU-PF members were arrested. The 24 detainees were granted bail, but the state used Section 121 of the Criminal Procedure and Evidence Act (CPEA) to suspend the bail order, and prolonged the detention by a further seven days. Section 121 of

the CPEA has been used in the past to prolong detention of perceived opponents of ZANU-PF.

■ On 10 July, Professor Welshman Ncube, leader of the MDC, the smaller of the two MDC parties, and several members of the party's executives, were detained in Hwange after being stopped at a police checkpoint. They were released after a couple of hours without charge.

■ Police in Matabeleland North province blocked two MDC-T rallies in Lupane and Victoria Falls on 29 and 30 October respectively. The rallies were to be addressed by Morgan Tsvangirai.

■ On 6 November, ZANU-PF followers disrupted a rally planned by the MDC-T at Chibuku Stadium in the town of Chitungwiza, and allegedly attacked supporters. Violence ensued and the meeting was abandoned. The police, who had been notified of the rally, were present but made no arrests. Following this incident, police spokespeople stated that they would not police MDC-T political activities, effectively preventing the MDC-T from holding rallies due to concerns about the safety of people attending. However, police subsequently provided a presence at an MDC-T rally at the same venue, effectively allowing it to go ahead.

Arbitrary arrests and detentions

Politically motivated arrests of senior members of the MDC parties persisted. Scores of MDC supporters were also arrested, some spending months in custody on politically motivated charges. Similar arrests over the years have ended in acquittals or the dropping of charges.

■ On 10 March, the Minister of Energy and Power Development, Elton Mangoma, of the MDC-T party, was arrested on trumped-up charges of corruption. He was later acquitted in court.

■ On 14 April, Moses Mzila, Minister of National Healing and Reconciliation and a member of the MDC, was arrested for allegedly failing to notify the police about a meeting held the day before in Lupane, Matabeleland North. On the same day, a Roman Catholic priest, Father Marko Mabutho Mnkandla, was arrested for holding mass in memory of the victims and survivors of the *Gukurahundi*, the atrocities committed by state security forces in Matabeleland in the 1980s.

■ In June, Jameson Timba, Minister of State in the Prime Minister's office, was arrested after allegedly writing in a local newspaper that President Mugabe had lied about the outcome of the SADC summit held in Johannesburg earlier in the month.

■ More than 25 people were arrested in connection with an incident in Glen View in Harare on 29 May, when a police officer, Petros Mutedza, was beaten to death by a mob. Without carrying out proper investigations, police issued statements blaming MDC-T supporters, and clamped down on the party's supporters in the area. Some of those arrested were tortured in police custody. Seven were denied bail and at the end of the year were still in remand prison. Cynthia Manjoro, a human rights defender, was arrested after her car was   reportedly seen being driven near where the violence took place; she herself was not in the area at the time and is not an MDC-T official.

Human rights defenders

Human rights defenders continued to face arbitrary arrests, unlawful detention, politically motivated charges, and even torture in police custody. Community-based activists faced harassment and intimidation by members of ZANU-PF because of their human rights work. Such threats and intimidation increased as ZANU-PF started making pronouncements of a possible election in 2011.

On 19 February, Munyaradzi Gwisai and 44 other activists were arrested by police in Harare while holding a meeting to discuss the implications of the protests in Egypt and Tunisia. They were detained beyond the 48 hours allowed by law and, just minutes before being taken to court on 23 February, told that they were being charged with treason. They were denied medical treatment and access to their lawyers and some reported being tortured by police. Thirty-nine of the activists were acquitted on 7 March. The treason charges were dropped in July but they continued to face charges of "conspiracy to commit violence or alternatively inciting public violence or participating in a gathering with intent to promote public violence, breaches of peace and bigotry."

On 28 February, seven members of the campaigning organizations Women of Zimbabwe Arise (WOZA) and Men of Zimbabwe Arise were arrested in Bulawayo. They were reportedly tortured at Bulawayo Central police station. Two days later they were released on US$50 bail and told to report to the police twice a week.

On 1 March, another 14 WOZA activists were arrested in Bulawayo while holding meetings on social issues. They were released the same day without charge.

Forced evictions

The government failed to provide education for thousands of children affected by the 2005 mass forced evictions, known as Operation Murambatsvina. In Hopley and Hatcliffe Extension, two settlements created by the government to rehouse the victims of the evictions in Harare, more than 2,000 children were attending unregistered primary schools, in inadequate buildings without trained teachers or stationery. More than six years after the forced evictions, most victims have been driven deeper into poverty because of the government's failure to find effective remedies.

Rights of lesbian, gay, bisexual and transgender people

Persecution of people based on their sexual orientation continued.

■ On 20 October two men, Lionel Girezha, aged 27, and Ngonidzashe Chinya, aged 28, were arrested in the suburb of Mbare in Harare and charged with sodomy. They deny the charges. They were beaten by the people who reported them before being taken into police custody. When the trial started, members of the ZANU-PF-linked Chipangano gang harassed and threatened the lawyers with violence for representing people suspected of being gay. Police failed to protect the lawyers, who had to appeal to the High Court to have the location of the trial changed from Mbare.

In October, Morgan Tsvangirai said in an interview with the BBC that he supported the rights of gay people. He was criticized by the state-controlled media, who tried to politicize the statement and incite hatred against "homosexuals".

Amnesty International visits/reports

🚌 Amnesty International visited Zimbabwe in January, August, September, October and November/December.

📄 Zimbabwe: Briefing to the pre-session working-group of the UN Committee on the Elimination of Discrimination Against Women – 51st Session (AFR 46/014/2011)

📄 Zimbabwe: Continued clampdown on dissent – Amnesty International submission to the UN Universal Periodic Review, March 2011 (AFR 46/016/2011)

📄 Left behind: The impact of Zimbabwe's mass forced evictions on the right to education (AFR 46/019/2011)

Z

Photos of the disappeared outside Benghazi North Court, Libya, April 2011. Al-Gaddafi forces engaged in an extensive campaign of enforced disappearances of perceived opponents across the country, including journalists, writers, online activists and protesters.

AMNESTY INTERNATIONAL REPORT 2012
PART THREE: SELECTED HUMAN RIGHTS TREATIES

12

SELECTED INTERNATIONAL AND REGIONAL HUMAN RIGHTS TREATIES
(AT 31 DECEMBER 2011)

SELECTED INTERNATIONAL HUMAN RIGHTS TREATIES

SELECTED REGIONAL HUMAN RIGHTS TREATIES

States which have ratified or acceded to a convention are party to the treaty and are bound to observe its provisions. States which have signed but not yet ratified have expressed their intention to become a party at some future date; meanwhile they are obliged to refrain from acts which would defeat the object and purpose of the treaty.

Indigenous and environmental protesters on their way to La Paz, Bolivia, to protest against a government-planned highway that would cut through Isiboro-Sécure Indigenous Territory and National Park, home to thousands. August 2011.

A Greek riot police officer kicks a protester during clashes in Syntagma Square, Athens, 15 June 2011. Protesters clashed with riot police in central Athens during a major anti-austerity rally.

	International Covenant on Civil and Political Rights (ICCPR)	(first) Optional Protocol to the ICCPR	Second Optional Protocol to the ICCPR, aiming at the abolition of the death penalty	International Covenant on Economic, Social and Cultural Rights (ICESCR)	Optional Protocol to the ICESCR (not in force)	Convention on the Elimination of All Forms of Discrimination against Women (CEDAW)	Optional Protocol to CEDAW	Convention on the Rights of the Child (CRC)	Optional Protocol to the CRC on the involvement of children in armed conflict	International Convention on the Elimination of All Forms of Racial Discrimination	Convention against Torture and Other Cruel, Inhuman or Degrading Treatment or Punishment
Afghanistan	●			●		●		●	●	●	●[28]
Albania	●	●	●	●		●	●	●	●	●	●
Algeria	●	●		●		●		●	●	●	●[22]
Andorra	●	●	●			●	●	●	●	●	●[22]
Angola	●	●		●		●	●	●	●	●	
Antigua and Barbuda						●	●	●		●	●
Argentina	●	●	●	●	●	●	●	●	●	●	●[22]
Armenia	●	●		●	○	●	●	●	●	●	●
Australia	●	●	●	●		●	●	●	●	●	●[22]
Austria	●	●	●	●		●	●	●	●	●	●[22]
Azerbaijan	●	●	●	●	○	●	●	●	●	●	●[22]
Bahamas	●			●		●		●		●	○
Bahrain	●			●		●		●	●	●	●
Bangladesh	●			●		●	●[10]	●	●	●	●
Barbados	●	●		●		●		●		●	
Belarus	●	●		●		●	●	●	●	●	●
Belgium	●	●	●	●	○	●	●	●	●	●	●[22]
Belize	●			○		●	●[10]	●	●	●	●
Benin	●	●		●		●	○	●	●	●	●
Bhutan						●		●	●	○	
Bolivia	●	●		●	○	●	●	●	●	●	●[22]
Bosnia and Herzegovina	●	●	●	●	○	●	●	●	●	●	●[22]
Botswana	●					●	●	●	●	●	●
Brazil	●	●	●	●		●	●	●	●	●	●[22]
Brunei Darussalam						●		●			
Bulgaria	●	●	●	●		●	●	●	●	●	●[22]
Burkina Faso	●	●		●		●	●	●	●	●	●
Burundi	●			●		●	○	●	●	●	●[22]

Optional Protocol to the Convention against Torture	International Convention for the Protection of All Persons from Enforced Disappearance	Convention relating to the Status of Refugees (1951)	Protocol relating to the Status of Refugees (1967)	Convention relating to the Status of Stateless Persons (1954)	Convention on the Reduction of Statelessness (1961)	International Convention on the Protection of the Rights of All Migrant Workers and Members of Their Families	Rome Statute of the International Criminal Court	
		●	●				●	Afghanistan
●	●	●	●	●	●	●	●	Albania
	○	●	●	●		●	○	Algeria
							●	Andorra
		●	●				○	Angola
		●	●	●			●	Antigua and Barbuda
●	●	●	●	●		●	●	Argentina
●	●	●	●	●	●		○	Armenia
○		●	●	●	●		●	Australia
○	○	●	●	●	●		●	Austria
●	○	●	●	●	●	●		Azerbaijan
		●	●				○	Bahamas
							○	Bahrain
						●	●	Bangladesh
			●				●	Barbados
		●	●					Belarus
○	●	●	●	●			●	Belgium
		●	●	●		●	●	Belize
●	○	●	●	●	●	○	●	Benin
								Bhutan
●	●	●	●	●	●	●	●	Bolivia
●	○	●	●	●	●	●	●	Bosnia and Herzegovina
		●	●				●	Botswana
●	●	●	●	●	●		●	Brazil
								Brunei Darussalam
○	○	●	●				●	Bulgaria
●	●	●	●			●	●	Burkina Faso
	○	●	●				●	Burundi

● state is a party

● state became party in 2011

○ signed but not yet ratified

○ signed in 2011, but not yet ratified

10   Declaration under Article 10 not recognizing the competence of the CEDAW Committee to undertake confidential inquiries into allegations of grave or systematic violations.

22   Declaration under Article 22 recognizing the competence of the Committee against Torture (CAT) to consider individual complaints.

28   Reservation under Article 28 not recognizing the competence of the CAT to undertake confidential inquiries into allegations of systematic torture if warranted.

12   Declaration under Article 12(3) accepting the jurisdiction of the International Criminal Court (ICC) for crimes in its territory.

124   Declaration under Article 124 not accepting the jurisdiction of the ICC over war crimes for seven years after ratification.

*   Signed the Rome Statute but have since formally declared their intention not to ratify.

**   Ratified or acceded but subsequently denounced the treaty.

	International Covenant on Civil and Political Rights (ICCPR)	(first) Optional Protocol to the ICCPR	Second Optional Protocol to the ICCPR, aiming at the abolition of the death penalty	International Covenant on Economic, Social and Cultural Rights (ICESCR)	Optional Protocol to the ICESCR (not in force)	Convention on the Elimination of All Forms of Discrimination against Women (CEDAW)	Optional Protocol to CEDAW	Convention on the Rights of the Child (CRC)	Optional Protocol to the CRC on the involvement of children in armed conflict	International Convention on the Elimination of All Forms of Racial Discrimination	Convention against Torture and Other Cruel, Inhuman or Degrading Treatment or Punishment
Cambodia	●	○		●		●	●	●	●	●	●
Cameroon	●	●		●		●	●	●	○	●	●[22]
Canada	●	●	●	●		●	●	●	●	●	●[22]
Cape Verde	●	●	●	●	○	●	●	●	●	●	●
Central African Republic	●	●		●		●		●	○	●	
Chad	●	●		●		●		●		●	●
Chile	●	●	●	●	○	●	○	●	●	●	●[22]
China	○			●		●		●	●	●	●[28]
Colombia	●	●	●	●		●	●[10]	●	●	●	●
Comoros	○			○		●		●		●	○
Congo (Republic of)	●	●		●	○	●	○	●	●	●	●
Cook Islands						●	●	●			
Costa Rica	●	●	●	●	○	●	●	●	●	●	●[22]
Côte d'Ivoire	●	●		●		●		●		●	●
Croatia	●	●	●	●		●	●	●	●	●	●[22]
Cuba	○			○		●	○	●	●	●	●[28]
Cyprus	●	●	●	●		●	●	●	●	●	●[22]
Czech Republic	●	●	●	●		●	●	●	●	●	●[22]
Democratic Republic of the Congo	●	●		●	○	●		●	●	●	●
Denmark	●	●	●	●		●	●	●	●	●	●[22]
Djibouti	●	●	●	●		●		●	●	●	●
Dominica	●			●		●		●	●		
Dominican Republic	●	●		●		●	●	●	○	●	○
Ecuador	●	●	●	●	●	●	●	●	●	●	●[22]
Egypt	●			●		●		●	●	●	●
El Salvador	●	●		●	●	●	○	●	●	●	●
Equatorial Guinea	●	●		●		●	●	●		●	●[28]
Eritrea	●			●		●		●	●	●	

SELECTED TREATIES

INTERNATIONAL

Optional Protocol to the Convention against Torture	International Convention for the Protection of All Persons from Enforced Disappearance	Convention relating to the Status of Refugees (1951)	Protocol relating to the Status of Refugees (1967)	Convention relating to the Status of Stateless Persons (1954)	Convention on the Reduction of Statelessness (1961)	International Convention on the Protection of the Rights of All Migrant Workers and Members of Their Families	Rome Statute of the International Criminal Court	Country
●		●	●			○	●	Cambodia
○		●	●			○	○	Cameroon
		●	●		●		●	Canada
○	○		●			●	●	Cape Verde
		●	●				●	Central African Republic
	○	●	●	●			●	Chad
●	●	●	●			●	●	Chile
		●	●					China
	○	●	●	○		●	●124	Colombia
	○					○	●	Comoros
○	○	●	●			○	●	Congo (Republic of)
							●	Cook Islands
●	○	●	●	●	●		●	Costa Rica
		●	●				○12	Côte d'Ivoire
●	○	●	●	●	●		●	Croatia
	●							Cuba
●	○	●	●				●	Cyprus
●		●	●	●	●		●	Czech Republic
●		●	●				●	Democratic Republic of the Congo
●	○	●	●	●	●		●	Denmark
		●	●				●	Djibouti
		●	●				●	Dominica
		●	●		○		●	Dominican Republic
●	●	●	●	●		●	●	Ecuador
		●	●			●	○	Egypt
		●	●	○		●		El Salvador
		●	●					Equatorial Guinea
							○	Eritrea

● state is a party

● state became party in 2011

○ signed but not yet ratified

○ signed in 2011, but not yet ratified

10 Declaration under Article 10 not recognizing the competence of the CEDAW Committee to undertake confidential inquiries into allegations of grave or systematic violations.

22 Declaration under Article 22 recognizing the competence of the Committee against Torture (CAT) to consider individual complaints.

28 Reservation under Article 28 not recognizing the competence of the CAT to undertake confidential inquiries into allegations of systematic torture if warranted.

12 Declaration under Article 12(3) accepting the jurisdiction of the International Criminal Court (ICC) for crimes in its territory.

124 Declaration under Article 124 not accepting the jurisdiction of the ICC over war crimes for seven years after ratification.

* Signed the Rome Statute but have since formally declared their intention not to ratify.

** Ratified or acceded but subsequently denounced the treaty.

	International Covenant on Civil and Political Rights (ICCPR)	(first) Optional Protocol to the ICCPR	Second Optional Protocol to the ICCPR, aiming at the abolition of the death penalty	International Covenant on Economic, Social and Cultural Rights (ICESCR)	Optional Protocol to the ICESCR (not in force)	Convention on the Elimination of All Forms of Discrimination against Women (CEDAW)	Optional Protocol to CEDAW	Convention on the Rights of the Child (CRC)	Optional Protocol to the CRC on the involvement of children in armed conflict	International Convention on the Elimination of All Forms of Racial Discrimination	Convention against Torture and Other Cruel, Inhuman or Degrading Treatment or Punishment
Estonia	●	●	●	●		●		●	○	●	●
Ethiopia	●			●		●		●	○	●	●
Fiji						●		●	○	●	
Finland	●	●	●	●	○	●	●	●	●	●	●22
France	●	●	●	●		●	●	●	●	●	●22
Gabon	●			●	○	●		●	●	●	●
Gambia	●	●		●		●		●	○	●	○
Georgia	●	●	●	●		●	●	●	●	●	●22
Germany	●	●	●	●		●	●	●	●	●	●22
Ghana	●	●		●	○	●	●	●	○	●	●22
Greece	●	●	●	●		●	●	●	●	●	●22
Grenada	●			●		●		●		○	
Guatemala	●	●		●	○	●	●	●	●	●	●22
Guinea	●	●		●		●		●		●	●
Guinea-Bissau	●	○	○	●	○	●	●	●	○	●	○
Guyana	●	●		●		●		●	●	●	●
Haiti	●					●		●	○	●	
Holy See								●	●	●	●
Honduras	●	●	●	●		●		●	●	●	●
Hungary	●	●	●	●		●	●	●	●	●	●22
Iceland	●	●	●	●		●	●	●	●	●	●22
India	●			●		●		●	●	●	○
Indonesia	●			●		●	○	●	○	●	●
Iran	●			●				●	○	●	
Iraq	●			●		●		●	●	●	●
Ireland	●	●	●	●		●	●	●	●	●	●22
Israel	●			●		●		●	●	●	●28
Italy	●	●	●	●	○	●	●	●	●	●	●22

Optional Protocol to the Convention against Torture	International Convention for the Protection of All Persons from Enforced Disappearance	Convention relating to the Status of Refugees (1951)	Protocol relating to the Status of Refugees (1967)	Convention relating to the Status of Stateless Persons (1954)	Convention on the Reduction of Statelessness (1961)	International Convention on the Protection of the Rights of All Migrant Workers and Members of Their Families	Rome Statute of the International Criminal Court	
●		●	●				●	Estonia
		●	●					Ethiopia
		●	●	●			●	Fiji
○	○	●	●	●	●		●	Finland
●	●	●	●	●	○		●124	France
●	●	●	●			○	●	Gabon
		●	●				●	Gambia
●		●	●				●	Georgia
●	●	●	●	●	●		●	Germany
○	○	●	●			●	●	Ghana
○	○	●	●	●			●	Greece
	○						●	Grenada
●	○	●	●	●	●	●		Guatemala
○		●	●	●	●	●	●	Guinea
		●	●			○	○	Guinea-Bissau
						●	●	Guyana
	○	●	●				○	Haiti
		●	●	○				Holy See
●	●	●	●	○		●	●	Honduras
		●	●	●	●		●	Hungary
○	○	●	●				●	Iceland
	○							India
	○					○		Indonesia
		●	●				○	Iran
	●							Iraq
○	○	●	●	●	●		●	Ireland
		●	●	●	○		○*	Israel
○	○	●	●	●			●	Italy

● state is a party

● state became party in 2011

○ signed but not yet ratified

○ signed in 2011, but not yet ratified

10 Declaration under Article 10 not recognizing the competence of the CEDAW Committee to undertake confidential inquiries into allegations of grave or systematic violations.

22 Declaration under Article 22 recognizing the competence of the Committee against Torture (CAT) to consider individual complaints.

28 Reservation under Article 28 not recognizing the competence of the CAT to undertake confidential inquiries into allegations of systematic torture if warranted.

12 Declaration under Article 12(3) accepting the jurisdiction of the International Criminal Court (ICC) for crimes in its territory.

124 Declaration under Article 124 not accepting the jurisdiction of the ICC over war crimes for seven years after ratification.

* Signed the Rome Statute but have since formally declared their intention not to ratify.

** Ratified or acceded but subsequently denounced the treaty.

	International Covenant on Civil and Political Rights (ICCPR)	(first) Optional Protocol to the ICCPR	Second Optional Protocol to the ICCPR, aiming at the abolition of the death penalty	International Covenant on Economic, Social and Cultural Rights (ICESCR)	Optional Protocol to the ICESCR (not in force)	Convention on the Elimination of All Forms of Discrimination against Women (CEDAW)	Optional Protocol to CEDAW	Convention on the Rights of the Child (CRC)	Optional Protocol to the CRC on the involvement of children in armed conflict	International Convention on the Elimination of All Forms of Racial Discrimination	Convention against Torture and Other Cruel, Inhuman or Degrading Treatment or Punishment
Jamaica	●	**		●		●		●	●	●	
Japan	●			●		●		●	●	●	●
Jordan	●			●		●		●	●	●	●
Kazakhstan	●	●		●	○	●	●	●	●	●	●22
Kenya	●			●		●		●	●	●	●22
Kiribati						●		●			
Korea (Democratic People's Republic of)	●			●		●		●			
Korea (Republic of)	●	●		●		●	●	●	●	●	●22
Kuwait	●			●		●		●	●	●	●28
Kyrgyzstan	●	●	●	●		●	●	●	●	●	●
Laos	●			●		●		●	●	●	○
Latvia	●	●		●		●		●	●	●	●
Lebanon	●			●		●		●	○	●	●
Lesotho	●	●		●		●	●	●	●	●	●
Liberia	●	○	●	●		●	○	●	○	●	●
Libya	●	●		●		●		●	●	●	●
Liechtenstein	●	●	●	●		●		●	●	●	●22
Lithuania	●	●	●	●		●		●	●	●	●
Luxembourg	●	●	●	●	○	●		●	●	●	●22
Macedonia	●	●	●	●		●		●	●	●	●
Madagascar	●	●		●	○	●	○	●	●	●	●
Malawi	●	●		●		●	○	●	●	●	●
Malaysia						●		●			
Maldives	●	●		●	○	●	●	●	●	●	●
Mali	●	●		●	○	●	●	●	●	●	●
Malta	●	●	●	●		●		●	●	●	●22
Marshall Islands						●		●			
Mauritania	●			●		●		●		●	●28

Optional Protocol to the Convention against Torture	International Convention for the Protection of All Persons from Enforced Disappearance	Convention relating to the Status of Refugees (1951)	Protocol relating to the Status of Refugees (1967)	Convention relating to the Status of Stateless Persons (1954)	Convention on the Reduction of Statelessness (1961)	International Convention on the Protection of the Rights of All Migrant Workers and Members of Their Families	Rome Statute of the International Criminal Court	
		●	●			●	○	Jamaica
	●	●	●				●	Japan
							●	Jordan
●	●	●	●					Kazakhstan
	○	●	●				●	Kenya
				●	●			Kiribati
								Korea (Democratic People's Republic of)
		●	●	●			●	Korea (Republic of)
							○	Kuwait
		●	●			●	○	Kyrgyzstan
	○							Laos
		●	●	●	●		●	Latvia
●	○							Lebanon
	○	●	●	●	●	●	●	Lesotho
●		●	●	●	●	○	●	Liberia
				●	●	●		Libya
●	○	●	●	●	●		●	Liechtenstein
	○	●	●	●			●	Lithuania
●	○	●	●	●			●	Luxembourg
●	○	●	●	●			●	Macedonia
○	○	●		**			●	Madagascar
		●	●	●			●	Malawi
								Malaysia
●	○						●	Maldives
●	●	●	●			●	●	Mali
●	○	●	●				●	Malta
							●	Marshall Islands
○	○	●	●			●		Mauritania

● state is a party

● state became party in 2011

○ signed but not yet ratified

○ signed in 2011, but not yet ratified

10 Declaration under Article 10 not recognizing the competence of the CEDAW Committee to undertake confidential inquiries into allegations of grave or systematic violations.

22 Declaration under Article 22 recognizing the competence of the Committee against Torture (CAT) to consider individual complaints.

28 Reservation under Article 28 not recognizing the competence of the CAT to undertake confidential inquiries into allegations of systematic torture if warranted.

12 Declaration under Article 12(3) accepting the jurisdiction of the International Criminal Court (ICC) for crimes in its territory.

124 Declaration under Article 124 not accepting the jurisdiction of the ICC over war crimes for seven years after ratification.

* Signed the Rome Statute but have since formally declared their intention not to ratify.

** Ratified or acceded but subsequently denounced the treaty.

	International Covenant on Civil and Political Rights (ICCPR)	(first) Optional Protocol to the ICCPR	Second Optional Protocol to the ICCPR, aiming at the abolition of the death penalty	International Covenant on Economic, Social and Cultural Rights (ICESCR)	Optional Protocol to the ICESCR (not in force)	Convention on the Elimination of All Forms of Discrimination against Women (CEDAW)	Optional Protocol to CEDAW	Convention on the Rights of the Child (CRC)	Optional Protocol to the CRC on the involvement of children in armed conflict	International Convention on the Elimination of All Forms of Racial Discrimination	Convention against Torture and Other Cruel, Inhuman or Degrading Treatment or Punishment
Mauritius	●	●		●		●	●	●	●	●	●
Mexico	●	●	●	●		●		●	●	●	●22
Micronesia						●		●	○		
Moldova	●	●	●	●		●	●	●	●	●	●
Monaco	●		●	●		●		●	●	●	●22
Mongolia	●	●		●	●	●	●	●	●	●	●
Montenegro	●	●	●	●	○	●	●	●	●	●	●22
Morocco	●			●		●		●	●	●	●22
Mozambique	●		●			●		●	●	●	●
Myanmar						●		●			
Namibia	●	●	●	●		●	●	●	●	●	●
Nauru	○	○				●		●	○	○	○
Nepal	●	●	●	●		●	●	●	●	●	●
Netherlands	●	●	●	●	○	●	●	●	●	●	●22
New Zealand	●	●	●	●		●	●	●	●	●	●22
Nicaragua	●	●	●	●		●	●	●	●	●	●
Niger	●	●		●		●	●	●		●	●
Nigeria	●			●		●	●	●	○	●	●
Niue								●			
Norway	●	●	●	●		●	●	●	●	●	●22
Oman						●		●	●	●	
Pakistan	●			●		●		●	○	●	●28
Palau	○			○		○		●		○	○
Panama	●	●	●	●		●	●	●	●	●	●
Papua New Guinea	●			●		●		●		●	
Paraguay	●	●	●	●	○	●	●	●	●	●	●22
Peru	●	●		●		●	●	●	●	●	●22
Philippines	●	●	●	●		●	●	●	●	●	●

Optional Protocol to the Convention against Torture	International Convention for the Protection of All Persons from Enforced Disappearance	Convention relating to the Status of Refugees (1951)	Protocol relating to the Status of Refugees (1967)	Convention relating to the Status of Stateless Persons (1954)	Convention on the Reduction of Statelessness (1961)	International Convention on the Protection of the Rights of All Migrant Workers and Members of Their Families	Rome Statute of the International Criminal Court	
●							●	Mauritius
●	●	●	●	●		●	●	Mexico
								Micronesia
●	○	●	●				●	Moldova
	○	●	●				○	Monaco
	○						●	Mongolia
●	●	●	●	●		○	●	Montenegro
	○	●	●			●	○	Morocco
	○	●	●				○	Mozambique
								Myanmar
		●	●				●	Namibia
		●	●				●	Nauru
								Nepal
●	●	●	●	●	●		●	Netherlands
●		●	●		●		●	New Zealand
●		●	●			●		Nicaragua
	○	●	●		●	●	●	Niger
●	●	●	●	●	●	●	●	Nigeria
								Niue
○	○	●	●	●	●		●	Norway
							○	Oman
								Pakistan
	○					○		Palau
●	●	●	●	●	●		●	Panama
		●	●					Papua New Guinea
●	●	●	●			●	●	Paraguay
●		●	●			●	●	Peru
		●	●	●		●	●	Philippines

● state is a party
● state became party in 2011
○ signed but not yet ratified
○ signed in 2011, but not yet ratified

10 Declaration under Article 10 not recognizing the competence of the CEDAW Committee to undertake confidential inquiries into allegations of grave or systematic violations.

22 Declaration under Article 22 recognizing the competence of the Committee against Torture (CAT) to consider individual complaints.

28 Reservation under Article 28 not recognizing the competence of the CAT to undertake confidential inquiries into allegations of systematic torture if warranted.

12 Declaration under Article 12(3) accepting the jurisdiction of the International Criminal Court (ICC) for crimes in its territory.

124 Declaration under Article 124 not accepting the jurisdiction of the ICC over war crimes for seven years after ratification.

* Signed the Rome Statute but have since formally declared their intention not to ratify.

** Ratified or acceded but subsequently denounced the treaty.

	International Covenant on Civil and Political Rights (ICCPR)	(first) Optional Protocol to the ICCPR	Second Optional Protocol to the ICCPR, aiming at the abolition of the death penalty	International Covenant on Economic, Social and Cultural Rights (ICESCR)	Optional Protocol to the ICESCR (not in force)	Convention on the Elimination of All Forms of Discrimination against Women (CEDAW)	Optional Protocol to CEDAW	Convention on the Rights of the Child (CRC)	Optional Protocol to the CRC on the involvement of children in armed conflict	International Convention on the Elimination of All Forms of Racial Discrimination	Convention against Torture and Other Cruel, Inhuman or Degrading Treatment or Punishment
Poland	●	●	○	●		●	●	●	●	●	[28] ● [22]
Portugal	●	●	●	●	○	●	●	●	●	●	● [22]
Qatar						●		●	●	●	●
Romania	●	●	●	●		●	●	●	●	●	●
Russian Federation	●	●		●		●	●	●	●	●	● [22]
Rwanda	●		●	●		●		●	●	●	●
Saint Kitts and Nevis						●		●	●	●	
Saint Lucia	○					●		●	○		
Saint Vincent and the Grenadines	●	●		●		●		●	●	●	●
Samoa	●					●		●			
San Marino	●	●	●	●		●	●	●	●	●	●
Sao Tome and Principe	○	○	○	○		●	○	●		○	○
Saudi Arabia						●		●	●	●	● [28]
Senegal	●	●		●	○	●	●	●	●	●	● [22]
Serbia	●	●	●	●		●	●	●	●	●	● [22]
Seychelles	●	●	●	●		●	●	●	●	●	● [22]
Sierra Leone	●	●		●		●	○	●	●	●	●
Singapore						●		●	●		
Slovakia	●	●	●	●	○	●	●	●	●	●	● [22]
Slovenia	●	●	●	●	○	●	●	●	●	●	● [22]
Solomon Islands				●	○	●	●	●	●	○	●
Somalia	●	●		●				○	○	●	●
South Africa	●	●	●	○		●	●	●	●	●	● [22]
South Sudan											
Spain	●	●	●	●	●	●	●	●	●	●	● [22]
Sri Lanka	●	●		●		●		●	●	●	●
Sudan	●			●				●	●	●	○
Suriname	●	●		●		●		●	○	●	

Optional Protocol to the Convention against Torture	International Convention for the Protection of All Persons from Enforced Disappearance	Convention relating to the Status of Refugees (1951)	Protocol relating to the Status of Refugees (1967)	Convention relating to the Status of Stateless Persons (1954)	Convention on the Reduction of Statelessness (1961)	International Convention on the Protection of the Rights of All Migrant Workers and Members of Their Families	Rome Statute of the International Criminal Court	
●		●	●				●	Poland
○	○	●	●				●	Portugal
								Qatar
●	○	●	●	●	●		●	Romania
		●	●				○	Russian Federation
		●	●	●	●	●		Rwanda
		●					●	Saint Kitts and Nevis
							●	Saint Lucia
	○	●	●	●		●	●	Saint Vincent and the Grenadines
	○	●	●				●	Samoa
							●	San Marino
		●	●			○	○	Sao Tome and Principe
								Saudi Arabia
●	●	●	●	●	●	●	●	Senegal
●	●	●	●	●	●	○	●	Serbia
		●	●			●	●	Seychelles
○	○	●	●			○	●	Sierra Leone
								Singapore
	○	●	●	●	●		●	Slovakia
●	○	●	●	●			●	Slovenia
		●	●				○	Solomon Islands
		●	●					Somalia
○		●	●				●	South Africa
								South Sudan
●	●	●	●	●			●	Spain
						●		Sri Lanka
		●	●				○*	Sudan
		●	●				●	Suriname

● state is a party

● state became party in 2011

○ signed but not yet ratified

○ signed in 2011, but not yet ratified

10 Declaration under Article 10 not recognizing the competence of the CEDAW Committee to undertake confidential inquiries into allegations of grave or systematic violations.

22 Declaration under Article 22 recognizing the competence of the Committee against Torture (CAT) to consider individual complaints.

28 Reservation under Article 28 not recognizing the competence of the CAT to undertake confidential inquiries into allegations of systematic torture if warranted.

12 Declaration under Article 12(3) accepting the jurisdiction of the International Criminal Court (ICC) for crimes in its territory.

124 Declaration under Article 124 not accepting the jurisdiction of the ICC over war crimes for seven years after ratification.

* Signed the Rome Statute but have since formally declared their intention not to ratify.

** Ratified or acceded but subsequently denounced the treaty.

	International Covenant on Civil and Political Rights (ICCPR)	(first) Optional Protocol to the ICCPR	Second Optional Protocol to the ICCPR, aiming at the abolition of the death penalty	International Covenant on Economic, Social and Cultural Rights (ICESCR)	Optional Protocol to the ICESCR (not in force)	Convention on the Elimination of All Forms of Discrimination against Women (CEDAW)	Optional Protocol to CEDAW	Convention on the Rights of the Child (CRC)	Optional Protocol to the CRC on the involvement of children in armed conflict	International Convention on the Elimination of All Forms of Racial Discrimination	Convention against Torture and Other Cruel, Inhuman or Degrading Treatment or Punishment
Swaziland	●			●		●		●		●	●
Sweden	●	●	●	●		●	●	●	●	●	●22
Switzerland	●		●	●		●	●	●	●	●	●22
Syria	●			●		●		●	●	●	●28
Tajikistan	●	●		●		●	○	●	●	●	●
Tanzania	●			●		●	●	●		●	
Thailand	●			●		●	●	●	●	●	●
Timor-Leste	●		●	●	○	●	●	●	●	●	●
Togo	●	●		●	○	●		●	●	●	●22
Tonga								●		●	
Trinidad and Tobago	●	**		●		●		●		●	
Tunisia	●	●		●		●	●	●	●	●	●22
Turkey	●	●	●	●		●	●	●	●	●	●22
Turkmenistan	●	●	●	●		●	●	●	●	●	●
Tuvalu						●		●			
Uganda	●	●		●		●		●	●	●	●
Ukraine	●	●	●	●	○	●	●	●	●	●	●
United Arab Emirates						●		●		●	
United Kingdom	●		●	●		●	●	●	●	●	●
United States of America	●			○		○		○	●	●	●
Uruguay	●	●	●	●	○	●	●	●	●	●	●22
Uzbekistan	●	●	●	●		●		●	●	●	●
Vanuatu	●					●	●	●	●		●
Venezuela	●	●	●	●	○	●	●	●	●	●	●22
Viet Nam	●			●		●		●	●	●	
Yemen	●			●		●		●	●	●	●
Zambia	●	●		●		●	○	●	○	●	●
Zimbabwe	●			●		●		●		●	

Optional Protocol to the Convention against Torture	International Convention for the Protection of All Persons from Enforced Disappearance	Convention relating to the Status of Refugees (1951)	Protocol relating to the Status of Refugees (1967)	Convention relating to the Status of Stateless Persons (1954)	Convention on the Reduction of Statelessness (1961)	International Convention on the Protection of the Rights of All Migrant Workers and Members of Their Families	Rome Statute of the International Criminal Court	
	○	●	●	●	●			Swaziland
●	○	●	●	●	●		●	Sweden
●	○	●	●	●			●	Switzerland
					●		○	Syria
		●	●			●	●	Tajikistan
	○	●	●				●	Tanzania
							○	Thailand
○		●	●			●	●	Timor-Leste
●	○	●	●				○	Togo
								Tonga
		●	●	●			●	Trinidad and Tobago
●	●	●	●	●	●		●	Tunisia
●		●	●			●		Turkey
		●	●	●				Turkmenistan
		●	●					Tuvalu
	○	●	●	●		●	●	Uganda
●		●	●				○	Ukraine
							○	United Arab Emirates
●		●	●	●	●		●	United Kingdom
			●				○*	United States of America
●	●	●	●	●	●	●	●	Uruguay
							○	Uzbekistan
	○						●	Vanuatu
○	○		●			○	●	Venezuela
								Viet Nam
		●	●				○	Yemen
○	●	●	●	●			●	Zambia
		●	●	●			○	Zimbabwe

● state is a party
● state became party in 2011
○ signed but not yet ratified
○ signed in 2011, but not yet ratified

10 Declaration under Article 10 not recognizing the competence of the CEDAW Committee to undertake confidential inquiries into allegations of grave or systematic violations.

22 Declaration under Article 22 recognizing the competence of the Committee against Torture (CAT) to consider individual complaints.

28 Reservation under Article 28 not recognizing the competence of the CAT to undertake confidential inquiries into allegations of systematic torture if warranted.

12 Declaration under Article 12(3) accepting the jurisdiction of the International Criminal Court (ICC) for crimes in its territory.

124 Declaration under Article 124 not accepting the jurisdiction of the ICC over war crimes for seven years after ratification.

* Signed the Rome Statute but have since formally declared their intention not to ratify.

** Ratified or acceded but subsequently denounced the treaty.

	African Charter on Human and Peoples' Rights (1981)	Protocol to the African Charter on the Establishment of an African Court on Human and Peoples' Rights (1998)	African Charter on the Rights and Welfare of the Child (1990)	Convention Governing the Specific Aspects of Refugee Problems in Africa (1969)	Protocol to the African Charter on Human and Peoples' Rights on the Rights of Women in Africa (2003)
Algeria	●	●	●	●	○
Angola	●	○	●	●	●
Benin	●	○	●	●	●
Botswana	●	○	●	●	
Burkina Faso	●	●	●	●	●
Burundi	●	●	●	●	○
Cameroon	●	○	●	●	○
Cape Verde	●		●	●	●
Central African Republic	●	○	○	●	○
Chad	●	○	●	●	○
Comoros	●	●	●	●	●
Congo (Republic of)	●	○	●	●	○
Côte d'Ivoire	●	●	●	●	○
Democratic Republic of the Congo	●	○	○	●	●
Djibouti	●	○	○	○	●
Egypt	●	○	●	●	
Equatorial Guinea	●	○	●	●	○
Eritrea	●		●		
Ethiopia	●	○	●	●	○
Gabon	●	●	●	●	○
Gambia	●	●	●	●	●
Ghana	●	●	●	●	●
Guinea	●	○	●	●	○
Guinea-Bissau	●	○	●	●	●
Kenya	●	●	●	●	○
Lesotho	●	●	●	●	●
Liberia	●	○	●	●	●
Libya	●	●	●	●	●
Madagascar	●	○	●	○	○

	African Charter on Human and Peoples' Rights (1981)	Protocol to the African Charter on the Establishment of an African Court on Human and Peoples' Rights (1998)	African Charter on the Rights and Welfare of the Child (1990)	Convention Governing the Specific Aspects of Refugee Problems in Africa (1969)	Protocol to the African Charter on Human and Peoples' Rights on the Rights of Women in Africa (2003)
Malawi	●	●	●	●	●
Mali	●	●	●	●	●
Mauritania	●	●	●	●	●
Mauritius	●	●	●	○	○
Mozambique	●	●	●	●	●
Namibia	●	○	●	○	●
Niger	●	●	●	●	○
Nigeria	●	●	●	●	●
Rwanda	●	●	●	●	●
Sahrawi Arab Democratic Republic	●	○	○		○
Sao Tome and Principe	●	○	○		○
Senegal	●	●	●	●	●
Seychelles	●	○	●	●	●
Sierra Leone	●	○	●	●	○
Somalia	●	○	○	○	○
South Africa	●	●	●	●	●
South Sudan					
Sudan	●	○	●	●	○
Swaziland	●	○	○	●	○
Tanzania	●	●	●	●	●
Togo	●	●	●	●	●
Tunisia	●	●	○	●	
Uganda	●	●	●	●	●
Zambia	●	○	●	●	●
Zimbabwe	●	○	●	●	●

● state is a party
● state became party in 2011
○ signed but not yet ratified
○ signed in 2011, but not yet ratified

This chart lists countries that were members of the African Union at the end of 2011.

	American Convention on Human Rights (1969)	Protocol to the American Convention on Human Rights to Abolish the Death Penalty (1990)	Additional Protocol to the American Convention on Human Rights in the Area of Economic, Social and Cultural Rights	Inter-American Convention to Prevent and Punish Torture (1985)	Inter-American Convention on Forced Disappearance of Persons (1994)	Inter-American Convention on the Prevention, Punishment and Eradication of Violence Against Women (1994)	Inter-American Convention on the Elimination of All Forms of Discrimination against Persons with Disabilities (1999)
Antigua and Barbuda						●	
Argentina	●62	●	●	●	●	●	●
Bahamas						●	
Barbados	●62					●	
Belize						●	
Bolivia	●62		●	●	●	●	●
Brazil	●62	●	●	●	○	●	●
Canada							
Chile	●62	●	○	●	●	●	●
Colombia	●62		●	●	●	●	●
Costa Rica	●62	●	●	●	●	●	●
Cuba*							
Dominica	●					●	○
Dominican Republic	●62		○	●		●	●
Ecuador	●62	●	●	●	●	●	●
El Salvador	●62		●	●		●	●
Grenada	●					●	
Guatemala	●62		●	●	●	●	●
Guyana						●	
Haiti	●62		○	○		●	●
Honduras	●62	●	●	○	●	●	●
Jamaica	●					●	○
Mexico	●62	●	●	●	●	●	●
Nicaragua	●62	●	●	●	○	●	●
Panama	●62	●	●	●	●	●	●

	American Convention on Human Rights (1969)	Protocol to the American Convention on Human Rights to Abolish the Death Penalty (1990)	Additional Protocol to the American Convention on Human Rights in the Area of Economic, Social and Cultural Rights	Inter-American Convention to Prevent and Punish Torture (1985)	Inter-American Convention on Forced Disappearance of Persons (1994)	Inter-American Convention on the Prevention, Punishment and Eradication of Violence Against Women (1994)	Inter-American Convention on the Elimination of All Forms of Discrimination against Persons with Disabilities (1999)
Paraguay	●62	●	●	●	●	●	●
Peru	●62		●	●	●	●	●
Saint Kitts and Nevis						●	
Saint Lucia						●	
Saint Vincent and the Grenadines						●	
Suriname	●62		●	●		●	
Trinidad and Tobago						●	
United States of America	○						
Uruguay	●62	●	●	●	●	●	●
Venezuela	●62	●	○	●	●	●	●

● state is a party
● state became party in 2011
○ signed but not yet ratified
○ signed in 2011, but not yet ratified

This chart lists countries that were members of the Organization of American States at the end of 2011.

62 Countries making a Declaration under Article 62 recognize as binding the jurisdiction of the Inter-American Court of Human Rights (on all matters relating to the interpretation or application of the American Convention).

* In 2009 the General Assembly of the Organization of American States (OAS) adopted resolution AG/RES.2438 (XXXIX-O/09), which resolves that the 1962 resolution that excluded the Cuban government from its participation in the OAS, ceases its effects. The 2009 resolution states that the participation of Cuba in the OAS will be the result of a process of dialogue initiated at the request of the government of Cuba.

	European Convention for the Protection of Human Rights and Fundamental Freedoms (ECHR) (1950)	Protocol No. 6 to the ECHR concerning the abolition of the death penalty in times of peace (1983)	Protocol No. 12 to the ECHR concerning the general prohibition of discrimination (2000)	Protocol No. 13 to the ECHR concerning the abolition of the death penalty in all circumstances (2002)	Framework Convention on the Protection of National Minorities (1995)	Council of Europe Convention on Action against Trafficking in Human Beings	European Social Charter (revised) (1996)	Additional Protocol to the European Social Charter Providing for a System of Collective Complaints (1995)	Council of Europe Convention on preventing and combating violence against women and domestic violence (not in force)
Albania	●	●	●	●	●	●	●		○
Andorra	●	●	●	●		●	●		
Armenia	●	●	●	○	●	●	●		
Austria	●	●	○	●	●	●	●	○	○
Azerbaijan	●	●	○		●	●	●		
Belgium	●	●	○	●	○	●	●	●	
Bosnia and Herzegovina	●	●	●	●	●	●	●		
Bulgaria	●	●		●	●	●	●	**	
Croatia	●	●	●	●	●	●	○*	●	
Cyprus	●	●	●	●	●	●	●	●	
Czech Republic	●	●	○	●	●		○*	○	
Denmark	●	●		●	●	●	○*	○	
Estonia	●	●	○	●	●	○	●		
Finland	●	●	●	●	●	○	●	●	○
France	●	●		●		●	●	●	○
Georgia	●	●	●	●	●	●	●		
Germany	●	●	○	●	●	○	○*		○
Greece	●	●	○	●	○	○	○*	●	○
Hungary	●	●	○	●	●	○	●	○	
Iceland	●	●	○	●	○	○	○*		○
Ireland	●	●	○	●	●	●	●	●	
Italy	●	●	○	●	●	●	●	●	
Latvia	●	●	○	○	●	●	○*		
Liechtenstein	●	●	○	●	●				
Lithuania	●	●		●	●	○	●		

SELECTED TREATIES

REGIONAL
COUNCIL OF EUROPE

	European Convention for the Protection of Human Rights and Fundamental Freedoms (ECHR) (1950)	Protocol No. 6 to the ECHR concerning the abolition of the death penalty in times of peace (1983)	Protocol No. 12 to the ECHR concerning the general prohibition of discrimination (2000)	Protocol No. 13 to the ECHR concerning the abolition of the death penalty in all circumstances (2002)	Framework Convention on the Protection of National Minorities (1995)	Council of Europe Convention on Action against Trafficking in Human Beings	European Social Charter (revised) (1996)	Additional Protocol to the European Social Charter Providing for a System of Collective Complaints (1995)	Council of Europe Convention on preventing and combating violence against women and domestic violence (not in force)
Luxembourg	●	●	●	●	○	●	○*		○
Macedonia	●	●	●	●	●	●	○*		○
Malta	●	●		●	●	●	●		
Moldova	●	●	○	●	●	●	●		
Monaco	●	●		●			○		
Montenegro	●	●	●	●	●	●	●		○
Netherlands	●	●	●	●	●	●	●	●	
Norway	●	●	○	●	●	●	●	●	○
Poland	●	●		○	●	●	○*		
Portugal	●	●	○	●	●	●	●	●	○
Romania	●	●	●	●	●	●	●		
Russian Federation	●	○	○		●	●		●	
San Marino	●	●	●	●	●	●	○		
Serbia	●	●	●	●	●	●	●		
Slovakia	●	●	○	●	●	●	●	○	○
Slovenia	●	●	●	●	●	●	●	○**	○
Spain	●	●	●	●	●	●	○*		○
Sweden	●	●		●	●	●	●	●	○
Switzerland	●	●		●	●	○			
Turkey	●	●	○	●		○	●		○
Ukraine	●	●	●	●	●	●	●		○
United Kingdom	●	●		●	●	●	○*		

● state is a party
● state became party in 2011
○ signed but not yet ratified
○ signed in 2011, but not yet ratified

This chart lists countries that were members of the Council of Europe at the end of 2011.

*   State is a party to the European Social Charter of 1961, which is gradually being replaced by the European Social Charter (revised). The revised Charter embodies in one instrument all rights guaranteed by the Charter of 1961, its Additional Protocol of 1988 and adds new rights and amendments.

** Declaration under Article D of the European Social Charter (revised) recognizing the competence of the European Committee of Social Rights to consider collective complaints.

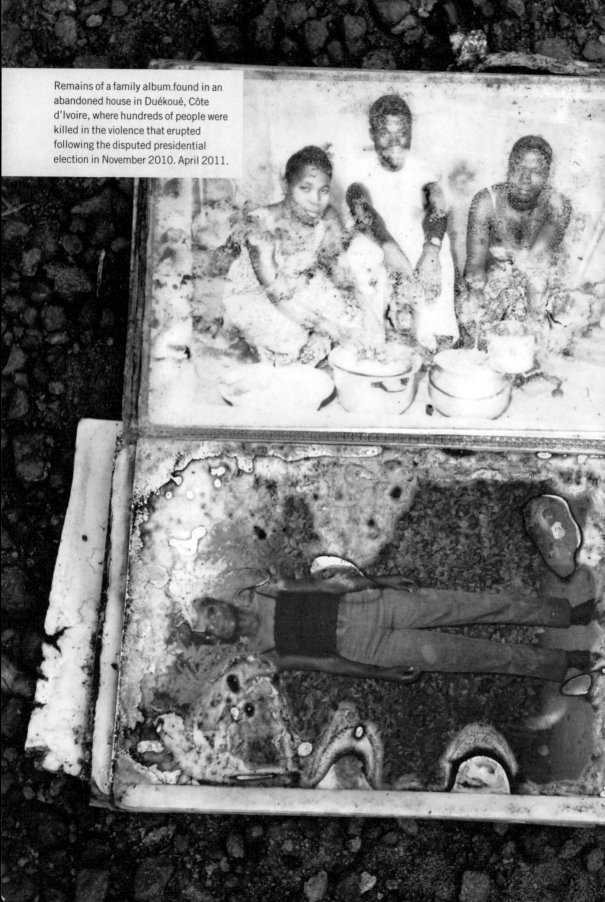

Remains of a family album.found in an abandoned house in Duékoué, Côte d'Ivoire, where hundreds of people were killed in the violence that erupted following the disputed presidential election in November 2010. April 2011.

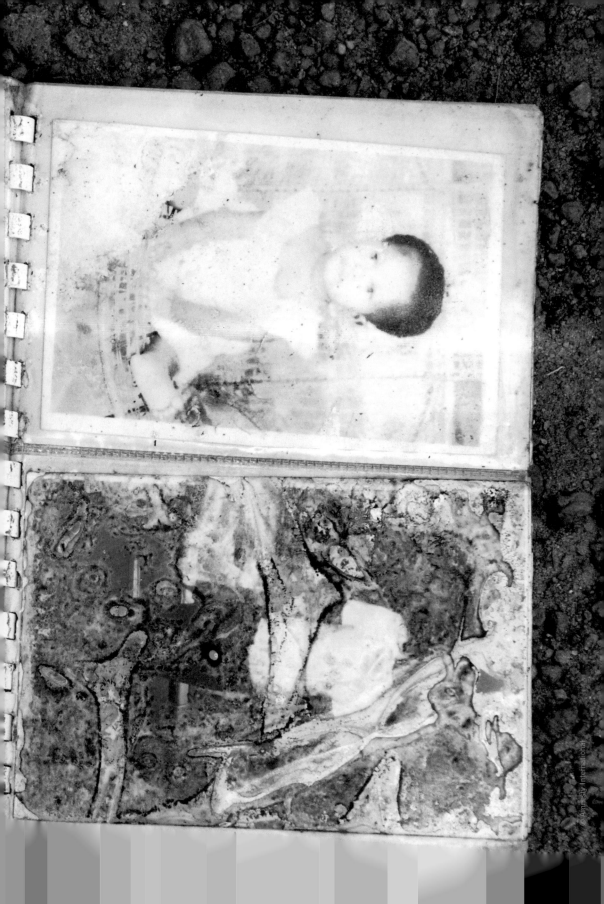

AMNESTY INTERNATIONAL REPORT 2012
PART FOUR

12

Martin Almeida
io 1975

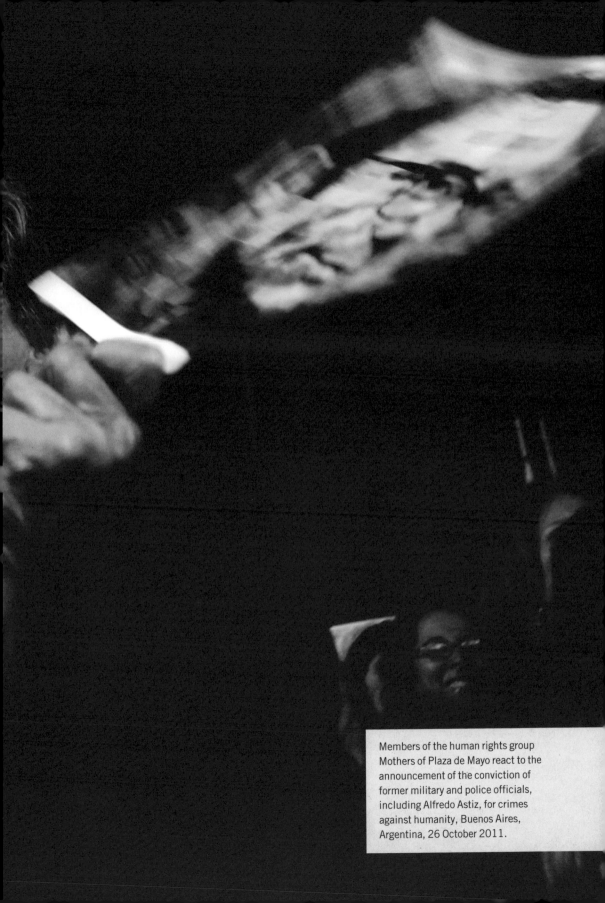

Members of the human rights group Mothers of Plaza de Mayo react to the announcement of the conviction of former military and police officials, including Alfredo Astiz, for crimes against humanity, Buenos Aires, Argentina, 26 October 2011.

AMNESTY INTERNATIONAL
SECTIONS

Algeria ❖ Amnesty International,
10, rue Mouloud ZADI (face au 113 rue Didouche Mourad),
Alger Centre, 16004 Alger
email: amnestyalgeria@hotmail.com

Argentina ❖ Amnistía Internacional,
Av. Pueyrredón 689, Piso 2, (C1032ABG) Buenos Aires
email: contacto@amnistia.org.ar
www.amnistia.org.ar

Australia ❖ Amnesty International,
Locked Bag 23, Broadway NSW 2007
email: supporter@amnesty.org.au
www.amnesty.org.au

Austria ❖ Amnesty International,
Moeringgasse 10, A-1150 Vienna
email: info@amnesty.at
www.amnesty.at

Belgium ❖
Amnesty International **(Flemish-speaking)**,
Kerkstraat 156, 2060 Antwerpen
email: amnesty@aivl.be
www.aivl.be
Amnesty International **(francophone)**,
Rue Berckmans 9, 1060 Bruxelles
email: amnesty@amnesty.be
www.amnestyinternational.be

Bermuda ❖ Amnesty International,
PO Box HM 2136, Hamilton HM JX
email: director@amnestybermuda.org
www.amnestybermuda.org

Burkina Faso ❖ Amnesty International,
BP 11344, Ouagadougou 08
email: aiburkina@fasonet.bf
www.amnesty-bf.org

Canada ❖
Amnesty International **(English-speaking)**,
312 Laurier Avenue East, Ottawa, Ontario, K1N 1H9
email: info@amnesty.ca
www.amnesty.ca
Amnistie internationale **(francophone)**,
50 rue Ste-Catherine Ouest, bureau 500, Montréal, Quebec, H2X 3V4
www.amnistie.ca

Chile ❖ Amnistía Internacional,
Oficina Nacional, Huelén 164 - Planta Baja,
750-0617 Providencia, Santiago
email: info@amnistia.cl
www.amnistia.cl

Colombia ❖ Amnistía Internacional,
On-line Action Platform
email: AlColombia.Online@amnesty.org

Côte d'Ivoire ❖ Amnesty International,
04 BP 895, Abidjan 04
email: amnesty.ci@aviso.ci

Czech Republic ❖ Amnesty International,
Provaznická 3, 110 00, Prague 1
email: amnesty@amnesty.cz
www.amnesty.cz

Denmark ❖ Amnesty International,
Gammeltorv 8, 5 - 1457 Copenhagen K.
email: amnesty@amnesty.dk
www.amnesty.dk

Faroe Islands ❖ Amnesty International,
Stephanssons Hús, Kongabrúgvin,
Fo-100 Tórshavn
email: amnesty@amnesty.fo
www.amnesty.fo

Finland ❖ Amnesty International,
Ruoholahdenkatu 24 , FI-00180 Helsinki
email: amnesty@amnesty.fi
www.amnesty.fi

France ❖ Amnesty International,
76 boulevard de la Villette,
75940 Paris, Cédex 19
email: info@amnesty.fr
www.amnesty.fr

Germany ❖ Amnesty International,
Heerstrasse 178, 53111 Bonn
email: info@amnesty.de
www.amnesty.de

Greece ❖ Amnesty International,
Sina 30, 106 72 Athens
email: athens@amnesty.org.gr
www.amnesty.org.gr

Hong Kong ❖ Amnesty International,
Unit D, 3/F, Best-O-Best Commercial Centre,
32-36 Ferry Street, Kowloon
email: admin-hk@amnesty.org.hk
www.amnesty.org.hk

Iceland ❖ Amnesty International,
Þingholtsstræti 27, 101 Reykjavík
email: amnesty@amnesty.is
www.amnesty.is

Ireland ❖ Amnesty International,
Sean MacBride House, 48 Fleet Street,
Dublin 2
email: info@amnesty.ie
www.amnesty.ie

Israel ❖ Amnesty International,
PO Box 14179, Tel Aviv 61141
email: info@amnesty.org.il
www.amnesty.org.il

Italy ❖ Amnesty International,
Via Giovanni Battista De Rossi 10, 00161 Roma
email: info@amnesty.it
www.amnesty.it

Japan ❖ Amnesty International,
7F Seika Bldg. 2-12-14 Kandaogawamachi,
Chiyoda-ku, Tokyo 101-0052
email: info@amnesty.or.jp
www.amnesty.or.jp

Korea (Republic of) ❖ Amnesty International,
Gwanghwamun P.O.Box 2045 Jongno-gu, 10-620 Seoul
email: info@amnesty.or.kr
www.amnesty.or.kr

Luxembourg ❖ Amnesty International,
BP 1914, 1019 Luxembourg
email: info@amnesty.lu
www.amnesty.lu

Mauritius ❖ Amnesty International,
BP 69, Rose-Hill
email: amnestymtius@erm.mu

Mexico ❖ Amnistía Internacional,
Tajín No. 389, Col. Narvarte, Del. Benito Juárez, 03020 Mexico D.F.
email: vinculacion@amnistia.org.mx
www.amnistia.org.mx

Morocco ❖ Amnesty International,
281 avenue Mohamed V, Apt. 23, Escalier A, Rabat
email: amorocco@sections.amnesty.org
www.amnestymaroc.org

Nepal ❖ Amnesty International,
PO Box 135, Amnesty Marga, Basantanagar,
Balaju, Kathmandu
email: info@amnestynepal.org
www.amnestynepal.org

Netherlands ❖ Amnesty International,
Keizersgracht 177, 1016 DR Amsterdam
email: amnesty@amnesty.nl
www.amnesty.nl

New Zealand ❖ Amnesty International,
PO Box 5300, Wellesley Street, Auckland
email: info@amnesty.org.nz
www.amnesty.org.nz

Norway ❖ Amnesty International,
Grensen 3, 0159 Oslo
email: info@amnesty.no
www.amnesty.no

Paraguay ❖ Amnistía Internacional,
Manuel Castillo 4987 esquina San Roque González,
Barrio Villa Morra, Asunción
email: ai-info@py.amnesty.org
www.amnesty.org.py

Peru ❖ Amnistía Internacional,
Enrique Palacios 735-A, Miraflores, Lima 18
email: amnistia@amnistia.org.pe
www.amnistia.org.pe

Philippines ❖ Amnesty International,
18-A Marunong Street, Barangay Central,
Quezon City 1100
email: section@amnesty.org.ph
www.amnesty.org.ph

Poland ❖ Amnesty International,
ul. Piękna 66a, lokal 2, I piętro, 00-672, Warszawa
email: amnesty@amnesty.org.pl
www.amnesty.org.pl

Portugal ❖ Amnistia Internacional,
Av. Infante Santo, 42, 2°, 1350 - 179 Lisboa
email: aiportugal@amnistia-internacional.pt
www.amnistia-internacional.pt

Puerto Rico ❖ Amnistía Internacional,
Calle Robles 54, Suite 6, Río Piedras PR 00925
email: amnistiapr@amnestypr.org
www.amnistiapr.org

Senegal ❖ Amnesty International,
303/GRD Sacré-coeur II, Résidence Arame SIGA,
BP 35269, Dakar Colobane
email: asenegal@sections.amnesty.org
www.amnesty.sn

Sierra Leone ❖ Amnesty International,
13B Howe Street, Freetown
email: amnestysl@gmail.com

Slovenia ❖ Amnesty International,
Beethovnova 7, 1000 Ljubljana
email: amnesty@amnesty.si
www.amnesty.si

Spain ❖ Amnistía Internacional,
Fernando VI, 8, 1° izda, 28004 Madrid
email: info@es.amnesty.org
www.es.amnesty.org

Sweden ❖ Amnesty International,
PO Box 4719, 11692 Stockholm
email: info@amnesty.se
www.amnesty.se

Switzerland ❖ Amnesty International,
Speichergasse 33, CH-3011 Berne
email: info@amnesty.ch
www.amnesty.ch

Taiwan ❖ Amnesty International,
3F., No. 14, Lane 165, Sec. 1, Sinsheng S. Rd,
Da-an District, Taipei City 106
email: amnesty.taiwan@gmail.com
www.amnesty.tw

Togo ❖ Amnesty International,
2322 avenue du RPT, Quartier Casablanca, BP 20013, Lomé
email: contact@amnesty.tg
www.amnesty.tg

Tunisia ❖ Amnesty International,
67 rue Oum Kalthoum, 3ème étage, escalier B,
1000 Tunis
email: admin-tn@amnesty.org

United Kingdom ❖ Amnesty International,
The Human Rights Action Centre,
17-25 New Inn Yard, London EC2A 3EA
email: sct@amnesty.org.uk
www.amnesty.org.uk

United States of America ❖ Amnesty International,
5 Penn Plaza, 16th floor, New York, NY 10001
email: admin-us@aiusa.org
www.amnestyusa.org

Uruguay ❖ Amnistía Internacional,
San José 1140, piso 5, C.P. 11.100 Montevideo
email: oficina@amnistia.org.uy
www.amnistia.org.uy

Venezuela ❖ Amnistía Internacional,
Torre Phelps piso 17, oficina 17 A,
Av. La Salle, Plaza Venezuela, Los Caobos, Caracas 1050
email: info@aiven.org
www.aiven.org

Zimbabwe ❖ Amnesty International,
56 Midlothean Avenue, Eastlea, Harare
email: amnestyinternational.zimbabwe@gmail.com

AMNESTY INTERNATIONAL
STRUCTURES

Hungary ❖ Amnesty International,
Rózsa u. 44, II/4, 1064 Budapest
email: info@amnesty.hu
www.amnesty.hu

Malaysia ❖ Amnesty International,
A-3-3A, 8 Avenue, Jalan Sungai Jernih, 8/1,
Section 8, 46050 Petaling Jaya, Selangor
email: aimalaysia@aimalaysia.org

Mali ❖ Amnesty International,
Immeuble Soya Bathily, Route de l'aéroport,
24 rue Kalabancoura, BP E 3885, Bamako
email: amnesty.mali@ikatelnet.net

Moldova ❖ Amnesty International,
PO Box 209, MD-2012 Chişinău
email: info@amnesty.md ,
www.amnesty.md

Mongolia ❖ Amnesty International,
Sukhbaatar District, Baga Toirog 44,
Ulaanbaatar 210648
email: aimncc@magicnet.mn
www.amnesty.mn

Turkey ❖ Amnesty International,
Abdülhakhamid Cd. No. 30/5, Talimhane,
Beyoğlu, Istanbul
email: posta@amnesty.org.tr
www.amnesty.org.tr

AMNESTY INTERNATIONAL
PRE-STRUCTURES

Croatia ❖ Amnesty International,
Praška 2/III, 10000 Zagreb
email: admin@amnesty.hr
www.amnesty.hr

Thailand ❖ Amnesty International,
90/24 Lat Phrao Soi 1, Lat Yao, Chatuchak,
Bangkok 10900
email: info@amnesty.or.th
www.amnesty.or.th

AMNESTY INTERNATIONAL
ENTITIES REPORTING DIRECTLY TO
THE SECRETARY GENERAL

Benin ❖ Amnesty International,
01 BP 3536, Cotonou
email: amnestybenin@yahoo.fr

Brazil ❖ Amnesty International,
email: contato@anistia.org.br
www.anistia.org.br

Ghana ❖ Amnesty International,
H/No. 347/7 Rolyat Castle Road, Opposite Havard College,
Kokomlemle, Accra
email: info@amnestyghana.org

India ❖ Amnesty International,
email: amnestyindia@amnesty.org

Kenya ❖ Amnesty International,
Suite A3, Haven Court, Waiyaki Way, Westlands,
P.O.Box 1527, 00606 Sarit Centre, Nairobi
email: amnestykenya@amnesty.org

Slovakia ❖ Amnesty International,
Karpatska 11, 811 05 Bratislava
email: amnesty@amnesty.sk
www.amnesty.sk

South Africa ❖ Amnesty International,
11th Floor Braamfontein Centre, 23 Jorrissen Street,
2017 Braamfontein, Johannesburg
email: info@amnesty.org.za
www.amnesty.org.za

Ukraine ❖ Amnesty International,
Olesya Honchara str, 37A, office 1, Kyev 01034
email: info@amnesty.org.ua
www.amnesty.org.ua

AMNESTY INTERNATIONAL
STRATEGIC PARTNERSHIPS

The Strategic Partnerships Project is part of the Growth Unit in Amnesty International. The project aims to grow human rights activism and impact in countries with no Amnesty International entities by establishing partnerships with local NGOs. It also aims to increase the visibility of Amnesty International and the strategic partner and create platforms for Amnesty International issues in the country. Amnesty International's Strategic Partnerships in 2011 were in Cambodia, Haiti, Indonesia, Timor-Leste, Latvia, Liberia and Romania. For more information on Strategic Partnerships, please contact: Strategic_Partnerships_Team@amnesty.org

AMNESTY INTERNATIONAL
INTERNATIONAL MEMBERSHIP

There are also International Members in several countries and territories around the world. More information can be found online at: www.amnesty.org/en/join
email: online.communities@amnesty.org

AMNESTY INTERNATIONAL
OFFICES

International Secretariat (IS)
Amnesty International,
Peter Benenson House, 1 Easton Street,
London WC1X 0DW, United Kingdom
email: amnestyis@amnesty.org
www.amnesty.org

Amnesty International Language Resource Centre (AILRC)
Head office
Calle Valderribas, 13, 28007 Madrid, Spain
email: AILRC@amnesty.org
Spanish: www.amnesty.org/es
Arabic: www.amnesty.org/ar
Amnesty International Language Resource Centre – French (AILRC-FR)
Paris office
47 rue de Paradis - Bât C, 75010 Paris, France
www.amnesty.org/fr

IS New York – UN Representative Office
Amnesty International,
777 UN Plaza, 6th Floor, New York,
NY 10017, USA
email: aiunny@amnesty.org

IS Geneva – UN Representative Office
Amnesty International,
22 rue du Cendrier, 4ème étage,
CH-1201 Geneva,
Switzerland
email: uaigv@amnesty.org

Amnesty International European Institutions Office
Rue de Trèves 35, B-1040 Brussels,
Belgium
email: amnestyIntl@amnesty.eu
www.amnesty.eu

IS Beirut – Middle East and North Africa Regional Office
Amnesty International,
PO Box 13-5696, Chouran Beirut 1102 - 2060,
Lebanon
email: mena@amnesty.org
www.amnestymena.org

IS Dakar – Africa Human Rights Education Office
Amnesty International,
SICAP Sacré Coeur Pyrotechnie Extension, Villa No. 22,
BP 47582, Dakar, Senegal
email: isdakaroffice@amnesty.org
www.africa-hre.org

IS Hong Kong – Asia Pacific Regional Office
Amnesty International,
16/F Siu On Centre, 188 Lockhart Rd, Wanchai,
Hong Kong
email: admin-ap@amnesty.org

IS Kampala – Africa Regional Office
Amnesty International,
Plot 20A Kawalya Kaggwa Close, PO Box 23966,
Kampala, Uganda
email: ai-aro@amnesty.org

IS Moscow – Russia Resource Centre
Amnesty International,
PO Box 212, Moscow 119019,
Russian Federation
email: msk@amnesty.org
www.amnesty.org.ru

IS Paris – Research Office
Amnesty International,
76 boulevard de la Villette,
75940 Paris, Cédex 19,
France
email: pro@amnesty.org

Protesters with pieces of bread shout slogans during a demonstration in the Syrian port city of Banias to show their solidarity with the protesters in Dera'a. 3 May 2011.

Anela Krasnic, her neighbour Zoran Durmisevic and his son Danijel, sit outside their former home in Belgrade, Serbia. Five Roma families living in privately owned buildings were forcibly evicted and left on the street with all their belongings.

INDEX OF SELECTED TOPICS*

extrajudicial executions

Bangladesh 76; Burundi 93; Guinea-Bissau 164; Libya 220; Pakistan 263; South Africa 307; Syria 325-6

F

forced evictions

Angola 63; Cambodia 95; Chad 105; China 108; Dominican Republic 132; Egypt 138; Ethiopia 146; Haiti 166-7; Honduras 168-9; Israel and the Occupied Palestinian Territories 187; Kenya 203; Nigeria 258; Serbia 293; Sierra Leone 296; Zimbabwe 373

freedom of assembly and association

Algeria 60-1; Angola 64; Armenia 66-7; Azerbaijan 70; Belarus 78-9; Burundi 93; Cambodia 96; Cameroon 98-9; Chad 104; China 110; Congo (Republic of) 116; Cuba 122; Egypt 137; Equatorial Guinea 142; Fiji 147-8; Georgia 154; Iran 177-8; Israel and the Occupied Palestinian Territories 189; Jordan 197; Korea (Republic of) 207; Kuwait 208; Malawi 227; Malaysia 227-8; Namibia 249-50; Nepal 251; Palestinian Authority 267; Russian Federation 280; Rwanda 285; South Sudan 310; Sudan 319; Taiwan 329; Uganda 346-7; United Arab Emirates 351-2; Zimbabwe 372

freedom of expression

Afghanistan 56-57; Algeria 60-1; Angola 63-4; Azerbaijan 70; Belarus 78; Burundi 93-4; Cambodia 96; Cameroon 98; Central African Republic 102-3; China 107-8, 110; Congo (Republic of) 116; Côte d'Ivoire 118; Cuba 122; Democratic Republic of the Congo 129; Dominican Republic 132; Ecuador 134; Egypt 137; Equatorial Guinea 141-2; Ethiopia 144-5; Fiji 147-8; Gambia 152; Guinea 163; Guinea-Bissau 164; Hungary 170; Indonesia 175-6; Iran 177-8; Iraq 183, 184; Israel and the Occupied Palestinian Territories 189; Jordan 197; Korea (Democratic People's Republic of) 205; Korea (Republic of) 206; Kuwait 208; Liberia 216; Macedonia 223-4; Madagascar 226; Malawi 227; Malaysia 228; Mexico 236; Montenegro 241; Morocco/Western Sahara 243; Namibia 249-50; Nepal 251; Nicaragua 254; Nigeria 259; Oman 261-2; Pakistan 264; Palestinian Authority 267; Panama 268; Poland 274; Puerto Rico 276-7; Qatar 277; Russian Federation 280-1; Rwanda 284-5; Saudi Arabia 287-8; Senegal 291; Sierra Leone 296; Singapore 298; Somalia 304-5; South Africa 306; South Sudan 310; Sri Lanka 316; Sudan 319; Taiwan 329; Tajikistan 330; Tanzania 331-2; Thailand 333-4; Tunisia 339; Turkey 342; Uganda 347; United Arab Emirates 351-2; Uzbekistan 361-2; Venezuela 364-5; Yemen 369; Zimbabwe 372

freedom of expression – journalists

Angola 63-4; Azerbaijan 70; Burundi 94; Central African Republic 102-3; Côte d'Ivoire 118; Democratic Republic of the Congo 129; Dominican Republic 132; Equatorial Guinea 141-2; Guinea 163; Guinea-Bissau 164; Iraq 183, 184; Madagascar 226; Mexico 236; Tajikistan 330; Uzbekistan 361-2

freedom of expression – trade unionists

Chad 104-5

freedom of movement

Korea (Democratic People's Republic of) 205; Turkmenistan 346

freedom of religion or belief

Algeria 62; China 108-9; Eritrea 143; Hungary 170; Iran 180; Laos 212; Maldives 229-30; Myanmar 247-8; Pakistan 264; Turkmenistan 345-6

H

housing rights

Albania 59-60; Brazil 89; Czech Republic 125; Ghana 157; Hungary 170; Portugal 276; Slovakia 299-300; Slovenia 301; Spain 313; Taiwan 329; Turkey 344

human rights defenders

Brazil 89; Burundi 93-4; Cambodia 96; Chad 104; China 108; Colombia 113-4; Cyprus 124; Democratic Republic of the Congo 129; Ecuador 133; El Salvador 140; Ethiopia 146; Greece 160; Guatemala 161; Honduras 168; India 173; Iran 178-9; Lebanon 213; Mexico 236-7; Namibia 250; Paraguay 269-70; Russian Federation 281; Rwanda 285; South Africa 308; Sri Lanka 316; Ukraine 350; Venezuela 363-4; Zimbabwe 373

I

impunity

Algeria 61-2; Argentina 65-6; Bolivia 82; Burundi 93; Cameroon 98; Chad 105; Chile 106; Colombia 114; Democratic Republic of the Congo 128; Dominican Republic 132; Ecuador 134; Egypt 138; El Salvador 139; Guatemala 161; Guinea 163; Guinea-Bissau 164; Haiti 167; Honduras 168; India 173-4; Indonesia 176-7; Israel and the Occupied Palestinian Territories 188; Kenya 201-2; Kyrgyzstan 211; Lebanon 214; Liberia 215; Libya 221; Mexico 235-6; Moldova 238; Mongolia 240; Myanmar 248; Nepal 250-1; Nigeria 258; Palestinian Authority 267; Paraguay 270; Peru 271; Syria 328; Tanzania 331; Thailand 333; Timor-Leste 335; Togo 336-7; Tunisia 340; Turkey 343; Ukraine 349; Uruguay 360-1

Indigenous Peoples' rights

Argentina 65; Australia 67; Bangladesh 76-7; Bolivia 81-2; Brazil 88-9; Canada 99-100; Chile 106; Ecuador 133; Guatemala 160-1; Mexico 237; New Zealand 253; Panama 268; Paraguay 269; Peru 270-1

internal armed conflict

Colombia 111-3; Myanmar 246-7; Philippines 272; Somalia 302; Thailand 333

international justice

Bangladesh 76; Bosnia and Herzegovina 83; Cambodia 95-6; Canada 100; Central African Republic 101-2; Chad 105; Côte d'Ivoire 118; Croatia 120-1; Democratic Republic of the Congo 129; El Salvador 140; Finland 149; Kenya 202; Malaysia 229; Moldova 239; Montenegro 241; Netherlands 252; Niger 255; Norway 260; Rwanda 286; Senegal 291; Serbia 292; Spain 313; Sudan 317; Sweden 323; Uganda 347-8

international scrutiny

Australia 68; Austria 68; Colombia 115; Germany 155; Italy 190; Korea (Democratic People's Republic of) 205; Mexico 238; Myanmar 248-9; Singapore 298; Uzbekistan 363

J

justice system

Australia 67; Bosnia and Herzegovina 83-4; Bulgaria 90-1; Burundi 93; Croatia 119-20; Georgia 154; Ghana 157; Haiti 167; Hungary 170; Jamaica 194; Japan 195; Liberia 215; Maldives 230; Mexico 235-6; Mozambique 245; Nigeria 258; Palestinian Authority 267; Poland 274-5; Rwanda 285; Sierra Leone 296; Swaziland 320; Taiwan 329; Trinidad and Tobago 337; Ukraine 349-50; Venezuela 364

L

lack of accountability
Serbia 295; Sri Lanka 315-6

land disputes
Brazil 88-9; Honduras 168-9

legal, constitutional or institutional developments
Austria 68; Belgium 80; Cambodia 97; China 110; Equatorial Guinea 140-1; France 149-50; Ireland 185; Mexico 237; New Zealand 253; Swaziland 320; Tunisia 339

M

maternal health
Sierra Leone 296

migrants' rights
Angola 64; Austria 69; Czech Republic 125-6; Dominican Republic 132; Germany 156; Jordan 198; Korea (Republic of) 207; Kuwait 208; Lebanon 214; Malta 231; Mauritania 233; Mexico 236; Nepal 251; Qatar 277; Saudi Arabia 289; Taiwan 329; United Arab Emirates 352; United States of America 359

P

police and security forces
Albania 58; Angola 63; Austria 69; Bahamas 71; Canada 100; Chile 107; Colombia 112; Cyprus 124; Dominican Republic 131; Ghana 156-7; Guyana 165; Honduras 169; Hungary 170; Ireland 185; Jamaica 194; Kenya 201-2; Liberia 215-6; Mexico 234-5; Puerto Rico 276; Sierra Leone 297; Timor-Leste 335; Trinidad and Tobago 337; United Kingdom 354; Venezuela 364

political prisoners
Eritrea 143; Laos 212; Mauritania 232; Myanmar 248; Syria 327

prison conditions
Albania 59; Benin 81; Brazil 87-8; Burundi 94; Chad 104; Democratic Republic of the Congo 128-9; Gambia 153; Greece 159; Ireland 185; Israel and the Occupied Palestinian Territories 188; Liberia 215; Madagascar 225; Poland 275; Sierra Leone 297; Tanzania 332; United States of America 358-9; Uruguay 361; Venezuela 364

prisoners of conscience
Angola 64; Armenia 67; Azerbaijan 69-70; Belarus 79; Central African Republic 102; Cuba 122-3; Equatorial Guinea 142; Eritrea 143; Finland 149; Guinea 162; Israel and the Occupied Palestinian Territories 189; Laos 212; Mauritania 232; Rwanda 285; Turkey 344; Viet Nam 366

R

racism
Austria 69; Bulgaria 90; Czech Republic 124-5; Greece 159; Hungary 169; Italy 190; Poland 274; Serbia 292-3; Spain 312

refugees, internally displaced, asylum-seekers and migrants
Afghanistan 57; Australia 68; Austria 69; Bahamas 72; Belgium 79-80; Bosnia and Herzegovina 85; Bulgaria 91; Canada 100; China 111; Congo (Republic of) 116; Côte d'Ivoire 118; Cyprus 123-4; Democratic Republic of the Congo 128; Denmark 130; Dominican Republic 132; Egypt 138; Eritrea 144; Ethiopia 146-7; Finland 148-9; France 151; Georgia 153-4; Germany 155-6; Greece 158-9; Haiti 166; Ireland 185; Israel and the Occupied Palestinian Territories 189; Italy 191-2; Japan 196; Jordan 198; Kazakhstan 200-1; Kenya 203; Laos 212; Lebanon 214; Libya 220-1; Macedonia 224; Malaysia 228; Malta 231; Montenegro 241-2; Mozambique 245; Myanmar 247; Nepal 251; Norway 260; Poland 275; Rwanda 286; Serbia 293, 295; Somalia 303; South Africa 306-7; South Sudan 310; Spain 313; Sri Lanka 314; Sudan 319; Sweden 323; Switzerland 323-4; Tanzania 331; Thailand 334; Tunisia 340-1; Turkey 344; Uganda 348; Ukraine 350; United Kingdom 355-6; Yemen 370

repression of dissent
Benin 81; Cuba 122; Gambia 152; Malawi 226-7; Morocco/Western Sahara 242-3; Oman 261; Saudi Arabia 288-9; Senegal 291; Swaziland 320-1; Syria 326-7; Turkmenistan 345; Venezuela 364; Viet Nam 366

right to education
Afghanistan 57; Czech Republic 125; Slovakia 299

right to health
Afghanistan 57; Guyana 165; Ireland 185; South Africa 306; United States of America 359

right to health – maternal mortality
Burkina Faso 92

rights of lesbian, gay, bisexual and transgender people
Bahrain 75; Bosnia and Herzegovina 85; Bulgaria 90; Cameroon 99; Croatia 121; Ghana 157; Guyana 165; Hungary 170; Iran 180; Italy 191; Jamaica 194-5; Lithuania 222; Malawi 227; Mauritania 233; Montenegro 241; Nigeria 259; Romania 279; Slovakia 300-1; South Africa 308; Swaziland 322; Turkey 344; Uganda 348; Zimbabwe 373

S

sexual and reproductive rights
Argentina 66; Brazil 89; Chile 107; Honduras 168; Indonesia 176; Mexico 237; Nicaragua 254; Peru 271; Philippines 273; Poland 275

T

torture and other ill-treatment
Afghanistan 56; Albania 58-9; Argentina 66; Armenia 67; Austria 68-9; Azerbaijan 70-1; Bahrain 74; Bangladesh 77; Belarus 78; Belgium 80; Bolivia 82; Brazil 87-8; Bulgaria 91; Burundi 93; Central African Republic 103; Chad 104; China 109-10; Congo (Republic of) 115-6; Democratic Republic of the Congo 128; Denmark 130; Egypt 135-6; Eritrea 144; Ethiopia 145-6; Fiji 148; France 150; Germany 155; Greece 158; Guinea 162-3; Guyana 165; Indonesia 175; Iran 179; Iraq 182, 184; Israel and the Occupied Palestinian Territories 188-9; Italy 192-3;

Jordan 197; Kazakhstan 199-200; Korea (Democratic People's Republic of) 205; Kuwait 208; Kyrgyzstan 209-10; Lebanon 213; Libya 219-20; Macedonia 223; Malaysia 228; Mauritania 233; Moldova 238; Mongolia 240; Montenegro 241; Morocco/Western Sahara 243; Mozambique 245; Nepal 251; Nigeria 257; Palestinian Authority 266; Paraguay 270; Philippines 273; Portugal 275-6; Romania 279; Russian Federation 281-2; Saudi Arabia 289; Senegal 291; Serbia 292, 294-5; Singapore 298; Slovakia 300; South Africa 307; South Sudan 310; Spain 311-2; Sri Lanka 315; Sweden 322-3; Syria 327; Tajikistan 330; Togo 336; Tunisia 340; Turkey 342-3; Turkmenistan 345; Uganda 347; Ukraine 349; Uzbekistan 362; Yemen 370

trafficking in human beings
Albania 59

transitional justice
Burundi 94; Morocco/Western Sahara 244; Nepal 250

U

unfair trials
Bahrain 73-4; Belarus 79; Egypt 136; Iran 179; Israel and the Occupied Palestinian Territories 188; Jordan 197; Kyrgyzstan 210; Lebanon 213; Moldova 238-9; Mongolia 240; Russian Federation 282; Turkey 343

unlawful killings
Democratic Republic of the Congo 127; Macedonia 223; Madagascar 225; Montenegro 241; Mozambique 245; Nigeria 256-7; Philippines 272; Swaziland 321; Uganda 347

V

violence against women and girls
Afghanistan 57; Australia 68; Bahamas 71-2; Bangladesh 76; Chad 103; Colombia 114; Côte d'Ivoire 118; Democratic Republic of the Congo 127; Denmark 130-1; Dominican Republic 132; El Salvador 139-40; Fiji 148; Finland 149; Ghana 157; Guinea-Bissau 164; Guyana 165; Haiti 167; Ireland 185; Jamaica 194; Japan 195-6; Jordan 198; Kenya 202-3; Mexico 237; Nepal 251; Nicaragua 254; Nigeria 259; Norway 260; Pakistan 265; Palestinian Authority 267; Portugal 276; Serbia 295; Sierra Leone 297; Spain 312-3; Switzerland 324; Tajikistan 330-1; Tanzania 331; Timor-Leste 335; Trinidad and Tobago 337; Turkey 344; Uganda 347; United Kingdom 355; Venezuela 365

W

women's rights
Algeria 61; Bosnia and Herzegovina 84; Canada 100; Egypt 137; Guatemala 161; Kuwait 208; Lebanon 213-4; Liberia 216; Libya 221; Oman 262; Saudi Arabia 289; Swaziland 321-2; Syria 328; Tunisia 340; United Arab Emirates 352; Yemen 370

workers' rights
Fiji 148; Kazakhstan 200; New Zealand 253

* This is an index of topics based around the subheadings that appear in the A-Z country entries. It should be used by the reader only as a navigational tool, not as a statement of Amnesty International's human rights concerns in a particular country or territory.

Mohd Rafiq Hakeem and Naseem Hakeem, parents of 14-year-old Faizan Hakeem, who was detained in Kashmir under the Public Safety Act in February 2011. He was released on 5 April 2011, following action by Amnesty International.